'As a fighter pilot and junior commander with a record of 420 operational sorties, first in the famous "Alsace" Squadron of the Free French Air Force in Great Britain, then with Royal Air Force Units, Pierre Clostermann was second to none'
Signe: A. M. Sir John Slessor CCB DSO MC Commandant en chef RAF

'Squadron leader P.H. Clostermann DFC and Bar, 30973 FF, is an exceptional fighter pilot who was in his third tour of operational flying at the cessation of hostilities. Apart from his personal victories recorded below, he is an extremely capable leader, whilst on the ground, his wide experience makes him an invaluable commander. He has been recommended for the award of the Distinguished Service Order'   Signe: Sir Harry Broadhurst KBE DSO DFC – AOC FAF 83 Group

'This officer has displayed outstanding courage and devotion to duty through his operational career in the course of which he has destroyed at least 11 enemy aircraft and damaged other military objectives'
Citation made by Air Ministry on 26 August 1944

'Since being awarded the DFC this officer has participated in 70 new operational missions during the course of which he has destroyed a further 12 enemy aircraft. Throughout Lieutenant Clostermann has displayed outstanding courage and ability and has proved to be an inspirational to all'
To FAF from Air Ministry, 28 May 1945

D1324194

Pierre Clostermann earned his pilot's licence in 1937, aged just sixteen. Studying engineering in the USA when France fell in 1940, he made his way to Britain and volunteered for the RAF. After the war he saw active service again in 1956–57 with the French air force in Algeria, eventually becoming France's most highly decorated citizen. He was married, with three sons. He died in 2006.

The Big Show

PIERRE
CLOSTERMANN

CASSELL

Cassell Military Paperbacks

an imprint of Orion Books Ltd,
Orion House, 5 Upper St Martin's Lane,
London WC2H 9EA

An Hachette UK company

First published in Great Britain by Chatto & Windus 1951
This Cassell Military Paperbacks edition 2005

British Library Cataloguing-in-Publication Data.
A catalogue record for this book is available
from the British Library.

Printed and bound in Great Britain by
CPI Mackays, Chatham ME5 8TD

The Orion Publishing group's policy is to use papers
that are natural, renewable and recyclable products
and made from wood grown in sustainable forests. The
logging and manufacturing processes are expected to conform
to the environmental regulations of the country of origin.

www.orionbooks.co.uk

CONTENTS

For my old team-mate Jacques Remlinger in memory of our two hundred missions together in the R.A.F.

For my friends Henri de Bordas and 'Jaco' Andrieux, Compagnons de la Libération, and brave and victorious fighter pilots of Free France.

For a thousand days, against Hitler and in the eyes of the allies and the world, with the F.A.F.L. it was on your shoulders alone that the honour of our Air Force was borne.

I dedicate this book to you, each line of which you have lived! My thanks also to the R.A.F.

'They are the last of the glorious tribe of the Mohicans. Their bones will whiten as their deeds are forgotten.'
— James Fenimore Cooper, *The Deerslayer*, 1841

INTRODUCTION TO THE
2004 EDITION

When I reread my notebooks upon which the *The Big Show* is based, the same feelings and all too often the same resentments come flooding back. How can I respond intelligibly to people who ask me questions about the war, always the same ones, wanting to know the motives and reasons for my actions? Perhaps Lartéguy had the right answer when he wrote in *Les Centurions*,

> He was like a bullfighter, asked by ignorant strangers to recount details of his fight that same evening, his emotions still heightened by fear, and with more fellow feeling for the beast he had killed in the heat of the ring than for those who were interrogating him.

Pride, sorrow and pity, fury, rage and shame are the feelings that evoke the 1939–45 period for me. Pride at having taken part in the crusade for a Free France, an episode in our history which has only been equalled by that of Joan of Arc and perhaps also Rossel. Sorrow and pity to have seen so many die in the flames and fury of combat, my brothers of the Forces Aériennes Françaises Libres (Free French Air Force) and my friends of the Royal Air Force. Today Ezanno, Andrieux, Fourquet, Bordas, Mathey, Poype, Albert, Leblond, Jacques Remlinger, Risso and other famous fighter pilots and fliers are living witnesses of the past. They stand like islands in a sea, all that remains of a continent engulfed by the ocean of the forgotten. Soon we will be no more than just a few lines in history.

I still feel fury at the immense waste of this war, this European civil war as De Gaulle once called it. We were forced to kill one other, to hunt down those fine German fighter pilots, so close to us in age and mentality, in love with life, with a passion for flying and from whom we were differentiated only by the colour of our uniforms and the markings under our wings. I was already writing such thoughts as these soon after the war

and I had good reason to do so, in spite of the insults and misunderstandings that arose as a result. And I repeat them today, in spite of the
revisionists.

I have often come across the word 'fear' in my notebooks from the war
years, because it is a constant in combat, an emotion that cannot be
ignored, upon which life or death depend and for the confrontation of
which nothing in our peace-time lives can ever prepare us. Why hide it?
So let us try to define fear, real fear, not the fear felt by the weak or the
anxiety of the uneasy. Fear is a cousin to courage. One does not go
without the other. It is obvious, but it is also a question of proportion. I
have frequently been asked about fear and it merits a lengthy response,
one on which I have often reflected. For the word itself, the French
language has only synonyms without nuance. The English language has
two words, each defining a level and an aspect of fear – the word 'fright'
means the immediate and physical shock of an unexpected event, while
'fear' defines the mounting anxiety that cripples, the slow psychological
process that destroys reason and paralyses action.

Experiencing a 20 mm. shell exploding 30 cm. behind your head on the
dorsal armour-plating of a plane is like receiving a punch in the solar
plexus. The mouth dries instantly and you have the horrible sensation
that you are suffocating in your oxygen mask, a red mist appears over the
eyes and your eardrums are traumatised, transmitting nothing but
deafening, crashing waves of sound to your brain.

It is at this moment that self-control must take the upper hand,
bringing you back to normality and enabling you to fight on. We can call
this simple courage. Action must continue, preventing any thought and
without leaving the time to weigh up the pros and cons of the situation in
an agitated state of mind from which the beginnings of panic sometimes
arise. Often, you have to decide instantly whether it is to be fight or flight.
At times, flight is the reaction to a fear that dares not speak its name, and
which frequently hides itself behind reason.

Worse still, fear can paralyse reflexes, putting the brain in shock so that
it momentarily freezes and ceases giving orders. I have often been a
witness to, taken part in or been the victim of the courage–fear
partnership. Thank Heaven I have never been afflicted as some have by
this paralysis in aerial combat. Instead, in me it releases a burst of energy
and aggression making me lose, I must admit, all sense of prudence and
discipline. My superior officers often reproached me for it and it was only
once I had attained the rank of squadron leader myself that I was able to
surmount it. Was it a simple reflex that made me throw all caution to the
wind at the sight of a Focke-Wulf 190? Could the lightning course that

the subsequent action took and the sudden rush of adrenalin that allowed no time for thought be qualified as courage? On the other hand, the 30 or 40 minutes of time spent flying towards an objective that you dreaded, such as to carry out a strafing run on an aerodrome, bristling with defences, knowing that in order to accomplish the mission you had to fly through a hail of small calibre shells, spat out at a demented rate by 20 mm. anti-aircraft guns, left you with plenty of time for reflection. This time lapse allowed first apprehension to mount and then among certain people – myself included – a certain form of anxiety to take hold. However, once the strafing run was underway, with the precision flying needed to hedgehop at maximum speed and the instantaneous search for a target while flinging the plane about without planting a wing tip in the ground that was shooting past at 200 m/s, fear was wiped away like the chalk from a blackboard. Then afterwards relief and a marvellous feeling of rebirth, while far behind you, flak, now harmless, hung in small white clouds of destruction in serried rows in the sky . . . I had been shot at and survived once more, but my relief had to mask one more erosion of my self-control.

For a time, the use of tranquillisers and amphetamines concealed the outward signs of fear, but once it had taken hold, only the total ceasing of the activity that caused it could save a pilot. That is why the roles of the commanding officer and the squadron doctor were of paramount importance – to detect the symptoms in a pilot in time and to send him for rest without delay. The R.A.F. had two or three nice properties in the country which they kept for this purpose.

Courage is neither acting recklessly nor out of bravado. Acting recklessly is less noticeable than acting out of bravado, which is a more conspicuous form of behaviour, constantly on show, both in combat action and in everyday life.

Lord Moran, personal physician to the royal family and Winston Churchill, whom he accompanied on all his travels, was given the task by the Ministry of Defence of studying the behaviour of men in combat in 1917. He returned to the subject in 1940 and subsequently wrote *The Anatomy of Courage* which was first published in 1945.

In 1917 Moran raised doubts about the inhuman practice of stamping the files of soldiers suffering from shell-shock L.M.F. (lack of moral fibre). This infamous phrase, noted by Moran in his role as medical officer, had been in use since the military campaigns in India and the Sudan, and in 1900 any unfortunate officer with his file marked thus had to choose between exile and suicide.

Lord Moran was the first to expound the theory that fear, as the opposite of courage which engages the will, is simply a reaction of the body's defence mechanism when the body is pushed to its limits by visual trauma – at seeing the bloody remains of comrades – and the physical aspect of battle. Consequently, what was all too easily termed 'cowardice' was, in most cases, an illness that should have formed a case for psychiatric examination rather than for a court martial.

To study the phenomenon of courage, Moran notably undertook clinical observations of fighter pilots, carrying out studies in 1917 as well as in 1940, particularly during the Battle of Britain, believing that it was among these men that courage could be found in its purest form, free from external influences. The fighter pilot in his single-seater aircraft, already vulnerable from the demands of his highly-pressurised profession, was alone in a vast sky with virtually no protection. He had to make his own decisions and decide to fight or retreat with no one to witness his action. The slightest wound could prove fatal. There was no help at hand should he be wounded and no hospital nearby to inspire hope of survival. He could not take comfort in the proximity of his fellow pilots, or from the pat on the back of a comrade or simply from being under the watchful eye of his commanding officer. Courage can also be collective, just as fear can be transformed into panic and cause a whole section of men to flee, a phenomenon that is well known. A key extract from Moran's writing is worth giving here:

> When I write of the birth of fear I have in mind something more deeply rooted that has nothing to do with the stage fright of the novice who does not know if he is going to act badly or well; something that is born of time and stress, which a man must watch lest it comes to influence what he does. It appears only in men that have been scarred by months of war. After the initial plunges into battle it may be months before the ordinary man has any trouble. His discovery of danger does not come at once. Often it does not come for a long time. At first he has a strange feeling of invulnerability, a form of egotism, then it is suddenly brought home to him that he is not a spectator but a target, that if there are casualties he may be one of them. ...

I would add to this that among the German fighter pilots there was also a fetishism of masculinity – the 'macho' complex, as we call it today – a blind Teutonic love of arms and the snobbery of belonging to what was the apolitical aristocracy of the armies of the fatherland, the general refusal to make the Nazi salute for example, even in the presence of Hitler.

What can I say in conclusion? Fear will always be the sword of

Damocles hanging above the head of every fighting man. Each test and every single combat in the skies snaps one more strand of the rope from which it hangs. Once in his seat, helmet adjusted, parachute strapped on, hood down, isolated in his own world, every pilot, no matter who he is, experiences the absolute solitude of the duellist of centuries ago, knowing that once his sword is drawn, there is no way out other than in a death. His own or that of his adversary.

Let me repeat that those men were few who, in the cold light of a dawn centuries ago, could flash the glint of steel into the eyes of the man that they were about to kill or who would kill them. Finally, few are the men who, in a pitiless and empty sky, can confront an enemy aircraft, as fast and silent as a hawk and as deadly as a cobra. That rare thing true courage will always separate the wheat from the chaff. You have to have lived this in order to be able to understand. My comrades, the fighter pilots of the F.A.F.L., and I lived it. *The Big Show* tells our story.

The world of the fighter pilot is strange and timeless, at once both enclosed and limitless. Is it the privilege of killing or being killed honourably which unites them in the unparalleled vertiginous drama of aerial combat? Is their kinship born out of a love of flying and a shared professional passion for high performance planes, be they Spads or Mig-21's, Fokker D VII's or Spitfires, or Messerschmitt 109's or F 105's? According to whatever story the propaganda departments wish to serve up, these pilots are either the heroes of good causes, or the most evil of all villains, but finish by meeting their end all too often in the smouldering debris of a plane on a hillside.

Thirty years to the day after my arrival at 341 'Alsace' Squadron of the F.A.F.L. at Edinburgh, I saw my son, Jacques, strap himself into his Mirage 3-E of 3/2 Squadron Alsace. There, on the base at Dijon, with the thunder of the Atar jet engines in my ears, I saw myself again in my Spitfire with the Cross of Lorraine, its fuselage too emblazoned with the arms of Alsace, heart beating and two fingers poised to bring its Rolls-Royce engine bursting to life.

In life's eternal cycle of renewal, the wheel had turned another 360 degrees. I was simply a survivor from the past with *The Big Show* as my testimony, which is why I wanted the text of this new edition to remain unchanged, exactly as my notebooks of 1942–45 – including any errors about which I could not possibly have known at the time. I have simply added all the previously unpublished pages from my notebooks, the ones that were omitted in 1947 due to a shortage of paper, bringing *The Big Show* of 1948 up to 350 pages. The preface from 1947 is now to be found as an appendix at the back of this new complete edition.

Like the bullfighter, I would like to dedicate this new edition to my adversaries of yesteryear, dead or alive, and friends today of whom Germany, now our ally, and even the whole of Europe can be proud ... Rudel, Galland, Gunther Rall, Priller, Barkhorn, Hartmann, Krupinsky and so many others.

I would also like the young readers of *The Big Show* to spare a thought for all the French fighter pilots of May 1940, the English pilots of September 1940, the Americans of January 1942 in the Philippines, the Luftwaffe of 1945 and the Argentinian pilots who flew in May 1982. They were all sacrificed and they had all inherited the mayhem left by others – pacifist politicians, incompetent generals, and indolent/negligent/lax nations. However, these pilots should be admired, not pitied, because in the final instant they were able to say, 'I experienced in my aircraft what others can never know.'

Pierre Clostermann
September 2003

PART ONE

The Free French

THE FALL OF FRANCE

October 1939

I was like a cat on hot bricks. Waiting for October 1941 to arrive when I would finally be old enough to enter the École de l'Air was like waiting for the turn of the next century. I flew every day at San Diego, I practised aerobatics, but the Ryan ST was not the Curtiss or the Dewoitine 520 of which I dreamt. . . . In principle, I still had another eighteen months to wait before I could obtain my qualifications.

June/July 1940

Everything had fallen apart. The taste of ash was in my mouth. With the news of the débâcle reaching us quickly from across the Atlantic came shame, the same shame that France was feeling and that was echoed in Claudel's tragic poem that De Gaulle would later quote with fury:

> I have suffered too much, too much has been done to me
> Yet all the knocks and blows count for nothing
> I am old, so much has been done to me in the past
> But I was still not prepared for the shame.

I too experienced this shame and the defeat that crushed my hopes of finally having the opportunity to serve my country.

It was then I received a letter from my father asking me to scour the American weekly magazines, *Life* and *Time*, and the daily papers for mention of a certain De Gaulle who was appealing from London for the fight to continue. I ended up unearthing a copy of the *Washington Post* in the library at my university from which I cut out a small article. The text was accompanied by a photograph of a man with a face that was at once both sad and severe beneath a *képi* bearing the insignia of a general. I sent the cutting to my father in Rio de Janeiro where he was posted. A month later, another letter arrived from my father telling me that he was going to join De Gaulle in Africa or London, with Commandant Valin, our air attaché in Brazil and entrusting me with the care of my mother and Madame Valin. I was instructed to dispatch them to Brazzaville which had become the capital of free France. As for myself, my father wrote that I was now a young man and that one does not often have the chance to do something for one's country and that he hoped I would join him in London. . . . He added that history doesn't give people second chances.

Seated on the beach at Malibu, I reread the letter. The war seemed so far away, but I knew now that I no longer had any choice. I owed it to my father* to go and to my mother to come back. I was an only child, what must she be thinking? Hailing from Lorraine and Alsace, my parents came from places where people had been used to such sacrifices for generations. I thought of the stone that I had been taken to see as a small boy, at the edge of the road near the De Dietrich factories at Niederbron. It was a modest ex-voto with an inscription to the memory of an ancestor, Lieutenant Colonel George Clostermann, killed at Reichoffen during a charge with the Brigade Michel in 1870.

I read about the exploits of the Royal Air Force in the press. My decision was taken. It would not be a Dewoitine 520, but a Spitfire. The excitement I had felt reading about the air aces, Guynemer, Fonk and Navarre, at school in Paris, was going to be revived for me, at least I hoped so. . . .

My decision made, I asked to see the Dean of CALTEC (the California Institute of Technology), where I was at university, and explained my problem to him. He welcomed me with a smile and was surprised because he had thought I was Brazilian.† He told me about his sympathy for the English – there were not too many Americans like him – and added that he would consult the board of education in order to find a solution for my degree. Besides, I had achieved practically all the credits I needed in all my subjects and had reached the Dean's list the previous year.

A week later, I had to sit a tough oral examination. The president of the jury was Donald Hall, the principal of Ryan College, the aeronautical department of CALTEC. Hall was the engineer who years previously had designed Lindbergh's *Spirit of St Louis* and was my professor of aeronautics and fluid mechanics. Everything went well and I was awarded my degree in aeronautical engineering. My commercial pilot's licence (the American pilot's licence of the period) was also stamped C.A.B. (Civil Aeronautic Bureau), and the 315 hours flying time was entered into my log-book.

There was now nothing to keep me in America any longer. I had to

---

* My father, severely wounded in the 1914–18 war – military medal, Légion d'Honneur, with three citations.

† Born in Brazil, was shown on my papers.

return quickly to Rio de Janeiro, which wouldn't be that simple, but Hall wrote to Lindbergh, Vice President of Pan Am, and a week later a free ticket from Miami to Rio arrived in the post. Pinned to it was the famous pilot's card bearing the words 'Good luck'.

The die was cast. San Francisco to Miami in an Eastern DC3, then Miami, Panama, Natal and finally Rio de Janeiro in a Pan Am Sikorsky seaplane. It was something of a leap into the unknown, and towards what future?

Four months later, I had organised the departure of my mother and Mme Valin for South Africa from where they would continue to Brazzaville. I passed a sad Christmas and finally, after various events, the English finally organised my departure for England, leaving Montevideo on a liner out from New Zealand.

ARRIVAL IN ENGLAND

I was on board the *Rangitata*, a liner belonging to the New Zealand Shipping Company with its two famous yellow funnels. There were as yet no escorts or convoys organised. However, it was the start of the great U-boat period and hundreds of allied ships had already been sunk. There were also one or two German merchant ships acting as surface raiders and the captain told me that our sister ship, the *Rangitiki*, had been sunk by the pocket battleship the *Graf Spee* which ended up being scuttled by its captain in the River Plate. So, for fast boats such as ours, the English began to take the precaution of devising different itineraries, such as reaching Europe via the South Atlantic. This involved dipping down below the level of Cape Horn to the edge of the Antarctic ice-field and well into southern latitudes, before rising once more to gain the tip of South Africa, from where they would head north via the Benguela Current, which, in principle, the South African navy patrolled.

For forty-five days I was the sole passenger on the *Rangitata*, whose hold was full of wheat and preserved meat. I had a sumptuous cabin and was the only pupil for the gymnastics teacher who wanted to make an Olympic athlete out of me. I swam in the warm seawater pool and lived like a lord dining on the ship's three-star cuisine. In short, the crossing was pure heaven.

The first port of call in Africa was Freetown, which had become a major allied port. I was heading down the gangway when I heard the velvet throb of a plane's engine. My heart stopped. My God, it could only be one thing, a Rolls-Royce engine. I hurried to the bridge and peering between the masts of the boats in the harbour I spotted a Hurricane. It was the first R.A.F. fighter plane I had seen in the flesh. It was climbing vertically into the sky and as I heard it roaring above me, the thought suddenly came to me, that's it, my youth is over, I have just jumped head first into the world of war where I will have to grow up quickly.

From then on, everything became very different. It was now another world, the war became more palpable and danger felt closer. We joined a convoy and I slept fully dressed, lifejacket to hand, my papers and money in a small waterproof bag that the ship's doctor had given me, attached to my belt.

The liner was suddenly invaded by soldiers and nurses. My life of tranquillity was over and I even felt a little apprehension at hearing, during the night, the muffled thud of depth charges, whose shock waves made the beakers on my washbasin rattle, and the strident noise of claxons on the escorting destroyers accompanied by the sound of orders being shouted through loudspeakers.

Finally, at first light one grey morning, we arrived in Liverpool. The city must have suffered a heavy bombardment the night before because the docks were in ashes. A large ship was lying on its side in the water, covered in oil, and a grey snow mixed with soot was falling from the sky. Watching the dreadful scene from the bridge, I saw the tangle of firemen's hosepipes, burnt-out trucks that were still smoking, cranes overturned on the quayside and people running in every direction. I went down to my cabin to fetch my things, my case and my fishing rods that I had also brought with me. A steward stopped me and told me to wait. I then saw two English officers from the security service accompanied by a policeman. They asked me if I were Pierre Clostermann and asked me to hand over my passport, which was just a travel document provided by the English embassy in Rio. Regarding me with a certain amount of amazement, they asked me what I was going to do with my fishing rod.

'It is proof that I believe in the final victory, otherwise I would have left it in Rio de Janeiro.'

Their British phlegm must have taken a bit of a blow. They were in little mood for joking surrounded by the docks in ruins and fires still burning. ... As for me, at that instant I was asking myself if I had been wise in leaving San Diego. I was thinking of the pretty girls in Malibu in the sun, as I stepped over the tangle of hosepipes with my 'guides', the clanging of fire engines in my ears, the cries and the noise of axes bringing down the burnt timber framework of the warehouses, and the smell of burning in the air.

They explained to me that we had to wait for the night train and so I acquainted myself with the very particular atmosphere of an English police station, the smell of a cold pipe, tobacco and beer. The day passed and I began to feel very hungry. The station sergeant, who lived on the floor above, asked his wife to bring me down a sandwich: a little margarine and a few bean sprouts between two slices of bread. I ate it without enthusiasm. Mentally I was still in the land of the hamburgers and steamed crabs served up on the pier in San Francisco!

Finally we boarded the train, with two police inspectors taking me by the arm. It was normal that they should take precautions and that before being vetted by security I should be considered a potential suspect and treated as such. The police evacuated a compartment: I had to travel alone with my escort without any contact from anyone outside, like a plague victim. All around me the train was packed with soldiers, standing crammed into the corridors on top of each other. Arriving at King's Cross station the sirens of London were howling; it was my first air raid warning. . . .

AN INTERVIEW

A car was waiting to take me, still under close escort, for interrogation by British Intelligence at the Royal Patriotic School, Wandsworth. All Free French and the thousands of patriots from occupied countries who had made their way to England to continue the struggle were required to go through this process from January 1941 onwards. Obviously, the Germans tried to slip in a few double agents among them: they succeeded, but the strict vetting process usually unmasked them pretty swiftly.

The interrogation methods used by the British were quite different to those of the Gestapo, and probably more effective. Torture had the drawback in most cases of traumatising the victim, paralysing the mind and producing a mental block. The British, on the other hand, attempted to win the confidence of the subject, with everything taking place over a cup of tea and a cigarette. The Luftwaffe, at Dulag Luft (their P.O.W. interrogation centre), were also more subtle than the Gestapo. They put to good effect statements from previous interrogations as well as their own files, in which they methodically classified every scrap of information – including, for instance, the name of a dog adopted as squadron mascot, discovered on the back of a photo. When a pilot of this same squadron was shot down and captured, the Luftwaffe interrogator would inform him, very courteously, that he already knew everything – like the dog's name or that of a barmaid at the unit's favourite pub. One can imagine how unsettling that was!

'Patriotic School', as it was familiarly known – I wonder what joker thought up the 'patriotic' bit – was a large, red-brick building, reminiscent of a public school, and very forbidding. At the solid-looking entrance gates, two old, leafless chestnut trees extended a mournful welcome in the rain to 'guests'.

Next morning I found myself attending my first interview in front of one of numerous whitewood tables in a classroom with its blackboard still on the wall. Appointed as my interrogator was a phlegmatic British officer wearing the ribbon of the Military Cross, very correct, very affable.

However, his eyes gave the lie to his smile as he offered me the traditional cup of tea. His questions, in an impeccable French, appeared quite innocent on the surface.

'So you studied in Paris?'

'Yes, sir.'

'Which school?'

'Notre Dame de Boulogne.'

'O.K., but where do your parents live?'

'When they were in Paris, at 23 avenue de Lamballe.'

'I see. Now where exactly was this school?'

'Porte d'Auteuil, sir.'

'Porte d'Auteuil, eh? What street? Can you show me on this map of Paris?'

'That's it – here.'

'What bus did you take to visit your parents and where did you alight? And in the U.S.A.?'

All of this took place like a conversation between friends. But the first trap soon materialised when he asked, with apparent indifference, if I went to the cinema on Sundays in Paris. I replied yes, to the Orphelins d'Auteuil or the Ranelagh.

'Ah, the Ranelagh, some friends in Paris have told me about it. I gather it's really palatial, on the *grands boulevards*, with the first giant screen in Paris.'

'No, no, quite the opposite, sir. It's very small, in the 16th *arrondissement*, and it's like an eighteenth-century private theatre inside.'

I was over the first hurdle!

It is extremely hard to hold out if you're not who you're pretending to be. Many an infiltrator had been weeded out using the trick question about a bus, the price of a Métro or cinema ticket, etc.

At length I was permitted to phone Commandant Valin. He had recently been promoted to colonel, replacing Pijeaud as C. in C. Free French Air Force (F.A.F.L.). (Pigeaud had died in combat over Libya flying a Blenheim of the Groupe Lorraine.) Valin had me out of there in three days. Before letting me go, the British very decently invited me to dinner, where I met an R.A.F. fighter pilot who, by his manner, might have been there merely for the conversation.

'Our air attaché in Brazil has sent us your C.V. With your record, you could just as easily go straight into the R.A.F., and you'd get a squadron much quicker than by the French route. You've also got talent as a journalist, and we're keen to put that to use. The Reuters Agency would like you to write some articles – paid, of course. That would eke out your flying pay, which wouldn't be very grand with our French friends. As you speak several languages, they'd be happy to have you on the B.B.C. now and again. Anyway, the going rate's £35 a broadcast. . . .' The Devil and all his works!

So, after the F.F.L. in Rio, I found myself, nonetheless, enlisted in the Free French Air Force. At this time the British were plugging the R.A.F., and weren't very keen on seeing De Gaulle's outfit grow bigger. The general, in turn, was on two of his hobby horses: the matter of uniform, and Frenchmen in French units! Unlike the Czechs, Poles, Belgians and the rest, he had never accepted us wearing British uniform. Cost what it might (and it did cost!) we had to wear the French uniform of our service arm so as to be highly visible despite our small numbers. . . . Condé used to say, did he not, that small armies win big battles.

As soon as I received my kit allowance and clothing coupons, I went to Lillywhites to get myself measured for a service dress uniform of the Armée de l'air. I had been promoted sergeant on the strength of my academic C.V. and my flying record. I left the store very proud, with the feeling that I was now a fully-fledged Frenchman, with the all the rights that entailed – provided I fulfilled my duties, as my father used to say. That was indeed my intention.

A MEETING WITH THE GENERAL

I didn't have to wait long for my first big excitement. The next day but one I found a note in my pigeon-hole at the small requisitioned hotel where I'd been billeted pending my posting: 'Report to Carlton Gardens; the General will see you today at 1730 hours.' The General? No need to ask which one. . . . De Gaulle!

I arrived with a dry throat. The aide-de-camp, Courcel I think, gave me a suspicious look before showing me in.

'You know how to salute, at least?'

I showed him.

'Well, not exactly. Look, like this. . . . Then, remain at attention, stand perfectly straight, remove your cap and put it under your left arm until the General tells you to sit down; if he doesn't, remain at attention. O.K.?'

In a sort of trance, I went in. The General was busy writing, and there was a large map of the world behind his desk. He looked up. I gave an impeccable salute, trembling and very emotional.

'Take a seat.' Then, with unexpected kindness, he added, 'I know your father; he's back home. I met him at Brazzaville and Fort-Lamy, and your mother, too. A very distinguished lady!'

A moment's pause. He stared at me attentively; there was a certain look in his eyes, sadness perhaps.

'I hear you're an experienced pilot already. How old are you?'

'Twenty, mon Général.'

An awkward pause. Then, 'Bien, très bien. Do your duty, but don't go and get yourself killed: France will need sons like you after the victory. I say victory, because we are going to win.'

I shall never forget that. He said a few words more; choking with emotion, I didn't take them in. I rose, replaced my cap, knocked it off, picked it up again, and somehow or other stumbled out of the room.

Such was my first meeting with General de Gaulle.

TRAINING AT CRANWELL

A week later, I underwent a long and gruelling R.A.F. medical. Next day, there was an interview to prove I could speak English. Well, with an American accent, maybe, but my syntax was correct! This was followed by an inspection of my pilot's log: 315 flying hours, cast-iron genuine, with the C.A.B. stamp. The people there were impressed, and began to talk about a posting to Rhodesia or Canada as an instructor. My refusal was categorical. I hadn't come halfway across the world for that; I demanded to be posted to a fighter squadron, to get to grips with the enemy. It was explained that things weren't quite that simple, and first I would need to submit to tests of my flying skill, the results of which would determine whether I was assigned to bombers or fighters.

So, to begin with, I was sent off to Sywell for elementary testing. There were already three French fliers there, including an instructor. Among the pupils was Jacques Remlinger, who would become my closest friend ever afterwards. He was a terrific character. My own C.V. was highly colourful, but his was not exactly run-of-the-mill either. His father was also from Alsace, an affluent businessman who had owned an import-export house in England since the Great War. Jacques had studied at Harrow, the famous public school attended by Churchill. He was a gifted rugger player, with the physique and speed to make a great wing-threequarter, and turned out for some very well-known sides in England. At eighteen, he had joined the Free French Air Force. On one occasion, he was questioned by General de Gaulle, along with other young volunteers from France, about how he'd managed to get to London: for some it had meant incredible risks and acts of courage. Embarrassed, Jacques had blurted out: 'By Tube, mon Général.' This, so I was told, took the Great Man aback somewhat! At Sywell, to start with, Jacques and I were mere nodding acquaintances. In any case, my stay there was brief, as I was only required to prove I could fly.

I was a bit miffed to be tested in a Tiger Moth, the *Tigre Mou* I had learnt to fly in five years previously. The chief instructor of the school took me up personally in a dual-control machine. Before we took off, he

turned to me and shouted down the speaking tube: 'Don't frighten me!'
Owing to the racket of the engine, I misheard this as 'Frighten me!'

So I cheerfully yelled back: 'I'll try, sir!'

We took off. 'Turn left, then right, climb to 3,000 feet, then do me a
loop followed by a spiral dive.'

I performed the required manoeuvres, pulling out of the dive like a
veteran. As our air speed was sufficiently low, I let him have a surprise
flick roll, finishing in textbook fashion, perfectly horizontal and under
control. . . . I heard some rumbling noises from the speaking tube. He
gestured to me that he was taking back the controls, then returned them
to me and indicated I should land. I put the crate down as if on eggshells.
He got out and took off his goggles, gloves and helmet.

'OK, that's enough. If I've got to die I'd rather do it later fighting Jerry!
You can go back to London. Oh, if it's of any interest, flick rolls are
forbidden on the Tiger Moth. The tail falls off.'

And in my brand-new R.A.F. log-book, on the first page of which was
entered my half-hour's flying time at Sywell, he wrote 'Above average' –
pretty churlish in view of my flick-roll and landing . . .

I spent another three weeks at Camberley, the transit camp for the Free
French Air Force, before being dispatched to Aston Down to be tested on
a more advanced aircraft. This was to be the Miles Master with its 600
h.p. Rolls-Royce Kestrel engine; it handled much better than the T-6 I'd
flown at San Diego and its controls were more sophisticated. Proceedings
began with a lengthy cockpit familiarisation, then, as before, it was aloft
for half an hour's varied manoeuvres and back down again.

'O.K.,' declared the instructor, 'I've got other things to do and more
pupils to test. You can go solo; play with her for an hour, keep your eye
on the petrol, don't get lost, and whatever you do, don't prang her.' As
happy as a sand-boy, I threw her around the sky without losing sight of
the field. They were watching me from the ground, and again I was
ranked 'above average'.

Next I was kept hanging around for two months at Camberley doing
drill, learning to march, salute, and use Morse. Goodness knows why
Morse: all communication between fighter aircraft was now by radio. I
waited and waited, my frustration mounting all the time. The English
girls I met were very nice, but I hadn't come thousands of miles to
improve the Entente Cordiale!

Finally, I was summoned to H.Q. at Queensberry Way.

'Well done! You're a lucky chap – the British have selected you to
become an officer in the R.A.F., and you're off to the Royal Air Force
College at Cranwell!'

So I wasted eight months – almost a complete year – at Cranwell, learning what I already knew. On the other hand, I recognised that British procedures, local navigational systems and how to map-read flying at tree-top level in the fog were new to me, and that knowledge of them was indispensable.

Having done most of my flying in the sunshine of California and Rio de Janeiro, I was glad I was taught how to cope with a pea-souper. . . . Ah, the joys of the British climate for three-quarters of the year! We were sent up – in an 800 h.p. radial-engined Miles Master II – when the weather was unfit for any sane person to fly in and even the crows were grounded. When the Americans finally arrived in Britain, they had the same problem. It was possible for a fog-bound B-17 pilot to remark: 'Visibility was so bad I couldn't even see my co-pilot sitting next to me.' We were also treated to formation flying ad nauseam.

What astonished me at Cranwell, among other British customs, was dinner. This was an elaborate ceremony which took place in the huge dining hall lined with carved wood panelling – at least what remained of it, as the school had been bombed and the entire wing to the left of the cathedral-like dome was still covered with tarpaulins stretched between the Corinthian columns! Perched on a balcony, a band played those extraordinary British marches which sound like slow waltzes. Dress uniform was worn at dinner, and in the mornings we played tennis!

I began to develop an admiration for the British way of life, and to realise that this was how the R.A.F. and the country coped with war. The Germans, for their part, could not understand. I sincerely believe that this is the reason they failed to win the Battle of Britain in 1940.

I passed out top of my class: not particularly meritorious considering my technical background and extensive flying hours. I was dispatched to O.T.U. (Operational Training Unit) No. 61 at Rednal in Wales for conversion to Spitfires. There it was that I met up again with Jacques Remlinger.

PART TWO

Pilot with the 'Alsace' Squadron

OPERATIONAL TRAINING UNIT
IN WALES

1942

The high Welsh hills, half-drowned in mist, glided to left and right of the railway line. We had passed Birmingham, Wolverhampton and Shrewsbury buried in greasy soot. Without exchanging a word, Jacques and I gazed indifferently at the depressing landscape, washed by an incessant drizzle, the dirty enervating mining towns crawling up the valleys, each one crushed by a pall of grey smoke anchored to the housetops, so dense that the wind, blowing in icy gusts, could not move it.

Our fellow-passengers gazed curiously at our navy-blue, gold-buttoned French uniforms. The pilot's brevet of the 'Armée de l'Air' gleamed proudly on our breasts, with the wings of the R.A.F. over our left pockets.

Barely a fortnight before we had still been pilots under training at the R.A.F. college at Cranwell, dragging round manuals on navigation and armaments and thick books full of notes.

All that was only a memory now. In a few hours, perhaps, we would be flying a Spitfire, thus clearing the last hurdle that separated us from the great arena.

A few minutes more and we reached Rednal, No. 61 O.T.U.* – for a conversion course on Spitfires before a squadron posting.

Suddenly Jacques pressed his face to the window:

'Look Pierre, there are our Spitfires!'

Sure enough, as the train slowed down alongside an airfield, a damp ray of sunshine succeeded in piercing the fog, revealing twenty or so aircraft lined up along a strip of tarmac.

The great day had come! It had snowed all night and the airfield was dazzling white beneath the blue sky. Heavens, how good to be alive! I filled my lungs with the icy air and felt the snow crunch under my feet,

* Operational Training Unit.

soft and yielding like an oriental carpet. It brought back many memories. The first snow I had seen for so long.

At the door of the flight-hut, where you shelter between flights, my instructor was waiting for me, smiling.

'How do you feel?'

'O.K., Sir,' I replied, trying to hide my emotion.

All my life I shall remember my first contact with a Spitfire.

The one I was going to fly bore the markings TO-S. Before putting on my parachute I stopped a moment to gaze at it – the clean lines of the fuselage, the beautifully stream-lined Rolls-Royce engine: a real thoroughbred.

'You've got her for one hour. Good luck!'

This thunderbolt was mine for an hour, sixty intoxicating minutes! I tried to remember my instructor's advice. Everything seemed so confused. I strapped myself in, trembling, adjusted my helmet, and still dazed by the mass of instruments, dials, contacts, levers, which crowded on one another, all vital, and which one's finger must not fail to touch at the psychological moment, I got ready for the decisive test.

Carefully I went through the cockpit drill, murmuring the ritual phrase, BTFCPPUR – Brakes, Trim, Flats, Contacts, Pressure (in the pneumatic system), Petrol, Undercarriage and Radiator.

Everything was all set. The mechanic closed the door behind me and there I was, imprisoned in this metal monster which I had got to control. A last glance.

'All clear? Contact!'

I manipulated the hand pumps and the starter buttons. The airscrew began to revolve slowly, and suddenly, with a sound like thunder, the engine fired. The exhausts vomited long blue flames enveloped in black smoke, while the aircraft began to shudder like a boiler under pressure.

When the chocks were removed I opened the radiator wide, for these liquid-cooled engines overheat very rapidly, and I taxied very carefully over to the runway, cleared by snow-ploughs, jet black and dead straight in the white landscape.

'Tudor 26, you may scramble now, you may scramble now!' Over the radio the control tower authorised me to take off.

My heart was thumping in my ribs. I swallowed the lump in my throat, lowered my seat and with a clammy hand I slowly opened the throttle. At once I felt myself swept up by a cyclone.

Snatches of advice came back to me.

'Don't stick the nose too far forward!'

In front of me there was only a slight clearance between the ground and the tips of the enormous airscrew which was going to absorb all the power from the engine.

Timidly I eased the stick forward, and, with a jolt that glued me to the back of my seat, the Spitfire started forward, then moved faster and faster while the airfield swept by on either side with increasing speed.

'Keep her straight!'

I ruddered frantically to check incipient swings.

Suddenly, holding my breath, and as if by magic, I found myself airborne. The railway line passed by like a flash. I was vaguely aware of some trees and houses, which disappeared indistinctly behind me.

I quickly raised the undercarriage, closed the transparent hood of my cockpit, throttled back and adjusted the airscrew pitch for cruising.

Phew! Drops of sweat ran down my forehead. But instinctively my limbs reacted like the well-regulated levers of an automaton. The long, tedious months of training had prepared my muscles and reflexes for just this minute.

How light she was on the controls! The slightest pressure with hand or foot and the machine leapt into the sky.

'Good heavens! Where am I?'

The speed was such that the few seconds which had elapsed had been enough to take me half a dozen miles from the airfield. The black runway was no more than a streak of soot on the horizon.

Timidly I hazarded a turn, passed over my base again and turned to left and right. I eased the stick back slightly and I climbed to 10,000 feet in the twinkling of an eye.

Gradually the speed went to my head and I got bolder. Moving the throttle the fraction of an inch was enough to unleash the engine.

I decided to try a dive. Gently I eased the stick forward – 300, 350, 400 m.p.h. The ground seemed to be hurtling towards me in a terrifying way. Scared by the speed I instinctively moved the stick back, and suddenly my head was driven into my shoulders, a leaden weight pressed my backbone down and crushed me into my seat, and my eyes blurred.

Like a steel ball falling on a marble block the Spitfire had bounced on the elastic air and, as straight as a rod, had shot up into the sky.

As soon as I had recovered from the effects of centrifugal force I hastened to throttle back, as I had no oxygen and the machine was still climbing.

Over the radio I heard Control calling me back. Christmas! an hour already! Everything seemed to have happened in one second.

Now I had to land.

I opened the radiator wide, throttled back, changed to fine pitch, opened my hood, raised the seat, and began my approach.

Once again I started to panic. The enormous engine in front of me with its broad exhaust pipes blotted out the whole runway. Blinded, my head kept in by the terrific pressure of the air, I was a prisoner in my cockpit.

I lowered the undercarriage and the flaps. The runway drew near at frightening speed. I would never succeed in putting her down. The airfield seemed to be getting simultaneously narrower and closer. Stick back, back desperately. The machine touched down with a loud metallic jolt which reverberated in the fuselage and – I felt her awkwardly rolling on the tarmac.

A touch of left brake, then a touch of right, and the Spitfire came to a standstill at the end of the runway. The throb of the engine ticking over was like the beating of a winded race-horse's flanks.

My instructor jumped up on the wing, helped me off with my parachute, smiling at my pale, drawn face.

I took a couple of steps, staggered, and had to hold on to the fuselage.

'Good show! You see, nothing to worry about!'

All the same, if only he knew how proud I felt. At last I had flown a Spitfire. How beautiful the machine seemed to me, and how alive! A masterpiece of harmony and power, even as I saw her now, motionless.

Softly, as one might caress a woman's cheeks, I ran my hand over the aluminium of her wings, cold and smooth like a mirror, the wings which had borne me.

Going back to the hut, my parachute on my back, I turned again and dreamt of the day when, in a squadron, I would have a Spitfire of my own, to take into combat, which would hold my life within the narrow confines of its cockpit, and which I would love like a faithful friend.

Those were, at O.T.U., two arduous winter months.

Course succeeded course, flying hours accumulated rapidly, aerial gunnery exercises over the snow-covered Welsh hills quickly mounted up in my pilot's log-book.

Not without losses and tragedies, however. One of our Belgian comrades' Spitfires exploded in mid-air during an aerobatics practice. Two of our R.A.F. friends came into collision and were killed before our eyes. Then Pierrot Degail, one of the six Frenchmen on the course, crashed one misty evening into an ice-covered hill-top. It took two days to reach the debris through the snow. His body was found in a kneeling position, his head in his arms, like a sleeping child, by the side of his Spitfire. Both his legs were broken and, unable to move, he must have died of cold during the night.

The burial ceremony, with military honours, was moving in its simplicity. Jacques, Menuge, Commailles and I carried the coffin, wrapped in the tricolor. God, how sad and weighed down we were, under the thin icy rain. The slow procession, one by one, before the pit filled with the sound of shovelfuls of British soil falling on the poor kid.

After five weeks at Rednal we spent the last three weeks of our training at Montford Bridge, a small satellite airfield lost in the hills.

Without interruption, as soon as the weather cleared somewhat, we flew. Formation exercises in threes, fours, twelves, emergency take-offs, dog fight practice, air-firing, course on tactics, on aircraft recognition, on elocution for speaking over the RT,* etc.

The cold was appalling. We lived in Nissen huts which had no insulating walls and keeping warm was a real problem. I used to go with Jean Scott, the baby of our team, who shared a room with me, and 'borrow' coal from a dump by the railway. John was very particular about his appearance, and it was a comic sight to see him, precariously balanced on barbed wire, passing greasy blocks of anthracite held distastefully between the thumb and forefinger of a carefully gloved hand.

Then followed the homeric business of lighting the diminutive stove which had the task of warming our hut. Pints of petrol – filched from the bowser – were necessary to excite the faltering enthusiasm of the damp coal and the wet wood. One fine evening, I remember, the stove, saturated with petrol vapour, blew up and Jacques, John and I were transformed into Zulu warriors of the darkest hue.

New Year's Eve came and went, very quiet and slightly sad in that remote corner. Then came the day of posting. Commailles, Menuge and I were to leave for Turnhouse in Scotland to join 341 Squadron, Free French Fighter Squadron 'Alsace', then in process of formation. Jacques, John and Aubertin were leaving for 602 Squadron in Perranporth.

The die was cast. The real war was beginning. At last!

* Radio telephony.

THE 'ALSACE' SQUADRON

Three young Sergeant Pilots disembarked in Edinburgh.
The world was theirs. They glanced absent-mindedly at the
'Princess of the North' bathed in sunlight, though she had
adorned herself with a resplendent snowy mantle.

They were very tired. They had just crossed the whole of England
diagonally from south-west to north-east. An exhausting night in the
train, with changes in the dark, jostling on damp platforms, mist forming
haloes round screened lamps, the panting of engines, the thronging crowd
of uniforms.

'The train for Leicester, please?'

Dazed by the noise, dragging their heavy kit-bags, they had vainly
searched for seats in crowded coaches with people sleeping on top of each
other – smell of soot, of sweat, of stale tobacco smoke.

The coaches had started moving. Then the alarming syncopated wail of
the sirens.

'Air raid on! Lights, please, lights, please!'

The jamming on of brakes, the hiss of compressed air, the impact of the
buffers jolting the dazed passengers, thin blue lights extinguished. A
quarter of an hour. Half an hour. One hour of cold and silence. A few
flashes in the sky. The distant hum of engines. Vague gleams of light on
the horizon, showing up for a moment the silhouettes of factories or
chimney stacks. Then the sirens again.

'All clear!'

A blast on a whistle, the squeaking of rusty chains, more jolts – the
engine skidding and racing. Vague impressions, drowned in an exhausting
and uncomfortable twilight sleep.

The bus stopped in front of the airfield guard-room. Miraculously, all
fatigue disappeared.

'Turnhouse!' cried the conductor.

We saw great hangars camouflaged with green and brown stripes, the
low buildings of the messes, the wooden Dispersal huts scattered round

the big tarmac runways which quartered the grassy surface of the ground. A few aircraft here and there.

The S.P. corporal on duty examined our papers, our identity cards, and had us escorted to the Sergeants' Mess.

Slightly cold greeting from the Station Warrant Officer.

'French Squadron? I haven't seen anybody yet.'

Good heavens! Perhaps it was a ghost fighter squadron? We began to sing a different tune. A utility truck deposited us with our baggage in front of a big, gloomy building. Dead silence. A smell of mildew, a large empty dormitory – iron beds, small grey cupboards. Not a soul about. The first impression was disconcerting. Where was the cosy, animated squadron bar, where were the gay, noisy comrades whom our imagination had showed us greeting us with open arms?

'Nom de Dieu! On ne peut plus dormir tranquille ici!'

The voice made us jump – an honest-to-goodness French voice, and from Paris, judging by the accent. And right at the far end of the room in a dark corner we made out a shape, lying on a bed and smoking a cigarette. Navy-blue uniform, gold buttons – a Frenchman! He got up languidly.

'Why, it's Marquis!'

We looked at each other and laughed. We four *were* 341 Squadron.

The days passed, and the 'Alsace' Fighter Squadron took shape.

Commandant Mouchotte,* one of the first to join the F.F.F., was to be in command. A tall, dark, slim man, with piercing eyes and a voice that snapped and admitted of no argument, but was followed by a warming, friendly smile. The kind of man for whom you get yourself killed without discussion, almost with pleasure.

Then Lieutenant Martell, who was to be my flight-commander, a blond giant with broad shoulders and enormous feet, and magic hands that handled a Spitfire with incredible power and flexibility.

Lieutenant Boudier – Boubou – a little wisp of a man behind a big pipe, with a heart of gold. He was an ace, with seven Jerries to his credit already. He commanded the other flight.

Then the pilots started arriving one by one, from the four corners of

---

* The French ranks, which were often retained, were as follows:
  Commandant – Squadron Leader
  Capitaine – Flight Lieutenant
  Lieutenant – Flying Officer
  Sous-Lieutenant – Pilot Officer
  Adjudant – Warrant Officer
  Sergeant Chef – Flight Sergeant

England, after tearing themselves away from the four corners of occupied France to come and fight. A natural selection brought about by will-power and patriotism; every social class, but an élite.

De Bordas, under a gay and carefree exterior, hid the tragedy of the loss of his best friend, killed at his side near Dieppe; Bouguen, a stiff-necked Breton; Farman, bearer of a name famous in the French air arm; Chevalier, calm, coldly determined; Lafont, one of the veterans of the G.C.1* in Libya; Girardon, one of our rare regular officers, full of banter and dry humour; Roos, who hid his bashfulness and his kind heart under a surly exterior; Mathey, who had crossed the Pyrenees on skis to join Free France; Savary, the poet of the party, subtle and cultured; Bruno, an experienced pilot and a wag; Gallet, his bosom friend, also a veteran from the heroic days with the G.C.1 in Libya; Pabiot, from the 'Ile de France' Squadron, who just wanted to continue the fight.

Gradually the team built up, and still they continued to come.

De Mezillis, from Brittany, who had lost an arm with the 'Lorraine' Squadron in Libya and, by an incredible effort of will, had learnt to fly with his artificial arm; Béraud, the 'steady type' of the gang, a sensible and studious pilot, whom you always went and consulted before you did anything silly; Laurent, meticulous, scientific, enthusiastic; Mailfert, that priceless practical joker; Leguie, another Breton, as phlegmatic as any Anglo-Saxon; Raoul Duval, hero of sensational escapes, a regular to his finger tips; Borne, friendly, self-effacing and discreet; Buiron, 'Bui-Bui and his pipe' to his friends; De Saxe, a walking skeleton who feared neither God nor the Devil.

One fine day, with a noise like thunder, our Spitfires arrived. Our English fitters took them over and we cleaned them up. Lorraine crosses appeared on the fuselages, with the markings of 341 Squadron, N and L.

Under the energetic leadership of Mouchotte and thanks to the experience of Martell and Boudier, the team of friends became a redoubtable combat formation. The planes were incessantly in the air – shooting, combat formation, dog fight exercises, scramble practice.

The British were amazed at how fast the unit got into shape and generously admitted that it certainly was an exceptional one.

One month later the 'Alsace' Squadron was posted to the Biggin Hill Wing. It was an honour, how great an honour we did not perhaps completely realise at the time. Biggin Hill, south of London, was the base with the highest number of victories to its credit and was reserved for the most select squadrons of the R.A.F.

* Groupe de Combat 1 – Fighter Squadron 1.

To go there we were to be equipped with Spitfire IX's, with Rolls-Royce Merlin 63 engines with two-stage superchargers, British aero technique's last word, parsimoniously distributed to a few outstanding units.

To celebrate the event suitably we threw a monster party for the Turnhouse personnel, from Group Captain Guinness, the Station Commander, to the last mechanic. I watched Mouchotte, in a corner, looking very calm but a little bit sad. I knew what he was thinking. He was wondering with bitterness in his heart how many of the kids in his squadron would survive to the end. Death had already struck. De Mezillis had been killed last week, when the wings of his Spitfire folded up in a dive. And only the day before Commailles and Artaud had crashed, the wrecks of their two aircraft interlocked, during a combat exercise.

A TOUCH OF PANIC

We arrived in Biggin Hill to find morale not particularly high. As the base covered south London, it had been a particular target of bombing during the Battle of Britain, so the facilities were spartan – just a few officers' dormitories in the mess building that had survived. We were allocated some small huts behind the Alsace Dispersal. We shared rooms with whomever we got on with best. Our engineers were already there, as were our planes. To our surprise they were the first Spitfire IX-Bs, the best Spitfires around at the time. It was a privilege for our squadron, as we were the only ones to get them that New Year.

Malan, the South-African ace with thirty victories under his belt, was the commanding officer of the base and Al Deere, another distinguished aviator, was the Wing Commander – that is to say, he had operational command over the two squadrons that operated out of Biggin Hill, where we had just relieved the Ile de France (340 F.F.) Squadron.

Someone told me why two of the R.A.F.'s most famous pilots had been sent here to command us. On 14 March, above Berk-sur-Mer, 132 and 340 had been engaged at 29,000 feet by the Focke-Wulf 190's of Priller's JG-26. After close combat involving 24 Spitfires and 30 Fw 190's, with an exceptional duration of almost 5 minutes, Wing-Co. Dickie Milne was shot down along with a guest, Wing-Co. Slatters, as well as Commandant Reilhac who had taken over from Schoesing, likewise shot down a few days previously. Three pilots were also reported missing. This was once again the work of JG-26, Gruppe II of which was commanded by 'Wutz' Galland, the younger brother of Adolf Galland. Our Spitfire IX-B's were in reality LF IX-C's with a Rolls-Royce Merlin 63-A engine that was greatly superior to the IX HF Rolls-Royce 61. This model allowed us to confront the latest Fw 190's of JG-26 and JG-2, who were to be our direct adversaries, below 25,000 feet. The IX-B's had a 28 m.p.h. advantage at maximum speed over the IX-A's and they also climbed better above 16,000 feet. The guns were heated so they no longer froze up and the

Bendix Stromberg carburettor prevented them from cutting out at inopportune moments. In short, they were magnificent combat machines.

In mid-April, we learned that Gruppen I and II of JG-2 'Richthofen' under the command of another great Luftwaffe ace, Major Walter Oesau, were leaving the Parisian region and setting up in Triqueville, right in the middle of our habitual hunting ground. The R.A.F. decided to take care of them at the earliest opportunity.

The bombing of the Amiens Glissy aerodrome by the B-17's of the 8th U.S. Air Force had been a complete failure – only two bombs out of 160 dropped fell on the runway and a herd of cows in a neighbouring field was obliterated. This time Triqueville was the target, but there would only be a low altitude fighter sweep. Oesau could not be expected to tolerate the sight of Spitfires flying insolently around his base.

Places on such a rare and ideal pure fighter mission were highly prized. Luckily, several candidates had had leave the previous afternoon and had been in London, returning in the small hours kicking up a great racket – they had been urged to stay in bed. Consequently, before I had the time to start canvassing for a place, Martell said to me,

'Don't start kicking up a fuss, mon petit Clo-Clo, you'll be my No. 2 and mind you cover me well as things are going to get hot!'

The briefing was simple – it was not the great mission expected – and very quickly carried out. Al Deere, code name Brutus, would command the affair at the head of 611 Squadron, and in case of any hitches Mouchotte would take over. 611 Squadron would attack by hedgehopping and firing on the Fw's that were parked or taking off. There would be just a single sweep and then we would head for maximum altitude as quickly and as far away as possible in order to take part in any possible combat if German reinforcements should appear. Meanwhile, 341 'Alsace' Squadron would patrol the south of the terrain at 3,000 feet to protect 611 just in case III Gruppen of JG-2 based in Évreux-Fauville, barely a few minutes' flight away, became involved. If this were to happen, it would quickly turn into a very dangerous hedgehopping shambles.

As I got into my plane, I was both nervous and excited at the thought of perhaps scoring my first victory. The idea that I might be killed during one of my first missions did not even cross my mind. My engineer, chamois leather and bottle of Clairol in hand, gave my hood and windshield a last polish. When I tightened the strap of my helmet and adjusted my headset, I suddenly found myself isolated from the rest of the world. I could no longer hear the put-putting of the engines that were starting up. Mine was running softly and regularly.

Forty minutes later, we crossed the coast between Dieppe and Saint-Valéry, at full throttle, just above the beach. A few sprays of 37 were the only signs of flak. Mouchotte gave the order, 'Open up, drop babies.' Hardly had we got back up to altitude than the calm voice of Mouchotte, who was observing the enemy aerodrome, announced, 'Brutus, there are planes taxiing on the ground at the end of the runway.' I glanced down and distinctly saw the first Focke-Wulfs taking off, their cockpits shining in the sunlight and the flares fired by the control tower to protect their pilots from danger. 611 Squadron emerged a minute or two later, but at least twenty Fw's had already taken off and were spiralling upwards. 611's Spitfires joined the mêlée and after a few seconds there was a fine old muddle of friendly and enemy planes above the big corrugated-iron hangars covered in camouflage tarpaulins.

Fascinated by the spectacle, we failed to notice the Focke-Wulfs of III Gruppen from Évreux arriving to the rescue. Fortunately, the ever-vigilant Bordas spotted them. Martell called, 'Turban Yellow break,' before Mouchotte could react. Breathless, turning desperately on the edge of blacking out, neck contorted by centrifugal force, I saw a Focke-Wulf opening fire on me, approaching fast, but failing to stay within my turning circle. Its tracers sprayed in luminous rain not far from my wing tips. Two Fw's joined it and homed in on me. Swallowing my pride I called for help, 'Turban Yellow One, Two calling, help!' The only response I received was a curt, 'Shut up.' The Fw 190 had gained so much on me in those few eternal seconds, that I distinctly saw the black eagle painted on its fuselage and yellow propeller spinner. I don't know why, but at that moment the Fw rolled to the left and slid under me before I could reverse my turn. Taking advantage of the speed he had acquired, he pulled up vertically, turned, and headed straight back towards me, skimming my plane and flying off accompanied by his wing-man just above the trees 3,000 feet below! The brawl was at its height when Al Deere, with an eye on his fuel gauges, gave the order to all the Turbans and Brutuses to break and rejoin the rendezvous point in Fécamp.

Mouchotte decided to take 341 back to Biggin Hill independently and we rejoined Al Deere who landed with 611. We took stock – we had lost two Spitfires when the Évreux Fw's had taken us by surprise. Two Fw's had been brought down. Two each then, but it could have been a different story had the 611 arrived two minutes earlier, surprising the Luftwaffe on the ground. Martell came towards me as I was tidying my parachute, 'So, mon petit Clo-Clo, did I detect a touch of panic?' I was mumbling a reply when Mouchotte who had heard, said to me, 'Don't worry about it, we've all been there in the early days. Sort yourself out, go and have some supper and a beer. It's over for today. Have a rest afterwards and we'll see each other again tomorrow morning!'

MY FIRST BIG SHOW OVER FRANCE

We were still 'in readiness'. All was calm in the Biggin Hill sector and the morning wore slowly on. Wrapped in blankets, the mechanics lay drowsily under the dew-covered wings of the Spitfires.

Time was hard to kill. In a corner of the Dispersal hut a gramophone was grinding out an old favourite, while Martell, Mailfert, Girardon, Laurent, Bruno, Gallet and I played a desultory game of Monopoly. Outside under the window, Jacques and Marquis, covered with grease, were fitting an enormous engine to a motor-cycle frame which they had dug up God knows where.

The telephone rang. Everyone looked up, with tense faces.

'Early lunch for pilots. There's a show on!' shouted the orderly from the booth. A very important sweep must have been laid on for early afternoon and the mess was preparing a special early lunch for the pilots taking part. Mouchotte had been warned and arrived at once, together with Boudier.

'Martell, detail your section, you provide Red 2 and Boubou will provide Red 3 and 4.'

We crowded round the board, studded with twelve nails on which would shortly hang twelve metal Spitfire silhouettes, each bearing a name. The squadron battle order was posted after a few moments' discussion between the two flight commanders.

Cdt. Mouchotte.

Lt. Boudier.	Sgt. Ch. Bruno.	Lt. Martell.
Sgt. Remlinger.	Lt. Pabiot.	Sgt. Clostermann.
S-Lt. Bouguen.	S-Lt. De Bordas.	Lt. Béraud.
Sgt. Marquis.		Sgt. Mathey.

Reserve: Sgt. Ch. Gallet.

Those left out muttered restlessly among themselves.

Rendezvous in the Intelligence Room at 1230 hours. Mouchotte went off in his Hillman utility with Martell and Boudier, while the other pilots piled into the mess truck. Quick meal with the pilots of 611; soup, sausages and mash. You could feel a certain apprehension in the air all the same. For most of us this was our first big operational flight, and it would probably take us far inside the enemy zone.

I felt very nervous. I was curious, and anxious at the same time, to know how I would react in the face of danger, a rather morbid wish to know what fear felt like – real fear, the fear of man, alone, face to face with death. And yet there remains deeply rooted, the old scepticism of the civilised human being; the routine of work, travel in comfort, the humanities, city life – all this, in truth, leaves very little room for a realisation of mortal danger or for any testing of purely physical courage. However, I would have liked to get right inside the mind of that Canadian from 611 Squadron, whose first operational flight this was far from being. He calmly asked the W.A.A.F. waitress for a second helping of mashed potatoes, while I was having difficulty in swallowing my first. And Dixon and Bruno, discussing football without pause, what were they thinking about, deep down?

It was at that moment, by association of ideas, that a certain Thursday at the Croix Catelan came back to me. I was keeping goal for my school football eleven, Notre Dame de Boulogne. The Albert de Mun centre-forward, a hefty chap who must have weighed at least 12 stone, had caught our backs off their guard and slipped past them. There was only one way of preserving my goal intact: to dive at his feet. Instinctively, I hurled myself forward with arms outstretched. Then, a fraction of a second before getting my hands to the ball, I twisted sideways. I was frightened of getting hurt by the studs on my opponent's boots. I was frightened, and the goal was duly scored. Ought I to be dreading a purely physical reaction of the same kind this afternoon? This sudden glimpse into the past finally killed my appetite.

It was 12.35.

'Come on chaps. Briefing!'

We moved in small silent groups towards the Intelligence Room. First, a room cluttered up with photos, maps, easy chairs, technical papers and confidential Air Ministry publications. In a corner a small low door gave access to the briefing room down a few steps. The atmosphere caught you by the throat the moment you put your foot inside the door. The first thing you saw was the big map of our sector of operations, completely covering the wall behind the platform; south-east England, London, the Thames, the Channel, the North Sea, Holland, Belgium, and France as far west as Cherbourg. On the map a red ribbon joined Biggin Hill to Amiens, turned back through Saint-Pol, and returned via Boulogne to Dungeness – our route for the day's sortie.

The pilots pushed in and found themselves somewhere to sit, amid the muffled stamping of flying boots and the scratching of matches. Smoke began to curl up from cigarettes held in nervous fingers. From the ceiling hung models of Allied and German aircraft. On the walls were pinned photos of Focke-Wulfs and Messerschmitt 109's taken from every angle, with diagrams giving the corresponding aiming deflections. The vital battle slogans were posted everywhere.

'The Hun is always in the sun.'

'Wait to shoot till you see the whites of his eyes.'

'Never go after a Jerry you have hit. Another will get you for certain.'

'It's better to come back with a probable than to be shot down with the one you've confirmed.'

'Look out! It's the one you don't see who gets you.'

'Don't dream about your popsie. If you don't see the Hun who is going to get your mate, you are a criminal.'

'Silence on the radio. Don't jam your RT channel!'

'If you are brought down over enemy territory, escape. If you are caught, keep your trap shut.'

The navy-blue French uniforms stood out among the blue-grey battledress of the British and Canadians, but the same hearts beat beneath them all. A sound of brakes was heard outside. Doors banged. Everyone got up noisily. Group Captain Malan, D.S.O., D.F.C., and Wing Commanders Al Deere and De La Torre came in, followed by Mouchotte and Jack Charles, O.C. 485 Squadron. Malan leaned against the wall in a corner, De La Torre and Al Deere went up on the platform.

'Sit down, chaps,' said De La Torre. Silence. He started to read Form D in his monotonous voice:

'This afternoon the Wing is taking part in Circus No. 87. H hour is 1355 hours. Seventy-two Flying Fortresses will bomb Amiens Glissy airfield.

'Close escort will be provided at 16,000 feet, by 7 Wings, i.e. 14 squadrons of Spitfire V's. The Wing from Kenley will provide advanced support and will operate at 20,000 feet in the vicinity of the target at H hours minus 5 minutes. Medium cover will be assured by 24 Spitfire IX's from West Malling and the 2 Wings of Spitfire IX's from Northolt will provide top cover at 29,000 feet.

'Two diversions have been laid on: 12 Typhoons escorted by 24 Spitfires will dive-bomb Poix airfield at H minus 20 minutes, i.e. at 1335 hours. Twelve Bostons escorted by 36 Spitfires will bomb the docks at

Dunkirk to H minus 10 minutes, after a feint on Gravelines. The diversions will have the effect of taking the German Radar's attention off the Flying Fortresses while they form up and of dispersing, at least we hope so, the efforts of the enemy fighters.

'The Biggin Hill Wing is to operate in the region of Amiens from H plus 5, i.e. 1400 hours, to cover the return of the Forts.

'The order of battle of the Luftwaffe relevant to this operation is as follows: 60 Focke-Wulfs available at Glissy – you'll probably have about 40 of them in the air. One hundred and twenty Messerschmitt 109 F's, and Fw 190's at Saint-Omer and Fort Rouge. You'll probably see a few of them coming back from Dunkirk where the Bostons will have drawn them. The 40 Fw 190's from Poix, stirred up by the Typhoons, will probably be the first to intervene over Amiens, but by the time you get there they will already have had a bone to pick with the escort proper. It seems probable that your immediate opponents will be the 60 Fw's from Rosière en Santerre, those from Glissy if they can get into the air before the bombing attack and, inevitably, your old friends the Abbeville Boys, whom you will be glad to see again.

'You will be controlled over the objective by Appledore, on frequency C, call-sign Grass Seed. Zona will control you on B up to that time. You will be the only formation on frequency C, so no interference to worry about.

'I am now going to hand over to Wing Commander Deere, who is going to lead the show.'

In a calm, measured voice, contrasting with his tough and dare-devil appearance, Al Deere gave us our final flying instructions:

'I shall lead 485 Squadron, whose call-sign will be Gimlet. My personal call-sign will be Brutus. Rene will lead 341, call-sign Turban. We shall take off in squadron formation from the north-south runway. Start up engines at 1320 hours for Turban and 1322 hours for Gimlet. Take off at 1325 hours. I will orbit base so that you can form up and at 1332 I shall set course.

'We will stay at zero feet until 1350, then we shall climb at full throttle so as to cross the coast at a minimum of 10,000 feet, and we shall rendezvous over Amiens, if all goes well, at 25,000 feet. On the way out Turban will fly 2,000 yards to my right. As soon as we gain height Turban will keep 2,000 feet above us and slightly to the rear. When we reach Amiens we will turn 90° port and steer a course of 047° for 5 minutes, unless Appledore gives us other instructions. In principle we will fly for 25 minutes on our auxiliary tanks. When I give the signal "drop your babies", you will take up battle formation.

'Absolute RT silence is compulsory until I give that signal. We are going to fly at sea level for 18 disagreeable minutes, so as not to be picked up by the German Radar – we can't have some clot wrecking the whole show by shooting off his mouth unnecessarily. If you have trouble and want to return to base, waggle your wings, pass over on to D frequency, but don't use it unless you are really in serious trouble. Otherwise, for Christ's sake, keep your trap shut.

'Now a final bit of advice. If your drop-tank doesn't come off, warn your leader and go home. It's useless trying to go on with that extra drag. You'll either handicap everyone else or you'll lag behind and be shot down as sure as fate.

'Give clear indications of the whereabouts of suspicious aircraft in relation to me by means of the clock code,* speaking slowly and clearly and giving your call-sign. If there's a scrap, keep together, and if things get very sticky, keep in pairs at least, that's essential. No. 2's must never forget that they are responsible for covering their No. 1. Always break towards the enemy. And mind your oxygen.

'If things go wrong, the direct course home is 317°. If you are lost somewhere over France and short of petrol, call Zona on frequency B. If you are more than halfway back across the Channel and in difficulties, but capable of getting back to base, warn Tramline on frequency A. If you can't get back to the coast, bale out after calling "May Day" on frequency D with, if possible, a transmission for a fix. As always, everything possible will be done to fish you out quickly.

'Don't forget to switch on your I.F.F.† as soon as you take off, and check your sights. Empty your pockets properly.

'Synchronise your watches; it is exactly 12 hours 51 minutes 30 seconds ... one ... two ... three ... it is 12 hours 52 minutes zero seconds. Keep your eyes open, and good luck!'

While Deere was speaking, the pilots had been scribbling the essential gen straight on to the skin of the backs of their hands: times, homing course, radio frequencies, etc. Then a rush for the door and the waggons.

The weather was superb, and for three days the sun had been unusually bright for the time of year. At the Dispersal everyone made a bee-line for his locker. I carefully emptied my pockets – no revealing bus tickets must be left, no addressed envelopes which might give away my airfield to the Hun. I took off my collar and tie and put on a silk scarf instead. I drew the thick white regulation pullover over a sheepskin waistcoat. I pulled on over my socks thick woollen stockings up to my thighs. Then on top of

---

* The clock code – normal way in the Services of indicating position relative to oneself. 12 o'clock is straight in front, 6 o'clock is behind, 5 o'clock is behind and slightly to the right, and so on.

† Identification Friend or Foe.

those my fleece-lined boots, tucking in my trousers. I slipped my hunting knife into the left boot, my maps into the right. I loaded my Smith and Wesson service revolver and passed the lanyard round my neck. In the pockets of my Mae West were my 'escape kit' and my emergency rations.

My fitter came for my parachute and dinghy, to place them in the seat of the aircraft, together with my helmet, whose earphones and mask the electrician would connect to the radio and the oxygen bottles.

1315 hours. I was already installed, firmly fixed to my Spitfire NL-B by the straps of my safety harness. I had tested the radio, the sight and the camera gun. I had carefully adjusted the oxygen mask and verified the pressure in the bottles. I had armed the cannon and the machine guns and adjusted the rear-vision mirror. Tommy was wandering round the aircraft with a screwdriver, getting the detachable panels firmly fastened. My stomach seemed curiously empty and I was beginning to regret my scanty lunch. People were busy all round the field. In the distance Deere's car stopped by his aircraft, under the control tower. He was wearing a white flying suit and he slipped quickly into his cockpit. The fire crew took up their positions on the running boards of the tender, and the medical orderlies in the ambulance. The hour was approaching.

1319 hours. Deep silence over the airfield. Not a movement anywhere. The pilots had their eyes glued on Mouchotte who was consulting his watch. By each aircraft a fitter stood motionless, his finger on the switch of the auxiliary starter batteries. Another stood guard by the fire extinguishers lying on the grass at the ready. My parachute buckle was badly placed and was torturing me, but it was too late to adjust it.

1320 hours. Mouchotte glanced round the twelve Spitfires, then began to manipulate his pumps. A rasping rattle from the starter, then his propeller began to turn. Feverishly I switched on.

'All clear? – switches ON!'

Kept in perfect trim, my Rolls-Royce engine started first shot. The fitters rushed round, removing chocks, dragging batteries away, hanging on to the wing tips to help the aircraft pivot. Mouchotte's NL-L was already taxiing to the northern end of the field.

1322 hours. The engines of 611 were turning and the twelve Spitfires beginning to line up on either side of Deere's in a cloud of dust. We lined up behind them in combat formation. I took up my position, my wing tip almost touching Martell's. I was sweating.

1324 hours. The twenty-six aircraft were all ready, engines ticking over, wings glinting in the sun. The pilots adjusted their goggles and tightened their harness.

1325 hours. A white rocket rose from the control tower. Deere raised his arm and the thirteen aircraft of 611 Squadron started forward. In his turn Mouchotte raised his gloved hand and slowly opened the throttle. Eyes fixed on Martell's wing tip, and my hands moist, I followed. The tails went up, the Spitfires began to bounce clumsily on their narrow under-carriages, the wheels left the ground – we were airborne.

I raised the undercart and locked it, throttled back and adjusted the airscrew pitch. We swept like a whirlwind over the road outside the airfield. A bus had stopped, its passengers crowding at the windows. I switched over to the auxiliary tanks and shut the main tank cocks. Handling the controls clumsily and jerkily, I contrived to keep formation. The Spitfires slipped southward at tree and roof-top level in a thunderous roar which halted people in the streets in their tracks. We jumped a wooded hill, then suddenly we were over the sea, its dirty waves edged with foam and dominated on the left by Beachy Head. A blue hazy line on the horizon must be France. We hurtled forward, a few feet above the water.

Some disconnected impressions remain vividly impressed on my memory – a British coastguard vessel with its crew waving to us; an Air Sea Rescue launch gently rocking with the swell and surrounded by a swarm of seagulls.

Out of the corner of my eye I watched the pressure and temperature – normal. I switched on my reflector sight. One of the 611 aircraft waggled its wings, turned and came back towards England, gaining height. Engine trouble, probably.

1349 hours. Over the radio we could hear in the far distance shouts and calls coming from the close escort squadrons – and suddenly, very distinctly, a triumphant: 'I got him!' I realised with a tightening of the heart that over there they were already fighting.

1350 hours. As one, the twenty-four Spitfires rose and climbed towards the sky, hanging on their propellers, 3,300 feet a minute.

France! A row of white cliffs emerged from the mist and as we gained height the horizon gradually receded – the estuary of the Somme, the narrow strip of sand at the foot of the tree-crowned cliffs, the first meadows, and the first village nestling by a wood in a valley.

Fifteen thousand feet. My engine suddenly cut out and the nose dropped violently. With my heart in my mouth and unable to draw breath I reacted instinctively and at once changed to my main petrol tanks. My auxiliary was empty. Feeling weak about the knees I realised that through lack of experience I had used too much power to keep my position and that my engine had used proportionately more fuel. A second's glide, a splutter, and the engine picked up again. At full throttle I closed up with my section.

'Brutus aircraft, drop your babies!' sounded Deere's clear voice in the earphones. Still considerably shaken, I pulled the handle, hoping to God that the thing would work ... a jerk, a swishing sound, and all our 24 tanks fell, fluttering downwards.

'Hullo, Brutus, Zona calling, go over Channel C Charlie.'

'Hullo, Zona, Brutus answering. Channel C. Over!'

'Hullo, Brutus. Zona out!'

I pressed button C on the V.H.F.* panel. A crackling sound, then the voice of Squadron Leader Holmes, the famous controller of Grass Seed:

'Hullo, Brutus leader, Grass Seed calling. There is plenty going on over target. Steer 096° – zero, nine, six. There are 40 plus bandits 15 miles ahead, angels† 35, over to you!'

'Hullo, Grass Seed. Brutus answering. Steering 096°. Roger out.'

Mouchotte put us in combat formation:

'Hullo, Turban, combat formation, go!'

The three sections of four Spitfires drew apart. Below to my right the Gimlets did the same.

'Brutus aircraft, keep your eyes open!'

We were at 27,000 feet. Five minutes passed. The cloudless sky was so vast and limpid that you felt stunned. You knew that France was there, under the translucent layer of dry mist, which was slightly more opaque over the towns. The cold was painful and breathing difficult. You could feel the sun, but I could not make out whether I was being burnt or frozen by its rays. To rouse myself I turned the oxygen full on. The strident roar of the engine increased the curious sensation of being isolated that one gets in a single-seater fighter. It gradually becomes a sort of noisy but neutral background that ends up by merging into a queer kind of thick, heavy silence.

Still nothing new. I felt both disappointed and relieved. Time seemed to pass very slowly. I felt I was dreaming with my eyes open, lulled by the slow rhythmical rocking movement up and down of the Spitfires in échelon, by the gentle rotation of the propellers through the rarefied and numbing air. Everything seemed so unreal and remote. Was this war?

'Look out, Brutus leader, Grass Seed calling. Three gaggles of 20 plus converging towards you, above!'

Holmes' voice had made me jump. Martell now chimed in:

'Look out, Brutus, Yellow One calling, smoke trails coming 3 o'clock!'

I stared round and suddenly I spotted the tell-tale condensation trails of the Jerries beginning to converge on us from south and east. Christ, how fast they were coming! I released the safety catch of the guns.

---

* Very high frequency.
† Altitude expressed in thousands of feet.

'Brutus calling. Keep your eyes open, chaps. Climb like hell!'

I opened the throttle and changed to fine pitch, and instinctively edged closer to Martell's Spitfire. I felt very alone in a suddenly hostile sky.

'Brutus calling. Open your eyes and prepare to break port. The bastards are right above!'

Three thousand feet above our heads a filigree pattern began to form and you could already distinguish the glint of the slender cross-shaped silhouettes of the German fighters.

'Here they come!' I said to myself, hypnotised. My throat contracted, my toes curled in my boots. I felt as if I were stifling in a strait-jacket, swaddled in all those belts, braces and buckles.

'Turban, break starboard!' yelled Boudier. In a flash I saw the roundels of Martell's Spitfire surge up before me. I banked my aircraft with all my strength, opened the throttle wide, and there I was in his slipstream! Where were the Huns? I dared not look behind me, and I turned desperately, glued to my seat by the centrifugal force, eyes rivetted on Martell turning a hundred yards in front of me.

'Gimlet, attack port!'

I felt lost in the mêlée.

'Turban Yellow Two, break!'

Yellow Two? Why, that was me! With a furious kick on the rudder bar, I broke away, my gorge rising from sheer fear. Red tracers danced past my windshield . . . and suddenly I saw my first Hun! I identified it at once – it was a Focke-Wulf 190. I had not studied the photos and recognition charts so often for nothing.

After firing a burst of tracer at me he bore down on Martell. Yes, it certainly was one – the short wings, the radial engine, the long transparent hood: the square-cut tail plane all in one piece! But what had been missing from the photos was the lively colouring – the pale yellow belly, the greyish green back, the big black crosses outlined with white. The photos gave no hint of the quivering of the wings, the outline elongated and fined down by the speed, the curious nose-down flying attitude.

The sky, which had been filled with hurtling Spitfires, seemed suddenly empty – my No. 1 had disappeared. Never mind, I was not going to lose my Focke-Wulf. I was no longer afraid.

Incoherent pictures were superimposed on my memory – three Focke-Wulfs waggling their wings; tracers criss-crossing; a parachute floating like a puff of smoke in the blue sky.

I huddled up, with the stick hugged to my stomach in both hands, thrown into an endless ascending spiral at full throttle.

'Look out! . . . Attention! . . . Break!' – a medley of shouts in the earphones. I would have liked to recognise a definite order somewhere, or some advice.

Another Focke-Wulf, wings lit up by the blinding flashes of its cannon firing – dirty grey trails from exhausts – white trails from square wing tips. I couldn't make out who or what he was firing at. He flicked – yellow belly, black crosses. He dived and fell like a bullet. Far below he merged into the blurred landscape.

Another one, on a level with me. He turned towards me. Careful now! I must face him!

A quick half roll, and without quite knowing how, I found myself on my back, finger on firing button, shaken to the marrow of my bones by the roar of my flame-spitting cannon. All my faculties, all my being, were focused on one single thought: I MUST KEEP HIM IN MY SIGHTS.

What about deflection? – not enough. I must tighten my turn! More ... more still ... more still! No good. He had gone, but my finger was still convulsively pressed on the button. I was firing at emptiness.

Where was he? I began to panic. Beware, 'the Hun you haven't seen is the one who gets you!' I could feel the disordered thumping of my heart right down in my stomach, in my clammy temples, in my knees.

There he was again – but a long way away. He dived, I fired again – missed him! Out of range. Raging, I persisted ... one last burst ... my Spitfire quivered, but the Focke-Wulf was faster and disappeared unscathed into the mist.

The sky had emptied as if by magic. Not one plane left. I was absolutely alone.

A glance at the petrol – 35 gallons. Time to get back. It was scarcely a quarter past two.

'Hullo, Turban, Yellow Two. Yellow One calling. Are you all right?' It was Martell's voice from very far away.

'Hullo, Yellow One, Turban Yellow Two answering. Am O.K. and going home.'

I set course 320° for England, in a shallow dive. A quarter of an hour later I was flying over the yellow sands of Dungeness. I joined the Biggin Hill circuit. Spitfires everywhere, with wheels down. I wormed my way in between two sections and landed.

As I taxied towards Dispersal I saw Tommy, with arms raised, signalling and showing me where to park.

I gave a burst of throttle to clear my engine and switched off. The sudden silence dazed me. How odd to hear voices again undistorted by the radio.

Tommy helped me out of my harness. I jumped to the ground, my legs feeling weak and stiff.

Martell came striding towards me, and caught me round the neck. 'Good old Clo-Clo! We really thought you had had it!'

We went over to join the group by the door round Mouchotte.

'Hey, Clo-Clo, seen anything of Béraud?'

Béraud, it appeared, must have been shot down.

Bouguen's aircraft had been hit by two 20 mm. shells. 485 Squadron had brought down two Focke-Wulfs. Mouchotte and Boudier had severely damaged one each.

I was now voluble and excited. I told my tale, I felt light-hearted, as if a great weight had been lifted from me. I had done my first big sweep over France and I had come back!

That evening, in the mess, I felt on top of the world.

Another day. Briefing after lunch. Take-off at 1525 hours. Escort of American Maraudeur B-26's which were once again to bomb Triqueville aerodrome, where two squadrons of Messerschmitt 109's and Focke-Wulf 190's were theoretically hidden. Not far away, in Évreux-Fauville, there were two other *Gruppen* of the same Geschwader, but equipped only with Focke-Wulf 190's. It was the latter of these we needed to be particularly wary, apparently. As usual I was Martell's No. 2, which by no means meant an easy ride! Barely were we above France than confusion crackled on the radio,

'Zona, Zona, Soda Yellow Four calling, homing please, homing please!'

'Shut up you clot. Steer three three oh. Zona is on channel D.'

Somewhere in the sky, some poor, confused lost soul on our channel C was brutally called to order by Soda Leader. He had forgotten that at this distance he needed to be at an altitude of at least 30,000 feet for our planes' radio to carry as far as England and that Zona on Channel D could give him a direct steer home.

Shouts and cries had been coming over the radio for 5 minutes. I craned my neck but could see nothing. I was sticking close to Martell. Below, the Yankee B-26's for which we were the high-level cover at 15,000 feet were imperturbable, in impeccable formation amid the explosions and black splinters of the 88's.

No Luftwaffe in our vicinity, unless perhaps very high, engaged in the mêlée of concentric white vapour trails of a spiralling combat.

Mouchotte, ever-prudent, snapped us back to reality, 'O.K. Turban aircrafts, open formation and your eyes!'

Barely had he given the order than, flying vertically, three Focke-Wulfs crossed our squadron like racing cars and disappeared below, into the low mist, without anyone reacting let alone trying to follow them.

In front of us, incongruously, a parachute appeared, swinging gently. Everyone avoided it. I passed within a couple of hundred feet, taking care not to catch him in my slipstream. . . . I didn't have time to get a good look, but the immobile body attached to the strings appeared only to have one leg. I put the aircraft in a side-slip to try and get a better view, but it was already too late. Distracted by what I thought I'd seen, the alert call made me jump, 'Turban watch out! Break!' and twenty-four Spitfires scattered across the sky. Using all my strength I tried to follow Martell as best I could but he pulled up hard, white vapour trails coming from his wing tips and I came close to blacking out. We found ourselves in a whirlwind of Messerschmitt 109's. How many were there? Thirty or forty. They seemed to be everywhere.

Dry-mouthed, I tried to get my breath back, surprised and also frightened in this muddle of friend and foe. This was the shambles typical of this type of combat. Theories on the blackboard, clever tactics, the 'remain grouped at least two by two', etc. all came to nothing within a maximum of 15 seconds – and that was a long time – and then it was every man for himself. Martell was now going like blazes in front of me. I was at full throttle but still unable to catch him.

The brutal jolt of a wake. A Messerschmitt 109 had skimmed too close to me. Watch out for collisions. It would never do for two aeroplanes to crash into each other. It was impossible to make out in the fireball and the resulting rain of unidentifiable debris whether they were ours or Germans – or both, united in death.

I tried to fire on a '109' that I spotted in the chaos. Not possible, I couldn't get the correct angle. My plane juddered on the edge of a stall. It was comforting that the Spitfire turned better than the '109'! Certainly at high speed – but not at low speed.

I had been freezing cold 30 seconds earlier and now I was dripping with sweat and my sunglasses were steaming up. To start with I fired a long burst at an out-of-range '109', obviously without result. Another swerved under my nose, perfectly within my sights, at 90° – I needed to keep him in the outer circle of the gun sight to allow for the angle. He passed too quickly. Snap shot and missed. I was never going to do it! I felt as though I were suffocating in my oxygen mask even though the valve was wide open and my heart was thumping under my parachute buckle. A plane suddenly danced into my rear-vision mirror and threw me into a panic, but it was a Spitfire. . . . Time to get a grip on myself. There was no one else in the sky apart from a few small shining crosses that vanished into the countryside and a cascade of black dots that trickled across the sun, very far away – too far away – to the left, probably Germans going back to their bases.

A Spitfire came up, waggling its wings. NL-T, it was Mailfert. Good, we could go back together, providing some mutual cover.

'Did you open fire?'

'Yes.'

Not another word, particularly in French which was forbidden on the radio – there was no point in attracting attention. We flew towards the coast, going into a dive to get up speed. What had become of the B-26's? I could make out the explosions of a carpet of bombs on what seemed to be an aerodrome in the distance. A glance at the map confirmed that it was not Triqueville, our good allies had made a mistake once again. We would have a laugh about it at the debriefing. Well, in a manner of speaking, for I saw the two vertical streaks of fire and smoke from a pair of B-26's that the flak had just brought down.

We passed the coast leaving Cotentin to the west. By the middle of the Channel we were no longer alone. Two other small groups of three or four Spitfires were heading for England. I had to keep an eye on fuel all the same. I landed gently at Biggin Hill. The typical English high tea – eggs and bacon (the bacon as thin as cigarette paper), tea and toast – the operational meal reserved for pilots returning from a mission. A beer at the bar and to bed. I was very disappointed. There had been a horde of German fighters and I hadn't brought down a single one. I still hadn't found the knack. In thirty missions I had fired a dozen or so times and nothing – not a single victory – it was depressing. On this occasion Mouchotte had brought down a '109', but Radudu, our colleague Raoul D, had disappeared over Le Havre and nobody could say what had happened to him. As always Jacques had the final word, 'It's a mug's game!'

Jacques was quite right. That morning when my mechanic arrived at the Dispersal he said, 'Come and look,' and took me to see my NL-B. To my surprise he showed me two impacts under the fuselage, one of which had only missed one of the controls support struts by a few centimetres. This was particularly surprising as an impact within the resonant box that the fuselage formed would make one hell of a noise. I showed the holes, two entries and two exits, to Martell who commented amiably that if I had followed him more closely it wouldn't have happened – I didn't see why – and he added, 'The reason you didn't hear anything, mon petit Clo-Clo, is that you were squealing like a frightened frog!' A profound thought accompanied by a big slap on the back. Thank you!

FIRST SUCCESSES

The merry month of May in Biggin Hill! When the weather deigned to smile on us in England, it was delightful, and despite the war, the British had continued to grow flowers in their gardens in the picture postcard villages. Light dresses and even the severe uniform skirts of the English girls started to flutter in the gentle breezes. What an evil influence spring exerts over the prudish Albion. . . . Love without any tomorrow!

For us the good weather meant two missions per day and sometimes three. As a result, each of our pilots did at least one mission a day, generally escorting bombers over France or Belgium. As there were very few clouds in the sky in this rather exceptional May, it was necessary to fly very high, at the limit of our operational ceiling, in order not to be too vulnerable. Consequently our sweeps took place at 30,000 feet in pure oxygen, which we found very wearing. Our eyes were ravaged by an implacable sun unfiltered by any clouds, and in the sub-zero temperatures – outside it was minus 50° and inside the cockpit minus 25° – even our tears froze.

On the 17th, we went to meet some Bostons returning from the Parisian region. We found them above Caen. They had taken a drubbing. In their reduced formation of seven over twelve there were gaps, trails of smoke, tattered propellers. As always, they attracted German fighters like bees to a honeypot, and it was while we were taking up our escort position that we suddenly found a couple of dozen Me 109's above us followed by some very aggressive Focke-Wulfs.

As Mouchotte's wing-man, I covered him as much as I could in the spiralling disorder, one eye on him and another on the enemy fighters. There was a call for help – I failed to properly identify the code, but the Commandant, who had understood, banked in the opposite direction and headed towards a 411 Spitfire that was in trouble. He was being engaged by a Messerschmitt that was following barely 60 yards behind him. Mouchotte was quickly on the tail of the '109' and fired in turn. I pulled away to avoid the rain of 20 mm. cartridge cases falling from the guns on his wings. At that moment, as a result of this manoeuvre I saw just below us two Focke-Wulfs climbing vertically towards Mouchotte. . . . I warned him and engaging the emergency boost, I kicked the rudder and stormed head-on towards the two Germans firing. . . . We crossed at over 600 m.p.h. They passed in a rush of wind within a hair's breadth of me, one to the right, another to the left. They were so close I could clearly see every detail of them. God, but the German aircraft were beautiful!

I took my place again to Mouchotte's right at which point the damaged '109' lost its hood – it smashed his tail fin, leaving him in an uncontrolled nose-dive. The 411 pilot managed with great difficulty to drag himself out of his Spitfire which was now on fire. I saw him tumbling downwards. He disappeared and I didn't see his parachute open.

It was over.

The surviving Bostons, although greeted by flak, had crossed the French coast without any problem, and the sky had suddenly emptied of both friends and enemies. I stuck close to Mouchotte who was making gestures with his hands that I could not interpret.

Hardly had we landed than Mouchotte came towards me as I was getting out of my aircraft with my parachute on my back, and put out a hand to help me. 'Clostermann, I was trying to signal thank you at you back there. I hadn't seen them coming.'

What could I say, other than that I had done my job as wing-man?

I then confirmed his Me 109 in writing at the bottom of Mouchotte's report, which would very probably receive official confirmation.

Note: On 17 May, Mouchotte described this fight in his journals published after the war and added, 'Without the presence of mind of my number two who confronted two Focke-Wulf 190's, I would have probably been shot down.'

Another day that smelled of powder. We bolted our lunch.

Briefing at 1430 hours.

That afternoon our objective was the airfield at Triqueville. It was going to be bombed in force by two waves of seventy-two Marauders.

Triqueville, near Le Havre, was the hide-out of one of the best Jerry fighter wings – the famous 'Yellow-Nose' Richthofen outfit. According to our information, they had recently been re-equipped with the latest model Focke-Wulf, the 190 A6, fitted with a more powerful engine and, it was said, flap settings which enabled them to do very tight turns.

All the Richthofen pilots were hand-picked. They were commanded by one of the aces of the German Air Force, Major von Graff, and with their new machines they had specialised – with a good deal of success – in attacks on our day bombers.

Bombing them on the ground and wiping out their airfield had of course already been tried. But every time they had taken off before the attack and landed unperturbed on one of their three satellite fields – Évreux/Fauville, Beaumont-le-Roger, or Saint-André.

This game had gone on for four months and the R.A.F. wanted to finish the business today, especially as the American Marauder H.Q. had given out that they would refuse to fly any more sorties in that sector unless the Richthofen crowd were polished off.

This afternoon, therefore, Triqueville and the other three airfields were going to be bombed simultaneously.

As for us, should the Jerries already be in the air, we were going to intercept them at all costs and teach them a good lesson.

Sure, but there was probably going to be the hell of a scrap.

At Dispersal a disappointment was in store for me – I was not down for the sweep. I made a scene, stamped, shouted it was unfair, made quite an exhibition of myself, in fact. Like a good scout, and also for the sake of peace and quiet, Martell allowed himself to be persuaded and took me as his No. 2.

My bad luck still held. We had scarcely left the English coast behind when my jettison-tank gave out – probably a vapour-lock in the feed pipes.

Damn! I knew perfectly well that this show might take us a long way south of Le Havre, as far as Rouen or Évreux. After the fight – if there was one – I might well be distinctly short of fuel.

To hell with commonsense. I was staying on!

The Channel was covered with mist, but 3,000 feet up the weather was marvellous. No trace of a cloud. Already, halfway between Le Havre and Rouen, you could distinguish under the layer of fog the Seine crawling like a big silver snake.

Breaking the silence, the controller's voice in the radio sounded very excited:

'Hullo, Turban Leader, Donald Duck and his boys are up already and climbing hard. Can't give you very definite information yet!'

Donald Duck was the cover name given to von Graff. Some humourist in the I. Branch must have nicknamed him that because, it appears, he spoke through his nose like his namesake, Walt Disney's creation.

The old bastard was up to all the tricks and knew that the best defence was attack. If we let him slip through our fingers, the Marauders would once again catch a packet!

Mouchotte, leading the wing on this show, was, as usual, perfectly self-possessed:

'O.K. Zona, message received and understood. Turban leader out.' Then for our benefit, 'Turban and Gimlet, open your eyes!'

I noticed with a certain amount of anxiety that Martell, leading our section, was imperceptibly drawing away from the rest of the squadron and beginning to climb. Soon we could only see the rest of the Turbans as bright dots lost in the blue of the sky.

'Come up a bit, Yellow Section!'

Mouchotte, calling us to order, was interrupted by a yell from the Gimlets, flying 3,000 feet above us to the right:

'For Christ's sake break, Gimlet aircraft!'

It was old Donald Duck, who had been waiting for us to pass him, tucked away in the sun with his gaggle of pirates. The 485 boys had nearly fallen for it and it was only by chance that one of the New Zealanders had seen them coming. He had warned them now and they turned to face Donald Duck as he swooped down at 450 m.p.h.

Everything happened in a flash. At the S.O.S. from 485 Mouchotte went into a climbing turn with Red and Blue sections to go and help. So we found ourselves all on our own, 5,000 feet below the main scrap.

Martell made us turn to the left and we climbed to take part in the battle. Suddenly I saw a dozen Focke-Wulfs coming out of the sun straight down on top of us.

'Focke-Wulfs 11 o'clock, Yellow!'

Led by a magnificent Fw 190 A6 painted yellow all over and polished and gleaming like a jewel, the first were already passing on our left, less than a hundred yards away, and turning towards us. I could see, quite distinctly, outlined on their long transparent cockpits, the German pilots crouching forward.

'Come on, Turban Yellow, attack!'

Martell had already dived straight into the enemy formation. Yellow 3 and Yellow 4 immediately lost contact and left us in the middle of a whirlpool of yellow noses and black crosses. This time I did not even have time to feel really frightened. Although my stomach contracted, I could feel a frantic excitement rising within me. This was the real thing, and I lost my head slightly. Without realising it I was giving vent to incoherent Redskin war-whoops and throwing my Spitfire about.

A Focke-Wulf was already breaking away, dragging after him a spiral of black smoke, and Martell, who was not wasting any time, was after the scalp of another. I did my best to play my part and back him up and give him cover, but he was far ahead and I had some difficulty in following his rolls and Immelmann turns.

Two Huns converged insidiously on his tail. I opened fire on them, although they were out of range. I missed them, but made them break off and make for me. Here was my opportunity!

I climbed steeply, did a half roll and, before they could complete the 180° of their turn, there I was – within easy range this time – behind the second one. A slight pressure on the rudder and I had him in my sights. I could scarcely believe my eyes, only a simple deflection necessary, at less than 200 yards range. Quickly I squeezed the firing button. Whoopee! Flashes all over his fuselage. My first burst had struck home and no mistake.

The Focke-Wulf caught alight at once. Tongues of flame escaped intermittently from his punctured tanks, licking the fuselage. Here and there incandescent gleams showed through the heavy black smoke surrounding the machine. The German pilot threw his plane into a desperate turn. Two slender white trails formed in the air.

Suddenly, the Focke-Wulf exploded like a grenade. A blinding flash, a black cloud, then debris fluttered round my aircraft. The engine dropped like a ball of fire. One of the wings, torn off in the flames, dropped more slowly, like a dead leaf, showing its pale yellow under-surface and its olive green upper-surface alternately.

I bellowed my joy into the radio, just like a kid:

'Hullo, Yellow One, Turban Yellow Two, I got one, I got one! Jesus, I got one of them!'

The sky was now full of Focke-Wulfs, brushing past me, attacking me on every side in a firework display of tracer bullets. They wouldn't let me go; a succession of frontal attacks, three-quarters rear, right, left, one after the other.

I was beginning to feel dizzy and my arms were aching. I was out of breath too, for manoeuvring at 400 m.p.h. a Spitfire whose controls are stiffened by the speed is pretty exhausting work – especially at 26,000 feet. I felt as if I was stifling in my mask and I turned the oxygen to 'emergency'. All I could feel was a hammering in my damp temples, my wrists and my ankles.

My Spitfire was standing up to it valiantly. We made an integral whole together, like a rider and his well-trained steed, and the engine was giving its utmost. I blessed Rolls-Royce, all the engineers and mechanics who, with loving care, had drawn, constructed and assembled this enormous precision instrument.

Defending myself to the best of my ability, and economising on my ammo., I fired away at any Focke-Wulfe passing within range. Out of the corner of my eye I saw Martell settling the hash of a second Jerry, whose tail plane floated off.

My somewhat crazy manoeuvring brought me immediately above a Focke-Wulf and I promptly dived down on him vertically, without worrying about anything else. I saw his outline getting bigger in my sights, short wings, yellow cowling and fuselage tapering off towards the tail. Through the transparent cockpit I glimpsed the white smudge of the pilot's face turned up towards me.

Two short bursts and I was on the mark. The cockpit flew into fragments and my shells chewed up the fuselage just behind the pilot. Carried away by the speed I was still going straight for him. Instinctively I pushed the stick forward, banged my head horribly against the bullet-proof windshield, but avoided a collision by a hair's breadth.

I pulled brutally out of my dive and saw my Jerry gliding down on his back, a trail of black smoke issuing from the engine. A dark shape detached itself from the fuselage, twirled through the air, followed the aircraft for a space as if tied to it by an invisible string, and then suddenly blossomed forth into a big ochre-coloured parachute, which remained suspended in space while the Focke-Wulf continued its last flight.

I was flabbergasted. I had shot down two Huns! Two Huns! I was at the same time bursting with pride and trembling with supressed jitters, my nerves all jangled.

What about Martell? What had happened to him? He would again think I had left him in the lurch. The sky was empty. Although I was beginning to get used to it, I was again taken by surprise by the phenomenon of this sudden disappearance of every aircraft. The Focke-Wulfs, who had perhaps had enough, were diving towards their base and already merging into the countryside, 10,000 feet below me.

All gone ... except one! Looking up, I could see, far above me, one Spitfire – Martell's, probably – and that notorious yellow Focke-Wulf. It was a fascinating display – the whole gamut of aerobatics; Immelmann turns, flick rolls – the whole shoot. But neither could gain an inch on the other. Suddenly, as if by common accord, they turned and faced each other. It was sheer madness. The Spitfire and the '190' firing with everything they had, charged each other head-on. The first to break would be lost, for he would inevitably expose his machine to the other's fire.

With bated breath I saw, at the moment when the collision seemed imminent, the Focke-Wulf shudder, shaken by the impact of the shells, then all at once disintegrate. The Spitfire, miraculously scatheless, flew through a shower of flaming debris, falling like rain.

Martell and I returned together, but I was very short of juice and had to land at Shoreham to refuel. I was still so excited and overwrought that I nearly pranged on landing. The airfield was very short for a Spitfire IX and I had to brake hard, practically collapsing my undercart.

I taxied up to the bowser near the control tower, switched off and jumped down with a very superior air, as if one could read on my face that I had just shot down two enemy planes.

I could not resist ringing up Biggin Hill from the Watch Office – partly to let them know that I was safe and sound, but mostly for the pleasure of announcing in an off-hand manner (with a covert glance round the people in the office):

'Oh, by the way, I bagged a couple of Focke-Wulfs!'

Slightly childish, perhaps, but not at all disagreeable.

I did my first victory roll over Biggin Hill in almost solemn mood. Martell confirmed my first success. He had seen the Focke-Wulf set on fire. The second would probably be confirmed by the film.

I could not sleep all night and in the Sergeants' mess I bored everybody to tears with the constantly repeated story of my fight.

This show had been a success for the 'Alsace' Squadron. Boudier had brought one Jerry down and Mouchotte and Bruno had fired on one together. Mouchotte, very decently, had awarded it to his No. 2. 485 had brought three down. By a miracle, apart from seven aircraft damaged, we had sustained no losses.

On the evening of 27 July we received a telegram:

'To the Alsace and 485 boys stop nine for nought is pretty good score stop keep it up stop.'

WINSTON CHURCHILL

To complete the picture, we heard over the German radio three days later that Major von Graff, Iron Cross with swords, oak-leaves and diamonds, had been wounded in the course of a heroic combat against an enemy force very superior in numbers!

After this confirmation of Martell's victory over the yellow Focke-Wulf, the poor chap had to stand an impressive number of drinks all round.

Later we learned it was not Graff, but maybe Oesau.

THE THOUSANDTH KILL

Biggin Hill was in a state of high excitement as we were approaching the base's mythical thousandth victory. Biggin Hill, situated to the south of London, en route for London when the Luftwaffe were attacking the capital, already held the record for the number of enemy planes brought down during the Battle of Britain. Great celebrations were planned. Vickers who built the Spitfires, Rolls-Royce who provided the engines and the various other suppliers were throwing themselves into the preparations. Things were moving fast. Cullins of 611 got the 996th on 13 May, Martell the 997th on 14 May and as things were hotting up a lot on the French coast, with daily skirmishes, the jackpot was expected at any time. On the afternoon of 15 May, I was once again Martell's No. 2 when we came upon some thirty Focke-Wulfs in single file, spiralling upwards in order to attack us. 411 Squadron was the first engaged and immediately a Focke-Wulf and a Spitfire dropped in flames. On the radio someone shouted, 'Nine nine eight. Two more to go!' Martell fired and missed a Focke-Wulf that escaped by a hair's breadth. I tried to get it again as it went past, but I missed even though I wasn't badly positioned. Would I manage to score another victory today? Mouchotte crossed us followed by his wing-man, and fired on a Focke-Wulf who banked sharply. At that moment, Jack Charles who commanded the 411 came over the radio, 'I got another one.' And we saw a parachute at the very moment as Mouchotte's adversary literally exploded. This was the 999th and finally the 1,000th.

The aircraft and component manufacturers had hired out the large halls of the Park Hotel for the memorable party. The bash made the front page of the press – honour to the French! There were two orchestras including a band with accordions, sent by the Free French Naval Forces. Vera Lynn, the famous singer and the Windmill Girls, Françoise Rosay, Anna Marly and other artists had all agreed to come. The Canadians sent us half a ton of lobster and the Americans contributed two black chefs who cooked up Southern fried chicken. The Scottish distilleries and the brewers were not to be left out. . . . For these years of deprivation and rationing, this was a most exceptional soirée, without precedent or sequel, alas.

As it was also the baptism of 341 'Alsace', all the big cheeses of the R.A.F. had come – even Archibald Sinclair, the Air Minister, put in an appearance. Mouchotte, always the grand seigneur, did the honours and insisted that Jack Charles be at his side to receive the guests. Corniglion-Molinier, Kessel, Druon and all the bigwigs of Carlton Gardens were there. All the ladies were in evening gowns. Halfway through the evening, the actor Stewart Granger, who was introducing the acts, calling for a moment's silence, asked Corniglion to come up on stage and read two telegrams, one from Churchill congratulating the Biggin Hill squadron and the 'Alsace', the other from De Gaulle addressed to Mouchotte informing him that he was awarded the Order of the Libération.

In the name of the squadron, Mouchotte thanked all those who had contributed to the success of this event that would go down in the history of the war. He announced that the taxi-drivers' union had delegated thirty of its members to wait outside and take the pilots of 411 and 341 'Alsace' back to Biggin Hill without charge at the end of the evening. He added that refreshments had been sent out to them! Thunderous applause brought this memorable night to a close amid some of the most famous press photographers such as Charles Brown, and we French were particularly interested in these since we considered ourselves particularly photogenic in our grand Air Force uniforms, surrounded by attractive girls in evening dresses and the semi-clad Windmill Girls.

THE YANKEES ARRIVE

I was often on readiness with Henri de Bordas. He was one of the 'boys in short trousers'– young men still of school age who had, like Roland de la Poype, joined De Gaulle in June 1940. Jacques had in the meantime been sent to 602 – I was still with the French – so I often flew with 'Poupy' as he was called because of his childish face. He was an excellent pilot.

It was set to be a lovely spring day, but as we were on the British side of the Channel, we could expect a thick morning mist. The 'Alsace' was on release, and those who had not gone to London were still in bed. One pair had to remain on standby just in case, so when I met Mouchotte and Bordas coming out of the mess – they were early risers – and as my funds were still low, I volunteered. Bordas said that he would stay with me, so we hopped on our bicycles and set off for the Dispersal. The engineers were warming up the engines and our parachutes, protected against the drizzle by a canvas, were ready for us to put on – the shoulder straps hanging down so they could be donned very quickly. My helmet with the headset and oxygen mask connected was hanging up over the rear-vision mirror. Everything was ready, so it was possible to have a little snooze in a chair after a cup of tea.

As always, Henri had hardly dropped off and I had only just begun to immerse myself in an enthralling chapter of *Anthony Adverse*, a long book by Hervey Allen, when the loudspeaker broke the trance, 'Turban Red section, scramble now, scramble now!' We dashed outside – oh no, the mist had thickened – the mechanics standing on the wings started up the engines, holding out their hands to help us climb in. As soon as we were in, we made out a green flare. Immediate take-off, right in front of us, wing to wing, position lights lit. One of the advantages of Biggin Hill was that it was big and flat so you could take off in any direction without needing to follow a taxi-way to a runway. As soon as the wheels were retracted, we were in a pea-souper. Radar control made us follow several headings while keeping us at under 1,000 feet then finally gave the order to land. We landed in Z.-Z. (zero visibility) which was always testing.

Henri's instrument flying was very accurate, but all the same we were totally dependent on the goniometer operator and the duty pilot at the end of the runway, who made us cut our engines the moment he heard us pass above him, still in the cloud! We could hardly see the illuminated runway lights.

Bump! Safe and sound on the ground, we drank a cup of tea but immediately there was a new alert, causing us to take off again without time to refuel our planes, though luckily we had only flown previously for 10 minutes. Another Z.-Z., this time in the rain, and the controller made us land once again by the skin of our teeth. . . . Our planes were refuelled on the turnaround and there was another green flare and the ground-crew who ran towards us shouting, 'There are Dorniers over London! Get moving!'

As soon as we were in the air, Bordas commented politely to the controller that he was not keen on circling blindly among the barrage balloons that ringed London. After several long minutes, they ordered us to return. False alarm!

One section of the 611 was then put on stand-by, and we were able to relax a little. Returning to the mess for breakfast, we were cycling along the valley when in a crash of thunder four Dorniers, heading southwards, flew past at full throttle 10 metres above our heads! Ops. told us that it was the famous Fink again, a sly old fox who had survived the 1914–18 war as the Commandant of a Dornier 215 Squadron, who was leading these audacious raids.

At the beginning of April, we were told that the advance American operational fighting group were to spend a month or two at Biggin Hill to find out a little of what went on there. On this side of the Atlantic, the first American fighter groups had been operating in North Africa since the beginning of 1943. They were equipped with P-39 Aircobras, a plane that couldn't really cut the mustard over the Channel and Germany. Other than the pilots who had fought in the Eagle Squadron of the R.A.F. made up of American volunteers, neither the bombers nor the fighters of the U.S. Air Force had any experience of real air combat . . . and this was not something they could learn in school. I remembered what Capitaine Martell had said when taking me into his squadron,

'Mon petit Clo-Clo, the ability to put on a reasonable show of aerobatics doesn't mean you know anything. This is war, so forget everything that you have learnt, fly by instinct, whether your head is up or down, don't look at the horizon, don't give a damn about it. Only one thing counts and that's the enemy plane. It's your artificial horizon and if you think it's 250 yards away, don't kid yourself, it's really 600. When you're just about scared you're going to crash into it, you can start firing, it will still be 200 yards away! This is what you will learn to your cost when, with embarrassment, you watch the machine-gun ciné films that come back from the claims commission, if you haven't been shot down before this point. So if you want to avoid all this, forget what you've been taught and listen to me!' Thank goodness I had listened to him up until now, but how would the Yankees accept the advice of the R.A.F.?

Equipped with the first version P-47 Thunderbolts – known as 'razor backs' because of their narrow backs, and also because they were as fat as pigs – armed at the time only with six machine guns, the 56th Fighter Squadron of the U.S. Air Force made a sensational arrival at our base. Perfect landings in impeccable three by twelve formation. We were given the job of welcoming them as they touched down on the runway that lay adjacent to our Dispersal, to the side of which they were to park their monsters – twice the size of the Spitfires. Their ground personnel had not yet arrived and so it was our mechanics who helped them down. Our Chieffy (R.A.F. Flight Sergeant Engineer) came back to us with his eyes as round as if he had met some Martians. Mouchotte, immaculately dressed as usual and very aristocratic with his elegant bearing and long cigarette-holder, approached our new allies, saluted their commander, recognisable by the white ribbon that fluttered behind his cap (the squadron leaders had blue and red ribbons, as in the famous 1929 film *Dawn Patrol*!), but when he came back towards us he had an expression on his face such as Stanley must have had when he came across the first Pygmies. With their tasselled leather jackets, decorated with multi-coloured studs, their squadron badge painted right across the back, the double revolvers with mother-of-pearl butts and spare bullets on the belt, it wasn't clear whether they were Sioux chieftains or *pistoleros* of the Far West. They were staggered to encounter some Frenchmen, and to top it all, ones that spoke their language. They were, however, very friendly, and after ten minutes the ice was broken. With a screech of wheels, the big boss's Humber drew to a halt, and out got Malan and Al Deere who looked stupefied for a moment by the sight of the new tribe and all the Hollywood commotion. Even their British phlegm was not a match for it.

After a week, our Yankees understood that they were now operating in the big boys' playground. The manoeuvrability of the Spitfire amazed them, but unfortunately one of them had already been killed trying to turn a Spitfire too low in a combat exercise.

We escorted them on their first mission to the Continent. It was difficult to make them understand that they would have to open their formation. We were not on parade, and twelve aeroplanes, three by four, should stretch a distance of more than 1,000 yards and stack up over 600 feet in order to see what was going on around. Luckily, the Luftwaffe stayed in their lair. The German listening service airways must have been completely overwhelmed by the strange version of English spoken by these chatty newcomers to their airways. . . .

When they got back, Mouchotte had to explain to them that radio silence was a matter of life or death.

It must be said that they learnt quickly. Unfortunately, their planes were useless, and they lost three pilots above Saint-Omer in the course of their third mission, despite Al Deere's efforts to come to their aid with 611 Squadron. We were told that new, better armed and higher performance P-47's with more powerful engines were to arrive to replace the 'razor backs'.

Later I became very good friends with 'Gaby' Gabrewski who had scored some thirty victories in his P-47 and finally against the Mig-15 in Korea. He handled that great brute of a Thunderbolt like a bicycle.

A FILM WITH WILLIAM FAULKNER

9 August. A very busy month.

We escorted 24 Marauder U.S. bombing Fort Rouge. The Saint-Omer Focke-Wulfs did not show up.

12 August

Covered 36 Marauder U.S. bombing Poix. The ever-lucky Kenley wing intercepted. We witnessed the fight from a distance.

17 August

Bombing of Poix again, this time by 48 B-17 Fortresses. Flat calm. The Focke-Wulfs of the JG-2 have definitely moved and must have laughed to see the flak bring down three B-17's. The return journey was quite risky as we were low on fuel and night was falling.*

18 August

This morning we had a visit from William Faulkner accompanied by Corniglion-Molinier. The great writer was a big aviation enthusiast. He enlisted in the Royal Canadian Flying Corps in 1917 as a pilot, and one of his best books, *Pylon*, tells the life story of pilots in the closed-circuit races prior to 1940 such as the Thomson Trophy or the Bendix. He chatted with me for a short while, flicking through our log-book that I had illustrated with sketches of events in the life of the 'Alsace'.

That afternoon, Al Deere and Mouchotte talked them through some of the machine-gun ciné films of the 27 July combats, copies of which had

* This was a diversion mission for the first American raid on the Schweinguer of Schweinfurt in order to fool the German fighters. In reality, the JG-2's had moved in the morning towards the north-east and were awaiting the B-17's on their way back from Germany in the dreadful conditions that are already common knowledge.

just arrived. These confirmed, among others, my two victories. The film of the first of my Focke-Wulfs showed the impacts and, what I hadn't noticed, the pilot in the process of bailing out. The second was what one would call a 'lucky strike' because I only got him the first time when I was firing at him vertically from point-blank range. Staggered, I realised that he was little more than 30 or 40 yards away, a hair's breadth at that speed, which was extremely stupid. Once again, the usefulness of films was clear, as you could see things that in the heat of the action you did not register. Once again the pilot bailed out.

Malan turned to me, 'Clostermann, you don't have much future if you keep doing that sort of thing!'

Martell, who was sitting next to him went one step further, 'Nice film, mon petit Clo-Clo, but don't get cocky because if you try another trick like that one for your second Fritz, you're in severe danger of finding yourself in the drink – collisions are inexcusable and flying into a Focke-Wulf is a loser's game!'

As usual he had immediately put me in my place.

These machine-gun ciné films were indispensable for many reasons. First, because people in combat situations were often prey to illusion, and there was nothing like some film footage to put them right. Next to the starboard gun on the Spitfire's wing was mounted a 16 mm. camera, running at 12 images per second and meticulously regulated by micrometric screws. It was set up to centre on the exact point where the aircraft's weapons converged, with the camera operating automatically when the guns were fired. The four machine guns and the two cannons fired from outside the diameter of the propeller, and fire was concentrated, depending on the pilot's preference, 200 or 300 yards in front of the aeroplane. It was this point, where the bullets should hit their target, that was filmed, with a fairly big image field to make allowance for angles of fire of up to 90°.

After the combat, the film was passed image by image through a special projector fixed to a long table – standard installation on all British fighter bases. A graduated copper rail extending from one end of the table to the other made it possible to slide along a rigorously exact 1:72 model of the enemy aircraft, mounted on a swivel, with a protractor showing the angles, all in front of a pivoting screen on which was drawn the circle of the collimator-sights. The model was moved in the illuminated beam of the projector until its shadow coincided exactly with the image on the screen. It was then possible to read the distance of fire on the graduation of a ruler and the protractor would give the angle. The combat report would give a rough indication of the speed at which things had happened, and so it was possible to judge whether the firing correction in relation to the trajectory of travel was good. It was diabolically precise and often the impact of explosive projectiles – machine-gun bullets and A.P. bullets did not always leave visible signs on the target – confirmed what this apparatus had indicated.

The films were also used to identify or even discover new enemy material – guns, targets on the ground, etc. – and this is why throughout the war, attempts were continually being made to improve the cameras. The Tempests had 35 mm. cameras with 36 images a second which gave us good slow motion and good definition. Having said that, for the confirmation of victories, unless there was total destruction, even if fire or explosion were perfectly visible on the image, witnesses or reports from the information service were needed. Sometimes you could press a 'camera only' button to film an enemy falling as you followed him, but this was at your own risk and offered too easy a target to the enemy.

A victory was classed as 'probable' when despite good film footage showing the enemy plane to have been hit and often visibly very damaged without hope of returning to its base, it had not been seen by witnesses or filmed crashing into the ground, or with the pilot jumping out with his parachute. Combats taking place at high altitude often did not provide the opportunity for official confirmation. What's more, it was rare for a pilot to risk following an aeroplane that had been hit in order to obtain ratification, and in any case, it was forbidden to do this. Under the R.A.F. system, a 'probable' was in practice a victory, otherwise it was classed as 'damaged'. The film footage provided the main, indisputable evidence.

Often, the best films did not necessarily mean a victory. Some of my best films showed misses. In 1944, after Normandy, I remember I spent a month at the Catfoss armament training school which was attended only by operational pilots with successful combats already under their belts, and here they showed students' films, by way of example, with commentary by the great 'Sailor' Malan. After showing several of my films that were more or less decent and worthy of official confirmation, Malan said, 'And now I'm going to show you the latest super-production of our brilliant François who demonstrates splendidly how to miss an unmissable plane,' and then my Messerschmitt 109 of 6 July over Normandy filled the screen, shot at from less than a hundred yards, every detail of it visible close up. Before he got away I had fired 120 20-mm. shells and several hundred 7 mm. at him without the shadow of an impact that would have certainly been visible at this close range . . . incredible! Malan then demonstrated, pointing out the trajectory angle of the '109' and the movement of clouds in my very tight vertical bank, that I was side-slipping, and, firing from too close, I skimmed my adversary without touching him. Malan added to my complete confusion, 'You claimed a "damaged", and quite rightly it hasn't been granted.' He consoled me the following day by showing the film of a Focke-Wulf 190 that was classified as 'probable' over Normandy on 2 July, commenting that I should have been granted a 'destroyed'.

Another advantage of the film was its educational aspect. It demonstrated very clearly the most serious error of a fighter pilot (after that of shooting from too far away), namely 'snap shooting' which it was very difficult to resist. This consisted of firing a burst as you flew past an enemy plane in the risky and never-fulfilled hope of hitting him, without trying to get yourself into a good position to fire by manoeuvring. Obviously manoeuvring makes you vulnerable for a few very dangerous seconds. If I had brought down the majority of aeroplanes on which I had fired I would have scored at least a hundred victories but unfortunately I too was inclined to use 'snap shooting' on too many occasions. Once again, the films provided ample evidence of this! By contrast, it was the cameras of Bruce Oliver and Jacques Remlinger, my comrade pilots in 602 Squadron, which provided the evidence that it was really they who had fired on Rommel's car on 17 July 1944.

19 August

Fighter sweep over Le Crotoy. We were pursuing invisible German fighters across the four corners of the sky. Radar control was not working properly.

23 August

34 Marauders bombed Poix again. We preceded them at low altitude – 10,000 feet – in the hopes of surprising the German fighters as they took off. No luck, but loads of flak! A B-26 hit full on to our left was transformed into a cascade of fire that trickled slowly down from the sky. No parachute.

24 August

60 Fortresses over Évreux. This time the Focke-Wulfs of Fauville were ready to defend their lair. A messy combat led us almost as far as the suburbs of Paris and we could see the Eiffel Tower rising up through the haze in the distance. Everyone was shooting randomly in all directions. 611 brought down two Fw's. We managed to cause some damage to two or three and I fired on one from far too far away to do him any great

harm. We returned just in time as fog was coming up over England. As we were short of fuel, there was plenty of moaning over the radio!

'WEATHER RECONNAISSANCE'

That lovely summer of 1943 was definitely not too bad for me despite the missions escorting U.S. bombers that failed to bring out the Luftwaffe. The Focke-Wulfs played a strange game – either they remained obstinately on the ground, camouflaged in a host of small French and Belgian airfields, or they'd suddenly leap into action and you'd have a hundred on your tail!

I was flying every other sweep as Martell's No. 2 and increasingly as Mouchotte's – especially after 17 May, when I had chased the two Fw 190's from Mouchotte's tail that he had failed to spot, involved as he was in firing at another. I hadn't had the time to get myself into a good position then, as they could have brought him down at any moment, so I threw myself on them like a madman, boost engaged and yelling a warning. They took me for a dangerous fool and out of fear of collision reversed their turn in the wink of an eye – ah, the marvellous ailerons of the Focke-Wulf 190 – and abandoned their potential prey. All the same, one of the two had still managed to give me a massive fright by firing on me from immediately behind, miraculously missing from a distance of less than a hundred yards.

25 August

This morning there was a fog you could cut with a knife, a result of the burning sun of that beautiful summer week heating the waterlogged British lawns! No show was planned for the day and we ate our breakfast calmly at 7 a.m. before setting off in small groups for the Dispersal.

As it was 611 who were on 30 minute alert, with a bit of luck we would have a day off. London beckoned for the adventurous souls with money in their pockets, and bed with a sweetheart or a good book for the others.

In fact, barely had a game of Monopoly been set out and some clandestine Poker game started up in a corner, than Ops. phoned at 8.30 a.m. to say, 'Squadron released.'

Relief and whoops of delight. The door of the Dispersal was too narrow for the noisy horde that it spewed out! Mathey and Marquis disappeared with a revving of motor-bikes.

We lived in small huts a few yards from our planes and I went for my bike to go back and change. What to do then? No question of going fishing as it was too late to warn the English friends who owned my favourite river and anyway it was too hot for the trout to bite! The remaining options were London or the Y.M.C.A. library in Bromley South that was well-stocked even with French books.

With one foot on the ground and another on the pedal of my bike, I was surprised when Commandant Mouchotte's small green Hillman stopped next to me.

There was an exchange of salutes.

'Clostermann, have you any particular plans for today?'

And before I had time to reply he added, 'If not, would you like to come with me to do a weather reconnaissance over France?'

Of course I would! And judging by his knowing smile he knew the answer.

'O.K., leave your bike, grab your maps, hop in and come with me to the operations room.'

Weather recce was a euphemism for calming the worries of the R.A.F. command who were not at all keen to see 'rhubarb' missions – too often improvised and untidy – spread out over the length and breadth of France.

As usual, Mouchotte had put a lot of preparation into his part of the business, but when we arrived at Ops. I quickly saw that the authorities had different ideas and objectives for this mission, so unfortunately there was no longer great scope for improvisation. The Commandant gestured at me to sit down and went into the Intelligence Officer's office, returning with him a few minutes later. Carrying a message slip in his hand, he went to the big wall map and called me over.

It was indeed a weather recce in principle but another duty had been tacked on which would restrict our liberty, and the basic attraction of the free mission for which we had been hoping. The I.O. (Intelligence Officer) explained that a train transporting the heavy equipment of a German armoured brigade on the move, had just spent the three preceding nights in the protection of a tunnel in Sommery on the Rouen–Beauvais line. Repairs to the track, that had been damaged by a bombing raid or sabotage, had been carried out, and the French Resistance, it seemed, had passed on the information. The convoy would surely take advantage of the cover provided by the bad weather to set off and travel down to the south out of reach.

I looked for Sommery on the big 1:50,000 map which covered the south of England as far as north London, France, Belgium, Holland, Brittany, the Ruhr, and as far as Paris to the south. I found it at last, in the middle of the square formed by Abbeville, Amiens, Beauvais and Rouen, right in the centre of a hornets' nest! The red marks on the map which represented the dangerous areas of flak and the aerodromes – God knows there were enough of them in that area – were each marked by a white square bearing the number and type of aeroplane and the number of the Luftwaffe unit based there.

Six months previously, there had been much more activity, but several units of Messerschmitt 109's had migrated towards the east and Russia had started to cost the Luftwaffe fairly dear. Nevertheless, there were still plenty of aircraft around, and flown by good pilots, totalling around 300 fighting planes – JG-26, the famous Schlageter of Galland and Oesau, currently commanded by Priller, with its yellow-nosed Fw's, was in this area, in Abbeville. 'Assi' Hahan and JG-2 were in Beaumont-le-Roger. Graff had returned from his adventure on 27 July in Bussac further to the south with JG-52, but several squadrons from this area were still detached in the north.

'So,' said Mouchotte, 'it is a recce on a rather special fixed itinerary. We will cross the French coast a little to the west of Tréport, fly along the Bresle valley which is a good reference for Aumale and, turning there, we will steer 270°. At Neufchâtel, we will turn to the left along the railway as far as Forges where we will find on the right, in the middle of a forest, another railway which will lead us to the hill that the Sommery tunnel passes through. There, just before or just after the tunnel we should find a long train of platform waggons transporting vehicles and particularly tanks. If the convoy is there as expected, call "Appledore" or "Grass Seed" on channel C and use the code "Big Boys". We will then try to immobilise the locomotive to gain time and allow a strike by Typhoons or Hurricane-Rockets if the weather is still bad this afternoon. Otherwise, the Bostons will take over the mission. The plan is to use a Mosquito for the radio relay.'

This was then the real aim of our excursion – verifying the presence of armoured vehicles on the waggons and above all trying to see if there were any new Tiger tanks among them.

I knew the Tiger, but even if I had never seen it in flesh and blood, I knew from Intelligence photos that it was an imposing Panzer. The Mark IV is shorter and set higher up.

As we got back into the car, Mouchotte added,

'Don't waste time firing on them – the 20 mm. won't do a thing against their armour-plating. If you are sure of having identified them, count them and announce briefly to "Appledore" on the radio "Big boys! Big boys!". As they've told us it's a brigade, there should only be ten or twenty Tigers among the armoured vehicles. If, and only if, you are well positioned, try and shoot the locomotive, but please, just one pass and then we must head home. O.K.?

'I'll fly just above the daisies while you stay at 150 feet and if visibility allows then at 300 feet, parallel, to my right, always 30 to 50 feet higher in case of obstacles. Keep an eye on me and another on the air, you never know, there might be a crazy, aggressive Focke-Wulf on the rampage!

'If we are separated after the objective or for any reason, wherever you are in France, steer 330° which will bring you back, and you'll always find a landmark on the British coast. If you're really lost, call ZONA on channel D and they'll bring you in to base. Whatever you do, stay under the ceiling, no instrument flying, and if you can't cross the Surrey hills without risk, land on the first airfield that you find – there are plenty between Plymouth and Manston.'

Mouchotte's briefings were always full and precise to the slightest detail. He preferred to repeat the same things one hundred times. With him, I was fully confident, because he would always ensure that everything had been carefully thought out, the alternatives prepared, the navigation memorised. This was not the flat-out charge of the Light Brigade that it was with Martell. It might well have been less amusing but it was certainly safer.

So, with everything said, we returned to our aeroplanes. I helped Mouchotte carry his parachute to his Spitfire and couldn't help commenting that he looked very tired, his eyes red and dark-ringed.

The previous week when I had been working on illustrating the group's log-book in his office, he had said, 'Once summer is over, I'll take some long leave. The Sinclairs (the Air Minister Sir Archibald and Lady Sinclair) have invited me to their house in Scotland and Martell or Boudier could easily replace me for two or three weeks.'

We took off wing tip to wing tip. The Commandant always had a light touch on the controls and the throttle; this made him easy to follow and it saved fuel.

In this kind of fog, I was always more frightened of the sea than the land, because the low banks of mist meant it was difficult to tell what was sea and what was sky. Crashing at 300 m.p.h. wouldn't give you much chance to get out!

We suddenly flew over a large trail of foam standing out against the bluish-green Channel. Detritus, rubbish and debris of all sorts was bobbing in this wash – probably from a big ship – attracting flocks of seagulls. They were on us before we had time to make any manoeuvre and it was only by a miracle that we passed them. I felt no more than a slight bump and a clump of bloody white feathers must have fallen behind my Spitfire. It was the radiators and the propeller – particularly the fragile blades – that were vulnerable. It was very rare to get away with a breakdown over the sea, and ditching a Spitfire meant guaranteed death 99 per cent. of the time. If you were unlucky enough to experience this, the drill was to turn the 300 m.p.h. speed into altitude without a second's hesitation, jettison the hood, and turn on your back without going into a spin while you still had enough airspeed for the ailerons to be effective. You would then let yourself fall out, immediately pulling on the rip-cord of the parachute, praying for it to open quickly.

Going over the manoeuvre in my head every time I crossed the Channel gave me no pleasure at all. It was always in the middle of the Channel, with the waves rolling just below the wings, that the marvellous sonority of the Rolls-Royce Merlin engine would suddenly take on a worrying tone, even though I knew that it was just the fruit of my imagination fed by apprehension.

Look out! I almost broke the sacrosanct radio silence – a dark, low silhouette with a narrow funnel and a mast loomed out of the fog. We avoided a British trawler that had no business to be in the area by an extremely narrow margin.

Flying over the sea, you should never arrive at full throttle over a convoy because it will always fire immediately at anything that flies. Ops. had guaranteed that there was nothing on our route . . . which was all very well but we could easily have happened upon a pair of German flak ships taking advantage of the fog to move from one continental port to another. Unless you were one of the dangerous maniacs of 91 Squadron, like Maridor or Jaco Andrieux whose job it was to hunt them out, it was better to avoid them. The Royal Navy likewise, because fireworks were always guaranteed whenever anyone went near them.

After 18 minutes crossing, the French coast not far away, we dumped our supplementary tanks. The throbbing zin-zin-zin of the German early-warning radar – the big new Wurzburg in Bruneval without doubt – started coming through our headsets. We were still too low for them to pin-point us exactly but the flak must be waiting for us. The long barrels of the 20 mm. anti-aircraft guns must already have been probing the fog through which we were slipping almost invisibly.

A beach appeared with anti-tank obstacles and a small hotel, with Le Tréport clear to the left. We remained at ground level, veering off to avoid the town and find the Bresle.

And there it was and, more than a stream, it was a string of ponds and marshland. The humidity was certainly not going to improve visibility in the valley, already poor with poplar trees everywhere. We also had to keep a careful eye out for the high-voltage power lines, running from one hill to the next, which could be fatal traps.

The cloud ceiling was barely 150 feet and visibility less than half a mile. We were flying at 340 m.p.h. – very little when it came to spotting, assessing and avoiding an obstacle. I tried hard to climb a bit, but was immediately in the cloud and had to go back down and stick by Mouchotte, making all cross-cover impossible. Luckily the weather meant the Messerschmitts would not be out of bed!

Aumale!

'Turning sharp right.' These were Mouchotte's first words on the radio since taking off. He rolled and slid under me and I turned sharply so as not to lose him from sight. If the Germans had located us – which I doubted – this manoeuvre would make them think we had turned back. Two minutes and 30 seconds from Aumale to Neufchâtel-en-Bray, then we turned left at 180°. Good timing! Sommery was a little over a minute away and we had to find the railway line to the east of the hill through which the tunnel passed. There it was. We crossed the rails at a right angle. Nothing on this side. A risky turn in the cloud and returning on the other side we saw, some 2,000–3,000 yards from the black mouth of the tunnel on the track towards Rouen, the white smoke of a locomotive dissipating into the fog, and the long convoy that it was pulling, snaking out behind, half-hidden by the embankment. It was not going in the direction expected.

Only Mouchotte was in a position to fire on it as he was coming out of a turn. I saw the stream of cartridge cases and the flash of his guns as he fired, and miracle of miracles, the impact of hits on the locomotive and the tender.

I didn't have time to see more because suddenly there was flak. Lights appeared in the middle of the train and others came from the embankment.

Too late to attempt the slightest avoidance manoeuvre, with my head sunk in my shoulders I passed through a dazzling spray of tracer shells and bang! Like a fist going into the pit of my stomach. I was hit by flak for the first time since I had flown in operations, with that terrifying noise of a shell exploding inside the resonant hollow of the wing, the clatter of splinters striking metal and the shock waves of enemy projectiles passing too close for comfort. I suffered a panic attack. How I failed to hit the signal post and control hut that disappeared underneath me, God only knows. I had the luminous imprint of the tracers in my eyes, like a necklace of golden pearls. Between each tracer there were four invisible shells. All the same, as I flew through a clear section in the fog, I managed to spot vehicles on the waggons: three or four enormous forms under tarpaulins in the centre of the convoy. I finally saw a Tiger tank uncovered. It was undeniably a Tiger, its imposing shape hanging over the platform, square, set very low on its broad caterpillar tracks, and its great long gun barrel finishing in a huge muzzle brake.

With a dry throat, I shouted into the radio, 'Appledore, Appledore! Big Boys, Big Boys!' and I heard Mouchotte repeat the message behind me.

From very far away but clear as a bell came the response, 'Appledore answering, message received with thanks!' Because of the V.H.F. range at low altitude, a Mosquito at 30,000 feet in the middle of the Channel had provided the relay.

My engine was still running, temperatures were normal and the controls still responded. It could not have been a serious impact.

But how many tanks had there been? I was incapable of saying, and there was no question of going back to count them. Everything had happened in the space of a few seconds, from which nothing remained but confused images, blurred by the blast of fear in my stomach.

The flak continued. There were tracer projectiles everywhere, in the form of small horizontal bursts that followed me and were then lost as they rippled through the low cloud.

Short of breath, a bitter taste in my mouth, I looked for Mouchotte and a slight clearing in the weather allowed me to gain a little height. I saw the Commandant's Spitfire and, turning to rejoin him, I could make out the locomotive, now stationary and enveloped in black and white smoke while human ants swarmed around on the ballast.

'Turban open up, going home!' Mouchotte said to me.

Little by little, I caught my breath and recovered some semblance of calm. The bursts of 20 mm. shells – surely a 37 mm. had hit me – had turned the leading edge around my left-wing cannon into a pepper pot. The impact must have been on the lower surface of the wing. The Spitfire is solid but even so, this is the place that houses the landing gear and wheels. Could they have suffered damage?

Heading due west took us towards the coast which we crossed at speed over Étretat. Finally the Channel! Luminous tracers ricocheted and disappeared in the sea of oil. It was an automatic flak post on top of the famous cliff that was shooting at us as we went past and accompanied us with little showers of foam until we were out of range. The clusters of cartridge clips from five or six bursts of German 37 mm. scattered in vain behind us. The weather lifted a little in the middle of the Channel and we steered north towards Beachy Head, passing over two French fishing boats whose fishermen gestured wildly and waved a tricolour flag.

Above England, the sun pierced the mist which was dissipating in places and Biggin Hill was the centre of a great pool of sunshine. Once in the circuit, I told Mouchotte that I had been hit and was concerned about my landing gear. He told me to lower it so he could take a look. 'Fly straight and level!' His Spitfire slid under mine, all seemed OK, and I got the green light.

All the same, I landed with care, my right wing low to take the strain off my left landing-gear leg and tyre. Everything was fine – phew!

The Spy (R.A.F. slang for the Intelligence Officer) was waiting for us. Our Chieffy helped Mouchotte get out and I went over to join them. Mouchotte didn't look too good, I was struck by his drawn, pale face, deeply marked by the oxygen mask. He must have seen it in my eyes, 'It's O.K., it's O.K. . . . that was very good, Clostermann.' Always a kind word.

While the I.O. debriefed him, we examined the damage sustained by my plane. We were astonished not to find any impact hole in the wing, but a multitude of tiny holes and cracks. It was a mystery. Was it the self-destruction of a 37 mm. that had exploded at the limit of its range? If the shell had hit me at full force, it would most probably have taken the wing off. Destiny. . . .

The mess telephoned to say there was a hot meal waiting for me if I wanted it.

Tea, sausages, and egg and chips – reheated unfortunately – in a mess that was deserted other than the W.A.A.F. serving, who chatted kindly to me. I managed to eat heartily.

Once again I experienced the sensation of being reborn into a civilised world – in the end, after the tension and stress of my mission, nothing but a slight acidity in the pit of my stomach remained. But I knew that in the future flak would always put the wind up me.

COMMANDANT MOUCHOTTE
FAILS TO RETURN

27 *August 1943*

The third show that day! The heat at Biggin Hill was stifling.

Briefing took place after tea. It was going to be an interesting sweep all right: four waves of 60 Flying Fortresses, each going to bomb a wood south-east of Saint-Omer, at 20 minute intervals. A German armoured division on manoeuvres had been reported there. Our Wing was to provide the sole escort for the first formation of American bombers; i.e. 24 Spitfires in all (12 from 341 Squadron, and 12 from the New Zealand Squadron, No 485).

As an escort, it was a bit thin. The strategists of 11 Group had decided that the Luftwaffe would not in fact have time to concentrate on the first box and that the main scrap would probably be with the second and third waves, which were going to be strongly escorted.

Taking part in the operation would be two squadrons of Spitfire XII's from Tangmere, eight squadrons of Spit VB's and the Hornchurch and Kenley Wings, together with a squadron of Spit VI's – 117 – due to follow directly behind us at high altitude. In addition four Thunderbolt squadrons from the American 8th Air Force were taking part as a strategic reserve.

When we got back from Dispersal the notice board had the final details up. I was Commandant Mouchotte's No. 2. Start up engines at 1803 hours. Take off and set course Hardelot at 1805 hours. There we were to meet the Forts at 18,000 feet at 1840 hours.

My old kite NL-B was by the Commandant's NL-L. Everything was ready, my parachute on the wing, my helmet slung round the control column and my gloves stuffed in between the throttle and the pitch control lever.

I settled in. A last look at the instruments. Tommy stuck his arm into the cockpit to set the camera-gun switch. He checked the runners of the hood. All set: oil temperature 40°C., radiator 10°C., trimmer tabs in position. I tested the sights.

It was close that day and I was stifling, trussed up in my Mae West, my parachute harness and my safety straps.

Commandant Mouchotte was beginning to strap himself in. For the first time since I had known him he had put on his uniform tunic over his white pullover. I heard Pabiot remark on it as he passed.

'Oh!' answered Mouchotte with a laugh. 'You never know. I want to look my best when I make my bow.'

Six o'clock less 2 minutes. I saw his emaciated figure slip into the cockpit and, before putting on his helmet and his oxygen mask, he did a thumbs up and smiled his irresistible friendly and encouraging smile at me.

1803 hours. The engines roared into life one after the other.

In the middle of the Channel I sensed that things were going badly.

'Hurry up, Turban Leader, the Big Boys are about to be engaged!'

Hell! The strategists had boobed. Not only were the Huns reacting, but on top of that the Forts, proverbially late, were 5 minutes early. They were flying desperately round and round in circles between Boulogne and Calais, not daring to commit themselves further south without an escort.

We accelerated, 2,600 revs. and plus 6 boost, and climbed.

At last I spotted the Forts in the distance, in impeccable formation as usual. Nothing abnormal at first sight, except possibly the pyramid of flak rising from Boulogne.

The controller was beginning to get on our nerves:

'Twenty-five Huns, over Abbeville, 15,000 feet, climbing.'

'Thirty plus over Saint-Omer, 20,000 feet, going west.'

'Fifteen plus 10 miles south of Hardelot, no height yet.'

'Forty plus 5 miles from the Big Boys, 25,000 feet, about to engage.'

The whole Luftwaffe was in the air today! Things were going to get warm.

We were almost immediately above Gris-Nez, at 22,000 feet when suddenly I saw the Jerries. About thirty Focke-Wulfs, in line astern, 900 yards above the Forts, were beginning to dive two at a time, and the mass of bombers lit up in a thousand points of fire – German explosive bullets striking, or Colt machine guns firing back. Higher up, lost in the light, you could guess there was a whole swarm of Focke-Wulfs, revealed from time to time by the flash of a wing catching the sun.

Calmly, as if on a training flight, Mouchotte began to give his orders:

'Come up, Gimlet Squadron!' to 485, thus placing them so as to cover us from any attack from the sun.

'Turban and Gimlet, drop your babies!'

We duly switched over to our main tanks and dropped our auxilliary tanks.

All was ready for the battle. With my thumb I released the safety catch of the guns and switched on the sight.

An electric current seemed to animate the whole squadron and the twelve Spitfires began to waggle their wings and swing to left and right restlessly. Everyone kept their eyes open.

The radio started getting jittery:

'Hullo, Turban Leader, 6 aircraft at 9 o'clock above!'

'Hullo, Turban Leader, Yellow One calling, about 10 Focke-Wulfs at 4 o'clock above!'

It was Captain Martell's calm voice. You could feel that he was hugging himself at the prospect of the big scrap coming.

We were now a good 20 miles inside France. To the left and below, the Fortresses were enveloped in a confused mass of Focke-Wulfs – about a hundred of them. So much the worse for them, nothing we could do about it. If it wasn't for us, there would be two hundred. We were keeping the rest at a respectful distance by our presence – but not for long!

'Turban, Red Section, break port!'

The sudden shout in the earphones pierced my eardrums. A glance to the left showed an avalanche of twenty or thirty Fw 190's tumbling down on us out of the sun. The first three were already 900 yards behind me, on my tail.

'Turban Squadron, quick, 180 port, go!'

A Hun opened fire; the tracers passed 15 yards from my wing tips. Decidedly unhealthy. I opened the throttle wide, pulled desperately on the stick to follow Mouchotte who was doing a very tight turn and climbing almost vertically.

I had pulled too hard. The engine cut out for one precious second and I hung there, with my nose in the air, while the first Huns began to flash like thunderbolts in between our sections.

My engine picked up, with a terrific jerk, but too late; I had lost contact with my section, whom I could see 100 yards further up, climbing in a spiral. Couldn't be helped. I did a wide barrel roll, which brought me within 100 yards of a Focke-Wulf at whom I let loose a long burst of 20 mm. with 40° correction.

Missed him!

A tight turn, to break away to the left, and I found myself parallel with two other Huns – two magnificent, brand-new glistening '190's', their cowlings painted red and their big fascinating black crosses standing out on the ochre and olive-green of the fuselage. Whang! Three others passed like lightning a few yards below me, waggling their stubby yellow wings.

Not too good! Up above me it was even worse. I could hear various people shouting over the radio. Captain Martell was handling his section in masterly fashion. Commandant Mouchotte's detached voice was trying to get the two squadrons to join up. There were shouts for help, New Zealanders yelling like demons, a few highly-seasoned Parisian oaths.

I began to struggle like one possessed, twisting and turning in every direction. I blacked out and my oxygen mask, dragged down by the g,* skinned my nose. I practically dislocated my neck keeping an eye on all the frightful jumble of aircraft passing within range.

Suddenly I found myself in a relatively clear bit of sky. Spitfires and Focke-Wulfs swirled all around. Four vertical trails of heavy black smoke that hung in the air without dissipating marked the fatal trajectory of four aircraft, whose debris probably blazed on the ground, scattered in the meadows 27,000 feet below.

Parachutes began to blossom on every side.

Why no reinforcements? What was the controller waiting for? Twenty-four against 200 didn't give us much chance.

Paradoxically, we got along quite well for a time. There were far too many Focke-Wulfs, and they got in one other's way. All the same, our retreat was cut off.

It would have been suicide to fly for more than 3 seconds without a violent turn first one way and then the other. What got me down was that, with so many Huns all round me, I could not shoot a single one down.

At last, an opportunity. Two Spitfires were diving hell for leather after a Focke-Wulf. Unnoticed another Hun slipped onto their tail and fired. I could see the whiffs of smoke from his cannon. Two New Zealanders evidently – lots of guts, but less sense. I tried to warn them:

'Look out, the two Spits following that Hun! Break!'

It was a bit vague, but I hadn't been able to read their markings. I turned quickly, a glance to left and right. I attacked the second Fw 190 from three-quarters rear. Just as I opened fire he saw me and broke right, diving.

I made up my mind I'd get him. The air-speed indicator went up and up – 420, 425 m.p.h. I pressed the firing button and the recoil of the guns made my Spit shudder. The Hun jigged about but I had him well in the sights – 5 degrees correction, range 200 – Bang! Bang! Bang! Bang! I fired in short bursts. Three explosions on the right wing between the fuselage and the black crosses.

* g = centrifugal force, measured in multiples of the force of gravity.

We were now doing over 430 m.p.h. A shell on his cockpit, whose perspex hood flew off and passed within a few feet of my aircraft. I was now gaining on him and went on firing at less than 100 yards. I distinguished the pilot's face turning round, looking like some queer insect with his flying goggles over his eyes.

We levelled out, and the chase went on. I pressed on the multiple button and this time fired all my guns at once – two cannon and four machine guns – to have done with it. Two shells exploded simultaneously just behind the engine and the cockpit belched forth a cloud of black smoke. The pilot disappeared. Slowly the Focke-Wulf turned over on its back. We were only 1,000 feet up. Roads and villages passed below our wings. Flames now gleamed through the smoke – the blow had been mortal. We went on down still further. A church steeple went by on a level with me. I had to throttle right back to avoid getting in front of my Hun. I had exhausted my ammunition and every time I pressed the button I heard nothing but the whistle of compressed air and the breech blocks clanking away.

But I had got him! At appalling speed the Focke-Wulf, still on its back, hit the ground and slid, scattering incandescent fragments everywhere, leaving a trail of blazing fuel, hurtled through two hedges and crashed against a road bank in a dazzling shower of sparks.

Fascinated, I only pulled out in the nick of time to avoid a row of telegraph poles. Climbing up in spirals at full throttle I cast a last look down. The petrol-sodden grass formed a fiery crown round the charred skeleton of the Focke-Wulf and the oily smoke swept by the wind drifted heavily towards the village of Hazebrouck.

But I hadn't finished yet: I had to get back to England. Quickly I pin-pointed my position: I was to the east of the forest bordering Saint-Omer airfield. I began to breathe again, but not for long. Up there the battle still went on. The radio told me that Buiron had shot down a Hun.

A few seconds later I heard, for the last time, Commandant Mouchotte's voice, calling:

'I am alone!'

What a hell of a fight for the Wing Leader – particularly the Biggin Hill leader – to find himself isolated! Where were Red Three and Four?

Things were still going badly above me, as I soon saw. I had just discreetly set course for England when a bunch of Focke-Wulfs decided to take an interest in my poor isolated Spitfire which seemed so ill at ease.

Stick right back, 3,000 revs., plus 20 boost, I climbed desperately, followed by the Fw's – two to the right, two to the left, a few hundred yards away. If I could reach the second stage of my supercharger before being shot down I would diddle them.

Six thousand feet. You need about 2 minutes at full throttle to reach 13,000 feet. In the present circumstances you might just as well have said two centuries.

Twelve thousand five hundred feet – I felt the sweat trickling down the edges of my oxygen mask and my right glove was absolutely sodden.

A roar, and my blower came into action before they could get into firing range. In desperation one of them sent me a burst but without touching me. I now easily drew away from them and was saved for the time being.

On the coast just above Boulogne I succeeded in catching up with four Spitfires in impeccable defensive formation. I drew near cautiously, announcing my presence. I identified them as NL-C, NL-A, NL-S, and NL-D, evidently Yellow Section, and Martell authorised me over the RT to join them.

For five more minutes the Germans went on attacking us. If this went on much longer, we had had it, as we would never have enough fuel to reach the English coast – and the Germans knew it.

Suddenly the sky filled with 'contrails' – a hundred perhaps, in fours, coming from the north. It was the Thunderbolts, at last. Still, better late than never, and they certainly saved our bacon.

The Focke-Wulfs, also short of ammunition and with tanks practically dry, did not insist. They all dived down and disappeared in the rising evening mist.

We landed on the first airfield on the coast – Manston. Chaos reigned supreme there. The Luftwaffe's reaction, in such an unfrequented sector, had disagreeably surprised everyone. Aircraft were simply piling up. A Fortress had crashed in the middle of the runway. The Thunderbolts, disregarding all the rules, were landing cross and down wind. The perimeter of the field was cluttered up with Spitfires, Typhoons and aircraft of every sort waiting for the bowsers. The poor ground-control chaps were rushing about with their yellow flags, firing red Verey lights in all directions, trying to park the aircraft from each flight all together.

We came across a few of our mates. Fifi had stood his Spitfire on its nose properly and it looked pretty comic, with its tail in the air and its propeller buried in the ground.

We counted heads – only ten. Commandant Mouchotte and Sergt. Chef Magrot were missing. We hung on the telephone. Biggin Hill had no information, the controller had lost all trace of Mouchotte, and none of the emergency fields had reported his arrival. Not much hope now, for his tanks must have been empty for the last quarter of an hour at least.

It was a tragic blow, and the world no longer seemed the same.

When we took off to return to Biggin the sun was beginning to slip down to the sea and, on the horizon, low mist hung over the battlefield where we had left two of our comrades.

We landed with navigation lights on, and we could make out a silent group in front of Dispersal. All the personnel of the squadron were there – those who had not flown today, the fitters, Group Captain Malan, Wing Commander Deere, Checketts – anxiously waiting for fresh news, a scrap of information, anything on which to build hope.

Commandant Mouchotte, Croix de Guerre, Compagnon de la Libération, D.F.C. . . . For us he had been the pattern of a leader, just, tolerant, bold and calm in battle, the finest type of Frenchman, inspiring respect whatever the circumstances.

Earlier that year Mouchotte, who had seen me drawing on the walls of our mess a cartoon that came out pretty well (buxom maidens chased by young bucks in Air Force uniforms), had asked me to illustrate the magnificent operations manual that Ida Rubinstein had presented to us and which nowadays is kept in the ante room of the Alsace Fighter Group in Colmar. To colour the drawings I borrowed his five-coloured Waterman propelling pencil every day. This propelling pencil was to play a significant part in events later on.

After the war, in early 1946, the Head of the R.A.F.'s Research and Identification services, Flight Lieutenant Noel Archer, came to see me in Paris and said, 'I have a problem, but I think you can help me. We've recovered from Midlekerque the body of an unknown man who was washed up by the sea 6 September, 1943. He was wearing a navy-blue uniform with four narrow stripes; here's one of his buttons.'

'But it's a Frenchman; this is an Air Force button!'

Several objects found in the pockets had been deposited at the local bank and he showed me the photographs. With a shock, I recognised the well-known propelling pencil, a round cigarette lighter, 'red with gold stripes', that I had often seen in Mouchotte's hands, and his waterproof, eight-day wrist-watch with a date display, stopped at 8.17, 3 September. The force of the waves flinging the body against the rocks had probably broken the mechanism. Mouchotte had always made a point of giving one or two turns to the winder when watches were synchronised at a briefing. Everything indicated that he had plunged into the North Sea, inexplicably far out according to our itineraries of 27 August 1943, but it would need a study of the currents, the chronology of events and the Belgian and German authorities' report of when the body was discovered to explain it. He was wearing only his lifejacket so he must have parachuted down, but why so far away? It was possible he had been feeling ill or faint, due to the terrible state of fatigue that he was in and, semi-conscious, might have let his plane drift almost 125 miles out over the North Sea, jumping instinctively when his Spitfire ran out of fuel and came down. Oddly, the medical report indicated that there was no water in his lungs, thus he was dead before his body drifted towards Belgium.

In his diary, published by his mother after the war, he wrote on 26 August 1943, 'The sweeps continue at a terrible rate. I am awfully tired. I feel worn out. The slightest effort exhausts me, I am desperately in need of rest!'

When a man of Mouchotte's calibre is reduced to writing such things, it is because he is at the end of his tether. What pilot nowadays would be willing to go up twice a day, almost every day, in an unpressurised plane, to an altitude of 30,000 or 40,000 feet in temperatures of minus 50°C, in a freezing cockpit where the temperature rarely exceeded minus 15 or 20°C? And to do this fifty, a hundred or two hundred times!

That was how I learnt the probable fate of Commandant Mouchotte, Compagnon de la Libération. How many of my comrades wound up in sanatoriums, before or after the end of the war, lungs burnt from inhaling the pure oxygen tasting of copper that we had to breathe every day?

RADAR AT DAWN

26 September 1943 – 4 a.m.

I groped my way out of my room, and made for the mess, where a sleepy
W.A.A.F. served me with eggs and bacon. When I came out again the sky
was still dark and a few stars twinkled in the glacial air. I could hear the
roar of an engine over by the Dispersal. Probably the ground crews
warming up my Spit.

On my way down I called in at the Intelligence Room for the final gen
on my mission.

I was to leave on my own on a calibration flight for the Radar stations
which controlled us. From the English coast I had to set a straight course
of 145 degrees, gaining the maximum height meanwhile, which would
bring me over Beauvais at about 33,000 feet. Then I had to come up as far
as Saint-Omer and give in clear over the radio my position in relation to
given landmarks.

My only chance of coming through without any bother was to get a
move on, to dawdle as little as possible on the way, so as to reduce to the
minimum the possibility of interception by an enemy force.

When I took off by the light of the flare-path and began to climb on
my course it was still pitch dark. I could dimly see the vague
phosphorescence of my instruments and the blue flames, punctuated by
red sparks, vomited by my exhausts.

I climbed hard and fast and crossed the English coast at about 22,000
feet. The fog was concentrated in the narrow valleys in long milky trails.
The atmosphere was so calm that I could distinguish in the shadows, over
there in the distance, the smoke of a train near Dungeness, motionless, as
if anchored to the ground. The Channel was but an indistinct opaque
mass with a vague silver hem along the cliffs. Not a cloud anywhere.

I climbed through the darkness embracing the earth towards the now
luminous sky and the dimming stars.

Suddenly, without any transition, I plunged like a diver into full golden
light. The wings of my Spitfire turned crimson. I was so dazzled that I had
to lower my smoked glasses over my eyes. Beyond Holland, far away over

there on the left, the sun emerged like a molten ingot from the inert leaden mass of the North Sea.

Beneath my wings was night – I was alone, 30,000 feet up in the daylight. I was the first to breathe in the warm life of the sun's rays, which pierce the eyeball like arrows. In France, in England, in Belgium, in Holland, in Germany, men were suffering in the night, whilst I, alone in the sky, was the sole possessor of the dawning day – all was mine, the light, the sun; and I thought with calm pride: all this is shining only for me!

Moments such as these compensate for many a sacrifice and many a danger.

I crossed the French coast on a level with Dieppe, and a few minutes later I had arrived over Beauvais. I could vaguely make out the airfield at Beauvais-Tillé and Mont Saint-Adrien surrounded by the forest of Fouquencies.

'Hullo, Dagger 25, Dagger 25, Piper calling. Orbit please, orbit please. A for able!'

A for able was the code-word for Beauvais. Control was ordering me to circle while they calibrated their instruments. It was very cold in spite of the sun and I began to feel drowsy as I mechanically went on flying.

'Hullo, Dagger 25, Piper here, what are your angels?'

The note of urgency perceptible in the controller's voice made me jump. A glance at the altimeter: 30,000 feet.

'Hullo, Piper, Dagger answering, angels X for X-ray.'

Something must be up for the controller himself to ask me to break the compulsory RT silence.

A minute passed.

'Hullo, Dagger 25, Piper here. Steer 090 degrees – zero, nine, zero.'

This time I twigged. There must be a suspicious aircraft somewhere about and the controller wanted to identify me for certain on his radio-location screen. I looked around me, waggled my wings to check on the blind spots – everything seemed quiet enough. If the Hun was above me he would doubtless, in this freezing cold, be leaving a condensation trail.

'Hullo, Dagger 25, Piper calling. Look out, you are being shadowed by a Hun. Look out at 5 o'clock!'

I immediately turned my head in the direction indicated and, sure enough, glimpsed a small brilliant dot slipping into a layer of cirrus cloud. It was too far for me to be able to identify him. If it was a fighter I was going to keep a discreet eye on him, keeping to my course in the meantime so as to make him commit himself. I switched on my reflector sight and released the safety catch of my guns.

Three minutes, and the dot had become a cross, about 2,500 feet immediately above me. At that height it was probably one of the new Messerschmitt 109 G's. He waggled his wings . . . he was going to attack at any moment, thinking I had not seen him. In a trice solitude, poetry, the sun, all vanished. A glance at the temperature and I pushed the prop into fine pitch. All set. Let him try it on!

Another minute crawled by. By dint of staring at my opponent my eyes were watering.

'Here he comes!'

The Hun embarked on a gentle spiral dive, designed to bring him on my tail. He was about 600 yards away and not going too fast, in order to make certain of me.

I opened the throttle flat out and threw my Spitfire into a very steep climbing turn which enabled me to keep my eyes on him and to gain height. Taken by surprise by my manoeuvre, he opened fire, but too late. Instead of the slight 5° deflection he was expecting, I suddenly presented him with a target at 45°. I levelled out and continued my tight turn. The '109' tried to turn inside me, but at that height his short wings got insufficient grip on the rarefied atmosphere and he stalled and went into a spin. Once again the Spitfire's superior manoeuvreability had got me out of the wood.

For one moment I saw the big black crosses of the '109' standing out on the pale blue under-surface of his wings.

The Messerschmitt came out of his spin. But I was already in position, and he knew it, for he started hurling his machine about in an effort to throw off my aim. His speed availed him nothing, however, for I had profited by his previous false move to accelerate and now I had the advantage of height. At 450 yards range I opened fire in short bursts, just touching the button each time. The pilot of the '109' was an old fox all the same, for he shifted his kite about a lot, constantly varying the deflection angle and line of sight.

He knew that my Spitfire turned better and climbed better, and that his only hope was to out-distance me. Suddenly he pushed the stick forward and went into a vertical dive. I passed onto my back and, taking advantage of his regular trajectory, opened fire again. We went down fast, 470 m.p.h., towards Aumale. As I was in line with his tail the firing correction was relatively simple, but I had to hurry – he was gaining on me.

At the second burst three flashes appeared on his fuselage – the impact visibly shook him. I fired again, this time hitting him on a level with the cockpit and the engine. For a fraction of a second my shell bursts seemed to stop the engine. His propeller suddenly stopped dead, then disappeared in a white cloud of glycol bubbling out of the exhausts. Then a more violent explosion at the wing root and a thin black trail mingled with the steam gushing from the perforated cooling system.

It was the end. A tongue of fire appeared below the fuselage, lengthened, licked the tail, and dispersed in incandescent shreds.

We had plunged into the shadows ... a glance at my watch to fix the time of the fight – twelve minutes past five.

As for the Messerschmitt, he had had it. I climbed up again in spirals, watching him. He was now nothing but a vague outline, fluttering pathetically down, shaken at regular intervals – an explosion, a black trail, a white trail, an explosion, a black trail, a white trail.... Now he was a ball of fire rolling slowly towards the forest of Eu, burning away, soon scattered in a shower of flaming debris, extinguished before they reached the ground.

The pilot had not baled out....

'Hullo, Dagger 25, Piper calling, long transmission please. Did you get that Hun?'

'Hullo, Piper, Dagger 25 answering and transmitting for fix.

'Got him all right. One ... two ... three ... four ... I am getting short of juice. May I go home?'

'O.K. Dagger 25. Steer 330 degrees – three, three, zero. Good show!'

The petrol was getting low in my tanks and the sun was climbing on the horizon. This spot was going to get unhealthy. Time I was getting back. I set course for England.

After several days – and especially having viewed my combat film footage which clearly showed the stricken Messerschmitt 109 catch fire – Malan summoned me to his office with Al Deere. He congratulated me on my '109', told me I was a lucky devil and said he hoped my luck would hold. Deere added that with a bit more discipline I had the makings of a very good fighter pilot but that, since Mouchotte's disappearance, it couldn't be within the French squadron. It is this kind of thing that marks out a good commanding officer: they know how to observe! To conclude our interview, he proposed to have me transferred to a squadron of my choice if the Squadron Leader was willing to take me. He gave me an envelope with a short note expressing his good opinion of me. I said that I wanted to join Jacques in 602. Why not?

Dupérier even lent me his own plane, a brand-new IX-B, to go courting the 602, the Scottish 'City of Glasgow' Squadron, who were naturally sympathetic towards the French. They were at Ashford, in an airfield with very primitive facilities. When I flew over, I wasn't thrilled by the planes I saw on the ground: old Spit V's. I couldn't resist giving a demonstration of my flying skills with my modest IX-B. I landed, they asked me to lunch and the Wing Commander Robert 'Bobby' Yule told me they already had two Frenchmen and that one more wouldn't make any difference. He shook my hand, adding that he would send the 83rd Group a message to this effect.

And so, without ceremony, I joined the 602, 125 Wing T.A.F.

PART THREE

Attached to the R.A.F.

'CITY OF GLASGOW' SQUADRON

28 September 1943

It was with rather a heavy heart that I left Biggin Hill and took my leave of the 'Alsace' Squadron, with whom I had fought my first battles and where I had met comrades whose patriotism, dash, and skill in combat made me proud to be a Frenchman.

As the truck passed the guard-room I saw the tricolor floating in front of Dispersal disappear among the trees.

Forewarned by Jacques, I had got rid of most of my kit. All the same, I was as usual cluttered up with suitcases, a parachute bag which seemed filled with lead (that blasted chute and its dinghy seemed to weigh a ton!), my revolver belt and cartridge pouches, my Irvine jacket – I presented a curious sight to the travellers gazing through the windows of their train while I stood on the platform waiting for mine.

At Ashford a lorry picked me up and a few minutes later I entered 125 Airfield.

Jacques introduced me. I met the whole perfect band of pirates of the air who composed 602 'City of Glasgow' Squadron – Scotsmen, Australians, New Zealanders, Canadians, one Belgian, two Frenchmen and a few Englishmen.

The Squadron Leader was an Irishman called Mike Beytagh, with a pink boyish face, a great drinker, a fine pilot and a good commanding officer.

The two flight commanders were both phenomenal types, each in his own way; 'A' Flight Commander had worked his way up in record time from Sergeant to Flight Lieutenant by sheer dash and courage. He was 6 feet 4 inches, as strong as an ox and always wore a gap-toothed grin. His name was Bill Loud. The other, Max Sutherland, was a typical English Public School product, complete with tooth-brush moustache; he was an ex-heavyweight champion of the London police. I was to be in his flight. A nice chap, slightly immature, inclined to be moody, capable of the most mulish obstinacy, as of the most extreme generosity. Nonetheless an excellent pilot, very experienced and as brave as a lion. We were to become fast friends.

After Biggin Hill, with its comforts and its glamorous status of world's premier fighter base, 125 Airfield gave a rather country-cousin impression. But it had an atmosphere of friendliness and jauntiness and of living with no thought for the morrow. 602 had been one of the brightest stars in the Battle of Britain but had been relegated to a secondary position for the two following years. It had then been one of the first units to be transferred to the Tactical Air Force and for some months had been moving up again under the impulse of Beytagh's drive.

The R.A.F. was to provide units to support the invasion of the Continent in close co-operation with the Army. To this end 602, with a dozen other squadrons, had been submitted to an intensive process of preparation: ground-level attack, machine-gunning of tanks, tactical reconnaissance, dive-bombing, etc.

Finally these units had been sent to airfields to complete their training. For four months the pilots had been living under canvas, learning to refuel, rearm and camouflage their aircraft and defend them, Tommy-gun in hand – leading, in fact, a real 'Commando' life.

Operating from fields similar to those which could be constructed in a few hours by the Engineers (two or three meadows joined up into a landing strip by laying steel mesh on the ground), Squadrons 602, 132, 122, 65 and a few others were at the same time participating in the current R.A.F. offensive. Equipped with Spitfire V-D's (technically, L.F.V.'s) with clipped wings, these squadrons carried out close escort missions for Marauders, Mitchells and Bostons.

602 shared Airfield 125 with another Spit unit, 132 'City of Bombay' Squadron, commanded by an old friend, Squadron Leader Colloredo-Mansfield, and an anti-tank Hurricane Squadron, No. 184. The airfield was on the sandy spit of Dungeness, and it was quite a pleasant spot in the glorious September sunshine.

Our tents were set up in an orchard. The atmosphere was delightful, more that of a holiday camp or a picnic than anything else. You could stuff yourself with enormous, sweet, juicy apples by just sticking your arm out through the tent flap. They may not have been quite ripe, but the open air and our youthful digestions allowed us to survive without discomfort. We ate out of doors or, when it rained, in a barn, all the pilots in a crowd together. I had no mess-tin and no 'irons', and so I used Jacques'.

Naturally I bunked in his tent too, shared with a Belgian – Jean Oste – and an absolutely charming Englishman called Jimmy Kelly, who was to become one of my best friends. He used to shout with rage whenever anyone started talking French. We slept on camp beds and we washed in the river – the water was very cold, and so we washed as little as possible.

The great problem was lighting. Candles were too dangerous because of the hay covering the floor. We were provided with storm lanterns from R.A.F. stores, but they never worked. When there were matches, there was no wick. When a wick had been unearthed (usually scrounged from the tent next door), there was no paraffin. When we had finally collected all the necessary and lit up with enormous care, the whole shoot would usually go up in flames, followed by a stampede and a battle with foam extinguishers. The whole tent would get a rocket from the squadron-leader and finally undress by the light of a cigarette lighter or the stars.

In the morning we were awakened by a soldier with a can of boiling hot tea who made such a racket that everybody was up in five seconds, tearing barefoot across the grass, mug in hand. After that we went to fetch water from the river in more or less watertight canvas buckets, washed extremely perfunctorily, slipped on a dirty battle-dress and flying boots, wound a scarf round our necks and galloped off to the mess for eggs and bacon, a cup of coffee, and a slice of bread baked in the farm nearby.

Then a crazy drive round the field in jeeps, as many as twelve precariously clinging onto each, tearing at full speed across the fields, jumping the ditches and crashing through the hedges.

Quickly we removed the camouflage nets from our aircraft, warmed up and checked over the engines, and prepared for the first show of the day.

Such was the daily life in my new squadron.

'Clipped, cropped, clapped' was the magnificent description of the Spitfire V-D invented by that great humourist in the squadron, Tommy Thommerson.

'Clipped' for its clipped wings. In order to increase its speed and its lateral manoeuvreability, the Vickers engineers had reduced the Spitfire's wing span by about four feet by suppressing the wing tips, which rounded off the ellipse of the wing so harmoniously.

'Cropped' for its Merlin 45M engine. It was only a Rolls-Royce Merlin 45 with a supercharger turbine reduced in diameter, allowing the power to be stepped up, below 3,000 feet, from 1,200 h.p. to 1,585 h.p. As the volume of supercharged air was much reduced however, the power curve fell rapidly from 8,000 feet up, until at 12,000 feet it produced only about 500 h.p. On top of that, these engines, artificially pushed up to plus 18 boost, had a very reduced life.

'Clapped' – which is self-explanatory – expressed the general opinion among pilots of the Spitfire V-D. For, though extremely fast at ground or sea level (350 m.p.h. straight and level) they became lumps of lead at

10,000 feet, the height at which we had to operate on our escort missions. The square wings also made them lose the Spit's main advantage, the ability to turn tight.

Our confidence in these machines was only limited – a feeling which was more or less justified by the fact that the airframes had all done about 300 hours and, graver still, the engines 100 to 150 hours. It is not always amusing to cross the Channel there and back twice a day on a single-engined aircraft of this sort! To cap all, the cannon only carried sixty shells each (as against 145 in the Spitfire IX!).

If one remembers that even in 1941 and 1942 Spit V's were easily outclassed by Focke-Wulf 190's, my very qualified enthusiasm can be imagined when Sutherland informed me that we were going to have to carry out another five or six sweeps on Spit V-D's before celebrating the arrival of our brand-new IX-B's.

THE *MUNSTERLAND* BUSINESS

The Germans, in war-time, raised obstinacy to the level of a national virtue. When Providence adds luck to this attribute, certain situations arise which defy logic. The *Munsterland* will certainly go down to posterity as a symbol of Teutonic stubbornness, and of British obstinacy too, if it comes to that.

The *Munsterland* was a fast ultra-modern cargo ship of 10,000 tons equipped with oil-burning turbine engines. She had been surprised in a Central American port by Pearl Harbour and had made for Japan. There she had loaded a precious cargo of rubber and rare metals and had then calmly sailed for Germany again.

Fortune favours the brave, and, by a series of incredible circumstances, she had succeeded in slipping through the air and naval patrols and making Brest. She was immediately photographed and dive-bombed three hours later by 24 Typhoons. Towards 6 p.m. on the same day, 32 strongly escorted Mitchells attacked her, still without appreciable results.

In the course of the night she made for Cherbourg at full speed and was again photographed as soon as she made port. A study of the prints showed that everything was ready for her to be discharged. Three flak ships from Havre and two from Saint-Malo had anchored off the Pelée at dawn and sizeable light and heavy flak units were in position.

Extremely unfavourable meteorological conditions led to the failure of a raid laid on at about eight in the morning.

Without medium bombers it was difficult to cope with a problem of this magnitude. The Beaufighters could not intervene as the layout of Cherbourg harbour did not lend itself to a torpedo attack. The Bostons might at a pinch have tried a low-level bombing attack, but the powers that be could really not send them in to be slaughtered at 250 m.p.h.

The weather was getting worse – rain, fog, low cloud.

At 0845 the flying personnel of the Wing were urgently summoned to the Intelligence Room. 602 and 132 were put at immediate readiness.

First Willie Hickson, in a speech improvised for the occasion, reminded us that the *Munsterland*'s cargo was of vital importance to German industry. The thousands of tons of latex she carried, suitably mixed with the synthetic leuna product, would enable no fewer than twelve armoured divisions to be equipped and maintained for two years. The special metals would be precious for German metallurgists producing jet engines. In addition the Kriegsmarine must not be allowed to get away with the moral fillip of such a flagrant breach of the blockade.

Thirty-six Typhoons equipped with 1,000 lb. delayed action bombs were to force an entry into the bay and try to sink the *Munsterland* or set her on fire.

A special dispensation of Command had bestowed the delightful task of escorting them on 602 and 132 Squadrons. Our role would consist in neutralising the flak ships with cannon and machine-gun fire and then covering the operation against the important German fighter forces massed in the Cotentin peninsula in case of need.

To increase our radius of action the Wing would put down at Ford, where the refuelling of the aircraft had been arranged, and from there we would take off again for the rendezvous with the Typhoons, over Brighton at zero feet.

Wing Commander Yule, prospective leader of the operation, reminded us briefly that flak ships were normally armed with four quadruple automatic 20 mm. mountings, and with four or eight 37 mm. guns, also automatic. The last P.R.U.* photos had revealed, along the mole linking the six forts of the roadstead, at least 90 light flak guns, probably reinforced and very active since our client's arrival.

In principle the two squadrons would split up into six sections of four which would each look after a flak ship, in order to reduce them to silence for the few seconds necessary for the passage of the Typhoons. After that, they were free to take such offensive action against any fighter formations as might be necessary.

Obliging to the end, Command had decided to lay on a special Air Sea Rescue service, the fast launches of which would be strung out between Cherbourg and the British coast along our track.

Even for the most enthusiastic amongst us, this last arrangement looked suspiciously like belated remorse on the part of Command and had a sinister implication which considerably chilled the atmosphere.

The last preparations before we took off were carried out in silence. Only Joe Kestruck made a disillusioned remark to the effect that every time the Navy made a balls of a job, the poor bloody R.A.F. had to clear up the mess. At Ford there was the usual panic about tyre bursts and flat starter batteries. Luckily Yule's long experience of advanced airfields had

* Photographic Reconnaissance Unit.

led to the provision of three reserve aircraft per squadron and at 0950 hours 602 and 132 took off at full strength.

I was flying as Blue 4, next to Jacques who was Blue 3, in Ken Charney's section.

On our way to the rendezvous we passed three Bostons whose task was to scatter, over a stretch of 20 miles towards Cape de la Hague, strips of tin-foil designed to jam the German radar. Thanks to this, and to the mist, we would probably reach the entry to Cherbourg without being picked up too much.

We joined up with the Typhoons at house-top level over Brighton and set off obliquely for Cherbourg, skimming the grey sea.

I loathe flying so low as that with all the paraphernalia of supplementary tanks and cocks. Somewhere or other there is always liable to be an airlock, enough to make the engine cut out for just the fraction of a second necessary to send you slap into the drink at 300 m.p.h.

We flew through belts of opaque mist which forced us to do some very tricky I.F.* a few feet above the sea, which of course we could not see. The Typhoons, in spite of the two 1,000-lb. bombs under their wings, were setting a cracking pace and we had a job to keep up with them.

Obsessed by the idea of seeing the red light on the instrument panel going on (indicating a drop in the petrol pressure to my carburettor), I began to sweat from head to foot. What would it be like when the flak started?

1015 hours. The fog thickened and it started to pelt with rain. Instinctively the sections closed up to preserve visual contact.

Suddenly Yule's calm voice broke the strict RT silence:

'All Bob aircraft drop your babies, open up flat out, target straight ahead in 60 seconds!'

Freed of its tank and drawn by the 1,600 h.p. of its engine, my Spitfire leapt forward and I took up my position 50 yards on Jacques' left and slightly behind him, straining my eyes to see anything in the blasted fog.

'Look out, Yellow Section, flak-ship, 1 o'clock!'

And immediately after Frank Woolley, it was Ken Charney who saw a flak ship, straight in front of us!

'Max Blue attacking 12 o'clock!'

A grey mass rolling in the mist, a squat funnel, raised platforms, a mast bristling with radar aerials – then rapid staccato flashes all along the superstructure. Christ! I released the safety catch, lowered my head and nestled down to be protected by my armour plating. Clusters of green and red tracer bullets started up in every direction. Following Jacques, I went

* I.F. = instrument flying.

slap through the spray of a 37 mm. clips which only just missed me – the salt water blurred my windshield. I was 50 yards from the flak ship. Jacques in front of me was firing; I could see the flashes from his guns and his empties cascading from his wings.

I aimed at the bridge, between the damaged funnel and the mast, and fired a long, furious continuous burst, my finger hard on the button. My shells exploded in the water, rose towards the water line, exploded on the grey black-striped hull, rose higher to the handrails, the sandbags. A wind-scoop crashed down, a jet of steam spurted from somewhere. Twenty yards – two men in navy-blue jerseys hurled themselves flat on their faces – 10 yards – the four barrels of a multiple pom-pom were pointing straight between my eyes – quick – my shells exploded all round it. A loader carrying two full clips capsized into the sea, his legs mown from under him, then the four barrels fired, I could feel the vibration as I passed a bare yard above – then the smack of the steel wire of the aerial wrenched off by my wing as I passed. My wing tip had just about scraped the mast!

Phew! Passed him.

My limbs were shaken by a terrible nervous tremor, my teeth were chattering. Jacques was zigzagging between the spouts raised by the shells. The sea was seething.

Half a dozen belated Typhoons passed to my right like a school of porpoises, bearing down on the hell going on behind the long granite wall of the breakwater.

I skimmed over a fort whose very walls seemed to be belching fire – a curious mixture of crenelated towers, modern concrete casements and Thirty Years' War glacis.

We were now in the middle of the roadstead – an inextricable jumble of trawler masts and rusty wrecks sticking out between the battered quays. The weather seemed to have cleared a little – look out for Jerry fighters! The air was criss-crossed with tracer, lit up by flashes, dotted with black and white puffs of smoke.

The *Munsterland* was there, surrounded by explosions, flames and debris. Her four masts bristling with derricks and her squat funnel well aft emerging from the smoke. The Typhoon attack was in full swing, bombs, exploding all the time with colossal bursts of fire and black clouds of smoke, thickening as they drifted away. A Typhoon vanished into thin air in the explosion of a bomb dropped by one in front. One of the enormous harbour cranes came crashing down like a house of cards.

'Hullo, Bob leader, Kenway calling – there are Hun fighters about, look out!'

What an inferno! I was close to Jacques, who was gaining height in spirals, making for the layer of clouds. Two Typhoons emerged from the cumulus, a few yards from us, and I just stopped myself in time from firing at them. With their massive noses and clipped wings they looked uncannily like Focke-Wulfs.

'Break, Blue 4!'

Jacques broke away violently and his Spitfire flashed past a few yards under my nose, a white plume at each wing tip. To avoid a collision I waited for a fraction of a second and a Focke-Wulf – a real one this time – flashed past, firing with all four cannon. A shell richocheted off my hood. As I went over on my back to get him in my sights, a second Focke-Wulf loomed up in my windshield, head-on, at less than a hundred yards. Its big yellow engine and its apparently slowly turning propeller seemed to fling themselves at me and its wings lit up with the firing of its guns. Bang! stars appeared all over my splintering windshield which became an opaque wall before my eyes. Thunderstruck, I dared not move for fear of a collision. He passed just above me. A stream of oil began to spread all over my hood.

The sky was now alive with aircraft and full of flak bursts. I let fly at another Focke-Wulf and missed. Luckily! . . . it was a Typhoon. Robson was circling with a German fighter. I saw his shells explode in the black cross on the fuselage. The Focke-Wulf slowly turned over, showing its yellow belly, and dived, coughing smoke and flames.

'Good show, Robbie! You got him!'

My oil pressure was disquietingly down. The rain began again and within a few seconds my hood was covered with a soapy film. I slipped into the clouds and set course north on I.F., first warning Jacques and Yule over the radio.

I reached Tangmere as best I could, with my oil pressure at zero and my engine red hot and ready to explode. I had to jettison my hood to see to land.

In this business we had lost two pilots, as did 132. Five Typhoons were destroyed, plus two which came down off Cherbourg and whose pilots were picked up by the launches.

As for the *Munsterland*, although seriously damaged and with part of her cargo on fire, she succeeded two nights later in sneaking as far as Dieppe. She finally got herself sunk off the coast of Holland by a strike of Beaufighters. So we were told!

BALL-BEARINGS AND FLYING
FORTRESSES

When the monthly 'Met' forecasts had come in, the directors of planning on the American staff had decided in extremis to take advantage of the last fine days of the year to bomb Schweinfurt. There, south-east of Bremen, in the heart of Germany, sprawled the enormous ball-bearing factory, the biggest in western Europe. It was a high-priority target.

If the 8th Air Force did not attack on 13 October, at least four long winter months would elapse before as favourable weather conditions occurred again. And in four months that factory would supply ball-bearings for thousands of aero-engines for the Luftwaffe.

It was an extraordinary race against the clock. The whole operation had to be organised inside forty-eight hours. It was no small task to impose absolute secrecy on a hundred airfields, to mobilise nearly 1,300 British and American fighters, to bomb up hundreds of Flying Fortresses and to prepare 10-yard long cartridge belts for each of their thousands of machine guns.

It was the first time, too, that Spitfires were going to fly over Germany. As the Forts would be over enemy territory for more than four hours, a formidable reaction on the part of the enemy fighters was anticipated. The Luftwaffe had about 3,000 Messerschmitts and Focke-Wulfs at its disposal between Belgium and Denmark. The American Air Forces, foreseeing that the Thunderbolts and Mustangs would have too much to do and would get too short of ammunition and fuel to be able to cope by themselves, had asked the R.A.F. for reinforcements.

But Spitfires – fast interceptor fighters – were not designed for long-distance escort duties and had to have special auxiliary tanks to increase their radius of action as far as Germany.

In three days, not an hour over, a Watford factory undertook to manufacture 800 90-gallon tanks. Close on 1,000 workmen worked day and night, and on the 13 October at dawn R.A.F. fitters were fixing them to the bellies of the Spitfires.

At the last minute, just as everyone was all keyed up, there was a counter-order: H-hour for us was put back to the next day at 12 o'clock.

14 October 1943

From 8 a.m. heavily laden Fortresses and Liberators began to take off from 27 airfields. For an hour they circled Hull, forming into four impeccable boxes of 70 machines each, wing tip to wing tip.

At 1040 hours 19 squadrons of Thunderbolts (15 from the 9th A.F. and 4 from the 8th A.F.) set off to join the armada and take up their escort positions, while the Spits turned about.

At 1115 hours 10 squadrons of Lightnings left to protect the big four-engined machines on their final approach to the objective.

The Spitfires – rearmed and refuelled – were due to take off again at about 12 o'clock to cover the return of the whole force, the rendezvous being fixed for 1315 hours at the northern German-Dutch frontier.

The eight Spitfire squadrons earmarked for the operation had massed on four airfields in Norfolk, the nearest point to our objective. The first take-off at 9 a.m. was awkward because the pilots were unaccustomed to the extra weight of their machines. Two Spitfires crashed. A number of others had tyre bursts, some had trouble with their tanks caused by air-locks.

Jacques and I were among the victims. Landing on our flimsy tyres, with 90 gallons of juice under the belly and 150 more in the wings and fuselage was tricky – like landing on eggs, as Jacques put it. Seething with rage, we watched the swarm of Spitfires disappear towards Germany in the morning mist.

The fitters immediately set to work, emptying and checking the tanks, while we slept under the wings, in preparation for the second mission.

At 1145 hours the Spitfire Wings came back and hordes of mechanics, perched on the bowsers, descended upon them to refuel them in record time, while the pilots, lurching on their stiffened legs, ate a sandwich and swallowed a cup of tea. They were surly and not inclined to talk.

Everything had gone off well, quite a lot of flak, but up to the time when they had left their charges – i.e. 1030 hours – not one German fighter had intervened.

A few minutes before 12 o'clock, just as we were settling down in our cockpits, the loudspeakers started blaring:

'Hullo, hullo, Station Commander calling all pilots. The big boys over Germany are being very heavily engaged by overwhelming enemy fighter forces. Squadrons are to take off immediately in order to relieve the present escort. Everything possible is to be done to bring the Fortress

Boys home safe. They've been doing a grand job today. Hurry up, and good luck to all!'

At 1204 hours, 132, 602, 411 and 453 Squadrons took off from Bradwell Bay. Jacques and I flew as 3 and 4 respectively in Yellow Section, led by Sutherland.

1315 hours. 'Attention, Clo-Clo, douze Boches au-dessus, 5 o'clock!' Jacques promptly got called to order by Maxie for talking French: 'Shut up, bloody Frenchman!'

Everybody's nerves were on edge. We had been flying at 30,000 feet in arctic cold for nearly an hour and a half now. All those instrument dials were dancing in confusion in front of my tired eyes – altimeter, artificial horizon, air speed and 'turn and bank' indicators, radiator, oil and cylinder-head temperature gauges, pressure gauges, warning lights – in a jumble of figures and needles.

I was obsessed by that tank weighing down my Spitfire. According to the clock I still had in theory about 7 minutes' worth of juice before I could jettison it. My back hurt, my toes were frozen, my eyes were watering, my nose running – altogether I felt in rotten shape and everything struck me as being in a complete mess.

The weather, which had been so fine till midday, had deteriorated and big banks of cloud and mist rose vertically from the ground like ramparts. Going through one of these big cumulus Jacques and I had lost contact with the rest of the squadron. Now we were lost in this inferno and we stuck frantically together, trying to get to the rendezvous.

But, in fact, we must be past that damned rendezvous, and how on earth could anyone recognise anything in this witches' sabbath of aircraft and clouds? It was quite impossible to pin-point our position. Below on our left the last Frisian Islands were outlines – yellow and arid on the grey sea. Somewhere on the right below the mist must be Emden and the rich canal-bordered pastures of North Holland. Far behind us already, the Zuyder Zee.

Up in the air it was a nightmare. I had never seen anything like it. Clusters of flak appeared from the void and silently hung on the flanks of the clouds. Space brought forth swarms of German fighters – a disquieting example of spontaneous generation.

We passed Lightnings and Mustangs hurrying home with empty magazines, their pilots worn out and dodging between the clouds to avoid combat.

At last, the bombers!

A scene of frightful panic. It was the first time that under the concerted efforts of the flak and the avalanches of Junkers 88's and Messerschmitt

410's armed with rockets, boxes of Fortresses had been broken up, dislocated, reduced to shreds. The big bombers were scattered all over the sky, vainly trying to bunch in threes or fours to cross their fire. The Focke-Wulfs were rushing in for the kill. And how many there were! They appeared from everywhere and, down below, on Dutch airfields, others were preparing to take off.

The Spitfires and the bombers were much too dispersed for an organised plan of defence to be possible. It was a question of everyone for himself and the Devil take the hindmost. The controller's voice in the radio had become so distant that it was imperceptible; without it, without its support and advice, we felt cut off from our world, all alone, naked, unarmed.

It was a miracle that we had not yet been brought down! Twisting and turning, firing off our guns, we had succeeded in gaining quite a lot of height over the main scrap. I had exhausted half my ammunition. I should have to find someone to go home with.

Suddenly Jacques spotted in the middle of the sky dotted with parachutes and burning aircraft about forty Focke-Wulfs pouncing on four Fortresses which were lagging behind trying to protect a Liberator, one of whose engines was in flames.

What could we do? – it was impossible to call for help in this infernal scrum. All the Spitfires, as far as the eye could reach, were whirling about in dog fights and seemed to be banging into the clouds and bouncing off again like boxers against the ropes of the ring. A glance at my petrol gauge. Only 2 minutes' worth left. Never mind, it wouldn't be much loss.

'Hallo, Jack, dropping my baby!'

I stooped down and vigorously pulled on the release, while Jacques kept watch. Freed from the load, my Spitfire bounded forward.

'O.K. Jack, your turn!'

Jacques' tank fluttered down in a shower of petrol.

'Attacking!'

Sights switched on, finger on firing button, together we rolled on our backs and dived on the Focke-Wulfs milling round the bombers. As I dived I kept a look out and tried to choose one. They were attacking from every side – front, side and rear. One of the Fortresses went into a spin, slowly. Another suddenly exploded like a gigantic flak shell, and the explosion tore a wing off the one to its right. A big dark mushroom spread out, incandescent debris dropping from it. The now asymmetrical outline of the Fortress grew smaller and fainter, falling like a dead leaf. Like shining new nails on a wall, one, two, four, six parachutes suddenly dotted the sky.

I passed a few yards from a disabled Focke-Wulf trailing a black veil – no point in wasting ammo., he'd had it.

I had the impression I was diving into an aquarium full of demented fish! Nothing but radial engines, yellow bellies, black crosses, and clipped wings beating the air like fins. The air was criss-crossed with multi-coloured tracer bullets, and instinctively I blinked.

Here we are! I tightened my stomach muscles, put my feet on the top pedal of the rudder bar to resist the centrifugal force, swallowed hard to get the bitter taste out of my mouth and pulled out violently. Before I had time to register, my finger had instinctively pressed the firing button. A burst at the Focke-Wulf, who for one second filled my windshield. Missed him! Surprised, he stalled and fell away. Jacques fired on him and missed him too – but a grey Messerschmitt, its wings edged with fire, was after him. I yelled:

'Look out, Jacques! Break right!'

Quickly, I put all my weight on the controls, the ground whipped round – but too late, the Messerschmitt was out of range. I was drenched in sweat.

In front of me two Focke-Wulfs were converging to attack a Fortress drifting like a wreck. A glance at the mirror: Jacques was there. The red filaments of my sight encircled a green and yellow Focke-Wulf – Jesus, how close he was! The wings of my Spit shuddered from the hammer-blows of my two cannon . . . three flashes, a belch of flame and a grey trail unfurled in his wake!

Then I saw a sheet of flame on the flank of a cloud, just where Jacques' aircraft was at that moment – my heart missed a beat – but it was his triumphant voice shouting in the radio:

'Did you see that, Pierre? I got him!'

Thank God, it was a Focke-Wulf, and out of the corner of my eye I saw his Spit swaying 50 yards away. What a relief.

Suddenly a thunderclap, a burning slap in the face. My eardrums were pierced by the shriek of air through a hole just torn by a shell through my windshield. Bang! another . . . I broke frantically, the Hun was so close that the flash of his guns made me shut my eyes. But Jacques was there, and the Focke-Wulf broke away.

For a time I lost all notion of what was going on. For 10 minutes I blindly followed Jacques' instructions over the radio; when I picked up the thread again we were in the middle of the North Sea. On my right was a Fortress, holed like a sieve but flying all the same, and on my left a red-nosed P-47 limped along.

England at last. Just inland I could make out four crashed Fortresses in the fields.

We landed at Manston after the Fortress, exhausted, drained. We parked by the Thunderbolt. Introductions. The pilot was the commander of a US fighter squadron. It was his last mission, for he was due to be repatriated to the States the week after.

'Jees,' he said, roaring with laughter, 'I hope I get sent on furlough, quick, against the Japs!'

The Schweinfurt factory had been razed to the ground, but out of the 280 Fortresses only about 50 were still airworthy. We had lost more than 100 crews; 197 German fighters had been shot down and 51 of ours.

DISCOVERY OF THE V-I

1 December 1943

I had the impression that the R.A.F. had a flying-bomb complex. Some weeks previously the Germans – with Hitler in the lead – had launched their secret weapons campaign and the neutral press was full of horrific stories of gigantic rockets controlled by radio, capable of carrying 3 tons of explosives 150 miles, etc., etc.

We read the papers and shrugged our shoulders. One fine afternoon, however, all the pilots were called to the Intelligence Room. Willie Hickson, the senior I.O., gloomily unveiled a large-scale map of northern France studded with little numbered flags.

'Gentlemen, the situation is grave!' and he began a by no means reassuring speech in which he outlined the following facts:

Either on the one hand the Hun was trying to bluff us, or, on the other, he had really succeeded in producing these contrivances, and we might very well learn one morning that half London had been pulverised. We were choosing to suppose that it was a bluff. But Air Ministry was taking it seriously and talking of switching our bombing offensive against all these spots marked on the map.

'In two months, the Todt organisation has begun the construction of nearly 200 sites. Not a single one must be allowed to be completed. The 18 you see there – marked by the red flags – where the work is most advanced, will be bombed tomorrow by 1,300 aircraft. We shall continue until they are all wiped out. Now, one last warning, the severest penalties will be imposed on the first one of you who mentions these facts to anyone at all. The public must not be given a chance to panic.'

The No-balls – that was the cover name given to these sites – multiplied like mushrooms: the more were demolished the more cropped up again. If it really was a bluff the Germans must have been having a good laugh.

Gradually, every type of aircraft was mobilised and thrown against the 'rocket coast' as the coast from Boulogne to Cherbourg came to be called. 184 Squadron with its old Hurricanes was soon sent into the fray. With their four 60 lb. rockets the miserable machines dragged along at 200 m.p.h. Exceptional nerve was needed to go and try conclusions with the German flak at ground level and at that speed.

With childish levity and spite we poked fun at the pilots and their misgivings. These were all the more comprehensible as they were beginning to receive their new Typhoons and it was really a bit hard for them to get shot down just as their dreams were about to be realised.

We didn't laugh long at their expense, anyway. On 4 December, eight Hurricanes had just crossed the French coast when ten Messerschmitt 109 G's attacked them. 184, Squadron Leader Rose at their head, defended themselves tooth and nail. Weighed down by their bombs and with only two 7.7 mm. against the Germans three 20 mm. and two 13 mm. the Hurricanes hadn't much hope of coming through. Six were brought down and the other two crashed on landing, their pilots both seriously wounded by enemy bullets. And we laughed quite on the other side of our faces when it was decided that in future the Hurricanes would be escorted at ground level by Spitfires.

15 December 1943

There was a mist and the damp clouds scraped the tree-tops. At least we would get some rest that day.

Sitting in front of bacon and eggs and several slices of toast done to a turn and dripping with margarine, I was having breakfast in the mess, at the same time arranging the programme for the day. There would certainly be a 'general release', I would have a hot bath, then, after lunch, Jacques and I would go – if his car had not fallen to pieces – to Maidstone. After a flick we would dine at the Star and, after a round of drinks, come back to bed.

'Hallo! hallo!' Damn! that blasted loudspeaker again. 'Operations calling. Will the following pilots of 602 Squadron report to Intelligence immediately!' Seething, I heard my name among the eight called. I gulped down my cup of coffee, spread a double layer of marmalade on my last piece of toast and scrammed. At Intelligence I found I was the last to arrive. Everyone else was already there and seeing their long faces I soon caught on.

'Surely those G.C.C.* types can't expect us to fly on a day like this!'

I noticed that eight pilots from 184 were there. All was now clear. One of those escorts we had been hearing about. Delightful!

The I.O. explained our mission on the map. The eight Hurricanes were to attack No-ball No. 79, south-east of Hesdin, with rockets. As our Spits

* Group Central Control.

did 350 m.p.h. while they could just make 200 m.p.h., an escort as usually understood was out of the question. They were to cross the French coast at 1012 hours and make straight for their objective. Simultaneously four Spits each from 'B' and 'A' Flights were to patrol Hesdin and Abbeville, ready to intercept any German fighter reaction.

On paper it looked harmless enough – but in practice....

At 0940 hours the Spitfires took off and plunged into the mist towards Dungeness. In mid-Channel, as 'Met' had predicted, visibility improved and the ceiling rose to 1,000 feet. The Channel was repugnant that morning. Its short foam-crested waves were cold, dirty and glaucous. As we were flying at sea level we had to look out for gulls, which have a nasty habit of flying slap into radiators at full speed or of crashing into the windshield and covering you with blood and feathers.

'B' Flight left us, making for Point-au-Blanc, more to the north-east. Soon, slightly to the right, the cliffs of Tréport reared up their mass of whitish chalk. We opened up flat out and the four Spitfires seemed to slide from one wave crest to the next. Suddenly we were over the estuary of the Somme with its sandbanks and marshes. The beach swept past beneath my wings and I gently eased my Spit over the bumps in the ground, flying as low as possible. We followed the course of the Somme as far as Abbeville. All was quiet at first, no flak, everything seemed deserted and asleep.

Suddenly the ball began. From each bank light flak opened fire. The air filled all at once with long incandescent trails, red and green 20 mm. tracers criss-crossed, giving the disagreeable impression of being about to hit you between the eyes and then at the last moment curving off to one side.

Clusters of luminous balls came up from carefully camouflaged sites, crossed over our heads or ricocheted off the river in front of us. The 37 mm. soon joined in and the venomous black puffs began to appear all round. In spite of violent swerves between the trees and even making use of the hedges as cover, we were relentlessly followed by the light flak. Scarcely were we out of range of one emplacement than we came under fire from another.

We turned 90° left; to maintain our line abreast formation we had to cross over at full speed. Suddenly I saw Ken coming straight for me and I pulled the stick to avoid him. For a moment, therefore, I was not protected by my closeness to the ground. Immediately three shells burst a few yards from me, one of them just over my wing; I could hear the shell fragments rattling on it like hail falling on a sheet of iron.

Right in front between two haystacks I made out some sandbags with the barrels of a multiple pom-pom emerging from them. All around vague grey shapes were rushing about frantically. A pressure on the button and my shells struck the flimsy parapet and my machine-gun bullets churned up the earth all round. One of the stacks caught fire, and I can still see with absolute clarity one of the loaders collapsing, mown down by the storm of bullets.

As I flew on, avoiding obstacles and watching out for high-tension wires which stretch their deadly snare 30 feet above the ground, I kept an eye on Jacques flying 200 yards to my right.

He was clearly in form. Several times I saw him go slap between two trees instead of over them. Knowing him as I did, I knew he must be revelling in it – whereas I would rather have been in bed or, at a pinch, doing a fighter sweep at 20,000 feet.

The difficulty about low flying at 350 m.p.h. is that your field of vision is very limited. You just have time to evaluate an obstacle or a target, you have a fraction of a second to avoid the one and aim at the other, and they have flashed by beneath your wings.

Every light flak post must have been alerted, for streams of tracer were coming up on every side. After a few minutes you get used to it. . . . Suddenly the obstacles disappeared and flattened out before what I took at first to be a big meadow. It was an airfield!

I was flying along the perimeter and Jacques straight down the middle! He must have realised the danger at the same time as I. An absolute wall of flak rose up all round him. At any moment I expected to see him crash in flames. But he was too busy to take any notice of what he calls 'those little details'.

He had just caught a glimpse, in a corner, of three Messerschmitt 109's under camouflage nets. Desperately he tried to get them in his sights. Taking his life in his hands he throttled right back and tried to do a tight turn, his wing practically touching the ground. No good, he was going too fast. Without much hope he fired a burst but it merely bespattered a boundary wall. On the other hand his manoeuvre brought him slap in front of the airfield control tower, a two-storied wooden building with wide bay windows like a belvedere. The effect of his two cannon and his machine guns on such a target was terrifying. The windows flew into fragments and the bullets wrought havoc within. I caught sight of shapes diving out of the door and even the windows. With his finger on the button, Jacques let them have it and went on firing point-blank, just dodging out of the way in the nick of time. The two Huns keeping watch on the roof, seeing the Spitfire coming straight for them, belching fire, did not hesitate; they simply jumped overboard. Everything happened in a flash, like a dream. I heard Jacques' triumphant voice over the radio:

'Hallo, Pierre, that shook 'em!'

For ten more long minutes we continued our patrol, and it was with relief that, unharmed – apart from a few gashes here and there in the Spits – we turned for home.

Drenched with sweat, swearing that we would never be caught at it again, we landed at Detling in pouring rain and a dense fog.

Home, sweet Home.

'Doulce France,' infested with Huns, was less and less welcoming!

20 December 1943

Out of the corner of my eye I watched the Hurricanes about to launch their attack. The target, carefully camouflaged against vertical photography, was visible in every detail at this angle: the high-tension cables to the transformer, the concrete block of the control room with its curious aerials, from which the flying bomb is controlled. On either side, cleverly hidden in the undergrowth, the curious low ski-shaped construction, whose function still baffled the R.A.F. technicians and Intelligence Officers for all their cunning, and, lastly, the launching ramp, 45 yards long, pointing straight at the heart of England. On the rails, a sinister cylinder, about 20 feet long, with two embryonic wings.

Things seemed to be devilishly advanced! All round the No-ball stretched a 20-yard wide barbed wire barrier and light flak posts – five in a radius of 800 metres, according to the interpretation of the latest photos taken by the P.R.U. Mustangs – all equipped with multiple pom-poms, and on the roof of the control block were two 37 mm.

The Hurricanes began their dive, slap into the machine-gun bullets. The tracer bullets formed a wall of steel and explosive round the target.

The inevitable happened. Powerless, I watched the tragedy. Flight Lieutenant Roughhead, just as he let go his salvo of rockets, was hit and killed instantly. His disabled Hurricane recovered with incredible violence and zoomed vertically upwards, its propeller stationary. At the top of the trajectory one wing dropped, the aircraft hung as on a thread suspended in space, motionless, then went into a spin.

As in a nightmare I saw Warrant Officer Pearce's Hurricane literally mown down by a burst of 37 mm. The tail came off, the machine crashed into a wood, scything down the trees, scattering jets of burning petrol.

The other two Hurricanes attacked simultaneously. Struck by a direct hit, Sergeant Clive's machine exploded and was soon nothing but an inchoate mass of flame, dragging a long trail of black smoke.

By a miracle, Bush the Australian was luckier; he succeeded not only in placing his eight rockets in the control room but even in extricating himself from the barrage of flak, in spite of an enormous gash in his fuselage, not to mention two bullets in the thigh.

I sat there petrified, flying mechanically. Everything had happened in a fraction of a second.

Still out of range of the light flak we completed our round and I prepared to set course for home. I heard Ken detaching Jacques and Danny to escort Bush and shouting to me in the radio:

'Hallo, Beer 2, attacking the bloody thing!'

My blood froze in my veins. Ken must be absolute crackers. If he wanted to commit suicide, he ought to do it on his own. I wasn't feeling at all good when Ken, after a long feint in the neighbouring valleys, brought me back on the objective.

'Line abreast, go! Attack!'

We charged, skimming the ground at 10 or 12 feet. Even before we were in position the flak had got our range. Their precision was diabolical. Two posts immediately caught me in their cross fire. With hammering heart I tried to put out their aim, kicking hard on the rudder bar to make my machine skid. No good. I got three direct hits which went slap through my main plane without exploding.

There was no question of attacking. All I could hope for was to save my own skin. Every flak post in the area was alerted by now. Dazzled by the showers of tracer, I crouched down and instinctively moved my head about, as if to avoid the bullets. I felt I was going to be hit any second and crash hopelessly, like the Hurricanes. Desperately I hurled my machine about. Taking my life in my hands I got right down on the deck, feinting violently to left and right. Too late I saw the obstacle – a row of poplars along a canal. I banked instinctively, putting on full left rudder. With a terrifying crash which reverberated through the fuselage and a jolt which nearly wrenched the control out of my hands, my starboard wing caught the tree-tops. Only the momentum of the 3 tons of my aircraft, hurled at 340 m.p.h. prevented me from crashing into the raised towpath on the opposite bank.

Dazed by the shock, paralysed by fear, that fearful physical fear which twists your guts and fills your mouth with gall, I felt my muscles liquefy. . . . I avoided a high-tension cable by a hair's breadth – passing like a flash under the gleaming steel wire.

My heart failed me then. Losing my head I pulled the stick back, seeking the refuge of the clouds rolling dark and grey about 2,500 feet above. I lost the protection of the ground and during the few seconds that my climb lasted I was hit five times – a shell exploding in my left aileron, three bullets in my elevator and another through one of the blades of my propeller. Never had the hollow damp shade of the rain-laden clouds been so welcome. It took me about a minute to go through the cloud layer, and I suddenly emerged in full sunlight, bathed in sweat as on awakening from a nightmare. The blue sky, the sun reflected in the sea of clouds passing beneath me – I was back at last in a glorious and reassuring world.

Timidly I tried the controls. My aileron had sprung its hinges and was held only by a thread of aluminium. The skin of the upper surface of my wings was crumpled like a piece of tissue paper and the shining metal showed through the cracks in the paint.

My jammed tail-trimmer was weighing on the stick.

Back at Detling I made a fairly sensational landing – two or three conspicuous bounces that I had to check violently. Ken had already landed a few minutes before me, writing off his aircraft in the process; his undercart, jammed by a bullet, had failed to come down, and he had had to land on his belly. Later, when we did a post-mortem on our aircraft, Ken discovered that an unexploded shell had smashed one of his magnetos to smithereens and gone through one of his exhaust pipes.

My old LO-D would be in dock for a week. In addition to the damage to the controls, the fuselage had been hit near the roundels by three shells. A bullet had ricocheted off one of my oxygen bottles. I had a fine retrospective fright at the idea that if the shell had hit that bottle fair and square the explosion of the gas under pressure would have turned me into heat and light.

RANGER OVER FRANCE

Half past six. The ringing of the alarm clock tore me out of bed. Christ, how cold it was! I peeped under the blackout curtain – low clouds, ceiling less than 2,000 feet, and what a wind! It screamed through the telegraph wires outside and every gust shook the twenty doors in our quarters.

I lit a cigarette and put the light on. Tom and Danny, my room-mates, had gone back to sleep; the fourth bed was empty – we had lost Croft three days ago. I hurriedly put on a couple of pullovers over my pyjamas, a leather waistcoat, my battle-dress, two pairs of long woollen stockings and my flying boots, into which I slipped my map.

The dark concrete bulk of the Ops. room loomed in the night. I could dimly hear the throb of the air-conditioning plant for the underground rooms. After the bitter cold outside, I felt as if I were plunging into a deliciously warm vapour bath as soon as I passed through the heavy metal doors. The room, lit by mercury vapour lamps, seemed like a scene from another world.

The Sergeant on duty was kept busy answering a dozen continuously ringing phones. Without even looking up he handed me the 'Met' report and the area controller's instructions. Ten-tenths cloud at 4,000 feet. Wind at sea level 320 degrees, 35 m.p.h.; 50 m.p.h. at 5,000 feet. Visibility moderate, dropping to 500 yards in the showers. Watch for twelve Typhoons, who were to carry out a sortie in the Chartres area from 0840 to 0850 hours at zero feet. A piece of cake, if it weren't for the wind.

I woke up the rest of the gang. Ken and Bruce were O.K. but Jacques proceeded to bind like hell. I shook him up. Five minutes later we were on our way over to Flight. On our way we checked the fixing of our big 45-gallon auxiliary tanks, slung like bombs between the Spitfires' two radiators. The mechanics lay on the ground, working away by the light of their storm lanterns. How can we ever thank them!

'Take-off at 8 o'clock sharp,' Ken shouted to them.

It was 7.25, just time to get a cup of coffee and a few biscuits. Time for breakfast proper when we got back – if we did get back.

Huddling round the miserable stove, Jacques, Dumbrell and I listened while Ken, map in hand, gave us the gen.

'We'll cross the French coast, either on I.F. or above the clouds, then we'll go as far as Amiens flying low. We'll turn left and patrol the area Saint-Quentin, Noyon, Beauvais, and we'll come back at 13,000 feet. Like that we'll stand a decent chance of intercepting a low-flying transport. Roughly line-abreast formation, 100 yards between aircraft, crossing over from left to right when we alter course. Every man for himself if it comes to a scrap. The first one who spots a target tells the rest and leads the attack.'

0750 hours. Strapped in our Mae Wests, cluttered up with our dinghy as well as the parachute, we climbed laboriously into our cockpits, helped by the mechanics. My breath immediately froze on the windshield. I switched on my radio, my camera-gun, the carburettor, pitot-head and gyro-intake heaters and the de-icing equipment. My fingers were numb under three layers of gloves – silk, wool and leather – and it was quite a business messing about with all those tiny buttons crowded together on the instrument panel.

0755 hours. I got them to properly adjust the rear-view mirror! A glance at the sight. I set the safety catch of the guns. All set. A glance towards Ken.

'All clear.'

'Contact.'

A whine from the starter. One cylinder fired, then two more. I pumped furiously and all at once the engine burst into life.

It was still very dark and the mauve flashes from the exhausts lit up the snow. It was two minutes past eight. Navigation lights on, wing tip to wing tip, we climbed through the black, threatening clouds.

We emerged at 13,000 feet above the thick layer of stratocumulus, over the Channel. At once we took up battle formation. Complete silence over the radio. In spite of icing we had switched over to our auxiliary tanks without anything going wrong. In the gathering dawn the clouds were edged with light.

The German spotters had probably picked us up. The usual irritating radar interference started up in our headphones, worse with each sweep of the beam. Suddenly Bruce Dumbrell waggled his wings and turned for home. The perfect ellipse of his wings was outlined against the pale sky for the space of an instant and I could make out a thin white stream flowing from his radiator. Glycol escaping. One aircraft less. In theory one of us ought to escort him over the sea but if we did that we should have to return to base without completing our job.

Ken said nothing and merely signalled to us to close up again for the dive through the cloud-layer. It was a tricky business. Ken had worked it out that if we didn't time it right there was a risk of coming out in the coastal flak belt. The 'Met' forecast had to be right too as, if the cloud base was lower than expected, we wouldn't have enough margin to rectify any error in our I.F.

We plunged into the opaque mist. Ken had his eyes glued to his instruments, Jacques and I desperately clung to his wing tips. Suddenly we found ourselves in clear air again, at less than 1,500 feet, over a cluster of little wooded hillocks intersected by a narrow marshy valley. A fine rain was falling, shreds of mist dragged over the ground, the light was glaucous, like in an aquarium. That awful curdling of the stomach muscles as usual. We must watch out now.

'Hullo, Skittles, Red Leader calling. Combat formation, drop your babies.'

Having got rid of our auxiliary tanks, we dived to get up speed. Ken was skimming the river in the middle of the valley; Jacques beyond him was following the road, keeping below the level of the telegraph wires. I was halfway up a slope, bothered by constant clumps of trees. I kept a cautious lookout for high-tension wires. One hundred and seventy-five yards a second. In that grisly visibility the fatal obstacle came on you in a flash. On the ground, apart from a glimpse through my hood of a couple of women, sheltering under an umbrella, there wasn't a solitary cart, nothing. A few roofs outlined against the horizon, a factory chimney or two. White smoke from a small marshalling yard approached rapidly. Doullens, probably. We veered towards the south, to leave the French town clear on our left. We had neither permission nor inclination to attack a train – no point in risking flak unnecessarily.

The rain started to come down in sheets. I must really watch out now. Amiens must be somewhere not far away in the murk.

'Look out, flak!'

A shout from Jacques over the radio. Instinctively, I turned. A fan-shaped cluster of white puffs spread in front of my windshield. Tracers started whipping through the trees. Then, under my wings, I saw roofs, allotments. In a rift the towers of the cathedral loomed up, too close. I roared over wet cobblestones, greasy macadam, dirty slates, clusters of grey houses. It was Amiens.

Skimming the chimney pots we veered to the left and emerged level with a station. A glimpse of a few railwaymen, rooted to the spot, caught between the trucks of a goods train, then flashes from a loco park as a battery of three automatic guns opened up, their stuttering barrels wreathed in smoke.

Each of us on his own, weaving, full throttle, we made off, pursued by orange tracer. It was only a few miles from the town that we formed up again. I discreetly checked on the course Ken was setting and studied the map as best I could. No doubt about it, Ken had boobed as we came out of Amiens, at the Langean fork. We were heading for Noyon and Compiègne instead of Saint-Quentin. The Canal du Nord passed beneath us, then the Oise. Sure enough, here was Compiègne forest, slashed by a bank of fog apparently anchored to the trees.

Suddenly we heard the controller's voice, very distantly as we were flying low:

'Hullo, Skittles, look out for Huns and Tiffie boys around.'

I wedged myself against the seat and tried to pierce the murk into which we plunged, 6 feet above the denuded branches. Suddenly all hell was let loose – we roared into a fearful madhouse of planes. Yellow cowlings marked with black crosses cut through the tracer trails. At least twenty Focke-Wulfs, all apparently gone berserk. With my thumb I immediately released the safety catch of my guns. My earphones were screaming.

I just avoided colliding with a Focke-Wulf. Glued to the back of my seat by the centrifugal force I did a tight turn behind another and let fly with my machine guns as I passed. Then, my finger still on the button, I had to break away violently. I could see another hovering just behind in my mirror, his wings lit up by the flashes of his cannon.

Having got rid of that one I drew a bead on another, who seemed to have lost his head and was waggling his wings. All of a sudden a Typhoon loomed up in my windshield, coming straight for me. I kicked the rudder bar desperately. I just about grazed him, and caught my wing tip a terrible crack in a branch. Sweating and holding my breath I righted my Spitfire, just as a Focke-Wulf in flames crashed in front of me, mowing down the trees in a fearful shower of sparks.

Stick right back I made vertically for the clouds, firing a burst of cannon on the way at a Focke-Wulf which was so close that the black crosses on his fuselage filled my gun sight. With his tail plane half torn off, he went into a spin and crashed into a clearing.

Once I got into the shelter of the clouds I breathed more easily. That bunch of pirates, 609 Typhoon Squadron, commanded by my Belgian friend Demoulin, must have dropped unexpectedly on a wing of Focke-Wulfs taking off from Compiègne airfield. We had landed in the middle of the party by mistake!

Nerves tensed, I came down into the scrap again. I saw three flaming masses on the ground and three thick columns of black smoke rose above the forest. Visibility was getting worse and worse. I caught a glimpse of a couple of Focke-Wulfs vanishing into the mist. No one left in sight. I could vaguely hear Ken and Jacques over the radio, excitedly chasing after a Focke-Wulf. They ended by shooting it down somewhere or other and then the wireless went dead for a bit.

I called Ken to tell him my juice was getting low and that I was going back to Detling. Half an hour's I.F. through cumulus with flanks heavy with snow and I found myself over the sandy spit of Dungeness, in a fog you could cut with a knife. I asked for a homing and was brought back slap over base by the controller. As I made my approach, skimming the tree-tops, I saw Ken and Jacques touching down, Ken doing a fearful ground loop. I taxied past him. He had caught a packet in his starboard wing from 20 mm., but he signalled that he had bagged a Jerry.

With the help of my mechanics I jumped down from my Spit, stiff and cold. Only to hear that immediately after breakfast I had to return to Dispersal on stand-by readiness.

ESCORTS

21 December 1943

Briefing at 10.30.

Superb weather, a temperature fit for brass monkeys – not a trace of a cloud in the sky. The Spitfires' wings were streaming with water, for the hot-air de-icing trailer had just passed. The runway was covered with ice.

I had to take off my gloves to do up my straps, and so my hands froze, and I couldn't get them warm again. I opened up the oxygen, to put a bit of stuffing into myself.

The ice on the runway these last days had produced a crop of accidents, serious and otherwise – smashed undercarts, taxiing accidents, etc. – and now we only had eleven serviceable planes left.

Dumbrell, Jacques and I were Max section, with the C.O. With 132 we were to patrol the Cambrai area, where German fighters had been particularly active recently. We climbed to 22,000 feet, then, as the cold was intense, we came down to 17,000.

The winter sky was so clear, so dazzling, that after a mere 20 minutes over France we were continually blinking.

The controller told us there was a strong enemy fighter formation not far off, but it was impossible to spot anything in the dazzling light. To be on the safe side, as Grass Seed was getting urgent, we gained height again.

Suddenly, woooof! Thirty Focke-Wulfs were on top of us. Before we could move a muscle, the brutes opened fire. A whirlwind of enormous radial engines, of short, slender wings edged with lightning, of tracer bullets whizzing in every direction, of black crosses all over the place. Panic. Everyone broke. In the space of one second the two flights' impeccable combat formation was disrupted, dislocated, scattered to the four winds. Too late! Old Jonah was on his way down in flames, and Morgan, the Scots Flight Sergeant, in a spin, one wing torn off by a hail of Mauser.

132 were no luckier. Three of their pilots were shot down. A fourth – as we learnt later – succeeded in bringing his badly damaged machine half

way back across the Channel, then baled out and was fished out an hour later.

Once the surprise had passed, we pulled ourselves together. Captain Aubertin, in command of Skittles, suddenly found himself isolated: his No. 2 and 4 had been shot down and his No. 3 had vanished into thin air – poor old Spence had got a 20 mm. shell 4 inches from his head which had smashed his radio to smithereens. Half knocked out, he had instinctively pulled the stick back and opened the throttle, and had woken up at 36,000 feet, absolutely alone in the sky.

A Focke-Wulf sneaked in behind the captain but missed him. The Hun overshot him. He was carried away by his speed and Aubertin settled his hash in no time at all; the biter bit. Unfortunately four other Focke-Wulfs engaged him and not only did he fail to see his victim crash but he himself only succeeded in getting away after an eventful 45-mile chase among the trees, round church steeples and through village streets. His Spitfire was hit seven times.

Meanwhile Jacques and I – contrary to our settled habits – followed on Sutherland's heels like faithful hounds and had the pleasure of seeing him liquidate another '190' at 600 yards range. The Hun disintegrated in the air, but the pilot escaped: a little later we saw a parachute open out below us.

Danny fired a sly burst at a '190' but missed.

If results were wanted, this sweep certainly produced them – out of 23 Spits, 6 were shot down, 8 others damaged, not counting Williams of 132, who was wounded and had to belly-land.

7 January 1944

A long trip this time. We were going to Rheims to fetch home a strong formation of Flying Fortresses and Liberators coming back from Germany. 602 was to cover the first three groups – 180 bombers in all – and 132 the three following.

We took off at 1210 hours after a rushed lunch, and we flogged our aircraft, weighed down by 45-gallon auxiliary tanks, up to 23,000 feet. After 30 minutes flying we passed Paris on our right, sensed rather than seen below a cloak of mist and smoke. On the way German heavy batteries loosed some beautifully aimed salvoes which burst very close – we immediately scattered about the sky. The black puffs appeared on every side. Climbing at full throttle with Thommerson, we succeeded in getting out of range and re-forming, not without difficulty.

1050 hours. The Jerries seemed to be reacting and the Focke-Wulfs must be taking off all over the place because control was beginning to get agitated. Still nothing near us.

Soon a cluster of black dots appeared on the horizon, followed by others. Our bombers!

The Thunderbolts and Lightnings whom we were relieving returned to base, and we took up our positions – in patrols of four on either side of the formation.

A show of Fortresses certainly is an impressive sight! The phalanx of bombers in impeccable defensive formation – several massive boxes of a hundred or so 4-engined aircraft in banks at 27,000 feet, each box bristling with 1,440 heavy .5 machine guns – spread out over 20-odd miles.

On either side the Spitfire escort stretched as far as the eye could see. The top cover of Spit VII's and IX's was only visible in the shape of fine white condensation trails.

The visibility that day was splendid. The sky was dark indigo blue, paler towards the horizon, passing from emerald green to milky white where it merged with the bands of mist over the North Sea.

Below, France unfolded like a magic carpet. The peaceful meandering Seine and its tributaries, the dark masses of the forests with their curious geometrical shapes, the multi-coloured checker-board of the fields and meadows, the tiny toy-like villages, the towns sullying the translucent sky with patches of smoke clinging to the warm layers of air.

The sun burnt through the transparent cockpits, and yet I could feel ice forming in my oxygen tube, and the exhaust gases condensed in a myriad microscopic crystals, marking the wake of my Spitfire in the sky.

Fatigue, stiffness, the painful cramp in my back, the cold searing my toes and fingers through the leather, the wool and the silk, all were forgotten.

Here and there in the Fortress formations there were gaps. From close to you could see machines with one, sometimes two stationary engines and feathered propellers. Others had lacerated tail planes, gaping holes in the fuselages, wings tarnished by fire or glistening with black oil oozing from gutted engines.

Behind the formation were the stragglers, making for the coast, for the haven of refuge of an advanced air base on the other side of the Channel, flying only by a sublime effort of the will. You could imagine the blood pouring over the heaps of empty cartridges, the pilot nursing his remaining engines and anxiously eyeing the long white trail of petrol escaping from his riddled tanks. These isolated Fortresses were the

Focke-Wulf's favourite prey. Therefore the squadrons detached two or three pairs of Spitfires, charged with bringing each one back safe: an exhausting task as these damaged Fortresses often dragged along on a third of their total power, stretching the endurance of their escort to the limit.

On this occasion Ken sent Carpenter and me to escort a Liberator which was only in the air by a miracle. Its No. 3 engine had completely come out of its housing and hung on the leading edge, a mass of lifeless ironmongery. His No. 1 engine was on fire, the flames slowly eating into the wing and the smoke escaping through the aluminium plates of the upper surface, buckled by the heat. Through the tears in the fuselage the survivors were throwing overboard all their superfluous equipment – machine guns, ammunition, belts, radio, armour plates – to lighten their machine, which was slowly losing height.

To crown all, there was a burst in the hydraulic system, freeing one of the wheels of the undercart which hung down and increased the drag still further.

At 1,800 revs., minus 2 boost and 200 m.p.h. we had to zigzag to keep level with him. We had been hunched up in our uncomfortable cockpits for two hours already, and we were still over France, 12 miles behind the main formation. Ten Focke-Wulfs began to prowl round us, at a respectful distance, as if suspecting a trap. Anxiously Carp and I kept an eye on them. Another B-24 courageously joined us to help our protégé.

Suddenly they attacked, in pairs. Short of juice as we were, all we could do was to face each attack by a very tight 180° turn, fire a short burst in the approximate direction of the Hun, and immediately resume our position by another quick 180° turn. This performance was repeated a dozen times but we succeeded in making the Focke-Wulfs keep their distance. They eventually tired of it – or so we thought.

Over Dieppe the fighters gave way to the flak. We were flying at about 10,000 feet. The German light flak opened fire with unbelievable ferocity. An absolute pyramid of black puffs charged with lightning appeared in a fraction of a second. Violently shaken by several well-aimed shells, Carp and I separated and gained height as fast as we could with our meagre reserves of petrol. The poor Liberator, incapable of taking any sort of violent evasive action, was quickly bracketed. Just as, after a few agonising seconds, we thought it was out of range there was an explosion and the big bomber, cut in half, suddenly disappeared in a sheet of flame. Only three parachutes opened out. The blazing aluminium coffin crashed a few hundred yards from the cliffs in a shower of spray, dragging down the remaining members of the crew.

With heavy hearts we landed at Lympne, our tanks empty.

Luckily we were often more fortunate than this and succeeded in bringing our charges back to our airfield at Detling, where their arrival always caused the greatest agitation – ambulances, fire service, curious onlookers. We felt fully repaid by the gratitude in the eyes of the poor exhausted fellows. In many cases it was only the moral support of the presence of a pair of Spits that gave them the courage to hold out to the end, to resist the temptation of baling out and waiting for the end of the war in some Oflag or other.

DEPARTURE FOR THE ORKNEYS

We were about to leave for the Orkneys. There was a regular pea-souper and the Harrows would be prevented from coming to fetch us.

Alea jacta est – we would go by rail. Just the job, something like twenty hours of more or less comfortable travel.

We piled our luggage into the lorries and went and had lunch at the 'Star' in Maidstone, where we found Jimmy Rankin and Yule. A few last rounds of drinks, promises. . . .

As usual I was cluttered up with a mass of belongings – mandoline, Irvine jacket, etc. Luckily Jacques was there to help.

On the way through London we dropped in in a body – twenty-four pilots – at the 'C—', a very swanky and exclusive club in Soho. After half an hour the manager, fearing for his interior decoration and seeing the alarm of his immaculately dressed clientéle, came and asked us to move on. A few well-chosen arguments, including the transfer of his magnificent white carnation to Ken's button-hole and a threat of public debagging, were enough to calm him down.

From 6 to 9.30 (our train was at 10.20) we drank hard – whisky, beer, whisky. By 9.30 we were bottled, and singing our squadron ditties. 'I belong to Glasgow!' followed 'Pistol-packing Momma' and 'Gentille Alouette', and gradually we embarked on the more lurid items of our repertoire. Our fellow-guests began to feel embarrassed, to blush, and some of them even discreetly made themselves scarce.

Robson climbed up on a table, upset a few bottles, and we began to intone in chorus 602's war-cry:

'Is it one, two, three?'
'No!'
'Is it one, two, three, four, five, six?'
'Siiiiiiiiix!'
'Oh?'
'Ooooooh!'
'One, two?'

'Twooooo!'

'One, two, three, four, five!'

'Six, hooooo! Twooooooo!'

At that point the captain very nicely reminded us that we had a train to catch. It was just as well he did, for as we were getting up, the proprietor burst in escorted by two policemen and half a dozen M.P.'s. After a few minutes of confused explanations we succeeded in getting rid of them, and surged down the Piccadilly Circus underground. A civilian permitted himself an out-of-place remark about 'those good-for-nothing R.A.F. blokes'. Robson and Bob Courly inserted his umbrella into the moving staircase, which jammed with a terrifying din. We took a compartment by storm, the passengers regarding us with a mixture of incredulity and horror, and finally we found ourselves at King's Cross.

We piled our luggage on the electric trolleys. Carpenter took over the controls and embarked on an epic dash along the platforms crowded with travellers, warning bell going full blast. It was such a riot that the stationmaster took a hand in person, followed by an imposing escort of Military Police. An unwise move on his part, for within a minute or two his beautiful cap covered with gold braid had mysteriously found its way into Tommy's suitcase. This cap now figures among the Flight's most valued trophies, together with a London policeman's helmet, a Canadian general's beret, a Panzer Grenadier colonel's forage cap, brought back from Dieppe by Bill Loud and Rudolph Hess's helmet.

The platforms were swarming with people and, what with the blackout, it was hard to find our way about. However, we did eventually succeed in finding our reserved compartment, at the door of which an M.P. and a railway official were mounting guard.

Our Pullman was divided into two, with a communicating door. The other half was occupied by 129 Squadron from Hornchurch, also going 'on rest'. We soon made friends. A terrific racket again, everyone singing, bottles flying. Round about 2 a.m. we organised a Rugger match, but it fizzled out, for lack of players.

By 3 o'clock everyone was asleep, on the seats, under the tables, on the carpet in the gangway, even in the luggage racks.

18 January 1944

It was a pitiful squadron which emerged from the train at Aberdeen at about 5 o'clock in the morning. Dishevelled, unshaven, covered with soot, our mouths like the bottom of a parrot's cage, we first had to unload our luggage and manhandle it over to the lorries and buses taking us to Peterhead.

There we embarked in two gigantic Harrow transports, piling our baggage in the fuselages. I noticed that each one of us unobtrusively sat down on his parachute bag. Some clot began repeating the story of how a Harrow had been shot down on this trip by a Junkers 88 a few weeks earlier.

During the take-off, we all clenched our teeth, but when we were airborne we heaved a sigh of relief and began to crack a few jokes. Not for long! The air was far from calm and the machine began to pitch and toss, shaken by air pockets.

The laughs soon gave way to a general mood of profound gloom. This pathological state was not unconnected with the state of our stomachs, which had not yet recovered from the corrosive mixture of beer and whisky.

Every pilot held his head in his hands, his elbows on his knees, and nobody thought of admiring the superb snow-covered country over which we were passing.

We reeled out of the Harrow at our destination with dry throats and asleep on our feet. We wished the Station Commander would go to hell as he did his utmost to make us welcome in a charming little speech, which we had to listen to standing in the open under the piercing blasts of the wind.

Skeabrae in winter might just as well be the North Pole. God knows what maniac at Air Ministry had the bright idea of setting up a fighter base in those god-forsaken islands. A few hours' daylight in the twenty-four; occasionally a gleam of sun pierces the wan clouds, disperses the arctic mist and reveals a desolate countryside, wind-swept rocks emerging from the thick snow.

A few miles away, sheltered by a group of islands similar to ours, was the great naval base of Scapa Flow where the Home Fleet lay, protected by mine barrages and anti-submarine nets.

602's role was to foil any attempts at bombing or aerial reconnaissance on the part of the Luftwaffe.

We found our aircraft sheltering against the ice-laden hurricanes in pens scattered all around the airfield. Seven or eight Spitfire V's, 'clipped, clapped, cropped', and in particular four magnificent Strato-Spit VII's, comprised our equipment.

Those Spit VII's were special machines. Their wing span had been increased and thanks to their Rolls-Royce Merlin engines with 2-stage superchargers, and their pressurised cockpits, they could go up to practically 50,000 feet. Only a dozen aircraft of this type had been built, and distributed to strategic points in Great Britain.

Our fitters quickly adopted them and furbished them with loving care.

We removed the two machine guns in the wings to lighten them, keeping only the two 20 mm. cannon.

From time to time the Germans hazarded a Junkers 88, which came over at sea level to try and observe the movements of the Fleet and, just recently, an aircraft of unknown type had succeeded in photographing Scapa from 47,000 feet. We therefore always kept a couple of Spit V's and two of our Strato-Spits at immediate readiness.

A most monotonous week passed. An over-daring Junkers 88 stupidly got itself shot down by a Bofors battery, under the nose of Carpenter and Ken Charney, who came back seething with rage.

To cap all, 'B' Flight was detached to the Shetlands, about 60 miles still farther north. They took some fitters and four Spit V's with them. We commiserated with them hypocritically – sooner them than us.

Jacques and I organised an egg-round. Using the little Tiger Moth attached to the Station, we raided the archipelago twice a week, landing near the farms and snaffling all the eggs. At the end of a fortnight of eggs for breakfast, lunch, tea *and* dinner, the very sight of an egg made our gorges rise. Ken even made out that feathers were growing down his back.

Snow fell, the wind blew, snow fell again for a change. We spent our days roasting our fronts and backs in turn round those little R.A.F. stoves. Our poor fitters had the hell of a time with engines freezing and spent hours and hours keeping the wings of the four aircraft in readiness free of ice.

Intercepting an Me 109 H at 40,000 feet is no joke, nor is chasing a Ju 88 slaloming along among the banks of mist over the small islands at the edge of a frozen sea. From the beginning of December, the weather forecast remained poor: visibility nil, snow and frost kicking in from take-off, if anyone was fool enough to attempt it!

Max Sutherland worried about ways to keep us busy. At first, being a hearty English physical exercise nut, he had us jogging or doing gymnastics, bare-chested in the snow. I respectfully explained that while the De Gaulle–Churchill Charter of August 1940 obliged me to obey an operational order, gym, half-nudity, bronchitis, etc., weren't included, and that furthermore I was allergic to the whole thing and consequently preferred to stay in my room writing my diaries. On the contrary, he told me, chuckling, escape exercises were considered to be 'combat training', impossible to duck. It was quite a business. We were transported blindfolded with only a compass and an unreadable map of the island, the size of a playing card, in a tarpaulin-covered truck that stopped at regular intervals. Two M.P.s – the Military Police, who organised these jolly pranks – grabbed one of us by the scruff and dropped him in the roadway. There you were supposed to count up to one hundred, honestly, like a good British gentleman, then take off your blindfold and get back to base before 1700 hours, i.e., before it got pitch dark. All the island's forces were out to capture us.

What a palaver! Finally, the M.P. sergeant took pity on us and dropped Jacques and me off together. It was forbidden to use the roads. Pure sadism: the snow was heavy, everything was white, the earth, the sky, the air we breathed. . . . Never mind, we found ourselves on the only remaining orientation point, the road, but the snow was so thick that we didn't know if we should go to the right or to the left! Sure, the compass showed us the north, but was the base east or west? We mentally tossed for it and began to walk. Every three minutes Jacques muttered, 'The bastards!' until at last we made out a little pub, one of those extraordinary shebeens of the Orkney islands that are built half-underground, like igloos, as protection from the cold. A few slippery steps to descend, a knock at the door and we entered a warm – at last! – tunnel, lit by a big chimney where a peat fire smoked. Beside it was an enormous copper cauldron filled with that black, thick Scottish beer, which was being ladled into pewter pint mugs. The next step, as the innkeeper explained, was to take a white-hot poker from the fireplace and plunge it into the beer. Froth immediately poured down the sides and the alcoholic level mounted dizzyingly – to 8° or even 10° – so as beer went this was really serious stuff. We ate two smoked red partridge to help the beer go down and began laughing when we thought of the M.P.s who would soon be searching for us in the snow and of the anxiety at the base. By the fourth pint we were euphoric, as tight as ticks. Jacques was recumbent in an armchair, eyes closed and smiling like the cat who got the cream; my tongue somewhat thickened, I managed to tell him, 'There'll be hell to pay when we get back.'

At 8 p.m. a Military Police jeep arrived. They had been searching for us for two hours and were beginning to think we had died of cold somewhere. They heaved a sigh of relief, we offered them a beer, which they refused virtuously and went off to send a radio signal that 'those damn Frenchies are alive, unfortunately!'

Their jeep wouldn't start. We helped them to push and when it took off I fell flat on my face. I felt so relaxed and it felt so soft and cosy! I could understand how people could let themselves die, numbed in the snow. . . . Jacques, no fool, had bought from the innkeeper a bottle of old pure local malt, that marvellous peat-smelling whisky. When we turned up slightly sheepishly at the mess bar Max advanced on us, eyes spitting fire, but before he had time to bawl us out Jacques held out the bottle to him with the air of a contrite cocker spaniel who had peed on the carpet. Max and Ken Charney were mollified, told the barman to bring four glasses and asked for our story and an explanation for why we had not played the game. Taking precautions, I got ready to duck, I told him that we had taken the exercise seriously, that it was important to remember we were French and that, as we nearly always operated over France, after parachuting in, we were, in theory, chez nous and therefore simply waiting for the Resistance to take us to England. . . .

This response subsequently did the rounds of the base to some success!

A MATTER OF LIFE AND DEATH

For several days I sensed that a storm was brewing up inside my partner-in-crime, Jacques. Depending on his mood it would be Shakespearean drama or Wodehouseian comedy.

He was a good-looking chap, a dead ringer for the actor Tyrone Power, a great lady-killer but very masculine; women adored him and fell into his arms. However, he was obsessed with the W.R.E.N.'s, the female auxiliaries of the Royal Navy – the 'sailorettes', as we nicknamed them.

With their seductive navy-blue uniform, tricorne hat perched on blonde hair – real or dyed – and, above all, the famous black stockings over their pearly British flesh, for Jacques they were completely irresistible. Briefly, for want of anything better, he had spent the last two months exchanging inflammatory letters with a W.R.E.N. who must have been more talented than the others; the billet-doux no doubt steaming with passion rather than romance. Two months of celibacy in that frozen universe was a long time. True, there was a big detachment of W.R.E.N.'s in the Scapa Flow base, but this was a camp fortified literally and figuratively by the Navy, to which we had no access.

That morning, at breakfast, the storm burst – this time it was Shakespearean. The postman had just arrived and I saw Jacques, crimson-faced, crumpling a letter into a ball and tossing it away!

'Oh, ho! What's happened to you?'

He answered, through gritted teeth, in the Franglais which he slid into when things went badly: 'They're all tarts. . . . They're all les mêmes!'

Finally he explained that his naval sweetheart, Vera – out of sight, out of mind – had made a conquest of a major in the Commandos who was about to leave for Burma and wanted to marry her at once.

'Rubbish, Jacques, one down and ten to go! Calm down, you can't do anything about it.'

I wished I'd never said it!

'I'm going to London to rescue Vera from that ape. I'd already seen him sneaking around her.'

'How? We're in the Orkneys, at the end of the world – and have you forgotten about the Royal Navy that we're supposed to be protecting?'

'I don't give a damn about the Royal Navy; it's Vera I'm interested in. I've worked it out; I'll have to catch the 10.45 train from Wick, which will get me to London around nine this evening.'

'And how are you going to do that? The ferryboat to Wick leaves at 10 a.m. You'll have to take the train tomorrow morning. Ask Max for a 48-hour pass. You know he'll give it to you.'

'Out of the question, that'll be too late. It's got to be the plane for Wick, it's do-able, and since no one will lend me a Spitfire for that, *you* are going to ask R.A.B. to lend us his little private plane.'

Good God, Jacques had a nerve! R.A.B. was our redoubtable Group Captain who commanded the base. His initials, we had been warned, were the first letters of the word 'rabies'. Quite a character. He was titled, a member of the upper aristocracy, a vague cousin of an uncle of the queen, and was allowed to keep and to use his peace-time plane, a Percival with a Gipsy Major engine, for trips to and from Scotland. The king kindly furnished the petrol and in exchange R.A.B. economised for His Majesty on the liaison planes. This Percival was the apple of his eye and you could always see mechanics polishing it in a corner of the principal hangar.

'Jacques, you're mad. He'll chuck me out.'

'Clo, you could at least do this for your best friend!'

Having received my epaulettes a fortnight before Jacques, in official correspondence of the F.A.F.L. H.Q. I was grandly categorised as 'Head of the French detachment with the 602 "City of Glasgow"', in the absence of Captain Aubertin who was on extended leave. Armed with this title, I cautiously approached R.A.B., who received me courteously. However, I realised anxiously that the more I elaborated on my request – 'it's a matter of life or death!' – the more stupefied he was by my audacity, so that in the end he could only choose between complete apoplexy and capitulation.

Permission granted, I saluted and executed a perfect about-turn, leaving him stupefied, but with bulging eyes.

Quickly, before he changed his mind, I got out the plane, checked the fuel levels and rapidly set a course, getting Jacques on board with his B.E.V. We rolled at top speed towards the runway between two banks of snow, and took off.

It was a 100-mile journey from the base to Wick, with a big detour around Burray and Berwick to avoid the alert and edgy anti-aircraft fire from the big naval base, which was encircled by a dense chain of barrage balloons. There was a lot of sea to cross during the trip, particularly the

15 miles of the Penland strait. To cap it all, after the majestic purr of the Rolls-Royce engines of our Spitfires, the motor of this old banger sounded like a coffee-grinder with its valves going like castanets. We had our lifejackets, of course, but in a water temperature of 2° or 3° they wouldn't be of much use.

At last the coast came in view and, with the first houses of Wick, alas, the smoke of the London train just leaving the station.

'Go on to Inverness! We can go faster than the train and I'll catch it there!'

A glance at the map. God! Another 60 miles to go. I wouldn't have enough petrol to return. I'd have to fill up on the spot. At Inverness Jacques hurtled out, with plenty of time to catch his train of destiny, and I found myself in front of the aerodrome's civilian fuel-pump, where no one would accept a voucher signed by me. I explained that I was in the Glasgow Squadron, hence a compatriot, they responded that was a good reason to refuse, and that moreover they were from Edinburgh and the east coast, and that the Glasgow folk from the west coast of Scotland were a bunch of bandits. Endless arguments ensued, but finally the local R.A.F. liaison settled the question after my explanations. So I flew back to the air base where I arrived dramatically after a delay of several hours. The Air Sea Rescue had been alerted and was looking for me. R.A.B. tore his hair and declared to anyone who would listen that 'those cretinous Frenchmen have dumped my plane in the water!' When he saw me return with his precious banger intact, he was so relieved that he didn't bawl me out – or not much. Not that he congratulated me either. Max, to whom I told the story in detail, howled with laughter, as did Ken Charney, and even bought me a drink.

Jacques finally resurfaced a week later and was very discreet about his all-important tryst. I learned that he had arrived too late to prevent the fatal step but that the poor little W.R.E.N. was so sad at the departure of her handsome officer that Jacques had to spend four days and nights consoling her.

THE *TIRPITZ*

everal days later, on 20 December, the 602 received a message from R.A.F. H.Q. that officer cadet Pierre Clostermann, Free French Air Force, was to present himself at a certain hour the following day at landing stage X of the Scapa Flow base. Dress uniform No. 1, battle-dress and change of clothing for several days.

At the designated hour I embarked on a launch that deposited me at the gangway of a very impressive aircraft carrier. I was given, with full silver service, a sensational breakfast – the like of which I had not seen or eaten for two years, confirming me in my opinion that the 'rowers', as we called them, knew how to live – and then I was asked to wait in a saloon. I was intrigued. I questioned the lieutenant who accompanied me and was told to wait for a surprise. After a while he got on the telephone and then said: 'Follow me.' We mounted to the snow-covered bridge, overlooking the plane-filled ship. I waited, and suddenly, through the sheet of low fog hanging over the water appeared the unearthly, imposing silhouette of a great warship, the long steel grey mass of a magnificent battleship slipping slowly and silently out of the fog as if emerging from the sea. Beside me, several Royal Navy officers were smiling and one said, 'Isn't she beautiful?'

She was indeed a great lady and I could not believe my eyes: it was the *Richelieu*, about to escort, together with the English and the Americans, a convoy bound for Murmansk: the bait to trap the big rat *Tirpitz* skulking in Norway. The *Nelson* was equal to the *Tirpitz* in terms of artillery, but could not match her for speed. The other ships of the line under the American Admiral Frazer were just good enough for close protection of the convoy but not for chasing after the swift and powerful *Tirpitz*. Only the *Richelieu* had the clout and the speed to go up against her. Our four escorting torpedo boats, including the Norwegian *Stord*, were there simply to try and slow her down if necessary. What was my role to be in all this? It was just after the business of the famous PQ 17 convoy, massacred by the Luftwaffe and the Kriegsmarine before limping on to Russia, where the few survivors were rescued from the polar ice-field.

So it was, without much enthusiasm, that I left for Russia on board the *Richelieu* . . . but I was very impressed. At the end of the 1930s the French Navy had built two super-battleships, the *Jean-Bart* and the *Richelieu*, that were technically ten years ahead of their English and American counterparts. Unfortunately, for three long years they had remained immobilised at Dakar – out of loyalty to Admiral Darlan and Vichy, and hatred of the English. . . . In short, after many miserable episodes, the *Richelieu* was refitted (most notably with anti-aircraft defences, in which it was lacking) in the U.S.A. and this masterpiece of naval architecture returned to the fray. It was a bit late, but never mind. (Better late than . . . etc., etc.) Besides, when I arrived in the lieutenants' quarters, I was welcomed joyfully with open arms and gallons of punch. 'You're from the Free French? You've seen De Gaulle? Do you know him? What do you think of him?'

I couldn't say as much for the superior officers, who received me as if I had the pox when I reported to them as a matter of courtesy. The Cross of Lorraine on my chest had the same effect on them as a crucifix upon vampires. After we had cast off I was invited to see a film where, by contrast, I received a warm reception from the sailors. 'Look, did you see, it's one of De Gaulle's flyers, look at his Croix de Guerre and the Cross of Lorraine. Bravo!' and lots of 'Tell me, Lieutenant, do you know my cousin, he's with your lot, he's called Le Guen . . .'. All these splendid Bretons had brothers or uncles in the Free French. I was moved to tears; here at last was the real France.

On the third day I was summoned by loudspeaker to the commandant's bridge. I had to follow my guide through a series of lifts and stairways. The ship was gigantic and I found myself in a hurricane of icy wind on the equivalent of the first landing of the Eiffel Tower. In the centre, out in the open, sitting on something resembling a tennis umpire's chair, was the ship's lord and master, Captain Merveilleux du Vignaux, enormous binoculars dangling from his chest. I saluted with one hand while holding my hat on with the other. Now I understood why sailors had chin-straps on their caps. He barely looked at me and acknowledged my salute with a nod of his chin. Bof!

I quickly saw that they hadn't much experience of war. An officer came up to me and said, '*What is it?*' (in English) pointing to a silhouette high in the sky.

I looked at him and answered, 'In the first place I am French and I speak it, secondly it's a Junkers 88; you know it, I trust?'

'Oh, really? It's been there a good 15 minutes.'

I gave a start. 'Well, in that case you are being amazingly patient. He is monitoring your position continuously and giving it to the Kriegsmarine.'

I assured him that it was indeed a German, not an ally, and I couldn't resist adding that it would have alerted the submarines and that consequently they would be wise to take some serious precautions. Being a pilot, I added, I didn't know much about torpedoes and it was up to them to worry about their tub. Smugly, I then descended to the lower depths, 30 feet below, to drink punch with the friendly lieutenants.

We escorted this convoy to within sight of the northernmost tip of Sweden, and apart from an attack by Heinkel III torpedo boats, nothing happened – to my great relief! – and we returned to Scapa Flow. We learnt that the four destroyers, three English and one Norwegian, had damaged the *Tirpitz*, which took refuge in a Norwegian fjord. Standing on the bridge while entering the harbour, we witnessed an extraordinary sight. Very slowly, almost side by side with our ship, the four destroyers sailed past, superstructures literally in shreds. They had just accomplished one of the Royal Navy's most remarkable feats. The *Tirpitz* for which we had lain in wait had actually left, then did a U-turn, no doubt alerted by the spotter planes (probably including my Ju 88). In a savage sea and a freezing temperature, those four little ships charged the 50,000-ton steel monster, bristling with heavy artillery, firing off their torpedoes three times and then falling on the German escort boats, which beat a retreat, leaving the battleship conclusively out of action.

What a sight! All the hundred or so ships in Scapa Flow let off their sirens at full blast to salute their return. The Commander on watch on his bridge in his khaki duffle-coat, the long row of coffins. . . . A triumphal entry like that would mark a man for life.

TUSSLE IN THE STRATOSPHERE

21 February 1944

In a Victorian novel this chapter would be sub-titled, 'Or the unexpected consequences of a game of chess'.

Jacques and Kelly were on 'readiness' from 1030 hours to 1400 hours. Superb weather, but bitterly cold. Not having anything much to do, Ian Blair and I were playing a game of chess. At 12 o'clock everybody went off to lunch, but we decided to finish our game. Kelly enviously watched the others going – this cold sharpened the appetite, and, as usual, he was famishing. We ended up by taking pity on him and offered to take their place. They accepted joyfully, for it must be admitted that this high-altitude readiness business was rather a bind.

They went. We slipped on our Mae Wests, put our parachutes and helmets ready in the two Strato-Spit VII's. Ian had not flown one yet and wanted the new one with the pointed tail fin. I gave way, after calling him every name under the sun, and we resumed our game of chess.

1222 hours. 'Your queen's had it,' said Ian. My queen certainly was cornered, but just as he stretched out his hand to take it, the air-raid siren went.

In the ensuing turmoil, queens, pawns, rooks, everything went for six. The fitters rushed into the corridor with a clatter of nailed boots. I dived for the door, shouting 'scramble, scramble!' Ian leapt out of the window.

In less than 50 seconds I was installed, strapped in, oxygen switched on, engine ticking over, while the fitters were screwing down the air-tight hood over me. Three white rockets from Control, showing that the runway was clear. The ground was frozen so hard that we could safely cut across the grass to get on the runway.

At 1223 hours 35 seconds exactly, we took off at full throttle, and already control was giving us our first instructions.

'Hallo, Dalmat Red one, Pandor calling, bandit approaching B for Baker, at angels Z for Zebra, climb flat out on vector zero, nine, five. Out!'

I fumbled inside my boot for my code card, which had got mixed up with my maps. I was so clumsy about it that I had to ask Pandor to repeat.

O.K. a Jerry was approaching Scapa Flow, at altitude Z – I looked it up on the card. Phew! Z meant 40,000 feet. I set my course, still climbing at full boost. Ian's Spit hovered a few yards away and I could feel his amused eyes on me under the sun goggles.

It was a wonderful winter's day – not a trace of cloud in the sky – and the arctic sun pierced my eyeballs. I switched on the heating and set the pressure in my cabin.

'Hallo, Dalmat Red one. Pandor calling, bandit now over B for Baker. Hurry up!'

'Hallo, Pandor, Dalmat answering, am climbing flat out on vector 095, am angels R for Robert.'

What did the controller take us for – rockets? In 5 minutes we had got to 23,000 feet; not bad going.

In the meantime I had been thinking: this Jerry must be a reconnaissance aircraft. In this weather he must be able to get perfect photos. The Fleet's ack-ack couldn't shoot because of us, naturally, and the Navy must be cursing. At all costs we had to get that Hun. If we didn't, the admirals would get us!

We passed Scapa and continued on course 095°. I glanced back and saw a white 'contrail' describing a wide circle over the naval base, about 10,000 feet above us. That must be him.

I wondered what kind of machine it could be – one of the new Junkers 86 P's? Anyway, he wasn't worrying in the slightest and calmly went on taking his photos.

'Hullo, Pierre, Red two here, smoke trail at 6 o'clock above!'

We were now at 33,000 feet, between the German and Norway. If we could climb another 7,000 feet without being seen, we would have cut off his retreat.

I opened up flat out, easily followed by Ian, whose Spitfire was superior to mine. The Jerry, still showing no sign of alarm – he probably thought he was perfectly safe at that height – started a second run. The heavy ack-ack opened up, but the black puffs were well below the white trail.

Forty-one thousand feet! The cold was really getting frightful and I turned the oxygen full on. Thanks to the pressurised cockpit the pain was bearable. From now on our exhaust gases left a heavy white trail which stretched out and widened behind us like the wake of a ship. We had the sun behind us.

The Jerry was now coming towards us. Either he had seen us and was trying to get by before we were in a position to intercept him, or else he had simply completed his task.

Our special engines were pulling beautifully and our lengthened wings supported us well in the rarefied air. Ian was parallel to me, about 900 yards away, and we had gained about another 2,000 feet, which brought us roughly 1,000 feet higher than our quarry, who was about 2 miles away and approaching rapidly.

He must be as blind as a bat.

'Tally-Ho, Ian, ready to attack?'

'O.K.'

He had seen us, but too late. We converged on him. To our surprise it was a Messerschmitt 109 G equipped with two fat auxiliary tanks under the wings. He shone like a newly-minted penny and he was camouflaged pale grey above and sky-blue underneath. He had no nationality marks.

First he turned left, but Ian was there, veering towards him. He reversed his turn, saw me, and, with a graceful continuous movement, banked more steeply, rolled gently over on his back, diving vertically in the hope of leaving us standing.

Without hesitating we followed him. He dived straight towards the grey sea which looked congealed, without a wrinkle. He was half a mile ahead of us, with his tanks still fixed to his wings. The speed increased dizzily. At these heights you have to be careful because you soon reach the speed of sound and then, look out! There is a strong risk of finding yourself hanging on a parachute, in your underpants, in less time than it takes to describe it.

The Hun made full use of his GM-1 booster and kept his lead. At 27,000 feet my A.S. indicator showed 440 m.p.h., i.e. a true speed of 600 m.p.h.! I had both hands on the stick and I leant on the controls with all my strength to keep the aircraft in a straight line. The slightest swerve would have crumpled up the wings. I felt my Spitfire jumping all the same, and I could see the paint cracking on the wings, while the engine was beginning to race.

The controls were jammed. We still went on down – 15,000 feet: Ian passed me; 10,000 feet: Ian was 200 yards ahead and 600 from the Hun. He opened fire – just a short burst. Perfect shooting!

The Me 109 suddenly tore in half like tissue paper, and exploded like a grenade. One wing flew off to one side, the engine and half the fuselage went on falling like a torpedo, while debris fluttered in every direction. One of the tanks went spiralling down leaving behind a trail of burning petrol vapour.

Eight thousand feet. I must straighten out. I pulled on the stick, gently but firmly. In the denser atmosphere the elevators reacted, and I saw the horizon beginning to slide under the nose of my aircraft – but the sea was already there! It was no longer the solid block I saw at 40,000 feet – but a moving greenish mass, fringed with foam, rushing towards me.

I pulled the stick again – no good, I felt I wasn't going to straighten out in time. Then, taking a chance, I gave the trim a full turn back. Immediately a veil of blood spread over my eyes, I felt my back and my bones twisting, my guts tearing, my cheeks pulling at my eye sockets, fingers tearing my eyes out. Everything went black. The whole aircraft creaked and groaned.

When I opened my eyes again the headlong momentum had carried me up to 13,000 feet. There was a warm trickle from my nostrils, dripping on to my silk gloves – blood. My head was swimming. I could vaguely hear the controller's voice in the headphones, but the centrifugal force had damaged the valves in my radio and I couldn't make out what he was saying.

I was alone in the sky, I couldn't see Ian anywhere. Down below, a large irridescent patch of oil and petrol and a puff of smoke wafted away by the wind showed the grave of the Messerschmitt.

I set course for the islands I could see on the horizon and soon I could make out the big Scapa Flow barrage with its balloons shining like a rope of pearls. Waves of sickness swept over me and I flew by instinct. Only the thought of our reception when we landed revived me a little. Just as I touched down, I thought I heard Ian over the radio. He was therefore O.K. thank God. I landed with the wind and taxied mechanically up to Dispersal. I hadn't even the strength to help the fitters unscrew my cockpit. Sutherland, warned by Control, was there with the Intelligence Officer. They told me straightaway that Ian was safe and sound. He had made a belly landing in a field on Stronsay, his aircraft damaged by the debris from the Hun. So everything was all right and this success got copiously celebrated in the mess.

The next day the London papers were full of it. You would have thought that we had saved the entire British Navy. We received telegrams of congratulation – from the A.O.C. 12 Group, from Admiral Ramsay, the C. in C.

Ian was brought back from his island in a motor boat, frozen to the marrow but as happy as a sandboy.

EVENTFUL LANDINGS

7 *March* 1944

What a day for the Flight! At 6.30 a.m. Oliver and Danny Morgan took off for the dawn patrol over the naval base. At 6.40 Oliver succeeded, with his oil pressure at zero, in getting back to the airfield and landing without an accident. He immediately changed aircraft and took off again. At 7.20 Ops. rang up in a flap to tell us that Oliver had made a forced landing on the tiny island of Shapinsay. Not his best day!

I was Joe'd for this job, as usual. I was detailed to go and collect him. I took an armourer with me in the Tiger Moth and succeeded in landing without mishap in the only possible field. It was covered with 8 inches of snow and mud, and there was a cross-wind. Ollie had pancaked on to it, undercart up.

I brought Ollie back, leaving the armourer to unload the cannon and machine guns and dismantle the secret equipment.

At 7.45 p.m. Jacques and I took off for the night patrol. The sky was cloudless, the moon was in the first quarter, but a very dense mist hugged the ground. For a quarter of an hour, at 7,000 feet, we circled the naval anchorage surrounded by a barrage of balloons.

'Look out, Dalmat Red One, bandit approaching H for Harry from East, 30 miles out, angels O for Orange.'

'Roger Novar, Red One out!'

Oh hell! Another game of hide and seek. We switched off our navigation lights. I could only place Jacques' aircraft by the slight glimmer from his exhausts.

By the dim light of a red bulb fixed in the side of the cockpit, I decoded the message with the help of the key for the day. From what we had just been told, the Jerry must be approaching the Fair Isle Radar station at a height of less than 1,000 feet.

'Hullo, Dalmat One, steer zero, six, zero – open up if you can, bandit very fast.'

We opened the throttle full out and, as soon as we passed the hills on the mainland, we came down to sea level, as in bad visibility it is easier to distinguish an aircraft from below upwards than vice versa – especially over water.

The controller didn't seem in form this evening and, after giving us a dozen contradictory courses amongst the little islands in pursuit of an elusive Junkers 88, he ordered us home. It was 8.30.

The visibility had got worse and worse and Jacques was obliged to follow me in close formation so as not to lose me. I concentrated on my instruments and called my radio station at regular intervals to get a fix. We ended up by finding ourselves over the base, sensed rather than seen, thanks to the regulation red lights indicating obstructions on the ground.

'Hallo, Control, Dalmat Red One calling, over base, about to pancake.'

The flare-path was immediately lit up. Its carefully screened flares twinkling in the mist – indistinct, but comforting.

The fog was getting thicker, but as long as I had those flares I wouldn't get lost. Cheered by this thought, I decided to add a quarter of an hour to my night-flying time and let Jacques land first. Ten minutes later I began my approach, opened my cockpit and a moist salt-laden mist swept in. I started on my last 90° turn, which brought me in line with the flare-path and I pushed down the undercart lever. I throttled back and immediately the alarm buzzer went off in my ears! Instinctively, keeping my eye on the runway coming towards me, I felt for the lever and pushed it right down. It gave and I immediately realised the position – the pneumatic system must have packed up and the wheels were not locked in the landing position.

This kind of accident is fairly rare and disagreeable enough in daylight. At night it assumes considerably graver proportions.

I immediately informed flying control of the position and, opening the throttle full out, gained height again, which would enable me to try and get my wheels down by some violent manoeuvre.

Commotion on the ground. Loudspeakers warned my C.O., the station C.O., the ambulance, the M.O., the fire tender, etc. In spite of my efforts nothing happened and, as a last resort, I tried the bottle of compressed carbonic gas, but with no result. Clearly not my lucky evening.

A glance at the gauges showed the radiator temperature going up alarmingly and my oil pressure beginning to drop: 110, 115 degrees – 80, 70, 60 lbs.

Christ! Spitfire V's have only one radiator, set asymmetrically under the right wing and the leg of my half-down undercart was masking the radiator air intake; 120°F. being the maximum temperature permissible, I had to take a quick decision.

'Hallo, Belltop Control, Dalmat Red One calling, will you put the floodlight on the patch of grass in front of the watch office – out.'

'Roger Red One.'

As I had to resign myself to landing wheels-up before the engine exploded, I couldn't do it on the concrete runway. With the sparks and the heat produced by the friction of 4 tons of metal going at 100 m.p.h., my machine could catch fire immediately.

The 30,000 candle power floodlight lit up a big triangle of grass in front of Control and I was going to try to land my Spit on it on its belly. Sweat began to trickle down my back and my vest stuck to my skin like a cold wet towel. I did my best to prepare myself for the formidable deceleration – from 100 m.p.h. to dead stop in the space of 30 yards and half a second. I tightened the straps of my harness, firmly fixing myself to the seat. I lowered the seat to protect my head, in case I turned turtle, and I slid back the hood and locked it tight; at least there was no risk now of being imprisoned in a burning box. I released my parachute, undid my oxygen tube and, before pulling out my headphones, I called control:

'Hallo, Belltop, Dalmat Red One Calling. Coming in now. Switching off to you now. Off!'

It was high time. A continuous stream of sparks was escaping from my radiator and noxious glycol fumes were beginning to invade the cockpit. I took in a big gulp of air and with a slightly shaking hand reduced throttle, set the propeller to fine pitch, lowered the flaps and began my approach.

The lamps marking the edge of the airfield shot past below me and the brightly-lit triangle rushed towards me. I levelled out at about 12 feet, still in shadow. Suddenly my aircraft flew into the blinding flood of blue light. Fumbling, I switched off the engine and the petrol. A cloud of smoke belched forth to left and right of the cowling.

I held my breath, my eyes fixed on the grass passing beneath my wings. I could sense the ambulance following me at full speed, followed by the fire tender. Gently, I eased the stick back, still more, still more, reducing my speed to the minimum – 90 m.p.h. – my propeller must be just about touching the ground, the aircraft began to tremble and, I pulled the stick hard, right back.

No longer held up by anything, the machine crashed to the ground with an appalling din. Bits of propeller blade flew about, my engine churned the ground, raising mounds of earth and grass. The port cannon twisted like a wisp of straw, tearing the wing.

The shock hurled me forward with incredible violence and the safety straps cut into my flesh, ripped my shoulders. The thought flashed through me that if they didn't hold, my face would be smashed against the sight. I felt a searing pain in my right knee, heard the slapping of the stick against my leg, when the aileron wires broke. Carried forward by its terrific momentum the aircraft stood up on its nose, rose up on one wing and, for one agonising fraction of a second, I was suspended in space, clinging desperately to the windshield, with one foot on the instrument panel, the ground standing up in front of my eyes like a wall. Would it land on its back? With a crash like thunder, which reverberated in the stretched aluminium box of the fuselage, the aircraft fell back on its belly. A last jerk, then silence ... which pierced the eardrums. A drop of sweat trickled down my cheek. Then suddenly the hissing sound of glycol and petrol vapourising against the white-hot metal of the engine. Thick smoke began to emerge through every chink in the cowling. The ambulance bell brought me back to my senses. I pushed open the door with my elbow, threw my helmet outside, jumped on the earth-covered wing, tore out my parachute and, forgetting the excruciating pain in my knee, I removed myself as fast as I could from the neighbourhood of the aircraft. I covered a few yards, staggered and collapsed in Jacques' arms. He had run all the way from our Dispersal 500 yards away and was completely winded. Good old Jacques! Leaning on his shoulder I limped to safety, to where the spectators were outlined in the glare of the floodlights, at a respectful distance. The fire crew were already sousing the aircraft with carbonic foam. I sat down on the grass. Somebody offered me a lighted cigarette and the doctor and his orderlies fussed over me. A screech of brakes and my Squadron Leader emerged dishevelled from his car – he had dashed out of the cinema when the loudspeaker announced that an aircraft was in difficulties.

'Hallo, Closter, old boy! are you O.K.?' I was bundled into the ambulance in spite of my protests and taken to the Sick Quarters where a cup of hot, sweet tea, generously laced with rum, was waiting for me. My knee was already all swollen and blue, but the M.O. said it was nothing. He then examined my shoulders where the straps had raised two painful purple weals.

By and large I had had a lucky escape.

8 March 1944

Immediately after breakfast I went and examined the traces of my eventful landing. The aircraft lay at the end of a deep furrow ploughed in the rich earth by the cowling. The oil and glycol radiators had been torn off on the way. The plastic propeller blades had snapped off flush with the spinner, scattering in a thousand fragments.

Afterwards I had to fill in a dozen 'crash reports' and, as usual, the technical officer tried to prove to me by A plus B that it was my fault. A heated argument followed until, disconnecting the hydraulic pump, he saw that its spindle was broken. As I really couldn't have broken it with my teeth he had to agree that I had done what I could. Sutherland and Oliver on their side fished out the 'pilot's notes' from the bottom of their drawers, to prove that I had acted correctly in the circumstances, and defended me energetically. After a lively interview with the Station Commander, whom I treated to a long technical dissertation (of which he didn't understand one word), I retired to the mess absolutely vindicated.

A CHANCE MEETING WITH
THE GENERAL

We returned to the south, to Detling, where we were delighted to find brand-new Spitfire IX-B's, and relieved to experience a more clement climate. We could lay aside our Eskimo garb and put on civilised uniforms without having to don two pullovers over two vests, in wool and silk, woollen stockings, a shirt, battle-dress and Irvine jacket on top.

As there were no opportunities to spend money at the Orcadian north pole, I had accumulated four months' pay, so when I saw in a shop-window boots laced '*à la Guynemer*',* I bought them and had some English-style riding breeches tailor-made. Now that I had gone up in rank, I also treated myself to an officer's bamboo cane . . . the epitome of London style. Whatever else, those dumb Americans out on the town would no longer take me for a hotel porter and ask me to call them a taxi!

Jacques and I had three days' leave, a fair amount of money (relatively speaking, with our pitiful Free French pay) and a promising long weekend ahead. Pomaded and perfumed, we left the hairdresser and strolled like fashion-plates, caps tilted, white scarf, brown gloves, to F.A.F.L. H.Q., the French Lycée, Queensberry Way, to collect our back pay. When we arrived, the sentry at the entrance executed an impeccable 'Present arms', something a pilot is not used to. Rather surprised, I suspected that something other than our elegance must have prompted this. I turned, in time to see two long grasshopper legs unfolding from a newly-arrived front-wheel drive Citroen, maroon stripe on khaki trousers, a general, then. Christ! Not just any general, THE GENERAL!

De Gaulle climbed the steps of the staircase four at a time. We froze to attention. He saw us, pivoted, looked more closely, motioned me to come forward. I advanced to the foot of the stairs, saluted him, stick under my arm: an impeccable salute, head high, eyes fixed 10 cm. above the two-star

---

* Georges Guynemer (1894–1917) was the biggest air ace of the French Air Service in WWI.

képi, hand slightly open – a text-book salute. I presented myself: 'Officer Cadet Pierre Clostermann, regimental no. 30973, my respects and at your orders, mon Général!' An eternity passed and I waited: perhaps a compliment for my Croix de Guerre was being framed . . . then it fell on me, and from a great height, since he was three steps above!

'Monsieur le cadet.' (I'd never been called that; it sounded good but the tone didn't bode well. Silence). 'Monsieur le cadet,' (another silence), 'where have you left your horse?'

I agonised. Next, jerking his chin towards my stick: 'Are you going fishing? Go and take off that ridiculous fancy dress!'

Then he made an about-turn and continued.

I heard Jacques, who exploded, bent double with laugher, saying, 'We'd better not follow him too closely inside.'

DIVE-BOMBING

The No-ball question was still giving the R.A.F. a considerable headache, and on our return from the Orkneys it was decided to equip some Spitfires with 500-lb. bombs and make them dive-bomb the flying-bomb sites. 602 and 132 Squadrons were to be the guinea-pigs in this experiment.

On 13 March we left with our Spitfire IX's, which we had recovered, for Llanbedr, on the North Wales coast, for the first trials.

Dive-bombing with Spitfires is a technique on its own, as the bomb is fixed under the belly of the machine, in the place of the auxiliary tank. If you bomb vertically the propeller is torn off by the bomb. If you bomb at 45°, aiming is very difficult. After various attempts Maxie evolved the following method:

The twelve aircraft of the squadron made for the objective at 12,000 feet in close reversed echelon formation. As soon as the leader saw the target appear under the trailing edge of his wings he dived, followed by the remainder, at 75°. Each pilot took the objective individually in his sights and everyone came down to 3,000 feet at full throttle. At that point you began to straighten out, counted three and let go your bomb. It was rather rudimentary, but after a fortnight the squadron was landing its bombs inside a 150-yard circle.

During the three weeks we spent at Llanbedr we were the object of visits from every V.I.P. from Inter-Allied G.H.Q., each time we staged a demonstration. They had their money's worth. At the first visit Dumbrell's bomb landed plumb on Fox at 450 m.p.h. and the poor blighter had to bale out in extremis. At the second visit one bomb, McConachie's, hung up. He decided to land with it and made a run over the airfield to warn them. As he passed the bomb came free at last and exploded bang in the middle of the airfield, covering the dismayed visitors with earth and mud.

Really, apart from Max and Remlinger, who were always eager beavers and dreamt of nothing but blood and thunder, nobody was very keen on this brand of sport. We preferred to await the first results against an objective well defended by flak before making up our minds.

In the meantime we had constant lectures on No-balls. After the first bombardments, in the course of which 16,432 tons of high explosive had been dropped on the launching sites in four months, the Germans had evolved a new type of much simplified installation. They were erecting more than fifty a month, very well camouflaged and hard to detect. The total German layout consisted of nine sectors, four directed against London and the other five against Southampton, Portsmouth, Plymouth, Brighton and the harbours of Dover and Newhaven respectively.

According to the latest information the Flying Bomb, or V-1, was a jet-propelled device capable of carrying about a ton of explosive a distance of 250 miles at roughly 425 m.p.h., and highly accurate, i.e. to within 1,000 yards.

We returned to Detling on 8 April and waited without exaggerated impatience for our first dive-bombing trip.

13 April 1944

The day before, for the first time, Spitfires had dive-bombed the continent. 602 and 132 had attacked the flying-bomb installation at Bouillancourt, 12 miles south of Le Tréport.

Although our objective was in an area crammed with flak, the Germans had been so surprised at the sight of twenty-four Spitfires, each carrying a 500-lb bomb, that they had opened fire only after we were out of range.

16 April 1944

We were going to repeat the prank on a big scale. We were to bomb Ligercourt, by the forest of Crécy. It was much less funny this time as in a radius of 2,000 yards round the target there were nine 88 mm. guns and twenty-four 20 and 37 mm. – not to mention the fact that we should be within range of Abbeville's formidable defences.

We took off at 1225 hours. We were to attack first, followed by an Australian squadron (453), while 132 covered us against possible enemy fighter reaction. We passed the French coast at 10,000 feet and Sutherland put us into our attacking positions:

'Max aircraft, echelon port, go!'

I was the tenth of the twelve and didn't feel at all happy.

'Max aircraft, target 2 o'clock below.'

I could see Ligercourt woods just under my wing and I recognised the target – another flying-bomb site cleverly camouflaged among the trees – from the photos we had been shown at briefing.

We were now immediately above it. With a turn of the hand I depressed the switch that fused the bomb and removed the safety catch of the release mechanism.

'Max, going down.'

Like a fan spreading out, all the Spitfires turned on their backs one after the other and dived straight down. This time the flak opened fire straightaway. Clusters of tracer began to come up towards us. Shells burst to left and right, and just above our heads a ring of fine white puffs from the 20 mm. guns began to form, scarcely visible against the streaky cirrus clouds. Our acceleration, with that heavy bomb, was terrific: in a few seconds we were doing well over 400 m.p.h. I had only just begun to get the target in my sights when the first bombs were already exploding on the ground – a quick flash followed by a cloud of dust and fragments.

Max and Skittles Flights were already climbing again, vertically, jinking hard, stubbornly followed by the flak.

My altimeter showed 3,000 feet and I concentrated on my aim. I pulled the stick gently back to let the target slip under my Spitfire's nose, following our technique – a tough job at that height. I counted aloud – one, two, three – and pressed the release button.

For the next few seconds, as a result of the effect of the violent centrifugal force, I was only dimly aware of what was going on. I recovered to find myself hanging on the propeller, at full throttle, at 8,000 feet. The flak seemed to have given us up. A turn left soon showed me why. 453 were beginning their dive. The aircraft went over like a waterfall and were soon only tiny indistinct patches against the ground.

The flak redoubled. Suddenly there was a flash and a Spitfire turned over, leaving a trail of burning glycol, and crashed into the middle of the target. A horrifying sight, which I couldn't get out of my mind.

A bitter blow, one of the dead pilot's friends told me back at the airfield. It was Bob Yarra, brother of the famous 'Slim' of Malta, also brought down by flak the year before. Bob had got a direct hit from a 37 mm. between the radiators as he was diving at well over 400 m.p.h. The two wings of his Spitfire had immediately folded up and come off, tearing off the tail plane on the way and spattering with debris the aircraft behind, which had to take violent avoiding action. Three seconds later the plane crashed into the ground and exploded. Not the ghost of a chance of baling out.

Those No-balls were certainly beginning to cost us dear.

THE *ENTENTE CORDIALE*

Interlude in London. Max got us a 48-hour pass. Jacques' mother had sent him a comfortable allowance this month, and I'd received a cheque for £22 – after tax – from the B.B.C. for a broadcast in Spanish. A fortune compared with our pay!

So we were flush. And money could only be for spending, seeing that at any moment we might disappear in a ball of flames! So we decided to head for London and after a quick call to our little hotel in Piccadilly, we were on the train to Waterloo.

We arrived in the capital at 6.30 that evening. First came dinner. Horsemeat steak – not yet rationed – and real French *frites* in the small Belgian bistrot Chez Rose in Soho. We shared a bottle of burgundy with Geerts and Demoulin, Belgians from 609. This was a rare substantial meal in those days of hard rationing, though it's true that no right-minded Englishman would countenance dining here and on a portion of one of Man's four-legged friends!

A meal in London would not have been complete without a visit to the bar of the S——. As everyone knows, fighter pilots are a gregarious bunch, rather like starlings. They frequent the same drinking places, sending anyone packing who clearly isn't of the same ilk. Impeccable credentials were required to get into the S—— in the evening, which meant being a member of a crack squadron in 11 Group or sporting the D.F.C. . . . You always bumped into chaps you knew, acquaintances or friends from this select little world. Always the same stories accompanied by the same hand gestures. Always pretty girls in uniform, too: the grey, khaki or navy-blue of W.A.A.F., A.T.S. and W.R.E.N. officers perched on bar stools. Everyone else would be standing, pint mugs were passed over people's heads, and there would be the inevitable chap in the scrum who spilt the gin-and-orange or Pimm's No. 5 he was bearing off to some charming creature. A waiter passed round a silver tray; we helped ourselves to small sausages in breadcrumbs, but no-one ever dared take more than one!

The barman had served everyone who was anyone in the Battle of Britain, and the fading poster asking the public for donations to the

Spitfire fund was smothered in pilots' signatures. Nine out of ten of these boys had bought it by now. Behind the barman on the wall was a notice: OUT OF BOUNDS TO DOGS, to which an anonymous hand had added AND PONGOS (infantry), and another, in black paint, YANKEES AND NIGGERS!

While I was chatting to Johnny Cheketts, who'd been returned home in record time by the French Resistance – a mere three weeks after being shot down over Abbeville – Jacques had moved in on a pretty W.R.E.N.

I could just make out his line of attack above the din: 'But, ma chérie, Queen Victoria had a crush on Napoleon III. They even fought the Russians in the Crimea side by side.' That was his invariable and often infallible take on the *Entente Cordiale*, generally leading to an update of the invitation to 'make war together'.

Knowing what to expect, I left him to it. Quite likely, I wouldn't see him again till breakfast next day. If all went well, he'd be over the moon all week and take more risks than ever during sorties. . . .

AN UNSAVOURY INCIDENT

Once again, we were escorting American B-26's on a raid against a Belgian factory. Compared with the B-17 Flying Fortresses, B-26's were on the whole easier to escort as they flew faster and the crews kept their nerve better: Fortress gunners had a nasty habit of letting fly at anything that hadn't got four engines, which was the case with most escorts. The only aircraft they seemed to recognise was the P-38 Lightning, because of its twin fuselages, but the first ones were only just arriving in England.

Unfortunately, the cruising altitude of the B-26 was critical for the superchargers of our Rolls-Royce 63 LF Merlins, which automatically switched between stages in response to atmospheric pressure. Retarding the throttle to the minimum had little effect, and the engines shuddered violently despite their solid construction as the boost ceaselessly cut in and out. The sun was rising on my left, cruelly blinding in the immaculate blue sky. Even with my Ray Bans, it was impossible to scan the sector from 30 to 60° east. To persist meant ending up seeing nothing but a black hole with red spots. Obviously, the Messerschmitt 109's always came diving out of the glare. They suddenly filled our windshields, enormous, in nose-to-tail formation, and then vanished just as fast: fleeting, ghostly shapes with their black crosses. . . .

Ten or so '109's' flashed across our formation's path in this manner, hitting Aubertin and holing Max's brand-new kite. He would be mad all week! In the same swoop they were on to the B-26's. Surrounded by lines of tracer, the bombers resembled giant porcupines. Everything was over in seconds: this job was all reflexes and quickness of eye. A B-26 broke formation and began to lose altitude, trailing heavy black smoke. Immediately it left, Max detached two machines to try and escort it back to England, as damaged aircraft attracted German fighters like flies. A few moments later, another B-26 went into a vertical dive and crashed close to a village. Five parachutes. The missing sixth man was probably the pilot, who would have struggled to keep the aircraft flying while his crew baled out. As the B-26's started their bomb-runs, we were relieved by

Typhoons. They were still relatively unfamiliar, and their arrival caused a certain chaos on the radio. It had to be admitted, though no excuse for trigger-happy gunners, that from a certain angle Typhoons could be mistaken for Focke-Wulfs, especially by a pilot not too hot on aircraft recognition.

We turned for home, with Bobby Yule leading the wing. Despite being an old hand, he managed to bungle his navigation and took us bang over Ostend – a well-known hotspot – where we were treated to a barrage of 88 mm. flak, something of an honour for fighters. . . . We found ourselves in the thick of big, black smoke-bursts illuminated by flashes; our attack formation degenerated into a headlong flight in all directions of the compass. We were not used to seeing flak batteries wasting good 88 mm. shells, nearly a yard long and no doubt very expensive, on Spitfires. Nonetheless, four of our machines were damaged by fragments of flak, and their pilots arrived back at base somewhat pale round the gills.

The next day we had escort duty again, but this time with B-17's. It was a real chore, as it meant flying slowly to hold our position protecting the bomber formation's flanks. If attacked, our Spits lacked the impetus and speed to manoeuvre. In any case, when on 'close escort', it was vital to keep a safe distance from those B-17's of the 8th Air Force; their gunners were quick on the trigger, as quick as their imaginations when it came to claiming kills the moment they landed!

The Yanks' objective was a marshalling yard at Rouen. The flak was no heavier than usual, but the lead bombardier appeared to lose his nerve; on his command the entire formation of 130 Fortresses dropped its bombs, laying down a deadly carpet of explosions and flame well before the left bank of the Seine and crossing it a long way south of the target. The rail yards were undamaged, but hundreds of wrecked houses were blazing right up to the foot of the cathedral. Its graceful spire, through some divine providence, appeared intact. How many of my fellow Frenchmen – all civilians – had died or would die for nothing before our eyes? A murderous rage exploded inside me. I started yelling over the radio, so everyone could hear: 'You American sons of bitches! You immoral bastards, you've got no feelings at all . . .'.

Max called me back to my senses with an order to button it and keep my place in the formation or return to base. He realised how close I was to diving and shooting at the B-17's. A moment's reflection, and I decided to return alone to Detling, choking with fury. With allies like that, who needed enemies? There could be no legitimate excuse for carpet bombing.

To make matters worse, it was about this time that we learnt through the newspapers that Roosevelt was engaged in a struggle with De Gaulle to reduce France's independence and assume control of our empire, of which he thought us unworthy.

A few days later, we dined out at the Coq d'Or in London. There we bumped into André Philip, who invited Aubertin and myself to his table. I told him about the Rouen business. He replied that it was not merely De Gaulle whom Roosevelt despised, but the French as a whole.

All the same, this was no reason to massacre our civilians and destroy our cities in a way even the Germans had not dared to. I have to say that my R.A.F. comrades who witnessed this last raid were as scandalised as I was. Fortunately, André Philip added, De Gaulle had things in hand in Algiers and the Resistance was behind him – though that would have been small comfort to the wretched people of Rouen. . . .

The opening in 1995 of archives relating to the Second World War has revealed secret documents of a terrifying nature, impossible to read without deep unease. One document is particularly disturbing, a key piece of the D-Day planning and connected with the bombing missions which so outraged my comrades. This is Directive RE 8 from Eisenhower, the Supreme Commander. It is one of those American studies where every possible eventuality is foreseen, itemised and evaluated in the minutest detail. Among others, the chapter entitled 'Transportation Plan' calls for the bombing of forty or so French populated areas – including major cities – with important road or rail junctions, barracks or reserves of equipment. One paragraph evaluates the possible losses of the 8th Air Force during these operations, with a footnote of a few lines warning of the inevitable deaths of 160,000 French civilians and a considerable number of non-fatal casualties, not to mention the enormous material damage resulting from carpet bombing, the only method which, by its sheer ruthlessness, would reduce the losses of B-17's and B-24's.

Churchill was outraged, demanding revision of the plans. He admitted, however, that a few thousand deaths were a necessary evil in such operations. He felt compelled to write to Algiers warning De Gaulle, and his letter ended by acknowledging that the French had been courageous and loyal friends of the Royal Air Force. Allied fliers had strict orders to do everything possible to avoid harming French civilians, who had consistently come to the aid of downed aircrew, including Americans.

The archives do not contain De Gaulle's reply, simply noting that he thanked Churchill.

Air Marshal Harris, chief of Bomber Command, was asked by Churchill what was his and his crews' viewpoint on the subject. He replied, 'I have no point of view. I receive orders and I give them.' Churchill, in a letter to Roosevelt dated 14 April 1944, declared that the results failed to justify either the massacre of

French civilians or the scale of the political damage. 'I beg you to put pressure on Le May, Eaker and Spatz about this.' (The commanding generals of the U.S. 8th Air Force.)

Receiving no reply, he repeated his appeal on 29 April 1944, stating that losses of French civilians exceeding 100–150 could not be tolerated unless a target overwhelmingly justified them. General Eisenhower had to realise that twenty-seven of the targets selected for destruction, in densely populated areas, simply could not be attacked. It was contrary to all ethical principles to deliberately terrorise civilians who were risking their lives to save downed aircrew.

Still with no reply from the President, Churchill telegraphed him a severe note on 7 May. What he said is not known, save that it was barely within the limits of politeness. Roosevelt finally replied on 15 May. 'Whatever is necessary for the safety of our boys is at the discretion of Ike (Eisenhower).'

So it was that at the end of the month Amiens, Angers, Avignon, Chambéry, Chartres, Grenoble, Nîmes, Saint-Étienne, Rouen, Cherbourg, Paris, Trappes, etc., were bombed by the U.S. Air Force. In the space of three days, 8,200 people were killed, 12,000 injured, 120,000 made homeless; 11 hospitals, 35 schools and countless other buildings were destroyed, totally needlessly in 80 per cent. of cases.

'Minimising American casualties' always seems to translate as the killing of hundreds or thousands of civilians. It was in this scheme of things that towns like Caen, Saint-Lô, Cherbourg, Avranches, Falaise or Villers-Bocage suffered appalling raids at the time of the Normandy landings.

A MEETING BY THE RIVER

The end of April, and I had three days off. The first mayfly were just hatching, and my intention was to try my luck with a few trout. (Jacques was away doing his own brand of fishing, i.e., for the female species.) There was more and more talk of a landing in June or July, so it was my last chance before the balloon went up. Not far from Detling is a very fine river, one of those 'chalk streams' every yard of which must have been leased out for a small fortune before the war and guarded by the owner like the crown jewels. By now there were no bailiffs – they'd all been called up, so I fished away with a true Frenchman's disregard for authority. But it wasn't exactly poaching: I was fishing like an English gentleman.... Had I been caught using maggots or a spoon bait into the bargain, instead of flies, goodness knows what the British would have had to say about those barbarians from over the Channel! I had managed to spend most of my leave for the last three years by the water, and, I must say, every time I'd needed to ask permission to fish, it had been granted, without exception. The only problem was equipment, and my stocks were running low. In London, the window of Hardy's, the famous manufacturer of fishing tackle, was empty. The old, very dignified salesman behind the counter had become a friend over the months; he often dug into his secret reserves to find me some Tortue line, a skein of silk, hooks now simply unobtainable or some amazing flies....

And the beauty of the river! The beds of water weed, the marsh marigolds, the reeds, the timid moorhen, darting dragonflies and mayflies, a cloud of midges caught in the rays of the low morning sun filtering through the branches.... There was a sense of peace and wonder which made the war seem so distant.

Two or three trout were rising, watched placidly by a heron standing motionless on one leg, and after two trial casts I managed to place my sedge in the middle of the ripples made by the largest fish. As the river was no longer fished, the trout had lost its wariness, and bit greedily. It put up a great fight, struggling upstream for some 50 yards before I managed to exhaust it. A second soon went the same way: enough for one day. I wrapped my catch in leaves of wild mint; it stains their bright, pearl-like scales, but lends the flesh a marvellous taste. Time to light up my pipe. Sitting on a tree-trunk, I reread for the tenth time a chapter of Maurice Genevoix's *La Boîte à Pêche*, which, to my eternal shame, I had pinched from the library of the Free French Volunteers in Bromley South.

Suddenly and almost blasphemously shattering the calm, a V-1 passed overhead in a clattering roar like that of a giant motor-cycle, and a few minutes later I heard the ack-ack trying to bring it down before it reached London. There was no escape from the war after all.

I delved in my knapsack for the spam sandwiches the W.A.A.F.'s from the kitchens had kindly – and surreptitiously – prepared for me. On the very point of opening a bottle of Bordeaux purchased at a pub en route, I realised I'd forgotten my corkscrew. As I hesitated whether to break the neck of the bottle, I heard a voice behind me.

'Why don't you borrow my corkscrew?'

A man had come up silently across the damp grass, proffering a Swiss Army knife. 'Those trout look quite nice. Congratulations!'

Seventy years old if a day, straight as a ramrod, with his gaiters, tweed jacket and white moustache, he looked every bit a retired general of the old Indian army. . . . Which he was!

He sat down beside me and took out a pipe. I offered him my tobacco; he sniffed it and said he didn't like the American stuff, it was too sweet. He preferred his own. I gathered he was the landowner, but he put me at ease and invited me to come and fish whenever I liked. He asked me about myself, intrigued by the fact that I was a fighter pilot, and obviously French to boot. He tried one or two casts with my rod, but declared it not up to scratch. 'It's American.' That hardly surprised him; on the other hand, he declared he had some perfect flies for this river, and would let me have them if I came to dinner tomorrow. He told me the address and how to find it.

All afternoon I worked my way along the stream, releasing two more trout. Evening arrived with a fresh little breeze, and I had to leave my little paradise and hitch-hike back to base. One of the trout I gave to a clergyman who very decently offered me a lift in his ancient Austin. The other one I got the mess chef to fry, and I ate it on the quiet in the pantry, strictly out of bounds to officers.

Finally I settled myself into a chair in the mess to update my diary, which I'd neglected somewhat lately. I began by describing the lovely day I'd just spent. Tomorrow, I would accept my old general's invitation.

After fishing his river and taking him a pair of fine trout on each occasion, I received regular invitations to visit and was treated to the privilege of his solitary friendship. He wore two wedding rings on his left hand and a mourning ribbon on the lapel of his town jacket. He always had a bottle of port tucked away somewhere.

One day I told him I was to be awarded the D.F.C. He wanted to go and fetch champagne from his cellar, but I declined. Then, making an excuse, he disappeared for a moment and returned with a long leather case which he set on the table in front of me.

'They're yours now.'

Reverently, I admired two wonderful, split-bamboo rods: one for trout, the other for salmon.

Before leaving for Ford, I wanted to say goodbye to him. But at Maidstone police station I learnt there had been a tragedy. A malfunctioning V-1 had fallen beside the little creeper-clad manor, quite destroying it. My old general was now reunited with his wife, a nurse who had been killed during a London air raid in 1940. It was only then that I learnt that his son, a fighter pilot and squadron leader of 601, had gone missing over the Channel in 1941. The father had never mentioned the fact. It was his son's rods he had presented me with. I admit I had tears in my eyes that evening as I brooded on the injustice of fate.

THE NORMANDY LANDING

The great moment approached. 4 May. 125 Wing left Detling for its new base at Ford, near Brighton.

The transfer of the aircraft took place in very bad weather and our patrol of eight, under Ken Charney, had to land on an American field near Dungeness in pouring rain and visibility zero. This field was occupied by Thunderbolt squadrons which had arrived from the United States the week before. It was the first time these Americans had seen Spitfires from close to. They were flabbergasted to see that people flew in weather like this (what did they expect? – England isn't California) and the manoeuvrability of our machines, our side-slips and S approaches gave them something to think about.

Towards evening the weather cleared and we gave them a demonstration of steep short take-offs. With our Spit IX's we were airborne in 50 yards while a laden Thunderbolt needs 600. Immediately after retracting my undercart I did a slow roll that cut the daisies.

There were already seven fighter squadrons at Ford. The runways and accommodation buildings were thoroughly congested, and we decided to sleep under canvas near our aircraft instead of lodging in a large requisitioned castle-building a couple of miles from the aerodrome, near Arundel.

Ford reminded me of the Place de la Concorde at 6.30 in the evening. It was now home to four R.A.F. squadrons, plus four American groups – two each of P-47's and P-51's. Our transatlantic allies were very kind, but extremely invasive. As the Brits put it: 'over-sexed, overpaid, and over here'. There were three servings at every meal, and one had to queue. The Yanks didn't take kindly to the mediocre portions and the British cooking.

We slept in tents hastily pitched to accommodate all this throng on a peace-time base designed for, at most, two or three fighter squadrons. Too many aeroplanes, too many men, too many jeeps. Amid the chaos, Jacques, who had his head screwed on, went exploring near the coast – an out-of-bounds area in view of the imminent invasion – and discovered a little pub that, in the circumstances, was generally empty. It was a delightful place, deep in an English countryside glorious with spring, with a comfortable lounge, flowery chintz armchairs and a bar that had acquired the patina of years. Jacques made short work of charming the lonely landlady, whose husband was away fighting in Burma. She let us in outside the statutory hours, fried us eggs (from her own hens, and thus, in theory, not rationed) and served us tea. We were utterly happy and flirted with her quite harmlessly. After every mission we headed straight there on Jacques' motor-bike, not even bothering to change from our flying kit.

One afternoon, after a particularly difficult sweep, we were washing down our eggs at the bar with a glass of Guinness when some other customers came in, and we heard French being spoken. Damn! So much for our peace and quiet! The newcomers sat down in the area used to serve tea. A tall beanpole of a fellow wearing the four *galons* of a French *commandant* appeared and began throwing his weight about. He turned towards Jacques, who was busy eating, and stared hard, taking in the shoulder-flashes – proclaiming 'France' – below our modest pilot officers' tabs.

'Are you French? Has no one taught you to greet a superior officer and salute? Haven't you noticed there's a French general behind you? Go and pay your respects to him!' This in a tone one might use to a couple of infantry privates. And we weren't exactly new recruits. . . . Like all good fighter pilots, we'd earned our share of gongs. (Those afflicted with jealousy put it rather differently.) Fifteen-odd mentions in dispatches between us, and we each had the French médaille militaire and were members of the Légion d'Honneur. Jacques rose, dragging his feet somewhat, made his way towards the general, saluted and stood at attention in the approved fashion. Unfortunately, he was wearing round his neck the infamous scarf which Tim, the caricaturist, had decorated for him with Indian ink. It was a large silk square, bright orange in colour, with a frieze running round the four edges. On this frieze were depicted some delightful nymphs in an advanced state of undress, holding each other by the hand as they danced; and in the middle, a callipygian young lady, naked and kneeling, in a rear view – and in great detail – bearing an Eiffel Tower on her back. Written in big letters was: 'Climb up here and see Montmartre!' Which, needless to say, added a somewhat colourful touch to a regulation uniform.

A peremptory voice addressed itself to Jacques in a tone that clearly admitted no reply. 'Right now, mon ami, stand up straight! And what's this round your neck? Show me. . . . You want to look like a dancing girl instead of a French officer? Then why not stick a feather in your arse!'

Poor Jacques – he had stumbled upon General Leclerc! The *comman-dant* was Guillebon, who later became one of my best friends . . . and has never forgotten this incident.

We were kept pretty busy. On 8 May two dive-bombing trips. On 9 May two dive-bombing trips including an attack against the famous viaduct at Mirville. There we got a very hot reception from automatic flak and the following official report was published in the press: 'Squadrons of Spitfires dived through a wall of flak to attack the big viaduct at Mirville on the railway line between Paris and Le Havre. The viaduct has 39 arches. The Spitfires hit it in the middle and at the northern end.'

For those who know the restraint of R.A.F. communiqués the term 'wall of flak' was no exaggeration. In fact the bombardment was rather pathetic and I don't know who were the heroes of 132 or 602 who scored hits. I know that my bomb at least fell over 200 yards from the viaduct. Gerald and Canuck were reported missing as a result of this affair.

On 10 May in the morning we carried out a sweep – Marauder escort – which lasted 2 hours 20 minutes. We met some very clever Germans in a mixed formation of Me 109's and Fw 190's. Maxie Sutherland got one, Jacques and Yule probably another each. As for me, my shooting was beneath contempt. In the afternoon of the same day another dive-bombing trip against No-ball 38.

On the 11th, dive-bombing of No-ball 27 (Ailly-le-Vieux-Clocher). On the 12th ditto of a railway junction at Steenbecque. On the 13th two dive-bombing trips, including one against No-ball 86 defended by a formida-ble array of flak. The constant-speed mechanism in my propeller packed up, which gave me a considerable fright at the time.

At this tempo we were quickly reduced to wrecks. Dive-bombing tests the body severely and we had some bad cases of internal lesions – haemorrhage in the pleura, abdominal ruptures and other disagreeable complications – at least, so the squadron doc said.

Today 145 Wing received a visit from Group Captain James Rankin, a top Battle of Britain ace and now rejoicing in the title of 'G.C. Tactics' at the H.Q. of 83 T.A.F., under Broadhurst, our C. in C.

His purpose was to find volunteers – in a very circumspect and roundabout way, of course – to train on the Hawker Typhoon; apparently the Typhoon squadrons were short of pilots – not to mention aircraft! Obviously, he was careful not to mention the savaging they'd taken or the technical problems and mechanical failures occurring during high-speed dives. Despite his enthusiastic address, he made few converts. He claimed that the Typhoons would play a major role against German armour in the forthcoming landings, that they were the fastest fighters currently in service with the R.A.F., apart from the Spitfire Mk XIV, and that they were already downing Focke-Wulfs by the dozen. . . .

Over lunch afterwards there was a lively discussion.

'Are you going?' Jacques asked me. 'If so, let's go together.'

I replied that I wasn't too keen. For a start, we were in clover in 602, and secondly, I was still allergic to flak. No amount of bull would lessen the risks – one only had to look at the statistics. Indeed, when we got back to the flight hut, Max called us together and declared that anyone who wanted to transfer to a Typhoon squadron must be off his head. He unfolded a paper and read us the notes he'd made from confidential documents in the Ops. Room after Rankin had left. Typhoon losses, in fact, were so shocking as to be unbelievable. He quoted several examples which I forgot by the evening, though one remains clear: during attacks on radar installations along the French coast, 18 out of 48 Typhoons were shot down in a single week. Max concluded with a memorable remark: 'If anyone wants to commit suicide, no problem: there's a Typhoon waiting!' He added: 'I'm not telling you this to stop you leaving. I'd be glad to see the back of you. How lovely to run a squadron without you lot of moaning, big-headed pilots!'

Rankin had little more success with 132 than 602, and went away empty-handed.

Since Leclerc's charming compliment, Jacques had been going into a sulk every time he spotted a French uniform. It so happened that a Boston from the Lorraine Group landed at Ford on 8 May, and over lunch we chatted with the crew, which included Tournier and our old friend Masquelier, who straightaway spotted the infamous scarf. Jacques repeated the story, and asked who was this General Leclerc with the earthy vocabulary. Tournier explained things to him, put him in the picture about Kufra and Tunisia and the formation of the 2nd DB, adding that he was a very big shot.

We'd just reached dessert – a sort of crumble with synthetic raspberry sauce – when the loudspeaker announced an alert and we were scrambled. It was quickly explained to us that a Typhoon from 183 Squadron had been shot down while attacking a radar post at Dieppe.

Flak again! The downed pilot was a Norwegian, the famed Wing Commander Erik Haabjoern, C.O. of 124 Wing; he had baled out and landed near the mole. He managed to climb into his dinghy, but right under the eyes of the Germans. They swiftly set up a machine gun on the mole and began firing at him. Before our eyes, and just as we were about to engage, one Typhoon blew the machine gun to smithereens with a salvo of rockets, while seven others which were circling around to protect their leader took out four A.A. posts, as well as using their cannon to sink a German patrol boat which had rashly ventured out towards the dinghy. It was a bloody good show, and once we'd regained some altitude, we contented ourselves with covering the boys from 124 who were running low on juice and needed to head back. They asked us to take over till they were relieved. Just at this moment, though, four Focke-Wulfs followed by several Me 109's dived down on them. I was Red 2. Max opened up on the lead Focke-Wulf from a head-on position, scoring a certain hit; as it passed at right angles to me from left to right, I gave it a burst of my own at point-blank range. It was an absolute sitting duck, but I'm not even sure I touched it. Anyway, it flipped over on its back and hit the drink with an almighty splash. Fortunately, the German fighters were more interested in the Spits than the dinghy.

Indifferent to the dog fight raging above it, a small Walrus seaplane arrived unnoticed in the confusion and put down quietly on the water. Despite a strong swell, it taxied over to the dinghy and picked up Erik with great sangfroid. Twice it failed to take off again, floundering in the devilish troughs, but in the end it miraculously made it, with us as escort. I hoped the pilot of the Walrus would get the D.S.O. at the very least for his amazing gallantry.

As usual, what promised to be a grand dog fight with the '109's' suddenly fizzled out. Within seconds, the sky was empty. . . .

We returned to base somewhat disappointed. On arriving, we were told that this was the second time Erik had parachuted into the Channel and got away with it. Max, in his report, gave me all the credit for our Focke-Wulf, which everyone had seen fall near the Dieppe mole. I protested that he had hit it first. At least we ought to share it. Not at all, replied Max, ever the chivalrous leader.

The Typhoons were the stars of the R.A.F. during the Normandy landings. Again and again they rescued Allied units from situations of dire peril by taking on the German Panzers. It is no exaggeration to say that it was in great part due to them that the operations of June, July and August 1944 went ahead without disastrous setbacks. Because of their supremacy in air-to-ground combat, the Typhoons attracted the full fury of the Wehrmacht's flak batteries as they frantically attempted to minimise the terrifying effect on armour and infantry alike. The aircraft boasted enormous firepower: four 20 mm. cannons and eight or twelve heavy rockets armed with either high explosive anti-personnel heads or hollow charges for piercing armour. The R.A.F., to be blunt, rescued Patton and his 3rd Army. The flamboyant American commander had extended his dash south too far, and at Mortain his tanks began to run short of fuel. He was in danger of sharing the fate of his predecessor (and personal hero!) General Custer – but in 1876, the latter lacked the option of air support. In August 1944 the place of the Sioux was taken by 200 or 300 heavy Tiger and Panther tanks aiming to cut off his inevitable retreat to the north. The Tigers of the 2nd Panzer Division, assisted by poor flying weather and the fact that the Americans had no specialised tank-busting aircraft, made short work of the lighter Shermans; with their 88's, it was a turkey-shoot. During the course of 8 August alone, Patton lost sixty tanks. Next morning, the American High Command sent an SOS to the R.A.F. requesting a massive and immediate intervention by the Typhoons.

21 Wing at once dispatched Nos. 174 and 181; 124 Wing followed and notably 123, which comprised two famous squadrons: 609, which had been absorbed by the Belgians and 198, commanded by a Frenchman, the celebrated Major Ezanno, who later attained the rank equivalent to Air Chief Marshal. By the evening of 7 August, eighty-four German heavy tanks had been knocked out and countless vehicles abandoned by crews cowering under the fury of the attacks.

As the flak batteries had been unable to keep up with the rapid movement of the Panzers – an error never to be repeated – only four Typhoons were brought down and ten or so damaged. Two Spitfires were lost during the evening when the Luftwaffe finally began to react. Four days of bad weather saved most of the surviving tanks of II Panzer. A week later, between Mortain and Falaise, the Typhoons and their rocket-salvoes crushed the last German hopes of a counter-offensive. From 16 to 18 August, however, their fighters exacted a terrible revenge.

Seventeen Typhoons of 84 Group were lost during 17–18 August in engagements with the Me 109's of JG-27, as well as eight from 183 Squadron. We know that III/JG-27 was commanded by Fritz Gomotlka, who achieved four kills. Next day – 19 August – Major Ernst Dullberg brought down another three, two from 184 and one from 266. Ezanno's 198 had lost eleven machines, and he himself was shot down twice in two days! In all, in ten weeks' fighting over Normandy, the R.A.F.'s tank-busting squadrons lost more than 150 pilots: some 66 per cent. of their total manpower. 609 was under the command of my Belgian friend, Major Charles Dumoulin, who was to become godfather to my youngest son Michel.

As for me, I was completely creased. Luckily, on 15 May, Group Captain Rankin was summoned to Allied Expeditionary Air Forces G.H.Q. at Uxbridge. He took me with him. My French uniform provided a bit of local colour, as he put it.

The concrete underground vaults at Uxbridge, which had sheltered

British Fighter G.C.C. during the crucial days of the Battle of Britain, had become the Allied air forces centre for the Normandy landing.

It was an absolute Tower of Babel, thronged with pink and olive-green American uniforms and the blue-grey of the R.A.F. I never in my life saw so many stars and so much braid – up to the elbows. The most insignificant little man you met was at least an Air Commodore. Air Marshals were thick on the ground.

There were Leigh Mallory of the R.A.F., who was C. in C., Quesada, the big noise in American fighter circles, General Arnold, C. in C. U.S. Army Air Forces, Doolittle, of Tokyo raid fame, etc.

Being in the secrets of the great is no joke. I had pocketfuls of passes and all day long I was challenged by hordes of M.P.'s cluttering up the entrances and the underground corridors lit by mercury vapour lamps.

It was difficult to get a general view of what was being hatched, but the invasion date seemed to have been fixed for the first few days in June and the zone too, the strip from Le Havre to Cherbourg. Things did not seem to be going too smoothly. There was a lot of friction between the R.A.F. and the American 8th Air Force.

In particular there were discussions where an attempt was made to decide the number of German fighters available. The production of fighters for the Luftwaffe, from the very accurate reports of the Intelligence Service, had been, from 1 November 1943, to 1 April 1944, 7,065 fighters; 150 jet-propelled, about 4,500 Messerschmitt 109 G's and K's, and the rest Focke-Wulf 190's, with a few twin-engined Messerschmitt 410's.

From 15 November to 15 April on the other hand, German fighter losses were estimated as follows: 678 destroyed, 102 probables and 347 damaged by R.A.F. fighters; 73 destroyed, 5 probables and 22 damaged by ack-ack.

The American 8th Air Force, however, claimed that its bombers (Fortresses and Liberators) had obtained the following results during the same period: 2,223 destroyed, 696 probables and 1,818 damaged; plus 1,835 destroyed by their fighter escorts.

The British regarded these figures as ridiculous. They admitted the right of the American press communiqués to produce such results to sugar the pill for the American public, which was finding the enormous Air Force daylight losses hard to swallow. But the R.A.F. categorically refused to base its plan of campaign on fancy propaganda figures.

The argument soon got heated. The British maintained that it was better to underestimate the number of successes, as they did, by means of a very strict method of confirmation by ciné-film, than to base them on individual verbal accounts which were hard to check. Naturally, when in a box of 72 Flying Fortresses you had 300 or 400 machine-gunners blazing away at 20 Focke-Wulfs, and 5 were in fact brought down, there were in the nature of things bound to be several dozen gunners who swore black and blue and in perfect good faith that they had brought one down.

In addition it seemed very odd that, in a raid like the one on Augsburg, 900 British and American escort fighters declared they had brought down 118 German aircraft while 500 Forts claimed 350 successes, i.e. almost a third of the German fighters in the air that day.

In a similar mixed show, for instance, on the same objective, after a very severe dog fight, an R.A.F. squadron (i.e. 12 Spits of the latest type) applied for the confirmation of 7 successes, while one single American fighter pilot claimed 6 successes, in circumstances which would have led to his being credited with scarcely one by R.A.F. standards.

It was finally decided to take as a working basis one third of the American figures for bombers and one half their fighter pilot claims, which still gave the fairly impressive figure of 800 successes for the Forts and 900 for the fighters, giving a grand total for the allied forces of 2,700 Me 109's and Focke-Wulfs out of action.

Taking into account inevitable wastage, losses in training and so on, that left the Luftwaffe about 3,000 first-line fighters, out of which a maximum of 600 could be operating on the western front.

Against these the Allied Expeditionary Air Forces could pit exactly 2,371 first-line fighters, of which 1,764 were R.A.F.

Next we were kept busy planning the preliminary fighter operations for the second fortnight in May. On the 21st a general offensive was laid on against railway locomotives in the whole of northern France and Belgium; 504 Thunderbolts, 433 Spitfires, 16 Typhoons and 10 Tempests took part in this simultaneous operation and, in the 'Nord' French railway system alone, 67 locomotives were destroyed and 91 seriously damaged.

From 19 May to 1 June 1944, there were 3,400 fighter sorties against locomotives in France, Belgium, Holland and Germany: 257 were destroyed and 183 seriously damaged. These unimpressive results were due to the pilots' lack of experience against this type of target.

At the same time the fighter-bombers had to carry out a very heavy programme of attacks against road and railway bridges; 24 bridges were put out of action over the Seine, 3 at Liége and others at Hasselt, Hérenthals, Namur, Conflans (Pointe Eiffel), Valenciennes, Hirson, Tours and Saumur.

I had the opportunity of seeing the aerial photographs taken after the heavy bombing raid by the R.A.F. on Trappes on the night of 6–7 March. This important marshalling yard had been completely destroyed. At least 240 one-ton bombs had hit the target. Two-thirds of the loco sheds had been razed to the ground; all the tracks destroyed, including the electrified Paris-Chartres track.

All the marshalling yards from Paris to Brussels were attacked and razed in the period from April to May. The plan to isolate the chosen landing zone was beginning to bear fruit.

We next had to prepare detailed plans for the air-cover of the landing proper which had by then been fixed for 5 June.

The task of the fighters was to destroy on the afternoon of 4 June the three chief German radar stations at Jobourg, Caudecote and Cap d'Antifer. On the 5th, the day of the landing, it was to furnish a permanent protection of 15 fighter squadrons for the convoys and the beaches. It was decided that on days D plus 1, D plus 2 and D plus 3 even the strategic reserve would be used, which would bring the number of fighters and fighter-bombers to 3,483, the R.A.F. providing 2,172 of them.

The programme of advanced bases for our fighters in Normandy was elaborated according to 'Shaef' estimates. Favourable sites had been worked out after careful study of P.R.U. photos and on day D plus 10 – i.e. 15 June – we would theoretically have at our disposal:

Three E.L.S. (Emergency Landing Strips), strips of more or less flat ground, 600 by 30 yards, with an ambulance and a fire pump capable of receiving aircraft in distress that had to do belly-landings.

Four R. and R. (Refuelling and Rearming), strips of well-rolled, well-levelled ground, 1,300 by 60 yards, with two dispersal areas well out of the way, each 100 by 50 yards. These runways were to enable fighters to land to refuel and rearm. Special 'R.A.F. commando' personnel were earmarked for these, with sufficient technical training to undertake these jobs.

Eight A.L.G. (Advanced Landing Grounds), provided with wire-mesh runways 1,300 by 60 yards with space prepared for the dispersal and protection of 48 fighters permanently based there. Arrangements were made for fixed ack-ack and also for the billetting of the ground and flying personnel. They were to be occupied by 8 fighter wings.

Special engineer units entitled Airfield Construction Units were to leave on D-day with their complete equipment of bulldozers, steam-rollers, tents, steel-mesh, etc., to carry this programme out.

The following spots were chosen: Bazenville, Sainte-Croix-sur-Mer, Camilly, Coulombs, Martagny, Sommervieu, Lantheuil, Plumetot, Longues, Saint-Pierre-du-Mont, Criqueville, Cardonville, Deux-Jumeaux, Azeville et Carentan, Chapelle, Picauville, Le Molay et Cretteville.

After a fortnight spent at Uxbridge in this way, I was not sorry to join my

Pierre Clostermann

Henri de Bordas

Jacques Andrieux ('Jaco')

Bruno

Bruce Oliver

341 'Alsace' Squadron at Biggin Hill in 1943. For a few hours the war seemed far away.

The Free French Air Force of 1941–42. From left to right: Bougen, de Daxé, Moinet and Guynamar.

Commandant Mouchotte and
Wing Commander Al Deere at
Biggin Hill.

'Alsace' Squadron, 1943. The
pilots in life jackets are, from
left to right, Laurent, Bruno,
Remlinger, the author, Mathey,
Farman and (on the wing)
Menuge.

Mouchotte, photographed just twenty minutes before his death.

Combat film: Clostermann scores a hit on a Focke Wulf, 2 July 1943.

After returning from a mission, the author helps the mechanics to rearm his Spitfire.

The author receives the D.F.C. from Sir Archibald Sinclair, while
Ken Charney keeps an eye on three Focke Wulfs.

Clostermann, wearing the First World War aviator boots that so irritated
General de Gaulle. His comrade on the right, Tournier, is wearing the regulation uniform.

Jacques Remlinger and Pierre Clostermann, July 1944. The two remained close friends for 60 years, until Remlinger's death.

The author examines his LO-D after an eventful landing.

Flak: the terrible German 20mm anti-aircraft guns.

Two flak ships after the armistice. They carry: 1. Two 20mm guns, 2. Two single barrel 37mm guns, 3. Two double barrel 37mm guns and 4. Two 20mm guns

Without enthusiasm, the author makes
the acquaintance of a Typhoon.

The great Belgian pilots Detal, van
Lierde, Geerts and Demoulin, who made
609 Squadron a legend.

The 'old hands' of 3 Squadron. *Sitting:* Gordon, Dug Worley, Wright, Torpy.
Standing: Hassal, the author, Walker, Peter West, Bruce Cole and Macintyre.

The Messerschmitt 109 – ever present, and always dangerous.

The Messerschmitt 262 – an aeroplane ten years ahead of its time.

On the way to Rheine. The author, photographed by Charles Brown,
flying 'Le Grand Charles' along the Dortmund-Ems Canal.

Leutnant Söffing and Oberleutnant Dortemann who, between them, shot down 14 Tempests in just 60 days.

Focke Wulfs, hidden beneath the trees at Evreux-Fauville.

The Messerschmitts of JG-2.

Walter Nowotny was decorated with the Knight's Cross with Oak Leaves, Swords and Diamonds. He died aged 24, at the controls of his Me 262 jet.

Priller, the German ace, after a solo reconnaissance flight over the Normandy beaches on 6 June. Two days earlier he had recorded his 98th kill, on a Typhoon.

Major Oesau, Commodore of JG-2. He reported 117 victories before being killed in France.

The author, sitting in 'Le Grand Charles' at Fassberg at the beginning of April 1945.

Pierre Clostermann says his farewells to l'Armée de l'Air in Alsace.

comrades at Ford again. As I had had to sign an undertaking not to breathe a word to a soul of what I might have seen or heard, I could not answer any of the thousand questions they plagued me with. I had also had to undertake not to fly over enemy-held territory until D-Day plus 10 hours. It is easy enough to see why. I might be shot down, and if ever my interrogators should suspect what I knew – in particular the place and the date of the landing – the Germans would stop at nothing to make me talk. To avoid any possible weakening the British, who wished to run no risks and had few illusions as to the ability of the human system to resist certain arguments, allowed no one who knew even a small part of 'Neptune' and 'Overlord' to cross the Channel and risk being taken prisoner.

As a result of atmospheric conditions D-Day was put back to 6 June. Bound by my oath, I had to wait until 5 p.m. before flying. That meant I was able to watch the formidable procession of gliders and paratroop-carrying aircraft which started at dawn and lasted for hours.

Everybody was worn out. 602 carried out a sortie at 0355 hours, another at 9 o'clock, one at 12 o'clock, one at 1730 hours and finally one at 2035 hours. I took part in the last two.

It is difficult to give a general impression of the landing as we saw it from the air. The Channel was congested with an inextricable jumble of warships, merchant vessels of every tonnage, tankers, tank landing craft, minesweepers, all dragging their little silvery barrage balloons at the end of a string. We passed half a dozen tugs sweating and puffing away, dragging a kind of enormous concrete tower sitting on a frame as big as a floating dock – one of the sections of the 'Mulberry' prefabricated harbour.

The weather was not very good. The Channel was angry and choppy and the smaller craft seemed to be making heavy weather of it. The low cloud made us come lower than altitude Z at which we should have been flying, and leave the safety corridors. As a result we flew slightly too close to a 10,000-ton cruiser, Southampton class, escorted by four big MTB's. The cruiser immediately started tacking desperately and signalling by Aldis lamp all sorts of violent things that nobody could understand. Personally I have never been able to assimilate morse, still less visual morse. To avoid unpleasantness from her ack-ack we turned our backs on her as fast as we could.

We flew along the Cotentin peninsula. There were fires all along the coast and a destroyer surrounded by small boats was sinking near a little island. Our patrol zone was the area between Montebourg and Carentan. Its cover name was 'Utah Beach'. We were covering 101st and 82nd American Airborne Divisions while the 4th Division which had just landed marched on Sainte-Mère l'Eglise. We couldn't see much. A few houses were in flames. A few jeeps on the roads. On the German side, to all intents and purposes nothing. Two cruisers were bombarding coastal batteries near the fort of L'Ilette.

The sky was full of American fighters, in pairs. They were wandering about rather haphazard, and showing a tendency to come and sniff at us from very close to. When they seemed too aggressive we showed our teeth and faced them. One Mustang coming out of a cloud actually fired a burst at Graham. Graham, whose shooting was as good as his temper was short, opened fire on him, but luckily for the Mustang, he missed.

Astonishing absence of reaction on the part of the Luftwaffe. According to the latest Intelligence gen they now had in France 385 long-range bombers, 50 assault aircraft, 745 fighters, 450 twin-engined night-fighters, plus reconnaissance aircraft – in all 1,750 first-line aircraft. This force would certainly soon be reinforced if the airfields were not bombed too much.

My second patrol was a dusk patrol over 'Omaha Beach'. It was a nightmare. The night was dark, with low cloud. In the gloom hundreds of aircraft were stooging about without being able to see each other, blinded by the fires raging from Vierville to Isigny. The battle seemed to be bitter in that sector. On the beaches high seas swept charred remnants of landing craft, lit up by salvoes from the batteries planted on the sands.

All the pilots concentrated on I.F. and tried in particular to avoid colliding. About twenty Junkers 88's – the first appearance in force of the Luftwaffe – took advantage of the situation to dive-bomb, rather at random, the concentrations of troops and material compressed on the narrow strip of the beachhead. I heard over the radio three pilots from 611 chasing six of these Ju 88's and I recognised Marquis' voice shouting:

'I got one of the bastards!'

Sure enough over there to the left a ball of fire fell down from the clouds.

The return to Ford in the inky darkness, and with the fog beginning to rise, was tricky. Four squadrons of Spitfires arrived in the circuit together. There was a confused medley of green and red navigation lights flashing past in every direction, swearing over the radio and general panic. Almost all the aircraft were short of juice and piled invective on the poor controller to get landing priority. As Jacques and I had carefully saved up our petrol with just this situation in mind, we left the far too crowded and dangerous neighbourhood of the airfield and climbed to 10,000 feet above the scrum. We landed after everyone else without any fuss and bother.

WE SHOOT UP SAINT-ANDRÉ

The first few days of the Normandy landing had not brought the expected swarms of German fighters in our gun sights. Jacques and I decided to carry out a little scheme that we had been hatching since the previous December.

At that time at Detling we had carefully prepared a shoot-up of the airfield of Évreux/Fauville. A P.R.U. Mustang had sown the seed. It had brought back a remarkable oblique photo showing the German base in minutest detail, including a row of Focke-Wulfs being serviced by a swarm of mechanics which had particularly arrested our attention. In theory it was pure madness – airfield flak almost always got you. In practice, with a bit of luck and a carefully managed element of surprise, we might easily get away with it.

The problem now was not quite the same as in December, as Évreux/Fauville was too close to the battle zone to be in permanent use. Failing Évreux/Fauville our choice fell on Saint-André-de-l'Eure and Dreux, further inland. We would let circumstances decide which to go for.

It was now a question of convincing Sutherland, who had been impossible to move the previous time over the Évreux business. We tackled him at breakfast, not too directly. We suggested he should let us go on a sort of free-lance sweep. We might take off as a kind of reserve for the morning's first beachhead patrol, and then, with his consent, break formation and take a turn round Caen at high altitude. Maxie was not very keen, but for the sake of peace and quiet he ended up by giving in.

We took off at 0950 hours behind the twelve Spits of the squadron. Half-way over we quietly gave them the slip and we at once gained height. We veered towards the south-east and the estuary of the Seine. Jacques was 400 yards to my right and slightly above. Like that we were mutually covered against any surprise. The weather was possible – four-tenths cloud at 7,000 feet. Naturally I would have preferred a layer of cloud further down which would have given us better protection against flak.

At 1020 hours we were immediately over Lisieux, its church tower standing out against the surrounding green. From 15,000 feet we could see the great German airfields at Fauville, Conches, Beaumont-le-Roger and Saint-André, with Dreux in the distance in a patch of mist. We circled for a quarter of an hour, scanning the sky. No one else in the air.

We listened in on the wavelengths of all the different controls. No information which might interest us.

O.K. then, let's go.

Conches was the nearest airfield. We gave it the once-over; at first sight everything seemed deserted.

Then Saint-André. Some sort of activity had continued there, according to the Intelligence reports. We must examine it from closer to. We went down in a wide spiral. The clouds intermittently hid the airfield, but on the other hand they prevented us from being observed by the watchful flak spotters.

Saint-André seemed to have had a terrible pasting – sticks of bombs criss-crossed over the runway, the hangars were in ruins. On the other hand, all around were trim villages and barns in clumps of trees, connected by little roads.

Mm! those roads seemed very straight. We came down to 10,000 feet. Just so! Those roads were taxiing-strips and the barns were hangars, perfectly camouflaged. We must look into this! Yes, sure enough, in front of what looked just like a farm a ray of sun projected the sharply defined shadow of two Heinkel 111's covered with nets.

'Look out, Jacques, two Heinkels down below!'

'O.K. Pierre, they're lovely!'

I opened the throttle and made another circuit, to get into position for the dive, sun behind us. I jettisoned my auxiliary tank. In the meantime those blasted clouds had made me lose the two Heinkels. I was almost in position for an attack but however much I stared and stared, it was no good. Only that ray of sun, throwing that revealing shadow, had given the game away. I simply couldn't dive down without a definite objective and risk getting shot up by the flak wandering about in the middle of the airfield at ground level, looking for something to shoot at.

I waggled my wings to warn Jacques of my indecision. He had come in close and we made signs at each other. It was really too silly. I looked at the airfield again. We were going to have to make our minds up quickly – everyone would be on the qui-vive if we went stooging around for hours.

'Look, Pierre, a Hun!'

Jacques and I saw him simultaneously – a small brilliant cross, skimming along the main runway, probably a fighter.

'Going down!'

'Look out, Jacques, your baby is still on!'

'I know!'

I had warned him, and now I had to work fast, before the flak got going. At full throttle, I dived down – 400 m.p.h. – quickly, because it would soon be getting unhealthy round here.

The details began to show up more clearly. Between the destroyed hangars there were others, of a different type, half-buried and covered with turf. Bomb craters, most of them filled in. The large main runway was carefully repaired and the craters which pitted it (as we thought, from 13,000 feet) were dummy ones, artistically painted to give the impression of an unserviceable runway. I caught a brief glimpse of men working and of lorries.

I levelled out 2 or 3 miles from the airfield and kept right down on the deck, to keep the flak off, roaring over the hedges. At the far end of the airfield I could now see the German in silhouette – it was a Messerschmitt 109. I skimmed along the edge of the field, registering what I could see. In the shade of a clump of trees about 20 brand-new emerald green Focke-Wulfs were warming up. . . . A pilot leapt off a wing on to his face in the grass. . . . More Focke-Wulfs along a hedge. . . . Some Messerschmitts in an orchard . . . some bowsers, covered by branches. . . . Variegated tents scattered about among the bushes. This airfield, which at 13,000 feet had seemed deserted, was simply swarming with aircraft and personnel.

My '109' was getting close – he turned left – I made for the centre of the field to cut him off – I climbed to 150 feet – the flak began, a clumsy cluster of tracer far away to the left. . . . I suddenly found myself nose to nose with another Messerschmitt which, intent on the other one, I hadn't seen. Too late to shoot. His undercart was down, perhaps even his flaps. His fuselage was grey, spotted with green and brown and he had big black crosses on a level with the cockpit.

I passed a few yards from him. He was probably landing, doing about 150 m.p.h. – I was doing 400. The pilot must have had a heart attack!

I was gaining on the other at amazing speed. The flak let fly with all it had, without bothering about him. He must have wondered what on earth was going on. I got him in my sights – only 500 yards – I pressed the button – cannon and machine guns – 200 yards, I went on firing – 50 yards. Before breaking I had time to see three of my shells burst; one between the engine and the pilot, another on the tail plane, and the third smashed one of the oleo legs of his undercart. I just avoided him in time, and as I cleared him I saw him turn over on his back and go into a spin.

The flak – and what flak! – was coming up in a sort of wavy curtain, shedding deadly little black puffs everywhere. I turned right and climbed desperately towards the clouds, 10,000 feet a minute, with full boost. It seemed to take ages.

Even when with a sigh I reached the haven of the clouds, the long red trails of tracer kept on stabbing the damp gloom round my aircraft.

What had happened to Jacques? Although he had failed to get rid of his tank he had followed me into the dive, but had lost me as we went through the cloud layer. He had found himself in the middle of the airfield at ground level a few seconds after me, and naturally he got the benefit of all the flak. Hampered by his tank he missed the second Messerschmitt, which landed under his nose. Keeping straight on through the bursting shells he spotted a row of mine-laying Heinkels which he machine-gunned. One of them collapsed in flames with a colossal explosion and another got a burst of 20 mm. and incendiary bullets at point blank range.

Hard pressed by the flak but, by a miracle, unscathed, he succeeded in joining me above the clouds. We once again passed over the airfield, now covered by an umbrella of black and white puffs, at 10,000 feet. The light flak persisted, in spite of our being out of range, and a salvo of 88 mm. burst far behind us.

My Messerschmitt 109 had crashed in a field at the southern tip of the main runway and the remains were still blazing away near a white ambulance. Trucks were tearing to the scene of the disaster in a cloud of dust. A column of thick black smoke rose from the direction of Jacques' Heinkels.

We came back via Évreux, turning right towards Le Havre, where we caught a glimpse of the concrete U-boat pens half wiped out in the recent Lancaster raid. Along the estuary were the oil refineries bombed by the Marauders – a large devastated stretch of land where only the round foundations of the storage tanks were visible. One or two still stood intact, like silver coins.

We climbed to 20,000 feet to avoid the flak, and to take a quick look at a nimbo-stratus layer where, a few hours previously, Johnson's Wing, 126, had shot down three Dorniers.

Going into a shallow dive we set course for Ford, where we landed at 1133 hours. As we taxied towards Dispersal we passed in front of the Intelligence Room. By the door was a deck chair with James Rankin in it, sunning himself. When he saw the black trails on our guns and wings he shot up and came running towards us. He climbed up on my wing and helped me to get unstrapped.

'Any luck, Clostermann?'

I was not too proud of our exploit, which constituted after all a serious breach of Control discipline, but I told him what we had been up to. Jacques joined us, bubbling over with joy. Rankin, for appearances' sake, greeted my account rather coldly, but he was not too displeased at bottom. Like a fool I mentioned the flak to Maxie, who landed a few minutes later with the squadron. He hated losing any of his chaps through flak and consequently tore me off a hell of a strip.

The Intelligence Officers were lukewarm, but when we described the rows of camouflaged German fighters they brightened up. G.C.C. was very interested by our report and shut its eyes to the escapade, and called us in after lunch for further information. We were asked to indicate on large-scale plans of Saint-André* the approximate layout of the camouflaged Dispersals and we were questioned as to the types of aircraft, etc.

The P.R.U. Mustangs would bless us for they would certainly get sent in the late afternoon to take low-level obliques and, after that morning's show, they would get a pleasant reception.

The next day we had the satisfaction of seeing our report confirmed by the daily Air Ministry secret bulletin, which added that the Luftwaffe had in fact reinforced that sector by withdrawing six Wings from the Russian front.

* N.B. – The author learnt after the war at Air Ministry that the airfield he had strafed was Dreux, not Saint-André.

PART FOUR

France

FIRST NIGHT IN FRANCE

11 June 1944

We were on 'readiness' after tea when suddenly we were informed that we were going to spend the night in France.

The 'Met' forecasted fog over the south coast for the next morning, which would immobilise the fighters. On the other hand the weather over France would be reasonable and, clearly, if the Spits did not patrol the beachhead the Luftwaffe would come out in strength over Normandy and make a nuisance of itself.

To avoid this, half a dozen squadrons were to take off that very evening, land as best they could on half-finished emergency fields, spend the night there and be ready at dawn for any eventuality. Each pilot must take two blankets and a box of K rations.

Jacques and I were distinctly excited at the idea of being the first French pilots to land in France. We decided to don our full regalia and Jacques took his flask of brandy to celebrate the occasion suitably.

A dash for the billets on our motor-cycles. We took off at 1830 hours and, after a normal patrol – nothing out of the ordinary to report – we met over Bazenville.

'Hallo, Yellow 3 and 4; hallo, Blue 3, you pancake first. Good luck!'

Sutherland was telling us, the Captain, Jacques and me, to land first. Very decent of him.

Jacques and I, in close formation, landed just behind the Captain in an impenetrable cloud of dust. Christ, what dust! It was white and as fine as flour. Stirred up by the slipstream of the propellers it infiltrated everywhere, darkened the sky, suffocated us, found its way into our eyes and ears. We sank in up to our ankles. For 500 yards round the landing strip all traces of green had disappeared – every growing thing was covered by a thick layer, stirred by the slightest breeze.

Two commandos whose eyes only were visible under a crust of dust and sweat, with Tommy-guns slung on their backs, helped me to jump down from my plane and laughed when they recognised my uniform.

'Well, Frenchie, you're welcome to your blasted country!'

Jacques emerged out of a cloud, a handkerchief over his face, and we shook hands – a moving movement all the same. We were treading French soil after four years' absence.

If the truth must be told, instead of the deep emotion I was expecting, what I felt most was profound regret at having brought my smart new 'best blue' uniform to such a dump. Already I looked much more like a powdered circus clown than an officer of the Armée de l'Air!

A Captain from the Canadian division stopped in his jeep on his way past to warn us:

'No straying from the airfield. No crossing from one side of the track to the other. Don't touch anything. Avoid areas marked by cloth strips, they are still mined. The Huns have left mines everywhere and only half an hour ago a man was killed and two others wounded by a German sniper hiding in a wood half a mile away who has got telescopic sights.'

We all met again behind a hedge where a mobile canteen gave us tea, biscuits and marmalade (all liberally sprinkled with that blasted dust).

Our strip was absolutely stiff with ack-ack – at least a dozen Bofors on the alert with the crews in position. When we expressed astonishment at the enormous quantity of empties round the guns a sergeant told us that if we waited until 11 o'clock that night, we would soon understand.

We spent the next two hours dispersing our planes and refuelling them with two-gallon cans; we puffed, we sweated, we coughed. I spent my time bemoaning my uniform's fate. When night began to fall we opened our rations, had a slice of ham and a few biscuits, then set off in search of a hole to spend the night in. Cautiously ferreting round in the orchard next door Jacques and I discovered a tent full of chairs, tables, coconut matting and large boards covered with maps. After a bit of rearranging we succeeded in dossing down with our blankets in reasonable comfort.

2230 hours. It was now quite dark. Jacques and I went off to have a smoke and a chat with two Canadian officers. A few stars were shining. To the south-east we could see the glow of Caen burning. All was quiet. Suddenly we heard the hum of an aircraft in the sky.

'Hallo,' I said, 'that's odd. It sounds like a twin-engine, but it certainly isn't a Mosquito.'

We looked up, trying to locate the sound. It seemed almost immediately above us.

'Don't worry, Pierre,' said Jacques after a moment's thought, 'if it was a Hun the ack-ack would already have opened fire.'

He had scarcely finished when a characteristic swishing sound disclosed the fact that a large bomb was coming straight down on us. In a fraction of a second the two officers evaporated. I dived under a lorry and Jacques, trying to follow me, tripped over an apple-tree root and fell flat on his face. There was a terrific crash. The earth quivered, a burning gust of air slapped our faces and glowing splinters bespattered the tent, the trees and the lorry and bounced back sizzling on the dew-covered grass.

At that moment the ack-ack opened fire. The sky above us turned into a moving mass of 40 mm. tracer shells rising in thick snaky clusters. It was as light as day. Our heads buzzed from the continuous roar. Shell fragments fell as thick as hail, bringing down branches and leaves from the trees, riddling the tents and clanging on the lorries and empty drums. Somewhere on the field a Spit caught fire and the flames brought the Junkers 88's clustering round like moths.

The bombs began to fall thick and fast. You could tell them apart by the sound – the big thousand-pounders went 'Frrrooommm' as they fell, while the medium ones whistled, phweephweephweeeeee – Bang! One fell so close that the impact threw me in the air and I gave myself a large bump against the lorry's differential. A Bofors, less than 10 yards away, was blazing away all the time in bursts of five shells. The barking noise pierced our eardrums. Deafened, battered, we crouched under our lorry, shivering with funk.

Round about 1 a.m. there seemed to be a lull. I sprinted across to our tent to fetch our blankets. I managed to find them under a pile of big boxes and boards, which had collapsed when the first bomb had gone off. If we had been there, we should have had all that down on our heads.

When I got back Jacques had crawled out and was dusting himself and swearing.

Suddenly a pyramid of tracer rose from Arromanches, where the convoys were concentrated, and, like a gas ring with jets lighting up in succession, the whole sky again flared up. The searchlights leapt out of the shadows and started probing the clouds.

Within a radius of 12 miles from our strip there must have been a good three thousand ack-ack guns. As the radar equipment was primitive and control non-existent, all those guns – Bofors, 3½-inch, 7-inch, etc. – fired away more or less haphazard, all at once. The ammunition seemed inexhaustible and the crews just kept their feet on the pedal.

The Junkers 88's and Dornier 217's came over in groups of about a dozen every five minutes or so and stooged around in the middle of this inferno, letting go their bombs more or less anywhere. It didn't really matter where, as the beachhead was so full of troops, ammunition dumps, convoys of lorries, concentrations of tanks and planes that they could scarcely fail to score a bull practically every time.

The nightmare went on until 3 a.m. Worn out, petrified with cold, we ended up by going to sleep, only to be awakened an hour later by the stand-to siren. We emerged from our lorry haggard, grimy, dusty, hirsute, with rings round our eyes and coated tongues and . . . we nearly passed out from the shock – we had spent the night under a lorry-load of 20 mm. shells!

Scarcely able to breathe, we staggered off to join our comrades (who were in no better shape) round the field kitchen where we queued up for a drop of tea. It took a long time as there were only five mugs, the tea was scalding and there were twenty-four of us. Our two Canadian friends from the evening before were there – we thought they had been pulverised by the explosion.

'Oh, you know,' said one of them modestly, 'we are now pretty hot at sprinting. We've been here a week and we're unbeatable!'

Just at that moment we heard the noise of several engines approaching. Everyone climbed the bank round the perimeter to get a better view. Bang! bang! bang! bang! three Focke-Wulfs jumped the hedge at the other end of the field and opened fire.

I remember hearing a few bullets whistling past, a few shells explode in front of us on the field, raising spurts of dust, and suddenly we found ourselves in the shelter, a good length ahead of the Canadians, in an avalanche of pilots, mugs, tea, biscuits and flying boots. After all that we didn't even have our cup of tea!

We went back to Ford in time for lunch – minus four aircraft destroyed or damaged during the bombing. We spent an hour sitting under a nice hot shower.

The A.L.G. programme had been considerably delayed in our sector by the unexpected resistance of the Germans in Caen, which, according to the plan, ought to have been taken in the afternoon of D-day.

In fact the three first landing-strips built were to all intents and purposes under the fire of heavy 88 mm. flak batteries. Bazenville, where we had landed four days before and which was to be our real A.L.G., had had to be abandoned.

In the end B11 at Longues was to be our field. Our ground staff, with our mobile echelon, our tents and our lorries, was embarking that evening to prepare our base and we were to settle definitely in France on the evening of 18 June and operate from there thenceforward.

Exactly four years to the day after General de Gaulle had said over the B.B.C.: 'Rien n'est perdu parce que cette guerre est une guerre mondiale. Les mêmes moyens qui nous ont vaincus peuvent faire venir un jour la victoire.' We were coming back weapon in hand.

17 June 1944

This time we were finally leaving for France. We were to leave at 8.30 a.m. Two minutes before, cheering news: three-quarters of our matériel had gone to the bottom when the L.C.T. carrying our advance personnel had been sunk by a torpedo. Squadron Leader Grant, the senior M.P., was reported missing, together with two 'H.Q.' officers.

Hell of a flap. I tore round on Jacques' motor-bike to collect my kit. Naturally, I had too many things to take, as usual; my mechanics kept on screwing and unscrewing all the panels of my Spitfire, trying to stow away the maximum amount of gear in the minimum of space. I scarcely had room to sit down. I hoped to God there wouldn't be a fight on the way over as I could only just move the controls. A clumsy mechanic smashed my superb thermos. I could have murdered him! I sincerely hoped my parachute bag, somewhat insecurely hitched to the wireless set, wouldn't come adrift; it would jam the controls for certain. The rear armour plate had been removed to make room for my sleeping bag and three extra blankets. My camera and my steel helmet were both slung over the hand pump. I had with me two enormous bolonies, a gift of the Ford cook, my revolver and ammunition and my Mae West stuffed with oranges.

Once I was inside and swaddled up in my cockpit, they went and bunged in a dozen fresh loaves of bread for the mobile echelon which had been existing on biscuits for a week.

We still didn't know where we were going to land. B5 had been intended for our airfield but it had been recaptured by the Germans. All night long work had gone on to make the biggest possible number of planes serviceable. As a result we had 18, 132 had 20 and 453 had 17. As best they could all these Spitfires crowded in disorder on to the runway. Miraculously there were no collisions.

Everybody took off without mishap and we succeeded in forming up in groups of four. I partnered the Captain but after a few minutes he had to return to Ford with engine trouble.

The trip was uneventful. Only a few minutes after we had landed at B9 – Bazenville – and had jumped into a trench to shelter from the usual cloud of dust, a dozen Messerschmitts came over the landing-strips to cover two Focke-Wulfs which were shooting up B7. A flight of Norwegian Spitfires joined the party and a '109' was brought down a few hundred yards from us. The Jerry baled out.

We spent all day at B9 – stifling heat, sand, dust in our eyes, our noses, our teeth. Nothing to eat, nothing to drink. We soon ran out of cigarettes. How I regretted the loss of my thermos full of delicious sugary tea! During 'readiness' I had a chat with a few peasants who had come to have a look at our aircraft. Really they gave the impression they couldn't care less about what we were up to. Their chief worry seemed to be our landing-strip encroaching on their fields.

In the afternoon we carried out a few patrols, four planes at a time, and dropped our bombs over a variety of objectives. I got rid of mine over the little bridge at Mézons.

At 5 we had a meal in a farmyard. We were famished. Some crafty fellow had unearthed a few highly welcome cartons of 200 Canadian cigarettes. The farm was on the edge of a small wood; everything seemed so calm, the war so distant. The boom of the artillery hammering Caen reached us in snatches like thunder on a summer's evening.

However in front of us in a fine, sloping golden cornfield were three charred Sherman tanks. Quite close in the shade of a flowering dog-rose hedge there was a freshly-dug grave, covered with flowers, with a simple board nailed to the wooden cross:

'Ici reposent les restes de neuf soldats et officiers
du Xe bataillon du Royal Armoured Corps.
Ils sont morts pour la France.
Priez pour eux.
13 juin 1944.'

A bit further on behind the hedge, enormous and as horrible as the corpse of a prehistoric monster, was a Tiger tank, the one which had destroyed the three Shermans. It had been hit by a rocket-Typhoon and at first sight it seemed intact. From closer to, however, you could see three small holes – two above one of the tracks and the other plumb in the middle of the black cross painted on the turret, under the long barrel of the 88 mm. gun. Impelled by curiosity Jacques and I went and examined the inside. A shapeless stinking black mass like molten rubber had flowed over the driver's seat and the ammunition boxes and covered the floor. I poked with a stick and a wave of nausea came over me when a shin bone came to light with a few shreds still adhering to it.

Towards dusk we received instructions to land at B11, i.e. at Longues near Arromanches, where our airfield was ready for us. Eight aircraft had to carry out the evening patrol in two sections. Ken led one, I led the other. The remaining planes left straight for Longues. Jacques undertook to get our tent in shape.

After an uneventful patrol, we landed at Longues and were very glad to see our ground crews again. They had been working for three days to get the base ready and were as hairy as savages.

Second night in France – four German raids during the night –

naturally we didn't sleep a wink. Out of curiosity we got up to see the firework display put up by the ack-ack boys.

We made the decision to have a right-royal celebration to mark our return to the Mother Country. Bayeux had been liberated, so we invited Max Sutherland to a civilised French feast by way of thanks for letting us be the first to land on home soil. The four of us hopped into a jeep and went down to the Lion d'Or, where they told us that all the tables for dinner were already taken.

'What about that one down the end?'

The maître d' replied that it was already reserved. Huh! As we were the masters of the skies, we went and sat down anyway. Someone must have tipped off the owner, a nice chap, who came out and explained that it was the liaison mission's regular table.

'Put them somewhere else, then. We've been out on the front line for years, so. . . .'

The dining room was completely full when four French colonels turned up. A civilian at the next table told us they were Colonel de Boislambert and Colonel de Chevigné, both working for De Gaulle. We carried on eating our artichokes, and when Boislambert, who wasn't at all happy, came up to our table, Max rose up to his full 1 metre 90. Standing head and shoulders above the man, he simply told him to 'fuck off'! It was only a whisker away from turning into a fight when the colonels left, fuming.

What a feast after being in England! We washed down the duck, the Camembert and the apple tart with Alsace beer, Burgundy, champagne, coffee and cognac. The owner came back out and said that the champagne and the liqueurs were on the house – which touched all of us, especially the squadron leader – and suggested that the next time, we should telephone to make a reservation. I fobbed him off with empty promises, just like the Americans, as De Gaulle would have said.

We set off again. Max was driving the jeep and I felt very uneasy. After five minutes of zigzagging along, Aubertin reached over and surreptitiously switched off the ignition. Max, who was as meek as a lamb when sober, turned into a wild animal with a drop too much inside him. And with what we'd had over dinner, he'd had several drops too much! He jumped down from the jeep like a mad man. I could see that he was on the verge of hitting our captain, and his friend – and a Metropolitan Police heavyweight boxing champion packs quite a punch. Aiming to stop any irreparable damage, Jacques, who was a rugby player, leapt out from the back seat and threw our pal Max to the ground, breaking his arm in the process. This sobered us up and we were left wondering how to explain this away when we got back.

The doctor looked after our boss, but when he came out of the first-aid tent, his arm in plaster, Max fell on Rankin and on A.C.S., our none-too-brilliant new Wing Commander. What would happen next? We found out the following day.

1730 hours. We were attacking a lorry convoy near Bény-Bocage, led by our new Wing Commander. With these low clouds and the flak I took a pretty dim view of the new system of flying in two sections – one of two planes and one of four. I was flying that day with an excellent section; Jimmy as No. 2, Bruce Dumbrell at No. 3, and Mouse Manson as No. 4. No need of long explanations over the radio with them. Just a waggle of the wings and they went into line abreast – pursuit and battle formation.

'Hallo, Pierre. Two aircraft at 11 o'clock!' came Jimmy's voice.

They were far ahead to the left, flying at tree-top level. At two miles range I could identify them as Focke-Wulfs. I warned the Wing Commander who didn't answer. My section dropped its auxiliary tanks and increased speed. We easily gained on the Jerries. They must be escorting something on the road, probably big priority convoys of petrol bowsers for the panzers hemmed in near Bény-Bocage. A thousand yards from them I left the shelter of the ground and went into a steep climb to put the section in battle formation. The Huns saw us and immediately climbed towards us.

At that precise moment the Wing Commander and his No. 2 cut slap into us and passed through us just as if we weren't there. To avoid a collision I had to break, but the formation of my section was shattered. The two Huns boldly attacked vertically from below. They were pretty hot stuff, those two. Their daring manoeuvre took me completely by surprise. I had meant to cut them off from the clouds, but I hadn't expected to see them on top of us so fast. The new wing-commander's boob had made me lose my initial advantage. Before I had time to take the slightest avoiding action an enormous radial engine appeared in my windshield and a stream of tracer came straight for me. Instinctively I pushed the stick forward and felt his slipstream on my tail fin. I just avoided a tree. I turned desperately, stick right back, in time to see a terrific flash on the ground near a farm and a big black cloud. A Spitfire wing bounced up into the air, torn off at the root.

The Wing Commander and his No. 2 had disappeared.

The second Focke-Wulf was chasing a completely panic-stricken Spit which succeeded in reaching the clouds but not without collecting three or four shells on the way. I engaged the Hun, who turned so tight that I almost touched him, without being able to get a sufficient correction to shoot him. A chap who knew the ropes.

'Hallo Max Red Section, Red Two here, please help me; I have had it.'

It was Jimmy calling for help.

The Focke-Wulf came back in a vicious side-slip and I had to break so violently that I stalled and only righted myself by a distinctly risky half roll just above the tree-tops. My heart was in my mouth. I now fired on the Focke-Wulf in my turn but the bastard cleverly skidded out of the way on his short wings and I missed him.

I gained height by an Immelmann. The flak began again – the usual tangle of red and green arrows. I climbed towards the clouds at full throttle. The Focke-Wulfs had disappeared; the engagement had lasted perhaps 60 seconds.

At that moment, in front of me, I saw a Spitfire coming down in a glide, its propeller scarcely turning. A long cloud of burning glycol trailed from its punctured radiators, I read the squadron letters and felt a punch in the stomach which knocked all the breath out of me – LO-S, that was Jimmy. I passed quite close to see – I called:

'Hallo, Jimmy, are you O.K.?'

No answer.

I wanted to do something, to help him, not just sit by horrified and impotent and watch the end of a good friend. In the cockpit I could only make out a vague crumpled shape collapsed over the stick and just behind, in the fuselage, a series of gaping holes regularly spaced.

'Bale out, try, please, for Christ's sake, Jimmy!'

Slowly the Spitfire went into a steeper and steeper dive as if it was trying to do an outside loop. I closed my eyes, feeling sick.

Nothing left but a blazing mass by a roadside.

Coming back I felt tears streaming down my nose. What was Max going to say?

I hoped to God Dumbrell had got back. To get shot to pieces in such conditions, four against two – what a disgrace! O God, grant that Bruce got back, I just couldn't explain it away on my own.

Bayeux. . . . Longues at last. There was a busy group round a Spit that had crashed on the edge of the runway. I flew over it to have a look. The pilot, thanks be to God, was waving his arm; it was Bruce, safe and sound.

When I landed I found Sutherland completely shattered. He had just heard that he had been posted, and the death of his friend Jimmy had finished him off. When he heard the circumstances he went into one of his berserk rages and we and the Captain had to restrain him forcibly, to prevent him from doing something desperate.

Ken Charney took over the temporary command of the squadron until Max could be replaced, and Jonssen, a Norwegian, took over 'B' Flight.

FIGHT IN THE FOG

29 June 1944

It was pouring with rain and on the rounded perspex of my cockpit flowed a thousand rivulets that seemed to appear from nowhere. Under the pressure of the air the water infiltrated through the cracks and collected in small streams which ran on either side of the sight and landed on my knees. A damp patch gradually spread on each of my trouser legs.

I came down lower still amongst the trees, which in the murk I could sense rather than see. Scraps of cloud hung on the hill-tops. Half-unconsciously I kept on repeating to myself: I am going to hit a high-tension cable. . . . I am going to hit a high-tension cable. . . .

Suddenly the fog receded and emerging from the rain-cloud I found myself in a gloomy cavern with greenish reflections like an aquarium, bounded by pillars of rain. A funereal light succeeded in penetrating through chinks in the clouds, producing tiers of rainbows hanging from the lowering cloud ceiling like spider's webs.

Then once again I plunged into a thick vapour which blurred the landscape and hid its dangers. Rivulets once again began to course over my cockpit. Each time I turned to avoid a shower I got more lost. My compass, shaken up by my violent manoeuvres, turned slowly and erratically like a diseased top, stopped for a second, then almost regretfully started off the other way. I no longer had the foggiest idea where the north was. My restricted horizon merely showed a row of unknown hills bathed in twilight; anonymous roads and cross-roads succeeded one another, villages drowned in the mist all looked the same. Through an open door I caught a momentary glimpse of warm firelight.

Impossible to get my bearings. I daren't ask for a course by radio. I expected to emerge into a flak zone at any moment or over an airfield or a strongly-defended marshalling yard. I began to feel the terror of being alone in a hostile world. I began to expect a deadly stream of tracer bullets from every hedge, every cross-road, every wood.

Lost . . . lost . . . lost.

Oh well, to hell with it. I began to climb through the treacle. My artificial horizon was still all of a dither but I had to risk climbing on I.F.

The cockpit was now quite steamed over. I climbed straight up, my eyes on my instruments. My aircraft was swallowed up. I couldn't even see my wing tips, though I could feel them shaken by invisible eddies of warm air. I came out at 10,000 feet into a maze of clouds. Enormous towering cumuli rose up in the blue sky to vertiginous heights, forming canyons, gigantic corridors walled in dazzling white. The shadow of my Spitfire, projected by the sun, looked like some frolicsome porpoise. It jumped from cloud to cloud, hugging the contours, came near, receded, disappeared in the crevasses, scaled the white ramparts.

Setting course on north and out of range of the flak I made for the coast, where it would be easier for me to pin-point my position. All the same I felt very alone, and the feeling of independence which you get when operating on your own gave way to a vague feeling of anxiety. The Huns had reacted strongly recently in this neighbourhood and, for once, I would have been glad of company.

I began to keep a close watch on the sun and the blue of the sky. To anyone above me my Spitfire must be visible miles off against this cloud background. A glance at the petrol – still about 50 gallons.

The minutes ticked by. I must now be fairly close to the coast, and on the whole I would rather come out under the clouds over France than risk coming out in the middle of the Channel above some trigger-happy naval convoy. I hadn't fired one shell yet and I might perhaps keep my hand in on a German lorry.

As I turned round a cloud I suddenly discovered a dozen black spots coming towards me at full speed – at such speed that they were on top of me before I could make the slightest move. They passed on my right. Jesus! Focke-Wulfs!

They had spotted me too, and broke up in perfect formation, two by two, to cut off my retreat. I was just cruising along, they were doing about 350 m.p.h. – no hope of getting away by climbing; in any case two of them were already immediately above me, waggling their wings. My only hope was to reach the clouds and throw them off by I.F. For one fraction of a second I found myself spiralling down with one pair of Focke-Wulfs above, another turning into me from in front, another one below me and a last one preparing to cut off my retreat. The bomb rack hanging between my two radiators was an unnecessary drag and reduced my speed. I must get rid of it. I pulled desperately on the emergency handle but it wouldn't shift – probably iced up. Sweating, I braced myself and tugged desperately – the handle came away in my hand with part of the cable. I avoided a lateral attack by a quick skid and before another section had time to attack, putting my whole weight on the stick I reversed my turn. Damn! My safety catch was still on, so although I instinctively pressed the button the Focke-Wulf in my sights slipped by 10 yards away. Christ! What about all those other Huns? I couldn't see more than four. Indistinctly I remembered the vital rule. Look out for the Hun you don't see; that's the one that will shoot you down!

I pulled so hard on the stick that I partially blacked out. I couldn't even turn my head, but I felt that those who had disappeared were up there, just waiting for the moment to pounce.

I just avoided a stream of tracer by breaking sharply upwards – unfortunately this manoeuvre put me back just as far from my cloud as I had been at the start. I was in a lather. A nervous tremor in my left leg made it useless. I crouched down in my cockpit with my elbows into my side and keeping my head down so as to be better protected by my back armour. My oxygen mask, pulled down by the g, had slipped over my nose, and I couldn't get it up again, as I had both hands on the controls. I tried breathing through my mouth and felt a trickle of saliva running down my chin into my scarf.

It was now only a question of time. They had me taped; their attacks, perfectly co-ordinated – one from the right followed by one from the left – were going to catch me flat-footed at any moment. My limbs stiffened, the muscles in my neck contracted, I felt the arteries thumping in my temples, in my wrists, under my knees. . . .

The dust, the earth accumulated under my seat, loosened by the violence of my manoeuvres, flew about in the cockpit. A drop of dirty oil went slap into my eye.

Suddenly a stream of tracer shot past, pretty close. I looked at the rear mirror and nearly passed out; a Focke-Wulf 190 followed by three others was less than 50 yards behind me, its wings lit up by the fire of its cannon. I vaguely remember being paralysed for a second, frozen to the marrow of my bones and then suddenly feeling a hot flush. The instinct of self-preservation had returned in a flash; a big kick on the rudder bar, stick right back, then sideways, in one continuous movement. The violence of the manoeuvre took me by surprise too. A black veil passed in front of my eyes. I felt something tearing into the fuselage and then an explosion. Luckily my back plate stopped the fragments.

I found myself on my back and saw my four assailants, surprised at my unexpected movement, pass by beneath me. Now or never. I pulled the stick and straightening out on the ailerons hurled myself vertically towards the clouds.

Saved! I stabilised my plane as best I could – none too easy: my instruments were completely haywire. I heaved a sigh of relief. I tried the controls. Everything seemed to answer. Normal engine temperature – nothing vital seemed to have been hit, at least not seriously.

I flew around for 3 or 4 minutes, changing course every 30 seconds. They must have been thrown off the scent by now; however, better come out under the clouds than above, where they must be waiting for me.

I was now rather worse lost than before and I only had 30 gallons of juice left. No possibility of pin-pointing my position as my map didn't cover the area I was over. I set course north-east, thinking I had drifted westwards during the fight. I crossed a broad river which could only be the Seine; but that didn't help much. The Seine meanders and the visibility was practically nil. I daren't risk following it down to Le Havre as the Germans had put up strong flak all along its banks, to protect the bridges against the constant attacks from Thunderbolts and Typhoons.

I had to make up my mind: the petrol was getting low. I reduced boost to the minimum and set my propeller to coarse. I had a vague idea I was about 30 miles south-east of Rouen. I flew just below the clouds so that I could nip back into them if any flak started firing at me, and followed a railway line which ought to get to Rouen without too much trouble. I might even, if a suitable opportunity arose, take a pot-shot at a locomotive.

I was mulling over this prospect when 1,000 yards ahead, an aircraft hove into sight, also following the railway line. I waggled my wings to have a better look at my find. It was a German plane, a Focke-Wulf 190.

I was sure he hadn't seen me. It was certainly one of the bastards who had put me through the hoop – he must have lost contact with the others in the fog.

A discreet glance round me to make sure I was alone. Cautiously, 'on tip-toe', I prepared to take my revenge. I daren't open up too much to catch him up, as I was short of juice. But I could turn my 1,300-feet altitude into speed by going into a shallow dive.

I got right behind him, 300 yards away, in the blind area behind his tail plane. The pilot, unaware of what was going on, was having a fine time, jumping over telegraph poles and hedges along the track and jinking to right and left, incidentally presenting me with a difficult target.

I pulled the stick slightly to get out of his slipstream and got him plumb in the middle of my sight. I really felt like a murderer when I pressed the button. The first burst – the only one – was a bull and the Focke-Wulf disappeared in a cloud of fragments. When the smoke cleared, I saw him go into a left-handed turn, one leg half-down, engine blazing. He mowed down a row of trees along a road by a level-crossing and crashed into the next field, where he exploded.

A couple of runs over the burning remains to photograph them – for confirmation – and then I made for home.

Return flight was a nightmare, as I only had just enough petrol. Wing Commander Yule encouraged me over the radio and gave me a direct course, adding that, if I'd rather, he could direct me towards a convoy where I could bale out.

I decided I preferred trying to get back. On the way I recognised the viaduct at Mirville, which we had dive-bombed a few weeks before. The Germans had begun to repair the two arches we had destroyed. As I passed I let fly at the scaffolding with a few shells.

I landed at B11 with just under a gallon in my tanks and had a large strip torn off me for wandering off so far by myself without letting anybody know.

A SUCCESS AND THE END

2 July 1944

'Scramble, south-east of Caen, as many aircraft as possible!'

Frank's shout tore us out of our lethargy. Great commotion! Where were the pilots? Were the aircraft ready?

Most of the pilots were having lunch and, as the squadron had just returned from a show, only a few of the aircraft were refuelled. I unhooked my helmet as I passed, looked for my gloves for a moment, then gave it up; as I hurriedly strapped on my Mae West I asked what wavelength was being used.

'Channel B! Hurry up, for Christ's sake!' shouted Ken who was already racing like a mad man towards his plane. Luckily my old LO-D was ready, and my mechanics, who had heard the scramble siren, were already on the wing, holding out my parachute half done up. I put it on like a jacket while Woody started up my engine. I strapped myself in in a hurry. Three aircraft from Flight B were already taking off in a cloud of dust and Ken was waiting for me, with his engine ticking over, at the edge of the track. I took up my position and we took off.

Queer sort of weather, eight-tenths cloud at 3,000 feet, five-tenths at 7,000 and a great bank of stratus covering the whole of our sector as far as the Orne canal. At 12,000 feet, there was a ten-tenths layer of nimbo-stratus. Ken and I managed to catch up with Frank, the Captain, and Jonssen the Norwegian over Caen at 6,000 feet. Control gave us vague courses to patrol, and told us to keep our eyes open for two unidentified aircraft moving about in the clouds near us. We climbed to 7,000 feet, just on a level with the second cloud layer. In the distance, out of range, a few suspicious black dots were moving among the cumulus. Suddenly Frank's voice sounded in the earphones:

'Look out, chaps, prepare to break port.' I went into a slight left-handed turn and looked up. A solid mass of forty German fighters was emerging from the clouds, 3,000 feet above us. We couldn't identify them yet – Messerschmitts or Focke-Wulfs – but one thing was certain, they were Jerries. The way they flew was unmistakable. The nervous waggling of the wings, their, at first sight, untidy formation. A heady feeling of elation swept over me and my hand trembled so much that I only succeeded in taking off the safety catch at the third attempt. I felt on top of my form. Instinct schooled by long practice functioned smoothly; I tightened my safety straps, huddled down on my seat and shifted my feet up the rudder bar. Excitement keyed my muscles to their highest pitch of efficiency, all fear vanished. My fingers were in harmony with the controls, the wings of my plane were extensions of myself, the engine vibrated in my bones.

I began to climb in a spiral. Now! The first fifteen Huns released their auxiliary tanks, fanned out, and dived towards us.

'Break port! Climbing!' Full throttle, 3,000 revs., we faced the avalanche.

They were Focke-Wulf 190's. My Spitfire was climbing at 45°, hanging on the propeller. I intercepted the first group, which was diving in line astern on Frank's section. Frank made the mistake of diving for the clouds, presumably to gain speed but forgetting the vital principle: 'Never turn your back on the enemy'. As we crossed I managed to get in a burst on the front Hun whose wing lit up with the explosions. Three or four puffs of white smoke appeared in his slipstream but they were just machine-gun bullets, my shells didn't touch him. Two Focke-Wulfs did a tight turn bringing them head-on to me, and the tracer from their 20 mm. Mauser 151's formed long glittering tentacles snaking towards me and curling down just under my fuselage. The sky began to be a whirling kaleidoscope of black crosses.

In a dog fight at over 400 m.p.h. you sense rather than see the presence of aircraft circling round, until suddenly your eyes fix on one of them.

I fixed one of them one! A Focke-Wulf. He was circling, his black crosses edged with yellow and his cockpit glittering in the sun. He was waggling his wings looking for an opponent too. Now I had him framed in my sights. Ought I to fire? Not yet. Patience . . . still out of range. But he had seen me, fell off to starboard and went into a tight turn. Two white 'contrails' appeared at his wing tips. He then began a vertical climb, straight up like a rocket. Suddenly he turned on his back with such violence that in spite of his change of attitude, his momentum continued to project his glittering belly towards the sun. Within range at last! I jammed my thumb down on the button and my wings shuddered with the recoil of the two cannon. With one motion of the stick I made the luminous spot of my gun sight travel along the Hun, through his propeller slowly churning through the air like some pathetic windmill. I was now so close to him that every detail was clear. I could already see the little blue flames of the exhausts, the oxide trail left by the burning gases along his fuselage, his emerald green back and his pale belly like the pike I used to fish for in the old days in the Mayenne. Suddenly the sharp clear picture shook, disintegrated. The gleaming cockpit burst into fragments. My 20 mm. shells tore into him, advancing towards the engine in a series of explosions and sparks that danced on the aluminium. Then a spurt of flame, thick black smoke mingled with flaming particles. I must get out of the way. I put all my weight on the controls and as my Spitfire flicked off I had a last vision of the Focke-Wulf, disappearing down below like a comet towards the shroud of clouds covering the Orne canal.

The whole thing had hardly lasted a few seconds. Never before had I felt to the same extent the sudden panic that grips your throat after you have destroyed an enemy aircraft. All your pent-up energy is suddenly relaxed and the only feeling left is one of lassitude. Your confidence in yourself vanishes. The whole exhausting process of building up your energy again, of sharpening your concentration, of bracing your battered muscles, has to be started all over again. You would be glad to escape, you hurl your aircraft into the wildest manoeuvres, as if all the German fighters in the entire Luftwaffe were banding together, and concentrating their threat exclusively on you. Then the spark strikes again, the partnership of flesh and metal reforms.

To my right a Spitfire broke off and dived behind a Focke-Wulf. I caught a glimpse of the markings – LO-B; it was Ken. I must cover him and, avoiding several determined attacks by Huns, I went into a tight spiral dive – they were moving too fast to follow me.

Ken fired; his wings disgorged long trails of brown smoke and a rain of empties. Intent on watching him I was paying no attention to anything else. A shadow formed, covering my cockpit. I looked up. A hundred feet above, a Focke-Wulf's enormous oil-bespattered belly passed me. He had missed me and opened fire on Ken.

Instinctively I throttled right back, pulled gently on the stick, aligned him in my sights and, at point-blank range, opened fire. The stream of steel belched forth by four machine guns and two cannon smacked into him at 150 yards range just where the starboard wing joined the fuselage. The Focke-Wulf, shaken in its course, skidded violently to the left and the right wing folded up in a shower of sparks, parted company with the fuselage, smashed the tail plane and whizzed past me in a hail of fragments. The film was going to be good.

I had scarcely recovered from my surprise when six other Focke-Wulfs attacked me. Turmoil ensued and I defended myself like one possessed. Sweat poured off me and my bare hand slipped on the stick.

Three thousand feet above, Frank's section was trying to hold its own in a whirling mass of Focke-Wulfs.

The only thing to do was to keep constantly turning, while the '190's' stuck to their usual tactics – diving attacks, followed by vertical climbs. We had one factor on our side; we were fighting 15 miles from our base, while the Huns were 150 from theirs. They would be the first to pack up.

All the same, I got a bit fed up with this rigmarole. I succeeded in nabbing one who was slow in straightening out from his climb: shells exploded under his belly. The usual spin, the usual tail of thick black smoke. It would have been hazardous to go down after him – I should immediately have had half a dozen others on top of me. Oh well, he wouldn't be a 'certain' but I should be satisfied to have him put down as a 'probable'.

No time for repining, anyway. Other things to think about. My port cannon jammed. I pumped my remaining twenty or so starboard shells into a Focke-Wulf whom I caught doing an impeccable roll. What an extraordinary idea to do a roll in the middle of a scrap! As the British say, there is a time and place for everything!

The Focke-Wulfs seemed to have had enough and showed signs of weakening. Apart from three or four who continued to attack, they set course south. I took the opportunity of sidling discreetly off to the clouds. I was exultant, for, in 40 minutes, I had scored three successes, two of which would be confirmed, and I had damaged two other planes. I indulged in the luxury of two victory rolls over Longues, to the joy of the country folk.

It's very bad for morale when you have a squadron leader in whom you don't have total confidence. A.C.S. was the kind of commander who would finished off his briefings with something along the lines of: 'Happy hunting, chaps. I'll be thinking of you' and then went back to his easy chair stroking his moustache. And when he went up himself, he was useless. What happened when we lost Jimmy shows exactly what I mean, even more so because the Luftwaffe had finally woken up.

The JG-2 and JG-26 Jagdgeschwader (fighter wings) and their brave pilots Oesau and Priller were no longer on their own. On 6 June, at the time of the Normandy landings, these were only two squadrons in France that were up to full strength. We had been warned, however, that starting on 8 June, about 600 fighter planes would be moved in from protecting the Reich. This was quite the opposite to press stories in London and in Washington and to reports from the B.B.C. of the Germans having only a modest number of aircraft available, perhaps a hundred. This was undoubtedly in order to demoralise the Wehrmacht. The Luftwaffe High

Command, and Galland, would still have a problem over fuel and accessible airfields. But it was true that, when added to the airfields in the Paris region, the airstrips at Saint-Omer, Abbeville and the numerous satellite airfields, which for the most part had not suffered much bombardment, would be able to accommodate a good thousand fighter planes. Intelligence told us that the Luftwaffe had been sending up 200–250 fighters every day, patrolling from Brittany to the Seine in large formations. This wasn't much, but we were continually finding ourselves ambushed and suffering a number of unbelievable and unaccustomed losses – 1,000 Spitfires and Typhoons since 6 June!

So it was that with their reinforcements, the Jagdgeschwader were sending out large fighter groups numbering twenty or thirty, to do a periodic quick sweep over the battlefield. The Allies had so many tactical aircraft in the air that the British radar monitoring couldn't make head nor tail of what was going on and weren't much use to us. This was bad luck for the small formations of four or eight Spitfires or Typhoons who fell into the clutches of the enemy. Since arriving at Longues on 12 June, Ken Charney, Jacques, another chap and I had found about three dozen Focke-Wulfs right overhead on two separate occasions, over Caen-Carpiquet. I still managed to bring down a Fw 190 in the run-for-your-life panic that ensued, and so did Ken. Jacques scored a likely hit, as one plane pulled away with flames streaming out behind. It was an indescribable muddle of friend and foe all mixed up together, as a group of Norwegian Spitfires came in to our rescue. On another occasion, in just the same circumstances and with the same fellows, we were on our way back from strafing a convoy of lorries when twelve tough Messerschmitt 109's took us by surprise. It was impossible to follow any of them for more than a couple of seconds without having another one on your tail shooting at you. Jacques and I got ourselves out of this mess with some difficulty only to find four Focke-Wulf 190's right on our backs. I had been firing at random all over the place at the Messerschmitts and was short of ammunition. I had a splendid Focke-Wulf in my sights. He would have been done for, but as they reloaded, my two gun breeches clattered empty and the few bullets that were left in the machine guns couldn't have done him much damage. When we landed, the press were determined to take photographs of Ken and me, insisting that I should put on my French officer's cap, to 'add a bit of local colour', I suppose. I climbed onto the wing of his aeroplane and we shook hands at least four times on the trot in order to get the perfect shot. I wondered what story they'd make up when it came out in the papers!

Every day, Jacques and I would go out on one or two strafing sorties behind the German lines. Any thing or any vehicle that moved, anything that could shoot, or even walk, was an authorised target, in a 60-mile-wide strip identified in our daily orders. This was to isolate the enemy from the rear, as well as from reinforcements and fresh supplies. The main roads were already impassable, encumbered as they were with a tangle of lorries, burnt-out vehicles, carts and dead horses. The bodies of dead soldiers has fallen into the ditches in their dozens and one day I even saw the body of a local peasant lying with his arms around the neck of his disembowelled horse. Poor man, to have ended up straying into such a hell as this. . . . The corpses had already started to swell in this end-of-June heat and there were swarms of flies buzzing around them. When we flew low, the crows, preying happily on the fruit of our strafing runs, flew up in clouds but soon settled down again to watch and wait. . . .

The German defences were increasingly in the hands of the anti-aircraft guns. These were 37 mm. twin-barrelled guns and 20 mm. quads that could fire at a rate of either 10 or 20 shells per second. Hidden under camouflage in the coppice hedges and along the strategic roads, these guns were a deadly trap that cost our Wing one plane a day.

At the 83rd Division Tactical Air Force General H.Q., the Head of Service for personnel marked the records of officer cadet Pierre Clostermann of 602 Squadron with a red arrow. His note in the margin read: *Awarded the Distinguished Flying Cross – operational rest from 7.7.1944.*

That same evening, a telegram reached the 125 Squadron Command Post:

30973 (F) P.H. Clostermann D.F.C. must be taken out of active service immediately tour of duty terminated stop he will return to United Kingdom stop seven days leave stop then report to inter-allied air liaison control and fighter command H.Q. for fresh assignment after consultation French Air Command stop effective on receipt stop confirm stop signed Vice Air Marshal H. Broadhurst A.O.C. 83 Group.

I had just returned with Jacques from a shooting-up trip in the Saint-Lô region. We had been greeted by dense flak along a sunken lane crammed with Jerry lorries. One run had been enough to put me off. A 20 mm. shell had exploded under the plate below my seat. I had prudently climbed to 3,000 feet and, in spite of my urgent calls, Jacques had made three attacks through a barrage of tracer. His plane was riddled with holes.

We were having a pint at the mess before getting outside our ration of corned beef and tinned carrots. Lapsley, who had been watching us in an

embarrassed way for several minutes, eventually joined us. He ordered a
beer from the barman and then hurriedly, like someone taking the bull by
the horns, blurted out that I had been recalled from ops., by superior
orders.

I had been half-expecting this for a fortnight, and dreading it. The wing
M.O. had found me out and had been surreptitiously doubling my dose of
benzedrine, so that my nerves should hold out a bit longer. The bastard
must have sent in a report.

After all, that was his job, and I was certainly in pretty poor shape.
Jacques himself had several times pointed out that I had a nervous tic like
a decrepit drug-addict. And I had certainly lost seventeen pounds in a
fortnight. *Sic transit*.

I hated leaving the Flight, particularly at that moment. I had reached
that stage of nervous depression when you are afraid of nothing, when
you are just not aware of danger. It is also the stage when your reflexes
disappear, when you fly mechanically in a sort of artificial complacency
produced by benzedrine and fatigue.

A few hours later a strongly escorted Dakota landed at B2. It carried Sir
Archibald Sinclair, Minister for Air, accompanied by Air Marshal Sir
Arthur Coningham, A.O.C. in C. 2nd Tactical Air Force, and Air Vice
Marshal H. J. Broadhurst, A.O.C. 83 Group. It was the classic morale-
raising inspection.

The Minister inspected us just as we were, dirty, bearded, covered with
dust, dropping with fatigue. The contrast between him in his impeccable
striped trousers and morning coat and us with our bedraggled uniforms
and our grimy scarves was absurd. The Minister showed true British
phlegm, particularly when a Focke-Wulf flew low over the airfield in the
middle of his speech. The ack-ack opened up, bits of shell fell like rain
and there was a general uproar, but he went on without even raising his
head. Jacques whispered that perhaps he was very deaf and very short-
sighted.

He took particular notice of the three French pilots in the party –
Jacques, Aubertin and I – and congratulated us on our successes. Then
taking a small box from his pocket, he discreetly handed me the D.F.C.

Later on I sat on my camp bed gloomily sewing the ribbon on my
uniform, surrounded by my untidy possessions, which I was going to have
to pack for the nth time.

ROMMEL

As I stood at the door of my tent at 1540 hours on 17 July 1944, I saw a 602 Squadron patrol taking off. On the engine cowling of a Spitfire is a red lion on a yellow escutcheon, and the coat-of-arms of Glasgow, the patron city of 602 Squadron, bears a red lion rampant on a cross of St Andrew, with the motto *Cave leonem cruciatum* (Beware the tormented lion). Jacques was among them. We should have been going off on leave together, but Staff H.Q. had other ideas. We had been flying as a pair and looking out for one another for such a long time that I had been feeling uncomfortable for a week seeing him going out with a makeshift team-mate. His tour of duty was to finish before the end of the month, but I always worried that the last missions were the ones that all too often brought rotten luck.

Chris Le Roux a South African and the new 602 Squadron Leader, replacing Max Sutherland . . . was leading this flight, which was made up of Jacques, 'Mouse' Manson, Jonssen the Norwegian, Robinson, and the New Zealander Bruce Oliver – all experienced pilots.

When they returned at 1650 hours, I went to the debriefing. Mouse was missing from the roll call and they were upset. I listened to their tale. That afternoon, things had been relatively quiet, with a bit of flak, obviously, but no real aggravation, and as often happened, one dangerous episode followed another with no rhyme or reason. It only took one brief glint of sunlight from the wing of a Messerschmitt, and Mouse Manson looking the right way at exactly the right moment, to make him call out 'Aircraft at 9 o'clock, slightly below!' Chris immediately dived in this direction, followed by Jonssen and Manson. At exactly the same moment, Bruce Oliver, who was teamed with Jacques, caught sight of a large convertible escorted by a couple of motor-cycles dashing along at break-neck speed towards Vimoutiers. He gave this out on the radio, but Chris was only interested in aerial victories, having fifteen already under his belt, and carried on charging towards the Messerschmitt 109's, who scattered. Oliver, followed by Jacques, did a 180° turn, heading straight for the target on the ground. Both of them opened fire on the car, which left the road and overturned. Then the battle with the Messerschmitts continued, and the last sighting of Manson's Spitfire was as it attempted a forced landing in flames. The flak then resumed, forcing everyone to separate as they gained height. The tally was one Me 109 destroyed, claimed by Chris Le Roux, and one damaged, this time by Jonssen. Jacques, just for a change, had been hit in the wing by a 20 mm. shell.

A few days later, he was awarded the D.F.C. Something was obviously afoot on the 17th, because a great bevy of Intelligence Officers arrived out of nowhere, including an Air Commodore, which was most unusual. Bruce and Jacques were questioned for a long time, but they were only able to repeat what they had already told our Spy at the time of the debriefing.

Many historians who were interested in the fascinating personality of Field Marshal Erwin Rommel – Hugh Trevor-Roper, Walter Gorlitz, Desmond Young, Liddell Hart and a few others besides – would not have known, when they were writing their biographies of Rommel in 1946–47, the details of how he met his end. These were not revealed until years later. In 1970, it was vaguely known that in Normandy in 1944 he had been seriously injured during an R.A.F. air attack. A rumour started to go round that this had been the work of the pilots of the City of Glasgow's 602 Squadron. A few years later, when the official archives were opened in 1975, it turned out that it was a 602 Squadron patrol led by Chris Le Roux, the South African Squadron Leader. A New Zealander and a Free Frenchman had also both played an important part in the action, which had happened thanks to a happy turn of fate.

So what happened?

Just before 1500 hours on 17 July 1944, Field Marshal Erwin Rommel had just left Saint-Pierre-sur-Dives, where he had met with Sepp Dietrich, the Commandant of the First Panzer Division 'Liebestandarte'. He was beginning the task of reorganising the Front, having obtained permission from Hitler to bring in the 21st Panzer Division's heavy Tiger and Panther tanks. He had turned down a lightweight Volkswagen in favour of his personal car, a heavy, powerful Horsch that had the advantage of being a convertible, which allowed him to watch the skies for any signs of an Allied air attack. A Military Police motor-cyclist rode in front.

To get back to H.Q. at La Roche-Guyon, Rommel's A.D.C. had suggested that they travel on the D4 then the D155. This would keep them off the Nationale 179 from Livarot to Vimoutiers, which was blocked with abandoned vehicles. It is likely that Sepp Dietrich had contacted the Luftwaffe and asked for a discreet air cover. Holker, the sergeant was sitting next to Daniel, the driver, in the place where Rommel usually sat, with Lang on a jump seat so he could keep an eye on the skies to the rear. On Rommel's left was Major Neuhaus, reading a map and giving directions to the driver.

At La Chapelle-Haute-Grue they had had to stop using the secondary roads, which also turned out to be blocked by vehicles, and took the N179. It was at this moment that six Messerschmitt 109's – probably the cover that Sepp had asked for – flew over Sainte-Foy, simultaneously crossing the path of Rommel's car and, in the air, the 602 Spitfire patrol led by Le Roux. The combination of smoke from the fires and a scattering of low cloud was letting very little sunlight through, and neither party had yet located the other, either in the air or on the ground. The '109's', the Horsch and the Spitfires would have continued on their way without seeing each other until Manson raised the alarm that would cost him his life. Holker and Lang saw two Spitfires coming straight along the road and closing on the car. With this forewarning, the driver accelerated in the hope of turning off, a little further on, onto a tree-lined path that led to the Laniel laundry. Oliver opened fire with his two 20 mm. guns and his four 303 machine guns. The driver's arm was torn off by a shell from the 20 mm., and he collapsed over the steering wheel as the heavy vehicle began to veer out of control. . . . A second shell hit the car at the height of Rommel's back, exploding in the folds of the hood and tearing it to shreds. If it had not been for the ultra-sensitive fuse designed to allow a gap of one-fiftieth of a second to penetrate the thin aluminium housing of an aircraft and explode within the fuselage, Rommel would have been killed on the spot. The Field Marshal had turned his head round to see what was going on, so the back of his neck was peppered with shrapnel splinters. On the left side, an open fracture to the skull left part of his brain exposed and a large piece of bone with part of the ear torn away. His cheek bone was broken, too, as a result of a fracture to the temple. Indeed, Jacques Remlinger, in the second Spitfire, also fired, killing the motorcyclist, who had come to a halt, and the car left the road, out of control. The vehicle had mainly been hit by a number of 303 bullets, one of which came off the barrel of Neuhaus' revolver and broke his hip. The Horsch touched a tree, bounced off and overturned. Lang and Rommel were thrown out, with Rommel hitting the trunk of an apple tree head first. Emerging unscathed, Lang, assisted by Holker who was only lightly wounded by shrapnel, extricated himself from the upturned vehicle and went to help the Field Marshal, who was unconscious and covered in blood. They watched as a Messerschmitt crashed and a Spitfire in flames was seen gliding some way off. . . . The events on the ground made the danger from the aeroplanes seem remote.

After a very long wait, Holker finally managed to flag down a military lorry, and Rommel was transported to a pharmacy at Livarot, guided by a labourer, Alain Roudeix, who had witnessed the scene. Finally, a French doctor arrived, one Professor Esch from a convent nursing home. Rommel was in a coma and the doctor dressed his wounds and administered first aid. Several hours had already passed since the attack, a delay that probably caused the fatal outcome. The doctor then told a shocked Lang that he doubted the wounded man would survive. It was almost midnight when an ambulance from the hospital at Bernay, which was run by the Luftwaffe, came to take the casualties to the place where Doctor Schenning would treat them. Daniel had died.

Rommel remained at the hospital at Le Vésinet for two weeks.

After that, and in spite of protests by the German Military Medical Team, he was taken back to Germany in a hedgehopping Ju 188. He was cared for at his home at Herrlingen by Professor Albrecht, from the university at Tübingen, who declared that 'It should not have been possible for anyone to survive such terrible injuries'. Still in a coma, Rommel hovered between life and death for several weeks, thanks to his robust constitution, and finally died on 14 October. Generals Burgdorf and Maisel, from High Command, had been notified, and made an official visit in order to certify the death and to take initial steps to prepare for the funeral. Some say that they arrived an hour before Rommel died – which opens the door to all sorts of hypotheses. Others say that they arrived after he died ... so his death was a natural one. Hitler ordered a state funeral.

The five 602 Sptifires got back to Longues at 1650 hours. One plane was missing – Mouse Manson's. It had been seen in flames, attempting a forced landing and exploding on the ground. Four pilots out of the five would never find out what had happened that day, and what a significant part their mission had played in the aftermath of the Normandy landings. Sheer statistics and the law of averages were unkind to this group of comrades from my former Scottish squadron. Chris Le Roux's plane crashed one month later, Jonssen and Robinson were brought down by anti-aircraft guns, and the last one, Bruce Oliver, went home to New Zealand and died in a crop-dusting accident. Only my friend Jacques Remlinger was to survive, and it was not until 1990 that he learnt what had happened on 17 July 1944 – the R.A.F. having always been very hush-hush about the Rommel affair – and who had been involved. I remember that he told me at the time that he would never boast about it.

THE BOAT BACK TO BRITAIN

Exasperating days passed waiting for a boat. There I was, sitting on the grass, while fight followed fight and my LO-D, now piloted by Jacques, took off in a cloud of golden dust, and bursts of 20 mm. ripped the air. It was then that I really understood what friendship meant. I saw an old pal, a comrade in arms, going off on ops. and had to wait for him to come back with my nerves on edge and a feeling of dread in the pit of my stomach. When we flew together it was quite different.

Jonssen got himself shot down, then Carpenter, then Connolly, one of the new arrivals. Jacques continued his series of daring flights.

Finally on 27 July in the evening, Frank Woolley and I left – he had just got his return ticket too – for Arromanches, our kit piled into a jeep. At 2130 hours we embarked on L.C.T. 322.

The Second Officer gave me his cabin. I was just about to turn in when a German raid of incredible violence began. I rushed on deck. The scene was lit up by the flashes from the angry Bofors guns. Columns of water thrown up by the bombs raised ghost-like shapes amongst the anchored vessels. A muffled explosion, like a heavy door closing in a cellar, a vast glow, flames rising to the moon, a monstrous pyramid of smoke. It was a tanker blowing up.

Then the hum of the Dorniers faded in the distance, the ack-ack was silent. I remained leaning on the rails, my eyes fixed on the Arromanches cliffs showing through the network of masts and funnels. Over there, from Longues, the clear note of a Spitfire engine rose in the starry night. The battle for Caen was in full swing, yet how calm everything seemed, how peaceful, how distant the sounds. Spasmodically the southern horizon lit up with flashes accompanied by a muffled growling. The town was enduring its martyrdom.

From time to time a cluster of tracer rose up in the sky and then vanished, like a handful of shooting stars. Round me the only sound was the lapping of the rising tide. The air was heavy with the smell of oil and brine. The black waters mirrored the red glow of the burning tanker.

It was all over. I felt in my bones that the liberation of France was now but the question of a few weeks and that by the irony of fate, I would only watch the liberation of Paris from afar.

The tide was up. The Diesel engines began to vibrate in the bowels of the L.C.T. and a big flower of white foam blossomed at the prow. The propellers began to beat their slow and monotonous rhythm, in tune with my heart, heavy with memories, friendship and mourning.

PART FIVE

Commands in the R.A.F.

THE TYPHOON

After mature reflection, I decided at the beginning of December to return to active operations. I didn't really breathe freely in that H.Q. atmosphere and the three months I spent there, in spite of the many nice people I met, were painful. I did a hop to Paris and the atmosphere there was, to say the least, unpleasant.

Through Jacques, who was now a squadron leader at 'Tactics', Fighter Command H.Q., Bentley Priory, I kept in touch with the latest phase of the war in the air. When I visited Pete Wyckham, the man most responsible for postings in Fighter Command, he promised to do what he could to help me quickly get into 122 Wing, which was due to return to the continent equipped with Tempest V's.

A few days later H.Q. French Air Forces in Great Britain received a courteous note from the Air Ministry:

> The R.A.F., at the express request of Air Marshal H. J. Broadhurst D.S.O. D.F.C., is most anxious to secure the transfer of Pilot Officer Pierre H. Clostermann D.F.C. (FF 30973) immediately on completion of his regulation rest period. The remarkable results he has obtained during his previous tours of operation mark him out as a future squadron commander in any unit he chooses. We therefore ask you to inform us whether you accept, in principle, the return of this officer to active duty with the R.A.F. under the conditions outlined above.
> — L. Herrera, Flight Lieutenant for Director of Allied Air Co-operation and Foreign Liaison

The Ministère de l'Air in Paris bluntly replied that there was nothing doing.

A few days later I met General Vallin and, as we strolled about, I put the question of my possible return to the R.A.F. to him. He very decently gave his consent in principle, observing, however, that I was on the list of pilots whom General de Gaulle wanted to retain and prevent from returning to operations. He promised to put in a word at the Ministère.

But time was pressing, and 122 Wing was making preparations to leave.

Then Colonel Coustey, O.C. French Air Forces in Great Britain, came to my rescue. When he saw the state I was reduced to, like a good commanding officer he took it upon himself to authorise my return to the R.A.F. At the same time, with that humour which characterised him, he begged me not to get myself killed, else he would get into trouble.

Quickly, to forestall a possible counter-order from Paris, I said good-bye to Monsieur and Madame Hermann – a French couple who had been living in London for over forty years, and who had looked after me and spoilt me with inconceivable kindness.

That same afternoon I reached Aston Down, where I was to do a quick conversion course on Typhoons and Tempests. Wing Commander Shaw, the Station Commander, when he saw my service flying log-book, decided to skip the formalities and to spare me the theory part of the course.

'All right, old boy, do a few circuits and bumps, and off you go to 83 Group Support Unit. If the weather's good, you can be in Holland within a week.'

That evening in the mess I plunged happily back into the clean, frank, open atmosphere of the R.A.F.

At last a ray of sunshine. In the afternoon I would therefore be able to have my first crack at a Typhoon.

I arrived at my flight with all my kit, and reported to my instructor, MacFar, an Australian, called 'Immaculate Mac' because of his scruffy appearance.

With my parachute on my back it took three people to help me up to the Typhoon's cockpit, which is 6 feet off the ground. As the plane is very streamlined there is nothing to hang on to. You have to get your fingers in hollows which are covered by metal plates on spring hinges. They close up again when you remove your hand or your foot, just like a rat trap. In the end they hoisted me up, settled me in, slapped me on the back, shouted 'good luck', and I found myself all alone inside the bowels of the monster.

I rapidly called back to mind all the gen. my instructors had given me. As the exhaust gases had a high carbon dioxide content, and seeped into the cockpit, you had to breathe oxygen all the time. I therefore hurriedly put on my mask and opened the intake valve. On take-off Typhoons swing hard right and I therefore adjusted the rudder trim very carefully. I opened the radiator wide. I checked the locking of the undercart – the lever looked uncomfortably like the one for the flaps. I lowered the flaps control to open up the pneumatic circuit in order to avoid ram effect just as I started up.

I switched on the instrument panel light. I regulated the throttle lever – open five-eighths of an inch (not one fraction more, otherwise the carburettor would flood and there might be a blow-back). I pushed the pitch control lever right forward, and then back an inch or so, to avoid run-away in the constant speed unit.

I verified that my tanks were full and selected the centre fuselage tanks for the take-off (gravity feed in case the pump packed up). I unscrewed the Wobble pumps; one sent a mixture of alcohol and either into the carburettor, the other a mixture of petrol and oil to the cylinders.

I inserted a cartridge into the starter. (The Koffman system, which uses the violent expansion of explosive gases to get the engine turning. If the engine doesn't start first time it will almost certainly catch fire, being bung-full of juice.) With one finger on the coil booster and another on the starter button, I fired the cartridge. The mechanic, hanging on to the wing, helped to 'catch' the engine and it started up with a deafening roar. The amount of noise seemed five times as great as in a Spitfire. After missing a few times, the engine settled down to a reasonably steady rhythm, though not without exuding oil at every pore. The sound of the engine and the way it vibrated struck me as suspicious. My nerves were very much on edge and I didn't feel at all easy in my mind. What on earth had ever induced me to return on ops.!

These reflections probably lasted some little time because, when I looked up, there were the mechanics looking slightly surprised and waiting for a sign from me to remove the chocks.

I began to taxi – a bit too fast. I must be careful not to over-work the brakes. They overheated very quickly, and hot brakes don't function.

That engine! You moved forward quite blindly, picking out the way like a crab, with a bit of rudder now left, now right, so as to be able to see in front. Once I was on the edge of the runway, before venturing further I cleared the plugs, as per instructions, by opening up to 3,000 revs., and a film of oil immediately spread over my windshield.

Two Typhoons who were in the circuit landed clumsily, but the controller seemed disinclined to give me the green light. I stuck my head out to make a sign, even though I would probably get a dollop of boiling oil in the eye. Still a red light. Christ, I must have forgotten something – and my confounded engine was beginning to heat. My radiator had already got to 95°. A glance round – my flaps were at 15° all right, my radiator was open. . . . Hell, the radio! I quickly switched it on and called:

'Hullo, Skydoor, Skydoor, Tiffie 28 calling. May I scramble?'

The controller replied by at last giving me a green light. Here goes! I tightened my straps, released the brakes, carefully aligned myself on the white line down the middle of the concrete and slowly opened the throttle, with my left foot hard down on the rudder bar.

I had been warned that Typhoons swung, but surely not as much as this! And the brute gathered speed like a rocket! I corrected as much as I could with the brakes, but even then I found myself drifting dangerously to the right.

Halfway down the runway my right wheel was practically on the grass. If I came off the concrete I would gracefully flip on my back!

To hell with it! I tore her off the ground.

This plane just had no lateral stability yet. I still went on drifting to starboard and, with those miserable ailerons that only 'bit' at speeds higher than 100 m.p.h. I daren't lower my port wing too much.

Luckily they had hauled F hangar down, after a series of accidents all due to the same cause, but even then I passed uncomfortably close to E hangar.

I retracted my undercart but forgot to put the brakes on. A terrific vibration which shook the whole plane from stem to stern reminded me that my wheels had gone into the cavities in the wings still revolving at full speed. I only hoped the tyres hadn't been ruined.

Really, it had been very pleasant behind that office desk. . . .

In the end I got my hand in a bit and felt better. There was a tendency to skid in the turns, but it wasn't too bad.

Just a wee dive to see what happened. Phew! With its 7 tons, the thing's acceleration downhill was simply fantastic. I realised with satisfaction that as far as speed was concerned this was much better than a Spitfire. What would it be like in a Tempest!

Half an hour quickly passed and I began to summon up courage for the landing. First a circuit at full throttle at 420 m.p.h., to clear those bloody plugs all over again. But after that I couldn't seem to reduce speed enough to lower my undercart with safety, even though I throttled back, fish-tailed violently, and lowered my radiator. One circuit, engine ticking over, at 300 m.p.h. Another circuit, at 250. In desperation I did a steep climb, without the engine. This took me up about 3,000 feet but it reduced my speed to about 200 m.p.h. At this low speed the machine was horribly unstable, and letting down the undercart had an unexpected effect on the centre of gravity. Once again, though I had been warned, I was taken by surprise, this time by terrific swings, more like incipient spins than anything else.

I asked for permission to land. Cautiously, nice and straight, and with a good reserve of speed, I made my approach, lowered the flaps, and everything went off fine until I tried to level out – those thick wings seemed to have plenty of lift, but they were treacherous. I had just begun to ease the stick back when the whole contraption stalled and dropped like a stone. Then it bounced back a good 30 feet with its nose in the air, amidst an appalling din.

I opened up like mad to break the fall, wrestling at the same time with the ailerons so as not to land on my back.

Eventually, after bucking two or three times like a mustang, my Typhoon finally calmed down and rolled drunkenly down the runway, which now looked distinctly short. However, I managed to stop before ramming the scenery, in a cloud of smoke and oil. A strong smell of burnt rubber rose from my poor tyres, which had stood up valiantly to 7 tons landing on them at 120 m.p.h.

Luckily my poor landing didn't seem to have attracted much attention – there had been such rotten ones that afternoon, including two involving serious damage, that, as long as the kite was still in one piece, it was considered as a good 'arrival'. My face was moist, but my morale was better.

A NEW PHASE OF THE
WAR IN THE AIR

The Hawker Tempest V, with its formidable Napier Sabre engine of 24 cylinders arranged in H-form, was the most modern fighter not only of the R.A.F. but of all the Allied air forces.

Sydney Camm, the chief designer in the firm of Hawker – he had already designed the famous Hurricane – had taken his latest creation, the Typhoon, which was an assault plane, heavy, massive, thick-winged, capable of carrying a good load, and after six months' work had transformed it into the Tempest. My impressions were as follows.

The fuselage was 2 feet longer, enabling it to house 80 extra gallons of petrol. The undercart was lengthened, to allow of the use of an enormous four-bladed propeller nearly 12 feet in diameter. The spread of the undercart was increased to 16 feet, to increase stability on the ground. Special ultra-thin tyres – they had to fit into the wings themselves – were evolved by Dunlop's. Indeed the Tempest's elliptical wings were so thin that special cannon (Hispano type V) had to be designed for them.

The cockpit was moved further aft, to improve downward visibility, and reduced in size to the strict minimum, until it was only a transparent plastic blister on the perfect stream-lining of the fuselage. The area of the tail fin had been doubled to ensure perfect stability at very high speeds, and flaps had been fitted along practically the whole of the trailing edge of the wings to give the maximum safety in landing. All the same, the landing speed was nearly 110 m.p.h.

Nothing was left undone to give the Tempest a maximum performance at medium and low altitudes. Special auxiliary tanks were designed even, with perspex connecting pipes, to fit under the wings. Quite extraordinary attention was paid to the rivetting, the joints and the surface polish. The result was a superb combat machine.

It had a thoroughbred look and, in spite of the big radiator which gave it an angry and wilful appearance, it was astonishingly slender. It was very heavy, all of 7 tons. Thanks to its 2,400 h.p. engine it had a considerable margin of excess power and its acceleration was phenomenal. It was pretty tricky to fly, but its performance more than made up for it: at 3,000 feet, at economical cruising speed on one third power (950 h.p.) with two 45-gallon auxiliary tanks, 310 m.p.h. on the clock, i.e. a true air speed of 320 m.p.h.; at fast cruising speed, at half power (1,425 h.p.) without auxiliary tanks, 350 m.p.h. on the clock, i.e. a true air speed of nearly 300 m.p.h.; maximum speed straight and level with + 13 boost and 3,850 revs.: 380 m.p.h. on the clock, i.e. a true air speed of 400 m.p.h.

In emergencies you could over-boost it up to nearly 3,000 h.p. and 4,000 revs., and the speed went up to 460 m.p.h. In a dive the Tempest was the only aircraft to reach, without interfering with its handling qualities to any marked extent, sub-sonic speeds, i.e. 550–600 m.p.h.

With its operational radius of 500 miles, its four 20 mm. cannon fed by 800 shells (almost 20 seconds of firing time) and 360 gallons in its tanks, the Tempest was the ideal fighter, a worthy companion to the nocturnal Mosquito.

The two first R.A.F. Tempest units (3 and 56 Squadrons) had been hurriedly equipped and hurled into the battle in June 1944, against the V-1's which were threatening London. Nearly 900 V-1's were exploded by these aircraft over the sea. American Mustangs and P-47 Thunderbolts and R.A.F. Spitfires could only catch these diabolical contrivances by diving on them, which reduced their chances of success. The Tempests, on the other hand, could stooge about on half-power, then, when they spotted a V-1, they opened up, got into firing position and fired in their own time, thanks to their overwhelming speed.

However, this hasty rushing into action had not been without its disadvantages. The Sabre engine found a diet of 130 grade fuel uncongenial. There were some serious accidents. Snags arose over the induction system (the Sabre was a sleeve-valve engine), over the lubricating system – the oil pressure sometimes suddenly dropped to zero – carbon dioxide found its way into the cockpit, etc.

The worst was the accumulation of petrol and oil fumes in the carburettor air intake, which led, we were told if ever the engine back-fired, to the plane bursting into flames, and sometimes exploding in the air in a matter of seconds.

As soon as the V-1 menace had gone, the Tempests were withdrawn from service. While the organisation of a Wing of four squadrons was put in hand, the technical experts from Hawker's and Napier's put their heads together to eliminate these faults. In the meantime, with the winter of 1944, the war had entered a static phase. The allied troops were re-forming and consolidating their positions on the left bank of the Rhine.

What was the Luftwaffe up to? For the general public, naturally,

Germany had no aircraft and no pilots left. This belief was carefully fostered by the Allied information services for a variety of reasons.

In the first place, the large-scale bomber offensive against the Reich's aircraft factories, in spite of the complete destruction of Warnemünde, Marienburg (Focke-Wulf factories), Wiener-Neustadt and Regensburg (Messerschmitt factories), didn't seem to have produced any visible reduction in the first line strength of the Luftwaffe.

This created an awkward situation, especially as the Americans published figures of German fighters shot down in the two or three hundreds after every raid over Germany. As these results were gained at the cost of colossal losses (87 Fortresses out of 642 engaged in the raid on Schweinfurt on 14 October 1943), which made the American public blench, a discreet veil had to be drawn over the activity of the Luftwaffe.

For us who were in daily contact with it and from whom it was obviously impossible to hide the real state of affairs, the optimism of American O.W.I. was not without a certain piquancy. The more Hun fighters the Americans shot down, the more there were!

One fact was certain: the offensive against the assembling factories and the repair workshops of German military aviation, although terribly efficient, had not prevented the production of fighters from going up substantially from July 1943 to March 1945. The Germans succeeded in maintaining a monthly production of 1,200 to 1,700 machines (2,325 in November 1944). It must naturally be added that, had it not been for this bombing, the Germans would have reached the expected production of about 3,000 machines a month in 1944 and 4,500 at the beginning of 1945.

This extraordinary vitality was due to two things: firstly the speed of reconstruction and rehabilitation of bombed factories; secondly the increasing number of invulnerable underground factories.

The Wiener-Neustadt factory for instance, six weeks after what seemed to have been total destruction, was turning out 2 Messerschmitt 109's a day. Two weeks later it was 9 and less than three months after the raid it was turning out its 10 Messerschmitt 109's per diem. It was a real tour de force, and another costly raid by Fortresses had to be laid on (about 100 never came back). The Germans couldn't keep this up indefinitely. Although the Fortresses' bombs were not heavy enough to destroy the machine tools, the buildings themselves became unusable in spite of makeshift repairs.

It was at that stage that the Germans began to bury their factories. Dr Kalmmler, in close touch with Goering and through Sonderstab H and Dr Treiber, took over the direction of the operation. It was an extraordinary feat. As early as January 1944, the Germans had taken a census of all quarries, caves and other suitable sites. They even went to the extent of diverting railways for dozens of miles so as to use the tunnels. The Berlin Underground itself sheltered some assembly lines. As early as April 1944 the R.A.F. and the British Information Services had conclusive proof that the Germans were producing in their underground factories at least 300 complete aircraft and a large number of engines a month.

It was only later, when Germany was occupied, that the full extent of this troglodyte activity could be assessed. In the middle of a large forest near Alt Ruppin the Russians discovered a clearing where nearly 100 Heinkel 162's and Fw 190's were lined up under the trees, carefully camouflaged. A little further on, following a railway line that seemed to lose itself in a clump of trees, they found the entrance to a subterranean factory, 6 acres in extent and with a production capacity of 4 fighters a day. The aircraft were transported in lorries as far as the Berlin–Hamburg autobahn, still under construction, a few miles away. One of the completed sections, 60 yards wide and 2½ miles long and perfectly straight, was used as a runway. The aircraft were then parked in, and sometimes even went on operational flights from, shelters spaced out along this magnificent improvised airfield.

In the Trier region several thousand workmen from Opel and Russelsheim worked in two of the tunnels on the Coblenz–Trier line, producing accessories, undercarriages for the Rochlitz firm, superchargers and turbines for jet aircraft for the Munsfeldwerke of Breslau.

In the great quarries of Halberstadt, near the airfield, wings and fuselages for Focke-Wulf Ta 152's were assembled and taken by lorry to the assembling plants.

In the Berlin underground, between Bergstrasse and Grenzallee stations, the Henschel factory had set up a construction belt for fuselages and tail planes for Junkers 188's. The completed fuselages, which would have been too bulky for the exits and the lifts, were built in two sections and assembled in the open. Up till the Liberation the joints had as a matter of fact been produced by a firm in Paris.

The galleries in the potash mines at Halle and Saale were widened and each sheltered 800 workmen working on pneumatic and electrical parts. The machine tools and assembly line of the Messerschmitt factory at Regensburg were, after two successive bombardments, transported in one week to a big road tunnel at Eschenlohe in Bavaria and were able, three months later, to turn out 10 Me 109's and 5 Me 262's a week. At Egeln the American troops found a gigantic underground factory which in December 1944 turned out 6 'long-nose' Fw's a day, and in March 1945 10 He 162's a day!

One could quote dozens of similar cases. The Germans were therefore able, contrary to all the estimates, to maintain a very high level of production, in spite of the bombing attacks, of the order of 2,000 aircraft a month.

What were these aircraft and what were they worth? The Germans were mass-producing:

(1) Two types of orthodox single-seater single-engined fighters – the Messerschmitt 109 series K and the Focke-Wulf 190 D9.
(2) Two types of single-seater jet fighters, the Messerschmitt 262 and the Heinkel 162 'Volksjäeger'.
(3) A bomber with a crew of three, the Junkers 188.
(4) A bomber-reconnaissance single-seater jet aircraft, the Arado 234.

The Focke-Wulf 190 D9 ('Long-Nose Dora') was a derivative of the classic Fw 190 but equipped with a liquid-cooled 12-cylinder in-line Jumo 213A engine (2,242 h.p.), with the benefit of water–methanol injection, instead of the radial BMW 801 engine.

This remarkable machine formed the equipment of about half the Jagdgeschwaders in January 1945. It was very fast (440–480 m.p.h.), very manoeuvrable, armed with a 30 mm. cannon mounted in the engine, two 20 mm. Mauser cannon in the wing roots. This Fw 190 D9 was a formidable opponent. Its general performance put it in the same category as the Tempest and gave it a very distinct edge over the American Mustang, Lightning and Thunderbolt, as well as the Spitfire XIV. The Messerschmitt 109 K, equipped with a Daimler-Benz 605 of 1,700 h.p. was a lighter equivalent of the Mustang and, in capable hands, could hold its own with the Tempest.

The Messerschmitt 262 jet, with its two Jumo 004-B1 and its four automatic 30 mm. cannon MK 108, was the most sensational fighter aircraft produced up till then. It was the first jet aircraft effectively used in combat. It was mass-produced, and used on a large scale from November 1944. It might have been the greatest fighter of all. Its speed was phenomenal, about 650 m.p.h., and it had a formidable armament with a useful range and 100 shells per cannon, and a very finely designed 89 mm. thick plating. This machine might have revolutionised aerial warfare, but unfortunately (or rather, fortunately), once more Hitler's intuition came into action. He intervened in person, after being present at a demonstration of the machine in April 1943, and forced the designer to modify it in order to turn it into a bomber for reprisals against England. After a year of alterations, discussions, orders and counter-orders, and in face of the growing Allied counter-offensive, O.K.W. ended up by convincing Hitler. The Messerschmitt 262 was restored to its original role of 'Kampfzerstoerer' ('destroyer of bombers').

The Messerschmitt 262 was very tricky to fly with a wing loading of 44 lbs. per square foot, a landing speed of just under 200 m.p.h. and a difficult take-off. The turbines also gave trouble and there were certainly high losses through accidents – JG-52, for instance, losing twenty-three pilots in three months. Nevertheless, the Luftwaffe had *in the line*, as early as January 1945, at least 200 Me 262's of which a third were based on the famous airfield of Rheine/Hopsten, where a concrete runway 3,000 yards long and 70 yards wide was built specially.

The 'Volksjäeger' – People's Fighter – Heinkel 162 was also a fascinating machine. It was specially designed for mass production, very easy both to build and to fly and equipped with the minimum armament necessary (two 30 mm. cannon and an endurance of 45 minutes). The 'Volksjäegers' were churned out like sausages from eighty-five factories scattered all over Reich territory.

The Junkers 188 was a fast long-range twin-engined bomber. Although more than 800 of them were built, indeed mass-produced, it was doubtless sacrificed in the last months of the war, since it could only operate with difficulty from improvised airfields, and the last stocks of C3 petrol (96 octane) needed for its BMW 803 and Jumo 213 engines were reserved for the fighters, and the last suitable airfields were turned over to the Me 262's.

The Arado 234 was a jet single-seater and built specially for reconnaissance and bombing. It was not so fast as the Me 262 (530 m.p.h.) but it carried, however, in addition to its two 20 mm. cannon, either 4,400 lbs. of bombs or several automatic cameras. At least three Aufklärungs-gruppen (recce. squadrons) were equipped with them by the end of 1944.

The Germans therefore had the machines, and good machines. What about their pilots? Were they up to the crushing task which was imposed on them? Generalisations on this point are more tricky. However, the question can be answered.

In the Luftwaffe there seems to have been no 'middle' and German pilots could be divided into two quite distinct categories:

The 'aces', 15 to 20 per cent. of the whole – pilots who were really superior to the average of allied pilots. And the remainder – not up to much. Very brave but incapable of getting the best out of their aircraft.

This hiatus was above all due to the hasty way in which new flying personnel – following on the heavy losses in the Battle of Britain and the Russian Campaign – were hurled into the fray. Their training was over-rapid and not very well balanced; an inordinate importance was given to morale, to the Greater Germany idea and to purely military theories, to the detriment of technical instruction proper. To these faults was added, from the end of 1943, an acute shortage of fuel.

So there was – gradually melting in the furnace of the skies of Europe – the heroic band of 'the old stagers' of the Luftwaffe, the real veterans, with three or four thousand hours of flying. These pilots, trained in the school of the Spanish Civil War, survivors of the successive campaigns of the Luftwaffe from 1940 onwards, knew their job inside out, with all the refinements. Both prudent and sure of themselves, masters of their machines, they were very dangerous.

On the other side there were the young fanatics with high morale and bound by an iron discipline, who were in many circumstances relatively easy prey in combat.

All in all the average standard of German fighter pilots was much higher at the turn of the year 1944–45 than at any other time since 1940. This can only be explained – apart from possible considerations of morale, such as the defence of the Fatherland – by the fact that the crack fighter units had absolute priority in everything, including personnel and also the handing out of fuel and lubricants. We were therefore very likely to meet in combat nothing but very experienced pilots, while in 1942, 1943 and early 1944 there had been a rotation of pilots between the Western and Russian fronts which often brought us in contact with units of very middling worth. These were later concentrated exclusively on the Eastern front. In principle the Russian front was a rest cure for the Luftwaffe, quantity mattering more than quality, and the best units were kept in reserve to face the R.A.F. and protect German towns against American daylight bombing. Such, *grosso modo*, was the situation of the Luftwaffe at the end of 1944.

There was one point on which all fighter pilots were agreed, whether British, French or Polish: the obvious superiority of the surviving Luftwaffe pilots in 1944 and 1945. The Americans, as always, considered themselves the best. But the kills they claimed for their P-51's and P-47's and the numbers of Messerschmitt 109's supposedly downed by B-17's and B-24's were the stuff of Hollywood movies, outlandish and ridiculous. We were amused by their naiveté, as were most likely the Luftwaffe. We realised, of course, that this was for public consumption back in the States: the authorities dared release only partial statistics of losses, thereby strengthening the national conviction of superiority.

After the war, specialist R.A.F. and Allied commissions carried out studies of Luftwaffe archives, combat film footage, and the records of the Jagdgeschwaders and supply services, which had been kept meticulously up to date until May 1945. From these they were able to obtain a precise estimate of German pilots' abilities. The Luftwaffe lost 25,525 daylight fighters and 4,881 night fighters. To these figures must be added 7,300 aircraft sustaining 10–60 per cent. damage and not necessarily repairable. Regarding pilot casualties, 11,300 were killed, 3,600 taken prisoner and 10,800 wounded; half of the wounded were unable to resume active service. Allied operational losses in Western Europe exceeded 40,000 aircraft. This figure includes losses in combat, from flak and all types of accidents, including crash-landings on return from missions. German fighter pilots claimed 25,000 confirmed, checked kills in the Western theatre; 105 German fighter pilots claimed 15,000 victories between them, three-quarters of them on the Russian front, where the Soviets admitted to losing 60,000 aircraft. The official figures for Russian production from 1941 to 1945 show a total of 113,735 machines. Taking into account the number of trained and available pilots and adding the 18,000-odd machines provided by the Allies, we arrive more or less at the Luftwaffe's total, which appears to be reasonably correct.

In 1964, the Allied historical services published, in an investigation into the effectiveness of fighter defence against bombers, the results obtained by one Luftwaffe unit (Jagdgeschwader 300) during the single month of July 1944. In this Wing, for instance, Konrad Bauer, leading Squadron No. 5, was shot down seven times and six times wounded. He downed 32 four-engined American bombers in three months.

JG-300, with its five squadrons each of two or three flights, could put up a hundred or so Focke-Wulf 190 A8's or D9's as well as 90 Messerschmitt 109 K's from three major aerodromes in North-West Germany as well as some six smaller dispersal fields.

On 3 July 1944, over Oscherbelen, 38 Fw 190's belonging to Squadrons I and II of JG-300 intercepted the 492nd Bomber Group of the US 8th Air Force.

In very tight formation they set about the two lower boxes of Liberators from the rear. In a few minutes, 26 bombers had gone down. A quarter of an hour later, II/JG-300 cornered another ragged group of B-24's as they headed back over Halberstadt; 8 were lost. During this action, W.O. Gausmaier, flying under the command of Kommodore Dahl, took on four P-38 fighters, destroying one before himself being shot down. He baled out, and was wounded by machine-gun fire from the American fighters: seventeen holes were found in his parachute. At this juncture the American escorts intervened. Despite being handicapped by the 30 mm. cannons mounted in gondolas below their fuselages, 38 Fw190 A8's along with 25 Fw D9's held out against some 150 P-47's and P-38's for more than 5 minutes. The Germans managed to shoot down 9 P-38's and 4 P-47's despite being almost out of ammunition. Against the loss of 34 four-engined bombers and 13 fighters on the American side, JG-300 lost only 12 aircraft, 6 pilots killed and 4 wounded. Another 14 Fw's were damaged, but repairable.

For the record, the gunners of the surviving B-24's and escorts claimed 83 kills for this engagement. I suppose a certain confusion is inevitable with some 300 B-24 gunners all targeting the same aircraft; when a Fw is hit, they all make individual claims in good faith. But an over-estimate of 71 seems a bit much!

On 18 July, it was the same story over Munich. II/JG-300, backed up by I/JG-3 under Heinz Bär – 69 Fw D9's in all – made a massed frontal assault on the Forts, while the Me 109's of IV/JG-300 took care of the escort. Panic ensued; 9 damaged bombers landed at Zurich Dubbendorf and their crews were interned in Switzerland for the duration; 37 were shot down, 18 crashed into the sea or over England.

On 27 July, I/JG-300 intercepted the 401st Bomber Group and downed 16 B-17's in a single pass.

It is impossible to close this catalogue without mention of 15 August, the date of what was a massacre pure and simple, meriting a special report by Gen. Eaker, C. in C. U.S. 8th Air Force. In this document he demanded a pause of two or three weeks and the reduction of aircrews' tours of duty to fifteen missions. His aim was threefold: to make up the losses in pilots and aircraft, allow the men the rest they needed, and restore morale, which had sunk to a low pitch. As proof of his sincerity, he informed the High Command that if these demands were not met, he declined all responsibility for the future operational use of the 8th Air Force!

On that fatal day, I/ and III/JG-300 intercepted 240 B-17's over Trier. Forty-one kills were claimed by III/JG, I/JG-300 claimed 36, and the Me 109's of JG-4 claimed 17 American fighter escorts. All these claims were later confirmed by comparing them with the losses recorded in official reports from 8th Air Force H.Q. JG-300 lost 16 aircraft, with a further 38 hit, including 20 which suffered 60 per cent. damage, in other words beyond repair. Pilot losses were 9 dead and 22 wounded. The film taken from Konrad Bauer's gun camera – he was an ace credited with 80 kills – was used to train new fighter pilots. His Focke-Wulf D9 had taken on 7 U.S. P-51's, shooting down 3. Despite being wounded in the hand and losing two fingers, he managed to bring back his damaged machine to his base at Nordhause. His claims were irrefutable.

Allied superiority in numbers was effective only as far as reserves were concerned, as there was not a sufficient number of airfields within a reasonable distance of the northern front to cater for the thousand or more aircraft comprising 83 and 84 Groups of the Second Tactical Air Force. The Luftwaffe on the other hand, skilfully scattered over a hundred small airfields grouped round the large major bases of the Arnhem–Osnabrück–Koblenz triangle, could operate in strength.

The Messerschmitt 262's could indulge in tactical reconnaissance over the entire Allied front with impunity, and once again we saw large German formations, sometimes 100 aircraft, machine-gunning and dive-bombing our troops and convoys in daylight.

The Allied reconnaissance aircraft and our fighter-bombers had a hard time. Typhoon formations frequently lost 2 or 3 machines out of 12 in encounters with Fw 190's and Me 109's. The Spitfires were powerless. There was only one Wing of three Spitfire XIV squadrons and the rest were equipped with Spitfire IX's or Spit XVI's (Spit IX's with Rolls-Royce engines built by Packard in the U.S.A.). In any case all the Spit IX squadrons operated most of the time as fighter-bombers. The Huns, knowing the Spit's quality in a dog fight, carefully avoided taking them on, and the poor Spits had neither the speed nor the range necessary to force the new German fighters to fight.

The Allied Staff was beginning to get seriously worried by this state of affairs. The situation was similar in the American sector round Luxemburg, but less acute, as the Germans knew that the final attack would come from north of the Ruhr, and they were concentrating on Holland.

The Rundstedt offensive had come as a surprise, and our Staffs for once were finding themselves less well-informed than the enemy. The Messerschmitt 262's had given the German General Staff a clear picture of the situation of our troops, while our reconnaissance aircraft were neutralised by the German fighters.

It was to remedy this state of affairs that 122 Wing of the R.A.F. was sent to Holland equipped with Tempests. It was a crack unit and on it depended the entire offensive and tactical system of the British front. Only pilots with at least one complete operational tour or who could prove they had had adequate experience were taken. The Wing comprised Squadrons Nos. 486 (New Zealand), 80, 56 and 274, and in addition No. 41, equipped with Spitfire XIV's.

The Tempests' performance being so sensational, a crushing task was assigned to them:

(1) Neutralisation of the German fighters, specially the jets.
(2) Paralysing of the Reich's railway system from the Rhine to Berlin by a systematic daylight onslaught on the locomotives.

With its morale sky-high, feeling it was the apple of the eye of the R.A.F., the Tempest Wing settled down at Volkel in Holland and was hurled into the fray.

It was pretty tough. Flying in twelves and twenty-fours the Tempests went and ferreted out the Focke-Wulfs even on their airfields. Sections of four flew at ground level as far as Berlin several times a day, leaving on their way there the railway lines blocked by locos holed like sieves, and on their way back pilitlessly ambushing the Luftwaffe. Pairs of Tempests were kept in a state of immediate readiness, pilots sitting strapped and harnessed in their cockpits, their finger on the starter, ready to take off as soon as an Me 262 crossed our lines.

In fifteen days, 23 German fighters were brought down, including 3 Me 262's, and 89 locomotives destroyed. We lost 21 Tempests.

Then came 1 January 1945, which was to treble Wing 122's task and its responsibility.

THE LUFTWAFFE'S LAST EFFORT

1 *January 1945*

When this day dawned the situation of the German armed forces was not exactly rosy. When the Rundstedt offensive petered out, the Nazis, hemmed against the Rhine and hard pressed by the Russians troops in Poland and Czechoslovakia, were reduced to the defensive.

However, at about 0745 hours strong formations of Focke-Wulf 190's and Messerschmitt 109's took off from twenty or more snow-covered airfields. At 0805 hours a tiny Taylorcraft 'Auster' artillery-spotting aircraft sent over the air a frenzied message: 'Have just passed formation of at least 200 Messerschmitts flying low on course 320°.'

At 0830 hours on twenty-seven Allied bases stretching from Brussels to Eindhoven, dozens of British and American aircraft were nothing but smouldering heaps. Everywhere tall columns of black smoke rose as straight as cathedral pillars in the still air, where the small grey and white clouds marking the bursts of thousands of ack-ack shells still floated.

General Sperrle had just risked a bold stroke which had no precedent in the entire war. On the airfields of Twente, Appeldoorn, Aldhorn, Hagelo, Munster, Lippstadt, Rheine, Neuenkirchen, Metelen, Harskamp, Teuge, and all their satellites he had massed ten élite Jagdgeschwaders. It was possible later to identify them as JG-2, JG-3, JG-4, JG-5, JG-26, JG-27, JG-52, JG-53 and a few others, in all about 650 Focke-Wulf 190's and 450 Messerschmitt 109 K's.

The evening before the German pilots did not know the aim of the operation. At twilight they had taken off from their usual bases and had concentrated on airfields. At 21 hours lights out – no staying up, no drinking, just a light but substantial meal for all the flying personnel.

At 5 a.m. on 1 January they were woken up and Sperrle's masterly plan was unfolded amid general enthusiasm. Goering himself did a lightning tour round the units to encourage them. Every pilot received a large-scale map on which all the Allied airfields and bases were clearly marked (the results of reconnaissance by Me 262's), together with return course, landmarks and detailed routing instructions. At H hour they took off, concentrated into three massive formations of 300 or 400 machines each, and these three forces, led by three Junkers 188's who were responsible for navigation, set course for the Allied lines.

One of them came down over the Zuyder Zee, skimming the waters and the beaches, and came up as far as Brussels. Another came at ground level through Arnhem down as far as Eindhoven, and the third, passing through Venlo, debouched on the American lines. The surprise was complete. For almost half an hour the Messerschmitts and Focke-Wulfs machine-gunned the Allied aircraft massed on the ice-covered perimeter tracks. A few isolated Spitfires succeeded in taking off while the shoot-up was actually in progress.

By an extraordinary twist of fortune 122 Wing was doing a sweep over Germany in force and, when they were called back, most of the Tempests were short of ammunition. By a miracle Volkel was one of the three airfields which were untouched. Everywhere else it was a catastrophe. At Brussels/Evère alone 123 transport aircraft, Flying Fortresses, Typhoons and Spitfires were wiped out. At Eindhoven a Canadian Typhoon Wing 124, and a Polish Spitfire Wing were nearly destroyed. In all nearly 400 Allied aircraft had been put out of action in a few minutes.

The few Tempests and Spitfires which managed to intervene shot down 36 Huns from the shoals while British and American ack-ack accounted for 157 more, i.e. about 193 German aircraft, whose remains were found after a week of search in our lines.

This operation had been brilliantly worked out and superbly executed. Allied public opinion would have been dealt a staggering blow if it had known of it. The American censorship and the Press services, in a flat spin, tried to present this attack as a great Allied victory, by publishing peculiar figures. We pilots were still laughing about them three months later.

The Luftwaffe's success, won at the cost of 280 or so machines, succeeded in nearly paralysing the tactical air force for more than a week. On the other hand, German losses in pilots killed or wounded were infinitely more serious: 251, including the commanding officers of 3 wings, 6 *gruppen*, and 18 flights. Operation Bodenplate had broken the back of the Luftwaffe.

On the Allied side, it was only thanks to the energetic action of Air Marshal Broadhurst, commanding 83 Group R.A.F. (the most battle-hardened) that a few combat groups were reorganised within 24 hours to hold the line. He immediately formed a central pool for all airworthy aircraft and called up reserves dispersed throughout Britain. I arrived at this juncture.

In the week following, 122 Wing in effect alone kept the aerial offensive going, from dawn to dusk, and in six days lost 10 pilots and 20 aircraft.

A DISAPPOINTING RETURN

I spent Christmas, my last remaining leave, in Jacques' company, before boarding the duty Anson with all my belongings.

The usual monotonous and uncomfortable journey on board the old crate. The duty Anson transported everything – pilots posted to units of 83 Group, the post, the newspapers, a bottle of whisky or two, laundry for a mess, somebody's uniform back from the cleaners, sometimes a dog or a mascot. All that piled up in a cabin 10 feet by 5 feet. Everything vibrated, icy draughts materialised from nowhere and, worst of all, you inevitably felt air sick within a quarter of an hour.

As I sat on my parachute bag, frozen to the marrow in spite of my Irvine jacket, I went over my conversation with Jacques again, full of a curious mixture of bitterness, fear, and haste to reach my journey's end. How hard this return to active operations was, compared with our arrival at Biggin Hill or 602 Squadron, two years ago. I was in a hurry to get back to the healthy, open atmosphere of a squadron, after four depressing months of offices and liberated France. But I also recognised again the old sinking feeling, the fear in the pit of your stomach before you take off for a fight.

Would I be able to take it?

After 300 operational flights, I was returning with neither the zest of the young pilot newly hatched from O.T.U. nor with the calm self-confidence which comes of long experience. I knew I had been pushed off in a hurry, as soon as permission had been obtained from the French, because flight commanders for Tempests were scarce. Pete Wyckham at Air Ministry had at least been frank with me – 122 Wing had lost on an average during the last two months one squadron commander and three flight commanders a fortnight.

'Good luck, Closter old boy. Bags of promotion over in 122 Wing!'

After being comfortably chair-borne for four months, going back on ops. on a type of plane I didn't know, after an hour and a half in a Typhoon and three brief trips in a Tempest, seemed not only risky but practically mad.

I saw myself back in Warmwell, not daring to do a barrel roll in a Tempest, not even a simple loop! How was I going to react to flak, which, according to Jacques, had got simply appalling? It had been tough enough in Normandy.

Oh well! At least now they would leave me alone! I wouldn't have to worry about the Ministère de l'Air in Paris, with its incoherence, its senile colonels, its 'members of the Resistance', its counter-orders, and all those fishy characters in their shady uniforms who had come to the surface over there, like the scum on boiling jam.

We of the Free French Air Forces, to whom the Armée de l'Air owed everything, especially honour, we who rushed into the holocaust one after the other, as happy as kids all the same – we, who were proud to start all over again, to mock the odds against us, wangling extra tours of ops., fagged out, dead beat, nerves in tatters, lungs burnt out with oxygen – we always got the thick end of the stick.

The rare survivors of this four-year-long effort had wanted more than anything else to go home, to tread French soil again, to see their loved ones again, to live again the life of the Paris streets, or of their peaceful native town. But they had quickly come back, bemused, uncomprehending, though as yet unembittered. They had been overwhelmed with Resistance stories, with tales of heroic deeds; the same words had been dinned into their ears a hundred times over:

'How lucky you were to be in London. Here, we suffered. If you only knew what risks we ran! In spite of all that, we kicked the Huns out.'

'You can't understand, you don't know what it was like. So-and-so was shot, so-and-so was tortured, deported.'

'What! You're a pilot sous-lieutenant? It's easy to see decorations weren't hard to come by in London!'

Pilots didn't understand all this. They had done their best. They didn't want flowers and jollifications. They expected no reward, except to see their homes again, even if they were in ruins. They preferred to keep quiet, but deep down there was a feeling of profound injustice. What had they gone through? They had only risked being roasted alive, trapped under the blazing remains of a Spitfire, or seeing the earth surge up before them when, imprisoned in the narrow metal coffin of a cockpit with its hood jammed, you count the four, three, two seconds left to you to live. Three times a day, for months on end, they had hurled their poor shrinking bodies into the flak, missing death by a hair's breadth, each time, until the last. . . .

War, for us, was not the desperate bayonet charge of a thousand human beings, sweating with fear, supporting and sustaining each other in a helpless, anonymous massacre. For us, it was a deliberate, individual act, a conscious, scientific sacrifice. Unaided, alone, each one of us had every day to conquer the stab of fear in our breast, to preserve, reform, our ebbing store of will power.

We had to do all that ten times, a hundred times, so many times, and then after each mission, take up again a normal healthy life – an appalling strain. The moment we stepped down from our planes, we found other human beings like us, the same flesh and blood, but who walked about, made love, went to the pictures, listened to the wireless as they smoked their pipes and read a book – and who knew they would be alive the next day!

What merely human nerves could go on standing up to this? L—, as brave as a lion for two years, had become a pitiful shadow of his former self. Gouby had crashed into the lorry he was machine-gunning, betrayed by his worn-out reflexes. Mouchotte, lungs burnt out by daily flights at 30,000 feet had collapsed in his Spitfire in the midst of the fight and disappeared.

There was no relief. It was always the same ones who flew to retain France's stake in the sky. While the others. . . .

After the liberation of France, we went on, to get away from the rank atmosphere of lust and hatred, of servility and haggling, and to preserve our remaining illusions.

For four hours I brooded. The Anson was now over Belgium. The pilot carefully kept to the safety lanes between the ack-ack zones, set up to protect Antwerp against the V-1 offensive.

After that, the south of Holland, monotonously flat, with its canals carving up regular squares of snow. Military convoys congested the roads. Suddenly a great airfield, pitted with craters, with two brick runways. Wrecked hangars, gutted buildings, here and there what looked like gypsy encampments – piles of empty petrol tins, camouflaged tents. Round each encampment, twenty or so Spitfires or Tempests in impeccable alignment. A snow-plough, surrounded by a cloud of powdered snow, was clearing one of the runways.

'Volkel,' said our pilot simply. A green rocket from the control tower and the Anson made its approach. The controller arrived in his jeep just as I was getting out.

'I'm Desmond. You're Clostermann, aren't you? We've heard about you from Lapsley. Yes, he's Kenway's Wing-Co. Ops. I'll take you to Wing H.Q. straightaway. Your kit will be taken to the mess.'

122 Wing was commanded by Wing Commander Brooker, D.S.O., D.F.C. He received me standing at the door of his command post trailer. I was introduced to him and handed him my posting order and my flying log. As he examined them in silence, I had a chance to have a good look at

him. He seemed very tired. He looked about thirty and, although his features still looked young enough, his eyes were bloodshot.

'Well, Pierre, I'm glad to have you here. As you know, we are having a pretty busy time. You'll be posted to 274 Squadron and command 'A' Flight. You've come at just the right moment, as Fairbanks, who's C.O., was wounded by flak this morning, and Hibbert, the senior flight-commander, left yesterday on ten-days' leave; so you'll be in charge until he comes back.'

As I climbed into the jeep, he added:

'Don't take too much notice of what the other pilots tell you. Their morale's a bit low, these last few days, because of losses and bad weather. Here are the ops. reports. Have a good look through them and give them back to me tomorrow morning. Get your stuff unpacked – we'll meet in the mess for dinner and I'll introduce your pilots to you.'

VOLKEL

Uden was a typical small Dutch town of 2,000 inhabitants, with clean, trim, brick houses, a church every 50 yards and two seminaries. We came back to the mess by jeep, jolting along through the snow and the mud, over the slippery cobble-stones, past an interminable convoy which filled the street with its roaring and clanking.

That convoy had become an obsession. When we left in the morning it was already on its way past, engines revving away and back-firing. When we came back in the evening it was still on its way past, a dangerous black mass punctuated by the glimmer of an occasional lamp. From time to time we passed a squadron of tanks, thundering to the front, with smiling crews hanging on to their monstrous steeds.

In the seminary courtyard were the electricity generators, their Diesel engines corrupting the air. Innumerable wires connected them to the dark building. The engineer officer watched over his dynamos with tender care, especially at night. That didn't prevent him, every time we had a breakdown or atmospherics in our radio receivers, from being abused by us all. Over the door of his trailer he had put up a notice:

'Don't shoot the electrician, he is doing his best.'

The officers' mess of 122 Wing was reached down a big school corridor with rows of coat pegs along the walls. On the right were the kitchens, the dining-room and the bar, on the left a ping-pong room and a library. The classrooms had been turned into dormitories. An appalling disorder reigned everywhere: camp beds at all angles, suitcases bulging with dirty clothes, period armchairs, oriental rugs, dirty crockery, cigarette ends, buckets of soapy water, dried mud, revolvers and ammunition, empty bottles, newspapers. On the first floor it was the same again, except in one room, 80 feet by 30 feet, divided up by wooden partitions like dormitories in public schools. A more or less decent order prevailed there.

The Unit Commanders and the old pilots lived there and the batmen had the situations more or less in hand.

The floor above was still inhabited by its rightful occupants and we sometimes passed them on the stairs on their way to the services in the church near by, silent, lost in a spiritual world which ignored our war and soared above its ills. Yesterday they shared the building with gunners from a German flak battalion, today it was an R.A.F. Wing, and tomorrow? Only God knew.

Life was very quiet at Volkel. Perhaps the atmosphere of the seminary had something to do with it. On Sunday evenings a curious scent pervaded the corridors – fried bacon, beer and incense!

After a frugal dinner the flight commanders put up on the big blackboard in the dining-room the list of pilots on dawn 'readiness' for the next day, who would have to be awakened.

The pilots off duty after tea had to dress up and shave for the evening. They queued up from 4.30 p.m., bucket in hand, in front of the only hot water tap. This was supplied by an oil furnace that was fed with 130-octane petrol. It couldn't take it and blew up every third day.

The others appeared at nightfall, returning from an alert or a trip, muddy, dead beat. They ate their dinner in silence, drank down a glass of beer by the corner of the bar and hurried off to turn in. For a mess bar ours was very quiet – too quiet. The bar is always a gauge of pilots' morale; here it was positively mournful. Yet it was very well stocked, thanks to what we had found in Jerry cellars, thanks to the lorry which the stores types took every fortnight to Naafi headquarters in Paris, thanks also to the arrangements which the more resourceful had made with breweries in Brussels. Never once did cigarettes, liqueurs, whisky, gin, champagne or beer give out.

However, on our Roll of Honour board, on top of an already long list of 113 pilots lost since the Normandy landing, there were now the names of 17 pilots killed or reported missing in the previous month. And February had started badly, with 8 pilots lost in less than ten days. As a result you saw only occasional pilots leaning against the bar, drinking their pint without a word, reading the previous day's London papers, brought by the duty Anson. One or two small groups in a corner were perhaps talking shop in a low voice, while a few more sitting on the floor by themselves, their glasses between their legs, read their letters. Occasionally one would burst in, pick up his chocolate and cigarette ration, hurriedly drink a glass of beer and go upstairs to bed without saying a word.

By 11 o'clock there was scarcely a soul. The barman dozed on his stool, a belated pilot still sipped his whisky, his back to the stove. The last B.B.C. programme could still be heard faintly through the heavy smoke-laden atmosphere.

4 o'clock. The beam from an electric torch seared your eye through the lids and a hand shook your shoulder.

'Time to get up, sir.'

The M.P. ticked a name on his list and noiselessly went off in his gumboots to wake up the other pilots on dawn 'readiness.' It was cold, you felt empty headed. Painfully you left the warmth of the blankets; you put on your battle-dress, your pullovers, your flying-boots, smoking a cigarette which made you feel slightly sick. Your Irvine jacket on your back, muffled up in a Balaclava, you went down to the icy dining-room. The frosted window panes gave back a pale reflection of the electric light bulbs. A half-asleep mess waiter brought grilled sausages and scalding tea, which you swallowed sitting astride the benches. Latecomers tore down the stairs, banged the doors, put a sausage between two pieces of bread and margarine, swore as they swallowed the hot tea, and rushed out to join their comrades in front of the entrance. The lorry was already there, the N.C.O. pilots sitting inside, smoking.

As Flight Commander I was entitled to the use of a jeep and a man from the transport section had brought one round for me. Accompanied by my two section leaders, my hands still numb with cold, I drove off, keeping my eyes on the red tail lamp of the lorry in front of me. There was ice on the road and as, since that 1 January show, headlights were not allowed, I had difficulty in following it.

An icy wind blew over the airfield, lifting the snow in damp clouds which pierced us to the marrow.

In the Dispersal hut the timekeeper had lit the stove and the kettle was beginning to sing on the Primus. Outside JJ-B – my aircraft – was so close that it seemed that its wing tip rattled against the boards of the hut. The wind found its way in in spite of the carpets hanging on the walls.

It was like being at a meeting of sleepwalkers. The pilots were doing two, and often three, very tough operations a day, and sometimes were ten hours on 'readiness.' They went to bed worn out and got up still tired. Numbed by the cold, their eyes heavy with sleep, they took down their parachutes, checked their helmets, staggered out and hauled themselves up on the slippery wings to get their planes ready.

The mechanics also led a dog's life. In that cold you had to have a night crew every 20 minutes to start up the engines and warm them up to 110°. It would have been catastrophic to let the oil in those sleeve-valve engines get too cold, as it was impossible to get the frozen oil feeds cleared. As a result the engines had to be run-up day and night.

0445 hours. The timekeeper rang through to Group Control to report that six Talbot aircraft were in a state of immediate readiness and would be called Blue Section. He then read out the names of the pilots with their call-signs and their positions in the section. He then passed me the telephone. It was Lapsley at the other end.

'Hallo, Pierre; got you up early this morning! The weather's pretty lousy but the Controller doesn't want to relax the state of readiness as one or two jets might very well try to slip through to take photos of our lines under that blasted cloud cover. All right? Cheerio; be on your toes, just in case.'

I hung up and went outside, shivering, to look round and see that everything was in order. Dawn was just breaking. The Flying Control lorries were picking up the night-flying flare-path.

With these low clouds, this sleet now coming down incessantly, not much chance of flying. Brr. . . . I nipped inside again. Complete silence in the hut. Sunk in their armchairs the pilots were all asleep. I took the opportunity of going through the order books, the RT procedure and the last battle reports, stuck up on the door.

The timekeeper noiselessly refilled his stove. The damp wood gave off an evil-smelling yellow smoke. I ended up by dropping off myself.

I was woken up with a start by the noisy arrival of the rest of the pilots, Squadron Leader Fairbanks at their head. A glance at my watch – already 8.15.

Fairbanks, an American who had joined up in the R.C.A.F. in 1941, was a tall fair, extremely pleasant fellow with delicate features like a girl. I got up and introduced myself. He had a frank firm handshake. In spite of his rather dreamy blue eyes he was an ace fighter pilot and a D.F.C. and bar adorned his chest. He had shot down 14 Huns, 12 in the previous month, including 2 jet Messerschmitt 262's.

He gave me a cigarette, we drank a cup of tea. I gave him the latest gen, and handed him the 'Met.' report, which needed no comment. We sat down and had a yarn. As usual we found we had a host of friends in common.

Fairbanks' tactics were very interesting and required a good deal of nerve. What a pity Jacques wasn't there! This would have been up his street. Broadly speaking, this was Fairbanks' technique.

The most frequented Jerry airfield was at Rheine, where a great many fighters were based. It took 8 minutes to get from Volkel to Rheine, thanks to the Tempest's colossal speed. Therefore Fairbanks had got into the habit of going there roughly once a day, generally round about 5 p.m. with only a section of four, sometimes even only a pair. When he got to the Rheine neighbourhood he kept just under cloud base – an average of 3,000 feet at this time of year – circling the airfield sometimes for as long as a quarter of an hour. Now and then, in spite of the flak, which was extremely dense and accurate just there, he dived to ground level, stayed on the deck for a few seconds then climbed back into the clouds fast. He used these few seconds to watch for any enemy aircraft in the circuit. He almost always managed to establish contact with a flight of Messerschmitts or Focke-Wulfs which he immediately attacked hell for leather, taking advantage of the element of surprise. Usually he shot one down and ran for cloud cover. To be objective it must be pointed out that these tactics had enabled him to run up a remarkable personal score. On the other hand, he often lost his No. 2.

'I'll make a milk-run to Rheine this evening if the weather clears a bit. If you'd like to see how I operate all you have to do is to come with my section as a reserve and you'll get the idea. I must get my hand in again; after seven days' leave you get a bit rusty.'

TEMPEST *V*. FOCKE-WULF

This afternoon the sky was an absolute death trap. We had been looking for trains in the Bremen area without much success. Fairbanks was leading a section of six Tempests – myself No. 2, Mossings No. 3, Inglis No. 4, Spence No. 5 and Dunn No. 6. I had pointed out before we started that his section was lop-sided – three young inexperienced pilots was too many. All the same we attacked a train in a marshalling yard. We were met by dense and accurate flak. Spence was hit in the port wing, and only just had time to jettison his blazing auxiliary tank. Fairbanks had dived to the attack rather steeply and I had had trouble in following him; the forty-odd shells I had scattered in the general direction of the locomotive couldn't have done it much harm. I had climbed up to the clouds again very quickly, with tracer all round me; it was obvious that my nerves couldn't take flak any more.

Fairbanks then led us in zigzags for 10 minutes as far as Osnabrück. Giving up hope of finding another train he set course 260°, which brought us back over the Ruhr. Two hundred Lancasters were carrying out a big daylight raid. There was a good chance of meeting a few Messerschmitt 109's round here.

The sky was still pretty bad. There was a thin translucent layer of ten-tenth's cloud at 10,000 feet and below a medley of small cumulus, between which we wended our way. Just the kind of position where you can't see anything but anyone can see you. Control called us:

'Hallo, Talbot leader? Canary please!'

'Hallo Kenway, Talbot leader answering, Canary coming up in 10 seconds!'

Canary was the cover name for the special secret apparatus which Tempests were equipped with. It sent out a certain radar signal when you pressed a yellow button on the right of the cockpit. This signal had the property of duplicating a radar echo and of changing its colour in cathode tubes. This enabled the Controller, with much greater precision than the old I.F.F., to identify such and such a formation from several others on a crowded screen.

'Hallo Talbot leader, Kenway calling – there are Huns around coming back from the Ruhr. Can't give you anything definite yet!'

I released the safety catch and checked my reflector sight. Hell! The bulb had burnt out. Feverishly I took off my gloves, fumbled in the little rack where the spare bulbs were clipped, and unscrewed the base of the sight.

'Look out for Huns coming down at 3 o'clock!' I swore under my breath and looked up, in time to see about thirty Focke-Wulfs peeling off less than 6,000 feet above and diving on us. Instinctively I stopped messing about with the sight and turned to face the attack with the other five aircraft. The base of my sight dangling on the end of the electric wire caught me full in the face, my gloves fell under my seat and a 30 mm. shell exploded in my starboard wing, riddling my fuselage with fragments. A poor start!

A 'long-nose' Focke-Wulf – it was the first I saw – nearly touched me and passed beneath me with a half roll.

Everything seemed to have got pretty confused.

'Good-bye chaps, I've had it.'

It was poor Spence's voice – his Tempest was spinning down, coughing oil and flames. Poor Spence, so proud of his new-born baby.

Now things really began to hum. The Focke-Wulfs, cleverly divided in groups of five or six, attached themselves to each of us. Without my gun sight, I fired away haphazard and unsuccessfully at a Jerry who jigged in front of me for a moment. I was disarmed and could take no further part in the show. I warned Fairbanks, who didn't answer, and decided to remove myself. My engine was beginning to heat alarmingly.

In front of me two Focke-Wulfs had collided and their entangled remains were slowly falling, throwing off a hail of flaming fragments. A parachute opened and disappeared at once into a cloud.

Followed by four Huns, I did a vertical climb and waited with my nose pointing up into the sky for the controls to slacken ... an anxious moment ... no drop in the speed ... my Tempest began to vibrate ... nothing for it! I kicked violently on the rudder bar ... the sky swivelled round – half roll ... I was upside down ... I pulled the stick back. ... What a ropy effort! I obviously wasn't handling my Tempest very well.

One of the Focke-Wulfs had followed my manoeuvre with the greatest of ease and his shells whizzed close by my hood. I now dived vertically. With my 7 tons I quickly reached 500 m.p.h. on the indicator and left the Focke-Wulf far behind. I must straighten out quickly as my damaged wing was vibrating and the skin, ripped by the shrapnel, was tearing dangerously. I crossed the Rhine at less than 150 feet, to the accompaniment of frenzied flak. Besides, I had chosen my spot badly and found myself on the left bank at ground level in the middle of the Wesel pocket. And what flak! Even the machine guns were taking a hand. I now understood why everybody made a detour over Goch. I missed Volkel in the mist and found myself Heaven knows where over the Dutch countryside. All the windmills, all the canals and all the towns looked alike – the map was no help. I asked Desmond for a fix and he brought me back plumb on the base with his first vector.

I made a very poor landing, as my flaps would only come halfway down and I was afraid they might pack up in the middle of my approach.

Inglis and Dunn had just landed, Mossings was in the circuit. Fairbanks and Spence had been shot down. Inglis and Mossings had each damaged a Hun and Dunn had scored hits on three. The violence of the scrap had prevented the results from being verified.

The mess was rather gloomy that night.

A TRAGIC LANDING

Through the dirty window-panes I was looking at Yellow Section of 274 Squadron returning from an armed reconnaissance. Only three aircraft in the circuit out of four ... and even then one of the three seemed to have been badly damaged by flak.

Desmond called me on the 'phone and asked me to come at once to the Control Tower. Just as I jumped into the jeep the two first Tempests landed in formation. A cluster of red Verey lights for the guidance of the third rose from the A.C.P.'s* trailer. Desmond was on the balcony of the tower, microphone in hand. Without bothering about the stairs I joined him quickly by shinning up the outside ladder. 'It's Alex,' he said, handing me his field-glasses, 'give him some advice.'

Poor Alex must have caught a packet from a 37 mm., and one of the legs of his undercart was dangling pitifully, the wheel half torn off. That leg must be got up at all costs; he would never succeed in landing on his belly like this.

'Hallo Alex! Pierre here, try to get your port leg up!'

No answer. I said it again, forcing myself to speak slowly and clearly. A few seconds later, at last, Alex's voice answered in the loudspeaker, hesitant and gasping: 'Sorry, I can't.'

'Try again,' I insisted.

The row of his engine at full throttle, the propeller in fine pitch, brought everybody out. I could see people climbing on the roofs of the huts and crowding at doors and windows. Hibbert and Brooker arrived, anxiously following the evolutions of the plane as it dived, climbed, waggling its wings to try and free that blasted wheel. Finally after a dive an object detached itself from the plane – it was the wheel – but there was still the oleo-leg.

'Alex, try your CO_2 bottle!' It was his last chance. With my glasses I could see the leg begin to come slowly up in jerks, almost into the cavity in the wing.

* Aerodrome Control Pilot.

'Hallo Pierre, I have used up my CO_2 and the leg isn't fully locked yet.'

His voice was trembling. Poor kid! How well I understood his panic, all alone up there, struggling with all that complicated machinery which had now become a death trap. I could almost see him, drenched in sweat, out of breath, desperately hammering at the undercart lever, still pushing on the CO_2 bottle lever although it was empty.

The ambulance started up and moved to the far end of the runway, keeping its engine ticking over. The fire tender followed; the crew on the running boards looking like deep-sea divers in their asbestos suits. The M.O.'s jeep arrived. Alex called me back.

'O.K. Desmond, coming in for belly landing. Switching off.'

'Christ! Clostermann, tell him to bale out!' shouted Brooker. Too late, he had switched off his radio.

The Tempest began its approach. I slid down the side of the ladder and leapt into a jeep. The fire tender got into gear and moved up to the front. People started running along the perimeter track. The Tempest lost height and quickly grew bigger. The brilliant disc of the propeller suddenly broke up as Alex switched off. He levelled out perfectly. Tail and flaps down, he approached the brick runway.

I trod on the accelerator, pursued by the fire tender's bell and the siren of the ambulance.

The Tempest was about to touch down – the transparent hood flew off through the air. Now! A terrific scraping noise, the propeller buckled up and the 8 tons fell at 150 miles an hour. With a crash like thunder the plane bounced a good 30 feet into the air before our horrified eyes, turned over and crashed onto its back, tail forward, in a sheet of flame. Bricks filled the air. A muffled explosion, a blinding light and, straightaway, terrible 20-yard tongues of flame, mingled with twisting spirals of black smoke scored with vivid flashes.

I jammed on the brakes 50 yards from the furnace and jumped out, while the fire-truck literally hurled itself into the flames, spitting carbonic foam through its six high-pressure nozzles. The fire crew leapt off, armed with axes, followed by the medical orderlies.

Thirty yards away the air was so hot that it burned your throats like spirits. White sparks began to spurt from the blaze as the ammunition caught. The dry crack of the explosions and the whistling of the fragments filled the air. Astonished, we could make out above all the racket a terrible scream – then an arm began to wave feebly amid the blinding flames and the creaks and groans of melting metal.

One of the firemen, trying to forge into the inferno, collapsed. He was hooked out from behind, like a blackened, smoking log. He climbed out of his asbestos suit bespattered with molten aluminium, staggered, and fell on his face, vomiting. The flames roared, the smoke stung our eyes. The firemen went on pouring gallons and gallons of milky liquid which splashed, turned into steam or ran over the bricks.

The heat was getting less all the same and the shattered carcase of the Tempest began to show through the tongues of fire – the disembowelled engine showing its copper viscera besmirched with earth, the skeleton of the tail plane, the fuselage broken up into three stumps, the wings ripped by the explosion of the belts of ammunition.

The fire was now almost vanquished. A vague shifting red glow could be seen beneath the boiling foam. Wading in up to our knees, we rushed in. The horrible stench of burning flesh and rubber caught our throats and made us retch. A fine white dust of powdered aluminium fell. Then the sound of axes breaking into the remains of the cockpit.

'Easy, chaps, easy!'

The gauntleted hands tore off the tangled fragments, threw back bits of white-hot metal that fell sizzling on the grass, and then . . . I don't know what impelled me to press on, closer.

Delicately, they eased out an inchoate red and black mass, to which scraps of charred cloth still adhered. The parachute and harness straps had burnt away, but underneath the bleeding crust you could imagine the white-hot metal buckles which had gnawed their way through to the bone. The doctor stabbed his hypodermic almost at random into what was a mere mass of burnt flesh, protecting his mouth all the while with a handkerchief. I don't know if it was our imagination, but we thought we could see a sort of irregular pulsing, as if the heart was still feebly beating above the gaping hole through which the pilots's insides had exploded. . . .

I felt the sweat congeal on my back. Completely unnerved, my legs gave way and I sat down in the slush of foam and cinders and, bent double, retched and retched.

25 February 1945

Another poisonous day. Snow, wind. Visibility nil; flying was quite impossible. However, G.C.C. maintained two sections of Tempests at immediate readiness – one from 486 and one from 56 – together with a section of Spit XIV's from 41 Squadron. These three sections had been taking it in turns, with no hope of flying, since dawn.

At about 15 hours the weather cleared slightly, and the six Spits were scrambled. In this appalling cold they had a job getting their engines started and we looked at them through our windows, jeering. In the end one pair took off, followed at least 3 minutes later by the rest. A quarter of an hour later these last four came back and landed, not having been able to join-up in the clouds. They told us, however, that the first two had jumped a German jet aircraft.

We got the remainder of the story that evening in the bar, when the pilots of 41 were distinctly pleased with themselves and let nobody forget it. Flying Officer Johnny Reid, D.F.C., shortly after he had scrambled and as he was patrolling Nijmegen bridge at 10,000 feet, had spotted one of the very latest and rarest Luftwaffe planes – an Arado 234 – sneaking into our lines at ground level. Diving straight down, flat out, ignoring the risk of his wings coming off, Johnny succeeded in catching the bastard in a turn, fired at him point blank and gently landed him in flames less than 100 yards from Broadhurst's H.Q. at Eindhoven.

We were told that the A.O.C. was delighted, as a group of American journalists had witnessed the operation, and it was the first Arado 234 to be destroyed for certain.

After this episode the pilots of 41 revived the good old Spitfire v. Tempest controversy, and pursued us with their jeers: 'You Tempests,' they said. 'You Speed Merchants, you think you're the cat's whiskers, you and your 7-ton crates, your 4 cannon, you've never managed to catch one of those things. You needn't have browned us off for days on end with yarns about your mighty dives and your terrific cruising speed!'

We naturally retorted that this particular Hun must have been very keen to commit suicide. Besides we'd seen Reid's plane after he landed: his poor Spit's wings were buckled like a concertina, all the paint had come off the surfaces, the rivets had sprung and the fuselage was twisted. Good for the scrap heap! And we closed the discussion by a conclusive argument that always annoyed Spitfire pilots considerably, i.e. that our landing speed was almost greater than their cruising speed.

As I was an ex-Spit pilot myself, Frank Woolley tried to drag me in as umpire. For 10 minutes I spouted feeble explanations and mathematical formulae and everybody was satisfied. Drinks all round settled it; we drank to the midges and they drank to the flying buses and we all went to bed in the best of tempers.

TEMPESTS *V*. MESSERSCHMITTS

ollowing on recent blows, particularly the shooting down of Fairbanks, Ops. and G.C.C. decided that only formations of at least eight aircraft might operate deep into enemy territory. In addition, two formations at a time would do sweeps following parallel courses and less than 60 miles apart, so that they could go to each other's assistance.

Leading Talbot, I was carrying out a sweep with eight Tempests of 274 in the Hanover area. 486 was operating somewhere not far off. At about 1505 hours, after having a look at the airfields at Hanover and Langenhagen, I set course 320° for Wunsdorf, from which two squadrons of Messerschmitts usually operated. Over the radio I warned Mackie who was leading 486:

'Hallo, Railroad, switching from H for Harry over to B for Baker.'

Wunsdorf with its two great runways in the shape of a St Andrew's cross, seemed deserted, though the field looked in pretty good shape. Leaving Steinhuder lake on my left, I came up towards Bremen.

1515 hours. We were within sight of Hoya, a night-fighter base. I decided on a 360° turn to have a look at the neighbourhood and to regroup my Tempests, who were scattered over about 3 miles of sky.

'Come on, Talbot, pull your fingers out, join up!'

During the turn I mechanically counted my aircraft. Hell! Where was the eighth? I waggled my Tempest about to look in the blind spot formed by my tail plane.

'Break port, Talbot!'

I just had time to shout it in the mike. There were the Wunsdorf '109's', 3,000 feet above, in impeccable formation; forty to fifty Messerschmitts.

'Climb flat out. Don't let your speed drop.'

They had seen us. A second of indecision, and they were now immediately above us, waggling their wings. They split up into two groups, one turning left, the other right.

'Hallo, Railroad, better come and give us a hand.'

It would be safer to have 486's help! It looked as if I was going to be caught, sandwiched between the two groups of Huns. Better try and get back towards Hanover and take no chances.

What were the Huns waiting for? They seemed to be anxious about something, to have smelt a rat. Now there were Blue 4 and Blue 3 lagging half a mile behind the rest of my formation.

'Join up, Blue 3 and 4, for Christ's sake!'

I had better try and maintain contact without fighting until Mackie turned up. I could hear Kenway bringing him along by radar.

'Join up, Blue 3 and 4!'

Those two idiots were going to spoil everything! There! About fifteen '109's' peeled off from the left-hand group and dived on them. Blue 3 must have gone blind, he just didn't seem to see them coming.

'Talbot Blue 3, break!'

O what the hell! I would have to attack.

'Talbot, break port. Attack!'

At full throttle, I cut short my turn and raced to help the two laggards. The first '109' fired a burst at Blue 3, as it passed. With one wing torn off by the 30 mm. shells the Tempest went into a spin.

I veered towards this Messerschmitt, who also turned towards me. He skidded, and I saw that his huge airscrew spinner bore the white spiral of the shock units of the German Air Force. I fired my four cannon together – one shell on his port wing . . . two more on the cowling . . . an explosion . . . the '109' passed 60 feet below me, dragging a trail of thick black smoke, and disappeared. My finger on the firing button, I flew straight on through the thick swarm of diving '109's'. I daren't attempt the slightest manoeuvre, afraid of a collision.

I kept on reminding my pilots to keep their speed above 300 m.p.h., for '109's' could turn better than we could at low speed, and you had to watch out for the 20 mm. cannon in their propeller – it didn't give you a second chance. The best technique was to do a spiral dive, work up to a speed of 450 m.p.h., do a straight vertical climb and then start all over again. The '109's' on the other hand, knowing that we dived faster than they did, tried to get us up to 16,000 feet, where our Tempests were heavy and our engines sluggish.

I made a false move and let myself get cornered by four aggressive '109's' who wouldn't let go. I outdistanced them on the way down, but when I levelled out they caught up with me and fired one after the other. This lift-like rigmarole might have a sticky end.

Most unpleasant, it was. You saw their propellers, the white trails at their wing tips, the big air-intake to their superchargers to the right of the cowling – then, suddenly, the staccato flashes of the 20 mm. cannon firing, with, in the centre, more sedate, firing in bursts of three shells, the

20 mm., whose fat tracer shells seemed to weave towards you in a most uncanny way. At the end of a few minutes the air was criss-crossed with a jumble of straight smoke trails left by the tracers. My engine was overheating as usual.

Sergeant Campbell stuck desperately to my tail and faithfully followed all my most violent manoeuvres. His life depended on it. However, he received a hit and, in a turn, I noticed oil streaking his fuselage. I shouted to him over the radio to go on with his turn normally while I passed behind him to cover him.

Pulling hard on the stick I did a half roll and he shot in front. This movement brought me cheek by jowl with a '109', slightly below him, at less than 30 yards distance. The sun reflected by the hood prevented my seeing the pilot's face. It was one of the latest Messerschmitt 109 K's with the new wooden rudder. He opened up flat out with methanol injection and tried to do a barrel roll round me. He slowly passed, on his back, above my cockpit and, looking up, I could see his yellow-edged black crosses. Trying to slip in his rear, I throttled back suddenly. But he was a crafty beggar and, before I had time to move a muscle, he swung away violently, then turned and let fly with his guns. One of his shells bounced off my cowling, exploded, and riddled my wing with shrapnel. At that same moment there were two explosions on the '109's' wing and he, surprised in his turn, broke away and went into a spin. It was Campbell, who had just winged him and got me out of a spot. Just in time!

A dozen '109's' had removed themselves from the scrap and were circling amongst the clouds above us, waiting for easy prey.

A Tempest caught fire and the pilot, W.O. Alexander, baled out. Another emerged from the dog fight and started tacking about aimlessly – it was that infernal Blue 4, fast asleep, as usual. Followed by Campbell, whose engine was missing badly, I made towards him at full speed, firing a burst on the Messerschmitt on the way. By the merest fluke I hit him, and he sheered off hastily, spouting glycol through his exhausts.

We were half a mile from Blue 4 when nine '109's' dived on him, three from each side. By a miracle he saw them coming, but in a panic he dived instead of climbing. The '109's', who had accumulated an adequate margin of speed, easily caught up with him.

'Turn starboard, Blue 4!' I shouted at him, so that he should pass under me and bring the '109's' within range of my guns. The Tempest, followed by three '109's', passed below and in front of me 50 yards away. One of the Huns opened fire. With a violent kick on the rudder bar I flicked off and engaged him at 45°. Concentrating on his target, he didn't see me coming.

Deliberately, I corrected my aim – two rings on the sight – a cautious glance behind me; Campbell was faithfully covering me. The shells from my four guns ripped the air: a flash under the Messerschmitt's belly, a shower of sparks, a jerk and he exploded into pieces, his wings torn off, his engine in flames. In the sky all that was left was a big cloud of black smoke and, down below, burning fragments framing a slowly falling parachute.

'Hallo, Talbot Red Leader, Red 2 calling. Going home; oil pressure.'

It was Campbell. His oil pressure packing up was not unexpected. Let's go home.

'Talbot aircraft, re-form!'

Just at that moment eight aircraft bobbed out of the clouds – a moment's flap. However, it was Railroad's Tempests. They immediately went for the Messerschmitts scattered about the sky. The Huns didn't stay to fight it out and began to make for the clouds, in pairs, in wide climbing spirals.

'Talbot, rendezvous over base, angels 10.'

On my way I dived down to have a look at an aircraft burning on the ground: it was a Tempest, which had turned over, trying to belly-land in a field of young wheat. I passed again to look at the registration letters. Christ, it was one of mine – JJ-Y – G—, who was Blue 1. No signs of the pilot.

I detached Red 4 to escort Campbell and bring him back to Volkel the quickest way, on course 265°. Then I came back via Osnabrück to cover them from a distance with my two remaining aircraft, plus a lost Railroad who had tacked on to us.

When I got to Volkel, Red 4 told me that Campbell's engine had packed up on him 3 miles from the Rhine, which he just managed to get across in a glide. He had apparently made a correct belly-landing near a field battery. Sure enough, after dinner Campbell turned up in a jeep with some artillery types. He was grinning all over his face, in spite of a bandaged head, a black eye and two stitches in his lip.

A DAY LIKE THE OTHERS

Curled up into a ball in bed, half-dressed and already wearing my Balaclava, overcoat and Irvine jacket beneath the covers, I was dreaming my favourite dream. There was a huge carp at my feet in the clear water of a lake about to rise to the bait. It opened its mouth and I felt my rod bend. Suddenly I woke up with a start. A hand was on my shoulder. Someone was shaking me. I glanced at my watch – its luminous hands showed ten minutes past five. Our watch started at 0600 hours. Not one more second could be spent in my warm, comfortable bed. God almighty, it was cold out there. I put on cotton socks beneath the thigh-length woollen stockings I wore with my battle-dress and then the heavy polo-neck sweater over the silk scarf that protected my neck when I was scanning the skies, head turning left and right. Laden with equipment like a deep-sea diver, I was about to enter a hostile world, where weather conditions, heavy cloud, flak and snow lay in wait. With a bit of luck I might come across one of the Messerschmitts that had become such a rarity since 1 January and *Bodenplate* – a day that had cost the allies dear, though even more so the Luftwaffe.

I rushed downstairs to meet the five other pilots who were due to share my watch, but the mess was still empty. Three swaying light bulbs cast a pale yellow light over the long, empty refectory tables and the small platform from which, in quieter times when used by the seminarians, an officiating monk would read from some edifying tome. The only ray of sunshine came from the gentle smile of the small Dutch serving girl who had looked after me very well since I had started saving my chocolate ration for her younger brothers. This particular morning she had hidden a precious egg under my navy beans – tinned American beans in tomato sauce with bacon – and the two breadcrumb sausages that comprised my breakfast.

She was pretty, with such lovely blue eyes. Ah, if only . . . but there was, as we all knew, 'a time for love and a time for war.'

The other pilots arrived noisily and destroyed the moment.

We had to get a move on. 'Come on chaps, hurry up!'

It was still dark outside and the soft snow that had fallen during the night had now frozen, turning the steps into an ice-rink. The cook brought out a huge thermos of boiling tea and three bags of stodgy scones.

'Where's my jeep?'

The lorry skidded to a halt and Chieffy, the Flight Sergeant who was in charge of maintenance for the squadron, jumped out and told me that some idiot from 56 had driven it into a ditch. It would be ready for action the next day.

We set off in a trance like sleepwalkers. The Naafi Woodbine that I lit began to choke me by the second puff. . . . God, it was cold. When we arrived at the squadron's hut we were literally paralysed. Not wishing to pull rank, I had stayed in the back with the pilots rather than travelling in the lorry's cabin.

Inside it wasn't much warmer than outside. Every now and then a frozen mechanic would come in and drink a cup of tea hunched over the feeble heat of a little stove. . . . The timekeeper gave me the weather forecast – foul – that had just come in on the teleprinter. It would have been better to leave us asleep in bed, conserving our energy. But, we had to be prepared. . . . We went out into the inky black night to put our parachutes in the cockpits ready for take-off. *Primum vivere* (enjoy life first)! Obey orders and don't think! Quite! Those damn Sabre engines had to be warmed up for 15 minutes every two hours to prevent the intake and exhaust gaiters from blocking up with solidified oil, so now the tanks had to be filled up. I pitied the mechanics who had to stand on slippery wings handling the 130-octane petrol that burnt like fire.

The JJ-Z's engine refused to start. We went outside to help, turning the enormous 4.40 metre propeller by hand. It took four of us at a time with one of us being lifted up to hang from a blade so that his whole body weight would shift it a quarter-turn. We tried again . . . and after turning it two or three complete revolutions with great difficulty, we got out of the way and Chieffy took over – Chieffy could do anything with Sabre engines, so they said – and indeed he succeeded with the second turn, and hanging on by the skin of his teeth, gave it a quick burst on the throttle when it was on the point of petering out. The exhausts spluttered irregularly, almost regretfully, and spat out an oily blue smoke for a couple of minutes until, at last, the engine began to turn with the deafening groan of its twenty-four cylinders.

There was always an icy fog, laying down a frozen film on the wings and deforming its contours. The de-icing truck did the rounds of all the planes, one after another. Often it had to return to the first Tempest, to clear off the layer of ice that had re-formed on its wings. The labour of Hercules.

A pathetic thread of light filtered over the Rhine under the thick leaden ceiling that hung over the ground. On the runway, a jeep followed phantom figures collecting the runway lights. Horizontal visibility was less than a hundred yards.

Right, that was enough! I telephoned control, waking all those fine fellows who snoozed snugly over their radar consoles. 'No dice!' it was out of the question to fly in this weather, and there was a good chance that it would be the same for the Focke-Wulf 190 D9's from Gütersloh that we had run into the evening before, lurking behind one of those clouds that were so handy for ambushes. We had each surprised the other and given ourselves a mutual scare. In the dramatic, overcast winter skies we had fruitlessly exchanged a few ragged bursts of gunfire. MacLaren was hit but succeeded in getting back. I had fired on a fine 'D9', but with a spot of MW5* it had slipped between my fingers, leaving me standing. It was an experience I preferred not to repeat.

My friend Lapsley, the controller in chief, woke up at last and asked what was wrong. I kept calm and told him that if he would kindly look out of the window he would see that the weather was too foul to send even a bicycle out, much less a Tempest carrying my precious skin. It was no good reminding him that we were short of planes since the Hawker strike. Group Support Unit had warned us of that.

'OK, Pierre, hold on.' And 5 minutes later: 'Squadron release'. Hurrah! The next day the weather was even worse.

That winter allowed us two days of respite, and the chance to spend an evening in the squadron bar. Here we would warm ourselves with a glass of Bols genever – a gift from the Dutch citizens of Uden – while we scrutinised the adventures of a scantily-clad Jane, the cult comic-strip heroine of the R.A.F., in a week-old copy of the *Daily Mirror*.

0755 hours

Dawn had barely broken when we heard the battery of Bofors guns from the military camp at Uden: the characteristic magazine five reports as their shells exploded somewhere up in the sky, invisible behind the clouds.

Then came the burst of a Messerschmitt 262's jet engines, increasing in an instant to the sharp whine of a circular saw slicing through a block of

---

* MW5: a system of methanol injection giving a brief but considerable boost to engine-power.

wood. We shot outside in time to catch a glimpse of it crossing Volkel like a rocket, close to the ground, trailing a fine line of grey smoke that wavered and dissolved in the fog. It was already far away when we heard the frozen air tearing like silk behind it. Our airfield's Bofors guns took aim in their turn but it was long gone. We remained rooted in the doorway, at once full of admiration and envy.

'Jesus Christ, that bastard is fast!'

On the third morning a '262' paid us a visit. We imagined it was making a photo-reconnaissance of Belgium and Holland's various neighbouring airfields. It was useless to give chase, and with that low cloud cover you couldn't patrol at 9,000 or 10,000 feet, which was the only solution, going into a steep dive with the vain hope of bringing it within range of our guns. We had to think of something else. We'd probably have to adopt Fairbanks' tactic of cornering them on approach, despite the risks, and brave the flak cover as they edged beneath it to land.

The Naafi waggon and the Salvation Army brought hot tea and biscuits. We always insisted our frozen mechanics were served first. The morning was too calm. To while away the time, I plunged into the R.A.F. 'intellectuals' favourite book, *No Orchids for Miss Blandish*.

Operation Clarion

With a great deal of publicity backup from the B.B.C., hundreds of planes attacked the rail networks and shunting yards in the west of Germany, in preparation for crossing the Rhine. The fighter pilots of the 2nd T.A.F. and the 83rd Group – in other words, us – were given the task of knocking out the trains running between Osnabrück and Hamburg.

Despite being far from keen on this kind of sport, that morning I had to lead a patrol of six Tempests from 56 Squadron, covered by six Tempests from 274.

Directly over Kassel, while all eyes were riveted to the ground looking for a train, around twenty 'long-nose' Focke-Wulf D9's surged out of those accursed low clouds and past our right flank. They were probably JG-26, which usually patrolled in that area.

'Talbot, break right.'

Suddenly there was a general mêlée in an area restricted by the low cloud. Not a good place to engage. However I had a splendid No. 2 who stuck with me, almost too closely, eyes fixed on me instead of watching my rear and his own. . . .

As soon as I managed to get myself at a good angle to line up a 'long-nose' I crossed a burst of tracer fire and took a hit on the right wing. I broke off in panic in a tight half roll, in time to see my team-mate literally

244 COMMANDS IN THE R.A.F.

explode. Two wings bearing roundels tumbled out of the ball of flames. I came out of my roll and, with the stick pulled back to my stomach for a power boost, rose above the clouds, followed by two Tempests. I was asking myself where those damn 274 pilots who were supposed to be covering us had got to, when the Spitfire XIV's of 41 Squadron that patrolled that area, alerted by the control tower, plunged into the fray.

'Talbot Red, let's get out!'

I beat a retreat. In the confusion we had veered towards a large airfield whose flak guns immediately opened fire on everyone, friend and foe alike. It was probably Rheine/Hopsten where, after all the bombardments they had endured for the last two weeks, the gunners were extremely edgy!

Three Tempests were flying due west at low altitude. I joined them to return in some company. They were aircraft from 486 Squadron. In the end, we had brought down two 'D9's' – one for 274 and another for the 56 Squadron – but lost four Spitfires. It was odd that our R.A.F. 56 Squadron was often up against the Luftwaffe's JG-56!*

Together with Cole, I went on a weather recce towards Rheine, hoping to pick up a '262' somewhere. I wasn't very keen. En route, we flew alongside the Dortmund–Ems canal, and came across a solitary Focke-Wulf that confronted us. 'Leave it to me!' shouted Cole, but he was dealing with a sharp pilot who handled his old Focke-Wulf A8 like a real expert. We tried to catch him in a pincer movement, but failed. Unhappily for him he tried to break away after 2 or 3 minutes and I had him for a fraction of a second in my sights. I fired without much hope and with odds of a million to one I hit him. He parachuted out in the nick of time.† So much the better! We made a half-turn, came across a flight from 56 Squadron escorting some Typhoons and were then attacked by a band of crazy American Mustang P-51's. Where did these dangerous lunatics come from? Before we knew where we were, they had shot down Flight Lt. Green of 56. We shook them off with superior speed, but the telephone line to the U.S. H.Q. in Brussels that day was red hot.

We learnt that these idiots who had no right to be in our sector had also brought down two Typhoons, the pilots of which let it be known that they'd fire on the first P-51 that crossed their path. When would they learn to identify allied aircraft?

The weather improved, and by 0800 hours the three squadrons of 122

* German archives revealed that during that particular fray Feldwebel Gertstensorer of the JG-56 was killed in his D9 and two other pilots wounded.
† The pilot was F.W. Erich Lange of III JG-54.

Wing were in the air in sections of four, in search of railway locomotives from the Rhine to Berlin. I led the Talbot Yellow section and 5 minutes after take-off, within sight of Cologne cathedral with its damaged spires standing out from the ruins of the city, we attacked three trains, one after another, running through a barrage of fireworks. Two of my planes were hit and returned to Volkel. We were now down to a pair. I searched in vain for another Tempest section to make me feel less alone, but everyone had disappeared. Never mind. I set a direct 90° course towards Berlin, hedgehopping all the way, and near Osnabrück spotted a long freight convoy coupled to two locomotives. It would be no picnic, relatively speaking, since it was stationary, probably having been warned of our presence, and it most likely contained at least three flak-waggons whose engineers were doubtless following us in their range finders. While I was trying to decide whether to attack or not, we were fallen upon by Focke-Wulfs. Peter West saw them in enough time and warned me that we'd better turn about and try to hide in the clouds, now alas a bit too high, before they cut off our route. Meanwhile, it was every man for himself. For a while a 'long-nose' flew a few metres parallel to me. It shone like a new penny and I recognised the black and white stripes of the JG-26 on its fuselage. We always encountered the same chaps! We looked at each other and broke away, me to the left, him to the right ... and then nothing, the sky was empty. I looked for Peter and didn't find him, but miraculously came across a section of 274 Squadron and together we tracked down three Dornier 215's flying in formation – a rare find. We shot them down, poor fellows, in the minutes that followed. I got the one that was trailing: my Tempest's four cannon didn't let up until the end. Peter was able to bring his damaged plane home, having shot down a Dornier himself.

By the end of the afternoon I led the Yellow and Blue sections just skimming over the tree-tops, while the others went off towards Rheine to search out and ambush a '262'. In passing we strafed several lorries on the Bremen autobahn.

Then the weather grew worse and visibility under the lowering sky quickly became poor. I thought it would be best to get back before it got even worse since I didn't fancy leading eight planes at 400 m.p.h. through those freezing clouds. I pulled the maps from my boot and looked down, trying to orient myself. When I looked up there was just time to shout 'Watch out, airfield ahead!' It was impossible to avoid it by swerving: I was right over a runway on which two Focke-Wulf D9's were taking off. Others were parked nearby. The control tower saw us, and the first Fw dodged by banking vertically but, finger on the button, I hit the second one as he was entering his landing pattern. My shells exploded on the runway and on the Fw that was taking off. One of its wings touched the runway and it foundered, leaving a long trail of flames from its auxiliary tank on the concrete.* Head down, I kept up the assault, firing on a half-dozen Ju 188's concealed among pine trees at the end of a well-camouflaged long taxiing-strip. I was going too fast to aim properly and got a 20 mm. in the left wing for my pains. On our return, we attacked a large convoy of at least thirty fuel tankers parked in a wood; unhappily for them the trees didn't yet have enough leaves! It was a gigantic bonfire, flames mounting to 100 metres. A Tempest passed through; it was MacIntyre. When he moved off, I thought for a moment that he was on fire and when he got back to Volkel we discovered that his plane's paintwork was blackened and blistered.

We got back, to learn with regret that Cole had been shot down as well as another of our planes; Rheine/Hopsten was not a profitable enterprise. Hibbert, being senior to me, took command of the squadron.

There was a big discussion at 122 H.Q. with Lapsley, the base and wing commanders and the other two group commanders. We were short of planes thanks to that scandalous strike at Hawker. 274 had pinched two Tempests from me and we had only about a dozen planes between us instead of the regulation twenty-six. I learnt that a second Wing of Tempests had been planned but it was cancelled. Tomorrow, 486 Squadron would in principle replace 274 or 56 who had been sent on leave, and several of their pilots would be distributed among the two remaining squadrons where there was a similar pilot shortage. 56 Squadron had only 14 out of the 24 pilots that were essential. Nine times out of ten, the reinforcements who arrived were inexperienced pilots although regulations stipulated that Tempests should only be flown by pilots with at least one tour of operations under their belts. The biggest inconvenience of this situation was that, since our squadrons could not fly in the most effective twelve-formation – the classic three by four – Wing Commander Brooker decided that from now on we would fly as they had done in Malta and for the same reasons, in a six-section – the 'fluid six'. In the end this wasn't such a bad idea, as it was a very handy little set-up for tackling an enemy superior in numbers.

After breakfast I was sent off to try the system out on a sweep over a very large area: Hanover, Magdeburg and Kassel, at 500 feet! Once again we were treated to rotten weather with a leaden sky and cloud. So I made a careful study of the flak zones, although these tended to change daily, always increasing in density.

---

* My airfield was Aldhorn and the German pilot, Obersleutnant Bott, although badly wounded, survived.

To my left in the formation were two pairs, one of which was led by Lieutenant Deleuze, one of the two Frenchmen who had arrived in the squadron the previous week. I was making a big detour to avoid the Langenhagen anti-aircraft fire – a large, well-defended base that housed '262's' – when suddenly a dozen Focke-Wulf D9's streamed past to my right, flying in the opposite direction. It was the classic booby trap. Everyone turned to look at them and it was at that moment that breaking cover from the left, almost behind us, four Focke-Wulfs attacked my two outer left planes. A Tempest hurtled straight down in flames, and crashed. Everything happened so fast that I didn't have time to react. Two more of my planes were hit, and one of them – a bad sign – trailed a trickle of white glycol-filled smoke. I decided to turn back to escort my crippled planes home.

On landing, I discovered that it was Deleuze who had been shot down.* He was an experienced pilot who had joined us after chasing V-1 flying bombs with 501 Squadron. On rereading his dossier, I discovered that on just his second Tempest flight, after having flown Spit V's, he had brought down the first of a series of eight V-1's during his tour of operations, and then in September a Messerschmitt 109. He was one of those young French pilots who, having arrived very early on in England before the formation of the F.A.F.L., had been taken in hand by the R.A.F., with whom he remained. When I asked him why, at our first meeting, he replied that in order to fight against the Germans, who by then were in Paris, he would even have signed up with the Eskimos!

* His body was recovered in Holland at the end of 1946, at the bottom of a deep crater carved out by his plane; it was identified thanks to the French flag that he carried rolled around his belt. It was the same flag that he had flown on the little boat in which he had crossed the Channel to escape to England.

'RAT CATCHING'

It was my 24th birthday. 274 Squadron, having lost half its strength, was sent to England to regroup. In the guise of a birthday present I was given command of a flight of 3 Squadron.

After a meal of congealed eggs and cold bacon in the mess – where was my little Dutchgirl? – I went to take up my position and to get acquainted with my new partners. These English pilots were astonishing. The same Wing comrades who used to call me by my first name now said 'Sir' quite unaffectedly. For them it was quite natural and they didn't care whether I was French or not – on the contrary, I think they thought that their Frenchman lent the squadron a touch of originality compared to the others!

The dreadful winter of 1944–45 ended, leaving traces of snow on the flanks of the Ardennes where the burnt-out carcasses of Tiger and Panther tanks still lay – remnants of the Runstedt offensive. Along the banks of the Rhine sheets of ice still clung to the wreckage of sunken barges.

I climbed onto the wing of my immaculate and shining new plane, which was resplendent in the G.S.U.'s new paintwork (Group Support Unit fitted out and checked the replacement planes as fast as they left the factory). It was registered JF-E.

The mechanics painted little black crosses on the cockpit to record the victories I had already achieved. I myself added a Cross of Lorraine on the nose, and decided to call it 'Le Grand Charles' in honour of De Gaulle (though I wasn't sure how much the dedicatee would have appreciated this if someone had told him!).*

The morning sky towards the west was clear, but to the east the wind was fanning the smoke from the fires, lit by the raids of Lancasters by night and B-17's by day. We had heard the thunder of bombs falling on the

---

* After the war I gave the General a photograph of my 'Grand Charles', which amused him greatly.

region's towns and cities throughout the previous day. The poor civilians were always victims. . . .

The wings of the aircraft were steaming in the dawn after the de-icing truck had been round. The firing of the Kaufman starters was followed by a hesitant backfiring, and the small blue flames in the exhaust pipes of engines that had been warming up for some time.

I wanted to test run my new Tempest and fire its guns to make sure that everything was functioning correctly. I felt sorry for the mechanic whose job it was to guide me down the narrow taxiing-strip, hanging on in the wake of the propeller's icy wind. He had a bottle of alcohol and rag at the ready, so that when we got to the end of the runway he could wipe the oil off the windshield that the Sabre engine had spat out as it ticked over. He then had to jump to the ground, bending down to pass beneath the wing before take-off. I had one of the new 2950 CV engines and a Rotol propeller with large blades that could really move!

I made off towards the Rhine to fire my four cannons over Germany, then to check the ammunition remaining in each casing. I was zigzagging between the low clouds, searching for the river, when below me three Me 109's emerged from a corridor of cloud, then a fourth, far behind. I sent an alert over the radio and fixed on the straggler, who had his eyes glued to his patrol and didn't see me coming. My four guns functioned perfectly. I hoped the camera had been properly set up! The '109' was now on its back, trailing grey smoke as the pilot jumped. He was pretty low and I didn't see a parachute open in the banks of mist. . . .

That afternoon the skies around Rheine were like a circus. The Focke-Wulf D9's of JG-26 were covering a pair of jet-engined Me 262's as they landed, making their way through a veritable tunnel of flak, 20 and 37 mm. shells exploding in the mêlée, menacing Focke-Wulfs and Tempests alike.

A pilot jumped from a flaming Tempest. He was low, but I was going too fast to see if he got out safely. On getting back we counted up, but it wasn't a great score for the first mission I had commanded with Filmstar (our code name for 3 Squadron). We had lost three planes and brought down two Focke-Wulfs – one by me and another by Ken Hughes. The machine-gun cameras attributed another two damaged planes to us. Quid pro quo.

The Messerschmitt 262's were becoming a distinct nuisance. These blasted jets were appearing on our front in ever-increasing numbers. Every day at dawn and at twilight they came over, singly, at ground level, to take their photographs. Every now and again, just for a change, patrols of three came and machine-gunned or bombed our lines.

For Kenway's controllers they were a difficult proposition. Radar couldn't pick them up properly as the posts swept the 360 degrees of the horizon too slowly to follow and fix the echo of a '262' batting along at nearly 600 m.p.h. at tree-top level.

The general of 216 U.S. Army Group didn't understand these technical subtleties and bombarded G.C.C. with peremptory notes, demanding immediate steps to have these armed reconnaissances stopped. Poor Wing Commander Lapsley cudgelled his brains to find some means of intercepting the '262's' with Tempests capable of only 490 m.p.h. Finally, he and Brooker worked out the 'rat code' (later called the 'bastard code' by the pilots).

The principle of the things was as follows. Two pairs of Tempests were permanently kept at a state of immediate alert – i.e. the planes were actually in scrambling position on the runway, with the pilots ready strapped in their cockpits, their finger on the starter, engines warmed up, radio switched on.

As soon as the '262' crossed the Rhine towards our lines, Lapsley sent out a warning in clear from his control post straight to the pilots, as follows:

'Hallo, Talbot Leader, scramble, rat, scramble, rat!'

The engines were immediately started up, three red Verey lights went up to clear the circuit and give the rat-catchers priority. The quarry being too speedy for any attempt to catch it to be worthwhile, the two Tempests immediately made for Rheine/Hopsten, the jet-fighters' base. Exactly 8 minutes from the sounding of the alarm the Tempests would be patrolling the approaches of Rheine at 10,000 feet, and trying to catch an Me 262 returning from his trip, when he would have to slow down to let down his undercart and his flaps before landing.

In one week we brought down eight 'rats' in this way. I was out of luck and missed two, who slipped through my fingers. The second one provided a complete triumph for the Volkel ack-ack boys. The 'rat-scramble' had just been given out. I was taking off, followed by my No. 2, when the '262' whizzed over the field about a hundred yards behind me. By the merest chance, and by an extra-special dispensation of Providence, the two Bofors of posts S.E.4 and 5 were pointing in the right direction with the crews in position. Each gun fired one clip, with the odds about a million to one, and the Me 262 stopped a 40 mm. and disintegrated into the air.

The Germans soon found the answer to 'rat-catching'. The Me 262's were told to return home at full speed and at ground level – which made them very difficult to spot, owing to their camouflage – and not to slow up until they got to the flak lane. Once there, they could land at leisure and in complete safety. In line with the main east-west runway at Rheine, over a distance of 5 miles there were many quadruple 20 mm. flak guns in a double line. These could put up an impenetrable curtain of steel and explosive, under which the Jerry could slip and land perfectly peacefully.

In one week we lost three Tempests which tried to attack an Me 262 in this flak lane. There was no point in persisting. Strict orders came out, absolutely forbidding any attack on a '262' within a radius of 6 miles of Rheine; which considerably reduced our chances of bringing any down.

On 7 March, 3rd Corps of the 1st American Army reached the Rhine at Remagen and by an extraordinary stroke of chance found the Ludendorff bridge intact. The 9th Armoured Division seized it in double quick time and General Bradley began to exploit the bridgehead. Within a couple of days this enclave on the right bank of the Rhine had become such a threat to the Germans that they made desperate efforts to cut the bridge. The Luftwaffe was hurled in and the American fighters, who had no suitable bases within reasonable distance, were soon overwhelmed. The R.A.F. was called in to help and, as Tempests were the only aircraft with a sufficient range to cover Remagen while operating from Holland, this task too fell to our lot.

I led the first of these protective missions, at twilight. Our eight Tempests flew up the Rhine, through Cologne, and reached Remagen, where we were greeted by virulent American ack-ack. The Yanks were in such a state of nerves that, even after we had made the usual recognition signals and they had been acknowledged, they continued to let off an occasional burst of Bofors at us. By the third salvo, which didn't miss me by much as I collected some shrapnel in the wing, I felt I didn't particularly want to go on giving these gentlemen target practice. I got my formation to do a 180° turn to make for home, when horrors! – We found ourselves face to face with an absolute armada of seven or eight Arado 234's escorted by a dozen or so Me 262's, diving down on that miserable bridge.

Full throttle I fell in behind them. Just as I was opening fire on an Arado 234 at over a thousand yards' range, twenty 'long-nose' Focke-Wulf D9's emerged from the clouds on my left. To hell with it! I warned my formation over the radio and kept straight on. The speed shot up frighteningly – 420 m.p.h. – 450 – 475. I was hurtling down at an angle of about 50°; the 7 tons of my plane, pulled by 3,000 h.p. had terrific acceleration. The Arado levelled out gently, insensibly, following a trajectory which would bring it down to the level of the Rhine a few hundred yards short of the bridge. I was 800 yards behind, but I daren't fire. Still behind my Hun, I flew into a frightful barrage of 40 mm. and heavy M.G. I saw the two bombs drop from the Arado quite distinctly. One of them bounced over the bridge and the other hit the bridge road. I passed over the bridge, 40 yards to the left, just as it exploded. My plane was whisked up like a wisp of straw and completely thrown off her balance. I instinctively closed the throttle and pulled the stick back. My Tempest shot up like a bullet to 10,000 feet and I found myself upside down right in the clouds, sweating with funk. A violent vibration – my engine cut out, and a shower of mud, oil and ironmongery fell on my face. I dropped like a plummet and then my plane went into a spin. A spin in a Tempest is the most dangerous thing on earth – after one turn, two turns, you get thrown about helplessly, you cannon into the walls of the cockpit in spite of the harness straps.

In a complete flap, I wrenched at the hood release; it came away in my hand. I tried to get up on my seat to bale out, but forgot to unstrap myself and succeeded only in giving myself a terrific bang on the head. When I came out of the cloud I was still in a spin – there was the ground, less than 3,000 feet below. I pushed the stick right forward and opened the throttle wide. The engine coughed and suddenly fired again, practically jerking itself out of the fuselage. The spin turned into a spiral; I gently tested the elevators, which responded all right – the fields however were rushing towards my windshield. I levelled out at less than 1,000 feet.

A close shave. I raised my helmet and felt my hair soaked with sweat.

I pin-pointed my position quickly. I was on the right bank of the Rhine to the north of the American bridgehead. I set course 310° for home and over the radio gave my patrol a rendezvous over Cologne at 13,000 feet. Just at that moment Kenway called me:

'Hallo, Talbot Leader, Kenway calling. What's your position? Over to you.'

I replied briefly: 'Hallo, Kenway, Talbot Leader answering, my approximate position is 20 miles north of Remagen, along Rhine. Out.'

It was Lapsley personally controlling at Kenway today, I could recognize his drawl.

'O.K. Pierre. Look out, there are a couple of rats around. Out.'

Right, I'd keep my eyes open. I was O.K. for juice and decided to do a quiet 360° turn under the clouds to try and spot the two rats in question.

A few seconds later some ack-ack tracers started coming up along the Rhine and I made out two long slender grey trails weaving just above the ground.

It was a '262'. It looked superb with its triangular fuselage like a shark's head, its tiny arrow-shaped wings, its two long turbines, its grey camouflage spotted with green and yellow. This time I wasn't too badly placed, I was between him and his base. Once again I dived hell for leather, to accumulate the greatest possible speed. He hadn't seen me yet. A slight turn on the ailerons and I got up to him at a tangent. I was making careful allowance for speed and bullet drop when suddenly two long flames spurted from his jets. He had seen me and opened up. I was in perfect position 600 yards away. I fired a first burst. A miss. I increased the correction and fired again quickly, for he was gaining on me. This time I saw two flashes on his fuselage, then one on the wing. The range was now 500 yards. An explosion on the right turbine which immediately vomited an enormous plume of black smoke. The '262' skidded violently and lost height. Our speeds evened out, with about 600 yards between us. The smoke got in my way and I missed him again. Curious red balls floating in this smoke dazzled me. Jesus! My two port cannon jammed. I aimed more to the right to correct the skid, and my two other cannon jammed too. The Me 262 flew on on one engine. I was mad with rage. There seemed to be a leak in my pneumatic system – no pressure showing on the gauge. I was simply livid with fury. I went on after the '262' in the hope that his second turbine would overheat.

After a few moments it was my own engine which began to heat. Regrettably I gave up, swearing to have that idiot's scalp who had written in the Air Ministry technical bulletin that an Me 262 couldn't fly on only one turbine (except when low on fuel – I had forgotten this detail).

Through all this I had clean forgotten my section, which must be getting somewhat restive over Cologne. Over the radio I handed over to MacCairn and we returned to Volkel separately at nightfall.

I was in a vile temper. Just to improve matters one of my tyres burst as I landed. I had to wait in an icy wind until it was changed before I could taxi to the parking place and get off to dinner.

TRAIN-BUSTING

In the grey dawn a column of smoke began to rise amongst the long wisps of mist over the monotonous snow-covered plain. Then another a little further along the black line which meandered through the immaculate whiteness of the countryside.

'Train, 2 o'clock, Talbot Leader!'

The four Tempests slid down to 3,000 feet in the frozen air and their polished wings caught the first gleams of a dingy dawn. We obliqued towards the second train and instinctively four gloved hands, benumbed by the cold, were already pushing the prop lever to fine pitch. We could now make out the locomotive and the flak truck in front of it and the interminable mixed train dragging painfully behind.

Without dropping our auxiliary tanks, we went into a shallow dive at full throttle ... 350 ... 380 ... 400 m.p.h. The blood throbbed in my parched throat – still that old fear of flak. Only about a mile or two now. I began to set my aim 20 yards in front of the locomotive.

Now! I leant forward, tensed. Only 800 yards. The first burst of tracer – the staccato flashes of the quadruple 20 mm. flak mounting – the locomotive's wheels throwing sparks, skidding with all brakes jammed on. 500 yards. I was skimming over the snow-covered furrowed fields. Rooks flew off in swarms. My cannon roared – the engine-driver jumped out of his cabin and rolled into the ditch. My shells exploded on the embankment and perforated the black shape which loomed in my sights.

Then the funnel vomited a hot blast of flame and cinders, enveloped in the steam escaping from the punctured pipes. A slight backward pressure on the stick to clear the telegraph wires, a quick dive through the smoke, then, once again, the sky in my windshield, covered with oily soot. Pulling hard on the stick I broke in zigzags. Live coals seemed to fly round my plane, 'le Grand Charles', but whether they were flak or ricochets from my No. 2, I couldn't say. The usual fiery white puffs began to hang in the air.

A glance backwards. The locomotive had disappeared, shrouded in soot and spurting steam. People were scrambling out of doors and tearing down the embankment like agitated ants.

Red 3 and Red 2 caught up with me, while Red 4 was still disentangling himself from the very dense flak spouting from the three flak trucks. I made my section do a wide climbing turn and we set course for the second train. It had certainly been warned by radio. It had come to a standstill and the smoke now rose vertically from it. I waggled my wings, unable to make up my mind. No point in attacking this one, as the flak crews must be expecting us, all set.

'Hallo, Talbot, no use, chaps, they've got the gen. Break away to starboard, one, eight, zero!'

Christ! Red 4 had gone crazy! 'Talbot Red 4, don't attack!'

The Tempest kept on down just the same, pointing at the locomotive. 'Come back. Break, you fool!'

The flak opened up, and I could see the trails of smoke from Red 4's wings as he fired. Then an almost imperceptible explosion along the fuselage, the Tempest slowly turned over, still keeping on its course. Almost on its back now, it just missed one of the trucks and crashed by the line. I could have sworn I heard the explosion. The inevitable mushroom of heavy black smoke, shot with burning petrol vapour immediately rose from the scattered debris.

'O.K. Talbot, going home.'

On the way home we attacked three more trains.

Another tragedy when we landed. My No. 3 had been winged by flak and was therefore landing first. A hundred yards from the airfield the duty Anson, doing a long flat approach, suddenly emerged under him. The two pilots couldn't see each other and blindly converged towards one another. Red 3 had obviously switched off his radio as he didn't hear the runway controller's desperate call. At the last moment the Anson sheered brutally off, but too late. The tangled remains of the two planes blazed in front of the control trailer. Seven dead. The Anson was bringing five new pilots to reinforce the Wing.

WALTER NOWOTNY

Walter Nowotny was dead. Our adversary in Normandy and in the German skies had died two days before in the hospital at Osnabrück as a result of burns. The Luftwaffe, whose hero he was, would not long survive his death, which was as it were the turning point of the aerial war. That evening in the mess his name was often on our lips. We spoke of him without hatred and without rancour. Each one of us recalled his memories of him, with respect, almost with affection. It was the first time I had heard this note in a conversation in the R.A.F., and it was also the first time that I heard, openly expressed, that curious solidarity among fighter pilots which is above all tragedies and all prejudices. This war had witnessed appalling massacres, towns crushed by bombs, the butchery of Oradour, the ruins of Hamburg. We ourselves had been sickened when our shells exploded in a peaceful village street, mowing down women and children round the German tank we were attacking. In comparison our tussles with Nowotny and his Messerschmitts were something clean, above the fighting on the ground, in the mud and the blood, in the deafening din of the crawling, stinking tanks.

Dog fights in the sky: silvery midges dancing in graceful arabesques – the diaphanous tracery of milky condensation trails – Focke-Wulfs skimming like toys in the infinite sky. We too, of course, were involved in less noble fighting: that strafing of trains in the grey dawn of winter mornings when you tried not to think of the shrieks of terror, not to see your shells smashing through the wood, the windows shivering in fragments, the engine-drivers writhing in the burning jets of steam, all those human beings trapped in the coaches, panic-stricken by the roar of our engines and the barking of the flak; all those inhuman, immoral jobs we had to do because we were soldiers and because war is war. We could rise above all this today by saluting a brave enemy who had just died, by saying that Nowotny belonged to us, that he was part of our world, where there were no ideologies, no hatred and no frontiers. This sense of comradeship had nothing to do with patriotism, democracy, Nazism or humanity. All those chaps that evening felt this instinctively, and as for those who shrug their shoulders, they just can't know – they aren't fighter pilots. The conversation had ceased, the beer mugs were empty, the wireless was silent as it was past midnight. Bruce Cole, who was neither poet nor philosopher, let fall these words:

'Whoever first dared paint markings on a plane's wing was a swine!'

We knew our habitual adversaries. In May 1944, Jacques and Yule had had a pretty lively encounter with Oesau and JG-2 over Le Havre. Many a time in Normandy, with 602 Squadron, we had had a bone to pick with him. He had machine-gunned our strip in the morning of 21 June, he had shot down over Bazenville three Dakotas ferrying loads of petrol and, a few days later, had had a scrap over Arromanches with a mixed formation of American Lightnings and Norwegian Spitfires which had lost three P-47's and two Spits, while one '109' crashed 100 yards from our mess.

At that time Priller was already a great ace of the Luftwaffe and was in command of the three fighter squadrons at Dreux. His sorties were easily identifiable as he always led his Me 109's in a Focke-Wulf 190.

Later we came across Nowotny, in command of JG-44 at Rheine/Hopsten, when we got to Germany. Since the 1st January show the Luftwaffe had had roughly speaking no central direction and Wings were left to their own devices. Apart from vague directives from above the commanders on the spot had complete discretion. Each group of units in the Luftwaffe gravitated round a main airfield to which several satellites were attached. These autonomous units had their own staffs, their own operational control, their own supply, flak and repair echelons and were only remotely dependent on G.H.Q.

At Rheine/Hopsten Nowotny was in sole charge of Jagdgeschwader 44, which was dispersed on various satellites: Nordhorn, Plantlünne, Neuenkirchen, Lunen, Hesepe and Bramsche. JG-44 effectives comprised about 40 Me 109's, 45 Focke-Wulf 190's and about 20 jet Messerschmitt 262's. A Staffel of Junkers 88 night-fighters was attached to it. This represented, with the tactical reserve, about 150 fighter planes under the orders of this twenty-two-year-old Lieutenant Colonel.

He was credited by Allied Intelligence with 60 confirmed victories on our front and more than 200 on the Russian front. He had succeeded in making himself respected everywhere. On the occasion of the shooting of 47 Allied pilots who had tried to escape from captivity, he had addressed a protest to Hitler himself, the echoes of which had reached even us.

On 15 March I was leading a section of four Tempests in a rat scramble over Rheine/Hopsten at 8,000 feet. Suddenly we saw at ground level a Messerschmitt 262 without any camouflage, its polished wings glittering in the sun. It was already in the flak corridor and about to put down. The barrage of tracers was already up to cover its approach. In accordance with the new orders I decided not to attack in these conditions, when, without warning, my No. 4 dived vertically towards the small bright dot which was nearing the long cement runway. Hurtling through the air like a bullet Bob Clark miraculously went through the wall of flak without being hit and fired a long burst at the silvery Me 262, which was in the final phase of its approach. The Messerschmitt crashed in flames just on the edge of the airfield.

A fortnight later we thought by cross-checking captured documents and prisoners' reports that that Me 262 had been piloted by Nowotny. Everyone had gone to bed. Bruce Cole, Clark and I had stayed up and we were glancing at an illustrated article on Nowotny in a review called DER ADLER which we had found at Goch. There was his picture, taken on the day he received the Iron Cross with swords, diamonds and oak leaves – the highest German military distinction. A face like that of a tired child, with a trace of sadness and a determined mouth and chin.

'All right now, time to go to bed. What a pity that type wasn't wearing our uniform.'

Gerhard Barkhorn, Gunther Rall, Walter Nowotny and Priller were well-known to us, because they had fought in Russia and in Western Europe, unlike Marseille and Hartman who had operated only in North Africa and in Russia respectively.

Nowotny – Novi to his friends – joined the Luftwaffe aged eighteen and on the morning of 29 July 1941 he scored his first three victories above the island of Oesel in Estonia. The afternoon of the same day, he was shot down into the sea by a Russian fighter. He spent the night on his raft, rowing with his hands, and got back to the coast where, fortunately for him, the German advance guard had just arrived! At twenty-two, he was a major and the first German pilot to achieve 250 victories and the ninth and last to receive the Knight's Cross with Swords and Diamonds. Galland, the Luftwaffe commander, gave him control of what became known as 'Kommando Nowotny' – fifty Messerschmitt 262 A1's based at Achmer and Hesepe near Osnabrück. Two other fighter squadrons were formed at Rheine, JG-7 and I-JG-54. Meanwhile, on Hitler's orders, this marvellous fighting machine was being converted into a bomber – a case of thoroughbreds being used as carthorses – in KJ-6, KJ-27, III Flight of KJ-54 and, in Prague, KJ-7. Since the only way to catch the '262' was to surprise it during take-off (and the Luftwaffe lost several decorated pilots this way), the '262's' were covered by the Fw D9's of JG-26 as well as by about a hundred Me 109's attached to that unit . . . not counting an unprecedented barrage of heavy and medium flak (at a level that would be unequalled even by that in Hanoi during the Vietnam war), defending the perimeter of the three airfields.

Nowotny had 255 victories to his credit when, having shot down three B-17's he was attacked by several P-51's. Running out of petrol, Novi was flying at low altitude towards Achmer when a bird got trapped in his left engine, which caught fire. He was probably then hit by a P-51 and plummeted to the runway crashing in flames. It seems that this is the correct version of what happened to him. In any case, that was the conclusion of the inquest ordered by Galland. The '262' that Bob Clark shot down at Rheine was probably piloted not by Nowotny but by Herman Buchner, who had brought down twelve B-17's and B-24's with his '262', which he still managed to land although it had been severely damaged. Clark's film footage backed up his claim to the victory, as the jet plane was undoubtedly irreparable.

THE RHINE

All week the squadron suffered hell. Its two flights lost 6 pilots. We had destroyed 14 German planes and 52 locomotives, but 274 Squadron was now down to just 11 pilots and 16 planes. We couldn't possibly keep it up. Group Support Unit could very quickly provide us with new aircraft but Tempest pilots didn't grow on every bush. On 20 March in the morning the duty Anson had brought us four Sergeant Pilots and one Warrant Officer. The last of these five new recruits got himself killed on the 23rd. The old hands, worn out by their three sorties a day, were already hard put to it to save their own skins, let alone look after the newcomers. These poor kids, fresh from O.T.U., had had just about three or four hours flying time on Tempests. Frightened by their machines, which they flew with great difficulty, they got themselves massacred by the flak and the Messerschmitt 109's.

Brown was one of these four Sergeant Pilots. As soon as he arrived at Volkel, at about 10 a.m. I had been obliged to put him through a firing test on one of our new Tempests before midday. He had then gone off to lunch on the mess with his kit and, before he could even unpack, he had been called back to Dispersal for an op.

Led by Hibbert, in a section of four, he had come up against a dozen Focke-Wulfs and, by the greatest luck, had succeeded in damaging one and getting home. But Hibbert and Humphries had been shot down.

That same evening, while my pilots went off for tea I had kept him with me for an immediate alert. Ten minutes later we were scrambled over Wesel at 10,000 feet. We arrived just in time to see a jet Messerschmitt 262 disappearing in the clouds. After a second's disappointment I broke, instinctively. Four Focke-Wulfs were on top of us and poor Brown went down like a torch on the banks of the Rhine.

The pilots' nerves seemed all in pieces, witness the uninterrupted succession of stupid accidents which were occurring – smashed under-carts, taxiing accidents, burnt-out brakes, punctures, bad landings, scrambles with propeller at coarse, etc.

The Wing couldn't go on like that. Between 15 February and 15

March we had had 31 pilots killed or reported missing. Out of all the pilots who made up 274 Squadron in Fairbanks' time, only two officers, a sergeant and myself survived. All I could do was to show the categorical orders from G.C.C. – we must hold on until the Rhine was crossed.

24 March 1945

First cover sortie at 3 a.m. over Wesel which was being attacked by the 1st Commando brigade. A thick pall of dust and smoke still hung over the town, which had been bombed by 186 Lancasters during the night.

In the airfield circuit there was a frightful mix-up of Tempests and Spitfires all flying round together at 300 m.p.h. Your nerve had to be good to last out 10 minutes' worth of this chaos of dancing green and red lights in which you had to try and form sections up in battle order. Nothing to report.

At 10 o'clock we took off again to escort the 669 aircraft and the 429 gliders from England which were carrying the Sixth British Airborne Division. It was an apocalyptic spectacle. Thousands of white parachutes dropped through an inferno of heavy, medium and light flak, while Dakotas crashed in flames and gliders rammed high-tension cables in showers of blue sparks.

The Typhoons were attacking every German flak emplacement with rockets. We were directed by the advanced radio control posts against Panzer columns coming up as reinforcements.

The Luftwaffe fighter force, broadly speaking, didn't interfere at all. The massive bombardment of Rheine and the tactical airfields the previous day had knocked it out temporarily.

We machine-gunned an armoured train near Ringerberg and a convoy of panzers at Bocholt in the streets of the town itself. It was a hair-raising business. We came down at roof level, all four cannon spitting fire. Tiles flew all over the place, flak shells exploded along the walls, lorries burned, the panic-stricken inhabitants ran in every direction and sheltered in doorways. Danny got a direct hit from a 37 mm. and crashed at 450 m.p.h. into a huddle of houses near the church.

After lunch, a third mission. I led a flight from 56 Squadron. We flew over the Bielefeld viaduct, pulverised some days before by the shock waves from fourteen block-busters. The craters were more than 100 yards across. Our main objective was to bring to a halt all road traffic in the Bielefeld–Altenbecken–Arnsberg triangle, and so I divided my planes into two pairs, each to act independently of the other.

I machine-gunned two lorries carrying troops – the poor devils didn't hear me coming owing to the noise of their engines. After two runs all that was left on the road were two flaming chassis and some bodies torn to shreds lying on the road. My No. 2 had lost contact and I found myself alone. I then fired a few shells at a locomotive sheltering in a marshalling yard and was greeted by terrific 20 mm. flak.

I circled over the rendezvous point for 10 whole minutes, waiting for my planes, and we went back to Volkel without Reg, shot down near Arnsberg by a free-lance Me 109.

1850 hours, 'phone call from Lapsley. He wanted a very experienced patrol of four planes to keep an eye on Rheine. It seemed that the Germans were going to try to evacuate their jet planes towards the interior, taking advantage of the last minutes of twilight. G.C.C. particularly wanted me to lead the patrol as our planes would be coming back after dark. Perhaps I felt flattered, anyway I accepted without giving myself time to think. Old Lapsley probably thought that quite normal – he had known me at Ashford in 1943, in Normandy in '44 and, as usual, he was banking on my willingness to take anything on. Yes, but after 40 sorties in 20 days my willingness had slightly cooled off.

Swallowing my pride I rang up the mess to try and get hold of Gordon Milne and get him to take my place. The orderly at the other end of the wire spent 5 minutes trying to find him and the time I was supposed to take off drew near. Oh well, to hell with it! I rang up the Flight Sergeant mechanic.

'Hallo Ron, stick JJ-B on the board, I'll fly her.'

I was very careful to choose a really good team: that extraordinary type Tiny, an Australian, was my No. 2, Torpy my No. 4 and Peter West No. 3. There were few instructions to pass on, it was a kind of roving free for all.

1910 hours. We were a few miles from Rheine, which was covered by scattered cumuli dragging their rain-swelled bellies. It was already getting dark and a long trail of milk-white mist hugged the Hopsten hills, hiding the Dortmund-Ems canal and its shattered locks.

Rheine seemed to have been very badly bombed – its three main hangars had collapsed and the familiar outline of the control tower flanked by its formidable flak emplacements had disappeared. It almost made me feel sorry – curiously enough – to see Rheine where so many of our friends had been brought down and where we had had so many scraps with JG-26, in such a state. It seemed now to be the scene of intense activity. In the woods and along the dispersal tracks we could see lights running hither and thither and those two long bright trails were probably the turbines of a Messerschmitt 262 about to take off. Probably quite a number of kites had already sidled off in the shadows.

'Hallo, Pierre, bloody silly, can't see a thing.'

I told Peter to dry up, but he was quite right, you couldn't see a thing. I decided to do a wide circuit over the airfield at 1,000 feet and then go home. My reflector sight was too high and was dazzling me. After a lot of fiddling about I managed to turn it down until all I could see in the windshield was a small red round filament.

A last look round. Suddenly, distinctly, two slender violet streaks, as of a twin-engined aircraft's exhausts, showed up to the left.

'Look out, Talbot Red! Attacking 9 o'clock!'

It was a Junkers 88 night-fighter. In the darkness it was impossible to judge proportions and distances and he loomed enormous in my sights. I fired a haphazard and rather ragged burst into the black moving shape and broke. Christ, what a fluke! Three quick explosions like morse dots, and then a sheet of flame poured out of the punctured tanks in the starboard wing, lighting up the long fuselage with its black cross. Then, very distinctly, superimposed on this luminous mass I saw the outline of a Tempest. A nightmarish fraction of a second, and a dazzling flash filled the sky. It was my No. 2, who had blindly followed me and, without having a chance to move a finger, had crashed straight into the stricken Ju 88.

Slowly the cascade of flaming debris from the two entangled aircraft scattered and settled in Mettingen forest. In a few seconds the night had swallowed up the scene.

Stupefied, panic-stricken, I lost for a moment all control over my plane and zigzagged about blindly, a few feet from the ground.

'Look out, Pierre, flak!'

Christ! I was flying over a grey strip pock-marked with craters and framed by buildings in shambles; by the light of the first tracer bullets I could see men running round in twos and threes, and a 'long-nose' Focke-Wulf, whose engine was ticking over.

It was Rheine. I had blundered straight into its terrific flak defences. In the night an impenetrable luminous web wove itself all round me. Glowing coals rippled towards me, lightning flashed angrily below the clouds, through the trees, round my wings. Desperately I opened the throttle wide and climbed, hanging on my propeller.

Suddenly, two stinging smacks – Bang! Bang! – shrapnel screaming through the aluminium plates, the stink of molten metal, burnt rubber and cordite. I was sick with funk and the thought flashed through my brain – This is it! This is the end! So this is what it's like.

I felt the blood thumping in my right leg. My toes were screwed up in a glutinous mess. My plane began to vibrate, shaking me, toppling my artificial horizon. No friendly voices in my earphones now – my radio was no longer a lifebuoy to a drowning man, it was a medley of cracklings and whistlings. I bit my tongue hard. My wits gradually collected themselves.

I reduced throttle and the vibration diminished. My tail plane must have caught a packet. An icy draught whistling through the cockpit finally woke me up. All was calm. The moon had risen and seemed to be rolling over the Dutch landscape. I must get home quickly – feel the ground beneath my feet, see friendly faces.

I set course on the conflagrations along the Rhine. I followed the course of the Twente canal, laboriously gaining height. For 10 minutes I concentrated on my instruments. They seemed to have gone haywire. Those faithful allies – altimeter, turn and bank indicator, pressure and temperature gauges – were now mocking me from behind their smashed dials.

Nijmegen and its new suspension bridge. The Rhine caught the last glow of the Arnhem fires and seemed to be clotted with blood. I tried my six wavelengths in turn, I called Kenway and Desmond – no answer. With my burnt-out circuits, no radio, no recognition lights, I was obviously going to get myself shot down by our ack-ack. I instinctively checked my parachute straps. I followed the Meuse and at Gennep picked up the railway line leading to Volkel.

The airfield was in darkness and the main runway scarcely visible. Jesus! What were they waiting for to light the flare-path? Couldn't those idiots at Flying Control recognize the sound of a Sabre engine? I did a dive over the control tower and waggled my wings. What the hell, surely those ack-ack types could tell the outline of a Tempest!

Suddenly, like a Christmas tree, Volkel lit up. At last! I passed over the field again slowly, waggling my wings to show I was in difficulties. I saw the headlights of the ambulance and the searchlight on the crash waggon.

I was going to land on my belly. I couldn't bale out because of my wounded leg and on top of that the left-hand runner of my hood had been buckled by a shell fragment. I pulled the lever to jettison it but nothing happened. The pain had now crept up to my hip, I couldn't feel the rudder bar any more.... I was very tired. Mechanically I began my approach – a quick one with 45° of flap. The plane answered sluggishly. I concentrated all my remaining strength on to bringing her in. Suddenly fear, naked fear, caught me by the throat. I wrestled with all my strength against the vision of Alex and his burning kite on this same runway – switched off and levelled out between the two rows of flares. At all costs I must keep calm! A lump in my throat threatened to stifle me ... careful ... the brute mustn't stall ... the flares passed by on either side ... I gingerly tried to put her down ... a bit more yet ... here was the first of the eight red lights which showed the end of the runway....

Now or never! I rammed down the nose to lift the tail and, with the aileron, deliberately stuck one wing in to take up some of the shock – like that perhaps I wouldn't turn over.

My poor Tempest, in spite of its 7 tons, was like a straw in a gigantic vice . . . a first, terrific, shock . . . the machine bounced up, hurling me against the side of the cockpit . . . the hood flew off . . . the wings were crushed like tissue paper . . . the metal plates were torn apart . . . I crossed my arms in front of my face . . . a fearful scraping screech, like Judgement Day . . . a jerk of such violence that the straps of my Sutton harness snapped. I was hurled forward, my face smashed into the sights . . . a sheet of red light . . . jaws gone . . . a taste of blood . . . tooth enamel grating in my mouth. . . .

A sudden stunning silence . . . a whiff of hot air in my face: the first shell going off in the flames.

A knife hacked at my shoulder, through the parachute straps, clumsy fingers caught me by my torn sleeves – 'my leg, look out!' the heat ate into my lungs . . . hands painfully wrenched me out of the shattered cockpit . . . foam extinguishers were gurgling, the fire pump in full swing. People were shouting. I was dragged on to the damp grass and wrapped in a blanket. Millions of dazzling red and green stars pressed into my eyes under the lids. The freezing air made me feel ill . . . a smell of ether – a sharp pain in the arm . . . oblivion.

I woke up again four hours after the morphia injection. My head felt empty and heavy and ached horribly. I tried to talk, but my lips were paralysed. The whole of my face except for one eye was in bandages. Was I in Eindhoven hospital? A night light showed white walls, a bedside table, a carafe and, in a saucer, a small rusty metal object on a piece of gauze.

'Ah, vous voilà réveillé,' it was Doc. Everald, who always insisted on speaking French in spite of his appalling Scots accent.

'Well, next time, try to land better. And don't go collecting scrap iron in your legs!'

Christ, what about my leg! Suddenly I got it . . . it was a piece of shrapnel I had picked up over Rheine. I felt more annoyed than anything else.

In any case it was going to be worth a week's peace and quiet to me! I was hungry and I was sleepy. The latter won and I fell peacefully asleep.

On 30 March, six days later, I came back to Volkel in time to go to Warmwell in the duty Anson to choose a beautiful brand-new Tempest with the new Rotol airscrew. Two days later I was posted O.C. 'A' Flight, No. 3 Squadron in 122 Wing (at B.112 Rheine).

CLOUDS, SNOW AND
FOCKE-WULFS

What a morning! We had been on 'readiness' since 4.30 a.m. My team was exhausted and all those tired youngsters stood the cold badly.

7.30 a.m. Order and counter-orders had succeeded each other and everything seemed to be going wrong this morning. It had started when the diesel generators had packed up, putting out the flare-path just as the first of three Spitfire XIV's of 41 Squadron, Yellow Section, was landing. The one behind him had stalled from a height of 30 feet, crashed and caught fire. The third, piloted by a young Pole called Kalka, had stayed up over the field for about 10 minutes; short of juice and diverted too late on Eindhoven, the pilot had baled out. Huddling round the door of the Dispersal we had vaguely caught sight of his Spitfire in the clouds with its undercart and flaps down; and the whirling black shape of the pilot falling. We had seen the parachute opening and had followed it as the wind swept it off. An hour later the jeep brought back his stiff body wrapped in the frosted silk of the parachute. The poor devil had fallen in the Meuse and its freezing waters had given him no chance, despite the courageous efforts of a Dutch girl who dived in to try and save him.

Just as the sullen day was unwillingly breaking, four Tempests had taken off, led by Wing Commander Brooker. An hour and a half later only two came back.

After machine-gunning a train in the Osnabrück region, with only half-hearted reaction from its flak, the section had re-formed. Suddenly Barry had seen a fine trail of smoke filtering from his chief's radiator. Brooker had been unaware of the danger and now waggled his wings to try and see. Even in the mirror the smoke was scarcely visible. Then suddenly the Tempest shook and a long slender flame unrolled in is slipstream. The other planes moved quickly out of the way and saw Brooker's gloved hands wrestling with the catches of the cockpit cover. Suddenly his face was lit up by a red glow – the fire had penetrated into the cockpit. The Tempest turned over violently, skidding on its back.

Appalled, Brooker's mates had eyes for nothing but his disabled machine. They did not see two shadows silently steal out of the iridescent mist. Just an incandescent trail of tracers and a glimpse of big black crosses on the wings of two Focke-Wulfs before they vanished again. A second Tempest went into a spin and its flaming fragments joined Brooker's alongside the autobahn.

This news provoked a fair bit of emotion back at base. Peter Brooker had been at the head of the Wing for such a long time that it was difficult to imagine 122 Wing without him.

At 8 o'clock, for the fourth time that morning, G.C.C. put us on immediate readiness – then countermanded it 10 minutes later. Every time we had to get out into the freezing cold, haul ourselves and our heavy parachutes up onto the slippery wing and take our gauntlets off to connect our helmets to the oxygen and the radio. We got back round the stove as fast as we could, our nerves on edge. We had another look at the map of the sector, with its black web of railway lines, which we were going to have to fly along at ground level, looking for those dangerous trains with their trigger-happy flak.

I kept an eye on my pilots – not a word passed between them, just an occasional move for a smoke or a light.

Suddenly the telephone in the orderly's cubby-hole tinkled thinly. Everyone was as if rooted to the spot, tense and dry-mouthed.

'Back to normal state, 15 minutes readiness.'

Shouts of rage, kicks at the unfortunate coal bucket – the feeling was not of relief so much as being tricked. I took my bad temper out on B—, one of the new pilots, who was timidly hiding his freckled, frightened face. The clot had dropped his parachute on a patch of oil yesterday or the day before and had failed to report it. Oil eats into tight folds of silk more surely than fire – a parachute in that state wouldn't stand up to the jerk of opening out, even at medium speed.

At 9.30 I took my chaps along to the mess for a second breakfast. In this weather I couldn't leave them on an empty stomach from 4 a.m. till lunch time. I had scarcely started on my porridge when the mess sergeant called me to the 'phone. My mouth full, I answered Lapsley's instructions – a patrol, Osnabrück–Münster–Bremen, with eight aircraft, priority for train strafing, naturally. Take off 0955 hours. O.K. I rang up Dispersal to warn them.

The weather had got worse, as foreseen. It was beginning to snow. The flakes stuck to the windshield and to taxi on to the runway we had to have a mechanic on the wing to guide us. With one hand he clung on to the freezing metal, slipping and with legs dangling, and with the other he showed us the way and wiped his streaming eyes.

My plane was continually skidding on the wire mesh of the taxiing-strip. Surely they weren't going to let us take off in this weather? I switched on my radio and called Desmond:

'Hallo, Desmond, Talbot Red Leader here; pretty sticky – any gen?'

'Hallo, Talbot, Desmond answering. Scramble!'

We had now reached the intersection of the taxiing-strip and the brick runway. The mechanics jumped down and started running back, bent double by the gusts, after the usual thumbs-up. My seven aircraft followed and took up their positions in pairs on the runway.

B—, nervous and upset, couldn't manage to line up properly next to me. He was maltreating his brakes and correcting with far too much throttle. I took off my oxygen mask and smiled at him encouragingly. If he panicked, with this cross-wind, he'd hit me when we took off.

The snow was now falling thick and fast. We could scarcely see as far as the end of the runway. I gradually opened the throttle and turned left as soon as I was airborne. I saw B—'s Tempest slip under my tail plane and skim the bare trees and the housetops.

On the runway my Nos. 3 and 4 were moving, trailing behind them the snow raised by their propellers, while behind them the first pair of Blue Section were getting under way.

After climbing through the frost-laden clouds for ten anxious minutes, we emerged, drenched with sweat, 7,000 feet above Münster. The black roads crossed and recrossed round the snow-covered houses. The wind whisked away the smoke and steam from the factories. The town seemed dead.

The cathedral was surrounded by bombed areas – blackened frames of houses, gaping cellar holes, mounds of debris. Serried rows of lorries and a few tanks were parked in the shadow of the towers.

On the other side of the canal jammed with ice-bound barges were the almost deserted marshalling yards. Bomb craters everywhere, burnt-out tank trucks and, in a corner near a turntable, two trains side by side, protected by automatic flak platforms. The flak crews were no doubt following our every move through their telescopic sights.

Suddenly I had an uncanny feeling that there was an 88 mm. battery in the vicinity.

'Talbot Red, quick, 180° starboard!'

I don't know why, but without waiting for the regulation second or two between command and execution, I at once did a tight turn. My planes, taken by surprise, started a rather ragged turn too. Just behind my tail and between me and B— – who had luckily lagged behind – appeared three flashes followed by tufts of black smoke. B—'s plane disappeared for a moment.

An anonymous voice cried into the radio: 'Christ, that was bloody close!'

My section were flying superbly. To be at the head of a formation was for me a constantly renewed source of naïve pride. On my left, impeccably spaced, Red 3 and Red 4. Close on my right was B—, Red 2. Five hundred yards farther away was Blue Section, MacCairn at their head, with his four aircraft in close formation.

The sky, under a very high vault of absolutely smooth cloud, was the clear luminous grey that you find only in winter. My Tempests were as if etched against the backcloth of cumulus. A bank of cloud drew near, fantastically floating on a layer of warmer air at 8,000 feet. I had the curious impression of hanging motionless between the grey stratus and the snowy plain while these indefinite, immaterial, flat-bottomed masses glided towards me. Enough of that! Was I going to pass above, or below them?

Calmly and methodically, I scanned the horizon all round me; I questioned the sky, dividing it up into neat strips by an upward and downward movement of my head. Nothing in the air.

Nothing on the ground either. I did catch a vague glimpse of a row of lorries parked along an autobahn – but I looked away again. I didn't want any fuss with flak before our auxiliary tanks were empty.

The radio was strangely quiet. We must be the only Kenway fighters in the air. Hardly surprising, in this weather. I felt a childish impulse to go romping among the clouds with my patrol.

'Priority for trains . . . priority for trains. . . .'

I could still hear Lapsley's voice on the telephone in my conscience. Naturally I wouldn't see any trains above a bank of clouds. I hoped to God there wouldn't be any trains down below either.

'Hallo, Talbot Squadron, keep just below cloud base.' We glided 30 feet below the translucent plateau.

Suddenly the radio rang with yells and curses. I jumped, surprised – thousands of pins seemed to be pricking my tongue, the back of my hands and my ankles.

'MacDuff Squadron BREAK!' – 'Help!' – 'Look out, Focke-Wulfs above!'—

'MacDuff Leader, you've got one of the bastards on your tail!'

A dog fight going on somewhere. Automatically my planes had taken up battle formation. From the waggling of the wings I could guess that seven pairs of eyes were tensely scanning the sky.

I didn't know 'MacDuff' – probably a squadron from 84 Group. I anxiously asked Kenway what was going on. Between two strings of shouts from the MacDuff boys, Kenway replied:

'Hurry up, Talbot Leader, there is a big do over Rheine, steer 275°.'

No need to warn my patrol, they had heard it too. We turned due west at full speed, our sights switched on, safety catches released. A glance at the map – less than 50 miles, so we would be over Rheine in 5 minutes, probably too late.

'Talbot, over to Channel C for Charlie – keep your eyes peeled!'

We changed frequency, as B was cluttered up by MacDuff. Like all raw No. 2's, B— began to lag. I was just about to call him up when I heard him excitedly shouting:

'Talbot Leader, aircraft just above the clouds, quick, they're Huns!'

Jesus! I looked up and saw, through the translucent layer, a dozen indistinct silhouettes each surrounded by an iridescent halo. I jettisoned my auxiliary tanks, changed to fine pitch, went through the emergency gate, and climbed vertically through the clouds.

I emerged into the clear sky hanging on my propeller, less than 300 feet below some Focke-Wulfs flying round in apparent disorder. In the luminous circle of my sights sprang the under-surface of a wing, the outline of an undercart, the black crosses and the pale blue belly of one of the Huns. I pressed the button and kept my finger down, shaken to the bones by the continuous discharge of my four cannon. A rending crash – a large metal plate fell off the 'long-nose' Focke-Wulf, which did two flick rolls, vomiting a sheet of flame and fragments. I just managed to avoid it. His tail, threshing the air, passed less than 5 yards from my rudder. Having lost speed, I desperately tried to complete my loop. Carried away by my reflexes I had got my plane into the most vulnerable of all postions, and that Focke-Wulf had not been alone! I found myself on my back, stupidly hanging by my straps, like a fly in a spider's web. I pushed the stick hard to the left but nothing happened. My Tempest shuddered violently, then stalled and dropped like a stone.

Bang! a blinding explosion just in front of my eyes burst my eardrums. I let go of everything and instinctively covered my face with my two arms. The smell of ozone and indiarubber from a short-circuit mixed with the acrid smell of cordite, filled my nostrils. Jolted above, my heart in my mouth, hanging upside down, I tried in vain to get my feet back on the rudder bar – my legs weighed a ton! One of the smashed instruments on the panel was hanging on the end of its wire in front of my nose, and I could see blue sparks on my contact box and hear their crackling in my earphones. It couldn't be anything else but a 30 mm. hitting my wing root.

Panting, I mechanically straightened out 1,500 feet below the clouds and my flooded engine started up again after a few noisy backfires – bloop! bloop! Bang!

What again! This time it was a 20 mm. in the fuselage. I felt the impact like a hammer blow through my back plate. Frantically, with both hands I put my aircraft into the steepest possible turn. The Focke-Wulf, spotted with green, flashed before my windshield, a white feather at either wing tip, and climbed vertically back into the clouds.

My radio was now dead, pulverised by that last shell. I hesitated – what ought I to do? I saw, emerging from the base of the cloud, in a shower of flaming fragments, a limp shape hanging on a half-opened parachute. Was it one of mine? Then I saw a Focke-Wulf dive vertically down at full throttle. The small glittering object hurtled towards the ground like a bullet – a fiery bubble burst on the snow, and the smoke bellied out immediately, mushroom shaped, but was soon swept away by the wind. A few little black crosses fading in the distance – then the sky was empty.

I decided to return to base. A quick glance around, and I lowered my head to readjust my gyroscope. It was then that I noticed that my legs were trembling and that, inside their fur gauntlets, my damp hands were frightfully painful, half-paralysed by the nervous vibration of the joystick and the throttle lever.

The return to Volkel was a nightmare. I wandered for 15 minutes, without radio contact, in a blizzard that blurred the outlines of the landscape and wiped out all orientation points. I lost my head a bit, crossed the Rhine twice, pursued by flak tracer fire, and finally wound up in an American airfield, 100 miles south of Holland. Landing blind, I skimmed the metal chimney of a hut and, badly damaged, my Tempest came to a halt without flaps within several yards of a Lightning. . . .

I was so exhausted that the American mechanics helped me out of my cockpit!*

---

* I still remember that day – 13 April 1945. We lost three out of six Tempests and brought down only one Focke-Wulf D9 – mine. This was, we learnt after the war, piloted by Leutnant Erich Asmus, aged twenty-three. His remains were found in the debris of his plane and buried without identification in the cemetery of the little village of Nadesdorf. It wasn't until 1955 that his mother was able to find his grave, thanks to his name being engraved inside his silver cigarette case, kept in a cupboard in the village archives.

It was small consolation to know that we had encountered twelve Focke-Wulf D9's that day, commanded by, among others, the aces of the JG-26, Söffing and Dortemann, who claimed one victory and shared another with Leutnant Konrad.

A NEW ENEMY

Flight Lieutenant Vassiliardes D.F.C., D.F.M. was killed this morning; he had commanded the second flight of 486 Squadron for barely three days. The doctor and the padre would be greatly saddened.

Poor Vass! However, he'd stuck his neck out and the extraordinary luck that had saved him from all his foolhardiness for so long must have finally deserted him. He stupidly let himself get caught in flak and on top of this he dragged Railroad Blue 2 and Blue 3 down with him.

We were on patrol that morning when it happened and were able to follow the whole thing by radio. Vass had quit his sector after several minutes. It was a boring mission, it had to be said, but providing cover for bridgeheads was an essential chore. Taking his four-plane section, he penetrated about 20 miles into the German lines and began attacking lorries in a zone well-known for its heavy flak.

There was a bottleneck at a crossroads. In order to machine-gun it, Vass had to run through a very heavy barrage of flak and his No. 2 crashed in flames. Prudently, his Nos. 3 and 4 refused to follow him.

Vass decided nevertheless to make another attack, bluntly ordering his No. 3 to accompany him.

'*For Christ's sake, Blue 1, don't go back in there! Too much flak!*'

Despite this desperate appeal from Blue 3, Vass made his pass. His plane must have taken a first hit, and we heard him shout over the radio: '*I've been hit!*'

Blue 4, who only narrowly managed to avoid the debris, told us later that Vass's machine had literally disintegrated in a sheet of flame. As for Blue 3 (Stanley), he never came back and his body was never found.

I was on patrol near the Elbe with Peter West, Longley and Don. We had machine-gunned a train in a small marshalling yard, without much result.

There was a lot of very accurate flak and Don's machine was hit. He baled out from his burning Tempest with some difficulty and landed on top of the flak battery.

Not much likelihood of being a prisoner long, as things were going. His chances of being alive to see the end were now better than ours!

As we passed we machine-gunned a few panic-stricken lorries on minor roads.

The three German airfields we saw seemed to have been deserted by the Luftwaffe. No trains running in the neighbourhood, either. No point in courting suicide for the sake of puncturing a few locomotives in well protected yards.

Germany was just lousy with flak. It was everywhere, even in the most unexpected places. You sometimes hit upon a peaceful country lane with a few lorries trundling along, you made your approach and whoooof! the sky was full of 20 mm. tracer.

German military road convoys now had to stick to roundabout routes, which had been carefully worked out in advance and were covered for the whole of their length by light flak batteries. The game was no longer worth the candle – there was no point in stupidly risking a Tempest for the fun of merely pulverising one Wehrmacht lorry.

Five other sections of four Tempests were also carrying out armed reconnaissance in the area, more for the look of the thing than anything else, as there seemed to be no interesting targets left. I stayed on the qui vive all the same, on principle: you never knew when you mightn't come across some marauding Focke-Wulf.

Apart from that I knew jolly well my pilots were not on top of their form. They had been worked to death for the last month and they had probably reached the stage of nervous depression when you don't much mind having to risk your neck over something but you don't actually look out for an opportunity of doing so. What confirmed my opinion was that whenever I came down below 2,500 feet to have a better look at the sunken lanes my three team-mates started zigzagging as if the entire German flak was after them. They came down with me unwillingly and hastened to get back to a safer height. Luckily it didn't prevent Peter West from keeping his eyes open.

'Look out, Filmstar Red 1, aircraft 4 o'clock!'

'O.K. Filmstar Red, breaking starboard and climbing.'

An aircraft became visible at tree-top level, approaching rapidly. A curious one, which I couldn't identify. He only saw us at the last moment, because we were just below the cloud base, in the shadows. He broke very quickly and for a moment I had a full view of him. He was obviously a Jerry – he had black crosses on the wings – but what an odd sort of bird!

Throttle full open, I tried to cut inside his turn, but he was moving astonishingly fast. Longley was better placed and fired at him, but without effect. The strange aircraft completed his turn and flew off at full speed.

He really was an extraordinary looking customer. His tail plane was cruciform, and it looked as if he had not only a normal propeller in front but on top of that a pusher propeller right in the tail, behind the rudder. His front engine was an 'in line', with a cowling like a DB 603 in a Focke-Wulf Ta 152C with a ring-shaped radiator; the other engine was buried in the fuselage, behind the pilot. The two long grey trails in his slipstream showed he was using a supercharger, and the thread of white escaping from his exhausts showed he was using GM-1. I toyed with the idea of bringing my overboost into action, but even with 3,040 h.p. we wouldn't be able to get him. We were doing nearly 500 m.p.h. and he was easily gaining on us.

I took a film of him, on the off-chance that there might be signs of jet-propulsion, but with this wan light the negative would be too under-exposed to show much. Longley kept after him for a bit, but he soon gave up. He fired one burst at extreme range, but the tracer bullets harmlessly bespattered the countryside.

'Hallo, Red 4, keep your ammo. No use shooting at the bastard.'

As a matter of form we pushed on as far as the Elbe. It was raining there and the visibility was very bad. We flew over a German pontoon bridge, maintaining itself with difficulty against the violence of the current. Not a soul about, but bags of flak. We moved on hastily. A lousy day, we must get back.

I pored over my maps, trying to pin-point our position, my two Tempests close by on either side. As our petrol was getting low, I finally made up my mind to ask Kenway for a course, but just then the wavelength was pretty crowded. Filmstar Blue Section were overusing it. From what I could gather from their infernal chatter they had cornered some unfortunate Ju 88 somewhere near Steinhuder and were murdering him.

For almost a minute the air was full of hounds yapping at the kill, then all was suddenly silent. The Ju 88 must be burning away in some field or other. As I called Kenway I made a mental note that I would tear them off a strip for their RT discipline.

Back at Rheine in the I.O.'s trailer we argued over our mysterious plane's identity for nearly an hour. In the end it was decided that its characteristics seemed to coincide with those of the Dornier 335, the latest German fighter. As it was the first time this type had been met on ops., I did several sketches from what I could remember for T.A.F. H.Q. I wrote a report for the Intelligence services on its probable manoeuvrability and performance.

I spent the rest of the afternoon putting my papers into some sort of shape. What a bind that sort of thing was.

Longley had gone off again on an armed reconnaissance with one of our sections. When he landed we heard that they had met – but this time maybe they had shot it down – another extraordinary plane.

He told me that, as they flew along a stretch of the Berlin–Hamburg autobahn that was in the course of construction, just where it hugged the shore of Neu-Ruppin lake they had seen a plane just over the water. This plane, with its undercart and flaps down, seemed about to land on the autobahn. In spite of the flak, Longley was sure he had shot it down.

It was a Heinkel 162, or 'Volksjäeger', jet-propelled. This seemed to confirm reports we had of the mass production of He 162's in underground factories near Neu-Ruppin. But up till now nobody had understood how these planes were tested. The only airfield nearby was the one at Ruppin itself, and care had been taken to bomb it and make it unusable. In addition, the bi-weekly photo cover had never once in the last three months revealed the presence of a single aircraft on this field.

We now had proof that a section of the autobahn, 3 miles long and 60 yards wide and perfectly straight, was being used as a trial runway. The machines were probably parked in camouflaged shelters in the woods on either side of the autobahn.

Life was full of surprises. The Jerries had succeeded in turning Germany into a regular conjuror's shop.

FLAMES AT DUSK

20 April 1945

G.C.C. were worrying us, as usual. They wanted us to fly a patrol that evening at dusk to cover the Bremen–Hamburg sector – because the Luftwaffe had been reacting in strength along the autobahn during the last few days, shooting up and bombing our advanced columns, considerably hampering their progress and their supply echelons.

We were quite agreeable, in principle, to flying a patrol, but G.C.C. couldn't seem to understand that Rheine/Hopsten had only one runway in good order, and a very short one at that, and no night-flying installation whatever. G.C.C. were also forgetting that the Jerries operated immediately after sun-down (if there had been any sun). Looking for small groups of Focke-Wulfs in the air in the mists that rose from the marshes of the Elbe and the low clouds which reflected the last glimmer of daylight was like looking for a needle in a haystack.

Besides, the aircraft situation was very tight. 'Chieffy', after we had made some diplomatic enquiries, hinted at only nine machines available – ten at the outside – during the next twenty hours. In the end we decided on a compromise; Bruce Cole kept six Tempests for normal armed reconnaissance, and I got the rest myself. As I didn't know my new pilots very well yet, I chose MacIntyre and Gordon, to help me with a difficult job.

We took off at 1636 hours. Gordon had difficulty in starting his engine and we lost 10 minutes of precious twilight circling round waiting for him.

At 1645 hours we set course for Bremen, flying at low level. Not much to be seen – in the distance a few vague bursts of tracer, dimmed by the summer light. Some houses on fire. In the vast pine forests a few fires glowed furtively.

We flew into driving rain which dragged down the clouds lower still. We went down to tree-top level. I could only just see Gordon's plane. The visibility was getting worse and worse. It was distinctly disquieting. The Huns were sure to come out, but I wasn't very keen on venturing at ground level over enemy territory in this sort of weather. I tried to pierce the mist. Hamburg, with its formidable flak defence, was somewhere quite close in the murk, straight ahead.

What the hell, let's go home!

'180° port, Filmstar, go.'

I kept my eyes on the dead straight autobahn as best I could. It was the only reliable landmark in this gloom, even though its white surface had been partially camouflaged by patches of tar. It marked our front line positions approximately.

It was about 1800 hours. The rain came down with redoubled vigour. We roared over British and American armoured columns, producing considerable panic. Those stupid 'pongos' never seemed to learn how to distinguish our aircraft from the Jerries'.

We flew over a squadron of Churchills scattered over a field, and the men ran all over the place, jumping for the shelter of the tanks, or under the caterpillar tracks or in the ditches. As they had been machine-gunned every evening recently in this part of the world – usually just about this time – they were taking no chances. Besides, we were probably the first R.A.F. fighters to operate round about there so late in the day.

Lousy weather. You might pass within 500 yards of a regiment of Focke-Wulfs and not see them. All the same, I kept a sharp lookout.

1810 hours. Out of the corner of my eye I saw somewhere behind my tail a red and green Verey light come up from our lines, followed immediately by an eruption of tracer, which disappeared into the clouds. Christ, something was up – Jerries, perhaps! I started a left-handed turn and warned the other two:

'Look out, Filmstar White – 180° port, and keep your eyes open!'

Just at that moment I felt a violent impact under my seat and at the same time a burning pain in my leg. Tracer bullets were whizzing up past my Tempest.

That really was too much! Those 'pongo' morons not only were shooting at us, but for once their aim was accurate. I broke and went into a tight turn, and poured some pretty varied invective into the radio. As they couldn't hear me anyway it was rather a waste of breath. The other two Tempests followed me in my turn, hotly pursued by increasingly heavy bursts of ack-ack. We waggled our wings, switched on our navigation lights, went right through the whole recognition rigmarole, all to no avail. As a last resort I was just going to let down my undercart when, like a shoal of fish passing under a skiff, thirty Focke-Wulfs appeared. They were hugging the ground and the rapid shapes seemed to slip through the trees, pursued by the flashes of their delayed-action bombs dropping on one of our tank parks.

'Focke-Wulfs 2 o'clock, Filmstar. Attacking!'

I heeled over and, at full throttle, dived towards the Huns. Just as my finger was hovering on the firing button something made me look round: a dozen Focke-Wulfs in close formation were emerging from the clouds, a hundred yards from my team-mates. In the meantime the ack-ack was increasing in fury – so was the rain. The Focke-Wulfs – they were magnificent 'long-noses' with the white spiral round the spinner – broke in every direction.

The visibility had by now got even worse, which didn't prevent two of the Huns from making a frontal attack on me – so close that I was left quite panting. My chief concern was not to get involved in a collision in the gloom. That really would be too stupid. In any case I hadn't had a genuine target yet.

Suddenly the radio blared. Gordon, in the hell of a flap, started shouting incoherently. He had just been hit by our ack-ack and a Focke-Wulf in quick succession. One of the Tempests – presumably his – was dragging a long trail of grey smoke and climbing straight for the clouds, followed by four Focke-Wulfs. Poor Gordon.

'Look out, Pierre, break! Break!'

Before I had even had time to realise this was meant for me, I had pulled hard on the stick – but too late. I was hit somewhere under my petrol tank. The impact was so violent that my feet jumped off the rudder bar. An acrid smoke filled the cockpit with the stench of cordite. A square wing bearing a black cross swept past in a flash only a yard or two away, and the Focke-Wulf's slipstream was so violent that this time the stick was nearly wrenched out of my hand.

Instinctively I completed a roll and levelled out just above the tree tops. The nausea of fear gripped my throat as a short bright flame licked my feet.

Fire! I felt the heat through my boots, quickening the first stabs of pain in my wounded right leg. I bent down and fumbled with my glove, trying to locate the course of the flame.

Bang! Bang! Two more shells smacked into my plane. This time my engine missed a beat – so did my heart. I hurled my Tempest into a violent skid which jammed me against the side of the cockpit, and at the same time retarded throttle. Then I slowly opened full out – the engine responded normally. Stick right back, I climbed back to the cloudbase. All around me in dismaying confusion were Focke-Wulfs machine-gunning, climbing, diving, turning.

In the half light one turned towards me, rapidly waggled its short wings and engaged me. I turned at once to face him, fired a burst from three-quarters front, but evidently missed him, and passed like a whirlwind just a few feet below him. I immediately brought the stick hard back, and put on full left rudder. My Tempest shuddered, showed signs of stalling, but completed an astonishingly tight turn all the same, two white 'contrails' at its wing tips. The Focke-Wulf seemed nonplussed – began to turn to starboard – skidded – righted itself – then turned to port.

That was a boob: now I in turn was in a good position, at less than 200 yards range. Quickly, before he had time to complete his manoeuvre, I corrected 10° – one ring of my sight. A long burst from my four cannon – lightning flashes lit up and seemed to bounce off his grey fuselage and his wings. Fragments were tossed about in a cloud of rapidly thickening smoke – the cockpit flew off and went spinning down, and I saw the pilot, his arms glued to the fuselage by the speed, trying to bale out.

Then the Focke-Wulf veered sideways at less than 150 feet, righted itself for a moment, hit the ground, bounced up, mowed down a pine tree in a shower of flames and sparks and finally crashed into a sunken lane. There was a terrific explosion which threw a lurid light like a magnesium flare for several hundred yards around.

The weather now seemed to be clearing a bit. Gaps appeared in the wall of mist, revealing a broad strip of moist, yellow horizon throwing a wan light over the pine forests and the marshes.

On the left a fire was raging; it was our tank park blazing, its tank trucks and its ammunition lorries in flames. Four Focke-Wulfs were flitting round like big moths, occasionally spitting a stream of bullets into the inferno. I daren't attack them – I could feel the others prowling round in the shadows.

Aha! I spotted a lone plane skimming over the tree tops in the direction of Bremen, whose tall chimney stacks looked positively mediaeval outlined against the dying sky.

Engine temperature 125°, oil pressure down to 55. Regretfully I opened the radiator and closed the throttle to 3,500 revs. Even then I went on gaining on the Focke-Wulf, who was probably making for home, his magazines empty.

We were now over Bremen, and he was still about 1,000 yards ahead. This business might take me rather far; I closed the radiator again and opened the throttle flat out. My 'Grand Charles' responded at once. We were now over the first docks on the Weser.

We roared between the shattered remains of the big transporter bridge. On either side rose the charred hulks of the warehouses; the few cranes and derricks still erect rose up like black skeletons.

Suddenly a salvo of flak shells blossomed between the Focke-Wulf and me – brief white flashes, mingled with brown balls which passed by on either side of me. More kept appearing miraculously out of the void. The automatic flak now chimed in and the orange glow of the tracer was reflected in the black oily water, from which overturned hulks emerged, like enormous stranded whales.

I concentrated on not losing sight of my Focke-Wulf – luckily he was silhouetted against the dying glow of the sky.

For a moment the flak redoubled in intensity. There was a sudden clang behind my back – then suddenly the tracers were snuffed out and disappeared. . . . A bit suspicious! A glance behind me explained this curious phenomenon: on my tail were six Focke-Wulfs in perfect close echelon formation – exhausts white hot – pursuing me at full throttle.

With one movement I broke the metal thread to enable me to go to 'emergency' and shoved the throttle lever right forward. It was the first time I had had occasion to use it on a Tempest. The effect was extraordinary and immediate. The aircraft literally bounded forward with a roar like a furnace under pressure. Within a few seconds I was doing 490 m.p.h. by the air-speed indicator and I simultaneously caught up my quarry and left my pursuers standing.

I had soon reduced the distance to less than 200 yards. Although in this darkness my gun sight rather dazzled me, I had him plumb in the middle and I fired two long, deliberate bursts. The Focke-Wulf oscillated and crashed on its belly in a marshy field, throwing up a shower of mud. He miraculously did not overturn. Without losing any time I climbed vertically towards the clouds and righted myself to face the others. They had vanished in the shadows. They must have turned about and left their comrade to his fate. I flew back over the Focke-Wulf I had shot down. The pilot was limping off, dragging his parachute and quite dazed by the shock. I bespattered the remains of his machine with shells and they caught fire at once. That made two!

It was now pitch dark. With my engine set to cruising speed (I had to cool it down and go slow on the juice) I slowly regained height, setting course south.

Minutes passed. I was trying to pick out a landmark when my engine cut out violently. A shower of sparks passed on either side of my cockpit. With beating heart I saw that the flame was intermittently reappearing beneath my feet. My hydraulic fluid tank, punctured by a piece of shrapnel, had leaked under my feet. The liquid had soaked one of the wires and produced a short between the pedals of the rudder bar. An acrid smoke caught my throat through my oxygen mask.

To add to my discomfort an allied ack-ack battery took this opportunity of opening fire and surrounding me with a dozen 76 mm. shells.

I decided to bale out immediately if the fire got worse, and quickly checked my straps. I gained height to have a good margin of safety and called Kenway to my assistance. Kenway luckily answered at once and gave me a course on Rheine. After ten difficult minutes, during which Kenway mothered me like an anxious hen, I finally made out two rows of luminous dots winking on the ground. A white Verey light came snaking up. Rheine at last.

Should I bale out? Ought I to risk landing on my belly?

My experience of 24 March ought to have put me off. But, stronger than my will, was that old pilot's instinctive reluctance to sacrifice his machine; I wasn't going to write off good old JF-E, which I had chosen at Warmwell so lovingly, without a struggle.

My hydraulic system was certainly out of action – no more fluid in the pipes – and I wasn't going to try and get my undercart down and find myself with a wheel half in and half out. Desmond finally helped me to make up my mind by telling me that the fire was getting worse, that the flames were visibly getting bigger. On top of that my engine was cutting out more and more frequently.

'Hallo, Desmond, Filmstar Leader calling, landing now.'

My voice probably wasn't very steady. Before switching off I heard Desmond wishing me good luck. I made a very straight approach, fast enough to give me a margin, jettisoned my cockpit hood and well in the middle of the flare-path, put my aircraft down.

Terrific row ... sparks ... jerks and jolts....

To my great surprise everything went off very well this time. After 30 yards of scraping and bouncing my Tempest stopped, lying slightly crooked between the two rows of lights. The ambulance and the fire tender arrived at once and I lost no time in jumping out of my kite.

My pilots came and picked me up in a jeep and I was surprised to meet the two reporters from *Aeronautics*, Montgomery and Charles Brown. They were still pale with emotion. They soon went back to the bar, while I went off to make out my report. I began by expressing to Higgins – our liaison boffin – just how well disposed the recent events had made me feel towards the army. The most comic part of the proceedings was that MacIntyre, who had got back first, reported that he had seen Gordon disappear in the clouds belching oil and smoke. Actually Gordon was there as large as life, having managed to get back somehow. He thought *I* was dead!

So we all three had occasion to rejoice. Result of our trip: two Focke-Wulfs destroyed by me, another damaged by Gordon – one Tempest lost and two Tempests category B damaged but also repairable by our maintenance services on the spot. Not a bad balance sheet.

In the 1952 official history of our adversary JG-26, whose two pilots, Waldemar Söffing and Hans Dortemann, had each brought down four Tempests in April (probably including those of McIntyre and myself), I found the following commentary. It related to what I had written about that 20 April mission in the original edition of *The Big Show*:

> Clostermann gives a good, if somewhat embellished, description of the JG-26 between Bremen and Hamburg in the dusk, and of the combat that followed. The pilots of the two D9's from 7th Staffel brought down by the Frenchman were Uffz Schumacher and Simmer. Since the battle took place in twilight, in very poor visibility and in the rain, it is difficult to know exactly what happened. Simmer was certainly the first to be brought down by the Tempest, near Holland, while he was machine-gunning an American column.

(NB: There is an error in the German archives: it was in fact a British armoured division.)

INTO THE INFERNO
OF FLAK

The Germans had thought up a new mode of operation for their fighter aircraft. All their large airfields had become rather unhealthy since our troops had crossed the Rhine – they had been bombed on a large scale. The Luftwaffe no longer had enough planes to be able to afford the luxury of having them uselessly destroyed on the ground. Now the Jagdeschwaders and the Jabos no longer had any fixed bases.

All along the right bank of the Elbe, carrying out Plan 1943 for the aerial defence of the Reich, the Todt organisation had built numerous secondary airfields, designed for defensive fighter operations against large-scale daylight raids by the Americans.

These bases were generally equipped with one good permanent runway (asphalt or concrete), 1,000 to 1,500 yards long, and excellent auxiliary hangars. They were ideal for the new 'general post' technique. Three-quarters of them were too far away to be bombed. They were only fleetingly occupied and therefore there was no justification for bombing them systematically, particularly in existing circumstances. About fifteen German fighter Wings – i.e. 1,200 ultra-modern fighters and fighter-bombers – led a nomadic existence between these bases. The motorised echelon moved off during the night, the mechanics got the hangars ready and the bowsers were hidden in the pine forests. The aircraft came in at dawn and took off again from their new home at about 10 a.m. for their operational trip. After a few days – never more than a week – the Geschwader again moved to another base.

Thanks to this technique the Germans succeeded in harrying our troops pretty efficiently, especially in the morning and the evening. An increasing number of supply convoys rushed towards our forward armoured columns were being intercepted and strafed or bombed to a standstill by low-flying Jerry planes.

The Army complained bitterly to R.A.F. Tac H.Q. The latter passed the baby to 2 Group but there was nothing Group could do about it: its

Mitchells and Bostons already had too much on their plate doing three sorties a day on tactical objectives, and maintenance was difficult. 2 Group in turn appealed to 84 Group, but the latter's fighter units were stationed too far to the rear to intervene.

In the end 83 Group found itself holding the baby. As usual it was our Tempest Wing which had this task palmed off on it as it alone was equipped with aircraft that were sufficiently fast (in theory) not to be massacred by flak; and it had sufficient radius of action to root out the Geschwaders from their most distant lairs.

We received from Intelligence plenty of gen on the new Jerry set-up, which was not calculated to increase our well-being.

In order to allow its fighters to operate in relative peace and quiet, the Luftwaffe had provided at least one Abteilung, i.e. battalion, of flak for each airfield. These Abteilungen were attached to the fighter Wings and generally comprised three batteries of automatic flak: one 37 mm. (9 single guns) and two 20 mm. (24 barrels in double or quadruple mountings). These Abteilungen followed the Geschwaders in their moves from field to field and were always the first on the scene. These formidable anti-aircraft defences manned by superby trained crews and equipped with gyroscopic sights and predictors made any attack extremely dangerous. The defences were always on the qui vive, helped by relays of experienced spotters over a radius of 6 miles. As a result an Abteilung could and did within a matter of seconds put up an impenetrable curtain of tracer shells over the airfield it was defending. Any aircraft caught flying at low level had a pretty slim chance of running the gauntlet of the 150 or so shells a second thrown up by the 33 barrels of the battalion.

All this didn't make us feel so good. Since our experiences over Rheine no one had the slightest wish to try conclusions with airfield flak again. I still had my morbid flak complex and as a result was in a poor position to improve my pilots' morale.

The two first airfield shoot-ups laid on by G.C.C. as a result of the new situation drew a blank: the airfields were deserted.

As a result of these checks G.C.C. thought up a new scheme to produce quicker action between the spotting of an inhabited 'Einsatz' (the name given by the Luftwaffe to these new fields) and an attack on it. The Canadian reconnaissance Wing (49 Wing) was to inform us direct, without going through G.C.C., of any interesting objective. We were to drop everything and go into action with whatever aircraft were available, at the same time informing G.C.C., which kept at our disposal a squadron of anti-flak Typhoons in immediate readiness.

The new scheme came into operation at dawn the next day. 56 and 486 Squadron had carried out the two previous fruitless sorties and so it was 3 Squadron which was on stand-by 'readiness'. The suspense was unbearable. I don't remember ever feeling more nervous, and the pilots, who weren't feeling too good either, told me I looked as happy as a dying duck in a thunderstorm.

When I had put up the dawn flying order, the seven chosen hadn't shown any marked enthusiasm, except Bay Adams, the Australian member of the party, who was quite imperturbable and feared neither God nor the Devil. Our nervousness finally infected even the mechanics. Every other minute the crew-room door would open and an anxious face ask whether there was anything doing yet.

12 o'clock struck. The situation was becoming intolerable. The weather was very stormy. I had absolutely forbidden any mention of the word flak – penalty a £1 fine. You could have cut the silence in the room with a knife. We had been on 'readiness' since 0355 hours. The consumption of tea and cigarettes was frightening, the floor was carpeted with cigarette ends. In the end I shut myself up in the office with Adj. near the telephone and tried to take my mind off it all by writing to my parents. I tore up three letters and gave it up.

'Adj., I'll take the jeep and pop over to Control to have a look at the last "Met" report. If anything happens in the meantime, fire a white Verey light.' I had just got into the jeep when I heard the phone go. I jumped out again. In Dispersal everyone was on his feet looking anxious. It was 49 Wing. I dictated to Ken Hughes:

'Schwerin airfield – 40 Messerschmitts seen by Spit Recco at 1140 hours, landing. About 100 A/C on base, 15 Arado two-seaters – refuelling point 500 yards S.E. of main hangar. Map 829 GA II – good luck!'

I glanced round at my pilots. For a moment no one spoke.

'Well, this is it!' sighed Wormsley philosophically.

'Quick, Adj., jump in the jeep and get hold of the I.O. and the German Airfield List, Volume 2,' I said. Ken Hughes had already found Schwerin on the wall map – 30 miles south-east of Lübeck – 150 miles for us to cover.

Adj. came tearing back with Spy, and handed me the List open at page 829: Schwerin, a fine big airfield by a lake, west of the town of the same name. I put up a rapid sketch on the blackboard: the three runways forming a triangle, the probable location of the aircraft, from 49 Wing report.

The Jerries had landed at 1140 hours. It was now 1210 hours. Refuelling and rearming the planes would take the Germans a good hour

– we just had time to catch them before they flew off, dispersed or hid in the pine woods.

I gave last instructions, while Spy phoned through to G.C.C. to tell them what we were going to do and to ask for the rocket Typhoons to be laid on.

'We shall attack from north to south, all eight together, in line abreast, with a 200-yard interval between aircraft. Speed 480–500 m.p.h. Each pilot will pick out his target as he dives – no last minute change of direction. Open fire at 1,000 yards and continue till point-blank range. Stay as close to the ground as you can, count up to twenty, and then break fan-wise and climb at full throttle.

'Rendezvous with the Typhoons is at 1300 hours – late, I'm afraid, but they can't get there any earlier. The Typhoons will come down from 8,000 to 3,000 feet 30 seconds before us and they will shoot up any flak posts they can spot with their rockets. Because there is bound to be some flak.' (Slightly forced smiles.)

'Remember that surprise, speed, and, especially, flying at zero feet, are our best defence. No point in waggling your wings and pretending you're putting off the flak boys – you'll lose a few precious m.p.h. and risk sticking a wing on the deck.

'One last bit of advice: if you are hit and have to bale out, the best way, let me remind you, is this: stick right back – jettison the hood – curl up in a ball – wait a few seconds – jerk the stick right forward. You'll have nine chances out of ten of being thrown clear of the cockpit. Naturally I hope it won't come to that!

'Any questions? O.K. then, let's go!'

'Hallo, Kenway, Filmstar Leader calling – what about the Tiffie boys?' I was beginning to get anxious. We had crossed the Elbe and we could already see Schwerin lake on the horizon quite clearly. No sign of the Typhoons. A few moments later Kenway answered apologetically:

'Hallo, Filmstar Leader, sorry old boy, there's a cock-up about the Tiffies. Do the best you can without!'

A pleasant prospect! Without anti-flak Typhoons, we were in for the hell of a time. My voice was probably not too steady as I got my flight into attack formation. A big blue lake edged with pine trees, cut in the middle by a peninsula on which stood the town of Schwerin, a picturesque little town with renaissance steeples and varnished tiles, clinging to the rock. To the west a fine airfield, intact, complete with buildings and camouflaged hangars – not many like that left in Germany.

We were at 14,000 feet and kept straight on over to the left, as if we had no intention of attacking. I took a close look at the field: the small dark crosses parked just where we had expected them showed up on the bright grass of early spring. I particularly noticed one, two, four, seven flak towers, their shadows clearly projected on the perimeter track by the sun. . . .

'Look out Filmstar Leader, flak at 6 o'clock!'

Sure enough, 200 yards behind us five big black puffs from 88 mm. shells had appeared. O.K.! five more seconds and then I would attack. The objective was behind us and we were facing the sun. Fear caught me by the throat and stopped me breathing. Aerial combat against fighters had always found me calm – after the early stages – but flak was quite different.

'Drop your babies, Filmstar.'

My stomach contracted and a wave of nausea swept over me – the advantage of a single-seater is that you can pass out with funk without anybody noticing.

'Quick, 180 port, go!'

This would bring us back facing the airfield, with the sun at our backs.

'Diving – full out, Filmstar!'

My seven Tempests were beautifully echeloned on my left although we were diving almost vertically.

'Smell of flowers,' came Bay Adams' voice mockingly in the earphones. Flak! Christ, what flak! The entire surface of the airfield seemed to light up with flashes from 20 mm. and 37 mm. guns. There must have been at least forty of them. A carpet of white puffs spread out below us and the black puffs of the 37's stood out in regular strings of eight.

What flak! Physical fear is the most terrible thing man can suffer – my heart leapt into my mouth, I was covered with sweat, with sticky, clammy sweat. My clenched toes swam in my boots.

We dived desperately into the smoke . . . explosions and tracer to left and right crossing over and under us . . . bangs round our wings and sinister dazzling flashes.

We were a mile from the perimeter, 150 feet from the ground. Men were running hither and thither.

'Lower, for Christ's sake,' I yelled hysterically. The broad expanse of grass, carved by the grey runways, tilted up before my eyes and rushed towards me. We were doing over 450 m.p.h. First a hangar . . . a bowser . . . then the Messerschmitts, perched clumsily on their narrow under-carts, about thirty of them, with men crouching under the wings. Too far to the left, unfortunately, outside my line of fire.

A group of a dozen Arados loomed up in my sight. I fired, I fired frantically, my thumb jammed on the button. My shells formed a ribbon of explosion worming its way between the Arados, climbing up the fuselages, hitting the engines . . . smoke . . . one of the planes exploded just as I was over it, and my Tempest was tossed up by the burning gust. A Tempest touched the ground and the fuselage bounded up in a shower of fragments of smashed wings and tail planes.

More hangars in front of me. I fired a second burst – it exploded on the galvanised iron doors and the steel stanchions.

'Look out, Red 2!' My No. 2 was coming straight for me, out of control, at terrific speed. His hood had gone. At 470 m.p.h., 200 yards to my right, he went smack into a flak tower, cutting it in two underneath the platform.

The wooden frame flew into the air. A cluster of men hanging on to a gun collapsed into space. The Tempest crashed on the edge of the field, furrowing through a group of little houses, with a terrific flash of light; the engine had come adrift in a whirlwind of flames and fragments scattered in the sky.

It was all over . . . almost. One, two, three . . . the tracer bullets were pursuing me . . . I lowered my head and hunched myself up behind my rear plating . . . twelve, thirteen, fourteen . . . I was going to cheat . . . a salvo of 37 burst so close that I only got the flash of the explosions without seeing the smoke . . . splinters hailed down on my fuselage . . . nineteen, twenty! I pulled the stick back and climbed straight up into the sky. The flak kept on.

I glanced back towards Schwerin, just visible under my tail plane. A thousand feet below a Tempest was climbing in zigzags, the tracers stubbornly pursuing him. Fires near the hangars, columns of greasy smoke, a firework display of exploding magnesium bombs. The lone Tempest caught me up, waggled his wings and formed line abreast.

'Hallo, Filmstar aircraft, re-form south of target, angels 10.'

'Hallo, Pierre, Red 3 here. You know, I think the rest had it!'

Surely Bay couldn't be right! I scanned the 360° of the horizon, and the terrific pyramid of flak bursts above Schwerin right up to the clouds, hanging in the still air. No one.

1304 hours. We had attacked at 1303 hours. The nightmare had lasted perhaps 35 seconds from the beginning of our dive and we had lost six aircraft out of eight. . . .

We crossed the Elbe again. I was beginning to relax and my legs stopped quivering. No point in thinking about the others. What good would it do?

One more trip done, 56 and 486 would do the next two. A day's respite perhaps.

Rheine again.

'Hallo, Desmond, Filmstar over base. May we pancake?'

Mechanically I lowered the undercart, reduced throttle. The usual sensation of being born all over again at the moment when your tyres screech on the concrete.

G.C.C. had just sent along the photos of the Schwerin show. They were very clear. A Canadian from 49 Wing had taken them three hours after the shooting up of the airfield and had been greeted by some very trigger-happy flak. He had had to come down pretty low to get his obliques and had been wounded. By sheer grit and will-power he had succeeded in bringing back his damaged Spitfire XIV and his photos.

We scrutinised the photos very closely. The game really wasn't worth the candle. Two Messerschmitts had apparently been destroyed by a bowser exploding, and you could see, between two sections of the Focke-Wulf repair plant, a tractor with another damaged one in tow. The only genuine havoc seemed to be in my group of Arados, five of which were clearly a total loss. However, that hadn't been the point of the trip, and it was pretty poor compensation for the loss of six Tempests and their pilots.

The flak really held too many trumps. I said as much in my monthly op. report and, for once in a while, G.C.C. took note. This type of show was given up.

We discovered later that Schwerin had a unique status and was to be used for special missions. The aerodrome harboured two special Heinkel III's, equipped with supplementary tanks and two bunks in the bomb bay. There were also three or four liaison Me 108 Taifuns. These planes were under the direct control of the German Chancellery and their main role was to facilitate the evacuation of regime personnel to Norway or Sweden and, in conjunction with the Heinkels, to South America via Spain.

It was from this very aerodrome that Skorzeny headed to Madrid, and from which Anna Reich and General Grimm took off in their Fieseler Storch bound for Berlin, besieged by the Russians in April 1945, in the hope of evacuating Hitler. The Focke-Wulf Kondor, Hitler's personal four-engined plane, used to be based at Schwerin. All of which explained the incredible amount of anti-aircraft defences protecting the base – at least three battalions of Vierlingsflak – the 4-barrelled 20 mm. automatic anti-aircraft gun!

The security chaps had just brought in a Luxemburger, caught hiding in a neighbouring farm. He had been an observer in the Luftwaffe. I listened to his interrogation. The poor fellow wasn't feeling too happy and made no difficulty about answering Abund's questions.

He was an interesting specimen, having served in Lechfeld as observer in KJG-40 from August 1943 to 25 September 1944. Lechfeld was the centre for the new jet Messerschmitt '262's', and the prisoner was a bosom pal of Fritz Wendel's, Messerschmitt's chief test pilot.

According to him the '262's' performance was as follows: maximum speed 610 m.p.h. at 23,000 feet, minimum landing speed 210 m.p.h. The '262' seemed to be equipped with a pressurised cockpit; anyway he had never seen Wendel wearing special flying clothes, although he had told him he had already been up to 42,000 feet.

All the aircraft of this type which the prisoner had seen had a white V painted on the grille of the turbine air-intake, followed by a number. He couldn't tell us whether this was a serial number. As the highest he had seen seemed to be V-15, the suggestion was that they were prototypes – V might very well stand for 'Versuchs', i.e. 'experimental'.

We found a lot of secret documents in his kit, which were duly passed on to H.Q.

'Curly' Walker had got his D.F.C. and we decided to celebrate the occasion in the customary manner. On top of that it was his birthday, and his mess bill by the time we were through was enough to swallow up at least three months' pay. He was called Curly because of his round, prematurely bald cranium. He was twenty-eight, but looked thirty-five. He was, with Ken Hughes, the senior surviving pilot in the squadron.

A LESSON FROM AN EXPERT

22 *April*

If you play with fire, you must expect to get burnt. It was 1 a.m. and the boisterous party celebrating my safe return was over, my mess bill having sustained some serious damage.

I was still in shock at having been made to look a fool – that's what one always thinks – by an expert Jagdgeschwader 301 pilot, probably from JG-26 Squadron. I had stumbled into his lair and my pride was well and truly dented. I had spread the word among my pilots, telling them to watch out, because in every Luftwaffe formation there were always two or three 'chibanis', crack pilots who had survived Spain, Poland, France, London and, quite often, Russia and had forgotten more about dog fights than we had ever learnt. I usually recognised them instinctively from the way they flew, zigzagging to avoid surprise attacks, their wings waggling as they manoeuvred to achieve maximum vision. There was only one way to handle them – simply not to engage them, but often to watch, powerless, while unsuspecting pilots who had not listened to such advice met their fate. In Kipling's *Jungle Book*, I read a phrase that is particularly appropriate to the Luftwaffe's ace pilots who had over a hundred genuine kills under their belt: 'The tiger has no smell and makes no noise, but you know he is there. There is something in the shadows – it's the tiger waiting for you.'

The tiger got me in the end – it had to happen one day.

So there I was, leading six aircraft in a routine patrol along the Osnabrück–Hamburg road. We were flying at 6,000 feet, too high for the 20 mm. guns and too low, in theory, for the '88s'. We were slaloming among cloud formations, some of which were beginning to cumulify, scouring the ground for a train or, even better, a pair of Dorniers flying at tree level, when a Focke-Wulf D9 suddenly appeared from behind a cloud flying at top speed. I scarcely had the time to turn my head, distracted by a streak of light bouncing off the glass on his cockpit, when he opened fire and hit my left plane, and then slid below me and opened fire on MacKenzie to my right, whose Tempest started spinning with half a wing torn off. . . .The Focke Wulf then continued its dive towards the lake so fast it was impossible to keep up with him. It all happened so quickly that we did not have time to react.

Suddenly, a mental picture of my chum MacKenzie and his wonderful dog sprang into my head and I was filled with anger. I was determined to get him. I flipped over on my back and dived down vertically towards the tiny shining cross below, now heading towards the Dummersee. I could not afford to lose sight of him. I engaged the overboost and with my 7 tons and boosted 3,000 h.p., the needle soon swung dangerously into the red section and the 'not to exceed 550 m.p.h.' mark. I felt the plane's nose become heavy and I pulled back the stick. 'Bay, Yellow 2 and Filmstar 3, give me top cover. I'm going to eat that bastard!'

I straightened up when I reached the lake, controlling the beginnings of a dangerous pitch resulting from my excessive speed. The Focke-Wulf was still there and it did not look as though he had seen me yet. He was balancing nearly half a mile in front, flying about 40 feet above the surface. The sun was setting behind me, perhaps making me too visible. I slowly moved to one side to avoid the eddy from his propeller and was now just about 1,000 feet behind him. He still had not seen me and I angled downwards to adjust the light on my collimator. I raised my eyes, my finger on the firing button of my four cannon, and . . . the Focke Wulf was gone! The sly fox had fooled me – he must have seen me out of the corner of his eye all along. I found him again, 1,600 feet above me, climbing vertically like a rocket. Twisting my neck, I pulled on the stick like a maniac and tried to follow him. We climbed higher and higher and I was pulling too hard to keep him in my sights. I felt the plane judder, a prelude to losing speed. Entering a tail-spin in a Tempest below 3,000 feet was not a good idea. Hell! I re-engaged the overboost and my Tempest teetered on a pin-head for a moment. I battled with the ailerons and scanned the horizon for the Focke-Wulf, which had vanished once again. Suddenly, there was a loud bang and my heart missed a beat as the propeller came to an abrupt halt. A shell had hit the engine which spewed oil all over my hood. My hood then took a hammering from the other 20 mms. I was too low to eject and my plane to glide down smoothly. I dived to conserve speed, having decided to land on my belly. I didn't have any other choice.

At the mouth of the small river that ran into the lake lay a large green meadow that I thought I should just be able to reach. A shadow passed above me briefly. A splendid 'long-nose' Focke-Wulf D9, on its back, was executing a roll over my plane. I could see the pilot watching me quite clearly and the small blue flames escaping from his exhaust. He slowed to a virtual standstill in order not to overtake me. I had enough time to notice the black and white stripe on his fuselage and his yellow-painted tail plane. I learnt later that those were the markings of the JG-26. He'd certainly made a fool of me.

I unhitched my parachute, tied the straps and safety belt around my body as tightly as I could and then jettisoned my canopy. It took just a few seconds. Miraculously, my flaps descended and I landed, wheels retracted, causing a cascade of black mud to gush over the cockpit and cover the plane. I had landed in a peat field, my Tempest sliding to a halt intact over the slippery ground.

I leapt up in panic, held back momentarily by the rubber tube of my mask that I had forgotten to remove. It broke and the copper nozzle bounced back into my face. I skidded on the mud-laden wing, fell into the sludge in a seated position and heard the sound of the Focke-Wulf engine coming back to me. It flashed past, a few metres above my head and then I saw its black and white spiralled prop hub heading straight for me. I covered my face instinctively but he did not fire, he simply waggled his wings in a goodbye salute and disappeared behind a row of poplar trees. A dozen or so Fw D9's heading east flew right over me.

Shocked and completely dazed, I could hear my Tempest flight in the distance, looking for me. Everything had happened so quickly that I was not sure if I was dreaming. I lit a cigarette, but my mouth was so dry that I spat it out. My heart felt as if it were going to explode in my chest and I couldn't catch my breath.

I had a problem: was I behind the German lines? There was movement all around me. Tanks were rumbling down the autobahn hidden behind the hill.

The thunder of artillery fire was continuous. I could hear a vehicle approaching on the small road that bordered the peat field. It was a jeep with three American soldiers who stuck a machine gun in my stomach as soon as they caught sight of me. The R.A.F. wings on my battle-dress, the word 'France' on my shoulder and the roundel clearly visible on my plane managed to convince them but not before they had taken my watch, wallet and revolver and given me a blow in the kidneys with a rifle butt. After finally being informed by the H.Q. of 122 Wing, a small American 105 Stinson arrived a couple of hours later, landing skilfully on an autobahn slip road that was under construction. After a few more dexterous manoeuvres, it lifted me out to safety and home.

It was time for dinner when I arrived, so I headed straight to the mess where I was greeted with a round of applause, two of my pilots brandishing a placard saying: 'Leave it to me, it's a piece of cake!' which is what Bay Adams claimed I said over the radio after ordering him to cover me. I was not convinced that those were my exact words, but they were to follow me everywhere until the end of the war!*

Our losses in the last three months had made us not just indifferent but immune. However, after that Fw 190 D9 had shot down MacKenzie's plane we were deeply touched, for the following reason.

In the previous December, MacKenzie had met a zoo keeper from Anvers. The war and the occupation had made it impossible for him to keep the carnivorous animals fed so they had to be shot, but the non-meat eaters posed no such problem. The keeper had rescued three Siberian husky puppies fathered by a Canadian grey wolf. Mac had bought one and brought it back in a parachute sack.

The dog was a real beauty – the most handsome I had ever seen. He quickly demonstrated both an exclusive loyalty to his master and an incredibly ferocious streak. Naturally he had inherited a set of very respectable fangs from his father and no one could stroke or even approach him. He did not leave Mac's side for a second, always slept under his bed, and would only be fed by his master. His name was Nook and when Mac was on a mission, he would lie near the chocks where the planes were parked, waiting for him to return.

On the day that Mac was shot down – and killed – Nook waited for him in his usual spot. He stayed in position, unapproachable, without moving, drinking or eating for four days and nights. On the morning of the fifth day, the Military Police found him on the runway. He had tried to return to his place of vigil but the shot from the German farmer's gun had proved fatal. The farmer denied having done it but we assumed that Nook had attacked his sheep. That evening, when we buried Nook, MacKenzie's faithful companion, there were tears in everyone's eyes.

In 1996 in Cologne at a fighter pilot reunion, I spent many hours talking with Werner Molge who commanded 7/JG-26 Squadron. He told me that he had tried to discover which pilot had shot me down in April, 1945 and had identified three possible candidates, two of them from JG-26 Squadron and one from 301.

There were two pilots in JG-26 with the reputation for 'killing'

---

* The R.A.F. published a confidential bulletin each month containing information, advice and so on, but it did not fail to include the mistakes and most idiotic deeds of its pilots. In each issue one of its 10,000 pilots received the 'Order of the Irremovable Finger', as in 'Take your finger out of your nose and pay attention to what is going on around you in the sky.' Another column contained famous last words of the month. In the late bulletin of June 1945 I had the honour of appearing under the heading – 'Our Forceful Frenchman ended his war with wit and grace by leaving the immortal words – Leave it to me, etc.' and that was how I went down in history!

Tempests. Their names were Söffing and Dortemann. The latter had shot down 8 of the 14 Tempests attributed to JG-26 between 28 March and 30 April – figures confirmed by R.A.F. archives. The date of my escapade also corresponds with a plane shot down by Rudi Wulf from JG-301 Squadron.

According to Molge the most likely candidate was Dortemann, leader of I Flight of JG-26 Squadron, who claimed to have shot down two planes and damaged one in the Dummersee area. In fact, he had shot down not two but three Tempests, believing that the first of my planes at which he shot was only damaged as he had not seen it in flames. This proved two things: firstly that German pilots, and in particular aces like Staffelkapitan Dortemann, only claimed victories of which they were wholly sure; and secondly that they were truly amazing pilots! The fun part is that he claimed two Spitfire XIVs instead of Tempests. Both planes, however, have the same eliptical wings.

THE LAST TEST

We had a very clear feeling that we were on the last lap. How long would German resistance last? If the Germans wanted to hold out on the Kiel canal line, in the Danish islands and in Norway, they certainly could for at least another two months.

The evacuation of the Luftwaffe was taking place in pretty orderly fashion. All the airfields in Denmark were full to bursting point with transport and combat aircraft. In every bight, in every estuary, along the beaches, were moored entire fleets of Blohm and Voss and Dornier flying boats. Their petrol stocks would certainly allow them to carry out effective defence for some time yet – at least in theory. Every hour the retreating movement on Norway became clearer. The big naval convoy in Kiel, the endless stream of aircraft across the Skagerrak, the obstinate resistance of the ground troops, all those were sure signs.

By the same token our bomber planes in the 2 Group area were outdistanced and could not operate from their bases carrying effective loads. Nor could we, for the same reason, rely on any effective help from the Marauders of the American 9th Air Force. Once again our poor 83 Group had to hold the baby.

This was confirmed by a phone message from Broadhurst, followed by one from Lapsley. As a sop we were told that all means would be taken to reinstate the airfields in the Lübeck area, once they were captured, so that our damaged aircraft should have somewhere to land. Belly-landing strips had already been installed at Ratzeburg and Schwartzenbeck and on the airfield at Lübeck itself. Ambulances were going to be permanently stationed there from 1330 hours that very day. If, by any chance, our troops were to occupy any airfields further north that were free of mines, the ends of the runways would be marked by 'electric red' strips.

Maintenance was a hard problem. Each flight could only collect at most three or four planes capable of flying. In No. 3 Squadron alone we had seven planes in the hangars (flak, oil leaks, plugs to be changed, flak again and yet again). Ken Hughes' aircraft looked more like a gigantic sieve than anything else with its leading edges, its airscrew spinner and its radiator riddled with shell splinters. Johnny Walker had a hole two feet across in his tail fin. My mechanics were just finishing rushed repairs to two holes the size of my fist in the fuselage of my 'Grand Charles'.

The personnel of the maintenance section hadn't half its equipment to hand, the hangars were open to the four winds, it rained into them and it was cold there. We were short of ammunition and guns, as the convoys had not been able to catch up with our rapid advance. All these details of base organisation were a big responsibility and the Squadron Leader Admin. of the Wing wasn't all that much help.

I was still uneasy about my new rank and therefore felt rather edgy. My position – if it hadn't been for the sporting attitude of the British – might have been awkward because after all I was only a Sous-Lieutenant though I was in command of English officers much higher in rank, 120 pilots and 900 men. I knew that the Air Ministry were doing their best to rectify the position but in Paris nobody cared a damn. There they thought only about politics, and whether those who were still fighting got promotion was a matter of complete indifference to them.

All the same I had done two trips that day and I was completely creased. In the course of the morning the Wing had lost six pilots, including 'Baby' Austin and Flying Officer Blee, the two best of the New Zealand 486 Squadron.

In the confidential information bulletin – *Tactical Air Force 83* – I read that 145 Wing was in Holland. It was a French Wing, made up of 341 'Alsace' Squadron lead by Jaco Andrieux, the 340 'Ile de France' and the 345 'Berry' Squadron under the command of Henri de Bordas. It contained a small core of surviving F.A.F.L. chums, most of whom had been re-grouped from the R.A.F. squadrons with whom they had been fighting for a long time – some having managed to survive since 1941.

My own squadron was on release for two days. There had been heavy losses and morale was low. The plan was to go to Brussels and take six rooms in a hotel in town, but the idea of Brussels did not excite me much, particularly since my funds were rather depleted! Instead, I wanted to try and see my French friends. I needed to find out where 145 Wing was located and spent an exasperating quarter of an hour on the mess telephone, being passed from one service to the next. Despite progressing from 'Please, could you be so kind as to . . .' to 'Don't be a bloody fool', I did not manage to find out where they were.

Our Spy watched me from his armchair, laughing at my efforts and told me not to waste any more time – he had all the information I needed in his case.

Ten minutes later he came back with the number and secret code for 145 Wing. It was now dinner time so I got Jaco on the line in ten minutes flat.

'Come and have lunch tomorrow!'

'Will do, but where are you?'

Jaco tried to spell out the multi-syllabled Dutch name – completely unpronounceable for anyone not from Holland. It sounded like Herto-something – on the edges of the Maas. Since Dutch was double to me, I asked Jaco to spell out its co-ordinates: 51° 42 N and 5° 18 E.

'See you tomorrow, then.'

I was flying at 6,000 feet when I finally spotted the airfield, where about fifty Spitfires were lined up alongside buildings and encampments. It was a perfect opportunity to show off a little. Lots of throttle, fine pitch propeller, engine at 3,000 revs, I dived at 40° and then straightened up at the last moment, very low, crossing the aerodrome level with the ground at 400 m.p.h. with the wind behind me. Pleased with myself, I had the time to see everyone rush outside. My show had been a great success. I did a graceful turn, reducing speed and, slowing further, lined up with the runway, my flaps down. Still pleased with myself, I began my landing when suddenly a red flare exploded, literally at the end of my plane's nose.

A red flare was an order to open the throttle immediately, which I duly did. I lowered my hand to raise my landing gear and . . . it was already raised! I was going to land with my undercarriage up, damaging both my ego and the Tempest. I would never have been able to live it down.

I completed the circuit and landed as if on eggshells, nothing to brag about. I was greeted on arrival by Jaco and Poupy, both doubled up with laughter.

'My dear Clo-Clo, what an amazing landing, but why didn't you go the whole hog? A Tempest on its belly is a rare sight. Bravo!'

Thankfully, Jaco had been waiting for me on the control tower balcony when I announced my arrival and saw my plane with its flaps down, engine slowed and ready to land without wheels. He grasped the situation immediately and pounced on the signal gun to warn me, sending up the red flare that saved me.

It was an emotional occasion and we enjoyed some good French food before I returned to Volkel in the rain, having had a quite excellent day.

The pilots had still not returned from Brussels and Nijmegen, which left me with a quiet day to myself. I took a jeep in which to explore the wonderful woods around Volkel. Suddenly, the war seemed a long way off.

That evening, after dinner in an empty mess, I sat at a table in the corner, lit only by a shaky bulb on the wall (our electrician had been at it again with the generators!), and wrote the previous week's story in my diary. It was not a sparkling entry and my heart was not in it. For some time I had been feeling as if I had only temporarily escaped that mad, seemingly endless world between life and death, constantly teetering on the high wire of chance, with no safety net and only courage, fear and nearly three years of combat experience to keep me balanced.

I knew that tomorrow I would have to make the effort all over again, reacting with perhaps slightly slower reflexes, weakened by fatigue . . . but I thought of my parents and felt stronger.

I could hear the airmen on leave returning in their lorry – they were shouting, singing and making a frightful noise. I finished my beer and discreetly made my way to bed.

Charlie, senior engineer officer of the Wing, had a list of our available aircraft. We had 27 – really 23 – out of the 95 that we ought normally to have at our disposal. He could promise four more for 1700 hours. It was 1530 hours.

Ken Hughes, Johnnie Walker and my two Australians Torpy and Bay, with Longley as reserve, went on a short armed reconnaissance in the Flensburg area. Ken was a careful type and wouldn't get himself shot down without good cause.

I went on studying the morning's pilot reports, cooking up the Wing's report for G.C.C. with Abund. No way of glossing over our deficiency in planes. The pilots' morale wasn't anything to write home about either, and I registered a devout hope that we wouldn't be sent on any anti-shipping strikes.

Flak was looming ever larger on my pilots' mental horizon. You could sense how it obsessed them in every conversation, at meals, at the bar, during briefings. To be convinced you had only to watch how sharply those who came back from a trip were questioned as to how dense the flak was, and where the posts were, by those who were about to set off. The word was on everybody's lips, all the time.

I chain-smoked cigarette after cigarette and drank innumerable cups of tea. My jaw and teeth still hurt from that belly landing on 24 March.

I had a somewhat lively argument with one of the liaison boffins from the 2nd Canadian Army – after that 20 April show I just didn't seem to cotton on to those khaki types. He didn't even seem to know what was going on on the ground. I had to go off and have a look at the teletypes myself to get up to date.

The ground situation seemed pretty confused – armoured thrusts towards Kiel and Elmshorn (north of Hamburg) against some strong nests of resistance supported by the airfields of Neumünster and Bad Segeberg and their satellites.

The Luftwaffe confined itself to covering the retreat of the ground troops and evacuating the staffs in Ju 88's and 52's, Heinkel 111's and particularly Fieseler Storchs, which sneaked off while layers of mist covered the Poner Lakes area at dawn and sunset.

The rather low clouds (ceiling less than 3,000 feet) which had covered the base of the peninsula of Denmark for several days militated against interception patrols on our part. The flak was so dense that as soon as one of our planes emerged below the cloud cover it was immediately caught in a cross fire by some of the hundreds of automatic guns covering the roads from Eutin to Kiel and especially the Neumünster–Rendsburg and Schleswig–Rendsburg autobahns.

All this was not very encouraging.

1720 hours. I went outside to watch 56 and 3 Squadrons landing on their return from a trip.

Poor Brocklehurst had been badly hit by flak as he was flying along the Flensburg autobahn. Rather than make a belly landing he had decided to bale out. He had got out all right, but the jeep sent out to bring him in had had the devil of a time finding him. The wind had carried him far into the forest of Orel.

Ken's section came back with the magnificent score of 23 lorries destroyed, plus 65 damaged – an absolute record – and, in addition, two Ju 52's brought down on the coast by Longley. Fine, that would look good in my report. On the other hand I was worried about Longley. He was getting increasingly rash. He knew that as soon as his tour of ops. was finished he would be repatriated to New Zealand, and he was devoting his last flying hours in an attempt to bag a D.F.C. I would have to apply the brakes a bit. I was going to ask Cole to put him up for it anyway as he had six confirmed Jerries to his credit.

All the planes except Brocklehurst's had come back. Six out of the nine would be rearmed and refuelled within 10 minutes.

Just as I was about to return to our Dispersal, a formation of torpedo-carrying Beaufighters passed immediately overhead in a roar like thunder, coming from the north. There were swarms of them, about three Wings. They were on their way back from the monster shipping-strike organised against the notorious convoy at Kiel.

One of them had an engine on fire – there was the tell-tale trail of black smoke – and tried to land on our field. He went into a spin about 500 yards off and crashed with a terrific explosion near the swimming pool. The fire tender and the ambulance tore off.

'Christ, what's all the hurry?' murmured Peter West. 'There can't be much left.' How right he was. Ten minutes later the ambulance came slowly back, bearing the pitiful remains of the pilot and the observer.

We were still talking about it at dinner, an hour later in the mess, when Spy rushed up:

'Scrambler, sir.'

Who on earth could be wanting me at this ungodly hour? I leapt into the jeep and tore off to the Intelligence Room.

The 'scrambler' was a new piece of ultra short-wave wireless telephony equipment that linked the squadrons to G.H.Q. It had the peculiar ability to scramble emitted waves and de-scramble received ones. Any information intercepted en route by the enemy was indecipherable gobbledygook. As a result, it was a speedy and practical means of communication that dispensed with the need to code messages.

Lapsley was on the line. The conversation was a short one.

'Pierre, how many planes do you have at your disposal?'

I glanced at the chart. 'Twenty-five, sir!'

'Good. Take down the following, for immediate action: The Germans are evacuating Grossenbrode air-naval base en masse, reference N.54.22 E11.05. Over 100 large transport aircraft loaded on beach and at anchor. Strong enemy fighter cover probable. Turn all available effectives on the designated objective. Strafe if possible. Actual method of execution left to your discretion. Inform Kenway of your plans at least 10 minutes in advance. I will try to give you anti-flak Typhoons. Do not rely on them too much. Good luck.'

I said thank you and hung up. This sounded exciting, but I was furious. How nice, after such a day, to be sent off again, at 6 p.m. on an objective like that!

'Orderly! Number One state of alert! Now!'

The orderly jumped to it and, a few seconds later, the roar of klaxons shook Fassberg.

I studied the wall map. Grossenbrode was about 90 miles as the crow flies, but the 'Met' reports said that Lübeck Bay and the Hamburg area were completely blocked. There was thundery cloud, with showers, up to 20,000 feet. We would have to make a detour to the north.

Tyres screeched on the concrete. The jeeps were beginning to arrive, carrying bunches of pilots. What with their interrupted dinner and the heavy day they had had, they were not in the best of tempers. A few were munching improvised sandwiches.

Everybody there? O.K. I quickly outlined the situation. We hadn't enough available aircraft to fly as a Wing, in formation by squadrons. So we would fly in twice three flights, each of four planes echeloned to starboard. I would lead the first formation of twelve Tempests and MacDonald, from 486, the second. Like that I hoped my twenty-four planes would be under control.

I couldn't then and there give precise details as to how the strike would be carried out; I would give the necessary orders on the spot over the radio. It would be more a question of what turned out to be advisable than of a premeditated plan. In any case I had neither the necessary data nor the time to elaborate a plan of attack.

'Synchronise your watches. . . . It's 2007 hours. Engine start-up at 1815 hours. I shall take off as No. 1, will do a wide circuit over the airfield to let the twenty-four planes get into proper formation, and I shall set course on the target at 1825 hours. Any questions? O.K. then, get weaving.'

For the other three in my section I chose F.Lt. Bone, F.O. Dug Worley and young Sgt. Crow, whose third operational trip this would be. Not a particularly experienced trio, but I had no choice. I couldn't decently ask pilots who had already had three trips that day, and who were completely creased, to do a fourth and certainly pretty tough one.

1800 hours. 'Grand Charles' was ready. The engine was already ticking over and Gray, lying on the wing, did a thumbs-up to show that everything was in order. The vast concrete expanse, framed by the great dark hangars, was alive with movement. As I strapped myself in I looked around. Engines ticked over, starter cartridges went off with a bang, mechanics rushed with maps or parachutes forgotten at the last minute. Pilots climbed awkwardly into their cockpits, festooned with Mae Wests and parachute harnesses.

1816 hours. 'Chocks away.' At 1825 hours, with the sun already low on the horizon and heavy cloud banks rolling eastwards, I set course north, slowly gaining height. The formation this evening was lousy – difficult to fashion a homogeneous team out of personnel from three different units.

'Come on, Filmstar, pull your bloody fingers out!'

Blue Section, which ought to have been on my left, was wandering about to my right 1,500 feet above me. Yellow 2, 3 and 4 were trailing along more than half a mile to the rear. I was on edge and called them to order without mincing my words.

We flew round Hamburg to avoid the clouds of dirty smoke rising from the burning buildings. My aircraft at last decided to fly in formation.

We flew over Neumünster at 10,000 feet and got shot at, very sloppily, by an 88 mm. battery. We veered to starboard and set course 052°. The weather was deteriorating and I had to zigzag to avoid the blocks of cumulus which rose high in the sky like white towers.

'Hallo, Kenway, any gen.?'

'Hallo, Filmstar Leader, Kenway answering, nothing at all.'

No sign of the recall I was secretly hoping for.

We were scarcely 20 miles from our objective when an impenetrable barrier of cloud blocked our way. I dived, followed by my formation, to try and find a way through underneath, but all we met was heavy rain and visibility zero. We quickly turned 180°, climbing, and then 180° again, bringing us back on our original course.

What was to be done? One plane by itself, or at a pinch a couple, might succeed in getting through, but for a compact formation of twenty-four to try it was not only a ticklish business, it was damned risky. I insinuated as much to Kenway.

'Hallo, Kenway, Filmstar Leader here. The weather stinks.'

Kenway's answer was straight to the point and his tone of voice left no room for doubt.

'Filmstar Leader, press on regardless.'

All right then; 'Cloud formation, go!'

I divided up my planes into independent sections of four, each one taking up close formation. We would have to try to get through the clouds on a set course and hope to join up again the other side.

We plunged into the storm and immediately lost sight of each other. Christ, it was pretty bumpy in there and I concentrated hard on my instruments, with an occasional eye open for my three unfortunate companions, who were keeping as close as they dared. The layer of cloud was luckily not very thick. After a very few moments we emerged over the Straits of Fehmarn, near Heiligenhafen. The sky was clear before us, all the way. My cockpit had got fogged up but now it cleared and I prepared to pin-point our position.

'Look out, Filmstar Leader!'

In a fraction of a second the sky had filled with a whirling mass of aircraft . . . an unforgettable sight!

Below, to the right, the big airfield of Grossenbrode, with its seaplane base and its runways crawling with multi-engined aircraft. Beyond, a calm sea with a few ships at anchor. Behind us, a solid wall of clouds from which my Tempest sections were just emerging haphazard and at various heights. All round us were massive groups of thirty or forty German fighters on patrol. One of them had already seen us and was swooping down on Yellow Section.

In front of us, either on the ground or just taking off, were more than

100 large transport planes – theoretically my primary objective. In the air, plenty of enemy fighters. One group at 1,500 feet, another at 3,000, a third at 4,500 and two others on a level with us, i.e. at about 10,000 feet. Above us there were certainly one more, perhaps two. And I only had 24 Tempests!

My mind was quickly made up. Filmstar Yellow and Blue Sections would attack the fighters above us, and Pink, Black and White Sections, commanded by MacDonald, would engage the Focke-Wulfs below us. In the meantime I would try to slip through with my Red Section and shoot-up the airfield. I passed this on over the radio and then, closely followed by the rest of my section, I released my auxiliary tanks and went into a vertical dive, passing like a thunderbolt at 500 m.p.h. through a formation of Focke-Wulfs which scattered about the sky like a flock of swallows. I straightened out gradually, closing the throttle and following a trajectory designed to bring me over the airfield at ground level, from south-west to north-east.

All hell was let loose as we arrived. I was doing more than 450 m.p.h. by the clock when I reached the edge of the field. I was 60 feet from the ground and I opened fire at once. The mottled surface of the anchorage was covered with moored Dornier 24's and 18's. Three lines of white foam marked the wake of three planes which had just taken off. A row of Blohm und Voss's in wheeled cradles were lined up on the launching ramps. I concentrated my fire on a BV 138. The moorings of the cradle snapped and I passed over the enormous smoking mass as it tipped up on the slope, fell into the sea and began to sink.

The flak redoubled in fury. A flash on my right, and a disabled Tempest crashed into the sea in a shower of spray.

Jesus! The boats anchored off shore were armed, and one of them, a large destroyer, was blazing away with all it had. I instinctively withdrew my head into my shoulders and, still flying very low, veered slightly to the left, so fast that I couldn't fire at the Dorniers, then quickly swung to the right behind an enormous Ju 252 which had just taken off and was already getting alarmingly big in my gun sight. I fired one long continuous burst at him and broke away just before we collided. I turned round to see the Ju 252, with two engines ablaze and the tail plane sheared off by my shells, bounce on the sea and explode.

My speed had swept me far on – straight on to the destroyer which was spitting away with all her guns. I passed within 10 yards of her narrow bows, just above the water and the thousand spouts raised by the flak. I caught a glimpse of white shapes rushing about on deck and of tongues of fire from her guns. The entire camouflaged superstructure seemed to be alive with them. Tracer shells ricocheted on the water and exploded all round over a radius of 500 yards. Some shrapnel mowed down a flock of seagulls which fell in the sea on all sides, panic-stricken and bleeding. Phew! Out of range at last!

I was sweating all over and my throat was so constricted that I couldn't articulate one word over the radio. Without realising it I had held my breath through the whole attack and my heart was thumping fit to burst. I regained height by a wide climbing turn to port. What was happening? The situation looked pretty grim. A terrific dog fight was going on above the airfield. Three planes were coming down in flames – I was too far to see whether they were friend or foe. Another, pulverised, had left a trail of flaming fragments in the sky and a fifth was coming down in a spin, followed by a white trail of smoke. Yet others were burning on the ground.

The radio was transmitting an incomprehensible chaos of shouts, screams and curses, mingled with the vibrations of cannon firing. Near the torpedo boat, in the middle of a patch of foam, the remains of a plane were burning and heavy black smoke curled up from the sheet of burning petrol.

What had happened to the rest of my section? Not a sign of them in the sky. I had seen a Tempest crash on my right when the attack began, presumably Bone's. The machine which had been shot down by one of the German ships was Crow's, I was sure. As for Worley, he was invisible.

I thought for a moment. Ought I to try to join in the fight against the German fighters raging above Heiligenhafen, or ought I to try a second run over the German base, taking advantage of the flap that was probably going on there?

Rather unwillingly I decided on the second course. I went down to sea level again and began to fly round Fehmarn Island at full speed. Suddenly I found myself face to face with three Dornier 24's, probably the three which had taken off from Grossenbrode a few seconds before our attack and whose wake I had seen. Do 24's are big three-engined flying boats of about 19 tons, fairly slow but well provided with defensive weapons.

When I had recovered from my surprise I sheered off to keep outside their crossed fires, opened the throttle wide and zigzagged back towards them, taking photos. Then, keeping out of range of their machine guns, I drew a deliberate bead on the first one. After two bursts one of his engines was on fire and another was coughing. He tried a forced landing, but as the sea was rough on this side of the promontory he capsized.

Immediately I made for the two others, who were skimming the water and attempting to get away. Long black trails escaped from their overworked engines. I felt almost sorry for them. With my 250 m.p.h. margin of speed and my four cannon, it was almost like potting two sitting birds. I chose the left-hand one, which was heavily laden and had lagged slightly behind the other. But this time, the bastard turned very cleverly at the last moment. Carried forward by my speed I found myself, like a fool, having to turn within point-blank range of his rear gunner who hit me with three bullets. Luckily they were only popguns of 7.7 mm. A side-slip brought me back into firing position and my shells ravaged his fuselage at less than 100-yards range. His wing tanks caught fire. The rear gunner shut up. Within a few seconds the machine was enveloped in flames. The pilot tried to gain height to allow his crew to bale out, but he was too low. Three men did jump, all the same. Only one parachute opened and that closed again at once, swallowed up by a wave. The big machine was nothing but a ball of fire rolling a few feet above the crests of the waves in a thick trail of black smoke. A few seconds later it exploded.

I looked for the third one. It had miraculously vanished into the landscape, probably behind one of the little islands in the strait. This business had brought me right round Fehmarn and I climbed to 10,000 feet. There was Grossenbrode behind the hill. I swallowed the lump in my throat, instinctively tightened my safety straps and once again dived for the airfield for another strafe.

This time I took them by surprise. The flak was otherwise engaged, firing rather haphazardly in the general direction of the swarm of German fighters and Tempests. I swept between two hangars and emerged over the airfield at full throttle. There were so many aircraft piled up there that I didn't know which to choose. Right in my sight there was a row of large transport Arado 232's. Before my shells exploded on the first two I had time to take in the curious fuselages, the big double-decker cabins and the 24-wheeled undercarts needed to support these gigantic machines.

A flak shell exploded within a few yards of my plane and shook it violently. Once out of range I broke away in a cimbing spiral and found myself plumb in the middle of a scrap, which by this time was beginning to slacken.

I tried to rally my aircraft, but in that confusion it was difficult. The first thing I saw was a Tempest in a dive. It was spinning, increasingly fast. Then both the wings broke off . . . a few seconds later a bright flame leapt up between two hedges . . . no parachute.

Two Fw's tried to engage me in a dog fight, but I quickly got rid of them by breaking away under them. JF-H, piloted by Bay the Australian, was in difficulties, its engine smoking. He was engaged with a Messerschmitt which was defending itself very cleverly, gradually reducing speed and beginning to get the upper hand. I roared towards the '109' and caught him by surprise, hitting him with at least two shells in the wing-root. The pilot, taken aback, instinctively reversed his turn and Bay, now in position, fired in his turn, hitting him again. Panic-stricken the Hun again reversed – I fired – he broke away – Bay fired – the Hun seemed to hang in the air for a moment, then one of his wings folded up in flames. The pilot managed to bale out all right, but his parachute screwed up.

At last the Tempests began to re-form and, two at a time, cautiously withdrew from the scrap. The Huns gave ground and turned back one by one. They dived towards Grossenbrode, from which a column of smoke rose up in the sky – probably the two Arados burning.

A belated Focke-Wulf had slipped in amongst us and was desperately waggling his wings. Followed by Bay, I immediately went for him. A long burst – then suddenly my guns rattled noisily – no ammunition left. However, the Focke-Wulf had slowed down and was beginning to smoke, so I must have hit him after all. Bay fired in turn, point blank, and pulverised him. He burst like a ripe tomato. This time the parachute did open.

The sun had now slid down, over there, behind the Danish islands. My patrol re-formed in the luminous twilight. I counted the planes; two, four, eight, ten, eleven – and then two others, lower down, laboriously catching up, probably damaged.

With navigation lights on we flew back towards Fassberg in the deepening night. Already the outlines of the landscape were becoming blurred. The warm evening air gently rocked my 'Grand Charles'. As we approached the airfield, undercarts and flaps down, I wondered what Mitchell, our engineer officer, would have to say when I brought him back thirteen planes out of the twenty-four.

A CASE OF 'FRATERNISATION'

Soon after that came the armistice, like a door closing. Eight days of bewilderment – an indefinable mixture of gladness and regret. Noisy jollifications, followed by long periods of calm, and, especially, a thick unaccustomed silence, which hung heavy on the airfield, on the tarpaulin-covered planes, on the empty runways. The snapping of the nervous tension was dreadful, as painful as a surgical operation.

That evening in the mess was like some extraordinary vigil over a corpse. The pilots were slumped in their chairs – no one spoke a word, or sang, or anything. Round about 11 o'clock Bay switched on the wireless. The B.B.C. were giving a running commentary on the scene in the streets of London and Paris, where the population was really letting itself go. All eyes turned towards the set, and in them you could read a kind of hatred.

It was so unmistakable, and yet so surprising, that I glanced enquiringly at Ken. I heard a crash of broken glass – someone had hurled a bottle at the set, at all this noise, at all those people shamelessly parading their sense of relief and deliverance before us.

One by one pilots got up and eventually only Ken and I and the sleepy barman were left in the silent mess. From the smashed wireless still came a feeble whispering noise.

I again looked at Ken. No need of words, we both understood. Half an hour passed, an hour perhaps. And then, suddenly, I swear I felt they were all there, round us in the shadow and the cigarette smoke, like kids who have been unjustly punished.

Mackenzie . . . Jimmy Kelly . . . Mouse Manson . . . young Kidd . . . Bone . . . Shepherd . . . Brooker . . . Gordon . . . dark uniforms too, with tarnished gold stripes . . . Mouchotte . . . Mézilles . . . Béraud . . . Pierrot Degail – all those who had set off one fine morning in their Spitfires or their Tempests and who hadn't come back.

'Well, Pierre, that's that. They won't need us any more.'

We went off to bed and I closed the door softly, so as not to awaken the barman, who had dropped off to sleep on his stool, and also so as not to disturb 'the others'.

It was 9 May and the war already felt distant. Pilots were starting to make plans for their return home. One of the A.D.C.s working for Broady, as we called him, told me discreetly that we'd not be going home as soon as we might think and that we should continue training flights – things were beginning to turn sour with the Russians.

We were in the middle of lunch when we heard the familiar, characteristic throbbing of the aircraft engines. We rushed outside to see an immaculate formation of five Messerschmitt 262's preparing to land after a long pause. The R.A.F. regiment A.A. officer came running.

'What shall I do? Open fire?'

'Don't be a fool, old chap, the war is over. We aren't going to start it again just for your pleasure.'

The '262's' landed faultlessly, except for the last of them, the leader, recognisable from the two black chevrons painted on his fuselage. He slewed round intentionally at the end of the runway, collapsing his undercarriage in order not to deliver his aircraft intact.

I rushed towards him in my jeep. The pilot was on his feet, checking his hair in the rear-vision mirror. His hair was too long, his helmet was broken and he was wearing a white silk scarf, a fine black leather flying suit at the neck of which was a Knight of the Iron Cross ribbon, with oak leaves. It was one of the Wehrmacht's highest decorations and he was doubtless an ace, but I could not recognise his rank from his epaulettes. I jumped out of the jeep and headed towards him and we suddenly, almost unconsciously, found ourselves shaking hands. He had undone his holster revolver and handed me the weapon. It was a rare, genuine pre-war Luger with a squared wooden butt. He took me by surprise, speaking to me in impeccable French.

'I suppose I should give you this.'

I asked him why he addressed me in French.

'I saw the word "France" on your shoulder and your helmet is not English. You are a lieutenant so why do you have different stripes on your battle-dress? We always used to speak French at home. We come from Cologne and live on the edge of the Rhine. We used to spend our holidays in France before the war.'

At this point, two flight commanders arrived in their jeep. 'Go and collect the others,' I told them, 'I don't know what we are going to do with them, but while we work it out, take them to the mess and let them have a drink and something to eat – the Officers' Mess of course.'

My Oberstleutnant told me he would like to wash. I took him to my room, gave him my razor and shaving cream and he took a shower, emerging with my towel wrapped round him. He was well-built but had scars all over his body. He explained that he had been shot down five times, wounded on four occasions and forced to bail out on three.

An hour had passed since the '262's' had landed and we suddenly heard the faint noise of a powerful engine. It was a small German four-seater liaison, a Messerschmitt 108, which landed without ceremony. It was the Oberstleutnant's orderly bringing his luggage. These Germans really were incredible. He had arrived from the besieged city of Prague, with two nurses whom he did not want to leave in the hands of the Russians.* He carried the luggage into my room with a clicking of heels and a faultless salute – not a Nazi one since fighter pilots in the Luftwaffe didn't do that – but a classic salute, hand raised to peak.

My Teutonic companion was still in his underwear as he unpacked his case, taking out a pair of polished shoes and an extraordinarily elegant white uniform jacket. In Germany, fighter pilots were the aristocrats of the armed forces. He rummaged around in his things and handed me his log book, decorated with a large gilded symbol of a pilot, eagle and swastika. I glanced at the final pages. It showed over a hundred victories. As I took him to the mess for a drink, as requested, I showed him a Tempest at close range. I chose mine so that he could see the black crosses on the fuselage. However, they appeared to make little impression. The plane, on the other hand, did. He thought it magnificent.

I drank a beer in the mess with the German, who sat in a chair looking extremely relaxed. I hung on the telephone, trying to reach the H.Q. of the 2nd Canadian Army in charge of the sector. I was just about at the end of my tether when finally somebody answered. It was probably an orderly and I could hear the armistice celebrations going on in the background, with people singing and shouting. The Lance Corporal at the end of the line, no doubt with his feet on the desk and a bottle of whisky in his hand, did not give a damn about what I was telling him.

'I have five prisoners. What should I do with them?'

He laughed and told me that they had five million prisoners of their own and I could go to hell. Then he hung up.

Given the circumstances, we invited the Germans to dine with our pilots and the beer flowed freely. Despite our lack of a common language, we managed to communicate with each other using the classic, universal gestures of fighter pilots recounting tales of combat. A large map of Germany was spread on the table to help. We pin-pointed where we had encountered each other and where we had engaged in combat. It was the private world of the fighter pilot in all its glory!

This went on for eight days, but we could not keep the Germans secret

* The 262 Squadron came from III KG (J) based in Ruzyne, near Prague.

any longer. All it needed was some idiot from ground crew who hadn't spent a single hour in the air in combat, but who now wanted to make up for it by at first protesting and then denouncing us. Two of the Germans asked for civilian clothes so that they could make their way home, and the others left for the prisoner of war camp, loaded down with oranges, chocolate and cigarettes. Why not? They had fought well and had always treated our downed pilots well. The war was over, and we had all survived with honour. In our swimming shorts in the underground swimming pool – we were in one of those wonderful peace-time Luftwaffe messes – you couldn't have told us apart.

12 May 1945

The war was well and truly over. Discipline was more relaxed despite the instructions issued from on high. One particular comic incident demonstrated that even orders on fraternisation with enemy citizens from the Supreme Commander himself (Ike Eisenhower) were not respected when a good opportunity presented itself. Ridicule never killed anyone. Our 'Supreme Chief' forgot to instruct pilots on how, in the huge brothel of 1945 Germany, to differentiate forbidden German thighs from the authorised ones belonging to deported women workers from Poland, Europe and the Balkans.

One morning, the doctor came to inform me, in the carefully-chosen, somewhat embarrassed words typical of an English gentleman broaching an unpleasant topic, that two pilots from our squadrons had got a dose of what he euphemistically called an S.T.D. Gracious me! What about penicillin?

'Yes, of course I can cure them,' he replied, 'but regulations demand a written report.'

I asked him to wait until the following week, but in the meantime to treat the men. I would advise him in due course.

He did not react but his tight-lipped air worried me. I had no intention of allowing H.Q. to take disciplinary action against pilots who had spent one rainy weekend relaxing in Brussels after six months of continual battle. I ran the risk of starting a scandal, though, because a very stern reminder of Eisenhower's orders had been posted in all messes just the previous week. Meanwhile, the question was: where did the silly devils catch it? I knew how, but where and from whom? I called in the guilty parties for interrogation – they marched in with trepidation. I told them they were lucky that I was a French scoundrel myself and that I found the whole thing very funny, and that Americans were uptight hypocrites, etc. I added that I planned, as much as possible, to stifle the affair, but that they had tell me all the details. Upon seeing them smile, I assured them that I had no intention of making any personal use of the information they imparted.

I found out that, while hunting deer with two friends in the magnificent forest belonging to Goering – a second activity that was prohibited – they had heard music deep inside and when searching for its origins, came across a wonderful private hunting lodge. In it were living a dozen or so young ladies who had probably been snaffled from the occupied territories for the recreation of German soldiers. The girls had taken refuge from the battles and chaos of war, living on the plentiful supplies of fine wine, champagne, luxury foods and caviar stored there. My 'explorers', not wanting to share their discovery, had kept it quiet and visited the chalet discreetly in the evening, joining in the good life that was being enjoyed there.

I explained to the doctor that he should keep the affair secret for the honour of the R.A.F., and that to thank him for his *esprit de corps* I granted him permission to spend a week in Paris or Brussels. As for my fornicating pilots, I imposed total silence upon them under threat of punishment ranging from being locked up in the Tower of London to being beheaded in Trafalgar Square!

A TRAGIC MISTAKE

Tragedy came hot on the heels of comedy. The shock of the Bremenshaven collision that took place on 12 May was to eclipse the affair of the hunting lodge completely, which no doubt would vanish amid the paperwork. Afterwards, I broke out in a cold sweat all over again as I committed to paper the drama of the day before, which I was still struggling to understand – both on a technical and personal level. I had never come so close to death.

Montgomery – our 83rd division of the T.A.F. supported his operations and covered his sector – had invited the Russian Commander in Chief, Marshal Zhukov, to visit what was left of Hamburg after the night raids of 24–25 and 28–29 July 1944. Virtually none of Germany's second largest city had been left standing. On this occasion, the R.A.F. was to make a show of force over Bremen, a useful exercise after the business with the floating bridges at Wittenberg on the River Elbe and the dispatching of 5,000 Russian paras to occupy the Danish island of Bornholm. Relations between the Soviets and the Allies were now on a mediocre footing.

It was an idea of major stupidity and one that was very tricky to execute in the way H.Q. demanded. We were to line up forty Wings, comprising a hundred squadrons of B-25's, Mosquitos, Typhoons, Tempests and Spitfires, and fly them in an airborne procession – an impossible task. An operational command – a form D – came through via the teleprinter indicating the tight schedule, the waiting areas, altitudes, the order of appearance, and the radio frequency for central control! I studied the order with two other squadron leaders. It was a highly demanding and dangerous command. To try to co-ordinate over 1,000 planes of such different performance in a relatively small amount of airspace was bordering on the foolhardy. What's more, the pilots had to face another challenge. The theory was that each Wing would assemble three squadrons of twelve planes in flight. Each squadron was to be given a number. We were given number 18 and had to insert ourselves between the Mosquitos, allotted number 17, and Spitfire XIV's, number 19.

Twelve assembly points had been designated – ours was at Winsen, a small village on a bend of the River Elbe south of Hamburg, with the code name Oscar. Everyone was to take his place in the procession according to instructions given by the controller, Jupiter. Over breakfast I learned that the new Wing Commander, Mackie – who had only arrived the day before to take over command – had been summoned to Schleswig H.Q., and could not get back in time. So I was to take over responsibility for directing our Wing's part in this crazy show. I only just had time to brief the thirty-six selected pilots, quickly explaining that we were to fly to the waiting area in open formation to avoid starting out with nerves already on edge before we took part in the fly-past itself. We would have to pay careful attention to the manoeuvres that we'd be called upon to execute – slowing down, speeding up or turning – none of which would be easy. I also recommended, most importantly, that they transfer to their main tanks when I gave the order: 'Close formation – Go!'

There was to be a vast number of Spitfires – perhaps five or six hundred in all. In order to fly past at exactly 1155 hours, as decreed in Form D, we would have to keep an eye out that we slotted in exactly behind number 17, the Mosquitoes (who fortunately were easily recognisable), and in front of number 19, one of the dozen or so other Spitfire wings. (When you considered how, in order to get their 300 B-17 Flying Fortresses in the air, the Americans would make sure their crews woke at 0345 hours and breakfasted between 0430 and 0500 hours, leaving them two hours to assemble in position before finally heading towards their target at 0700 hours, you can understand how, on so many occasions, the German radar managed to alert the Luftwaffe's defences in time.)

As the hour for take-off approached, I felt increasingly anxious. However, the take-off and assembling in formation passed off without problem. As we approached Winsen, Control contacted me.

'Hello, Filmstar, there is some delay. The new timing is 1205 hours. Orbit Oscar until we call you.'

'Some delay' turned out to be a euphemism, and the invective I heard over the radio told its own story. I had to lead my team in a slow, careful 360-degree turn, around a 6-mile radius.

At 1210 hours control ordered me to head towards Hamburg. Like dozens of swarms of bees, the squadrons attempted to fall into line – each one in its correct place – in a huge single file. Finally I spotted Hamburg, two of its factory chimneys miraculously still intact, and the walls of the bomb-damaged cathedral with which I aligned myself in order to make for Bremenshaven. I scanned the sky for the number 17's.

'Filmstar Leader, Blue 1 calling. Mosquitos at 10 o'clock, slightly above!' said Ken Hughes, alert as ever. They were indeed the number 17's and we were to move gently to the left and slide into the formation.

I was sweating as the sun streamed in through the perspex hood. I proceeded nervously, aware that I had to slow down very gently. I opened my cockpit. Not an easy task since I was too close to the Mosquitos and had to deal with their slipstream. However, we were correctly in formation and flying directly above a huge avenue, from which debris and ruins had been bulldozed clear. As we crossed the city, I thought of the tens of thousands of bodies that lay under all that rubble, blackened by fire – during the two dreadful Operation Gomorrah raids 5,000 tons of bombs were dropped here, resulting in almost 100,000 victims.

The quay at Bremen harbour was littered with cars and I could see the troops parading around the platform on which the American and English were escorting Zhukov. It was for the benefit for these people that we were sweating. I only just had the time to see the harbour literally strewn with the wreckage of destroyed hangars and collapsed cranes.

Phew – we overflew, a little low, but the accuracy of the formation was confirmed by the official inquiry later. We regained altitude by gently turning towards Volkel beacon. At 3,000 feet I gave the order to open up the formation in order to soothe everyone's nerves. The planes started to move apart, sunlight flashing off their wings, against the backdrop of a beautiful blue sky.

A sudden scream came through the headphones: 'Christ!' At that moment to my total disbelief, I saw plane debris floating through the air and heard a dreadful crashing sound resonate through my fuselage.

According to witness statements and the report made by the commission of inquiry, what probably happened was that my No. 2 had omitted to transfer to his main fuel tank, so that when his supplementary tank ran dry the engine cut out. He was in close formation, just 2 yards from my own plane. His Tempest literally fell on top of No. 3, which nosed up violently, sending No. 2 hurtling into the air. The propeller of the latter then sliced into my fuselage. The shower of debris crippled No. 4. It was a miracle that, given the instant breaking out of formation of no fewer than thirty Tempests, there were no other collisions.

I was absolutely terrified and was to relive this moment for years in my nightmares. The small cloud I had selected to help me stay on course, so that I didn't have to keep checking my position on my gyro-positioner, disappeared in a flash above my head, replaced in my line of vision by fields, and a large red cross between the tents of a field hospital. Everything was swirling and jostling in front of me. My instinct for survival kicked in. I felt like a mouse being shaken in the jaws of a cat. What on earth had happened? If I didn't get out now, I would die. Quick, action – move, now. The savage tailspin glued me to the edges of my seat. My arm felt like lead as I tried to release the canopy, and suddenly I was ejected violently by the centrifugal force. One of my boots was still hooked to the seat and my helmet was ripped off my head by the wire of my headphones, which were still connected to the instrument panel.

My fingers fumbled on my chest, searching for the release button for my parachute. I panicked. The earth was hurtling towards me. My parachute opened with a booming sound like two cannons going off and catapulted me violently over a hedge onto my back. The canopy of the parachute then dragged me to a barbed wire fence to which it attached itself tight. I undid my harness automatically, trembling all the while. I remained seated, my throat blocked, breathless and feeling the ground shake as planes crashed into it. Four columns of black smoke mixed with flames were visible. I stood up, a bitter taste in my mouth, dry with panic. Where were the others? I spotted a twisted torch-shaped parachute, only half open, in the neighbouring field, not far away. I stumbled towards it and found a body, intact, with its arms crossed and smashed into the ground. My God, it was Peter! Planes flew overhead. Two left the formation and passed above me, wings waggling. My legs gave way and I fell to my knees, frozen and vomiting. All I wanted to do was stretch out on the ground and go to sleep. A voice spoke to me in German. I vaguely grasped the word '*Krankenwagen*' (ambulance). A woman leant over and took my hand to support me and help me stumble my way to a farm. My bootless leg was bleeding beneath my torn trousers. She gave me a glass of schnapps and I quickly felt better. She sent a small boy to keep watch on the road. Three-quarters of an hour later, alerted by the child, a jeep came looking for me, together with an ambulance. It was Group Captain Jamieson himself, looking distraught. He informed me that the three others were dead. Peter had jumped out too low and Campbell and Robertson were unable to extricate themselves. Such a terrible fate for these boys, after a long, hard year spent in battle.

What was I supposed to write to their mothers, who had lived through anxiety day after day, only to find their relief at the end of the conflict shattered by the arrival of my news?

The Wing left for Copenhagen, charged with the mission of escorting General Dempsey, Commander of the British Second Army, who was to receive the surrender of the German forces on Copenhagen island. The surrendering troops were to be protected by the huge cruiser *Königsberg*, which threatened to open fire on the town if the Resistance touched so much as a hair on the head of a single German soldier. Dempsey's plane was a Dakota that crawled along at 180 m.p.h. Despite the order not to land in Copenhagen, I decided that we would have to do so, since we did not have enough fuel to complete the return journey at the Dakota's slow speed. The seven pilots that I selected for this mission were very keen to take it on. The reputation of the Danish girls was well-known. No sooner said than done, and after a cautious passage flying level with the *Königsberg*, which carried a huge war flag with a swastika, we landed at Kaastrup, the capital's airport. While we awaited the arrival of the special 130-octane fuel that we needed for our engines, we were gripped for a few days by the intoxicating atmosphere of the liberation.

Two weeks later our squadron was invited by King Christian to be guests of the city of Copenhagen. The R.A.F. decided to organise a huge air display for the international press on 1 July. I was given the task of making a solo display in a Tempest. Had I known how to read the omens, I would not have gone against my instincts. The 'Grand Charles' had an oil leak – as it had had on the morning of 12 May. However, stubbornly and in order not to let anyone down, I borrowed Bruce's new plane for the occasion.

The planes completed an impeccable formation, flying low over the crowd and the fluttering red flags with white crosses that decorated the town. Fate then intervened to produce the outcome that I had dreaded, but which I had foolishly believed was unlikely. It was a stupid error of judgement. Everything seemed to go wrong, my landing gear dropped only halfway and the engine would not respond to my desperate opening up. At 200 m.p.h., the Tempest finally gave up and disintegrated, leaving the debris of its smashed wings, engine and tail plane strewn over half a mile.

The ambulance picked me up unhurt but dazed, and I finally understood that this was fate's supreme effort on my behalf, its last miracle and last warning. Fate had grown weary of protecting me.

For the record, the ambulance that collected me from the debris of my Tempest, which had crashed between the 'tiger teeth' of the anti-tank defences on the shoreline bordering the aerodrome, was halted by the Military Police in front of the VIP stand. Air Marshal Broadhurst and the King of Denmark wanted news of my condition. Reassured, the King shook me by the hand and said in French, 'Good luck.' Broadhurst, who had known me since 1943, leant towards me and said in a low voice, an ironic smile upon his face, 'Well, Clostermann, you never miss an opportunity to liven things up.'

A few days later, I was invited to the royal castle in Copenhagen, where King Christian X decorated me with the Order of Dannebröd!

A FINAL FAREWELL

27 August 1945

I had applied for immediate demobilisation and it had been granted. I had that morning gone to say my farewells to Broadhurst and to the R.A.F. The New Zealander Mackie was then commanding 122 Wing. I had made a point of going to H.Q. at Schleswig in my 'Grand Charles'. Coming back I had taken him high up in the cloudless summer sky, for it was only there that I could properly say goodbye. Together we climbed for the last time straight towards the sun. We looped once, perhaps twice, we lovingly did a few slow, meticulous rolls, so that I could take away in my finger-tips the vibration of his supple, docile wings.

And in that narrow cockpit I wept, as I shall never weep again, when I felt the concrete brush against his wheels and, with a great sweep of the wrist, dropped him on the ground like a cut flower.

As always, I carefully cleared the engine, turned off all the switches one by one, removed the straps, the wires and the tubes which tied me to him, like a child to his mother. And when my waiting pilots and my mechanics saw my downcast eyes and my shaking shoulders, they understood and returned to the Dispersal in silence.

I sat next to the pilot of the Mitchell which was to take me back to Paris. As he taxied towards the runway he passed in front of the aircraft of the Wing, smartly lined up wing tip to wing tip, as if for an inspection. By them stood the pilots and the mechanics, waving.

Slightly to one side stood my 'Grand Charles', my old JF-E, with its red spinner, the black crosses of our victories under the cockpit, compact, determined and powerful-looking with its big motionless four-bladed propeller, which would never again be started by me. It was like the turning of a page in a book.

To the accompaniment of the strident howl of its American engines, the Mitchell gathered speed and rose into the air. I glued my face to the window for a last glimpse behind our tail of Lübeck airfield, of the tiny glittering crosses on the grass, growing smaller and indistinct in the evening mist. The pilot, embarrassed, turned his head the other way.

It was all over. No more would I see my flight of Tempests line up behind my 'Grand Charles', clumsy looking on their long legs, offering the yawning hole of their radiators to the wind from their propellers, with the trustful faces of their pilots leaning out of the cockpits, waiting for my signal.

But pride welled up within me when I thought of you, my planes, and above all of you, my dear R.A.F. friends, whom I had had the privilege of knowing and living amongst, with your uniforms the colour of your island mists.

The Big Show was over. The public had been satisfied. The programme had been rather heavy, the actors not too bad, and the lions had eaten the trainer. It would be discussed for a day or two more round the family table. And even when it was all forgotten – the band, the fireworks, the resplendent uniforms – there would still remain on the village green the holes of the tent pegs and a circle of sawdust. The rain and the shortness of man's memory would soon wipe out even those.

APPENDIX A
PREFACE TO THE ORIGINAL EDITION

For four years my parents and I – their only child – were separated by many thousands of miles. Between London and Brazzaville the mails were erratic, and any reference in letters to military matters were heavily censored. It was possible to send them a monthly air-letter, but that was too cramped for any description of my life in England with the Free French and the R.A.F. Yet I did want to make my father and mother understand this new life and the mingled feelings it aroused, a life that was unforeseen, often harsh but deeply satisfying. I wanted them to live it with me, day by day, even if I did not come back to describe it myself.

So every evening I used to write down for them the events of the day in a fat Air Ministry notebook, stamped 'G.R.' In an old envelope, stuck to the cover, I put my will; it was rather an absurd gesture, for General de Gaulle's 'mercenaries' had no goods and chattels to dispose of except their faith in France and their uncertain dreams of home. On the flyleaf I wrote: 'In case I should be killed or posted missing, I want this book to be sent to my father, Captain Jacques Clostermann, French Headquarters, Brazzaville. 10.3.1942.' This notebook went with me everywhere, crumpled by the weight of my parachute in the cockpit, stained with tea in the mess, or beside me at Dispersal during the long, dull hours of readiness. From the Orkneys to Cornwall, from Kent to Scotland, from Normandy to Denmark through Belgium, Holland and Germany, these notes – by the end of the war they filled three books – were always with me.

Fate, so cruel to most of my friends, decreed that I should survive 420 sorties and that one day I should be able to tell my father, in my own words, the story of those four years. The notebooks remained unread for two years. In that time, with the other few survivors of the Free French Air Force, I had the painful task of visiting the families of our friends who had not come back and giving them the bitter consolation of hearing of their sons' deeds. We also met a number of Frenchmen who had no idea of what had happened on the other side of the Channel, and who – in some cases – didn't want to learn. But equally we knew that there were many who were trying to find out, in the hope perhaps of being reminded of their own hopes and loyalties.

It is for them that this book is published. Change the dates and a few minor details and it is a record of the daily life of every fighter pilot. Any of my comrades could produce similar episodes by looking through his log-books.

I ask the reader not to expect a work of literature. I simply jotted down day by day the impressions, the fleetingly-caught incidents so sharply imprinted on my memory. It would require a remarkable talent to reproduce with truth and at the same time with literary grace the life of a fighter pilot in the last war. It is precisely because they are *true*, because they were written in the flush of action, that I have made no attempt to retouch these notes.

PIERRE CLOSTERMANN

APPENDIX B

NOTES ON THE ORGANISATION OF THE R.A.F.

The R.A.F. was divided into four commands: Fighter Command, Bomber Command, Coastal Command, and Training Command. Before the Normandy landings, this organisation changed slightly with the creation of the Tactical Air Force.

Each Command was comprised of Groups. In Fighter Command, No. 11 Group, for example, was in charge of defending South East England and London.

Each Group was divided into Wings. In the beginning, and up until 1943, the Wings belonged to an airfield, for example the Biggin Hill Wing, Kenley Wing, Tangmere Wing, etc.

Each Wing consisted of three or four Squadrons. Each Squadron had a number ('Alsace' Squadron, for example, was called No. 341 Free French Squadron in the R.A.F.) and the aircraft were identified by a group of letters. For example, 'Alsace' Squadron's aircraft had the letters 'NL', No. 602 Squadron the letters 'LO', No. 274 Squadron 'JJ', No. 3 Squadron 'JF', and so on. Each aircraft in each squadron also had a personal identification letter. The various aircraft in the squadrons that I belonged to were, for example: NL-B, LO-D, and my beloved 'Grand Charles' was JF-E.

Each Squadron was composed of two Flights: A and B. In the Fighter Squadrons, each Flight usually had twelve aircraft.

A Fighter Group was commanded by a Vice-Air Marshal. A Wing of single engine fighters was commanded by a Wing Commander, a Squadron by a Squadron Leader and a Flight by a Flight Lieutenant. A Group Captain commanded each air base.

Each Squadron had an average of 24 aircraft and 30 or 32 pilots, of which at least a third were non-commissioned officers (NCOs). In addition, there was a Warrant Officer, an Engineer Officer, a Flight Sergeant (traditionally called 'Chieffy' – a very important person) who in turn commanded a Sergeant Armourer, a Sergeant Radio Mechanic and a Sergeant Aircraft Engineer. Then there were forty or so ground staff: mechanics, armourers, airframe, engine and radio specialists. All in all, air and ground staff together came to around one hundred men.

Each Squadron had a radio code name: for example 'Alsace' Squadron's code name was *Turban*, and No. 3 Squadron's was *Filmstar*. In order to identify the aircraft in flight, in combat formation the codes were as follows:

Blue Section	Red Section	Yellow Section
T	T	T
T 1 T	T 1 T	T 1 T
3 2	3 2	3 2
T	T	T
4	4	4

A Squadron's combat formation comprised twelve aircraft divided into three sections of four aircraft. The Squadron Leader's code name was Turban Leader. Flight B's Flight Leader: *Turban Yellow Leader* and Flight A's Flight Leader: *Turban Blue Leader*, or *Blue 1*. The other pilots were called by their position number: *Turban Blue 4*, for example.

	CODE				DECODE	
135						
Abbeville	W	Dunkirk	D	A	Beachy Head	N	Bandit
Beachy Head	A	Gravesend	R	B	Pancake	O	Convoy (S)
Biggin Hill	Q	Gris Nez	F	C	Le Touquet	P	Hawkinge
Boulogne	J	Hawkinge	P	D	Dunkirk	Q	Biggin Hill
Calais	G	Le Touquet	C	E	Fr'dly Bomber	R	Gravesend
Chatham	U	Maidstone	X	F	Gris Nez	S	Fr'dly Fighter
Dover	L	Manston	K	G	Calais	T	Convoy (W)
Dungeness	Z	St. Omer	I	H	Pancake	U	Chatham
Convoy (E)	M	Convoy (N)	V	I	St. Omer	V	Convoy (N)
Convoy (W)	T	Convoy (S)	O	J	Boulogne	W	Abbeville
Fr'dly Bomber	E	PANCAKE	B	K	Manston	X	Maidstone
Fr'dly Fighter	S	PANCAKE	H	L	Dover	Y	Pancake
Bandit	N		Y	M	Convoy (E)	Z	Dungeness

0	1	2	4	6	8	10	12	14	16	18	20	22	24	26	28	30	32	34	36	38	40	45	A/c	B/c	I/c
D	G	B	X	H	Y	V	O	Z	M	T	K	S	I	W	L	J	N	R	F	P	E	A	C	U	Q

A	B	C	D	E	F	G	H	I	J	K	L	M	N	O	P	Q	R	S	T	U	V	W	X	Y	Z
45	2	A/c	0	40	36	1	6	24	30	20	28	16	32	12	38	I/c	34	22	18	B/c	10	26	4	8	14

Reproduction of one of the code cards used by R.A.F. controllers and pilots to communicate by radio. The numbers indicate the altitude in thousands of feet. Thus, for example, the controller might have ordered a pilot to go to W to intercept five N at altitude K. This meant: 'Rendezvous over Abbeville, five German aircraft patrolling at an altitude of 20,000 feet.' These cards were changed every week.

For individual flights, or for strictly personal calls, each pilot had his own code name; for example in the Alsace Squadron, my code name was *Turban 25*.

The Groups were divided into sectors, and tactical air control was entrusted to a G.C.C. (Group Central Control). G.C.C.'s headquarters was in a large underground concrete bunker overhung by glass-fronted balconies where the controllers worked. This was Fighter Command's nerve centre. It was here that all the radar information was received, and immediately transferred onto an enormous map that covered the bunker floor. On the walls were huge boards showing the state of each Flight, the number, name and code name of all its pilots, its position, the number of aircraft in flight, on the ground, rearming or refuelling.

Small signposts and different coloured arrows were placed on the big map indicating at 30 second intervals the position, altitude, course and strength of the formations in flight, both allied and enemy.

A W.A.A.F. (a member of the Women's Auxiliary Air Force) with a telephone headset on, in direct contact with the radar stations, was allotted to each of these signposts, which she moved around the map with a long croupier rake.

In his glass cage, the senior controller therefore had an immediate and comprehensive view of everything going on in his sector, from London to Chartres, and as far afield as Denmark. On his table were a dozen telephones connected to short circuit radio, enabling him to communicate with all of the Flights, even far into enemy territory.

There were two types of radar stations: early warning and ground control interception stations, which were extremely powerful and could track a German aircraft over Paris to within just a few of hundred yards of its precise location. The girls indicated the positions of the Luftwaffe formations to its flight units, moving them around the map like chess pieces. The flight units were only given complete freedom of action once they engaged with the enemy aircraft. Loudspeakers on the walls enabled them to hear all that was being said in the air, the pilot's remarks, responses to orders, and even swearwords uttered in combat.

The controller determined the state of alert for the squadrons on the ground:

Immediate readiness: four, six or twelve aircraft ready to depart, their pilots seated and strapped in, with motors running. This way, twelve aircraft were ready to take off 30 seconds after the 'scramble' signal.

Stand-by readiness: four, six, or twelve aircraft with motors running, ready to take off in one minute.

Readiness: six aircraft, pilots ready, motors running, ready to take off in 2 minutes.

Fifteen minute readiness: pilots in the airfield within earshot of the loudspeakers (either in the mess or in their rooms), ready to take off 15 minutes after the 'scramble' signal.

Available: a group whose aircraft had just landed and were resupplying, but were ready to take off again in 30 minutes.

At the G.C.C., they planned the 'sweeps' (sweeping action against enemy fighters, carried out exclusively by the fighter pilots), 'circuses' (bombing with a powerful escort of fighter planes, aimed at forcing the German fighters to engage in combat) and 'rhubarbs' (a kind of armed reconnaissance mission led by sections of two or four fighters, hedgehopping in enemy territory). Orders were sent to the Intelligence Officers of the various Wings via teletype and an operation order was called a 'D Form'.

At the G.C.C. there were also claims boards, where tactical experts, aeronautical engineers and other qualified staff used special projectors to examine videos of combats in order to decide whether to attribute kills. An enemy aircraft was considered 'Destroyed' when filmed exploding in the air, when its pilot was filmed parachuting from his aircraft or when the debris was filmed on the ground. It was considered 'Probably Destroyed' when it was filmed on fire, severely hit in its vital parts but, for one reason or another, the pilot was unable to film the debris on the ground. And it was considered 'Damaged' when severely hit and put out of combat, but not presumed to have been completely destroyed.

Attached to the wings of all R.A.F. fighter planes was a camera linked to the gun trigger, and carefully aligned with micro-metrical screws to the intersection of the wing guns' projectiles. This way, the pilot could bring back unquestionable proof of his gunfire, his tactical ability and the results he obtained. This was essential for the confirmation of kills.

The British military decorations were awarded very parsimoniously.* A Distinguished Flying Cross was awarded after five kills in around one hundred missions. A Bar to the D.F.C. was given between the tenth and twentieth kill and finally, the Distinguished Service Order was given to Wing Commanders or Squadron Commanders after twenty kills or three hundred missions. The Victoria Cross, the highest award for bravery in the British armed services, was only awarded to one fighter pilot throughout the Second World War: Squadron Leader J.B. Nicholson.

The French pilots seconded to the R.A.F. received these decorations just like the British subjects. With the usual British 'fair play', there was an extraordinary impartiality concerning these awards, which were overseen by the King himself and, consequently, we Frenchmen attached great value to these distinctions.

The R.A.F. motto was, and still is: *Per ardua ad astra*.

The R.A.F.'s 2nd Tactical Air Force was organised to follow and directly support the efforts of the British 21st Army Group under the orders of Field Marshal Montgomery as well as providing close support for the 1st U.S. Army. The II T.A.F. was divided into five Groups:

No. 83 Group, under the orders of Vice-Air Marshal Broadhurst, was mainly comprised of fighters.

No. 84 Group was mainly comprised of Wings of fighter-bombers.

No. 85 Group represented the strategic reserves, with a number of Fighter Wings and Night-fighter Flights.

No. 2 Group was composed of two Wings of medium-range bombers and a Wing of light bombers (Mosquitos).

No. 1 Group was in charge of communications and transportation, equipped with Dakotas and Ansons. (This group changed code name at the end of 1944, and became No. 38 Group).

Therefore, the front line (not including the reserve) aircraft of each unit was comprised of:

---

* The author received his first D.F.C. after 8 confirmed kills and almost 300 missions, his second D.F.C. after 370 missions and 20 kills and finally a D.S.O. after 420 missions, 33 kills and the successful command of a Squadron and a Wing.

70 Mitchell medium-range bombers
38 Mosquito light bombers
1,764 fighter and fighter-bomber aircraft (Tempests, Spitfires and Typhoons)
156 strategic and tactical reconnaissance Spitfires.

APPENDIX C

RAIDS BY R.A.F. FIGHTER PILOTS ON GROUND TARGETS IN OCCUPIED TERRITORY

Air raids on various ground targets in enemy occupied territory (France, Belgium and Holland) was strictly regulated in the R.A.F. and harsh disciplinary action was taken against pilots that were guilty of misconduct. Later, when the U.S. Air Force started to operate from British air bases, the British Air Ministry demanded that the U.S. pilots comply with the same regulations, but this was to no avail.

Here is a fairly interesting document responding to complaints that I regularly heard being made about 'R.A.F. aircraft gunning down women and children'.

SECRET

```
For immediate insertion into the Pilots' Order book
From: Headquarters No. 11 Group.
To: All Fighter Sectors
Ref: 11G / S.500/39/OPS 1
Date: 17th April 1943
```

AIR RAID REGULATIONS

Various breaches of discipline have recently taken place, concerning pilots engaged in offensive action against targets forbidden by the terms in memorandum 53/1942 from Headquarters No. 11 Group and by memorandum 96 dated 12th November regulating 'Rhubarb' operations.

Although we might understand that certain pilots returning from offensive action or engaged in 'Rhubarb' operations may feel inclined to attack all targets that seem to be of military interest, it is crucial we remind these pilots that the priority and choice of these targets are established with the greatest concern for the well-being of the populations that inhabit these territories. Pilots who do not observe these regulations will be subject to severe disciplinary action. In addition, it must not be forgotten that these oppressed populations provide tremendous aid to our pilots who are forced to parachute from their aircraft or make emergency landings in enemy-controlled zones.

Therefore, we would like to draw everyone's attention once again to appendix A3 part II of memorandum 96, which gives an easy-to-remember list of forbidden targets.

Signed: Air Commodore E.H. Stevens
Senior Staff Officer
No. 11 Group, Royal Air Force

Appendix A3
The following objects must not be attacked at any cost:
In enemy occupied territories.
1. Non-military targets (factories not individually specified and indicated by written order for attack – villages, houses, animals, civilians and private property in general).
2. Camps and barracks – unless they are occupied by enemy forces and written orders to attack them have been issued by the Air Ministry.
3. Lighthouses.
4. Castles (unless under special order from Fighter Command).
5. Windmills.
6. Electrical power plants in Holland.
7. Water towers.
8. Passenger trains and engines attached to passenger trains except for:
   a. in France at night
   b. in Holland and Belgium between 2300 hours and 0400 hours and south of the river Waal-Rhine.
9. Fishing boats.
10. Radio stations and pylons – including radar stations (apart for on special order from Fighter Command).
11. Targets in the Channel Islands (apart for on special order from Fighter Command).
12. Buoys and other maritime navigation signals.
13. Gas plants.
14. Alcohol distilleries.

German and Italian territories.
All of the targets forbidden by the Red Cross conventions.

APPENDIX D

CAPTAIN PIERRE CLOSTERMANN'S VICTORIES

Confirmed kills in aerial combat:
19 Focke-Wulf 190
7 Messerschmitt 109
2 Dornier 24
1 Fieseler 156
1 Junkers 252
1 Junkers 88
1 Junkers 290
1 Heinkel 111

Enemy aircraft probably destroyed or severely damaged during cannon raids on airfields:
7 Junkers 88 and 188
6 Dornier 18
4 Heinkel 177
3 Arado 232
2 Focke-Wulf 190
1 Junkers 252
1 Blohm & Voss 138

Enemy aircraft severely damaged or probably destroyed during aerial combat:
6 Focke-Wulf 190
6 Messerschmitt 109

Various confirmed ground and sea targets:
62 locomotives and around 100 trains destroyed
125 trucks and other road vehicles, among them some 30 fuel trucks
5 tanks
2 motor torpedo boats
Various targets attacked and destroyed with bombs and cannons, including an oil refinery in Gadesbuden, where 150,000 gallons of aviation fuel were destroyed, etc.

Number of completed missions:
   293 long-range offensive missions
   67 attack missions, cannon attacks and dive-bombings against ground targets
   42 defensive missions

APPENDIX E
COMBAT REPORTS

COMBAT REPORT 122/3347/83/II T.A.F.

Flight Lieutenant P.H. Clostermann D.F.C.
No. 56 Squadron – Tempest V – take-off: 1115 hrs – landing:
1318 hrs – combat location: Hameln – altitude 4,000 feet –
enemy losses: 2 'long-nosed' Focke-Wulf disabled

Personal report:
I was leading No.56 Squadron's Green section in a patrol of the
Osnabrück-Uchte region. At approximately 1210 hours, in the
Osnabrück region, we heard via radio that the Squadron code
named 'MacDuff' had met with enemy aircraft in the Rheine
region.
  A few minutes later, whilst making a 180° turn, I sighted
seven 'long-nosed' Focke-Wulf 190's, flying eastwards at 3,700
feet.
  There was 6/10° of cloud cover at around 3,000 feet and we
were flying just below it. I reversed my turn immediately,
followed by my section, and we jettisoned our reserve fuel. I
was now above the clouds, 2,000 yards behind the enemy formation. At full speed, I managed to get within 1,000 yards'
range. The Fw then saw me and veered off to the left. I made a
frontal pass then pulled up to within 200 yards and 25° from
the enemy patrol leader. I fired three bursts and the third
produced explosions on the wing root and along the aircraft's
fuselage. The Fw dived towards me and I lost sight of it. I made
a half roll and dived at 90° on another Fw. I fired a long and
continuous burst, reducing the deflection from 80° to 50°, and
hit his right wing. A dozen other Fw's then appeared from the
west and I pulled back towards the clouds, followed by my three
comrades.
  – The video camera worked.
  – The four cannon respectively fired 82, 84, 81 and 83 20 mm.
    shells.

COMBAT REPORT 122/3475/83/II T.A.F.

No. 3 Squadron – Tempest V – take-off: 1808 hrs – landing: 2003 hrs – combat location: Aldhorn airfield – altitude: 0 – enemy losses: 1 Focke-Wulf 109 D9 destroyed in the air, 2 Junkers 188's disabled on the ground.

Personal report:
I was leading *Filmstar* Yellow section on armed reconnaissance over the Bremen-Hanover region. We attacked a number of motor vehicles on the main road between the Cloppenburg and Aalhorn airfields. As I rolled out of my first strafing pass, I sighted two enemy fighters taking off from Aalhorn whilst a barrage of flak came at us.

I warned my section, and dived from 4,000 feet onto the second aircraft as it was lifting its landing gear. Skimming the runway, I attacked from the rear at 5° and below 30 feet. I fired a 30-second burst, opening fire at 400 yards and ending at 50 yards. I saw the impacts of my shells on the concrete runway below and around the aircraft that I identified as being a 'long-nosed' Focke-Wulf 190 D9. Severely hit, the enemy aircraft swerved off to the left and crashed against the airfield, scattering burning debris all over the place. My aircraft was covered with sprayed oil from the Fw's burst fuel tanks.

The other enemy aircraft was still in the vicinity, but I could not make a tight enough turn to engage with it. Since the flak was violent, I decided to stay close to the ground and in passing I fired at a group of 5 Junkers 188's parked in a small wood at the end of the runway. I concentrated my fire on the first two. My shells hit the motors and the cockpits, but neither caught fire.

Then my aircraft was hit by a 20 mm. flak shell. I headed back to base and destroyed 3 trucks and trailers on the way back.
  – The video camera worked.
  – The four cannon respectively fired: 146, 185, 184 and 150 20 mm. shells.

COMBAT REPORT 125/541/83/II T.A.F.

Pilot Officer P.H. Clostermann
No. 602 Squadron – Spitfire IX B – take-off 1105 hrs – landing 1157 hrs – combat location: Caen region – altitude: between 2,100 feet and 7,000 feet – enemy losses: 1 Messerschmitt 109 G probably destroyed, 1 Focke-Wulf 190 destroyed.

Personal report:
At 1105 hours No. 602 Squadron's Red section took off on alert, lead by me.

At 1107 hours Longues D.A.C. opened fire on twelve German fighters patrolling our base above the clouds at around 3,000 feet. Followed by my No. 2 Pilot Officer Kidd (R.C.A.F.) I headed straight up through the clouds.

Just as I came out of the clouds, a Messerschmitt 109 made a frontal pass at us. My No. 2 then engaged two Me 109's, 500 yards above to my right, whilst I attacked four Messerschmitts that were threatening our left flank. After a few preliminary passes I opened fire on one of the Me 109's and, after two bursts of 20 mm. shells and machine-gun fire, the enemy aircraft nose-dived into the clouds, leaving behind a trail of thick black smoke and a shower of debris. I followed it into the cloud, just firing my machine guns. Suddenly the Me 109 made a violent reverse turn at 700 feet and disappeared. Caught up in his turbulence, I lost control of my aircraft for a moment in a stall. Then I headed back up to 6,000 feet alone, following the controller's announcement of a strong formation of Germans concentrating behind Caen.

Just as I arrived above Caen Carpiquet, I was engaged by four Focke-Wulf 190's, whose patrol leader zoomed up to attack me from below. I faced them, opening fire with a continuous burst at a range of 800 yards to 40 yards. There was a series of explosions along the Fw's left wing leading edge. The engine cowling came off, breaking the vertical rudder. The enemy aircraft went into a spin, and despite the pilot's obvious efforts, crashed near to the airfield's south-west hangar. I then managed to disengage from the three others.

- The video camera worked: 6 feet of film.
- The two cannon respectively fired 75 and 76 20 mm. shells.
- The four machine guns fired 299, 300, 300 and 300 7 mm. bullets.

COMBAT REPORT 125/612/83/II T.A.F.

Pilot Officer P.H. Clostermann
No. 602 Squadron – Spitfire IX B – take-off 1520 hrs – landing 1635 hrs – combat location: Saint-Lô region – altitude: 1,200 feet – enemy losses: 1 Messerschmitt 109, probably destroyed.

Personal report:
I was flying as No. 2 to Flt. Lt Charney D.F.C in the Saint-Lô region around 1600 hours. After having attacked two trucks, we were engaged by four Messerschmitt 109's. I broke off from the attack and following four 360° turns I managed to place myself

at the rear of a Me 109 which I fired at from a range of 200 yards to 120 yards.

I saw a number of serious impacts on the engine and the cockpit. There was a thick cloud of glycol pouring out of one of the punctured radiators. Twice there was a sort of explosion from under the engine, followed by a shower of debris.

Before I managed to finish him off, I was hit by two incendiary bullets fired by another Me 109 and I had to break off and fire three quarters in front, to no avail.

- The film camera worked.
- The two cannons respectively fired 60 and 60 20 mm. shells.
- The four machine guns fired 223, 14 (it jammed), 222, 223 bullets respectively.

APPENDIX F

NOTES ON THE LUFTWAFFE

The Messerschmitt 109

The Messerschmitt 109, despite the introduction of the Focke-Wulf 190, formed the backbone of the Luftwaffe's *Jagdgeschwader* throughout the war.

A contemporary of the 'Spitfire' (both these aircraft were designed in 1934–35), it was constantly being improved by Germany's engineers.

Its main characteristic was its speed. Thanks to various improved features (GM-1, methanol injection in the cylinders, for example) which were easily adaptable to its Daimler Benz 605 1,800 h.p. in-line engine, the last Me 109 models such as the 109 K-14, came close to flying at 450 m.p.h.

Its very small dimensions (area 172sq.ft wingspan 29½ ft and length 29ft), and light weight (just over 7,000 lbs.), helped it to climb admirably. However, it had one serious fault: at high speed the controls jammed, which made it extremely difficult to handle. It was usually armed with three 20 mm. cannon, one firing through its propeller boss, and two light machine guns. Certain German pilots preferred the centrally-mounted cannon and two heavy machine guns on the cowling. In the last two months of the war this solution became standard, sometimes with a 30 mm. cannon, instead of the 151/20.

Although it was faster than the Spitfire, it was much less manoeuvrable. Later, in spite of our superior speed, we had to be very careful with our Tempest against the 109, because under 450km/h they turned better than us, especially at medium altitude.

For the Germans, the great advantage of the '109' was the ease with which it could be manufactured – almost 30,000 Me 109's were built during the war, in twenty-seven factories, the most famous of which was Regensburg.

An interesting detail: all the great German 'aces', with the exception of Walter Nowotny and Hermann Graf, always preferred the Me 109 to the Fw 190, probably because of its speed and its rate of climb (23,000ft in 6 minutes). However, in contrast to the Fw 190, it was not pleasant to pilot, with a narrow cockpit, whose interior was cluttered with fixtures and bracing struts, fragile and dangerous landing gear and an immense vulnerability.

The Messerschmitt 262

The Messerschmitt 262, the first jet fighter to be used successfully and in large numbers in the Second World War, was a splendid machine, whose aerodynamics were unequalled, even in the products of the Anglo-American technical advances of 1946–47.

Designed in 1941, and shrouded in secrecy, the first '262' flew at the end of 1942 with two Jumo 004 turbines. Following various trials and tribulations, due to the untimely interventions of the Luftministerium and Hitler himself, manufacturing was launched at the beginning of 1944. The lack of special metals for the axes and turbine bearings led to many setbacks. However, despite the limited power of the Jumo 004 B, the '262' reached a speed of 575 m.p.h., and was armed with four 30 mm. cannon.

This was revolutionary in aviation tactics, and it is certain that the appearance of the '262' in the fighter units aroused serious concern in the allied staff. Some '262' were especially effective against Flying Fortresses. In March of 1945, for example, six Me 262's left from Oberammergau test centre under the command of General Gollob and Nowotny, who piloted two of the aircraft themselves. They downed 14 Flying Fortresses in a single flight. These Me 262's were each equipped with 48 RM4 rockets, constructed in the R.W. factories at a rate of 25,000 per month. Luckily, it was too late.

The Me 262 had the following characteristics: wingspan, 41ft; length, 35ft; wing area, 226sq.ft; total weight, 17,600 lbs.; length of take-off on a concrete runway in 12 m.p.h. winds, 1,100 yards.

On the evening of 5 May, a few hours after the 'cease-fire', five Messerschmitt 262's appeared in the Fassberg circuit. They were coming from Prague, which was under Soviet siege, and after having strafed the Russian lines, they headed our way. These were the first '262's' captured intact, with all of their combat equipment.

A few days later, when they were taken by convoy to Lübeck in order to transport them to the R.A.F. test sites in England, it was the German pilots, almost with tears in their eyes, that had to give us the necessary instructions to pilot them. We were amazed by the beauty, and the technical prowess and progress behind these admirable machines.

'Somky' Schraeder, who commanded No. 616 squadron of Meteors, skilfully lifted one of them off the ground, and by some miracle, everything went smoothly, with the first four aircraft at least. The last of them obstinately refused to start.

The Focke-Wulf 190

We encountered two main models of Focke-Wulf: from 1941 to the end of 1943 with a radial engine (Fw 190 A9); from the end of 1943 to 1945 with an in-line engine ('long-nosed' Fw 190 D9).

Almost 15,000 Fw 190's were built in the thirteen main factories run by the Focke-Wulf company, of which the most renowned were Marienburg, Halberstadt, Wismes, Cassel, Sorau and Schwerin.

A single-seater aircraft with a single engine, entirely built in metal, fast and smooth to pilot and very well armed, in good hands the Focke-Wulf was a formidable adversary. With its 14-cylinder 1,875 h.p. radial engine (BMW 801 TS), this compact machine could reach speeds of up to 420 m.p.h. Weighing 4 tons, its wing area was 194sq.ft, its wingspan 33ft and length 29ft. It was powerfully armed with four 22 mm. MG 151 quick-firing cannon and two 13 mm. heavy machine guns. Thanks to its weapons' rate of fire, it had double the firing capacity of the Spitfire IX.

It could dive very quickly, and its ailerons were phenomenally supple, giving it a definite advantage in combat when it came to vertical manoeuvres. However, the Spitfire banked much better, which balanced out its chances in combat. Nevertheless, the Focke-Wulf 190 always had the invaluable capacity to break off an engagement thanks to its acceleration.

The 'long-nosed' Focke-Wulf 190 was an improvement on the classic 190. The first were identified in combat in the summer of 1943, and by the end of 1944, it had replaced the Focke-Wulf A9 in most of the Luftwaffe's squadrons. Its 2,000 h.p. cylinder engine gave it a slim shape, which was a great improvement in aerodynamic terms, enabling it to reach speeds of over 450 m.p.h. It was 6ft longer, and in the last phases of the war – with the exception of the Tempest – the 'long-nosed' Focke-Wulf proved to be far superior to the other allied fighter planes in low and medium altitude combat.

Its weapons had been revised – three 20 mm. cannon, one of which fired through the middle of the propeller (this 20 mm. cannon was occasionally replaced with a 30 mm. MK 103 cannon) and two heavy machine guns on the cowling. Its climbing power was a considerable 26,000ft in 10 minutes. Lighter than the Tempest, slightly less fast when flying level and especially when diving, the 'long-nosed' Fw 190 nevertheless climbed a little better and retained a certain superiority in terms of aileron roll. The performance in combat of the two machines was practically the same, the Tempest's only advantage being its acceleration.

All the allied aviators who had the chance to try out the Fw 190 were unanimously of the opinion that it was extremely pleasant to pilot. Its remarkable visibility, good protection thanks to the well-distributed armour-plating, a very comfortable piloting position, with feet high up, which helped greatly to resist against the deadly centrifugal force at high speed – all these qualities, combined with an extremely smooth manoeuvrability, even at high speed, made it a very dangerous adversary.

The Dornier 335

A small number of these aircraft were built from the end of 1944. Its design was strange, with a tractor engine at the front and a pusher engine at the back. The Dornier 335 could be used as a one-seater for fighting by day or as a two-seater for night combat. It was a large machine, 45½ft long, with a wingspan of 42½ft, a surface area of 377sq.ft, and weighing 6 tons. With two 1,700 h.p. Daimler Benz 603 engines each, it comfortably reached speeds of 470 m.p.h. It was armed with three 30 mm. cannons and two heavy machine guns on the cowling.

In reality, the Do 335 had been designed as a mixed-powerplant heavy fighter plane, with a Daimler Benz engine at the front and a jet engine at the back.

The Do 335 was hardly ever used in active operations.

The Arado 234

The first Arado 234, a reconnaissance jet plane, was first flown in December 1943 and mass production was started in the factories at Warnemunde in June 1944.

It was used for high altitude reconnaissance and especially for the tactical bombing of a number of very well-defended targets. This aircraft (the Arado 234 B) can be considered as the first jet bomber. It carried a 1,100 lb. bomb under its two turbines and a one-ton bomb under its fuselage. It flew at speeds of up to 490 m.p.h. Bigger than the Messerschmitt 262 (wingspan 49ft, length 42½ft, surface area 290sq.ft), it weighed almost 10 tons when loaded. It was extremely hard to take off when loaded, and it needed a runway of at least a mile and a quarter. Later, the Germans installed a jettisonable undercarriage and four rocket-assisted take-off boosters, thanks to which the take-off distance was reduced to around 650 yards.

The Arado 234 had a shape similar to that of the U.S. B-26 Marauder, and this similarity often led to confusion. Around 350 of these Arado were brought into service.

The Arado 234 C had four turbines and was designed to replace the A model in the squadrons. Only a very small number were delivered before the Armistice, but nevertheless, this aircraft appears to have been a first rate technical success, with a speed of 560 m.p.h. and remarkable stability.

The Arado 232

The Arado 232 was a transport aircraft, designed exclusively for that use. It had a very peculiar shape, with its four Bramo engines, its boom-type configuration and especially the eleven pairs of wheels under the fuselage.

It was used for the transportation of spare parts, fuel, engines and frequently as a troop carrier. Quite a large number of this aircraft were built and most of them were used to evacuate the officers to Norway in the last few days of the war. Its characteristics: maximum speed, 210 m.p.h.; wingspan, 110ft; length, 77ft; surface area, 1,930 sq.ft; total weight, 22 tons.

APPENDIX G
SOME OPINIONS CONCERNING THE GERMAN FIGHTERS

Group Captain Leslie E Simmonds, director of the technical and ballistic research services of the laboratory in Aberdeen (British Army G.H.Q.):

> German fighter planes were always first class. Although they were not without defects, their jet planes had a demoralising impact on the allied staff. The Messerschmitt 262 and the last Focke-Wulf models posed a real threat for the allied aviation supremacy up until the last days of the war. They flew at exceptional speeds, and the German fighter planes' weapons were far superior to ours.
>
> (Report to S.H.A.E.F. on German Research.)

Professor O.P. Fuchs, from the Zurich Institute (Switzerland), weapons expert assigned to the North American Committee for Aeronautics in the U.S.A.:

> Whilst during the period of July-August-September 1944 the reports of losses on either side was 1 to 1 (i.e. for the total losses recorded in combat on the German side, the same number were recorded on the allied side, especially the fighters, and a small proportion of bombers), from 22 February to 26 March 1945 (reliable data can only be given for this period) the ratio was 1 to 7.5, due to the use of the new Gollob gun/rocket combination. So, for *the total of German fighters destroyed, there were seven and a half times as many allied losses* (this time with a large proportion of four-engine bombers). These figures speak for themselves.
>
> (*From the estimate of onboard weaponry efficiency. Interavia*, 1/48.)

Samuel W. Taylor, former commander of the Tactical Bureau in the G.H.Q. of the 8th U.S. Air Force:

> We have always regarded the Luftwaffe as a very dangerous and technically superior adversary. The Luftwaffe might have indeed lost ninety-nine per cent. of its best pilots in action since 1939, and it may also have been obliged to put together a front line of inexperienced fighters. However, it

has always managed to develop offensive and defensive tactics that have proved to be highly efficient.

(Report for the year of 1944 – 8th Air Force.)

APPENDIX H

FRENCH CITATIONS CONCERNING THE AUTHOR
(MENTIONS IN DISPATCHES)

Amongst the French citations that have been awarded to Pierre Clostermann, the editor has thought fit to cite the following, which are related to a number of events in the text.

Flight Sergeant Pierre Clostermann – 'Alsace' Group.
'A valiant pilot, gifted with remarkable virtuous qualities. An ardent and very enthusiastic fighter. He has participated in twenty-two offensive missions over enemy-occupied territory. In an act of hardy determination, he gained two victories during a combat against Focke-Wulf 190's on 27 July 1943.
'This citation carries the award of a Croix de Guerre with palm.'
General order 13 of 15/09/43.

Flight Sergeant Pierre Clostermann – Fighter Group 'Alsace'.
'A fiery young pilot full of energy. He gained his third official victory on 27 August 1943, after having single-handedly attacked an enemy formation of Fw 190's.
'This citation carries the award of a Croix de Guerre with palm.'

Acting Pilot Officer Clostermann Pierre – on detachment to G.C. in the R.A.F.
'A pilot of great distinction, with remarkable energy and virtuosity, he is an exemplar cadet. Totalling over 184 war-time flight hours in the course of 125 missions of which 105 offensive missions over enemy occupied territory and five successful dive-bombings of particularly well-defended coastal batteries. Three Fw 190's destroyed in combat, two Me 109's and a Fw 190 damaged during air combat, a locomotive destroyed and numerous targets damaged, all to his credit.
'This citation carries the award of a Croix de Guerre with palm.'
Decision 14.344/S/DPM/I.

Acting Pilot Officer Clostermann Pierre – No. 602 Squadron of the R.A.F.
'A remarkable pilot. His courage and skill uphold the prestige of the French within the English group that he has served with for the past ten months. On 7 January 1944, when attacked alone above Abbeville by a formation of three Fw 190's, he damaged one of them.
'This citation carries the award of a Croix de Guerre with palm.'
Decision 08/09/44.

Acting Pilot Officer Clostermann Pierre – on detachment to G.C. in the R.A.F.
'A brilliant fighter pilot who, on 15 June 1944, during a free fighter mission, destroyed a Fw 190 on the Normandy front.
'This citation carries the award of a Croix de Guerre with palm.'

Decision No. 109 of 30/10/44.

Acting Pilot Officer Clostermann Pierre – on detachment to G.C. in the R.A.F.
'A young, courageous and thoughtful fighter who has once again distinguished himself on the Normandy front by destroying a Focke-Wulf 190 after having probably destroyed a Messerschmitt 109 during the same sweep on 26 June 1944.
'This citation carries the award of a Croix de Guerre with palm.'

Decision No. 109 of 30/10/44.

Acting Pilot Officer Clostermann Pierre – on detachment to G.C. in the R.A.F.
'A young flying officer who has again distinguished himself via his brilliant abilities as a fighter by shooting down a Fw 190 on 29/06/44. On 30/06/44, during his 200th offensive mission, he attacked and probably destroyed a Me 109 and set alight three enemy vehicles, two of which were fuel tankers.
'This citation carries the award of a Croix de Guerre with palm.'

Decision No. 109 of 30/10/44.

Acting Pilot Officer Clostermann Pierre – on detachment to G.C. in the R.A.F.
'An excellent officer and fighter pilot whose remarkable qualities of dexterity and courage are only equalled by his fighting mettle. During a particularly violent and prolonged combat against an enemy force far superior in number, managed to destroy a Fw 190 and damage four others, thus bringing the total number of his victories to six Fw 190 and one Me 109 destroyed, two Me 109 probably destroyed and five Fw 190 and two Me 109 damaged.
'This citation carries the award of a Military Medal.'

Decision No. 109 of 30/10/44.

Flying Officer Clostermann Pierre – on detachment to G.C. in the R.A.F.
'A flying officer in a Group for over two years, he has shown remarkable daring and courage. Driven by the purest patriotism, he has upheld the prestige of the French aviation within the ranks of the British fighters. He has a total of eight official kills, four probable kills, five enemy aircraft damaged and numerous ground targets destroyed.
'This citation carries the award of a Croix de Guerre with palm.'

Signed: Charles de Gaulle

Flying Officer Clostermann Pierre – on detachment to G.C. in the R.A.F.
'A flying officer with unrivalled mettle in combat. Imbued with the highest traditions of French aviation, he has recently returned to battle as Flight Leader in an elite group of the R.A.F. equipped with Tempest aircraft. On 5 March, during a patrol in the Hanover region, he attacked four Messerschmitt 109, managing to shoot one of them down. In the period of 1 to 6 March, he also destroyed a large number of engines.
'This citation carries the award of a Croix de Guerre with palm.'

Decision 950/17/07/45.

Flying Officer Clostermann Pierre – on detachment to the R.A.F.

'A very valuable officer and remarkable pilot with tireless devotion. Risking his life in all circumstances and spurning danger, he continues to fight against the enemy with extreme determination. When No. 274 Squadron was sent on leave following major losses, he asked to remain on the front line and was thus assigned to No. 56 Squadron of the Royal Air Force. On 14 March, during a fierce combat against 40 enemy fighters in the Hanover region, he obtained the following results: one Me 109 destroyed, one Me 109 probably destroyed, one Me 109 damaged.

'This citation carries the award of a Croix de Guerre with palm.'

Decision 950/17/07/45.

Flying Officer Clostermann Pierre – on detachment to the R.A.F.

'A brilliant flying officer with exceptional energy and sang-froid, who continues to demonstrate the greatest example of heroic courage. He particularly distinguished himself during numerous cannon raids made perilous by the density of the anti-aircraft defences. On 21, 23 and 26 March in particular, he personally destroyed 16 engines and damaged several others, as well as several fuel tankers. On 28 March, during a reconnaissance mission over the Rhine, he shot down a Fieseler 156, then disabled a tractor-drawn heavy artillery battery. On the same day, during another mission, he attacked a column of tanks, destroyed one and damaged four others. During this raid he was wounded in the right leg by a bullet and his aircraft was hit several times.

'This citation carries the award of a Croix de Guerre with palm.'

Flying Officer Clostermann Pierre – on detachment to the R.A.F.

'A flying officer of great merit, with remarkable dexterity and fighting spirit. Continuing his raids, he particularly distinguished himself on 31 March leading a patrol in the Hamburg region, personally destroying six engines despite very precise flak. During this raid, two of his comrades were shot down and his aircraft was seriously damaged. On 2 April, above Aalhorn airfield, he attacked two Focke-Wulfs that had just taken off, downing one in flames and seriously damaging two Junkers 188s on the ground. His aircraft was seriously hit four times by flak. On 3 April, during three missions, he personally destroyed six engines and seven trucks, one of which was a tanker, losing four of his comrades.

'This citation carries the award of a Croix de Guerre with palm.'

Flying Officer Clostermann Pierre – on detachment to the R.A.F.

'A magnificent leader of men with a high notion of duty. He particularly distinguished himself when leading patrols on 5 April. At dawn, he personally shot down a Junkers night-fighter in flames over Wunsdorf airfield, despite violent flak. He then strafed the airfield and damaged three other Junkers 88. During this operation, the patrol's four aircraft were hit by flak.

'On the same day, during another mission with his patrol, he engaged in combat with sixteen enemy fighters. He personally damaged two Fw 190 and shared in destroying two Messerschmitt 109. He managed to return in his aircraft to the base, despite damage by three successive 20mm. and 30mm. shells. He landed without landing gear and crashed his face into the gun sight, and the aircraft caught fire.

'This citation carries the award of a Croix de Guerre with palm.'

Flight Lieutenant Clostermann Pierre – on detachment to the R.A.F.

'An outstanding flying officer. He continues to give the best example of courage and drive. Once again, he particularly distinguished himself on 19 April, during armed reconnaissance in the Hamburg region. Despite violent flak, he personally destroyed seven trucks. Out of the eight aircraft engaged in his patrol, three were damaged and one shot down.

'The same day, with two volunteers, during another mission at dusk, he strafed Rottemburg airfield and personally destroyed two Heinkel 177's and damaged two others. On 20 April he shared in destroying a Junkers 290 over Skagerrak.

'The same day he led a night patrol in the Hamburg region where he engaged in combat against 30 Focke-Wulf 190's. Hit by flak, his aircraft on fire, he continued to fight and downed two Fw 190's. He then returned 200 miles to his base, with his aircraft still on fire, and crash-landed.

'This citation carries the award of a Croix de Guerre with palm.'

'A highly distinguished flying officer, combining his extensive knowledge of aviation with the highest qualities of leader and fighter. Always volunteering for perilous missions, he leads his group to battle with tireless ardour.

'He particularly distinguished himself on 3 May. During a reconnaissance mission, at dawn, in the Kiel-Lübeck region, he personally destroyed a Focke-Wulf 190 in air combat and damaged two others. He led another reconnaissance mission on the coast of Denmark and following seven consecutive passes with his patrol, he forced a 500 ton submarine to run aground, completely crippled.

'This citation carries the award of a Croix de Guerre with palm.'

Flight Lieutenant Clostermann Pierre – on detachment to the R.A.F. – was promoted to Commandeur in the order of the Légion d'Honneur with the following citation:

'Flying officer, who embodies the greatest traditions of patriotism, whose action in combat will always deserve to be cited as an example. On detachment to the R.A.F., he brilliantly contributed to the high renown of the French allies. He led a flight, then a group of Tempest aircraft, with extraordinary audacity.

'He particularly distinguished himself during the third mission carried out on 3 May 1945. At dawn, at the head of No. 122 Squadron of the R.A.F., he attacked Grossenbrode naval air base in Denmark, despite the fact that it was defended by 200 German fighters. He personally destroyed a Junkers 252 that had just taken off, followed by two Dorniers over the Fehmarn strait. During another strafing pass, he seriously damaged two Arado 232's on the ground and two Blohm and Voss in the water. He then shared in destroying a Messerschmitt 109 and a Focke-Wulf 190 in aerial combat. During this action, 14 enemy fighters were downed for a total of 10 allied losses.

'On 4 May 1945, during an attack on Schleswig naval air base, he destroyed two

Dornier 18's in the water and two motor torpedo boats. He ended this prestigious campaign aged 24 years, having totalled 2,000 flying hours of which almost 600 were combat sorties, after having gained 33 aerial victories, which ranks him as France's number one fighter pilot.

'This citation carries the award of the Distinguished Flying Cross with a Bar.'

The citation elevating Pierre Clostermann to the grade of Commander of the Order of the Légion d'Honneur, decision no. 208 J.O. of 6 June 1946 signed by De Gaulle, reads as follows:

'Pierre Clostermann is a fighter pilot whose action in combat will always serve as an example to others. Detached to the R.A.F. in a squadron of Tempests, he flew with a rare audacity and contributed substantially to the great fame of the French fighter squadrons. He finished his remarkable career aged just 24 with a total of 600 combat flying hours, and having scored 33 kills, which gives him the title of France's premier fighter pilot.'

Signed: Charles De Gaulle

PRIMARY EDUCATION

The Key Concepts

Denis Hayes

Routledge
Taylor & Francis Group

LONDON AND NEW YORK

First published 2006
by Routledge
2 Park Square, Milton Park, Abingdon, Oxon OX14 4RN

Simultaneously published in the USA and Canada
by Routledge
270 Madison Ave, New York, NY 10016

Routledge is an imprint of the Taylor & Francis Group

© 2006 Denis Hayes

Typeset in Bembo by Taylor & Francis Books
Printed and bound in Great Britain by TJ International Ltd, Padstow, Cornwall

British Library Cataloguing in Publication Data
A catalogue record for this book is available from the British Library

Library of Congress Cataloging in Publication Data
Hayes, Denis, 1949-
Primary education : the key concepts / Denis Hayes.
p. cm.
Includes bibliographical references and index.
ISBN 0-415-35482-X (hardback : alk. paper) – ISBN 0-415-35483-8 (pbk. : alk. paper) 1.
Education, Elementary–Great Britain. I. Title.

LA633.H39 2006
372'.941–dc22

2005018538

ISBN10 0-415-35482-X (hbk) ISBN13 9-780-415-35482-0
ISBN10 0-415-35483-8 (pbk) ISBN13 9-780-415-35483-7

Taylor & Francis Group is the Academic Division of T&F Informa plc.

CONTENTS

LIST OF KEY CONCEPTS

Ability
Accountability
Achievement
Activities and tasks
ADHD
Anxiety
Appraisal
Assembly
Assessment
Assistants

Behaviour
Behaviourism
Body language
Bullying

Caring
Celebration
Childhood
Circle time
Citizenship
Class size
Code of Practice
Collaboration
Collegiality
Communication
Competition
Concepts
Constructivism
Context
Control
Creativity

Cross-curricular work
    (curriculum integration)
Curriculum

Decision making
Differentiation
Dilemmas

Early years
Educational visits
Effectiveness
Emotion
Encouragement
Enjoyment
Enquiry
Equal opportunities
Expectations
Extra-curricular

Feedback
Friendship

Giftedness and talent

Health and safety
Homework
Humour

Imagination
Inclusion
Induction
Inspection

INTRODUCTION

Background

The idea of bringing children together for the purpose of formally educating them has its roots deep in history. Some historians claim that English education began with the arrival of Christianity to Kent in AD 597 and the subsequent establishment by St Augustine of the cathedral church at Canterbury. By the end of the seventeenth century the newly formed Society for Promoting Christian Knowledge was encouraging church parishes to set up their own schools. The movement was extended throughout Wales by the Reverend Griffiths Jones through a large number of 'Circulating' schools, staffed by peripatetic teachers, principally to teach children (and adults) to read in the Welsh language. There followed a series of voluntary schools, often led by teachers who were little better educated than the pupils.

In addition to the formal church-based initiatives, pioneers such as Robert Raikes, the founder of the Sunday Schools' movement (in 1780), Charles Gordon, who built 'ragged schools' to educate and provide sustenance for the destitute, and Charles of Bala in Wales were convinced about the inseparability of education and social action. The first publicly funded schools in the UK were founded in the mid-nineteenth century to give a basic education to children from poor families and teach them to read the Bible. Over succeeding years, control of education gradually switched from the Church to the state, though provision was uneven. Between 1846 and 1848 the Welsh Education Committee and the Cambrian Society were formed, which evolved into national schools. In Scotland, the 1867 report of the Royal Commission on Education led to the Education Act of 1872 that resulted in improvements in primary education for every child in Scotland and not merely for the labouring classes, as implied in the equivalent English reforms of the time. In the period running up to the setting up of the Northern Ireland state in 1920, education became one of the battlegrounds between Ulster unionism and Irish nationalism. Before partition the overwhelming majority of

Irish schools were under denominational control, even though they were financed chiefly by the state.

Following the 1870 Elementary Education Act in England, education was gradually provided free of charge for all pupils, though the government's obligation was at this stage merely to 'fill the gaps' where voluntary provision did not exist. Reforms were slow in being implemented and even at the commencement of the twentieth century schooling was inconsistent and attendance spasmodic. By 1926 the Hadow Report was recommending that the 'primary' phase of education in England should conclude for pupils at age 11 and secondary schooling commence. There were many important Education Acts over the following years, including the highly influential 1944 Act, but it was not until 1989 that a national curriculum was introduced into maintained schools (i.e. schools that are funded out of general taxation) in England, Wales and Northern Ireland.

Although most of today's primary schools are similar in physical layout, they have not always existed in such a form. Separate classrooms of the size and shape we recognise today did not become common until the late 1800s. In many elementary schools prior to the end of the nineteenth century, children of all ages were put together in a single large room with one teacher and a variety of helpers, some of whom were older pupils. Many of the teaching approaches commonly used by primary teachers today, such as grouping pupils by ability and encouraging children to talk about issues, were largely unused until the mid-1900s. Most teaching was dominated by instruction, memorising and reciting facts, learning to read in unison from words written on the board and learning to write by copying from an original.

The evolution of formal schooling gave rise to the concept of a body of knowledge that had to be mastered (a 'curriculum') and words like 'pupil' and 'scholar' were introduced to describe those who attended school, and 'master' or 'mistress' for those who taught them. Today, it is normal for children in primary schools to be referred to as pupils and young people in secondary education as students. Agreement about the need for a general education for children up to the age of 11, subject-specific teaching up to the age of 16 and selection of specialist subjects thereafter has become deeply rooted in the national system. However, during the last decade of the twentieth century and into the twenty-first century, primary schooling became more subject focused, with the introduction of standard lessons of fixed duration located within a predetermined timetable. Despite the additional resources that have been allocated to primary schools in recent years, there is a concomitant increase in the number of children that are educated at home and through alternative forms of independent schooling.

The majority of primary schools in the UK are for children aged 4 or 5 to 11 years; in Scotland, the primary age profile is from 4 to 12. Children aged between 4 and 5 years are educated in foundation classes in mainstream primary schools, where teachers follow specific curriculum guidance that emphasises social as much as academic development. A smaller number of schools are designated infant (ages 5 to 7) or junior (ages 7 to 11). A very small number of schools are deemed middle (ages 8 to 12 or 9 to 13) or first (ages 5 to 8 or 9). At the start of the twenty-first century the vast majority of primary schools cater for children aged 5 to 11, after which they move on to secondary education. Small village primary schools in sparsely populated areas may have only a handful of teachers, one of whom is a 'teaching head' (i.e. with part class responsibility). Smaller schools often have to be organised so that there is more than a single year group in the same class and tend to be more flexible about teaching arrangements and timetables.

The governing body ('school board' in Scotland) for each school consists of elected parents and staff members with representatives from the local community. The members have a special responsibility to represent and communicate with parents and deal with matters as diverse as:

- Appointment and dismissal of staff
- Repair and maintenance of school buildings
- Approval of head teacher's spending proposals on books and equipment
- Use of school premises outside school hours
- Discussing matters of interest to parents such as homework, bullying or school uniform

Increasing recognition has been given to the vital role played by parents as the 'first educators' and as co-educators with teachers. Head teachers and school governors are anxious to improve community links and satisfy parents, and many primary schools are categorised as community schools to emphasise this priority. In some parts of the country there are large numbers of schools that were founded by the established church, where governors have more control over religious education (RE) and, therefore, the spiritual and moral ethos of the school. Foundation schools are broadly of two types: Aided and Controlled. The Aided schools are more closely attached to the Church/Mosque; their representatives on the governing body are in the majority and responsible for monitoring the teaching of RE. In Controlled schools, links with the Church are less tightly bound. Over recent years there has been an increase in the number of foundation schools based on different world faiths. However, the principle of segregating children on the basis of religious belief has created active debate on the possible destabilising effect that this policy might have on society.

Despite the additional funding made available to schools in recent years, teacher recruitment and retention is still an issue in some parts of the country (notably where housing and living costs are high). Teacher shortages at the end of the twentieth and start of the twenty-first century have meant that newly qualified teachers' job prospects are better than they were in the past. However, the falling birth rate in the UK is resulting in the need for fewer primary teachers. For this reason and (more particularly) the heavy workload they carry, only about half of all newly qualified teachers are in permanent posts after five years' service.

Further reading

Campbell, R. J. (2005) 'Primary education or primary schooling?', *Education 3–13*, 33, 1, pp. 3–6.

Clegg, A. (1980) *About Our Schools*, London: Blackwell.

Cunningham, P. (2002) 'Primary education', in R. Aldrich (ed.) *A Century of Education*, pp. 9–30, Abingdon: Routledge.

Richards, C. (1999) *Primary Education: At a Hinge of History?* London: Falmer.

Thomas, N. (1990) *Primary Education from Plowden to the 1990s*, London: Falmer.

Woods, P., Jeffrey, B., Troman, G. and Boyle, M. (1997) *Restructuring Schools; Reconstructing Teachers: Responding to Change in the Primary School*, Maidenhead: Open University Press.

PRIMARY EDUCATION

The Key Concepts

ABILITY

Ability is variously defined as competence, power or talent, and indicates a capacity, expertise or proficiency in a defined area of learning. Ability is also affiliated to concepts such as flair, skill, aptitude and intelligence. At one time it was believed that ability was fixed, and people either possessed it or did not. However, it is now generally accepted that far from being innate (i.e. fixed at birth) ability develops in response to the environment in which children are nurtured (i.e. the specific and particular human and material influences affecting them). Educationists have come to acknowledge that a number of other variables influence progress and attainment, including adult/child relationships, the child's motivation, **creativity**, personality and peer pressure. The concept of a single fixed ability has been modified to encompass an understanding that people are capable of increasing their capacity for certain kinds of intelligent behaviour and attainment over time, providing the conditions are suitable.

Many teachers and adults working in school tend to categorise people according to their perceptions of their abilities and identify pupils by using labels such as 'good' or 'naughty' or 'clever' or 'fast' or 'slow'. Some educationists argue that ability labelling is unnecessary and may actually damage children's learning owing to its potential negative impact on pupils and the way that it influences teachers' **expectations**. An alternative approach to ability-based teaching is posited on a belief that pupils' capacity to learn has no limits, providing they are given relevant work, imaginatively presented and rooted in their interests.

While primary teachers carry out an initial **assessment** of children when they enter school to gain a better understanding of their **knowledge**, understanding, **skills** and potential, the process carries with it a danger of stereotyping pupils. Teachers may build a mental image of a pupil's ability that fixes what they believe a child is capable of achieving. Although assessments at all stages of primary school are helpful for teachers in setting work appropriate to the needs of the child, they can also establish arbitrary boundaries for **achievement**. Pupils then carry the 'limited ability' label throughout their school life so that teachers do not expect them to achieve anything of note, and the negative image continues into secondary education. As a result, pupils do not fulfil their potential and may become disenchanted with school or accept their lowly status.

Exceptional ability is frequently equated with **giftedness and talent**. Gifted pupils are defined as those who excel in academic subjects such as mathematics and English. By contrast, talented pupils excel in subjects like physical education, art and drama. Some gifted children struggle to complete their work on time because they want to try out their own methods or simply like to spend time pondering issues. At the start of lessons, teachers clarify their **expectations** for pupils of different abilities, taking account of the fact that all children are stimulated by opportunities to consolidate their learning through open-ended **activities**, problem-solving tasks and investigations. If pupils are all engaged in the same task, teachers take account of the child's ability when evaluating the quality of the work and providing **feedback**.

Further reading

Eyre, D. (1997) *Able Children in Ordinary Schools*, London: David Fulton.
Hart, S., Dixon, A., Drummond, M. J. and McIntyre, D. (2004) *Learning Without Limits*, Maidenhead: Open University Press, chapters 1 and 2
Ireson, J. and Hallam, S. (2003) 'Ability grouping in schools: Does it matter?', *Psychology of Education Review*, 27, 1, pp. 3–17.

ACCOUNTABILITY

Accountability has been central to the educational reforms that have been introduced in recent years, particularly since the highly significant Education Reform Act of 1988 that heralded the arrival of a national curriculum in England and Wales. As a considerable amount of public money is allocated to education and it has importance for the economic prosperity of the country, education providers (teachers, lecturers, etc.) are accountable to the taxpayer. Although some educationists argue that teachers should be much freer to exercise professional choice about what they teach and how they do it, teachers have had to adjust like other professions to the new demands placed on them by their clients.

The monitoring of teachers and schools takes various forms but is broadly considered with regard to financial accountability and professional accountability, the former rooted in value for money and the latter in pupil progress. Financial accountability is ultimately invested in the school governors/school board, the body that has responsibility for safeguarding the interests of the school. The role and purpose of governing bodies is to monitor education provision, advise and support the head teacher about key decisions and make a public response to inspection reports about the school. Governors themselves are also accountable to the parents and local community through the local education authority.

A problem with accountability is that of choosing the criteria for successful teaching to which a teacher can be held accountable. Most discussion has settled on pupil **achievement** as the chief measure of teaching success, but the relationship between achievement and teaching quality is inconclusive. Educational research is unable to show significant differences between teaching methods and their impact on cognitive and affective learning. The aggregated grades from national **testing** of pupils at age 11 years contribute to school performance tables, which are used for a yardstick for accountability to the local community. However, there has been considerable disquiet among teachers about whether test scores should be used as an indication of teachers' **ability**, as many other factors such as home circumstances and the work of previous teachers influence pupil performance.

Further reading

Ditchfield, C. (2004) 'Assessment, recording and reporting on children's work', in K. Jacques and R. Hyland (eds) *Professional Studies: Primary phase*, pp. 51–62, Exeter: Learning Matters.
Drayton, M. (2002) 'The role and purpose of school governing bodies', in M. Cole (ed.) *Professional Issues for Teachers and Trainee teachers*, 2nd edn, London: David Fulton.
Wrigley, T. (2003) *Schools of Hope*, Stoke on Trent: Trentham.

ACHIEVEMENT

Achievement is important in all areas of life and people are often judged on their public successes, particularly in academic and sporting fields. Children revel in the thrill and excitement of winning a race, being awarded a certificate for good work, earning a star after helping the teacher with a job or colouring in a square on a chart for finishing another **reading** book. It is less fulfilling for children whose achievements are limited, who struggle to finish the race, complete the work or compete with their illustrious classmates. An emphasis upon matching tasks and activities against pupil capability ('differentiation') to ensure that children succeed with their work cannot conceal the reality that there are winners and losers in school life as elsewhere. Adults involved in educating primary-age pupils have to be sensitive to the fact that pupils are not participating in an adult game known as 'school' but trying to understand life's complexities and their own place in it.

Achievement in learning is the ultimate goal for everyone involved in primary education, but identifying the nature of the achievement is problematic. In its simplest terms, pupils achieve when they gain measurably good results in their academic work. Most children are willing to persevere with their work for three reasons: to gain satisfaction from it, to contend with their friends and to please the teacher. Children are motivated to a different extent by each of these three factors, depending on the relationship they have with others and the interest they possess in the subject matter. Some children are strongly self-motivated and show a relentless determination to do well and find fulfilment in completing a task to their own satisfaction. Other children are highly competitive and view every piece of work as a challenge to outperform everyone else. While competitiveness can act as a spur to achievement, it can also lead to an unhealthy and strained classroom climate if it becomes the dominating factor. Educators have an essential role in encouraging pupils to feel proud of their achievements and to affirm children's successes warmly, while allowing a degree of competitiveness without tolerating rancour.

Achievement plays a big part in motivating pupils to learn and progress. It is good for children to do well and for their successes to be appreciated by adults and their peers. Many children work extremely hard and strive to attain their goals; they rightly receive recognition and praise. Nevertheless, children who equate achievements with evidence of their personal worth will become dissatisfied when the cheering fades, certificates crinkle, sparkling reports become an archive and others receive more approval. To base the worth of individuals solely on certificated or measurable successes while overlooking their personal qualities runs the risk of burdening children with the need to gain further achievements as a means of recognition.

In reality, success is judged not only through identifiable and visible outcomes but in how the outcomes affect the child's character, aptitude to cope with life, confidence and attitude to others. For young children in particular, both the winners and losers deserve praise: winners because of their victories, losers because of their tenacity and determination. Achievement is kept in perspective when the genuine efforts of every child are recognised and acclaimed, regardless of the child's place in the order.

Less able children will normally need more time to reach the same point in their learning than more capable ones. A small number of capable children are slow and methodical in their work, not because they lack the **ability** but because they are conscientious and anxious to avoid making mistakes. Some less able children complete work quickly because they can only engage with the concepts at a relatively superficial level and need to be encouraged to try more demanding tasks. More able children need opportunities to extend their **thinking**, rather than merely doing more of the same activity. Teachers try to ensure that every child gains initial success before progressing to tasks that require greater determination and knowledge to complete.

While pupils need to be encouraged to achieve the highest standards of which they are capable, low-attaining children need help if they are to avoid spiralling into an attitude of negativity towards learning. Some pupils seem to find everything a constant struggle, unable to compete, fearful and defensive lest they receive criticism from adults and always struggling to make an impression. It is unsurprising if, after a few years of this experience, they decide that they are not prepared to make an effort to try any longer. Such children prefer to put their efforts into other more disruptive behaviour over which they have some **control**. Treating children as individuals and sensitivity with regard to their emotional as well as their academic needs plays a major role in preventing these unhelpful attitudes from taking root. Caring adults in school help alleviate children's anxieties by being calm when dealing with their fears, sensitively encouraging pupils to confront their doubts and view the route to achievement as an exciting challenge.

Further reading

Gray, J., Schagen, I. P. and Charles, M. (2004) 'Tracking pupil progress from key stage 1 to key stage 2: how much do the route taken and the primary school attended matter?', *Research Papers in Education*, 19, 4, pp. 389–413.

Lloyd, G. (ed.) (2004) *Problem Girls*, London: Routledge.

Walker, S. O. (2004) 'Nature, nurture and academic achievement: a twin study of teacher assessments of 7-year olds', *British Journal of Educational Psychology*, 74, 3, pp. 323–42.

Wegerif, R. and Dawes, L. (2004) *Thinking and learning with ICT: Raising achievement in primary classrooms*, London: Routledge.

ACTIVITIES AND TASKS

An activity is a practical or reasoning task engaged in by one or more pupils to enhance and enrich learning. Activities are used in primary classrooms for one or more of four purposes. First, they help to reinforce pupils' **knowledge**. Second, they extend pupils' understanding. Third, they allow pupils to explore through problem solving and investigation. Fourth, they promote social contact (such as through the medium of **play**) and illuminate moral **dilemmas** (such as through the use of drama).

There is no sharp distinction between a task and an activity, but whereas the former tends to be associated with evaluating individual pupil performance, the latter often involves two or more children working cooperatively or collaboratively to achieve a common goal. Effective learning is assisted by meaningful activities that are relevant, interesting and motivate the children, with a teacher or assistant on hand to offer guidance, advice and **encouragement**. The activities that best motivate children include investigations, problem solving, making posters, writing short plays, creating poems, devising experiments and producing drama or dance routines. In many cases pupils like to demonstrate the final product or outcome to other members of the class or in **assembly**.

In determining which activities are suitable for pupils of a particular age and experience, teachers take account of the children's academic strengths and limitations. Suitable activities for younger pupils often require more direct adult involvement and structuring than those for older children who exercise greater flexibility. However, it cannot be assumed that children have the cognitive or social **skills** to engage with a group activity effectively. The best activities do not merely keep the children occupied but utilise their previous learning and extend their experiences.

Pupils often have interesting ideas about activities that will assist learning and will, if asked by a teacher, make sensible suggestions. Whereas in systematic **instruction** it is the teacher who makes decisions about the content of activities, in a project (**topic**- or thematically based) approach the children's preferences feature far more significantly. The teacher does not abdicate responsibility in the matter but acts as an adviser to help children make appropriate choices about the activities in which they engage until they become more independent in doing so. The difference between the project approach and more formally designated task allocation based on **ability** groupings is that children do not feel compelled to work constantly at the upper limits of their potential. In such instances, children select from a range of options rather than being given a set task that corresponds as precisely as possible to an identified learning needs. The advantage of using a flexible approach is that children are more likely to be motivated by being able to do things they enjoy using a variety of learning options. The disadvantage is that children may not engage with more challenging tasks that stretch their minds. The availability of adequate resources is also a factor, as structured activities that are planned in advance allow the teacher to organise resources, whereas spontaneous ideas may be problematic owing to resource limitations.

Further reading

Dawes, L., Mercer, N. and Wegerif, R. (2000) *Thinking Together*, Birmingham: The Questions Publishing Company.

Dickinson, C. (1996) *Effective Learning Activities*, Stafford: Network Educational Press.

Katz, L. G. and Chard, S. C. (2000) *Engaging Children's Minds: The project approach*, Stamford, CT: Ablex, chapter 3.

ADHD

ADHD (Attention Deficit Hyperactivity Disorder) was first described by Dr Heinrich Hoffman in 1845 and is a condition that becomes apparent in pre-school children or soon after they begin school. The principal characteristics of ADHD are inattention, hyperactivity and impulsive behaviour. Typically these children struggle to **control** their behaviour and have short attention spans. Since Hoffman's original study and the work of George Still around the start of the twentieth century, ADHD has received considerable attention and been the focus of numerous studies about its nature, cause and treatment.

ADHD is primarily a condition of brain disorder and is seen in a variety of forms depending on the situation and the child's temperament, but is commonly manifested through difficulties in concentration, rule-governed behaviour, variable motivation and lack of awareness of time factors. The wide variation in symptoms means that any restless children will soon come to the teacher's attention, while the constant daydreamer may be ignored as merely inattentive. Similarly, the impulsive child may be viewed as a discipline problem, while the passive or sluggish child, who also suffers from ADHD, may simply be thought of as unmotivated. It is likely that every class contains one pupil with ADHD, but because many children without the condition show some signs of the symptoms, teachers can wrongly attribute erratic or mischievous pupil behaviour. All children are occasionally unsettled or act unthinkingly or daydream; it is when the extent of distraction, poor concentration and impulsiveness affect performance in school and social relationships with other children that ADHD is likely to be relevant.

Pupils that suffer from ADHD present parents and teachers with a range of challenges. When children begin school it is likely that there will already be a case history of inappropriate behaviour and limited concentration in pre-school settings. Depending on the amount of help and advice that they have received, parents may not have been able to provide their children with the usual basic **skills** that would be anticipated in school-age pupils or the necessary social skills for them to orientate to mainstream primary school life.

If children suffering from ADHD are doing something they really enjoy, they are capable of concentrating for a considerable length of time; by contrast, giving specific attention to organising and completing a task or learning something new often proves difficult for them. They struggle to follow instructions and often lose or forget common items that are required for their work. Maintaining high levels of motivation by involving them in relevant and interesting work is therefore a priority for teachers and teaching **assistants**. The setting of **homework** produces particular challenges, owing to the high degree of organisation and self-discipline involved.

Hyperactivity is one of the most critical features of many pupils with ADHD, characterised by fidgeting and unpredictable movements around the room, and touching or playing with accessible items. In addition, children may move different parts of their body, tap on the table or **talk** incessantly; these actions make simple tasks, such as sitting still for a meal or concentrating during a school lesson or listening to a story, a considerable challenge. Impulsive behaviour may also be manifested through inappropriate comments, exhibiting extreme **emotion** or acting without regard to the consequences to themselves or other pupils. In the classroom, the impulsiveness may make it hard for children to wait for things they want, take their turn in games or line up patiently. Hyperactive pupils prefer to engage in activities with short-term **rewards** rather than persevere with those that take more effort yet provide them with more substantial long-term benefits.

By contrast, pupils with the *inattentive* type of ADHD are seldom impulsive or hyperactive, but struggle to pay attention. They appear to be daydreaming, easily confused, slow in reacting and rather lethargic; they also have difficulty processing information as quickly and accurately as other children. Although the inattentive group of children cannot easily grasp an adult's oral or written instructions and make frequent mistakes, they tend to be unobtrusive and may appear to be working well. In this way they tend to avoid adult intervention. These pupils socialise better than do children with the more impulsive and hyperactive type of ADHD; because their behaviour is less intrusive and disrupting, their problems can be overlooked.

Pupils with ADHD prosper in schools where they are encouraged to learn in a variety of ways with an emphasis upon a practical approach and the opportunity to be spontaneous and use their intuition. It is essential for adults to maintain a calm, encouraging and consistent approach, with well-structured (but not rigid) routines, clear **rules** and standards of work. During **lessons**, children benefit from having opportunities for active participation and plenty of opportunities to develop their non-academic strengths. As with all emotionally vulnerable children, pupils with ADHD are unpredictable and adults working with them in school require infinite patience and access to specialist advice.

Further reading

DuPaul, G. J. (2004) *ADHD in the schools : Assessment and intervention strategies*, New York: Guilford.

Kewley, G. D. (1999) *Attention Deficit Hyperactivity Disorder*, London: David Fulton.

Wang, X., Bernas, R. and Eberhard, P. (2004) 'Engaging ADHD students in tasks with hand gestures', *Educational Studies*, 30, 3, pp. 217–29.

ANXIETY

Anxiety is common to adults and children in every walk of life, but school can create the circumstances for additional concerns because of the specific and identifiable goals that confront both children and adults and the high **expectations** placed on them by parents, teachers and the local community. Children become anxious for many reasons, not all of which are directly related to school life. Circumstances at home, ill-health and feuds sometimes affect children adversely; they carry these concerns into the classroom with them and, inevitably, their work is affected. As one of the most significant adults in children's lives, each teacher or assistant has a considerable responsibility to ensure that a **learning climate** is provided in which pupils can be safe, motivated and supported in their learning. Although a few pupils are careless about their attitude towards their school work and appear disdainful of teachers' opinions, the overwhelming majority benefit from reassurance that the teacher is pleased with them and enjoys their company.

Extremes of anxiety may result in a child being unwilling to attend school, a condition sometimes known as 'school phobia'. Younger children may refuse to come to school because they are unwilling to be separated from a parent and feel more secure at home. School phobia tends to be most prevalent in pupils between the ages of 8 and 13 years with sensitive natures, who struggle to control their emotions. As a result of their emotional vulnerability they fear ridicule, criticism and work assessment (marks, grades, written comments, etc.). In a few cases, children have a specific anxiety, such as about going swimming or sitting with other children eating their lunch; consequently, they pretend that they hate school in general when, in reality, it is the specific event that frightens them.

Adults in school have to look out for children with weak interactive and social skills, as these inadequacies may signal deeper anxieties or previous negative experiences that have not been dealt with satisfactorily. In the most severe cases, children exhibit symptoms such as moodiness, withdrawal or even aggressive behaviour. Memories of a traumatic event in school can continue to haunt children for a long time unless there is appropriate intervention and counselling.

While the large majority of primary-aged children relish a degree of challenge, there are limits to their success in being able adapt to changing circumstances. Pupils who are weak in a subject areas used as a benchmark for school success (such as **reading**) may encounter demands that exceed their power to cope and result in anxiety or paranoia about the subject. Close liaison between school staff and parents of young children is essential if extreme forms of anxiety are to be dealt with satisfactorily, avoiding the onset of school phobia and the truancy that may follow later in the school career.

Adults in primary school are also subject to anxiety, especially during formal **inspection** of educational provision. School inspections provide schools with their greatest challenge, not only ensuring that standards of teaching and pupil attainment are satisfactory or better, but in the emotional and physical demands that they make of staff. Effective **leadership**, self-confidence and a positive whole-school spirit mitigate the worst effects of an inspection, though many teachers find it unnerving to be observed and assessed by an external person, especially when the stakes are high in terms of the school's reputation and its future.

For teachers in training, the requirements of a school placement create emotional tensions and fears that may detract from the job of teaching and hinder progress. Excited anticipation is healthy; darkening fears that undermine confidence and erect a wall of doubt instead of providing a path of certainty are not. Trainee teachers in particular have to adopt a resolute approach to their school placement and not allow themselves to be overwhelmed by the challenge. Although there are no short-term remedies to dispelling anxiety, novice teachers can position themselves into a more positive frame of mind, resisting the temptation to be gloomy and refusing to allow their past failures to hinder future success.

Even at the best of time, teaching is emotionally draining as well as liberating and there are few practitioners who do not suffer from occasional anxiety. Working with active youngsters each day has the potential to wear down even the most assured and confident teacher. It is therefore important for all teachers, regardless of their experience, to keep the job in perspective and remember that they have an identity outside school, as parents, sisters, brothers, neighbours and friends. Success as human beings does not reside solely in their achievements as teachers.

Further reading

Brown, E. (1999) *Loss Change and Grief*, London: David Fulton, chapter 5.

Hayes, D. (2003) *A Student Teacher's Guide to Primary School Placement*, London: RoutledgeFalmer., chapter 3.

Heyda, P. (2001) *The Primary Teacher's Survival Guide*, Portsmouth: Heinemann, chapter 7.

Woods, P. and Carlyle, D. (2002) 'Teacher identities under stress: the emotions of separation and reward', *International Studies in Sociology of Education*, 12, 2, pp. 169–89.

APPRAISAL

Appraisal for adults working in primary schools is a means of identifying good practice and areas for further development and forms an integral part of staff development. Appraisal is a method by which an individual's work, commitment and aspirations are formally recorded. The process involves noting areas of strength and areas for development, followed by a formal interview with the head teacher or nominee in which priorities for the year are agreed. In the case of teachers applying for promoted posts, an integral element of the appraisal may require a designated external assessor to evaluate evidence of proficiency provided by the individual being appraised.

Appraisal is posited on a belief that although some teachers have a surfeit of natural talent, all teachers benefit from identifying professional goals to which they can aspire. Newly qualified teachers (NQTs) in their first (**induction**) year will be appraised by a mentor (induction tutor) about once every half-term for the purpose of noting progress and setting targets for **achievement**. If the NQT has encountered significant difficulties, it may be appropriate for a designated person from the local education authority to take part in the appraisal. All teachers in their first year of teaching or its equivalent must undergo a final appraisal so that they can be recommended for full status as a qualified teacher. It is normal for the NQT being appraised and the appraiser to meet beforehand to discuss priorities, aspirations and the NQT's perceptions of his or her progress, needs and concerns.

For classroom teachers, observation of their teaching forms part of an appraisal. Both the appraiser and the person being appraised have to discuss the criteria involved in the observation and agree on what constitutes satisfactory practice. Correct interpretation of a classroom situation requires the appraiser to gain accurate perceptions from what is seen and interpret classroom events fairly. In doing so, the appraiser normally uses a checklist as a **memory** aid. However, itemising every aspect of a teacher's classroom behaviour runs the risk of being unmanageable and is open to the charge that a sum of the individual components does not necessarily equate to the outcome. A teacher may satisfactorily meet the criteria, such as employing good **time management**, providing well-differentiated tasks for pupils to complete and offering appropriate **feedback** on work, yet be uninspiring and fail to capture children's imaginations. Furthermore, the use of lists of criteria assumes parity across each criterion when in reality some things (such as maintaining discipline) are essential, whereas others (such as providing adequate resources) are fluid. Even allowing for the fact that criteria can be agreed, their interpretation may not prove straightforward. Post-session discussion between appraiser and appraised is therefore an essential part of the process in evaluating the impact of the lesson or session.

The word appraisal is not generally used when viewing pupil progress, though the use of the associated term 'conferencing' is fairly widespread in primary schools. Conferencing is a designated time when the teacher speaks individually to each child, examines a range of work, takes account of the child's view of his or her strengths and weaknesses and establishes learning targets. The conference is intended to act as a staging post in the overall assessment of progress and may contribute to the end-of-year report.

Further reading

Bartlett, S. (2000) 'The development of teacher appraisal: a recent history', *British Journal of Educational Studies*, 48, 1, pp. 24–37.

Campbell, R. J. (2004) 'Effective teaching and values: some implications for research and teacher appraisal', *Oxford Review of Education*, 30, 4, pp. 451–65.

Montgomery, D. (1999) *Positive Teacher Appraisal Through Classroom Observation*, London: David Fulton.

ASSEMBLY

An assembly is an occasion when some or all of the school community meets together to share and celebrate worthwhile and praiseworthy areas of living; it also provides a medium for communicating matters of significance. Assemblies have the potential to affirm the school's identity, develop a positive learning ethos and create and enhance a sense of community. In England, an act of *collective worship* is often incorporated into an assembly as it has been a legal requirement since the 1944 Education Act.

An effective school assembly offers an opportunity for pupils to consider significant human **values**, such as love, peace, truth, cooperation and respect, and has the potential to touch children's inner being and nurture their intrapersonal skills. In turn, the development of values acts as a foundation for religious education; personal, social and health education (PSHE); **citizenship**; and the spiritual, moral, social and cultural (SMSC) elements of the **curriculum**. Assemblies offer support for the school's fundamental ethic in as much as pupils are influenced by the attitudes, involvement and contributions that each staff member makes during these occasions. In this way every adult becomes a role model for the pupils to admire and imitate.

It is a prerequisite that any member of staff who leads an assembly is convinced that developing and deepening the spiritual dimension of children's lives helps them to mature into considerate and well-adjusted young people. The head teacher or teacher that takes responsibility for an assembly is also conscious of the need for pupil and adult comfort and creating the right atmosphere in the room to help children focus on the benefits that they enjoy. The use of genuine **reflection** (as opposed to hypnotic practices that limit thought rather than allow it to expand) allows children to tap into their **imaginations** and stimulates the creative part of their brains. The imposition of assembly on pupils by a reluctant and unenthusiastic staff is likely to create negative attitudes that impact unhelpfully on the rest of school life. Parents can request that their children do not attend assemblies of which an act of worship is a part.

Further reading

Hawkes, N. (2000) *Being a School of Excellence: The role of the school assembly.* On-line. Available http://www.livingvalues.net/reference/assembly.html (accessed April 2005).

Leicester, M. (2004) *Stories for Inclusive Schools*, London: Routledge.

Peirce, E. (2003) *Multi-faith Activity Assemblies*, London: Routledge.

ASSESSMENT

The assessment of children's progress in learning is a key element of educational practice at all levels. It is based on the assumption that it is possible for teachers to be able to identify what pupils know and understand. Assessment is used in three principal ways. First, teachers assess how well pupils cope with the **activities and tasks** they undertake as a means of evaluating how much support and guidance is required, a process sometimes referred to as 'formative' assessment. Second, teachers assess diagnostically by taking note of the extent of understanding and misunderstanding that pupils expose in regular classroom work. Third, teachers assess by marking and evaluating pupils' completed work, a process sometimes referred to as 'summative' assessment.

The assessment of children has to serve a variety of purposes, but it is principally to inform decisions made by the teacher about what work a child is capable of managing. This process places a considerable onus on the teacher to make an accurate evaluation of progress so that there is a reasonable match between the work and the child's capability. In addition, assessment is a means of providing information for pupils, parents, the next teacher, professionals such as educational psychologists and, indirectly, the general public, by using data from national test results. Assessment takes account of a pupil's previous attainment and potential and is therefore a strategy for identifying individual learning needs and offering direction for the future (a strategy commonly referred to as **target setting**). Teachers also use assessment opportunities to celebrate progress and sincere endeavour.

Assessment relies on evidence, but not on proof in the way that (say) a court of law demands. The evidence is normally accumulated over a period of time rather than relying on a one-off snapshot of attainment by scrutiny of a single piece of work. Most assessment evidence is drawn from what children say, what they write and record during regular classroom activities, and the way they answer questions during sessions or formally in a test.

Assessment has to be manageable for teachers and relate to what they are trying to teach the children. In offering summative **feedback** on work, teachers have to use comments and grades consistently and ensure that pupils understand their significance. Whereas older children may receive a mark (especially in mathematical computations) or a grade on an A to E continuum, it is more common for teachers to offer a written or spoken summary. Ideally, children are given the time to think and respond to the teacher's comments and be involved in the assessment process rather than passive recipients, as this gives them a sense of ownership over their learning. Teachers encourage children to self-evaluate their work and, for older children, sometimes respond to the teacher's written comment with a written comment of their own.

In addition to assessing **reading**, writing and mathematical **ability**, teachers have to take account of younger primary pupils' personal, social and emotional well-being and their attitude and disposition to learning. Consequently teachers assess pupils' social skills, their attention skills and persistence, and their language and **communication** competence. Children's understanding of their own and the wider world, and their physical and creative development, are also included in an assessment portfolio for new entrants to school.

When marking work and making suggestions about how it might be improved, teachers like to take account of the effort made by the pupil as well as the outcome. If teachers mark work with the child present, verbal explanation can accompany the written comments. The child's presence also facilitates praise and **celebration** of achievements that are balanced with critical ones to ensure that children are encouraged yet motivated to address shortcomings. Teachers take account of children's attitude towards their work and the way they persevere, reflected in the level of their enthusiasm and motivation, the extent to which they become self-sufficient and independent, and their growth in confidence. Errors are viewed as opportunities for restructuring work and making improvements rather than punitive. Judgements of attainment take account of practical factors, such as the time available for completion of the task, the level of difficulty of the work and whether the child was trying to be innovative or simply following the prescribed method.

Further reading

Black, P. and William, D. (1998) *Inside the Black Box: Raising Standards Through Classroom Assessment*, London: King's College School of Education.

Briggs, M., Woodfield, A., Martin, C. and Swatton, P. (2003) *Assessment for Learning and Teaching in Primary Schools*, Exeter: Learning Matters.

Clarke, S. (2001) *Unlocking Formative Assessment*, London: Hodder & Stoughton.

Drummond, M. J. (2003) *Assessing Children's Learning*, London: David Fulton.

ASSISTANTS

The use of paid assistants to support children's learning and help the teacher to organise and manage the classroom is common in primary schools. Voluntary help from parents and people on work experience also makes a significant contribution to the process of teaching and learning. If assistants are paid, they are normally referred to as teaching assistants (TAs) and have a job description to guide them. The title of Learning Support Assistant (LSA) is often applied to someone who is working one-to-one with a child who has been identified as having **special educational needs** (SEN). TAs have been employed in most primary schools over many years to undertake general duties but they are gradually assuming more responsibility for pupils' learning and there has been a large increase in their numbers to support the work of class teachers. The introduction of Higher Level Teaching Assistants (HLTAs) to take a more active and direct role in pupils' teaching is a key initiative in England, though their role is under negotiation with teaching unions. The Training and Development Agency has published a set of professional standards for the award of HLTA status (TTA 2004) under the headings of professional **values** and practice, **knowledge** and understanding, teaching and learning activities.

The UK government is keen to recruit tens of thousands of support staff and exploit their expertise in the classroom. Increasing the number of assistants is supposed to mirror the situation in hospitals where a senior professional (such as a consultant) is involved only with key **decision making** and advanced practice, leaving the subordinates (junior doctors, nurses) to carry out the orders and perform most of the regular work. Using this analogy, the teacher represents the consultant and the TA represents the junior doctor.

The number of assistants is affected by the size of the school. Small schools with fewer than a hundred pupils do not have the infrastructure, physical space or finance to operate like larger schools, with dedicated spaces and specialist support staff. Small schools are more likely to utilise voluntary adult help or employ part-time assistants, often shared across several classes. Consequently, the deployment of support staff involves considerable flexibility and close teamwork to ensure equity.

Increasingly, TAs possess a qualification and attend further in-service courses to develop their expertise. Some assistants are former teachers who no longer wish to teach, but the majority are people drawn from the local community who enjoy working in school, have their own children there and have been appointed to support the work of teachers. Owing to funding limitations, assistants are often employed on temporary contracts.

Primary education specialist Mike Waters suggests that adult assistants can be used in one or more of seven ways. (1) Being involved as a genuine participant in pupils' activities. (2) As a detached observer of how pupils cope with tasks. (3) As a scribe for pupils who struggle with writing. (4) Doing a variety of menial tasks. (5) Checking what pupils are doing. (6) Listening to what pupils want to read to them, tell them about and discuss. (7) Helping pupils to review their work. Although some assistants have their own clear view of what they are and are not prepared to do, it is up to the teachers to be specific about their requirements, especially in **early years'** classes where additional adult support is often interwoven into the fabric of the teaching day. There are numerous routine tasks that teachers have always carried out in the classroom that are now deemed more suitable for support staff, though not all of the tasks are equally important or relevant to primary education. The most appropriate responsibilities for TAs (apart from assisting pupils in class) include collecting money, collating pupil reports, stocktaking, bulk photocopying, record keeping and filing, putting up displays, carrying out minor repairs for ICT equipment within **health and safety** guidelines, ordering supplies and equipment, issuing and maintaining equipment and materials, seeking and giving advice to pupils, managing and inputting pupil data.

Employment of TAs is intended to lead to more flexible models of teaching and learning. In practice, this means that teachers have become principally responsible for ensuring that pupils achieve learning outcomes than taking responsibility for every aspect of the teaching and learning process. In theory, being freed from more routine tasks means that teachers can concentrate on the more specialised elements of their role, especially the planning, preparation and assessment (referred to as PPA) of pupils' learning. The application of this strategy necessitates that assistants are suitably trained to ensure that they possess the appropriate **skills** to complement the work of teachers. The relationship between teacher and TA must be harmonious to maintain the delicate balance of trust and mutual support that exists between them.

The involvement of large numbers of TAs to support children's learning requires teachers to develop new management acumen, in knowing how both to relate to TAs and use them profitably. If teachers fail to offer adequate support and direction, assistants understandably become frustrated or insecure and begin to create their own patterns of working which may not suit the teacher. Many teachers try to set aside a time each week to discuss matters of mutual concern and take every opportunity to thank assistants for their efforts and recognise their contribution to the life of the class. TAs become irritated if teachers make unjustified assumptions about their capability and level of responsibility or take advantage of their goodwill. Assistants expect appropriate respect and understanding from teachers, clarification about the nature of their work and being kept informed about timetable alterations. If the assistant is a parent, the teacher's reputation can hinge on the informal conversations that the assistant has with neighbours and friends about school life.

Further reading

Blatchford, P. (2004) *The Role and Effects of Teaching Assistants in English Primary Schools*, Research Report RR605, Nottingham: Department for Education & Skills.

Campbell, A. and Fairbairn, G. (eds) (2005) *Working with Support in the Classroom*, London: Paul Chapman.

DfES: www.teachernet.gov.uk/remodelling

Kay, J. (2002) *Teaching Assistant's Handbook*, London: Continuum.

Waters, M. (1996) *Managing Your Primary Classroom*, London: Collins.

Watkinson, A. (2003a) *The Essential Guide for Competent Teaching Assistants*, London: David Fulton.

Watkinson, A. (2003b) *The Essential Guide for Experienced Teaching Assistants*, London: David Fulton.

BEHAVIOUR

Every living thing 'behaves' in as much as it responds to changes generated both internally and externally. Behaviour does not depend solely on stimuli, though in the absence of stimuli a sentient being will actively seek to be aroused. Thus, in a school situation, a bored pupil will look for sources of amusement; a mischievous pupil will enjoy bating a teacher. It is perfectly normal for children (and adults) to seek the establishment and maintenance of active, continuous and gratifying transactions with those around them. In classroom life this gratification is likely to include creating friendships, responding to what people say, looking at pictures and graphic information, asking questions, catching someone's eye, laughing, responding to teachers' comments, and so forth. Children do not necessarily misbehave because they are under-stimulated, but if teachers fail to provide a medium in which this need for internal fulfilment is satisfied, children will seek other means to do so.

Behaviour is closely allied to discipline. Behaviour is a term that relates to pupil conduct, whereas discipline is the rule framework for behaviour imposed by the responsible adult. Thus, adults explain and reinforce for children the parameters, **rules** and regulations governing their behaviour. In turn, the children learn to modify their behaviour to conform to the agreed discipline structure. In this respect, it is not really possible for a teacher to 'make' a pupil behave, inasmuch as behaviour is based upon children's decisions about their own actions.

Appropriate behaviour should emerge naturally from effective discipline but in reality the maintenance of active, continuous and satisfying adult–child transactions means that the situation is much less settled. Two children may behave similarly but a teacher will employ different approaches according to the specific circumstances and the individual's experience, history and emotional state. For instance, the significance attached by a teacher to a child calling out in the middle of a maths lesson is different from the same pupil calling out in the middle of a sports' day race. Similarly, two children may snap a pencil: the first child accidentally, the second child through carelessness. In such circumstances, the teacher's response is likely to be different for each child despite the identical outcomes.

Children learn about appropriate ways to behave through trial and error, observing and imitating, discovering what actions are rewarded and being given direct guidance by an adult. Consequently, the adult–child relationship is crucial to the speed and efficiency with which children learn to behave appropriately. A teacher's authority is not ultimately found in formulaic approaches or implementing agreed school strategies but in effectively organising learning, presenting information with spirit and sensitivity to pupils' needs, communicating ideas using appropriate terminology, and monitoring pupil progress fairly. Most pupils respond well for the large majority of the time in school when treated firmly, but also with kindness and respect. They appreciate boundaries of acceptable behaviour that are consistently maintained by adults in school. Primary-aged pupils respond better to praise than to criticism and are more willing to persevere when the content is interesting and worthwhile.

The establishment of rules and **expectations** that can be explained to children and understood by them helps to promote a harmonious classroom climate, so that the imposition of rules does not mean that children are prevented from expressing their opinions and offering their ideas and perspective on situations. It is not always easy for teachers to balance individual choice with the demands of the statutory **curriculum**; nevertheless, choice with responsibility is the principal objective for all teachers to inculcate in their pupils. The teachers who incur fewest discipline problems are those who are willing to review procedures regularly, ensure that resources are available and fairly distributed, and willing to explain to children rather than harangue them. Pupils are drawn to adults who speak naturally, avoid nagging and keep things in proportion. Every child wants to be reassured that the teacher is concerned with his or her welfare and willing to make learning relevant and fun.

Many teachers use noise level as an indicator of whether pupil behaviour is acceptable, though this yardstick is a rather crude measure as some children naturally speak loudly and young children in particular may need numerous gentle reminders to moderate their tone of voice. Teachers have to distinguish between intrusive forms of noise that come from inappropriate behaviour and constructive forms of noise due to an engagement with the task. Teachers use a variety of strategies to keep noise levels in check, including having a 'tiptoes time' for younger children (tiny voices and quiet movements) or a 'lost in space' time for older pupils, both of which signal that children must work quietly. If the **activities** require **collaboration**, some noise is inevitable while children discuss and grapple with the problem or investigation. To improve their authority in a situation, many teachers deepen their voices and speak more slowly rather than raising the pitch and occasionally punctuate their normal way of speaking with short bursts of staccato speech to emphasise a point. Deepening the voice is particularly important for women, as their higher-pitched voices tend to blend with the children's voices and lose their distinctiveness. If teachers shout or attempt to over-speak the pupils it merely adds to the cacophony.

Inexperienced teachers may unintentionally invite poor behaviour by becoming too informal. Any mention of birthdays, children's parties, outings, sports' days and concerts evokes interest but also invites excitement and distraction. If one of these subjects emerges unexpectedly, experienced teachers allow the initial wave of chatter to be expended before insisting that the children give their full attention to the work. Inexperienced teachers are more inclined to panic when there is a flurry of spontaneous chatter because they imagine that they are losing **control** of the class. Teachers require a considerable amount of confidence before they can enjoy a few moments of **celebration** with the children without being sucked into the maelstrom, knowing that they can quickly retrieve the situation.

The transition times between different phases of the lesson test the quality of pupils' self-control as they move about, access their trays or lockers and settle to the new task. These changeover times benefit from very specific teacher direction, ensuring that the children know precisely what they are supposed to do. It is essential, though far from easy, for teachers to balance the need for speedily explaining the next stage of the lesson sufficiently thoroughly, and keeping the children for too long, thereby inviting restless behaviour.

Further reading

Behaviour4Learning: http://www.behaviour4learning.ac.uk

MacGrath, M. (2000) *The Art of Peaceful Teaching in the Primary School*, London: David Fulton, chapters 4 and 5.

Roffey, S. and O'Reirdan, T. (2003) *Plans for Better Behaviour in the Primary School*, London: David Fulton.

Visser, J. (2000) *Managing Behaviour in Classrooms*, London: David Fulton, chapter 6.

Wyse, D. (2002) *Becoming a Primary School Teacher*, London: Routledge.

BEHAVIOURISM

The behaviourist theory is based on an assumption that an external stimulus produces an inner reaction in a person that then results in an outward response. According to behaviourist theory, terms such as mind, sensation and feelings should be discarded in favour of things that can be readily observed and measured. Early behaviourists such as B. F. Skinner emphasised the way in which it is possible to condition animals to behave in certain ways through a process known as 'conditioning'. The process of conditioning is commonly seen during adult–pupil classroom **interaction**, in which teachers respond approvingly or disapprovingly to children's comments, answers or responses. In the classroom, the teacher's tone of voice and **questioning** elicit observable responses from the children, as witnessed by their facial expressions, the things they say and how they react. Satisfying the teacher therefore becomes a critical factor in the way that children behave.

Teachers make use of behaviourism in emphasising the place of **instruction** and the way in which adults monitor children's learning. In turn, learners assume a relatively passive role, responding to the teacher's instructions with regard to the content, pace and evaluation of the lesson. The teacher transmits information to pupils in a systematic way, using rituals, **rewards** and sanctions as appropriate. Such a **teaching approach** emphasises repetition, rehearsal, revision and regular practice until the teacher is satisfied that mastery has been achieved. Teachers also develop **skills** of close observation of children's actions, making painstaking records of those actions and utilising rewards and sanctions as a means of altering pupils' **behaviour**.

Adopting a behavioural approach to teaching rests on a number of assumptions. First, it deals with what can be observed, such that teachers concern themselves with what a child actually does as opposed to speculating about the underlying causes. Second, it assumes that ways of behaving are learned, so although adults in school are unable to influence pupils' upbringing and social background, they can nevertheless influence their behaviour by controlling the learning environment. Third, it anticipates that learning will involve a change in action as evidenced by applying specific criteria. Fourth, it presumes that the changes are strongly influenced by consequences; actions that lead to reward are likely to become more persistent, whereas those that lead to sanctions are likely to diminish. Finally, it supposes that all behaviours are governed by the contexts in which they take place, so children do learn not only how, but when and where to invoke a particular way of behaving.

Further reading

Davies, N. (1998) 'Teaching for self-esteem versus behaviourism and competition', *Prospero*, 4, 1, pp. 18–27.

Potter, R. (2003) 'An introduction to children's learning', in K. Jacques and R. Hyland (eds) *Professional Studies: Primary phase*, 2nd edn, pp. 63–73, Exeter: Learning Matters.

Wheldall, K. and Merrett, F. (1984) *Positive Teaching: The behavioural approach*, London: Allen & Unwin.

BODY LANGUAGE

Body language is a term used to describe the non-verbal signals that one person gives to another, either deliberately or unintentionally, and exercises a significant part in social **interaction** within the classroom. Pupils closely observe their teachers' body language; they take close note of facial expressions and the attention that is paid to them when they speak, and draw conclusions about their teachers' feelings towards them.

Pupils receive information from both auditory and visual sources. The auditory sources consist of not only the words that are spoken but the sound of the voice, which may be an even more significant factor than the specific words used. The visual sources are most forcefully conveyed through facial expressions, especially the use of the eyes. Although words can be falsified, the eyes cannot easily lie, so they are the principal means of communicating an intention from adults to pupils. Teachers also use hands and face gestures to communicate a variety of messages, including the use of signals to support class discipline. Posture, clothes and grooming are also important visual factors. As children gain experience in the classroom, they become skilled in interpreting the way that teachers respond, look and stand, and adjusting the way they act accordingly. Positive non-verbal affirmation from teachers in the form of nods of the head and non-threatening body stance lets children know that they are being acknowledged and approved. Teachers adopt an open body position when addressing pupils one-to-one, rather than a closed one, based on the principle that facing pupils directly aids communication. That is, they adopt a 'face-to-face' rather than a 'side-to-face' orientation.

Pupils also use a variety of signals to indicate the extent of their involvement in a session. The most common example is the use of a 'hands-up' to communicate to an adult that a child has something to contribute to the proceedings or wishes to ask a question. There is some evidence that physical passivity may indicate a lack of engagement with the lesson content and a refusal or inability to think. Whereas flapping hands, pulling faces, running fingers through hair, grimacing and similar actions, often accompanied by grunts and groans, may be delaying strategies to convince the adult that they are close to reaching an answer or solution, it can also assist some pupils to think. The belief that children are only being serious about learning if they are sitting still and silent does not accommodate the needs of those who prefer a more active mode.

Further reading

Bolton, R. (1979) *People Skills*, New York: Simon & Schuster, chapter 6.
Neill, S. and Caswell, C. (1993) *Body Language for Competent Teachers*, London: Routledge.
Robertson, J. (1996) *Effective Classroom Control*, 3rd edn, London: Hodder & Stoughton.

BULLYING

In primary education, the word 'bullying' is normally used to describe a range of situations in which a child's physical or mental welfare is threatened by the deliberately vindictive actions of another child or group of children. The circumstances that give rise to bullying are a form of disruptive **behaviour** whose effects can be long term and deep rooted, in extreme cases resulting in self-harm. It takes various forms, from name calling, teasing and physical abuse, to intimidation, extortion and serious physical assault. Bullying includes spoken insults, racist remarks, physical spite, such as hitting, and indirect manifestations, such as spreading rumours.

Lawson (1994) suggests that there are three types of bullies: aggressive bullies, anxious bullies and passive bullies. The *aggressive bully* is the most serious type, as children may be physically injured. Aggressive bullies are often badly behaved in school and require close supervision and monitoring throughout the day. Controlling aggressive bullying requires all adults to ensure that the malefactors are made to adhere to a strictly enforced set of **rules** governing their actions. **Parental involvement** is also essential in setting targets for improvement.

Anxious bullies see themselves as failures and vent their frustrations on other children by making cruel comments to them and undermining their achievements. It is often younger, vulnerable children who are subjected to their taunts, as they are unlikely to retaliate. Although anxious bullies create distress for other children, the bullies also need to be helped to gain **self-esteem** by placing them in a position where they can succeed. For instance, they may relate well to younger children in a structured environment, supervised by an adult who can monitor the situation and offer **encouragement** and direction.

Passive bullies are the support members of bullying gangs but not the principal perpetrators. The expression 'passive bully' is not wholly satisfactory as it implies that such types are less culpable. It is probably true to say that many passive bullies do not particularly relish their role and would prefer to expend their energies in other ways. Their fear of losing credibility with the aggressors, and perhaps becoming victims themselves if they do not conform, deters them from breaking free. Adults can help them to develop a new identity by providing them with positive alternatives and ensuring that they have a busy, interesting schedule, especially during break times. The process of restoration is often a long one and the adults involved in finding a resolution have to take into account the fact that bullying habits often continue after school as well as during it.

It is not always easy for adults to discriminate between high spirits and bullying, as all children occasionally have squabbles that to adult eyes look more serious than are truly the case. The animosity soon passes and the two opponents resume their **friendship** as if nothing had happened. On the other hand, conflict situations can create the circumstances for distress and unhappiness for children, so adults in school have a responsibility to be vigilant and intervene to prevent suffering. Racist bullying is a particularly unpleasant area of school life that has received a great deal of attention in recent years. All schools have to demonstrate that they not only have a policy to combat racism, but are also active in ensuring that it is implemented and monitored. Teachers have a duty of care towards pupils and have to take reasonable steps to prevent pupils from being verbally or physically abused. If they fail to do so it not only puts children at risk but also opens the teacher concerned to being accused of negligence. New teachers to a school have a responsibility to become familiar with its anti-bullying policies and procedures for dealing with incidents.

Common signs that children are victims of bullying include regular headaches, stomach aches, **anxiety** and irritability, and parents who suspect that bullying is contributing to the symptoms in their children are advised to contact the school immediately. It is important to deal with bullying because it can adversely affect children's mental and psychological health, induce social maladjustment and even be the cause of physical illness. Physical bullying is thankfully rare in primary schools, but unless it is dealt with during time in primary school, it is likely to continue once the pupils transfer to secondary school and perpetuate the climate of fear and uncertainty for the victims.

Teachers make a considerable difference to pupil attitudes by modelling a caring attitude, valuing each child as an individual and listening carefully to explanations. They can also promote opportunities for children who have been bullying others to become involved in positive, supportive activities that are more worthwhile than the bullying. The victims, as well as the perpetrators, need to be monitored, as there is a tendency for those who have been bullied to bully others in turn. Consequently, some children are victims, some are bullies and some are both victims and bullies.

One of the problems facing teachers is that bullying becomes a habit that eventually acts like a stimulant, such that the act of bullying becomes enjoyable for the perpetrator. If bullying is not dealt with sooner rather than later, it becomes habit forming and intervention to stop it being repeated becomes more difficult. Although pernicious bullying that brings distress to other pupils cannot be tolerated, the children concerned must also be shown that there are benefits attached to kindness, consideration and self-sacrifice that cannot be matched by tormenting a weaker child. The involvement of parents at an early stage normally falls under the head teacher's remit, supported by the Special Educational Needs Coordinator (SENCO) and, where appropriate, advice from external bodies, including the DfES web site on bullying, 'Don't suffer in silence' (www.dfes.gov.uk/bullying).

Further reading

Beane, A. L. (1999) *Bully Free Classroom*, Minnesota: Free Spirit.
DfES web site: www.parentcentre.gov.uk
Lawson, S. (1994) *Helping Children Cope With Bullying*, London: Sheldon Press.
OFSTED (1993) *Achieving Good Behaviour in Schools*, London: HMSO.
Rigby, K. (2001) *Stop the Bullying*, London: Jessica Kingsley.
Sharp, S., Thompson, D. and Arora, T. (2002) *Bullying*, London: Routledge.
Varnava, G. (2002) *How to Stop Bullying: Towards a non-violent school*, London: David Fulton.

CARING

All adults with responsibility for children have a duty of care placed upon them to ensure that, within their means, they do not suffer physical, emotional or psychological hardship that is incompatible with their age and maturity. The exact nature of this **accountability** is defined in law but can broadly be thought of as teachers exercising judgements in respect of a child's welfare that could be expected from a responsible parent. Primary schools are havens from the uncertainty of the world and offer a settled environment for young lives to be nurtured and developed.

Teaching **assistants** often have a designated caring role in dealing with personal and social needs and the majority are skilled at getting alongside children, advising them about decisions, comforting them in times of distress and offering an encouraging word. Their non-official status allows pupils to feel easier about approaching them and gaining a sympathetic hearing about issues that affect them.

Care is an approach that goes beyond a tender emotion or sympathy. It reflects a desire to seek the emotional and academic good of pupils and other adults in school and to behave in such a way that they are able to learn and develop without undue hindrance. This process requires that teachers explain their decisions (but do not try to justify them) and persevere to promote equality of opportunity and affirm children's genuine efforts. In turn, pupils can be helped to develop a sense of compassion through taking care of a younger child in the school, helping in charity fund-raising events or befriending elderly members of the community.

One of the reasons that people elect to become primary teachers is that they value the caring dimension of their work, which makes them feel positive about their teaching and sustains them during periods of difficulty. It is important for pupils to know that adults are considerate and want the best for them. Care lubricates adult–child relationships and enhances both pupils' and teachers' feelings of self-worth and respect. This form of caring is different from pampering the children or 'smothering' them and restricting their independence or hindering them from making their own decisions. Premature **intervention** and high levels of support to pupils brings great satisfaction to adults but may stifle initiative and make children overly dependent on assistance. Intervening in such a way that pupils have insufficient time and opportunity to grapple with problems does not help children to become self-sufficient or foster perseverance in them. Schools are social settings and although teachers are not social workers they work within a social climate that is created through the agreed priorities of the staff. Teachers have a professional responsibility to intervene in such a way that children's problems are lessened or solved and to intercede to resolve conflicts.

Unless teachers distance themselves from the children and become mere agents for delivering **lessons**, they cannot avoid being influential and significant. A school world in which teachers and children never spoke of birthdays, outings, brothers and sisters, world events and relational tensions, as well as fears and disappointments, would be a bleak one indeed. In March 2004 the Department for Education and Skills published *Every Child Matters: The next steps* (DfES 2004a) stressing the importance of establishing a framework to protect, to promote the well-being of, and to support all children and their families. At about the same time the government published its strategy for pupils with special educational needs, entitled *Removing Barriers to Achievement* (DfES 2004b) in which it accepted that children's emotional and mental health needs and family circumstances may have a significant impact on their capacity to make the most of their opportunities in school.

In every school there is a designated senior teacher for child protection and a deputy for occasions when the designated person is absent. Each school produces a child protection policy and procedures; monitors and maintains a confidential **recording** system; and produces information for parents in the prospectus, brochure and (in many cases) home/school agreement document. Child protection issues are also addressed through the curriculum, particularly in the areas of personal safety, **self-esteem**, relationships, **bullying** and safe access to the Internet.

Despite the timely warning issued by the noted education writer and researcher, Jennifer Nias – that it may be unhealthy for teachers to care too much owing to the heavy demands it places on them to the detriment of intellectual aims – it is undeniable that the caring attitude that inspires primary teachers is rooted in a desire for the good of humanity in general.

Further reading

Department for Education and Skills (2004a) *Every Child Matters: The next steps*, London: The Stationery Office.

Katz, L. G. (1995a) *Talks With Teachers of Young Children*, Norwood, NJ, Ablex.

Nelson-Jones, R. (1988) *Practical Counselling and Helping Skills*, 2nd edn, London: Cassell.

Nias, D. J. (1997) 'Would schools improve if teachers cared less?', *Education 3–13*, 25, 3, pp. 11–22.

Noddings, N. (2002) *Starting at Home*, Berkeley, CA: University of California Press.

Shaylock, G. (1998) 'Professionalism and intensification in teaching: a case study of care in teachers' work', *Asia-Pacific Journal of Teacher Education*, 26, 3, pp. 177–90.

CELEBRATION

There are many occasions when the staff and pupils in primary schools have cause to celebrate, some of which coincide with religious festivals; other times are to indicate milestones in the schools' history, such as a centenary or the opening of new buildings. Yet other celebrations are to signify special achievements, such as a successful school inspection or gaining a coveted trophy. Celebrations are sometimes intimate, involving a class or small group of children, but in primary schools they are more often whole-school events.

Celebration is often associated with academic or sporting success. Teachers who focus on positive aspects of children's work and celebrate success are more likely to enjoy a strong rapport with pupils and fewer **control** problems. Children that are well occupied with interesting work in an upbeat working environment provide less challenge than those who are trapped in a mundane one. Pupils who can ask for clarification about the work from teachers without fear of being criticised, supported in trying things for themselves and congratulated for making a genuine effort are usually contented.

In most teaching sessions, but notably during **literacy** and **numeracy** lessons, the final few minutes are frequently used by teachers to review the lesson, point out common misconceptions and indicate ways forward. This **lesson review** time (often referred to as the 'plenary') also provides an opportunity for teachers to celebrate children's achievements, salute the effort they have made and create a positive end to the session.

Pragmatic considerations about preparing and teaching **lessons** and striving to keep pace with the heavy demands of school life can cloud teacher memories of being a child. Celebrating the regular features of **childhood** experience, such as the excitement generated by a special school event, being in school after hours for an **extracurricular activity** or hearing the class sing a birthday song, reinforces the fact that a rounded education is composed of more than academic success.

Further reading

Brown, T., Foot, P. and Holt, P. (2001) *Let our children learn: allowing ownership, providing support, celebrating achievement*, Nottingham: Education Now.
Burton, A. (1996) *Children's Pleasures*, London: V & A Publications.
Jackson, M. (1987) 'Making sense of school', in A. Pollard, (ed.) *Children and Their Primary Schools: a New Perspective*, Lewes: Falmer.
Smith, J. and Lynch, J. (2004) *The Primary School Year*, London: Routledge.

CHILDHOOD

The United Nations Convention on the Rights of the Child defines a child as a person under the age of 18 years. The concept of childhood involves the separating of two phases of life, pre-adulthood and adulthood, but has not always been defined by reference to age. The difficulties involved in identifying childhood as something distinctive is underlined by the fact that eighteenth- and early nineteenth-century concepts of childhood applied only to children under the age of 5. Those over 5 years of age were often economically active in factories and mines alongside adults until the pioneering work of social reformers in the 1800s. During the latter part of the nineteenth century younger children were increasingly viewed as vulnerable and in need of adult protection. Regulation of the workplace introduced their right to a systematic education and social welfare. Concern about the moral development of children and the changing patterns of work and family life led to a fresh understanding about the responsibility of parents and the importance of privacy, morality and a settled home life in the development of the child. However, regulation also introduced the notion that the state has the right to intervene within the family to protect the child from parents and to ensure that the child has access to education. Perceptions of the position of children in society is seen by some as precarious owing to the increase in divorce rates, irresponsibility by absent fathers, larger numbers of mothers in full-time employment, sexual abuse and the rise of the single-parent family that requires children, especially elder siblings, to take a lot of domestic responsibilities from an early age. Some social observers even argue that the whole concept of childhood is under threat.

Childhood is not a universal phenomenon but a socially constructed one that regulates and reproduces the language, **expectations** and nature of the relationship between adults and children. In Western society the concept of childhood is reflected in the legal requirement for children to undertake compulsory schooling and to be protected from economic, sexual and other forms of exploitation. Adults working in school have a duty of care which includes showing patience and sympathy towards children's failure to understand and make mistakes, and their vulnerabilities. Childhood is important as a time when children find their own individuality so that they can stand firm when challenges arise later in life. The security and confidence gained during childhood allows children to reach the end of their primary years feeling comfortable with their place in the world prior to the demands of the teenage years. Ideally, this sense of self-belief can be translated into a positive attitude towards other people and a sympathetic approach to human relationships. Every adult in school has a measure of responsibility to contribute to the development process.

Teachers are influential in helping to shape and direct the way in which pupils mature and understand the world and themselves, so teachers have to be sensitive to the way in which their attempts to influence children may unintentionally upset the fine balance that always exists between natural development and adult intervention. Different cultures, religions and races also have particular priorities for their children to which teachers and other adults in school must be sensitive.

In the UK, the Children Act 2004 provided a legislative spine for the wider strategy for improving children's lives, covering the universal services to which every child has access and more targeted services for those with additional needs. The overall aim is to encourage integrated planning, commissioning and delivery of services, as well as strengthen multidisciplinary working, remove duplication, increase **accountability** and improve the coordination of individual and joint inspections in local authorities. The legislation is intended to be enabling rather than prescriptive and provide local authorities with flexibility in the way that they implement its provisions.

Further reading

Alderson, P. (1999) *Young Children's Rights: Beliefs, principles and practice*, London: Save the Children/Jessica Kingsley.

Bowlby, J. (1953) *Child Care and the Growth of Love*, Harmondsworth: Penguin.

Corsaro, W. A. (2003) *We're Friends, Right?* Washington, DC: The National Academies Press.

Masheder, M. (2004) *Positive Childhood: Educating young citizens*, London: Green Print/Merlin Press.

Postman, N. (1982) *The Disappearance of Childhood*, New York: Vintage.

Stern, D. N. (1998) *The Interpersonal World of the Infant*, London: Routledge.

CIRCLE TIME

Circle time is a group activity in which children sit down together with the purpose of better understanding themselves and one another, building relationships and facilitating dialogue between pupils and teachers, and between pupils and pupils. Circle time is an opportunity for children to learn the skills they need to prosper socially, including effective communication, emotional literacy, anger management and conflict resolution. The development of these skills may subsequently have a positive impact on pupil behaviour but this outcome is not the principal purpose of circle time and even the best-behaved pupils benefit from involvement. The experience is not a subtle form of coercion, reprimand or correction, but aims to create a space in which pupils can discuss, reflect, probe their emotions and feel empowered. At its best, circle time helps children to celebrate their personal identity.

Teachers create the atmosphere of circle time events by setting up an open circle of chairs or cushions for everyone to sit on, so that there are no barriers between pupils. One common activity is for an object (such as a toy or familiar object) to be passed around the circle with only the person holding it being allowed to speak about the topic at any time. Adults also sit within the circle and may participate as a member of the group or act as a facilitator. Most pupils enjoy circle time, as it gives them an opportunity to talk about themselves and one another, but rules have to be established and enforced if the time is to be effectively spent. The rules may include only one person to speak at any one time; that no one is obliged to contribute; and that comments must be temperate, free from personal slights. The rules help the children to feel secure so that they can express themselves freely and without fear of rebuke.

Topics for sharing or discussion during circle time depend on the age of the children and the existing relationship within the group. Many teachers of younger children use the opportunity to celebrate special occasions, share ideas and hobbies and even commiserate with a child who has undergone a miserable experience. Naturally, teachers have to be extremely sensitive that circle time does not become too intense or a time-filling activity. Some teachers use the time to select children who take it in turns to be 'special' for the day and receive small privileges as a result.

Further reading

Collins, M. (2003) *Enhancing Circle Time for the Very Young*, London: Lucky Duck/Paul Chapman.
Taylor, M. (2003) *Going Round in Circles: Implementing and learning from circle time*, Slough: National Foundation for Educational Research.

CITIZENSHIP

Citizenship education in primary schools offers pupils opportunities to grapple with difficult life issues and **dilemmas** through discussion, collaborative activities and problem solving. In most schools attention is given to ways in which pupils can make a difference in the world (locally or globally) and they are encouraged to take an active role in fund raising for poor communities, befriending the elderly and recycling materials. The principle underlying social action is to ensure deeper and lasting change in pupils for the benefit of everyone.

In the UK the development of citizenship for pupils of primary age is non-statutory but is nonetheless followed by every primary school in one form or another. The Qualifications and Curriculum Authority (QCA) provides a scheme based on twelve individual units, including topics such as 'choices', 'people who help us' and 'local democracy for young citizens'. Under the banner of PSHE (Personal, Social and Health Education) and citizenship, the national non-statutory guidelines provide a framework under two main headings of (1) **knowledge, skills** and understanding and (2) breadth of study. The first category focuses on developing confidence and responsibility, helping pupils to make the most of their abilities, preparing them to undertake an active role as citizens, developing a healthy, safer lifestyle, securing good relationships and respecting the differences between people. Aspects of citizenship are frequently introduced and promoted during occasions such as a whole-school or class **assembly** to share and discuss ideas about appropriate personal conduct and ways to be a responsible member of society, especially at local neighbourhood level.

Citizenship education is a means through which teachers help pupils to orientate towards a world in which there is a surfeit of information, yet little wisdom about its use or guidance about making sound choices. The successful preparation of children as responsible citizens depends to an extent on the moral lead that teachers are willing and able to provide for them, not only through formal citizenship **lessons** but in the way they behave and put their words into action.

Further reading

Bloomfield, P. (2003) 'Local, national and global citizenship', *Education 3–13*, 31, 3, pp. 59–67.

Bottery, M. (2000) 'Values education', in R. Bailey (ed.) *Teaching Values and Citizenship Across the Curriculum*, pp. 3–13, London: Kogan Page.

CITIZED: http://www.citized.info

Farrer, F. (2000) *A Quiet Revolution: Encouraging positive values in our children*, London: Rider.

Hicks, D. (2001) *Citizenship for the Future: A practical classroom guide*, Godalming: World Wildlife Fund.

Wilkins, C. (2000) 'Citizenship education', in R. Bailey (ed.) *Teaching Values and Citizenship Across the Curriculum*, pp. 14–27, London: Kogan Page.

CLASS SIZE

Class size has always been an important issue for teachers. Numbers of children in infant (**Key Stage** 1) classes have been reduced over recent years and are normally fewer than thirty; numbers in junior classes (Key Stage 2) have changed little for a generation. Today in nearly all maintained (state-funded) primary schools there is considerable use made of teaching assistants (TAs), increasing the frequency of child–adult **interaction**, though children may become unduly dependent on their support. The concept of one teacher being wholly responsible for the education of one class has gradually been replaced by more emphasis on specialist teaching, especially for older primary children. At the same time there has also been a slight increase in numbers attending private school, where the pupil–teacher ratio tends to be much better than in state schools. Although the majority of teachers welcome moves to reduce class sizes, the restriction on numbers has led some parents to complain that it has worsened the problems they have experienced of trying to get places for their children in popular, over-subscribed schools.

Common sense suggests that smaller classes must inevitably lead to higher standards and greater pupil **achievement** because teachers have more time to spend with each individual child. However, other factors impact upon attainment, including pupils' academic **ability**, level of motivation for the subject and availability of adult assistance and resources. The clearest evidence of positive effects of smaller class size is found among infant children; reducing class size can be especially helpful for disadvantaged and minority ethnic pupils.

The positive effects of small classes diminish if teachers persist in using instructional methods and formal classroom procedures that are more suited to larger, whole-class teaching styles. The greatest potential benefit to pupils in smaller classes is the quality of teacher–pupil **interaction**, facilitated by the teacher's insights into the children's educational and social needs. For new school entrants, a more favour-able adult–child ratio increases the likelihood that the children will adjust rapidly to the requirements and routines associated with school.

There is some disagreement among educationists about the length of time that the positive effects of smaller classes persist after pupils move to larger classes, but there is a consensus about the fact that class size reduction for new entrants to school (aged 5 years) facilitates greater academic success. The impact of smaller classes for older primary-age children (aged from 7 to 11 years) is less clear, though when class size drops below twenty there appears to be a sharp accompanying improvement in attainment, especially for less confident pupils.

Class size has implications for the type of **teaching approach** used by teachers dealing with larger and with smaller classes. Smaller clas-ses offer the chance of a more relaxed classroom atmosphere, due in part to the individual attention that each pupil receives, thereby reducing the frustrations in waiting for help from an adult. Further-more, in whole-class discussions and times when pupils are brought together, children are statistically more likely to be chosen to answer questions and given greater opportunity to contribute ideas than pupils of similar age in large classes. The smaller the class size, the greater the chance that pupils receive a high proportion of educa-tional resources. Teachers are likely to spend more time in larger classes on non-teaching activities and have to deal with more com-plex issues regarding classroom management owing to the logistics of coping with more pupils.

Larger class sizes do not necessarily disadvantage pupils but they make a teacher's life more onerous owing to the heavier workload of marking and report writing. Teachers dealing with larger numbers of children have to employ teaching and management strategies that allow them to avoid an excessive workload. For example, they may make greater use of pupil self-assessment (to reduce the extent of marking), more straightforward **homework** tasks, employment of computer software in producing reports, and collaborative learning. A study commissioned by the DfES in December 2004 (DfES 2004c) indicated that test results in mathematics, English and science were not appreciably different for children in larger and smaller classes, though the demands on teachers of large classes were considerably heavier.

Further reading

Blatchford, P. (2003) *The Class Size Debate: Is smaller better?* Maidenhead: Open University Press.

DfES: www.ed.gov/pubs/ReducingClass/Classsize.html

Department for Education and Skills (2004c) *The Effects of Class Size on Attainment and Classroom Processes in English Primary Schools (Years 4 to 6) 2000–2003*, Brief No. RB13–04, by P. Blatchford, P. Bassett, P. Brown, C. Martin and A. Russell, Institute of Education, University of London.

Robinson, G. E. and Wittebols, J. H. (1986) *Class size research: A related cluster analysis for decision-making*, Arlington, VA: Education Research Service.

CODE OF PRACTICE

The duties of schools and teachers are clearly laid out in the **special educational needs** Code of Practice and the Special Needs and Disability Act (http://www.dfes.gov.uk/sen/). The Code outlines the framework for identifying, assessing and making provision for children's needs, though the actual assessment and teaching measures used are left for individual teachers and schools to devise. The Code sets out a graduated approach to the identification, assessment and provision based on pupils' special needs. It makes clear that the Code is only concerned with interventions that are additional to or different from those provided as part of the school's normal differentiated **curriculum**. The Code sets out the framework in an accessible form for all teachers, who may also need to involve and inform the Special Educational Needs Coordinator (SENCO). In addition to the main document, teachers also use accompanying support materials (known as a 'toolkit'), consisting of a set of practical pamphlets on implementing the Code.

The Code describes two stages at which a more focused assessment and provision operate, referred to as School Action and School Action Plus. At the level of *School Action*, teachers decide on the basis of working closely with a particular child and consultation with parents that further support is required for him or her to make satisfactory progress in learning. The SENCO may advise that short-term support from outside agencies such as an educational psychologist or speech therapist is appropriate. Information about the child's academic progress is accumulated and evidence collected about previous educational initiatives. All the information is recorded on the child's personal record and an individual education plan (IEP) is produced specifying the educational strategy for the next stage of the pupil's education. *School Action Plus* involves a request for longer-term assistance from external agencies following a decision made by the SENCO and colleagues, in consultation with parents. Subsequently, a range of specialists may be approached and involved, depending on the nature of the need, and a new IEP is produced.

As the IEP is reviewed and monitored, the school may request a statutory assessment from the local education authority if the pupil has demonstrated a significant cause for concern. This assessment process may lead to a formal statement of special educational needs that will specify the additional support required or, in some cases, a move to specialist provision from outside the school. At this stage it is necessary to define more specifically the nature of the child's special need to facilitate decisions about the most suitable level of provision.

Further reading

Beveridge, S. (2004) *Children, Families and Schools: Developing partnerships for inclusive education*, London: Routledge.
Hayes, D. (2004a) *Foundations of Primary Teaching*, 3rd edn, London: David Fulton, chapter 9.

COLLABORATION

Collaboration is the process by which pupils work together to reach a specified and predetermined **learning objective**. Collaboration is different from cooperation, which is a general term for courtesy and thoughtfulness. Consequently, children may be cooperative while not collaborating, though effective collaboration relies on a high level of cooperation between pupils. Work-related collaborative **interaction** between primary-aged pupils accounts for less than 15% of the total time they spend on learning, and much of the collaboration takes place in pairs rather than in larger groups. In a collaborative enterprise, each member of the group fulfils a particular role; for example, one child may be leader and orchestrate the proceedings, while another child may say little but contribute practical **skills**. Teachers have to determine how much pupils should record in writing or pictorially and make decisions about seating arrangements for the groups and the identification of targets for **achievement**. Teachers also think ahead about the way in which ideas might be disseminated after the end of the session and the next steps in the learning process.

One of the key issues in collaborative learning is the amount that pupils contribute to the discussion and how much being part of a group enhances the quality of their **thinking**. Dividing children into groups can be an organisational device to expedite the allocation of activities of differing levels of difficulty, each group containing children of similar **ability** ('differentiation') or for the purpose of combining pupil expertise. Teachers of young pupils often use group collaboration to promote social awareness and develop interpersonal sensitivity, expressed through listening to one another, taking turns, showing consideration, and so on. For example, children may work in groups to solve a mathematical problem, act out some improvised drama or produce a complex piece of artwork. Younger pupils might also be encouraged to **talk** about ways to ensure that every child is included in playground games during break (recess).

With older pupils, the teacher sometimes presents an ethical dilemma (based, perhaps, on an aspect of **citizenship**) in which the members of the group have to discuss the options and arrive at an agreed solution or position. The teacher outlines the issues, invites preliminary comments from the children and presents them with the problem to be discussed in groups of four or five children. Pupils may also collaborate to discuss an issue about which they, rather than the teacher, feel strongly. For example, children have firm opinions about **friendship** patterns, **homework**, children's television programmes, playtime, school **rules** and associated topics, all of which provide fertile ground for exploring important principles. Separate groups may address the same issue and later combine to contribute their ideas; after further discussion a consensus is reached across the groups or, if not, the teacher summarises the conflicting positions to show children that having different views about issues is acceptable, providing there is evidence to support the assertions.

Teachers are not able to assume that children are capable of instant collaboration simply because they are put in groups to work together. Collaboration, like any other skill, has to be explained, developed and practised so that it can become refined into a powerful learning tool. While freedom of expression is important, children have to learn to show respect for other people's opinions while, as far as possible, expressing their own ideas openly. One of the most difficult attitudes for children to develop is having an open mind, such that they do not summarily dismiss views, pour scorn on unusual suggestions or marginalise other children in the group. Teachers stress with children the need for careful and respectful listening when working in pairs and in small groups, and as part of this preparation children are taught to summarise what others have said and ask sensible questions about their ideas. Meanwhile, adults enthuse about children's verbal contributions, offer new perspectives and add occasional comment to reignite discussion or provide a moderating influence when pupils make unbalanced statements.

The process of engaging mentally with a subject before offering an opinion or suggestion is a related skill that pupils need to develop before they can make an effective contribution to a collaborative venture. Younger children find this process difficult because they struggle to formulate ideas in their heads. Allowing children opportunities to **talk** to others enables them to move outside their immediate world, to recognise life's complexities, to gain self-confidence, to learn from sharing ideas, to evaluate opinions and to find ways to offer support to their classmates.

Adeptness in collaboration is also an essential skill for teachers as they liaise with colleagues to discuss educational issues and make decisions. The process helps teachers to explore and interrogate taken-for-granted aspects of practice and provides opportunities to challenge the prevailing orthodoxy. Teacher collaboration has to be authentic and not contrived, conducted within agreed professional boundaries and pedagogically sound; that is, it must be manageable and beneficial for teaching. Much of what passes for collaboration may lack rigour and lapse into low-level debate when it has the potential to offer opportunity for enquiry into aspects of practice and agreed strategies to enhance the educational provision within the school. It is even possible that a group of teachers' desire to conform or worries about upsetting colleagues may suppress more creative and spontaneous teaching ideas and suggestions for innovative practice that collaborative decision making could provide.

Further reading

General Teaching Council for England (2004) *Grouping pupils and students: what difference does the type of grouping make to teaching and learning in schools?* On-line. Available: http://www.gtce.org.uk/research/abilityhome. asp (accessed April 2005).

Hallam, S., Ireson, J. and Davies, J. (2004) 'Grouping practices in the primary school: what influences change?', *British Educational Research Journal*, 30, 1, pp. 117–40.

Hargreaves, A. and Dawe, R. (1990) 'Paths of professional development: contrived collegiality, collaborative culture, and the case of peer coaching', *Teaching & Teacher Education*, 6, pp. 227–41.

Kauchak, D. and Burbank, M. D. (2003) 'An alternative model for professional development: investigations into effective collaboration', *Teacher and Teacher Education*, 19, 5, pp. 499–514.

Minnett, A. M. (2003) 'Collaboration and shared reflections in the classroom', *Teachers and Teaching*, 9, 3, pp. 279–85.

COLLEGIALITY

The concept of collegiality, based on the root word 'college' to signify a society of scholars or an association of likeminded people, has
become an integral feature of school life. Since the early 1980s the
role of parents and school governors/board members in helping to
shape priorities and determine the direction of education has been
enshrined in legislation. A belief that the head of the school has to
take the full responsibility for all the decisions that take place in a
primary school is an outdated one. In fact, head teachers require and
seek as much assistance as possible in the complex task of leading a
school and ensuring its success.

Crucial to the ultimate success of any organisation is the commitment, motivation and satisfaction of the people who work there. In a
primary school there are many more adults involved in educational
provision than in the past, each person with a stake in its future and a
specific contribution to make. Thus, teaching and ancillary staff,
administrators and parents are invited to contribute directly (through
attendance at meetings) or indirectly (through informal contact with
the head teacher or one of the governors) when key decisions are
being made.

Collegiality goes deeper than the mere establishment of systems
and hierarchies. It is primarily rooted in the active participation of
staff members in such a way that they feel that their views on school
priorities are welcome and taken seriously. Most primary head teachers actively promote dialogue with colleagues: sharing plans, soli-
citing ideas, reviewing procedures and discussing the implications of
proposed innovations, such as changing the structure of the school
day.

It is not practical or desirable for every decision to be discussed and
affirmed by every member of the staff. However, primary schools in
which collegiality is genuinely espoused ensure that all major decisions are taken with full or majority support. Teachers are comfortable with a collegial approach if they feel that their views are not
only sought but also taken into account when decisions are being
made. Teachers are unimpressed with a situation in which a head
teacher declares an intention to involve everyone but to all intents
and purposes makes the decision in isolation.

Effective schools are places where teamwork and staff loyalty are
embedded into the fabric of everything that takes place and teachers
therefore need to be as sensitive to corporate endeavour and teamwork as to the technical competence to teach. All teachers have

responsibilities to children, parents, governors, members of the community and colleagues, and are required to demonstrate a willingness to support one another in the educational endeavour. Adults in school respond to genuine expressions of appreciation and considerateness from colleagues, thereby creating a bank of goodwill and strong feelings of camaraderie that are essential for effective teamwork.

Trainee teachers contribute to the collegial atmosphere by displaying a willing, enthusiastic approach to the job, doing their best to value those around them and being patient with situations that they find irritating or frustrating. While a head teacher may strive to enhance the level of participation and involvement among the whole staff, trainee teachers need first to demonstrate their sense of vocation, professional attitude and teaching potential before they are fully accepted into the discussion and **decision making** forum. Most schools have methods for canvassing pupils' views by establishing forums, school councils (composed of pupil representatives) or in-class discussions and feedback.

Further reading

Fielding, M. (2005) *Factors Influencing the Transfer of Good Practice*, Research Report RR615, Nottingham: Department for Education & Skills.

Mills, J. and Mills, R. W. (1995) *Primary School People: Getting to know your colleagues*, London: Routledge.

Nias, D. J., Southworth, G. W. and Yeomans, R. (1989) *Staff Relationships in the Primary School*, London: Cassell.

COMMUNICATION

Every adult working in primary education needs to possess strong interpersonal and communication **skills** exercised within a climate of patience, flexibility and dependability. Effective communicators are characterised by being able to make decisions with confidence, demonstrating a willingness to ask for help when needed and being open to suggestions and ideas to help their teaching. Teachers, trainees, ancillary staff and pupils have to persevere to interact with one another using supportive comments and showing a proper sense of decorum. They avoid confrontation by being sensitive to other people's viewpoints and showing sympathy for a position even if disagreeing with it, recognising that impressions are constantly being created through use of voice tone, gesture and attitude to what is being said. Class teachers and **assistants** learn children's names as quickly as possible, aware that the use of a name is a powerful tool in establishing and maintaining strong links with the individual concerned. In communicating with pupils, adults take account of their age and maturity and try to explain things calmly and carefully.

Every adult encounter with pupils in school involves establishing a rapid rapport with them. Teachers and assistants need to have insight into the things that children find significant if they wish to create effective communication networks that will enhance learning and maintain good relations. Children appreciate teachers who are fair, interested in them as individuals, transparent in their dealings, clear about their intentions, helpful in their explanations, non-judgemental in their attitude, yet unflinching in confronting unsatisfactory situations. They benefit from teachers who are prepared to listen carefully to what is said to them, leading to improvements in **self-esteem**, motivation and academic success.

To communicate well, teachers have to take account of the speed with which they **talk**, the frequency and length of pauses and the smoothness of their delivery. In this regard they have to bear in mind the likely significance of, and differences between, fast and confident speech. Fast speech can be used to disguise adult insecurity as it discourages interruptions and overwhelms the pupils with a flow of words, whereas confident speech is rich in character and interest. Effective teachers vary the speed of their delivery and use deliberate pauses while they establish extended eye contact pauses. Whatever the nature or intention of the communicative act, all teachers benefit from giving careful attention to a range of practical considerations, the first of which is audibility, which can be impaired by slurring of words and poor articulation. Careful articulation, firm use of consonants and the correct forming of vowels assist audibility.

The second skill relates to pace of speech. Inexperienced teachers sometimes speak too quickly owing to nervousness; others speak too slowly and solemnly in an effort to be precise. Some change of pace to emphasise specific points and variations in inflection to indicate a conclusion (downward inflection) or invite speculation (upward inflection) can also be used to good effect. The third skill is the selective use of pauses that offer pupils the opportunity to think and capture pupils' attention if mixed with regular speech. However, the excessive use of pauses and hesitations, such as 'uhm' and 'like er' and 'you know' irritates children. The fourth skill is injecting enthusiasm, transmitted through physical and mental energy, accompanied by appropriate gestures and the employment of dynamic verbs to inspire pupils rather than bland ones. The fifth skill is using 'bright' eye contact to engage pupils, demonstrating a personal interest in them and inviting their participation. The final communication skill is adopting an upright stance with good posture to indicate alertness and a resolute disposition.

Communicative acts are important in **behaviour** management and discipline. Children are very observant to variations in teachers' moods and the way that this impacts on their attitude and behaviour. Children favour teachers who do not resort to sanctions without first exploring other avenues of dealing with a situation, those who allow pupils to talk without interrupting them and those that explain work clearly without sounding irritated if the explanation has to be repeated. Children like teachers who are friendly and sympathetic, have a sense of **humour** and are interesting people, while still able to maintain class discipline without employing fierce methods. Teachers that use sarcasm and hectoring are particularly disliked. Thankfully, the use of **encouragement** and praise forms the bulk of adult–pupil verbal communication in school.

Communicating with parents is an essential element of the educator's role, both formally through planned meetings to discuss pupil progress and give information about proposed events, and informally through casual encounters that happen before and after school. Parents, guardians and relatives of younger primary-age pupils are most likely to have regular informal contact with teachers and support staff as they accompany the children to and from school. Parents of older primary-age children are more often constrained by work commitments. The growth in 'dawn until dusk' schools that provide extended childcare facilities in addition to the regular teaching day might increase the frequency of contact with parents. One measure by which parents judge school staff, especially teachers, is the quality of their receptiveness, pleasant manner and willingness to offer helpful comment about the child's progress.

Further reading

Barnes, D. (1975) *From Communication to Curriculum*, Harmondsworth: Penguin Books.
Gardner, S. (2004) 'Four critical features of teacher-guided reporting in infant science and literacy contexts', *Language and Education*, 18, 5, pp. 361–78.
Hayes, D. (1998) *Effective Verbal Communication*, London: Hodder & Stoughton.
Qualifications and Curriculum Authority (1999) *Teaching Speaking and Listening in Key Stages 1 and 2*, London: QCA Publications.

COMPETITION

Competition has always existed between pupils in school and out of school and will continue to do so. Parents contribute to this competitive element when, for example, they ask their children which book they are **reading** and how it contrasts with those other pupils are reading in the class, compare reports with other parents, scan lists to see where a particular school is placed in a league table of performance and urge their children to work harder to gain better grades. During sports' days, parents cheer and urge their children to run faster, jump higher or get ahead of the others. Pupil **activities** are often naturally competitive, but sometimes adults and older children can become extremely intensive about winning; for example, junior-age children become animated and exuberant about team games.

Although competition provides an important element of a pupil's desire to accomplish more and aspire to greater heights of scholastic and sporting **achievement**, children also need time to relax and have fun. Many parents want their children to develop their experience beyond the realm of academic subjects, which is partly the reason why so many children study dance, singing, piano, painting and so on, even though only a very small number of them will become professional artists or musicians etc.

The introduction of extra classes to refine and rehearse and reinforce **knowledge** is commonplace in school, especially sessions that are run after hours for children to master weaker areas in English and mathematics and help them to improve their national test results. In addition, most pupils receive regular **homework** from the time they enter the formal school system. Out of school some children are encouraged and cajoled by parents to undertake additional academic activities to ensure that they are one step ahead of their classmates and better placed to claim a place in the best schools, colleges and universities. Even very young children soon detect that one way to gain adult approval is to be performing near or at the top of the class. While excessive competition may be unsatisfactory, it is equally true that a lack of competitive stimulus often leaves pupils intellectually dissatisfied and underachieving.

Further reading

Davies, N. (1998) 'Teaching for self-esteem versus behaviourism and competition', *Prospero*, 4, 1, pp. 18–27.

Lewis, A., Simonds, L. and Maras, P. (1999) 'Elephants, donuts and hamburgers: young children co-operating to co-operate and co-operating to compete in two primary schools', *Educational Psychology*, 19, 3, pp. 245–58.

CONCEPTS

A concept can be defined as the idea a person possesses about a particular class of objects (animate or inanimate) or events, grouped together on the basis of their common characteristics. A child initially makes sense of the world through concepts such as big things, small things, wetness, dryness, and so forth. Children also classify things that they like and dislike, and make sense of new situations by referring to concepts that they already hold. For instance, very young children may begin to cry and repeat that they do not like something because they are unable to make sense of it using their existing experience of life. Thus, the presence of a real circus clown making squeaky noises, for example, may initially frighten a 3-year-old girl because she has never had such an experience other than via the medium of television in the safety of the home. The parent, laughing gently at the child's disquiet, may attempt to reassure her by saying things like: 'It's only a man dressed up.' However, if 'pretending' or 'dressing up' are unfamiliar concepts to her, she will still take a lot of convincing.

Concepts compose the main ideas and principles that are important to a learning experience, often referred to as 'understanding'. In lesson preparation, teachers identify the concepts from previous teaching that require reinforcing or revising, and those that are being developed or introduced. Conceptual development is difficult to pinpoint in a lesson plan, as it encapsulates a large number of variables and modes and reinforces the principle that understanding is gained over time. Deep understanding of a concept is promoted through careful explanation, engagement with practical tasks, discussing the relevant issues, trying things out, making errors, adjustments, revision, rehearsal and repetition. Every teacher has experienced the frustration that comes when pupils, especially younger children, appear to understand the work one day, only to have forgotten by the next.

It is important for primary teachers to understand concept formation because it provides four pieces of vital information that impact on learning. First, children's failure to understand something may be borne of the fact that they have not yet reached the point where they can make sense of the situation or event. Teachers have to be careful not to confuse children's unwillingness to think with their inability to think in particular ways that are necessary for understanding the problem. For instance, 7-year-old pupils can observe and accept that white light splits into a rainbow of colours but be unable to grasp the key concept of refraction or offer any explanation for the phenomenon. Similarly, understanding concepts like 'guilt' and 'innocence' are grasped slowly through repeated exposure to illustrative examples that provide children with a structure within which to explore the concept. Second, children are often helped by visual aids, the opportunity to work practically or experiment. Teachers are faced with the difficult choice about how much to allow children to investigate new experiences and how much to inform them directly. Third, appropriate use of vocabulary performs a vital role in assisting children to grasp a concept. The use of advanced terminology will only serve to confuse children, whereas straightforward language, while not necessarily conveying the complete meaning, will allow children to begin the mental processing that ultimately leads to understanding. Fourth, children need time and space to grapple with difficult concepts. The pace of interactive teaching that characterises so many **lessons** in primary schools does not allow for the **thinking** time needed for deeper understanding. When a teacher asks a class whether they understand something and they chorus 'yes' in return, each child will understand in ways substantially or subtly different from every other child.

Concept development is closely related to children's age but also to their maturity and life experiences. Pupils in the same class may be of similar age but have greater or less understanding because of their educational and socialising experiences in and out of school. Some young children have a profound grasp of moral **dilemmas** and societal challenges that are normally equated with much older pupils. Other young children make astounding progress in formal learning and tackle work that would tax someone a number of years their senior. These variations in conceptual sophistication may be attributed to an innate **ability** (i.e. a belief that some children are more able because they were born with superior brains) or they may be seen as a consequence of a child's access to informed adults and opportunities to benefit from a variety of enriching life experiences.

Further reading

Fontana, D. (1988) *Psychology for Teachers*, 2nd edn, Basingstoke: Macmillan, chapter 3.

Gunning, S., Gunning, D. and Wilson, J. (1981) *Topic Teaching in the Primary School*, London: Routledge, chapter 1.

McGilly, K. (ed.) (1996) *Classroom lessons: Integrating cognitive theory and classroom practice*, London: MIT Press.

Merry, R. (1997) 'Cognitive development 7–11', in N. Kitson and R. Merry (eds) *Teaching in the Primary School*, pp. 48–64, London: Routledge.

CONSTRUCTIVISM

Constructivist theory suggests that pupils learn best when thought and experience interact, resulting in the sequential development of more complex understanding (referred to as cognitive structures). The most influential constructivist was Jean Piaget (1896–1980), the Swiss psychologist and teacher who argued that children accommodate their existing **thinking** into new experiences and gradually assimilate aspects of the new experience to construct a more detailed and accurate understanding. Piaget suggested that the construction of these stages follows a distinctive sequence, characterised by the type of thinking the child uses at each stage.

Pupils' learning needs vary with age and are characterised in specific ways. Younger primary children tend to learn through concrete (hands-on) experiences, be less aware of other people's perspectives and the consequences of actions, and more egotistic. Older primary children tend to be more flexible, accommodating of other people's opinions, sensitive to the way things relate to one another and able to extract principles from a series of instances.

The impact of constructivist theory in classrooms has been to emphasise the need for children to **play**, discover things for themselves and carry out practical investigations. The notion of 'child-centred' learning, the integrated day (where subject boundaries and timetables are flexible) and stimulating classroom environments are, in part, based on constructivist theory. Constructivism puts children into the role of active participants in learning in which they exercise some choice about the work they do and how they carry it out.

During the mid twentieth century one of the unfortunate consequences of constructivist theory was in restricting the progress of more able primary children because teachers did not consider them 'ready' to progress to the next stage. In fact, although conceptual sequencing is ordinal (i.e. sequential) children move through the stages at different rates. Consequently, teachers now encourage pupils to reach their full potential by giving them opportunity to progress as far and fast as possible, providing their present understanding is secure and they know how to transfer it to new situations.

Constructivist theory is also associated with a form of teaching in which the teacher takes on the role of facilitator in meeting the children's resource needs, advising them about alternatives and steering them into new areas of learning. Critics point to this teaching approach's lack of structure, the level of responsibility entrusted to the children and the difficulty in monitoring subject coverage. Most recently, one casualty of this widespread criticism has been a reduction in the amount that children have been allowed to experiment with practical and cerebral ideas and learn through discovery. However, if children are given the opportunity to construct their understanding through practical and experiential means it stimulates their curiosity, enhances their motivation and can lead to innovative approaches when solving problems.

Further reading

Beetlestone, F. (1998) *Creative Children, Imaginative Teaching*, Buckingham: Open University Press.
Selley, N. (1999) *The Art of Constructivist Teaching*, London: David Fulton.
Williams, J. (2003) *Promoting Independent Learning in the Primary Classroom*, Maidenhead: Open University Press.

CONTEXT

Learning does not take place in a vacuum. It relies on a purposeful **learning climate** to motivate children and make them feel that the effort is worthwhile. Context refers to the prevailing physical, practical and emotional circumstances that influence pupils' capacity to learn and develop. Identifying the contextual factors that contribute to, or detract from, effective learning is difficult, owing to the distinctiveness of each situation. For example, a child in class A with teacher X may do better or worse than in class B with teacher Y depending on the nature of the work, the adult–pupil relationship and the home circumstances.

The most significant contextual factor is the person of the class teacher, whose influence pervades every aspect of classroom life. Thus, one teacher's approach inspires and encourages a class, while another teacher creates unease and restless behaviour with the same class in the same room. Teachers are obviously interested in creating an environment that facilitates learning rather than detracts from it.

They have a major role and responsibility to provide these conditions but some elements are not within their influence, such as the impact of **friendship** patterns, family events and health.

Apart from people and facilities, the most important parts of a school system that create the context are its organisation, **curriculum** and instructional materials and technologies. Decisions about the use of time and the allocation of room space and personnel are made to benefit pupils' learning; however, learning can equally be constrained by their lack of availability. Consequently, the context that an individual teacher tries to establish is directly affected by whole-school decisions (how time is configured, space allotted, staff hired and assigned) as well as the availability of resources (learning materials) and instructional technology (IT support).

The vast majority of primary schools promote active learning for all pupils in a caring environment and are committed to equity, empowerment, independent **thinking**, excellence and individuality. The key purpose of each school is to promote learning and teaching in a safe and supportive environment, supported by policies and practices with regard to monitoring pupil progress, behaviour management, countering harassment, monitoring pupils' attendance and ensuring their safety.

Further reading

Kershner, R. and Pointon, P. (2000) 'Making decisions about organising the primary classroom environment as a context for learning: the views of three experienced teachers and their pupils', *Teaching and Teacher Education*, 16, 1, pp. 117–27.

Le Cornu, R. and Collins, J. (2004) 'Re-emphasizing the role of affect in learning and teaching', *Pastoral Care in Education*, 22, 4, pp. 27–33.

Pointon, P. and Kershner, R. (2000) 'Children's views of the primary classroom as an environment for working and learning', *Research in Education*, 64, pp. 64–77.

Sarason, S. B. (1999) *Teaching as a Performing Art*, New York: Teachers College Press, chapter 6.

CONTROL

The terminology used for class control issues varies. The word **behaviour** tends to be used with respect to the child's actions and 'control' and 'discipline' with respect to the teacher's actions. That is, the teacher attempts to influence the child's behaviour through effective discipline in the belief that this is the most effective way of exercising control. However, the imposition of external constraints may have limited long-term value inasmuch as children ultimately need to exercise self-control rather than have it imposed on them. Teachers have an obligation to maintain discipline in the classroom and provide an environment for pupils to exercise self-control, but this is different from coercion. The only exception to this principle is in matters of **health and safety**, where adults often need to insist on rigid conformity to **rules** and procedures.

There are a number of negative terms associated with control, such as 'indiscipline', which occurs when children know what they are doing and choose not to do it, and 'bad behaviour', which occurs when children do not know *how* to behave. In the latter case, it is pointless for a teacher to tell a child to behave unless the child understands what behaving means. Teachers try to operate within a rule framework that can be enforced and easily understood by pupils and through which children can gradually strengthen their own self-control. Nevertheless, adults and pupils have to interpret rules within a particular classroom and school **context**, and effective teachers take time to explain and discuss the degree of latitude permitted.

The vast majority of children want to behave well but adults do not help this process if they are harsh, unreasonable, condescending or insincere. For instance, a teaching strategy that teachers can use for maintaining control is through the use of bogus questions, by employing the word 'really' in phrases such as 'Do you really need to chat to Imogene?' where the intended meaning is 'Stop talking to Imogene.' Similarly in 'I am not really sure that it is really that important, is it?' where the intended meaning is 'I do not think that it is important.' The improper use of a question can even be used to avoid confronting poor standards of work. For example, 'Have you really done your best?' is an indirect way of stating displeasure. Although every teacher occasionally employs questions as a control strategy, its excessive use can lead to children becoming confused and uneasy about the genuineness of all the other questions they are asked and invokes stagnation rather than fostering effective **communication**. The teacher who asks if the child really needs to chat to a friend is better advised to make a direct statement, such as 'Amy, please don't talk to Abigail, and finish your writing. Do you need any help?'

Classroom control is assisted by teachers being firm but tolerant, natural and sincere. Teachers win pupils' cooperation when they take a genuine interest in them, listen to what they say and respond appropriately, praise, explain calmly, avoid nagging and trust children to be sensible. Although such an approach takes longer to secure order than coercion does, it provides for a more secure **learning climate** and stores up a bank of pupil goodwill from which teachers can draw throughout the year.

Many control problems are avoided through thorough lesson preparation and by teachers practising the art of mentally envisioning the session from start to finish, as a lesson cannot run smoothly if it is punctuated by stops-and-starts in dealing with trivial matters that should have been foreseen. Not only do diversions disrupt the lesson, but also they exhaust the teacher and create an unsettled atmosphere. Teachers have to strike a balance between allowing pupils 'freedom to' attempt something and 'freedom from' constraints of any kind. Obvious contraventions of rules have to be dealt with but wise teachers find that it pays to take time finding out the facts before making accusations. Most incidents can be dealt with without causing humiliation or loss of face for child or teacher.

Further reading

Dreikurs, R., Grunwald, B. B. and Pepper, F. C. (1998) *Maintaining Sanity in the Classroom*, London: Taylor & Francis.
Hook, P. and Vass, A. (2002) *Teaching With Influence*, London: David Fulton, chapter 1

CREATIVITY

Creativity releases pupils from the rigid constraints of a formalised scheme of work to explore and investigate by active participation in genuine events and enterprises that delight them. Primary children of all ages are stimulated by hearing stories from real books, purely for pleasure, without then having to complete a worksheet. They prosper when they meet poets and authors instead of just seeing photocopied extracts of their work. Theatre attendance, visits to art galleries, museums, exhibitions and concerts all help to stir pupils' enthusiasm, promote purposeful conversation, excite their emotions and extend their horizons. Primary-aged children develop a sense of wonder by spending regular time outdoors to appreciate seasonal change, by tending a garden and by collaborating on projects. Methods for creative teaching and learning therefore include imaginative use of the school grounds, close involvement with the local community and an emphasis on children gaining direct experience of people, places and events.

There has been a lot of debate about whether creativity is an innate **ability** that is possessed or not possessed, or a skill that can be developed, caught, taught or wrought. Two key issues underpin a search for answers: first, whether a creative child behaves non-creatively in particular situations and creatively in others; second, whether an apparently non-creative child can discover a reservoir of creativity that no one (including the child) realised existed until that moment.

Teachers are sometimes categorised as creative types and non-creative types but this simple polarity fails to recognise the complexities involved in defining creativity. Teachers may find it easy to introduce creativity into their teaching in one school situation but fail to do so in another owing to the prevailing conditions that release or suppress their creative tendencies. A popular view among education specialists is that creativity is not a fixed entity but one that relies upon judgement, discernment and confidence to produce new and original ideas.

Creativity does not occur in a vacuum, but relies upon a framework of understanding, skill acquisition and **knowledge** that facilitates and supports a climate of problem solving, investigation and experimentation. True creativity is characterised by teaching that takes account of every child's interests and styles of learning and encourages them to employ their abilities in new contexts. Creativity is therefore closely linked to **thinking**, which in turn is related to freedom of opportunity, for thinking can start at any time and lead in many directions if given opportunity. Creativity can therefore flourish in any subject area, providing the conditions are suitably unconstrained by external demands and requirements (such as preparing for national tests).

The very best primary education is rooted in maintaining a sensible balance between mastery of essential **skills** and promoting activities that allow children to explore and interrogate ideas actively. Two of the most influential educationists in the UK with respect to creativity, Bob Jeffrey and Anna Craft, argue that there is a need for not only teaching creatively and teaching for creativity but also creative learning. That is, that children are liberated to engage with learning in such a way that it allows for their proclivities and instincts. This issue is of particular relevance to boys, of which a sizeable minority will happily discuss, experiment and compute, but may show a reluctance to work systematically and provide a written record of their findings.

Views about the factors that characterise creativity vary, though it is often thought of with regard to arts' activities (painting, drawing, making models, ceramics, and so forth) and examples of creative practice are often found in non-core areas; that is, all subject areas apart from mathematics, English and science that were formerly and rather oddly known as the 'foundation' subjects. Creativity seems to lend itself more naturally to subjects that are not desk-bound owing to the problem-solving component that often characterises work in these areas. Thus, children express their feelings in drama, experiment with models in technology, work out solutions in PE and pour out their inner consciousness through painting.

It is in the day-to-day business of teaching primary mathematics and **literacy** that the biggest challenge lies for teachers to sponsor and encourage creativity. First and foremost, teachers have to ensure that the work is interesting for the children, with the potential to be inspiring. Second, teachers have to offer pupils clear direction in their learning without unduly constraining their enthusiasm and thirst for understanding. Third, teachers open up possibilities for children to think deeply, engage with challenges and use their ingenuity to solve problems. A systematic approach to teaching does not exclude promoting imaginative engagement with the lesson content; on the contrary, it stimulates expressiveness and awareness of possibilities.

Creative accomplishment is facilitated by good teaching, rather than hindered by it, as children need both opportunity to explore and adult guidance to exploit their creative potential. Merely being given opportunity to experiment with ideas without basic skills and adult intervention is more likely to lead to chaos than to facilitate creativity. Too little guidance may lead to aimlessness. Too little opportunity will almost certainly lead to pupil frustration. On the other hand, too much skills training runs the risk of divorcing the child from the circumstances in which the skills are employed. Too much guidance can reduce self-sufficiency. Too much opportunity may give children the impression that learning is a random process.

Further reading

Diakidoy, I. N. and Kanari, E. (1999) 'Trainee teachers' beliefs about creativity', *British Educational Research Journal*, 25, 2, pp. 225–43.

Jeffrey, B. and Craft, A. (2004) 'Teaching creatively and teaching for creativity: distinctions and relationships', *Educational Studies*, 30, 1, pp. 77–87.

Jeffrey, B. and Woods, P. (2003) *The Creative School: A framework for success, quality and effectiveness*, London: Routledge.

Jones, R. and Wyse, D. (eds) (2004) *Creativity in the Primary Curriculum*, London: David Fulton.

OFSTED (2003a) *Expecting the Unexpected: Developing Creativity in Primary and Secondary Schools*, Reference HMI 1612, London: The Stationery Office.

CROSS-CURRICULAR WORK (CURRICULUM INTEGRATION)

Most definitions of cross-curricular work, also known as curriculum integration, emphasise how combinations of subjects are used within project or thematic work, incorporating a wide range of sources, related **concepts** and flexible schedules. Cross-curricular work is closely related to interdisciplinary teaching, thematic teaching and synergistic teaching. The integration element emphasises the fusion of ideas and concepts within and across subject areas and broader life experiences in an attempt to make education more relevant and meaningful for children.

By teaching the **curriculum** as an integrated whole, pupils' view of learning is likely to be more rounded, whereas if teachers emphasise the separation and discreteness of subjects, it can establish artificial barriers in younger children's minds and they may fail to make secure connections between knowledge components. Cross-curricular work is seen as a way to make education relevant for pupils by establishing links between the humanities (history, geography, RE), communication arts, natural sciences, mathematics, social studies, music and art. The things that pupils learn and apply in one area are then used to reinforce and expand their learning in other areas, organised in such a way that it cuts across subject barriers, affiliating fragments of subject curricula into a composite whole.

Supporters of an integrated approach to teaching and learning reject a philosophy of education that is rooted in **memory** and recitation of isolated fragments of **knowledge** and promotes the construction of more meaningful concepts and connections between them. They argue that crossing and combining traditional subject boundaries into one active project reflects pupils' experience of the world and goes beyond a superficial understanding of isolated facts to create insights that are established through seeing the interconnectedness of all learning. The increase in the world's complexity means that pupils need to develop an adeptness to draw from different areas of knowledge and solve problems that involve many and various factors. Pressures on primary school teachers have tended to result in subject-specific teaching, rigid timetables and teacher-directed learning, and treating subject areas as discrete learning units has sometimes made it difficult for teachers to relate the content to pupils' whole-life experiences. By contrast, an integrated view of learning enables children to make sense of complex issues and information by seeking solutions located in familiar life contexts.

A cross-curricular approach has the potential to offer pupils greater opportunities to explore, imagine, deviate from the norm and engage with concepts that span subjects, supported by: (1) Good quality **communication** through speaking, listening, **reading** and writing. (2) The practical application of number, involving a range of mental calculation techniques and the **ability** to apply them within a variety of contexts. (3) IT, using a range of information sources and ICT tools to find, analyse, interpret, evaluate and present information for a range of purposes. (4) Collaborating with other pupils by way of paired, group and whole-class discussions. (5) Reflecting on and critically evaluating work to ascertain what has been learned and what remains problematic. (6) Problem solving expressed through identifying and employing key strategies in finding answers. An integrated approach offers children more space and opportunity to pursue their interests and enthusiasm, allowing maximum freedom to explore ideas, as well as the motivation and capacity to grasp interrelated information, systems and structures. Proponents of integration argue that it is the most effective means of developing abilities that children will need in the future, and that integration based on these principles is an educational approach that prepares children for lifelong learning.

Opponents of integration argue that it is insufficiently rigorous, especially in ensuring that children have focused and regular opportunities to gain fundamental skills in key subjects. They insist that too much choice allows pupils to avoid areas of learning that they find hard, thereby inculcating poor work habits and attitudes.

Further reading

Burgess, H. (2004) 'The primary strategy: a chance for a whole curriculum', *Education 3–13*, 32, 2, pp. 10–17.

Fogarty, R. (1991) *The Mindful School: How to Integrate the Curricula*, Palatine, IL: Skylight.

Lake, K. (1994) 'Integrated curriculum', *School Improvement Research Series*, North West Regional Education Laboratory. On-line. Available: http://www.nwrel.org/scpd/sirs/8/c016.html (accessed March 2005).

CURRICULUM

It is far from easy to find an agreed definition for 'the curriculum' other than as the sum total of what pupils need to learn. The term derives from a Latin word meaning a racing chariot, based on the notion of a racetrack or course to be run and, by association, a course of study. Over the past century a variety of definitions have been proffered, including one in the 1904 *Suggestions for teachers code*:

> The curriculum of the primary school ... should provide a training in the English language ... handwriting to secure speed as well as legibility; arithmetic, including practical measurements; drawing from objects, **memory** and brush drawing ... geography, history, music, hygiene and physical training ... and moral **instruction**, given both directly and indirectly.

By 1931 the Consultative Committee was suggesting that the curriculum should be thought out in terms of **activities** and experience rather than facts to be stored. In 1985 Her Majesty's Inspectorate of Schools offered a sweeping definition, claiming that a school's curriculum 'consists of all those activities designed or encouraged within its organisational framework to promote the intellectual, personal, social and physical development of its pupils' (para 11). More recently, curriculum guidance for the Foundation Stage (QCA/DfEE 2000) offers a very broadly based definition: 'The term curriculum is used to describe everything children do, see, hear or feel in their setting, both planned and unplanned' (p. 1).

The scope and content of the school curriculum has also changed over the years, as have the names of the different government organisations regulating national policy. Only a generation ago, teachers were broadly at liberty to make their own decisions about what to teach and how to teach it. In fact, the freedom that teachers enjoyed to organise learning in a way that suited the classroom circumstances was considered to be an essential element of their professional autonomy. Since 1989, the National Curriculum (NC) has operated in all state-maintained schools and many private ones in England, Wales and Northern Ireland (through the Department of Education in Northern Ireland, DENI).

In Scotland there are national, non-statutory guidelines for Scottish local authorities and schools. They cover the structure, content and assessment of the curriculum in primary schools and in the first two years of secondary education (ages 5 to 14 years). The curriculum is divided into five broad areas: language, mathematics, environmental studies, expressive arts, and religious and moral education. For each curricular area there are broad attainment outcomes, each with a number of strands or aspects of learning that pupils experience. The aim of the 5–14 programme is to promote the teaching of a broad, coherent and balanced curriculum that offers all pupils continuity and progression as they move through school. The curriculum in Scotland is not set by law. It is a flexible system that places responsibility on individual education authorities and schools. National guidelines direct teachers by describing the subject areas which are to be covered but they do not give detailed instructions about exactly what and how these areas are to be taught to pupils.

The reason for the introduction of national curricula is three-fold. First, to ensure that learning is systematically structured and not randomly designed. Second, to ensure that those children who move school are able to continue their education without repeating work they have already covered. Third, to ensure that children's progress can be closely monitored through national tests. There have been a number of versions of the NC for England, Wales and Northern Ireland since 1989 and the present edition is referred to as NC2000 to signify the year of its adoption. In particular, there has been considerable emphasis upon the teaching of English (through **literacy**) and mathematics (through **numeracy**). In 1999 a Foundation Stage curriculum was published for children aged 4 and 5 in nursery and reception classes.

Mathematics in the NC2000 has three elements for pupils aged 5 to 7 years: (1) using and applying mathematics, (2) number and algebra, and (3) shape, space and measures. In addition, children aged 7 to 11 have to study a fourth element: handling data. There are also four elements in science: scientific **enquiry**, life processes and living things, materials and their properties, and physical processes. All other (non-core) subjects have a single element. Guidelines about personal, social and health education, and about **citizenship**, are also provided in the NC document. At Key Stages 1 and 2 the **knowledge, skills** and understanding that all children should gain include developing confidence and responsibility and making the most of their abilities, preparing an active role as citizens, developing a healthy, safer lifestyle, good relationships and respecting the differences between people.

National curricula are explicit about the overall aims and **values** of primary education in that the school curriculum should aim to provide opportunities for all pupils to learn and to achieve, promote pupils' spiritual, moral, social and cultural development, and prepare all pupils for the opportunities, responsibilities and experiences of life. In the UK (with the exception of Scotland) the curriculum contains a common structure and design for all subjects divided into **Key Stages**, for which there is a *programme of study*. This programme sets out what has to be taught in the subject to equip children with the necessary knowledge, skills and understanding and the **context**, activities, areas of study and range of experiences through which learning should take place.

Together with the programmes of study, notes of guidance, definitions and links with ICT and with other subject areas are appended. In addition there are *attainment targets* for each subject, setting out all that pupils of different abilities and maturity are expected to have gained by the end of each Key Stage. At the primary phase, each attainment target consists of six *level descriptions* of increasing difficulty; at secondary school level the number increases to eight. English has three attainment targets for children at Key Stages 1 and 2: speaking and listening, **reading** and writing. Each level description describes the types and range of understanding that pupils working at that level should demonstrate. On the basis of children's attainments, teachers have to decide which description best fits their performance. It is anticipated that the majority of children aged 7 years will reach level 2 and the majority of 11-year-olds will reach level 4 in English and mathematics, though there is government pressure for more able children to attain higher grades. Many primary teachers complain that an emphasis on improved test scores narrows the curriculum at the expense of the more creative elements such as drama and art. In the Scottish 5–14 curriculum, most strands have attached to them attainment targets at five or six levels: A–E or A–F. Assessment to attain these target levels can be taken by individuals or groups as and when their teacher considers them ready. Whole classes or year groups do not sit tests; they are designed such that teachers can use them as a confirmation of the progress that pupils have made.

The curriculum requires teachers to have due regard for **inclusion** principles that incorporate setting suitable learning challenges for all pupils so that they can experience success. This process necessitates that teachers respond to children's diverse needs and facilitate learning and assessment for individuals and for groups of pupils. These requirements mean that those children with learning difficulties and disabilities, and those for whom English is an additional language, are equally entitled to a relevant, broad and balanced curriculum. Children from all social backgrounds, gender and races must receive the highest quality of education, regardless of their physical and mental condition.

Further reading

Blenkin, G. M. and Kelly, A. V. (eds) (1983) *The Primary Curriculum in Action*, London: Paul Chapman.

Department for Education and Employment/QCA (1999) *The National Curriculum for England and Wales*, London: The Stationery Office.

Qualifications and Curriculum Authority/DfEE (2000) *Curriculum Guidance for the Foundation Stage*, London: QCA Publications.

Edgington, M. (2004) *The Foundation Stage Teacher in Action*, 3rd edn, London: Paul Chapman.

Ross, A. (2001) 'What is the curriculum?', in J. Collins, K. Insley and J. Soler (eds) *Developing Pedagogy: Researching practice*, pp. 122–31, London: Paul Chapman/Open University.

Sassoon, R. (2003) *Handwriting*, 2nd edn, London: Paul Chapman.

DECISION MAKING

The governing body/school board and head teacher, supported by the local education authority and, in the case of church foundation schools, the appointed religious representatives, make most of the major decisions that impact upon the school community. Decision making tends to fall into one of two broad types, the first of which concerns how to implement statutory requirements (such as **health and safety** legislation), the second of which concerns internal school matters (such as organising the curriculum or the structure of the school day). Most primary head teachers involve staff, parents and pupils in making decisions wherever appropriate, in the belief that collaborative decision making is more effective than single decisions. Many primary schools promote the involvement of the children in making procedural and practical decisions that have a direct impact upon their lives (such as where to site a school garden or games suitable for the break time), often by establishing a 'school council' that consists of delegates drawn from each class.

Teachers make hundreds of decisions every day about how to allocate their time, express ideas to pupils, introduce new concepts and teach fresh **skills**. They have to decide when to assist pupils and when to leave them alone, where to store resources, which teaching strategies to employ, how to handle a recalcitrant child, and so on. Other decisions involve judgements about the allocation of grades or marks, classroom management, **curriculum** implementation, task **differentiation** and pupil assessment.

The decisions that teachers make are rooted in their beliefs and **values** about educational provision and professional conduct. The wisdom and efficacy of moral choices that teachers make to ensure fairness and equity, the majority of which have to be made rapidly, are major factors in determining the quality of a teacher's relationship with pupils and colleagues. There are also four considerations that teachers are sensitive to when making decisions about classroom practice. (1) Whether the decision reflects their beliefs about education. (2) Whether the decision is pragmatic and results in greater efficiency. (3) Whether the decision is supported by empirical evidence; for example, data from formal tests to support a particular **teaching approach**. (4) Whether the decision takes sufficient account of external requirements. Teachers' decisions are not only based upon their ideals but need to be set against a variety of constraints, such as the views of the head teacher, government stipulations and community priorities.

Trainee teachers also have to make numerous daily decisions but they are constrained by the beliefs and value-system of the class teacher and the school policies about (for instance) discipline and pupil work habits. For inexperienced teachers the process of decision making requires thoughtful engagement with the issues through discussion and analysis of issues, informed by personal experience and advice from others. Teachers in training tend to draw insights about teaching from other practitioners and gradually develop a framework for action honed by time spent in school. In situations where qualified teachers have convictions that differ from those of the trainee, active dialogue and a degree of compromise are necessary to maintain consistency and harmony in the classroom.

Further reading

Alexander, R. J. (1997) *Policy and Practice in Primary Education*, London: Routledge, chapter 4.

Deuchar, R. (2004) 'Reconciling self-interest and ethics: the role of primary school pupil councils', *Scottish Educational Review*, 36, 2, pp. 159–68.

Hammond, M. (2002) 'Why teach? A case study investigating the decision to train to teach ICT', *Journal of Education for Teaching*, 28, 2, 135–48.

DIFFERENTIATION

All classes and groups of pupils contain children of mixed **ability**, slower and faster workers, less and more intelligent, keen and apathetic, confident and insecure. Regardless of the basis on which pupils are divided, each group will contain children whose varied learning and academic needs have to be taken into account in planning and teaching. Differentiation is based on the belief that pupils differ in the extent to which they can absorb information, grasp ideas and apply themselves to a task. Some children have sharp minds and mental agility; others are ponderous and slow. Some children are fascinated by facts; others need to be inspired before they demonstrate any interest in a topic. A small number of children are exceptionally clever and capable of high **achievement** or find learning difficult and require additional adult support. Some children are talented in areas such as music, art, drama or PE; others excel in mathematics and English but have little natural **ability** in other subject areas; yet others are good at everything or, if they are not, possess the character and perseverance to succeed. It is not easy for teachers to ensure that their teaching and the tasks and activities they set pupils to complete will meet the diversity of learning needs because the extent of a pupil's knowledge can never be fully understood by any teacher. The best that teachers can do is to monitor pupils' progress, talk regularly to them about the subject content and assess their progress systematically through formal and informal means.

There are two main types of differentiation used by primary teachers. The first type is where all pupils are given similar tasks to do but the expectation differs according to the pupil's academic competence. The second type of differentiation is where pupils of different academic proficiency are given distinctive tasks and activities on the same subject but with differing levels of challenge. This second form of differentiation often involves pupils of similar competence across several parallel classes being taught together ('setting'). Setting allows the planning to be more specifically targeted towards the academic needs of a narrower ability range of pupils, though even within a single group there will still be considerable variation in aptitude for learning.

Every teacher has to take account of the resource and time implications of trying to develop too many tasks and activities for children in an attempt to cater for everybody's individual needs. An individually tailored **curriculum** is impractical other than for classes numbered in single figures. Differentiated planning must rely on a satisfactory grouping of children such that each individual child in the group can cope with the demands of the work provided.

Further reading

Edwards, N. (2003) 'Planning for all abilities: differentiation', in K. Jacques and R. Hyland, (eds) *Professional Studies*, 2nd edn, pp. 33–50, Exeter: Learning Matters.

Harlen, W. (2000) *The Teaching of Science in Primary Schools*, London: David Fulton.

McNamara, S. and Moreton, G. (1997) *Understanding Differentiation*, London: David Fulton.

O'Brien, T. and Guiney, D. (2001) *Differentiation in Teaching and Learning*, London: Continuum.

DILEMMAS

Every day teachers face numerous problems and challenges that cannot easily be solved because competing influences produce a situation where straightforward solutions are not available (a 'dilemma'). The polarised language used to describe dilemmas that exist for teachers in areas of their work such as **teaching approach** and discipline can set up unhelpful dichotomies that oversimplify the intricacies of classroom life and the many stark choices facing teachers at each point of the day. However, although they can lead to inertia, dilemmas can also help to promote an understanding of issues impinging upon educational decisions because they help to clarify competing views. The unpredictability of school life means that it is preferable to view dilemmas as a vehicle to accommodate and explore uncertainties and contradictions in education. Every class of children, staff and school ethos is different and every working environment influences, and is influenced by, the unique characteristics of the situation. Consequently, the **context** in which teachers work must be taken into account when interpreting situations, allowing for a consideration of the larger issues that are embedded in everyday experiences of adults and pupils.

Teachers face numerous emotional dilemmas in their work. They gain immense satisfaction from teaching, yet they are aware that they can never give to the job what it demands. The tension between gaining satisfaction and the limitations imposed upon staff by time factors, deadlines and competing commitments is an issue faced daily by everyone who works in primary schools. Despite the commendable aim of achieving a work–life balance through remodelling the workforce, it is common for primary teachers to admit that the energy they expend in performing the job prevents them from leading a normal life outside school. Teachers are also subject to the aspirations and desires of other interest groups, including the head teacher, governors, community, and local and central government. They have to accommodate the competing demands made by these groups while remaining true to their personal and professional convictions.

Dilemmas exist for teachers in that the majority of them make their career choice based on a desire to make a difference to the lives of children by having the opportunity to show initiative and employ a high degree of autonomy through the medium of teaching. On the other hand, they are also conscious of the constraints placed upon them from the agreed programmes of study, internal school guidelines, parental demands and government legislation that stress the importance of test results. Thus, teachers have a personal agenda for teaching and know what they would like to achieve, but at the same time they have to take close account of other competing agendas.

Further reading

Berlak, A. and Berlak, H. (1981) *Dilemmas of schooling: Teaching and social change*, New York: Methuen.

Hargreaves, L., Hislam, J. and English, E. (2002) 'Pedagogical dilemmas in the National Literacy Strategy: primary teachers' perceptions, reflections and classroom behaviour', *Cambridge Journal of Education*, 32, 1, pp. 9–26.

McDiarmid, G. W. and Kelly, P. P. (2002) 'Decentralisation of professional development: teachers' decisions and dilemmas', *Journal of In-service Education*, 28, 3, pp. 409–25.

EARLY YEARS

Early years is a term used to describe children who are not yet of formal school age but are receiving a recognised form of education in nurseries, playgroups or pre-school centres. The development of a Foundation Stage **curriculum** for pre-school pupils in most parts of the UK (QCA/DfES 2000) and the accompanying handbook of guidance is recognition of the fact that young children require a special type of education that forms the basis for all that follows. The justification for the large amount of funding that has been allocated to this phase of education is underpinned by a belief that pre-school education intervention is amply rewarded by later academic success and increased social stability.

Children who start primary school with significant disadvantages in areas such as language and **communication**, attention span, **reading** and writing, and social finesse receive additional support through the UK government's Primary Excellence in Cities project that focuses on working closely with parents. The project is linked to another initiative, *Sure Start*, a programme that aims to achieve better outcomes for children, parents and communities by increasing the availability of childcare for all children and improving the emotional development of young children. *Sure Start* also aims to support parents in their aspirations towards employment by the development of helping services in disadvantaged areas, alongside financial help for parents to afford childcare. Primary Excellence in Cities has four main objectives:

- To target the most needy children and build on the work of the *Sure Start* scheme, involving parents as much as possible.
- To bridge the transition from early years' settings to primary school, and from the Foundation Stage to **Key Stage** 1 (KS1, for children aged 5+ to 7 years) by offering needy children extra support.
- To utilise the expertise of experienced teachers in training and equipping other teachers and other staff in early years' settings
- To support parents in developing their children's **skills**, making packs and videos available for parents to explain what children are learning at school and how they can be helped at home.

Six developmental priming mechanisms to enhance learning have been suggested for young primary-age children. First, encouraging them to explore their environment. Second, close involvement of adults to assist with basic intellectual and social training. Third, celebrating new expertise that children acquire. Fourth, rehearsing and expanding their new skills. Fifth, protecting children from inappropriate **punishment** or ridicule for developmental advances. Sixth, stimulating language and **communication**.

In the UK, discussion about formalising further the assessment of children at the Foundation Stage is ongoing. For example, the DfES is promoting the use of an assessment framework to include personal, social and emotional development. Improvements in young children's language and **literacy** involve teaching strategies and learning opportunities to stimulate thought, link sounds and letters, and gain mastery in reading and writing. Mathematical development includes using numbers as labels for counting, calculating, shape, space and measures, **knowledge** and understanding of the world, physical development and creative development. Practitioners working with disadvantaged young children need to show their achievements in percentage form, using the following scale ranges: 0–3, working below the goals; 4–7, working within them; 8–9, meeting or exceeding them.

A Foundation Stage *Profile* (QCA/03/1006) was published in January 2003 to build on the existing curriculum guidance for teachers, emphasising the key role of skilful and well-planned observations in providing reliable assessment information on young children and setting out a way of summarising young children's achievements at the end of the Foundation Stage. These data provide information for parents and teachers of 5-year-olds (new entrants). The document contains guidance on how teachers can develop a broad curriculum, respond flexibly to children's needs and track their progress. It also outlines areas of learning, assessment scales and how to record children's development in the form of a profile.

Further reading

Aubrey, C. (2004) 'Implementing the foundation stage in reception classes', *British Educational Research Journal*, 30, 5, pp. 633–56.
Broadhead, P. (2004) *Early Years Play and Learning*, London: Routledge.
Hargreaves, L. M. and Hargreaves, D. J. (1997) 'Children's development 3–7', in N. Kitson and R. Merry (eds) *Teaching in the Primary School*, pp. 27–47, London: Routledge.
Hirst, K. and Nutbrown, C. (eds) (2005) *Perspectives on Early Childhood Education*, Stoke-on-Trent: Trentham.
Katz, L. G. (1995a) *Talks With Teachers of Young Children*, Norwood, NJ: Ablex.
Riley, J. (2003) *Learning in the Early Years*, London: Sage.

EDUCATIONAL VISITS

Educational visits are the most exciting part of the school year for many children and schools usually have a well-ordered programme of visits to museums, landmarks, ancient monuments and adventure courses. Careful planning and organisation is essential and the energy expended on making the appropriate practical arrangements is considerable. Strict rules govern charges made to parents for curriculum visits arranged by schools and no child may be excluded for financial reasons. Many teachers use a visit as a starting point for the production of stimulating displays and investigative work. Trainee and newly appointed teachers normally collaborate with a more experienced colleague jointly to plan the enterprise.

Educational visits and other field activities provide a wonderful opportunity for children to learn things first-hand and to seal adult–pupil relationships in an informal setting. Trip organisers have to send letters home detailing the itinerary, receive permission slips from parents, order transport, check out insurance and liaise with colleagues whose lessons are going to be affected by pupil absence. A good practice guide, *Health and Safety of Pupils on Educational Visits* (DfEE 1998a) is designed to help head teachers, teachers and governors to safeguard pupils from potential hazards. The guide includes chapters on legal responsibilities and a number of model forms that can be copied or adapted. A three-part supplement to the good practice guide was produced in 2002 (www.teachernet.gov.uk/healthand safety):

- *Standards for local education authorities in overseeing educational visits* sets out good practice for local education authorities in overseeing educational visits carried out by schools, youth services and other organisations.
- *Standards for adventure* is aimed at the teacher or youth worker who leads young people on adventure activities.
- *A handbook for group leaders* is aimed at anyone who leads groups of young people on any kind of educational visit. It sets out good practice in supervision, ongoing risk assessment and emergency procedures.
- *Group safety at water margins* is aimed at anyone who organises learning activities that take place near or in water, such as a walk along a river bank or seashore, collecting samples from ponds or streams, or paddling or walking in gentle, shallow water.

Even when all the planning and organising is complete, teachers have a lot of work to do in ensuring that the day runs smoothly, including carrying out an assessment of potential risks and trying to anticipate problems, together with the appropriate action needed to respond to particular situations. For instance, teachers should not only have access to a mobile telephone for making contact with emergency services, but also carry a list of key contacts, including direct-dial numbers for children with health problems.

Thorough preparation is essential if the trip is to be a success. Some visits are not viable because of the cost of travel or entrance fees. Coach travel is slower than travelling by car because the coach driver is obliged to follow a prescribed main-road route. Coaches must conform to minimum safety standards, such as the requirement to fit safety belts. If private cars are used, a list of experienced drivers with current licences has to be compiled and checked with the head teacher. If the venue involves any activity that carries some risk (such as an adventure course) basic health and safety regulations must be strictly observed and the activity centre's own safety procedures verified.

Local authorities have guidelines for the amount of adult help required for an educational visit. Younger children require a higher level of supervision than older ones and under-5s need one adult per two or three children. The experience and competence of the adults involved also has to be taken into account when responsibilities are drawn up and every helper has to be fully briefed before the visit.

Parents must be notified well in advance of the proposed visit about the purpose of the visit, suitable clothing, eating arrangements, and the physical demands being made of the children, together with an invitation for parents to contact the teacher in charge should they have any queries. The permission slip has to include space for the child's name, address and a contact number, and for the parent to mention any special circumstances, such as the child's need to carry an inhaler or fear of heights/water. Schools often send out two letters: a preliminary note with the basic details requesting parental permission and, nearer the time, more detailed information.

Timings for each stage of the visit have to be allotted and given to parents in advance of the visit: the departure, stops and starts, breaks and anticipated time of arrival. Parents also have to be told if the visit is likely to continue beyond normal school hours; this helps to facilitate arrangements for children being picked up after returning to school. Clipboards, paper, pencils, activity sheets, maps, measuring tapes, cameras and other necessary equipment have to be gathered in advance, using the help of teaching assistants where possible. In most schools, caterers and the teachers who normally hold extra-curricular activities have to be informed that children will be away during the day. A playground duty may have to be swapped. Children whose parents do not have to pay for meals are entitled to a packed lunch on the day of the visit. All these details have to be sorted out in advance to avoid misunderstanding, annoyance and complication.

The purpose and place of the visit will determine the practical arrangements and level of direction provided for children. If the visit is to an established and supervised venue, the pattern of the day is normally quite predictable, though the majority of visits incorporate a degree of freedom for children to explore and exercise autonomy, a fact that must be taken into consideration with regard to safety and supervision. Depending upon the age of the children and the purpose of the visit, most teachers prepare worksheets for completion or guidance about information to be noted by pupils in their notebooks. Larger venues (such as zoos) normally have an education department, appropriately staffed and resourced. In the days and weeks following the visit there is opportunity for children to draw upon their experiences or utilise their new-found skills, understanding and knowledge in a variety of learning contexts. Educational visits are frequently linked to **topic work** and result in the production of displays and other artistic outcomes (such as a drama sketch for an **assembly**).

Further reading

Department for Education and Employment (1998a) *Health and Safety of Pupils on Educational Visits*, Sudbury: DfEE Publications.
DfES (2002): www.teachernet.gov.uk/healthandsafety
Zucker, J. and Parker, D. (1999) *A Class Act*, London: Sapphire, chapter 13.

EFFECTIVENESS

Effectiveness in education has become equated with practitioners meeting predetermined performance targets; consequently, close monitoring of their performance has dominated education discourse in recent times. For qualified teachers, the implications of effectiveness are significant for their salary and promotion prospects; for trainee teachers effectiveness is measured by the level of their success on school placements for work experience. National criteria for teacher effectiveness rely heavily on pupil test results and what is referred to as the 'value-added' factor; that is, the measurable improvement that pupils make from the time they enter a teacher's influence to the point at which they leave it. Though logical, the value-added approach to judging effectiveness is crude and has severe limitations, as progress in learning cannot be itemised and checked off like a shopping list. Furthermore, an instrumental view of teaching, in which **skills** and strategies are identified, isolated and implemented as part of a seamless robe, belies the complex nature of the job and the many other influences outside the teacher's **control** that influence attainment (notably, home circumstances). Nevertheless, a belief that attainment is directly attributable to the effectiveness of teaching underpins the production of the numerous competence statements that have characterised teacher education and training in recent years. There are implications for trainee teachers in acquiring good grades for their school experience, the quality of their reports, getting a teaching post and coping with the demands of the first (**induction**) year of teaching. Furthermore, parents are greatly influenced by schools that are officially pronounced good or excellent by inspectors, reflected in the house prices in areas where school test results are strong and the clamour to get their children into schools perceived to be the best.

Effective teachers have open and accessible paths of **communication** to colleagues, parents and pupils, and succeed in making each child feel valued, happy and confident. They use techniques that motivate children and maintain discipline while demonstrating genuine care, and adapt their teaching methods to suit and satisfy children's varying needs. Effective teachers enjoy working with children and have patience to help and encourage them in their learning. They look beyond pupils' immediate abilities and see the potential in every child. They observe and listen to children in the class, both as individuals and within a group, assessing the academic needs of each one and organising the learning to give everyone a chance to succeed. They help and encourage the children to become independent thinkers and self-motivated learners, providing the necessary resources and support for learning. The effective teacher needs to possess solid subject **knowledge**, but also to be adept at putting across information in an accessible way such that the child will remember the facts and be enthused to find out more.

Effective teachers build on the knowledge and understanding that children already possess instead of focusing on their inadequacies. They make a conscious effort to be liked by the pupils but do not try to ingratiate themselves, as children work better with teachers they admire and respect. Effective teachers have clearly established classroom routines with manageable procedures that make sense to the pupils, who are not afraid to approach them for academic or welfare support. Ultimately, the best teachers succeed in making the children think for themselves and thereby extend their ownership of new learning instead of making them passive recipients of information.

Even when set criteria are used to measure effectiveness, they still need to be interpreted with a high degree of professional judgement and awareness of the prevailing school and classroom climate. Teachers and trainee teachers who are grappling to engage with heavy workloads, demanding pupils and challenging situations, or struggling to move beyond 'coping' and reach new heights of expertise, may initially underachieve and require additional support from the head teacher and colleagues. Many educationists have pointed out that a teacher may achieve miracles in motivating a group of underprivileged children who, nonetheless, perform quite poorly in formal tests. Different governments have made a good job of convincing the public that the only success criteria that warrant serious consideration are measurable ones, despite the self-evident truth that (non-measurable) moral and social factors are immensely important in creating a civilised, peaceful society. Parents are interested to know that their children are valued, that teachers are doing their best for them, and that their sons and daughters are happy, well adjusted and fulfilled. The need to conform to externally imposed stipulations means that inexperienced teachers and those in demanding situations sometimes hesitate to employ more innovative teaching methods for fear of disapproval or recrimination or lower grades in formal tests.

Effectiveness in teaching is ultimately posited on a belief that all children should have the opportunity to succeed at their own level of understanding and feel fulfilled and satisfied. Teachers act as guides inasmuch as they can show pupils that learning is exciting and worthwhile, thereby promoting a spirit of **enquiry**, offer tantalising glimpses into fresh areas of knowledge and actively encourage children to think laterally by posing problems and setting up challenges for them to overcome.

Further reading

Browne, A. and Haylock, D. (eds) (2004) *Professional Issues for Primary Teachers*, London: Paul Chapman.
Davis, A. (2001) 'Can we pick out good teachers by discovering what they have taught their pupils?', *Education 3–13*, 29, 3, pp. 33–8.
Gipps, C. and McCallum, B. (2000) *What Makes a Good Primary Teacher?* London: Routledge.
Hayes, L., Nikolic, V. and Cabaj, H. (2001) *Am I Teaching Well?* Exeter: Learning Matters.
Muijs, D. and Reynolds, D. (2005) *Effective Teaching: Evidence and practice*, London: Paul Chapman.

EMOTION

Emotional experience is integral to all life experiences and the significance of emotions in the work and motivation of teachers has long been recognised, but the theory that there is a separate type of social intelligence, unrelated to traditional abstract intelligence, is a relatively new idea. The concept of *emotional intelligence*, drawn from the work on multiple intelligences by the American psychologist Howard Gardner, has been made popular by another American psychologist, Daniel Goleman. Emotional intelligence as defined by Goleman is basically another name for the personal intelligences observed by Gardner.

Gardner initially formulated a list of seven intelligences (he has subsequently extended the number). Linguistic intelligence involves sensitivity to spoken and written language, the **ability** to learn languages and the capacity to use language to accomplish certain goals. Logical–mathematical intelligence consists of the capacity to analyse problems logically, carry out mathematical operations and investigate issues scientifically. Musical intelligence involves skill in the performance, composition and appreciation of musical patterns. Bodily–kinaesthetic intelligence entails the potential of using one's whole body or parts of the body to solve problems. Spatial intelligence involves the potential to recognise and use the patterns of wide space and more confined areas. Personal intelligence includes two separate categories: interpersonal intelligence and intrapersonal intelligence. Interpersonal intelligence is concerned with the capacity to understand the intentions, motivations and desires of other people. Intrapersonal intelligence entails the capacity to understand oneself, to appreciate one's feelings, fears and motivation.

Goleman has been instrumental in alerting educationists to the central role played by the emotions in decisions and actions. He argues that human competencies like self-awareness, self-discipline, persistence and empathy are of greater consequence than IQ in much of life, and that we ignore these competencies at our peril. Research about the demands made on teachers suggests that their emotional condition has a major role in the ease with which they handle pressure. It is important, therefore, for teachers and pupils to understand and manage their emotions, learn how to communicate effectively and gain insights from a range of life experience. Such emotional **literacy** includes reflective listening, focusing on non-verbal clues and becoming more imaginative.

It is in the classroom that the impact of a teacher's emotional sensitivity is most readily exposed, as the basis of effective teaching is located in communicating and connecting with pupils through care, trust, mutual respect and establishing a rapport. The best primary classrooms are those characterised by purposeful work that is also enjoyable and motivating for children. The emotional attachment that exists between teacher and the children and the sense that they are doing a significant job is a strong motivating factor and provides everyone involved with a sense of purpose and fulfilment.

Emotionally sensitive teachers make an effort to engage with children at two levels. (1) They seek to understand the way children think and demonstrate a genuine interest and concern in their welfare. (2) They offer direction through suggesting possibilities and alternatives. Emotional intelligence also alerts a teacher to the motives that underpin a pupil's behaviour, including non-verbal clues such as facial expression (especially use of the eyes), gesture, breathing, voice tone, speed of speech and pacing of speech. Thus, a pupil's distorted facial expression may indicate that the pupil is trying to make sense of a problem. Poor eye contact may mean that the child is feeling alarmed, guilty or under-confident. Rapid speech can indicate enthusiasm, commitment or confusion, whereas hesitant or slow speech indicates confusion or mental overload. One of the many challenges facing teachers is rapid **decision making** about what is genuine and what is contrived emotion. These insights are gained through becoming familiar with the children's dispositions and backgrounds, identifying their individual needs and responding appropriately to their disparate behaviours.

As emotions are central to teachers' work and lives, they merit a significant place in the mind of every aspiring teacher. This fact is especially significant for trainees on work placement as they enter a school that is largely unknown to them in respect of its ethos, interpersonal relationships and patterns of behaviour. Trainee teachers have to cope with adjusting to the prevailing norms; establish and maintain relationships with staff; learn procedures and adapt to the school's priorities, some of which may be abstruse and difficult to interpret.

The impact of emotion has implications for children's learning. Some pupils fear failure and worry about getting things wrong and being in trouble as a result. Other pupils are unwilling to persevere when faced with challenges, either because they are unable to cope with the situation or because they avoid making more than a nominal effort to achieve a satisfactory outcome. As these negative responses are the result of emotional insecurity, teachers spend a lot of time seeking to understand the root causes of behaviour and strengthening each child's sense of well-being. Teachers encourage pupils to persevere with work and not be afraid of making genuine errors; they also use mistakes positively by explaining the alternatives and using the opportunity to deepen children's understanding of concepts.

Further reading

Bocchino, R. (1999) *Emotional Literacy: How to be a different kind of smart*, Thousand Oaks, CA: Corwin Press/Sage.

Corrie, C. (2003) *Becoming Emotionally Intelligent*, Stafford: Network Educational Press.

Gardner, H. (1999) *Intelligence Reframed: Multiple intelligences for the 21st century*, New York: Basic Books.

Golby, M. (1996) 'Teachers' emotions: an illustrated discussion', *Cambridge Journal of Education*, 26, 3, pp. 423–34.

Goleman, D. (1999) *Working With Emotional Intelligence*, New York: Bantam Books.

Hargreaves, A. (1998) 'The emotional practice of teaching', *Teaching and Teacher Education*, 14, 8, pp. 835–54.

Nias, D. J. (1996) 'Thinking about feeling: the emotions in teaching', *Cambridge Journal of Education*, 26, pp. 293–306.

Sharp, P. (2001) *Nurturing Emotional Literacy*, London: David Fulton, chapter 4.

ENCOURAGEMENT

Encouragement and praise are both important strategies to promote pupils' enthusiasm for learning. Encouragement can be given to children to help them improve a draft version of their work or complete a difficult piece of work or concentrate harder in order to achieve a higher standard. Praise, on the other hand, is offered for good-quality work, real effort, sensitivity and responsibility. Encouragement recognises that the present level of attainment is acceptable but that there is even more to achieve. Praise recognises that the very best outcome has been achieved in the circumstances. When encouraging children, teachers use a variety of expressions to cajole, chivvy, motivate and offer support, often accompanied by bright eye contact, congratulatory claps, smiles, open faces and close (but not inappropriate) body proximity. Both encouragement and praise open dialogue that helps pupils to evaluate their present attainment and monitor their own progress.

Adults that encourage children in the primary classroom help to create a **learning climate** in which **creativity** and problem solving can flourish because pupils know that they are going to be supported in their endeavours. Such positive encouragement allows children time to think, defers judgement, promotes independence, actively listens, follows the child's interests, uses mistakes constructively and promotes imaginative **play**.

Children do not accept encouragement or praise from an adult they do not respect, but perceive it as being a subtle form of coercion. Even young children are quick to spot insincere encouragement and praise. The unthinking 'That's good' or dismissive 'Yes, fine' (without paying any real attention to what the child has done or said) is likely to lead to reduced motivation as children see how little they can get away with and still receive teacher approval. Consequently, praise has to be merited and not offered lightly. Experienced teachers bide their time and are gently approving rather than letting loose a flood of commendation prematurely. Inexperienced teachers sometimes expend too much encouragement and offer praise for work and effort that does not merit it.

Encouragement is most effective when it is used constructively, without rancour and with reference to clearly defined tasks and **expectations**. Praise, publicly and sincerely given, is reserved for genuine instances of quality work and effort. For children who trust their teacher, there is no greater source of satisfaction.

Further reading

Houghton, S., Williams, S. and Bain, A. (1991) 'The effects of a school-wide behaviour management programme on teachers' use of encouragement in the classroom', *Educational Studies*, 17, 3, pp. 249–60.

Merrett, F. (1993) *Encouragement works best: Positive approaches to classroom management*, London: David Fulton.

Spinrad, T. L. (1999) 'The relation of parental affect and encouragement to children's moral emotions and behaviour', *Journal of Moral Education*, 28, 3, pp. 323–37.

ENJOYMENT

The UK government has been so keen to advance the notion that learning can be enjoyable that one of its most influential documents is entitled *Excellence and Enjoyment* (DfES 2003a) to convey the impression that high standards and pleasure in learning are compatible. Pupils are engaged with work by learning in such a way that it expands their **thinking** and promotes their inventiveness. As a result, children enjoy the diversity of their learning, both in the variety of topics that are presented to them, but also in the different ways that they learn, such as in small groups, through the arts, **extra-curricular** activities and the involvement of parents and friends at home. Part of the enjoyment is gained through the interactive nature of learning and the excitement that comes from mutual discovery and **collaboration**.

Enjoyment is a prerequisite for making optimum progress in learning. There are two principal forms of enjoyment: enjoyment *of* learning and enjoyment *in* learning. Enjoyment of learning involves a **passion** for finding out and discovering new things. Enjoyment in learning means that the processes used in finding out are satisfying and meaningful. The two forms of enjoyment, though distinctive in character, form two sides of the same coin, as children who enjoy learning for its own sake will find satisfaction in reaching their goal by whatever means is necessary; similarly, children who enjoy what they are doing are likely to learn more. Teachers who are able to inspire a love of learning in children and provide interesting and relevant ways of helping them to do so provide the best possible **learning climate**. By contrast, teachers who present pupils with unimaginative and tedious means to address the lesson content are in danger of squeezing the enthusiasm from them. Some pupils, especially older ones, become disillusioned with learning in school if they are bored and it then takes perseverance for even the most talented teacher to reignite the spark.

Enjoyment of learning is sometimes confused with casual and random **teaching approaches**. The belief that children do not come to school to 'have fun' but rather to take their work seriously – a view popular among some politicians and parents – may be borne of such confusion. While a combination of attractive lesson content and a persuasive teaching approach creates the best circumstances for enjoyment, not all content is intrinsically enjoyable, so the challenge for every practitioner is to find ways to present **knowledge** in ways that inspire and motivate pupils. In recent years there has been a considerable emphasis placed upon the importance of adjusting the teaching approach to accommodate the learning styles of the pupils. Thus, some children particularly benefit from visual support, others from illustrative stories, yet others from detailed verbal explanations.

Studies show that the majority of any school staff finds work enjoyable and fulfilling. Teachers, administrators and ancillary workers are agreed that their role is significant and that they benefit from the companionship and sense of mutual endeavour that working in primary schools offer them.

Further reading

Alexander, R. J. (2004) 'Still no pedagogy? Principle, pragmatism and compliance in primary education', *Cambridge Journal of Education*, 34, 1, pp. 7–33.

Department for Education and Skills (2003a) *Excellence and Enjoyment: A strategy for primary schools*, London: The Stationery Office. Web site: www.dfes.gov.uk/primarydocument

Moyles, J. (1997) 'Just for fun?', in N. Kitson and R. Merry (eds) *Teaching in the Primary School*, pp. 11–25, London: Routledge.

ENQUIRY

Enquiry-based learning is closely related to problem solving and investigation, two terms that share common features. Both processes involve finding solutions to an aspect of knowledge that is unknown or problematic, but they can be distinguished on the basis of the methods used to arrive at a result and the diversity of solutions. The term *problem solving* is frequently employed when there is a single solution, whereas *investigation* tends to be used when there are a variety of possible outcomes. Both terms, however, are subsumed within the umbrella term 'enquiry'.

Enquiries can be conducted by individual pupils but are generally more effective as a group effort, as the opportunity for pupils to cooperate in solving problems contributes to academic advancement, social development and increased **self-esteem**. Interacting with children of their own age fosters a climate in which active discussion about issues is more natural for the pupils concerned. Furthermore, the existence of disagreement forces the children to attend to aspects that they will miss if they are working alone. The search for clarification and truth during an enquiry allows pupils to reconstruct their present understanding and adjust their perspectives on issues.

Enquiry-based learning relies on pupils as active learners, who exercise some ownership of the activities (rather than being wholly directed by the teacher) and have the opportunity to reflect upon the processes that contribute towards their grasp of the things they learn. Janet Moyles, the noted educationist, offers an eight-point approach to promote this sort of active learning. (1) An entering strategy, consisting of starting points and introduction. (2) An exploration mode, where pupils engage with the task supported by adequate resources and directed by adults. (3) Consideration of content in respect of the subject, processes and **skills** that the children are intended to learn. (4) Clarification about ownership and responsibility, especially the presence or absence of adult supervision. (5) Adult intervention, **interaction** and level of support for children. (6) Evaluation and analysis of children's learning. (7) Opportunities for children to reflect on their learning. (8) Justification for the work completed and its outcomes. Failure to provide opportunities for this type of experiential learning can result in uninspired pupils who comply with the teacher's wishes but have little understanding of the lesson purpose or their own responsibilities as learners.

Enquiry-based learning is constrained by the need to address stipulated schemes of work and timetable factors. However, the use of unstructured days and an emphasis on **topic work** rather than single-subject work, with timetable barriers relaxed, allow pupils to probe and explore areas of knowledge more freely.

Further reading

Johnston, J. (2004) 'The value of exploration and discovery', *Primary Science Review*, 85, pp. 21–3.

Katz, L. G. and Chard, S. C. (2000) *Engaging Children's Minds: The project approach*, Stamford, CT: Ablex, chapter 3.

Kellett, M. (2004) 'Just teach us the skills, please, we'll do the rest: empowering ten-year-olds as active researchers', *Children and Society*, 18, 5, pp. 329–43.

EQUAL OPPORTUNITIES

Nursery and primary education provide a starting point for meeting the needs of individual children and groups of children. Teachers aim to offer every pupil the opportunity to experience success in learning, setting high but sensible **expectations** for each boy and girl, pupils who have special educational needs and those with disabilities, pupils from different social and cultural backgrounds, ethnic groups, refugees and asylum seekers. The essence of equal opportunity is to provide a more inclusive **curriculum**, available to as wide a range of children as possible, founded on three tenets. First, to set pupils suitable and relevant learning challenges. Second, to respond to their diverse learning needs. Third, to overcome potential barriers to learning that may hinder optimum progress.

In attempting to ensure that all pupils experience success in learning and feel confident about themselves, teachers have to take account of unusual circumstances, such as extended absence, and the need for **differentiation** of tasks and activities to provide appropriate work for children with exceptional learning difficulties or abilities. For example, a child who has been away from school for several weeks may need to be given an individualised work programme to allow for 'catching up' and regaining momentum in learning.

In responding to pupils' diverse learning needs, the aim is to provide equal opportunity for all children, regardless of gender, race or disability, by motivating them to work hard, make regular assessments of their progress and set appropriate targets for learning. Particular care has to be paid in communicating effectively with children for whom English is an additional language. In such cases, strategies include the use of steady, well-articulated speech, a good range of tactile experiences and making a special effort to involve all the children in creative activities where spoken language is not necessarily essential to complete the work. As some children from atypical cultural backgrounds may be frustrated by their inability to conform and contribute to classroom discussion, enlisting the help of a sympathetic child (a 'buddy') to help them find their way around, and the close involvement of teaching **assistants** who possess appropriate language proficiency, are significant strategies. Teachers are also aware of the potential value of support agencies, such as social services and the educational psychologist.

The principle that every person deserves to receive a good education is reflected in official documentation. The National Curriculum 2000 for England and Wales (DfEE/QCA 1999) insists that:

> When planning, teachers should set high **expectations** and provide opportunities for all pupils to achieve, including boys and girls, pupils with special educational needs, pupils with disabilities, pupils from all social and cultural backgrounds, pupils of different ethnic groups including travellers, refugees and asylum seekers, and those from diverse linguistic backgrounds.
>
> (p. 31)

A raft of legislation in recent years, supported by active public debate of the issues, has emphasised that unfair discrimination is not allowed in schools on any basis whatsoever. The principle is well expressed in the following: 'Our education system must support all pupils well and unintentionally discriminate against any particular group of pupils' (DfES 2003a, p. 42). Furthermore, all qualified teachers must recognise and respond effectively to equal opportunities issues, and challenge incidents of bullying and harassment. Deliberate or unintentional bias towards pupils which can be construed as discriminatory leaves teachers open to charges of unprofessional conduct, so it is important that they are as impartial as possible at all times. Not only must all children be granted the same opportunities, support and **encouragement**, but it is not appropriate to label children owing to circumstances such as home background or physical appearance. A teasing pleasantry about a child's looks or domestic circumstances may be more hurtful and inflict greater damage than a teacher intends or imagines. A useful antidote to discriminatory attitudes is for adults to develop a positive attitude towards what can be accomplished and to adopt an 'all things are possible' **learning climate** in which all children can fulfil their potential. One way and another, it is part of every teacher's responsibility to treat children respectfully, regardless of the provocation or the need for firmness.

In a DfES publication dealing with raising the achievement of minority ethnic children (DfES 2003b) three characteristics are identified as significant for helping to improve the educational attainment of minority ethnic pupils. The first is establishing an agreed strategy that applies across the whole school. The second is to strive for effective learning and teaching, including support for bilingual pupils. The third is to create an ethos of respect, with a clear approach to issues relating to racism and behaviour. In addition, parents and the community are encouraged to undertake a full part in the life and development of the school. The study revealed a complex picture of minority ethnic attainment and participation. In broad terms, black, Bangladeshi and Pakistani pupils perform less well than other ethnic groups during the time of compulsory schooling; by contrast, Indian and Chinese pupils perform better than any of the other ethnic groups included in the survey. Proportionately more black, Pakistani and Bangladeshi pupils were recorded as having special educational needs, though regional variations were apparent.

The reason for underachievement of some minority groups is partly explained by the social and material deprivation that characterised those groups, as indicated by the incidence of free school meals. For instance, over 30% of Pakistani and black pupils, and over half of all Bangladeshi, Gypsy/Roma pupils were eligible for free school meals, compared with 14% for white pupils. However, there was not found to be a simple relationship between these figures and academic progress, as the biggest gap in attainment was between white pupils with and white pupils without free school meals. Clearly, then, there are other factors that need to be taken into account when addressing issues of under-performance.

There has also been a great deal of discussion about the challenges facing educators to ensure that pupils receive a full and appropriate education, regardless of gender. Concerns have been expressed about the limitations that teachers sometimes place upon girls in subjects like science and the tendency for them to direct more time and attention towards boys. However, results from national tests indicate that the position is more complex and that girls are forging ahead of boys in most areas of work, especially in language-based topics. A report by the Office for Standards in Education (OFSTED) found that although girls outperformed boys in almost every area of academic work, some schools and teachers were able to help boys achieve their potential, especially in the problem area of writing (OFSTED 2003b). In such schools there was a culture where intellectual, cultural and aesthetic accomplishment was valued by boys as well as by girls. In schools where boys perform well, they are encouraged to read widely and offered choice about the content of their writing, even when the form (genre) is prescribed. Teachers in such schools make every effort for children to write to 'real' audiences where possible. Effective planning and teaching are accompanied by frequent and formative assessments of boys' writing, and a culture that enables them to take pride in what they produce. There appears to be a clear link between the development of independent **reading** habits and enthusiasm for writing on the part of the teacher and the pupils.

While it is necessary that impartial decisions are needed as far as possible when dealing with children, male and female, the principle must not be confused with a need to take account of individual differences. Children respond differently to situations and circumstances, and adults must be prepared to adjust their responses and actions accordingly. A **dilemma** exists for teachers because on the one hand it is necessary for them to be consistent in their treatment of children, but on the other hand children respond differently to similar treatment. For example, being stern with one child may have little effect, but may be upsetting to another child in the same class. Teachers have therefore to be wise in the way that they approach all interpersonal encounters. However, blanket stereotyping of children on the basis of gender or any other defining characteristic is deemed unacceptable. For example, studies have shown that adults tend to expect tall children to be more emotionally mature than small children of the same age.

A teacher's assumptions about children's potential to learn and make progress may have a direct influence upon their attitude to school in general, their willingness to cooperate and persevere, and ultimately their achievements. Attention to equal opportunity provision improves the **learning climate**, eases classroom management and enhances **pupil motivation**.

Further reading

Brown, B. (1998) *Unlearning Discrimination in the Early Years*, Stoke-on-Trent: Trentham.

Commission for Racial Equality (2002) *A Guide for Schools*, London: CRE.
Department for Education and Skills (2003b) *Aiming High: Raising the achievements of minority ethnic pupils*, London: The Stationery Office.
MULTIVERSE: http://www.multiverse.ac.uk/
Skelton, C. and Francis, B. (2003) *Boys and Girls in the Primary Classroom*, Maidenhead: Open University Press.
Suschitzky, W. and Chapman, J. (1998) *Valued Children, Informed Teaching*, Maidstone: Open University Press, chapters 1 and 2.
Yelland, N. (1998) *Gender in Early Childhood*, London: Routledge.

EXPECTATIONS

Expectation is a more involved concept than it may initially appear to be, consisting of an amalgam of teacher and pupil aspirations, attempts to achieve the lesson purpose and account taken of individual pupil targets for improvement, time constraints, adult support and resource factors. One of the requirements for qualified teacher status is to demonstrate high expectations of all pupils, to respect their social, cultural, linguistic, religious and ethnic backgrounds and be committed to raising standards. It is taken for granted that every adult wants pupils to succeed in their academic work and mature in their social development; to achieve this aim teachers have to transmit a positive message to their pupils about the quality of work that has to be attained and the effort that has to be expended to reach the expected standard. Putting these worthy aspirations into practice is not always easy because sophisticated judgements are needed to strike a balance between high and unreasonable expectations, especially for pupils who possess limited intellectual capacity. Teachers also have to take account of the possibility that a highly demanding expectation for a pupil working alone may become manageable for (say) a pair of children cooperating or a collaborative enterprise involving four or five pupils. Expectations therefore vary depending on the demands of the task, the time available for its completion and the extent of adult support offered to the child.

Expectation may relate to a specific aspect of learning, depending on what has been identified by the teacher as especially significant (the learning objective). For instance, in a piece of extended writing the emphasis may be upon developing a storyline or constructing the piece in a prescribed manner using a predetermined framework or writing neatly or inserting a creative element or enthralling the reader or accurate grammar or a combination of several things. Teachers have a responsibility to clarify their expectations and involve children in determining what is particularly important to their individual learning. Thus, in the same piece of writing, a child may have struggled with conveying meaning and the need to concentrate on rectifying the deficit; another child may have lots of good ideas but write incoherently; yet another may need to improve handwriting. Within a single session, therefore, there may be general expectations for all pupils but also a specific target for an individual child to succeed in a particular aspect of the work.

Expectation does not just apply to academic attainment. A key element of primary education is to work with parents in the task of developing confident and well-adjusted children who are capable of exercising a mature role in society. To assist in the process, all primary schools emphasise the need for pupils to exercise self-discipline and take responsibility for their actions. School governors and staff draw up a general **behaviour** policy for the school and each class teacher establishes and reinforces discipline through class **rules**, with sanctions for flagrant and persistent violation of the agreed code of conduct. Despite the efforts of teachers to impress on pupils the importance of high expectations, their quest is sometimes undermined by an increase in the number of emotionally unsettled children in mainstream primary education and the eclectic range of moral norms in society.

Further reading

Cassidy, M. (2004) 'Fitting in? Scottish primary teachers' expectations of school entrants', *Scottish Educational Review*, 36, 2, pp. 191–205.

Tauber, R. T. (1997) *Self-Fulfilling Prophecy: A practical guide to its use in education*, London: Praeger.

Wrigley, T. (2003) *Schools of Hope*, Stoke on Trent: Trentham, chapter 5.

EXTRA-CURRICULAR

The expression 'extra-curricular' denotes the fact that activities are outside the remit of the prescribed **curriculum**. Primary teachers have always been involved in providing educational and recreational opportunities for children outside school hours and extra-curricular activities play an important part in the life of most primary schools. However, the close regulation of teachers' working conditions in recent years and the additional demands made of them to maintain detailed records, carry out extensive assessment procedures and provide justification for every aspect of pupils' learning have led to a general curtailment of voluntary activities. Issues of **health and safety**, child protection and increase in litigation have also contributed to a situation where teachers are more cautious about committing themselves over and above the demands of regular teaching. The introduction of financial incentives for teachers to undertake extra duties, the increase in the number of ancillary staff, together with the provision of pre-school and after-school opportunities, have helped to ease this situation.

The use of the expression 'extra-curricular' has broadened in recent years and now incorporates a range of activities and opportunities for both children and adults that transcends the more familiar after-school football practice and lunchtime recorder club. Depending on the size of the school, the age of the children and the availability of staff, a range of opportunities, covering musical, sporting, academic and more general interests, are offered. The artistic, musical and dramatic talents developed during extra-curricular sessions are sometimes employed for school productions and seasonal celebrations. As part of the extra-curricular dimension, schools run 'booster' classes and additional **lessons** that take place outside the regular school day to improve pupils' academic performance (such as **homework** clubs). Some schools are designated 'community school' owing to their close ties with the neighbourhood and the use of their premises for a variety of activities for local residents. Some schools open early to provide breakfast for children and continue until early evening by employing ancillary staff to provide childcare facilities.

ContinYou is a UK learning charity that has played a role in shaping the out-of-school hours learning and study support movement in education, striving to ensure that extra-curricular activities are kept at the centre of the education and policy agenda. They support and promote out-of-hours opportunities (known as Extra Hours) through programmes such as breakfast clubs. Their aim is to enrich the lives of children and young people, provide new opportunities for learning, enable them to develop new skills and build on existing provision. Many educationists believe that out-of-hours activities help to raise attainment, improve attendance, increase aspirations, build confidence and remotivate disaffected pupils.

Recently qualified teachers seeking employment are frequently asked what additional contributions they can make to school life and the appointing panel are usually keen to hear that candidates are willing to commit themselves to the school over and above their immediate contractual obligations. However, head teachers are keen for new teachers to settle into the regular pattern of teaching and learning before extending the range of their responsibilities.

Further reading

Byard, K. (2003) 'Where have all the clubs gone? The decline in extra-curricular activities', *Education 3–13*, 31, 2, pp. 60–3.
ContinYou: http://www.continyou.org.uk
Department for Education and Skills (2004d) *Work with Children in Out-of-School or Holiday Clubs*, Ref. 1226, London: The Stationery Office.

FEEDBACK

The process of evaluating the merits and limitations of pupils' work, approach to task completion or finished product, where an informed adult offers constructive comment to a pupil, is usually referred to as 'feedback'. High-quality feedback informs children in such a way that they are left more confident about the way to achieve greater success by better comprehending how they can improve their work. Pupils rely heavily on teachers to provide them with good-quality feedback such that they can adjust their priorities, correct misunderstandings and advance their knowledge and thereby proceed with assurance. Poor-quality feedback leaves pupils dissatisfied, unclear about the task requirements and unsure about methods to enhance their output. The act of providing feedback is, therefore, an essential skill for every teacher and assistant who works with children.

The type of feedback given to pupils tends to fall under one of three broad categories: instructional, procedural or advisory. Instructional feedback occurs when the adult gives the child unambiguous commands about what needs to be done to improve, remedy or enhance work. Procedural feedback clarifies the teacher's **expectations** about how, why and when the task is done; it does not concern itself with the quality of the work directly. Advisory feedback offers suggestions about options and alternatives available to the children; the onus is placed on pupils to determine the most appropriate course of action. Teachers have to ensure that children are clear about which type of feedback is being given or pupils may (for instance) interpret advice about ways to proceed as an **instruction**.

The content of the feedback to pupils from adults depends upon five factors. First, the **learning objectives** act as a beacon for the advice and guidance that is offered, as the tasks and activities with which children engage are inevitably closely linked to what children are learning. Second, the relationship between teacher and pupil will influence the tone of the feedback, as the more intimate the relationship, the more relaxed and interactive the exchange is likely to be. Third, the working **context** is important, as a more formal situation (such as a test or a specific task undertaking requiring silence) will limit the extent of the feedback; such feedback is likely to be more procedural than instructional. By contrast, an informal collaborative task provides for a great deal of spontaneous feedback of different kinds. Fourth, the nature of the work will have a bearing on the specificity of the feedback. Open-ended tasks (especially investigative and problem-solving ones) require the teacher to 'stand back' and allow pupils to persevere without excessive guidance, whereas situations in which there is a defined and single answer or solution requires close monitoring. Fifth, the confidence of pupils and their experience in the area of learning dealt with will affect the composition of the feedback. Thus, confident children with a strong track record in coping with the demands of the work benefit from questions from the teacher that extend their **thinking** and cause them to reflect more deeply on the issues attached to the work. On the other hand, timid children or those with little experience in the area of work require more specific direction until they gain confidence.

Teachers have to exercise fine judgement when offering feedback to children about their work and effort. At one level there is a need for them to explain to children how things can be improved. At another level there is a pressing need, especially with children who have experienced limited academic success in the past, to encourage, praise and celebrate small achievements. Consequently, successful feedback is a skill that requires considerable sensitivity and professional adeptness if it is to be fully effective.

Further reading

Chalk, K. and Bizo, L. A. (2004) 'Specific praise improves on-task behaviour and numeracy enjoyment: a study of year four pupils engaged in the numeracy hour', *Educational Psychology in Practice*, 20, 4, pp. 335–51.

Clarke, S. (2003) *Enriching feedback in the primary classroom: Oral and written feedback from teachers and children*, London: Hodder & Stoughton.

FRIENDSHIP

Helping children to develop friendships is not the principal purpose of primary education, but attention to the implications arising from good relationships is important in the quest for a positive teaching and learning environment. Children attach great importance to learning alongside their friends, so teachers have a responsibility to identify and promote such groupings, though friends do not necessarily work well together. When establishing groups, teachers may take pupils' views into account with regard to their academic and social compatibility, as children usually know who they work well with and their comments can usefully inform decisions about grouping. These decisions are often far from straightforward, as teachers need to distinguish between friends who work well together and friends who are a distraction. Most pupils want to have friends in the same class but they are not always strong-willed enough to resist the temptation to divert from the task and chatter to them.

Strong friendships between children bring them joy and satisfaction and impact positively upon their attitude to learning. There is a growing concern about the loss of **childhood**, as reflected through the reduced amount of time that children spend with parents, the flood of media images that saturate their minds and the speed with which children are expected to absorb adult perspectives and practices. Sincere friendships between adults and children can have significant benefits far beyond the immediate situation and offer hope and security for children. In a time when there is often a suspicion of adults who express a loving interest in children's welfare, positive teacher–pupil relationships provide considerable reassurance for those who view compassion as a key dimension of their role.

Teachers work hard to build a rapport with children and thereby place themselves in a much stronger position to influence pupil attitude and behaviour, as the extent of their influence is severely curtailed if they are emotionally detached. While it is not necessary for adults in school to be friends with pupils, it is essential for them to be friendly, warm and accessible. At the heart of the friendship between an adult and a child is a question of trust, for which a prerequisite is that the adult proves to be reliable, consistent and fair.

Pupils may be without friends for a variety of reasons. Sometimes a child has recently moved to the school or has joined mid-year at a time when friendships are already well established. Sometimes a child is different from the majority of pupils in ways that other children find it hard to accept. Sometimes a personality quirk creates problems and invites ridicule that may verge on **bullying**. Most teachers help new pupils to find their feet and make friends by pairing them with sensible and helpful members of the class. Friends offer one another mutual support, so when friendships go wrong they often need adult support to resolve the matter. Girls tend to have two or three very close friends while boys tend to have a larger and more fluid group of friends. Whereas breakdowns in friendships between boys are normally short and quickly resolved, breakdowns in friendships among girls tend to be more prolonged owing to the emotional intensity of the relationships that may intrude on their classroom work.

Further reading

Clarke, S. (2003) *Enriching feedback in the primary classroom: Oral and written feedback from teachers and children*, London: Hodder & Stoughton.

Peters, S. (2003) 'I didn't expect that I would get tons of friends: children's experiences of friendship during the transition to school', *Early Years*, 23, 1, pp. 45–53.

GIFTEDNESS AND TALENT

There are numerous definitions of the terms 'gifted' and 'talented'. However, a commonly held view is that *gifted* denotes an exceptional **ability** in English or mathematics. Gifted children are characterised by being able to apply their **knowledge** widely and utilise a variety of resources, ideas, methods and tasks. The word *talented*, on the other hand, tends to be reserved for children who display exceptional skill in other **curriculum** areas where there is more of an arts or public performance element. Gifted and talented pupils typically comprise between 5% and 10% of the population; consequently, in a class of thirty children there is likely to be between one and three children in the gifted or talented category. Over recent years, a lot of attention has been given to the needs of less able children in school but rather less time has been allocated to the needs of the more able. This imbalance is gradually being rectified in primary education and there is now more attention given to the potential of gifted pupils by setting more challenging tasks and providing **extra-curricular** classes to help children achieve optimum success in formal examinations.

Both talented and gifted children tend to possess similar attributes. They are creative and imaginative, possess keen insight and intuition and can work independently of others. Gifted and talented children often have a good, if sometimes unconventional, sense of **humour** and are highly motivated (particularly in self-selected tasks), demonstrating exceptional critical **thinking** and **skills** for problem solving. Gifted pupils will often have widespread interests, superior powers of reasoning, intellectual curiosity, a broad attention span and a superior vocabulary. They are capable of employing advanced **reading** strategies (such as the ability to scan text) and possess strong powers of observation and originality in their approach to solving problems. Gifted children tend to respond quickly to new ideas and memorise facts quickly. They may demonstrate maturity beyond their years, expressed by an interest in people and the way that situations interrelate.

Helping children who are gifted in English and mathematics is fairly straightforward for teachers in that there is a considerable amount of time spent in schools on **literacy** and **numeracy**, so it is easier to spot exceptional capability and adjust the demands of the work accordingly. By contrast, talented children may remain 'hidden' owing to the small amount of time allocated to other subjects in the primary curriculum. For both gifted and talented pupils, the teacher has to take account of the learner's own interests and preferred style of learning, and provide opportunities to be independent and autonomous. There is also a need to make it possible for pupils to share ideas and initiatives with others and find connections across areas of learning through engagement with **cross-curricular work**, projects, themes and topics. It is particularly important that children are encouraged to think deeply about the process of learning in such a way that they are not merely complying with adult demands but actively interrogating the implications of their actions and decisions. A teacher's good practice with very able pupils provides a model for effective practice with all children.

The learning environment has an impact on the emergence of the gift or talent. A creative **teaching approach** is likely to draw out children's best endeavour, whereas a rigid one is more likely to suppress it. It is essential for teachers to ask searching questions that force able pupils to apply their reasoning and logical powers. While non-gifted pupils may not be able to employ such abstract thought, they can learn from the astute comments and insights provided by their more illustrious classmates.

Experience suggests that teachers are sometimes tempted to leave bright pupils alone to work independently or simply give them additional work to keep them busy while attention is given to slower learners. In fact, the highest levels of academic performance are achieved when teachers interact with pupils in a way that encourages them to grapple with demanding concepts and levels of under-standing. The imposition of artificial ceilings in the level of difficulty of tasks can lead to gifted children becoming dissatisfied and fru-strated. Capable pupils find fulfilment through active dialogue with the teacher and prefer to be challenged within the regular teaching programme rather than by being given special provision outside it. They do not benefit from being isolated from the regular tasks and activities but prosper when they are given the opportunity to explore ideas and be innovative. Gifted and talented pupils are more moti-vated by a teacher's honest evaluation of their work (written or spoken) than by the provision of grades, providing the **feedback** is constructive and challenging.

Most exceptionally able pupils take their work seriously and want to do well. Their attainment can be suppressed by adult insensitivity, a preponderance of mundane tasks and being made to feel different from everyone else, thus gaining a reputation as a 'swot', 'nerd' or 'square'. Able pupils can underachieve in the same way as other children, especially if they lack motivation or if teachers consider them to be uncooperative instead of welcoming their perceptive contributions. The challenge of presenting academic success as desir-able is most challenging among a small percentage of older primary-age boys, though a competitive climate may help to offset this tendency.

Some gifted and talented children are unconventional; their **behaviour** may be interpreted as being anti-social by adults because they ask probing questions and insist on using their own ideas rather than familiar ones. Talented children may not shine at mathematics and **literacy**; as a result they can be made to spend additional time on these subjects, thereby reducing the opportunity for them to dis-play their creative abilities in the areas in which they excel. Others pupils do well in every subject area (including sporting **activities**) and thereby attract considerable admiration from their peers. Yet other children have latent talent that requires a stimulus before it is released. For example, children from less affluent homes may not have a chance to attend out-of-school ballet, dance, craft or sporting sessions, at which they might have excelled had they been offered the opportunity to do so.

Further reading

Eyre, D. and McClure, L. (eds) (2001) *Curriculum Provision for the Gifted and Talented in the Primary School*, London: David Fulton/NACE.

Haylock, D. (2004) 'Gifted and talented pupils in primary schools', in A. Browne and D. Haylock (eds) *Professional Issues for Primary Teachers*, pp. 150–65, London: Paul Chapman.

Hymer, B. and Michel, D. (2002) *Gifted and Talented Learners*, London: NACE/David Fulton.

Smith, C. (2005) *Teaching Gifted and Talented Pupils in the Primary School*, London: Paul Chapman.

HEALTH AND SAFETY

In recent years there has been a considerable amount of attention given to ensuring that pupils are protected from hazards and avoidable injury at school, through carelessness, neglect or ignorance. Sensible health and safety precautions are not intended to limit pupils' learning or their participation in practical activities, but to liberate the children to work confidently and assuredly. The increase in litigation and highly publicised cases of teachers and local education authorities being taken to court by parents over health and safety issues has heightened awareness of the need for increased care. It has also created a climate of extreme caution about pupils undertaking any **activity** that carries a risk. Most lesson plans used by teachers in training include a 'risk assessment' category, where potential dangers to pupils have been identified beforehand. These issues are particularly relevant for vulnerable pupils, including the very young, those with disabilities and children with allergies.

Considerations about children's well-being have to take account of both emotional and physical factors; there are at least ten health and safety rules that teachers are constantly alert to. First, pupils and adults must be able to walk around the room unhindered by obstacles such as poorly positioned furniture or articles lying on the floor. Second, pupils carrying out activities that require large areas must be given the appropriate space in which to work and not expected to squeeze into a confined spot. Third, equipment and resources have to be stored so that they can be reached without having to stretch or pull items down from the shelf. Fourth, wet activities have to be restricted to a designated area away from main walkways, and sink areas are kept free from furniture. Fifth, pupils must be taught how and when to wash their hands thoroughly before meals, after messy activities and after contact with soil, flora or fauna. Sixth, teachers need to ensure that pupils' view of the board and other visual aids is unhindered and does not require children to twist unnaturally or squint. Seventh, seating has to be organised in such a way that pupils do not sit next to a draughty window, hot radiator or a tall piece of furniture with free-standing objects resting on top. Eighth, pupils must only use specialist equipment with adult supervision and after appropriate training. Ninth, pupils must be regularly reminded not to suck or put small objects in their mouths. Finally, class rules need to stress that pupils walk and do not run in the classroom.

The use of computer equipment raises specific issues with regard to electrical safety, ensuring that children are properly supervised, liquids are not permitted in the area of the machines and attention is given to the possible hazards from trailing leads and flexes. Teachers are also careful that pupils do not spend an excessive amount of time in front of a computer screen and that chairs are correctly positioned and suitable for the purpose. The danger of repetitive strain injury caused through excessive keyboard work is not a serious problem for pupils in school, though it may be a problem in the home if adult supervision is slack. Teachers, too, have to be cautious that when they spend time entering data into a computer or (especially) writing reports they abide by the same safety considerations that they enforce with pupils in the classroom or computer suite.

Healthy eating, personal hygiene and awareness of the dangers from drugs form an important element of primary pupils' education. All children require nutritious food, regular exercise and appropriate amounts of rest and sleep to function efficiently during the day and make the best use of the learning opportunities provided in and out of school. Schools promote healthy eating, encourage children to eat fruit rather than snacks, and pay close attention to the nutritional value of school meals. School safety programmes tend to reflect adult concerns about children's safety, such as accident prevention, ensuring that pupils are taught about hazards from traffic and roads, trains and railway lines, electricity, fire and heat, machinery, sharp objects, medicines, poisons, and so forth. Danger from strangers is also commonly emphasised in primary school safety programmes. Children, however, may harbour more concerns about burglars and violence. Younger children may be worried by imaginary dangers, especially those that result from exposure to unsuitable television programmes.

Inexperienced teachers tend to take advice from senior colleagues about health and safety issues, especially when using specialised equipment and during apparatus work in the gymnasium. Should an injury occur then national laws about appropriate adult and child behaviour and relationships, regional guidelines about procedures and agreed school policies are activated, depending upon the nature of the incident. In situations where a number of different activities are taking place in the room simultaneously, teachers have to ensure that sufficient adult help and supervision is available. In large-space activities involving heavy or potentially hazardous equipment (in aspects of physical education, for instance) teachers carry out safety checks beforehand and monitor pupil access closely. Teachers generally use a limited range of equipment safely than attempt too much at one time, which might create unsafe working conditions.

Further reading

McWhirter, J. M. (2000) 'Evaluating Safe in the Sun: a curriculum programme for primary schools', *Health Education Research*, 15, 2, pp. 203–17.
Wetton, N. (2003) 'Growing up safely in a changing world', *Wired for Health*, NHS Health Development Agency, London: The Stationery Office. http://www.wiredforhealth.gov.uk (accessed April 2005).

HOMEWORK

Most primary teachers provide relevant forms of homework and other out-of-class tasks for pupils that help to consolidate and extend the work that has been carried out during the school day, involving parents where possible. The homework has to be manageable, as there is little point in setting work that is impossible for the children to complete or that requires expensive ICT resources that may not be available at home. Government guidelines suggest that children as young as 5 should spend up to an hour a week doing homework on **reading**, spelling and number.

Homework is particularly useful if it builds on previous school-based work or teases open intriguing new avenues of learning, with tasks organised in such a way that children can cope unaided if necessary and directly linked to the **learning objectives** that the teacher has established for the lesson. Some homework consists of 'finishing off' incomplete work from the day; however, this penalises slower workers and does little to extend the more able. Commonly, children are given a number of activities that have to be completed over a period of time (a half-term, say) in addition to short-term tasks such as learning how to spell a list of words. Homework can provide a starting point for discussion and sharing experiences, and a useful spur in promoting dialogue in learning.

Typical homework tasks include giving the children work to do that is based on observation, consulting with an older adult about 'living history' (events that occurred during the lifetime of the adult) or paper and pencil activities, such as completing a set of mathematical computations. The simplest form of homework is when the same task is given to all the children such that they are all able to engage with it at their own level, and where the end product can be marked easily or shared with others. For younger children, additional reading is frequently used, with a parent signing in a reading record book to confirm that it has been completed. Homework has to be monitored and assessed by the teacher if it is to be fully effective, so the more elaborate it is, the more time and effort has to be expended in dealing with the outcome. Some teachers use teaching assistants to monitor completion and check accuracy.

There is general support among primary educationists for homework as a method of enhancing learning but a few studies suggest that it might have a negative impact because it places a strain on family relationships that may outweigh the educational benefit. Research at the University of London's Institute of Education found that helping pupils with homework can exacerbate or create family tensions (http://www. literacytrust.org.uk/Update/homework.html). One of the study's conclusions was that parents may inhibit learning by exercising strict **control** over the way homework is done, instead of helping the children to interpret for themselves. The authors conclude that the most effective help that parents can provide is in offering moral support to children, but only helping them directly when specifically asked to do so. The study acknowledges that homework can have modest benefits for academic progress but that brighter pupils and older pupils are the main beneficiaries. The author of the London Institute research, Susan Hallam, claims that 'homework clubs' in school give pupils the benefits of homework without creating antagonism in the home. In addition, children also have access to resources and informed adults.

Further reading

Department for Education and Employment (1998b) *Homework: Guidelines for primary and secondary schools*, Sudbury: DfEE Publications.
Hallam, S. (2004) *Homework: The evidence*, Bedford Way Papers 21, London: Institute of Education.
Kidwell, V. (2004) *Homework*, London: Continuum.

HUMOUR

The word humour derives from the Latin term *humourem* and has many potential benefits in promoting classroom harmony and enhancing adult–pupil relationships. Humour can lift spirits, increase enthusiasm for learning, act as an antidote for stress by stimulating the immune system and empower pupils and adults in school by giving them a different perspective on familiar situations. Other claims for the value of humour include helping to create a positive classroom environment, reducing pupils' **anxiety**, holding their attention and encouraging their involvement in lessons. With regard to learning outcomes, there is some evidence that humour can promote comprehension and retention and foster cognitive development. It may also help in managing undesirable behaviour and building self-confidence. Despite the potential benefits, some teachers are reluctant to use humour for fear of creating a climate of indiscipline or appearing unprofessional and not taking their work seriously enough. By contrast, other practitioners believe that laughter serves to bring about a closer working relationship between pupils and adults in the classroom.

Although humour is important in teaching, teachers have to be careful in its use, as too much of it can prove unhelpful if children find it difficult to distinguish between the serious and the trivial. Adults have to be careful to ensure that pupils know when humour is being employed or the children may respond by being silly or acting inappropriately. The most effective form of teacher humour is when it is integrated within the fabric of the lesson rather than presented as a series of jokes. Teachers also have to be wary of humour that may be construed as coarse or misinterpreted by children. In a settled classroom environment, pupils are often encouraged to develop a sense of humour by enjoying the time they spend with adults and other children, sharing amusing incidents, telling jokes and having opportunities to express their joy. Respectful humour between adult and children signals an appropriate and comfortable relationship and is wholly different in kind from cynical forms of humour used as a subtle form of coercion or ridicule. Unkind jesting between pupils (especially older ones) that seems to be targeted at a particular pupil is construed as **bullying** and treated as such.

Further reading

Atherton, J. S. (2003) *Learning and Teaching: Humour*. On-line. Available: http://www.dmu.ac.uk/~jamesa/teaching/humour.htm (accessed February 2005).

Kaufman, D. M. (2002) Using Humour in Teaching, Learning and Instructional Development Centre, Simon Fraser University, Burnaby,

BC. On-line. Available: http://www.sfu.ca/lidc/research/kaufman/UsingHumour.html (accessed July 2005).

Powell, J. P. and Andersen, L. W. (1985) 'Humour and teaching in higher education', *Studies in Higher Education*, 10d, pp. 79–89.

Woods, P. (1990) *The Happiest Days?* London: Falmer, chapter 7.

Ziegler, J. B. (1998) 'Use of humour in medical teaching', *Medical Teacher*, 20, 4, pp. 341–8.

IMAGINATION

Stimulating pupil imagination is seen by many teachers as a prerequisite to making an activity of educational worth. Authentic imagination prompts positive action and differs from hopeful imagination characterised by a passiveness that leaves the active work to others. Imagination provides pupils with a vehicle to visualise new possibilities and prompts educators to visualise and shape their ideas to make them into something workable. The power of imagination creates vision that empowers pupils and adults to act resolutely and achieve the desired goal, regardless of setbacks and disappointments. Stimulating children's imaginations through stories, songs, visual resources and other means taps a rich source of learning in primary-age children.

In an education climate that increasingly advocates high standards through standardisation of **teaching approach** and **pupil learning** style, the promotion of imagination and **creativity** is an alternative means of achieving rich forms of learning. A political climate in which evidence of success relies on measurable outcomes does not encourage teachers to use their imaginations or encourage children to use theirs, because imagination is a quality that is impossible to quantify. Although a small proportion of primary teachers prefer being told what to do and how to do it rather than being given freedom to be innovative, the majority of educators prefer greater flexibility in covering the curriculum so that they can foster imaginative practice. In preparing pupils for tests and examinations there is little manoeuvrability within the timetable to give pupils the time and space they need to explore and imagine.

Kieran Egan, a noted education thinker, claims that imagination is not a desirable-but-dispensable frill and should form the heart of any truly educational experience. Consequently, imagination should be integral to basic training or disciplined thought or rational enquiry, as it gives them life and meaning. Furthermore, imagination is not the sole province of the arts in education or a leisure **activity**, but is central to all areas of learning. Egan goes so far as to say that imagination is the hard pragmatic centre of all effective human thought.

Within the constraints of working within a national curriculum framework, imagination is seen as a means of supporting and sustaining the kind of enterprising approach that is needed to invigorate learning and raise standards of **achievement**. Such a philosophy requires a fresh understanding of ways in which children are motivated to learn. Imagination is therefore not in opposition to the practical demands faced by teachers and learners but a way to energise them.

Further reading

Greene, M. (1995) *Releasing the Imagination: Essays on Education, the Arts and Social Change*, San Francisco: Jossey-Bass.

Kieran E.: http://www.educ.sfu.ca/kegan/MemoryIm.html

Trousdale A. M. (2004) 'Black and white fire: the interplay of stories, imagination and children's spirituality', *International Journal of Children's Spirituality*, 9, 2, pp. 177–88.

Tyrrell, J. (2001) *The Power of Fantasy in Early Learning*, London: Routledge.

INCLUSION

Inclusive education is concerned with minimising barriers to learning and participation in educational settings, including primary schools, in terms of both the adequacy of provision and issues of equity. Schools are charged with offering an education to all pupils by modifying the way that practitioners approach their work such that no child is excluded who could, with appropriate human and practical resources, be incorporated into the warp and weave of regular school life. Schools that formerly excluded pupils with particular disabilities and learning needs (including children with emotional vulnerabilities) are now obliged to include them whenever the resources are available to make it possible. It is no longer acceptable that children with disabilities who have the intellectual capacity to learn are hindered from doing so on the basis of their physical limitations.

Three principles underpin the provision of effective learning opportunities for all children in school. The first is that teachers are required to set suitable challenges for all pupils, including less able and more able ones. The second is for teachers to respond to pupils' diverse needs by creating a productive learning environment, offer all children an equal opportunity to access resources and participate in activities, assess their progress and set them suitable challenges. The third is for teachers, in conjunction with other colleagues where necessary, to combat potential barriers to learning for individuals and groups of pupils with disabilities and those for whom English is an additional language.

Whereas the majority of physically disabled pupils can be comfortably incorporated within mainstream activities, teachers find the presence of emotionally vulnerable children to be a much greater challenge. There is an increasing body of evidence to show that disruptive pupils tend to affect adversely the education of other children, even with the presence and involvement of an assistant to provide learning support. Although the pupils that experience the greatest difficulties in learning and conforming to behavioural norms provide a useful barometer for teachers about the quality of their organisation, clarity of explanations and relevance of **lessons**, they also absorb a considerable amount of time and energy. Nevertheless, teachers that succeed with pupils experiencing the greatest difficulty in concentrating find that they can use the same principles of curriculum relevance, clarity of expectation and calmness of approach to improve learning for the rest of the children.

The involvement of Learning Support **Assistants** is important in helping to meet the learning needs of included pupils, though there is always a risk of the child becoming too dependent on the adult or, especially in the case of older primary children, feeling resentful about the constant close attention they receive that highlights their different status. To combat the 'exclusive attention' factor, an assistant is sometimes deployed to oversee the work of a group of pupils, of which the special needs child is one. Pupils are most likely to require additional support at the beginning of lessons and when they move away from whole-class to small-group situations. Adult intervention is also necessary to redirect children's attention and energies when they are wandering off task, especially pupils diagnosed with **ADHD**.

Supporting pupils with special needs necessitates cooperation with a range of other professionals from outside the school, such as the educational psychologist and local authority advisory teachers. Specialist expertise is normally available in teaching the hearing impaired and visually impaired and a range of paraprofessionals such as speech therapists and physiotherapists, social workers, educational welfare officers and medical services are occasionally involved in providing support to teachers, pupils and their parents. The Special Educational Needs Coordinator (SENCO) is often the person in school who liaises with these agencies, as well as providing ongoing support for class teachers. All adults in school have to be alert to ways in which they are able to assist in servicing an inclusion policy, not only for pupils' benefit but also to ensure that each adult in school feels significant and valued by being 'included'.

Further reading

Department for Education and Skills (2001) *Inclusive Schooling*, London: The Stationery Office.

Fox, S., Farrell, P. and Davis, P. (2004) 'Factors associated with the effective inclusion of primary-aged pupils with Down's Syndrome', *British Journal of Special Education*, 31, 4, pp. 184–90.

Nind, M. (2005) 'Inclusive education: discourse and action', *British Educational Research Journal*, 31, 2, pp. 269–75.

Nutbrown, C. and Clough, P. (2005) *Inclusion in the Early Years*, London: Paul Chapman.

Thomas, G. (1998) *The Making of the Inclusive School*, London: Routledge.

INDUCTION

Induction refers to the process by which pupils and new teachers are inculcated into the working practices of a school and become, through structured support and guidance, better able to understand and cope with the procedures, routines and covert agendas that exist there. For children who have never been to school it can be a shock for them to discover that the freedom and spontaneity of pre-school is curtailed and they have to conform to specified practices. To reduce the impact of the change there is normally close liaison between reception teachers (who teach new school entrants), pre-school workers and parents, and between teachers teaching pupils in their final year at primary school (year 6) and staff in the receiving secondary school. Thus, year 6 pupils meet their future secondary teachers and spend some time in the new school during the term preceding transfer. Brand new school entrants ('rising fives') may spend half a day in school initially, increasing to full time after a suitable period of time (a half-term, say).

Arrangements exist to provide all newly qualified teachers (NQTs) with a bridge from initial teacher training to regular teaching. An induction programme to provide well-targeted monitoring and support within the framework of a reduced timetable and to help embed an ethos of continuing professional development and career development during the first year of teaching facilitates this process. At its best, induction helps new teachers to show their potential, make rapid progress in becoming effective practitioners and exert an impact on the school's overall development and progress. NQTs are expected to benefit from and contribute to the sharing of effective practice, extend their vision of the **teacher role**, experience opportunities for subject specialist and classroom-focused development, contribute to the workforce reform agenda and begin developing **leadership** qualities. Naturally, these qualities are not present in every NQT to the same extent at the same time and require nurturing if they are to mature over the months and years as experience is gained in the job.

National standards for new teachers are not dissimilar to those for qualified teacher status. Thus, a new teacher needs to be able to demonstrate competence in planning, teaching, class management, monitoring, assessing, **recording** and **reporting**. A vital element of demonstrating this competence is for the teacher to take close account of the needs of individual children and ensure that every one is offered the best chance to be exposed to the full **curriculum**. There are also demands made of new teachers with regard to deploying and working with other adults (including parents), implementing school policies (such as dealing with bullying and racial harassment) and taking responsibility for their own professional development.

As part of a new teacher's development, a fellow staff member is allocated as mentor (officially known as the *induction tutor*). In a larger primary school the induction tutor is likely to be a senior teacher; in a smaller school it may be the deputy head or head teacher. In addition to offering general advice and **encouragement**, the tutor encourages the new teacher to contribute to working parties and visit other local schools to enhance his or her experience of primary education. The induction tutor is also available to offer advice about diverse aspects of school life, such as **time management**, handling paperwork, dealing with troublesome children, relating to parents and maintaining a reasonable work/home balance. By the end of their induction year, all new teachers must have demonstrated that they can teach on a consistent and sustained basis, with the direct and personal responsibility and **accountability** for pupil performance that accompanies it. They must also show that they have made progress in key areas such as managing pupil behaviour and contributing to pupils' learning, and to planning and attaining the school's performance targets.

NQTs will not normally be expected to endure excessive demands by (say) having to take a very large class or a group of particularly difficult pupils. They should only teach for only about 90% of the time to give them opportunity to gain wider experience by working alongside colleagues, observing successful teachers at work and attending courses to enhance their knowledge and understanding of primary education issues and practices.

Further reading

Bubb, S. (2003) *The Insider's Guide for New Teachers*, London: Kogan Page.
Department for Education and Employment (1999a) *The Induction Period for Newly Qualified Teachers*, Sudbury: DfEE Publications.
Hayes, D. (2000) *The Handbook for NQTs (Primary)*, London: David Fulton.
Simco, N. (2003) *Succeeding in the Induction Year*, 2nd edn, Exeter: Learning Matters.

INSPECTION

Inspection is a formal procedure, funded by the government, to determine the value for money of schools and colleges (including pre-school and nursery units). The quality of teaching, **leadership**, management and partnership with parents is graded according to set criteria and a report is provided for the school governors/school board and subsequently made available to the general public. In England, the Office for Standards in Education (OFSTED) is officially the Office of Her Majesty's Chief Inspector of Schools. It is a non-ministerial government department set up in 1992, principally for the management of the independent system of inspection of all schools that are wholly or state funded. A similar system of inspection applies to all institutions in receipt of public funding providing education for children under 4 years old. Similar bodies exist in Wales, Scotland and Northern Ireland, though the criteria used by inspectors differ slightly from country to country. All inspections involve observations of teachers while they are teaching, scrutiny of documentation, a discussion with parents, and interviews with governors, staff and head teacher. Older pupils may also be asked to offer a perspective on school life, though this practice has been criticised by some teacher unions as potentially divisive.

Inspectors are looking for schools that are well led, creatively follow the prescribed **curriculum** and possess a strong sense of purpose to achieve high academic standards and inculcate positive qualities in children. Head teachers and subject leaders are questioned to ensure that there is whole-staff agreement about issues as diverse as resources, **teaching approach**, assessment procedures, and ways of **recording** pupils' achievements and progress systematically.

The announcement of a coming inspection has a dramatic impact on school staff and during this period of time head teachers have a crucial role in maintaining stability and providing **leadership**. Inspections have an impact on teachers' professional relationships inside school and on their personal and social relationships outside school. Many teachers view inspections as a necessary evil and a distraction from children's learning, and conscientious teachers seem particularly vulnerable to suffer **anxiety**.

The experience of class teachers being observed teaching by an external evaluator whose judgements have great significance for the reputation of the school is emotionally stressful and professionally demanding. The ordeal is less severe if teachers are used to being observed by a colleague or the head teacher, so a team spirit needs to be embedded in school life long before the inspection takes place, to ensure smoother liaison across the staff members when the pressure becomes intense during the period of the visit. Inspections are also mentally and physically exhausting for teachers and even a successful inspection often has a debilitating influence on staff efficiency for some time afterwards. Some head teachers equate the inspection aftermath with post-traumatic stress disorder. Staff absences through illness tend to rise and it usually takes a school some months to recover fully and return to normality. Primary schools that receive a good report are not inspected as often as those deemed to be weaker.

The stresses created by having a long period of time between the announcement of the inspection and the event occurring are such that the notice of inspection is being reduced considerably for successful schools. Schools in which standards are judged to be unsatisfactory can be placed under a series of special measures in which their progress is closely monitored until they rectify the shortcomings (frequently identified as one or more from: weak leadership, indiscipline, low expectations of pupils). In a small number of cases a school regarded as failing is closed and reopened with a new head teacher and under a different name.

Further reading

Hayes, D. and Bennett, G. (2004) 'The impact of an Ofsted inspection before it begins: a primary teacher's experiences', *Primary Practice Journal*, No. 37, pp. 12–15.

Kenyon, P. (1998) *Ready for Inspection*, Leamington Spa: Scholastic.

Newton D. P. (2003) 'Ofsted doesn't work', *Managing Schools Today*, 12, 6, pp. 16–18.

Richards, C. (2001) 'School inspection: a re-appraisal', *Journal of Philosophy of Education*, 35, 4, pp. 655–65.

INSTRUCTION

Instruction is an essential component of effective teaching and a necessary skill for every teacher, both in learning and in maintaining discipline. As a component of learning, instruction takes a variety of forms: explanation, exposition and demonstration. *Explanation* is a method by which a teacher offers information, explores situations and justifies decisions or positions in a rational, structured manner. It is a technique that frequently employs examples to illustrate key points. Explanations take account of the age of the children and teachers adjust their language and terminology accordingly, such that children are given time to absorb what is said, think about the implications and ask questions of clarification. Like all good teaching, explanations build on the children's existing **knowledge** and understanding.

Exposition is a more complex form of explanation, involving graphic illustrations, critique or commentary on an aspect of work or a specific occurrence. Exposition is literally an 'exposing' or revealing a situation or value position as viewed from a variety of perspectives. During exposition, teachers use persuasion, project their personalities into what they say and often exhibit a little flamboyance. For instance, an exposition to older primary children might highlight the harmful exploitation of indigenous populations. In this case, illustrations may include statistical details of economies before and after foreign intervention and a critique of the benefits and losses that accrued. The teacher might encourage the children to raise their own questions after carefully considering the issues. With younger children, an exposition might deal with issues of road safety, healthy eating or moral issues such as kindness.

Demonstration includes elements of exposition but makes use of more varied resources and equipment, together with presentations of the techniques, **skills** or procedures associated with the task. For instance, a teacher may demonstrate the correct handling and techniques associated with a variety of percussion instruments or the way to access an index or employ strategies in a sport. Demonstration depends on the teacher having a firm grasp of the processes and being able to show them to the pupil audience at the same time as talking to them about the conceptual or practical stages involved.

Pupils need help from adults to distinguish between instructional and invitational comments. Thus, the instructional comment anticipates compliance, whereas the invitational comment is a recommendation rather than a command. Inexperienced teachers sometimes present children with a choice when they intend to project a command and find that they have to revert to a formal instruction after initially using an invitation. It is possible for what is intended as a command to end up sounding like a choice or an aspiration. For example, there is a significant difference between statements such as 'Can you sit still, please?' (choice) and 'I would be pleased if you sat still' (aspiration) and 'Please put your pencil down and sit still' (command).

Primary teachers make increasing use of computer technology to aid instruction, notably *interactive whiteboards* that provide access to the Internet and in-school computer systems. The technology allows teachers to draw from a wide range of information, including charts, diagrams, photographs and other data, and also to display an example of a pupil's work on screen for the attention of the whole class (by employing a digital camera). Children's work that would have been erased using a conventional board can be saved on the computer for future use.

Further reading

Bennett, R. (2004) *Using ICT in Primary English Teaching*, Exeter: Learning Matters.

Gagne, R. M. (1985) *The Conditions of Learning and Theory of Instruction*, New York: Holt, Rinehart and Winston.

Hardy, C. A. (1990) 'Pupils' understanding of teachers' instructions', *Bulletin of Physical Education*, 26, 3, pp. 17–22.

Scott-Evans, A. (2003) 'A critical study of effective ways to teach instructional texts', *Education 3–13*, 31, 1, pp. 53–60.

Williams, J. and Easingwood, N. (2004) *ICT and Primary Mathematics*, London: Routledge.

Yates, S. M. and Yates, G. C. R. (1990) 'Teacher effectiveness research: towards describing user friendly classroom instruction', *Educational Psychology*, 10, 3, pp. 225–38.

INTERACTION

It is no exaggeration to claim that adult–child interactions lie at the heart of effective primary education. Interaction is a broad term to describe the numerous instances when adults in the classroom make some form of verbal or non-verbal connection with pupils, or pupils with adults. The formality or informality varies as the circumstance dictates. Thus, in a teacher-led lesson phase the interaction is normally initiated by the adult and is closely controlled by the adult. By contrast, out-of-lesson interactions are frequently informal (unless discipline needs to be exerted) and may be initiated by adult or child.

Teachers work to produce a purposeful **learning climate** in which they can exert a positive influence on the way that pupils react and behave, taking special care over their words and the way in which they respond to children's comment. In particular, the provision of direct information and instructions to children forms a key part of the interaction process. To ensure that pupils hear and understand what is said, teachers have to be clear about the information and **knowledge** they want to convey and to engage the children's interest as they do so. Careful sequencing of points is important, especially for less able children and younger children, as this offers them a framework within which they can build their understanding. There is also a limit to the amount of information that children can hold in their minds at one time; so visual supports such as a picture, chart or summary sheet are often used as memory aids. In the richest form of interaction, children are given an opportunity to ask questions, both to clarify what has been said and to expand the scope of their ideas.

Teachers commonly interact with pupils by asking a question, affirming the response, commenting further on the points that have been raised or alerting the children to the errors in their reasoning. Sometimes a teacher asks another child to provide an answer or offer a perspective. The need to teach **lessons** within a given time frame means that there is a limited amount of time available for child-initiated conversations; this time limitation has the effect that adults initiate nearly all the verbal exchanges and restricts pupils' opportunities to respond. Some educationists argue that teacher-dominated sessions are unhelpful, as pupils learn more effectively when they are given the opportunity to **talk** about their work, express their feelings and freely offer comment on relevant issues. Teachers of younger children, in particular, tend to employ a 'circle time' approach in which every child has a chance to speak and contribute in an affirming atmosphere.

Interactive teaching in which extended forms of pupil–pupil or adult–pupil dialogue are involved has become less common in primary teaching because teachers have been encouraged to inject 'pace' into the sessions, reducing the opportunities for reflective dialogue. As a result, some teachers do not feel comfortable in allowing children room to pursue an argument, explore an issue or express an opinion unless it can be done succinctly. In addition, some younger children speak slowly and others need to ponder, pause and retrace the steps of their thinking, so that even more time is needed to complete what they want to say. If time is absorbed by a child's extended verbal contribution, the squeeze on the remaining lesson phases becomes a serious factor in fulfilling the intended learning outcomes. Teachers wishing to develop children's verbal competence sometimes use the strategy of 'tell a friend what you think before you tell an adult' during interactive sessions and make stronger use of collaborative work, whereby a number of children work together initially to discuss ideas and formulate suggestions that are then more widely shared.

On the occasions when pupils initiate a conversation with an adult about learning, they tend to do so by asking one or other of two types of work-related questions. By far the most common type of question is about work procedures to clarify what they are meant to be doing. However, less confident children sometimes prefer to struggle on uncertainly rather than risk a teacher's wrath by asking about an aspect of the work that they feel they should already have grasped. Teachers find that there is less need to repeat what has been said if information and instructions are given precisely to pupils in the first place. The second type of query that children frequently raise is uncertainty about how to work something out or the way to employ essential **skills**. Teachers are regularly faced with a choice about whether to tell children, encourage them to try and find a solution for themselves or give them general guidance in the expectation that they will gradually make sense of the problem with which they are grappling.

Teachers have to master a variety of interactive techniques, not least the use of demonstrating skills, strategies and practical procedures to pupils. There are a number of instances when demonstrating techniques can be a highly effective way of introducing ideas, reinforcing learning and motivating children. For example, a demonstration and explanation of the correct usage and limitations of equipment or resources is often necessary in advance of a practical lesson. Demonstrations for the purpose of reinforcing learning can be linked with the children's wider experiences, using familiar situations from everyday life. If a demonstration requires the use of specialist equipment or is potentially hazardous, then teachers have to take close account of **health and safety** considerations before and during the lesson.

Further reading

Bearne, E., Dombey, H. and Grainger, T. (2003) *Classroom Interactions in Literacy*, Maidenhead: Open University Press.

Hardman, F., Smith, F. and Wall, K. (2003) 'Interactive whole class teaching in the National Literacy Strategy', *Cambridge Journal of Education*, 33, 2, pp. 197–215.

Hook, P. and Vass, A. (2002) *Teaching With Influence*, London: David Fulton, chapter 3.

Moyles, J., Hargreaves, L., Merry, R., Paterson, F. and Esarte-Sarries, V. (2003) *Interactive Teaching in the Primary School*, Maidenhead: Open University Press.

Smith, F., Hardman, F., Wall, K. and Mroz, M. (2004) 'Interactive whole class teaching in the National Literacy and Numeracy Strategies', *British Educational Research Journal*, 30, 3, pp. 395–411.

INTERVENTION

An integral part of a teacher's classroom work is monitoring pupil progress by keenly observing how the children are coping with the set tasks and activities, and then intervening by offering appropriate support to them. Teacher intervention is necessary for any one of at least five reasons. First, the teacher's poor initial lesson introduction, organisation or resources mean that further explanation is necessary. Second, poor matching between child and task results in confusion or uncertainty. Third, the child's lack of confidence creates tentativeness. Fourth, a child's failure to grasp what is required results in uncertainty about how to go about the task. Fifth, the child's lack of concentration necessitates regular reminders from teachers about remaining on task. The majority of pupils let a teacher know if they have concerns or questions about what they are doing. However, teachers and assistants have to develop the skill of monitoring that consists of scanning the room to gain clues about the way that children are attending to their work and the level of adult support that needs to be provided.

The relationship between monitoring and intervening is fluid. Sometimes a teacher may be aware that a child is struggling but decide to delay intervening to allow opportunity for the child to think and engage with the problem. On other occasions the teacher may decide to be highly specific and tell the child precisely what must be done. Awareness of children's progress through observation of behaviour and information from their written work provide numerous insights into a child's conceptual grasp of the task, confidence in tackling the set work and, ultimately, the nature of his or her achievements. In this regard, all primary teachers need to be skilled observers of children and keen judges of how much support to offer.

The extent of adult intervention depends on the specificity or flexibility within the task, the teacher's knowledge of the child's willingness to persevere and how much the work has been understood. If the pupil is unwilling to persevere, it may signal a poor attitude or a weak aptitude towards learning. If pupils lack understanding, it may be that the teacher has assumed too much or failed to explain adequately. If the pupil lacks confidence, adults have a significant part in helping to build **self-esteem** by using praise and **encouragement**. If the end product is still disappointing, teachers have to give serious attention to issues of task clarity, lack of understanding, poor attitude and lack of self-confidence as they make instant judgements about the type and quality of their intervention.

Unless the occasion is a formal test in which assistance is not permitted, every teacher has to balance the importance of offering guidance to children against intervening to such an extent that the child loses ownership of the task. Consequently, part of a teacher's skill in knowing when to intervene is discerning when it is better *not* to intervene. Experienced teachers develop an aptitude for spotting events and noting pupils' comments and behaviours that require immediate attention, those that can be left for a while and those that are best ignored. Sometimes teachers find it useful to allow time for the pupil to self-correct rather than rushing in immediately, particularly if the lesson purpose is principally about allowing pupils to grapple with problems rather than providing immediate solutions. The principle underpinning 'standing off' from children as they struggle is that they need to be taught self-sufficiency rather than promoting their over-reliance on a teacher.

Some children are happy to be told the answer by an adult instead of putting their minds to a problem. A pattern of behaviour emerges whereby the child engages with a task, encounters difficulty and immediately asks for assistance and advice, which the teacher dutifully provides. However, the behaviour pattern can be gradually changed, such that the child engages with the task, encounters a difficulty, thinks intently about solutions, seeks advice from a friend and only as a last resort seeks advice from an adult. A delayed intervention strategy is supported by phrases such as 'try it yourself first and I'll come back in a moment if you are still stuck' or 'ask a friend first then ask an adult'. However, leaving a child to flounder for too long without adult help is counter-productive if it leads to disillusionment or creates restless behaviour.

Further reading

Doll, B., Zucker, S. and Brehm, K. (2004) *Resilient classrooms: Creating healthy environments for learning*, New York: Guilford.
Myhill, D. and Warren, P. (2005) 'Scaffolds or straitjackets? Critical moments in classroom discourse', *Educational Review*, 57, 1, pp. 55–69.
Roffey, S. and O'Reirdan, T. (2003) *Plans for Better Behaviour in the Primary School*, London: David Fulton.

KEY STAGES

Since the introduction of the National Curriculum in England and Wales, coverage of the curriculum has been divided into four Key Stages. Key Stage 1 (KS1) is designed for children aged 5 to 7 and follows on directly after the Foundation Stage; it applies to pupils in year 1 (5 to 6 years of age) and year 2 (6 to 7 years). Key Stage 2 (KS2) is designed for children aged 7 to 11 years and follows after KS1; it applies to pupils in year 3 (7 to 8 years), year 4 (8 to 9 years), year 5 (9 to 10 years) and year 6 (10 to 11 years). Key Stage 3 (KS3) and Key Stage 4 (KS4) are the curricula for secondary-aged pupils: KS3 for pupils aged 11 to 14 and KS4 for pupils aged 14 to 16. Statutory examinations exist for pupils at the end of each Key Stage (in England); Wales, Scotland and Northern Ireland have slightly different systems but the concept of a 'key stage' is implicit throughout the UK.

Further reading

Hayes, D. (1997) *Success on Your Teaching Experience*, London: Hodder & Stoughton, chapter 4.

KNOWLEDGE

There is a lot more information available to pupils today than a generation ago, so they face both immense opportunities and challenges in negotiating the available knowledge. As the amount of information in the world is estimated to double approximately every seven years, this fact has implications for **curriculum** content and selection. There are many different forms of knowledge relevant to primary education, including knowledge of facts, practical **skills**, controversies, situations, procedures and people; each form of knowledge can be transitory or deeply embedded in a pupil's mind. Knowledge of facts involves more than memorising; it also needs to take account of new understanding. Knowledge of skills requires tuition and opportunity for careful practice. Knowledge of controversies requires an awareness of key facts and opinions that impinge on the dispute. Knowledge of situations demands a wide view of related factors and the capacity to make judgements about their relevance and importance. Knowledge of procedures is necessary for task completion. Knowledge of people is required to negotiate social situations. Knowledge evolves and deepens with age, experience and increased language acumen.

Most knowledge needs to be immediately accessible, such as remembering a multiplication table to employ in solving a mathematical problem; but children sometimes seem to be locked in a transitory knowledge zone, apparently learning something one day and seemingly forgetting it by the next. Sometimes the knowledge is locked into a child's recall system but cannot be accessed, either because it is too deeply stored and requires a verbal or visual stimulus to extract it, or because the child is tired or circumstances (such as stress) create a barrier to recall. Primary-age pupils also need to gain wisdom about the appropriate use of knowledge, its relevance and its function in life. Teachers face the interesting challenge of helping children to apply what they learn to a variety of contexts.

Although at one stage of a child's development it may be sufficient to 'know something is true', it is necessary for adults to point out that things are not always as straightforward as they appear. For example, 7-year-old children may be told that all solid objects fall towards the ground at the same rate, but 11-year-olds also need to be aware that the principle only holds under constant atmospheric conditions. Pupils therefore acquire knowledge at a variety of different levels. They may know something because they are able to repeat what they have been told or read. They may know because they can explain why something happens or because they can observe, describe and comment on an event.

Most powerfully, children can apply their knowledge to other situations (knowledge in use) of which three types have been identified:

knowledge by association, knowledge through replication and knowledge through application. Knowledge by association allows links to be made with previous learning. Knowledge through replication is being able to remember and reproduce facts when required to do so. Knowledge through application is for use in solving problems and is the most significant of the three as it necessitates making connections between what presently exists and what might exist. Consequently, the most powerful forms of knowledge facilitate understanding across a variety of contexts rather than being restricted to the understanding that is attached to it by the learner in the present situation. Primary teachers that espouse such a view are likely to promote **enquiry**-based learning in which children have to apply their knowledge to solve genuine problems. The most effective teaching incorporates both the transmission of knowledge and its application.

Further reading

McKeon, F. (2004) 'Teacher autonomy and subject knowledge', *Education 3–13*, 32, 3, pp. 32–7.

Walker, D. F. and Soltis, J. F. (1992) *Curriculum and Aims*, New York: Teachers College Press.

LEADERSHIP

The senior primary school leader is normally designated 'head teacher' (or 'Principal'). He or she is a person appointed to manage the day-to-day running of the school and ensure that staff behave in accordance with professional codes of conduct. The head teacher has the final responsibility for managing the **curriculum**, finances and teacher and pupil activities, and for maintaining school property. The head teacher must also build and enhance the reputation of the school with respect to academic standards and the service it provides to the community. Primary school head teachers are both the professional leaders and managers of primary schools and are assisted by the governing body, consisting of volunteers who carry ultimate responsibility for education provision at an executive level. Head teachers have had to oversee and implement the vast array of government initiatives that have impacted on primary education over recent decades, including the government's strategy for primary schools launched on 20 May 2003 through the document *Excellence and Enjoyment* (DfES 2003a).

Primary school head teachers are guardians of the reputation of the teaching profession by ensuring their staff deliver high-quality education. Consequently, they are leaders of learning (both within individual classrooms and at a school-wide level), the assessment of pupil **achievement**, innovations and improvements in classroom practice, and the monitoring and evaluation of teacher performance.

All teachers in primary schools other than newly qualified ones are expected to be subject leaders, though sometimes a new teacher will help a colleague in a supportive capacity. Over recent years the role has changed from one of being a subject *coordinator* who is only responsible for maintaining an overview of what is being taught in the school, to one of subject *leader* who is actively managing the subject. Subject leadership in primary schools is generally exercised in two ways. (1) By controlling resources and offering advice about their implementation. (2) By promoting curriculum development and change. The national standards for subject leaders (Teacher Training Agency 1998) state that they should aim to provide professional leadership and management for a subject (or area of work) and to secure high-quality teaching, effective use of resources and improved standards of learning and **achievement** for all pupils. Subject leaders are most effective if:

- They possess a high level of subject **knowledge**.
- They are able to relate their subject to other subject areas.
- They have a secure grasp of the strategic development needs of the school and their subject.
- They are very good teachers who can and do model good practice.
- They can lead staff by inspiring them to believe pupils can achieve better results.
- They can communicate effectively and build good relationships with staff, pupils and parents.
- They know how to plan and implement change.
- They manage resources effectively.
- They monitor staff and pupil performance and give objective **feedback** whenever possible.

Leaders strive to ensure that they remain at the cutting edge of their subject and promote its ongoing development through staff development and guidance to colleagues. They keep abreast of local and national initiatives and practices and keep colleagues in touch with new educational initiatives that may impact upon their work. The best leaders foster excellence in teaching, facilitate discussion and advise about particular **pupil learning** needs. Many primary leaders are given a small amount of relief from regular timetable commitments to pursue their extra responsibilities, though balancing class teaching and subject leadership can be onerous and demanding.

Further reading

Bell, D. and Ritchie, R. (1999) *Towards Effective Subject Leadership in the Primary School*, Maidenhead: Open University Press.

Boyle, M. and Woods, P. (1996) 'The composite head: coping with changes in the primary head teacher's role', *British Educational Research Journal*, 22, 3, pp. 325–44.

Buster, H., Harris, A. and Wise, C. (2000) *Subject Leadership and School Improvement*, London: Paul Chapman.

Dean, J. (2003) *Subject Leadership in the Primary School*, London: David Fulton.

Farmery, C. (2004) *Successful Subject Co-ordination*, London: Continuum.

Hallinger, P. (2003) 'Leading educational change', *Cambridge Journal of Education*, 33, 3, pp. 329–51.

Harrison, M. and Theaker, K. (1999) *Curriculum Leadership in the Primary School*, Dunstable: Folens.

Teacher Training Agency (1998) *National Standards for Subject Leaders*, London: TTA.

LEARNING CLIMATE

A learning climate is also referred to as a learning 'environment' or an 'atmosphere'. Positive learning climates lead to motivated pupils and optimum attainment; negative learning climates tend to have the opposite effect. When the learning climate is relaxed yet purposeful, there is a strong sense of expectancy among the children and they do not have to expend energy on worrying about whether or not they are doing the right thing. When the relationship between adults and children is mutually respectful and everyone knows where the boundaries of appropriate behaviour lie, it saves having to waste time on constantly exploring what is and is not acceptable behaviour. Where children can take risks without fear of being censured and ideas can be exchanged in the certainty that they will be treated seriously, a fertile environment for innovation exists and creativity flourishes. A learning climate where mistakes are not tolerated and boundaries are blurred leaves children feeling vulnerable and restricts their curiosity and imagination, as instead of channelling their energies into creative approaches to work they spend their time acting defensively to avoid blame or recrimination.

The bedrock of academic success is found in creating a learning climate in which pupils have self-confidence, feel relaxed in the company of other children in the class and enjoy an easy relationship with the teacher. Pupils not only need relevant work but also positive experiences of their engagement with learning that will equip them with the skills they need to prosper in the future. Teachers facilitate these positive experiences by establishing and maintaining a calm and expectant climate, within which a variety of learning approaches is encouraged. Pupils help themselves by being taught the skills of conflict resolution, collaborating, reflecting, discriminating, listening and sitting quietly. Teachers promote pupil satisfaction by ensuring that lessons are relevant, accessible, engaging and interesting, and organising the classroom such that children are so engrossed in the tasks that they have no desire to be mischievous.

The most productive learning climate is one in which each child is valued and accorded the same chances to achieve success, where competition is with the self as much as with others, and one pupil's triumph is shared by all. Teachers help to promote a healthy learning environment through their own positive attitude, striving to be fair, promoting equal opportunity and considering children's emotional as well as their academic needs. New teachers soon discover that speaking to children warmly whenever possible, valuing their efforts and encouraging them to reach their potential, all contribute towards the positive climate that they seek. Consequently, teachers enhance the climate by showing a personal interest in individuals, communicating in ways every pupil can understand and encouraging everyone to do their best. Learning is promoted as a worthwhile and collaborative effort that allows children to build high self-esteem and make best progress within a supportive environment, whether in the classroom or in other areas of the school.

A thoughtfully arranged and clean classroom in which children are helped to value the physical environment is more inviting than one with an air of disarray and dowdiness. Small adjustments can make a considerable difference to the ambience; for instance, checking that tables and chairs are of suitable size for pupils and that trays, books and resources are clearly marked and accessible. Rooms that look cared for and give the impression that they are places where everyone can work safely and efficiently and with a sense of purpose are likely to be enhanced by interactive displays, with examples of good-quality children's work on the walls. Displays, paintings, models and exhibits enliven many primary school classrooms. Some corridors are festooned with colourful motifs and stimulating pictures, all of which take considerable time and energy to produce, mount and maintain.

Despite the orientation of modern primary school life, in which competence is judged largely by academic outcomes, many teachers extol the need for colourful and well-displayed classrooms and invest a lot of energy into ensuring that pupils' work is prominent. Teachers of younger children often establish different areas in the classroom to stimulate the children's imagination, such as a story corner surrounded by lavishly painted pictures of characters from fairy tales, a writing corner separated from the rest of the room by curtains from which hang samples of completed stories and pictures, a mystery corner with unusual items of interest and a home corner full of household items. The same classroom may have a number of tables with specimens collected during walks, mathematics equipment and small-scale construction materials to handle, **play** with and enjoy. Cards with carefully framed questions or challenges to find out more are placed alongside the displays, prompting children to engage with the theme by handling the objects and talking about them to their friends. The pupils in these classrooms encourage their parents to come and admire their contributions. The class teacher is known throughout the school as having a 'fantastic classroom', though it is not intended to be a **competition** between teachers and some head teachers worry that time spent on display can mean time lost in promoting standards in the core subjects. In fact it is sometimes the teaching assistant that takes the main responsibility for displays, though the TA may not receive the public credit for doing so.

Further reading

Department for Education and Skills (2005) *The Importance of Emotions in the Classroom*, Primary National Strategy, Ref. 0640, London: The Stationery Office.

Dyer, A. and Lewis, J. (2001) *Personal, Social and Health Education in the School Grounds*, Crediton: Southgate.

MacGrath, M. (2000) *The Art of Peaceful Teaching in the Primary School*, London: David Fulton, chapter 1.

LEARNING OBJECTIVES

The term 'objective' in the phrase 'learning objective' derives from the root word 'object', one definition of which is an intention or target. In education parlance it has come to mean the product of a learning experience. Thus, a learning objective represents the focal point of teaching, by which the teacher organises and manages pupils' learning in such a way that they gain new or deeper levels of insight in the subject.

The process of identifying pupils' present state of **knowledge**, then teaching and setting tasks with a view to improving their learning, evaluating the outcomes through assessing progress and organising activities to take account of this information underpins much of mainstream primary education today. Each lesson or session is characterised by the establishment of clearly defined learning objectives followed by systematic teaching to achieve the intended outcomes. However, primary education that is based on this objectives-led model of teaching and learning has to be reconciled with the well-established fact that children learn best when motivated, given some choice about their activities, encouraged to explore and investigate phenomena and use spoken language in natural settings. As a result, objectives-led teaching and the need for flexibility in learning sit uneasily together.

Learning objectives that are expressed in terms of desirable learning outcomes for pupils, while promoting a systematic approach to teaching and learning, have also attracted criticism. Concerns are rooted in a belief that too much precision about the things pupils must learn leads to having an unmanageable number of objectives that, if pursued laboriously, create a pedestrian approach to learning. There are three specific concerns attached to reservations about the efficacy of learning objectives. First, many objectives can only be loosely described. For instance, the intended learning outcome may be for children to understand how to employ adjectives as a means of describing nouns with greater accuracy. However, the understanding may reside at the level of knowing that adjectives are also known as add–nouns (adding to the meaning of the noun) or may involve familiarity with a range of adjectives to provide a choice when describing the noun or may incorporate subject-specific adjectives (e.g. the *evaporating* liquid) or colloquialisms (such as 'the *cool* attitude'). Again, the concept of 'greater accuracy' in writing is a subjective judgement, requiring an understanding of audience and the meaning that is being conveyed. Consequently, what appears to be a straightforward learning objective is extremely sophisticated and requires considerable skill in interpreting and managing.

The second concern associated with the identification of specific learning objectives is that it is difficult for teachers to quantify pupils' existing learning, as all tests and measures are subject to the limitations of the measure being employed. There are also many aspects of learning that defy straightforward evaluation, such as innovation, insight, wisdom and team membership. Objectives-driven learning is based on an assumption that it is possible not only to specify what children presently know but also to direct their learning so precisely that they will learn exactly what the teacher intends. The implication is that if teachers fail to discern pupils' needs precisely, they cannot possibly provide a matching set of tasks and activities to promote their learning. In fact, such precision between needs and tasks is very difficult to achieve.

The third issue raised by an objectives-driven process is the fact that children are capable of learning many things over and above the intended outcomes that have not been anticipated by the teacher. By strict adherence to the approach of establishing objectives, designing work through which children attain them and monitoring their progress towards the narrowly stated objectives, teachers may inadvertently suppress or restrict unforeseen learning opportunities.

The establishment of learning objectives offer teachers a useful means of controlling lesson content, covering the curriculum and focusing pupils' thinking on an identified area of knowledge and understanding. Objectives also facilitate closer monitoring of the curriculum because they provide a straightforward means of checking what children have learned and what remains to be learned. However, strict adherence to this approach tends to oversimplify the intricate nature of learning.

Further reading

Hughes, P. (2002) *Principles of Primary Education Study Guide*, 2nd edn, London: David Fulton.
Popham, W. J. (2004) 'Objectives', in D. J. Flinders and S. J. Thornton (eds) *The Curriculum Studies Reader*, pp. 71–84, London: Routledge.

LEGALITY

Over the past twenty years or so a considerable amount of legislation has been passed that is specific to education. Other legislation outside the immediate field of education, such as the Children Acts of 1989 and 2004, have also had an impact on the way that adults in school relate to children. In addition, there has been a substantial increase in the amount of litigation in society and this trend has impinged upon the work of adults in school. Consequently, all teachers are obliged to keep abreast of the way in which laws and codes of practice impact upon their classroom and teaching. They must also conform to their professional duties as required by the head teacher, as explicitly stated in their contracts of employment. A refusal to do so can be interpreted as a breach of contract and invite disciplinary procedures. In this regard, all new teachers receive a letter of appointment from the school governors/school board specifying matters such as salary, duties and tenure.

Common law requires that teachers have a duty of care towards pupils in a way that reflects the behaviour of sensible parents. It is assumed that teachers will conduct themselves while they carry out their professional duties in a way that benefits the children and the other adults in the school; for example, being honest and protecting vulnerable pupils from harm. In extreme circumstances this duty may extend to administering medicine or taking action in an emergency, though teachers are not contractually required to act as medics. They can, however, volunteer to occupy such a position if the local education authority indemnifies them. Primary teachers may be responsible for children of 4 or 5 years of age, with the attendant close level of care and supervision that is necessary to ensure their safety and welfare. Teachers of older pupils have to be particularly aware of the sensitivities and privacy issues relating to fast-maturing young people, and adjust their words and actions to take account of the possibility that their actions might be misconstrued or their comments misinterpreted. Teacher concerns about litigation and culpability have resulted in a curtailment of outdoor activities and **educational visits**, especially those involving an element of risk.

Workforce remodelling is having an effect on the role and responsibility of teachers. Teachers' contracts now state that teaching **assistants** rather than teachers should undertake routine clerical and administrative tasks (e.g. extensive photocopying), though this rule is deemed normal rather than inviolable. Space in the school day must also be found for teachers with special responsibilities to carry out their roles and, in theory, all teachers should have adequate preparation, planning and assessment (PPA) time. Head teachers in smaller primary schools especially (with number of pupils on roll fewer than 100) often struggle to provide substitute teacher cover from their budgets.

Further reading

Ford, J., Hughes, M. and Ruebain, D. (1999) *Education Law and Practice*, London: Legal Action Group.

Gibley, P. (2004) 'Primary school teachers and the law', in A. Browne and D. Haylock (eds) *Professional Issues for Primary Teachers*, pp. 58–70, London: Paul Chapman.

Ruff, A. R. (2002) *Education Law: Text cases and materials*, London: Butterworths.

LESSONS

A generation ago, the word lesson tended to apply to secondary education where different subjects were taught within an allocated time frame. Primary education was based largely on integrating subjects within a 'topic' (**topic work**) or 'thematic' framework (laying the stress on one particular subject above others) that emphasised the interconnectivity of learning through **cross–curricular work**. Nevertheless, mathematics and English were taught separately as well as being incorporated into the topic. In recent years, the emphasis upon **literacy** and **numeracy** (and to a lesser extent, science) as subjects in their own right has given rise to the term 'lesson' being applied to distinct subject sessions. A lesson has thereby acquired dual meaning: (1) the subject content covered over a given period of time; (2) the time allocation for content coverage specified within a set timetable.

Lessons have to be manageable, with clearly identified **learning objectives** that are normally linked to the requirements of a nationally monitored system. Most teachers share the intended learning intentions with the pupils, either verbally or through a written reminder, or both, so that pupils are aware that lesson tasks and activities do not constitute an end in themselves but are part of a larger educational endeavour. The concept of a lesson is therefore based on the assumption not only that teaching should focus on identifiable learning outcomes during the period allotted to it, but also that the process can be precisely planned, organised and monitored to correspond precisely with the allocated time period.

Lesson content is determined by what the teacher intends that pupils should learn and understand and must be straightforward to teach, allowing the teacher to introduce the aspect of learning, supply children with tasks to complete and rapidly evaluate their progress. Lesson structure has to take account of the pace at which pupils learn and the manner in which they do so, as some children work quickly and efficiently, while others work laboriously. Some children like to think deeply before proceeding, others are spontaneous and (sometimes) over-eager to complete the work. Some pupils can think abstractly (i.e. they can figure things out in their heads); other children require visual, verbal or even kinaesthetic resources (such as materials of different textures to assist partially sighted children) to assist them in their work. Teachers also have to ensure the proper **differentiation** of the tasks and activities undertaken by pupils to allow them to finish the allocated work within the lesson time frame.

The most productive lessons are those in which teachers have high (but sensible) **expectations** of the children; offer clear instructions; help them to identify their own learning targets; and encourage an active, purposeful dialogue about the content. By contrast, weaker lessons are vague, teacher dominated, routine or repetitive and badly paced. The best lessons are those in which the teacher uses an appropriate range of teaching strategies (giving information directly, using IT resources, employing question and answer, making children think and reflect, etc.), sets appropriate challenges with respect to the **ability** range of children, monitors progress and intervenes sensitively. Effective teachers provide pupils with stable learning conditions under which they can prosper by organising work that is based on their present knowledge and understanding, and within the time and resource constraints that operate. The majority of lessons conclude by spending a few minutes reviewing what has been learned, a time that is commonly referred to as a plenary or **lesson review**.

Further reading

Butt, G. (2003) *Lesson Planning*, London: Continuum.
Hughes, M. (1997) *Lessons are for Learning*, Stafford: Network Educational Press.
McCallum, B., Gipps, C. and Hargreaves, E. (2001) 'The structure of lessons', *Education 3–13*, 29, 1, pp. 33–7.

LESSON MANAGEMENT

There are different ways to understand the term 'management'. The most immediate definition for teachers is with respect to managing a group or class of children, which has practical implications for the satisfactory running of sessions, efficient organisation, provision of resources and negotiating the direction of **pupil learning**.

Effective management ensures that pupils understand the procedures attached to the process of learning, which is made more likely when teachers are explicit with their instructions, explaining precisely what is expected of the children and involving them in decisions where appropriate. Teachers improve the **effectiveness** of their management by starting **lessons** promptly, showing enthusiasm for their content, checking that pupils have the necessary information to cope with the work tasks and making resources easily available to every child. Good class management is enhanced when the lesson is carefully paced and teachers insist upon careful work and enthuse about children's effort and successes.

Good class management involves taking practical considerations carefully into account. For example, teachers do not keep children sitting for too long on the carpet at the start of the lesson or organise too many messy activities at one time or work up to the last moment, thereby failing to leave sufficient time to clear up and discuss the lesson, all of which might invite unsettled behaviour. During the session it is also possible for adults to give too much time to one group of pupils and neglect others that require guidance. Although some tasks require more adult involvement than others, smooth management necessitates that teachers are careful not to become indispensable to pupils, but rather encourage them to be curious, imaginative and independent as much as possible.

Well-organised teaching leads to satisfied children and thereby improves the learning experience. Inexperienced teachers sometimes leave insufficient time during one lesson to achieve all that they planned or fail to sort out in advance the activities that different children will be involved in doing. More experienced teachers know that there are likely to be interruptions during the lesson that need to be taken into account in the planning and that lessons immediately before or after any events (such as **assembly**, singing practice or rehearsals) might affect the time available or pupils' concentration levels.

Good management is particularly important towards the end of the lesson, as poor use of time may mean that the lesson overruns and children have to leave the room before it is tidy or are delayed from going out to the playground or late starting the next lesson. An orderly exit is essential, both from a discipline and a **health and safety** perspective.

Further reading

Hayes, D. (2000) *The Handbook for NQTs (Primary)*, London: David Fulton, unit 5.

Hayes, D. (2004a) *Foundations of Primary Teaching*, 3rd edn, London: David Fulton, chapter 6.

Merry, R. (2004) 'Are we allowed to ... ? Teacher autonomy and interactive teaching in the Literacy Hour', *Education 3–13*, 32, 3, pp. 19–23, 31.

LESSON PLANNING

The ultimate purpose of lesson planning is to produce plans that facilitate the implementation of a systematic teaching programme. Specific lesson plans relate to a particular class or group of children, requiring teachers to give careful thought to the pupils' learning needs and the circumstances in which they take place. Although all teachers are pleased to have lesson ideas and topics, they take ownership of the plan by mentally rehearsing the planning process and adapting it to their situation. Thus, teachers must know something about the origin of the plan, where it fits into the longer-term learning aims, what it assumes of children and what modifications are necessary to accommodate the needs of individual pupils. Lesson plans are formulated with an awareness of pupils' previous learning and longer-term goals. In addition to the formally prepared content, effective teachers ensure that unpredicted opportunities for learning that emerge during the lesson are seized and exploited.

A lot of the preparation that contributes towards effective teaching happens away from the classroom, which can make it appear to an observer that the teacher has some innate qualities that make things run smoothly with minimum effort. In reality, the lesson planning is an active process, requiring a familiarity with the school's broader educational priorities and children's individual learning needs. In drawing up successful lesson plans, teachers do so with reference to the school's existing medium-term **curriculum** plans (often spanning half a term) and through working closely with other teachers who have responsibility for the same age group or subject (often meeting fortnightly to formulate plans and share ideas).

A lesson plan can be compared with a map of an underground railway system that offers guidance about going from one place to another with minimum delay by using a net of coloured lines between stations. The map does not give or intend to give any information about the state of the trains, the exact distance between stations or the air quality in the tunnels; it simply points the way to get from the start to the finish most efficiently. A lesson plan parallels the principle of a tube train map by setting out the chronological steps in such a way that the session runs smoothly. It does not contain details of how the children will behave, make predictions about whether the equipment will prove to be satisfactory or describe the nature of the classroom climate, and is not intended to do so. However, if the 'journey' through the lesson is to be a success, the planning must take account of time constraints and anticipate factors that may detract from learning or enhance it. The more thoroughly teachers think through and prepare for the predictable elements, the easier they find it to cope with the unexpected events.

Every lesson plan is based on specified **learning objectives**, though learning *intentions* is sometimes a preferred term, as it is not always possible to predict precisely what children will learn and sometimes the same objectives apply to several consecutive sessions, requiring only minor adjustments in the focus of teaching. Although the objectives apply to every child in general terms, the specific needs of particular children have to be taken into account through **differentiation** of the vocabulary, questions and tasks that are used to reinforce learning. Lessons do not take place in isolation and a lesson plan has to indicate the links with previous lessons to strengthen continuity and the developmental nature of learning. Pupils are not involved in lesson preparation, so teachers have to explain to pupils what is happening in the lesson if the children are to engage fully with it.

Children take differing amounts of time to grasp concepts and remember facts, so in addition to addressing the needs of less able and more able pupils, lesson plans have to make allowance for faster and slower workers. Plans differ according to the subject matter, location and age of children. Thus, a shortened maths lesson with bright 11-year-olds following an unexpectedly long **assembly** makes different demands from a lengthy outdoor games' session or a period of adult-directed **play** for 5-year-olds.

Experienced teachers make far less detailed plans than a trainee or new teacher would be expected to keep but still have to be conscientious in preparation. They can only teach efficiently and respond adeptly to unexpected events because they have got other aspects of the lesson firmly under control, using techniques gained from hard-won experience. By contrast, inexperienced teachers rely heavily on the lesson plan and cannot imagine teaching without it. As they become more confident, they are able to set the plan aside and concentrate on improving their lesson presentation, interaction with pupils and promoting effective learning.

Teaching and learning are a continuous unfolding of **knowledge**, **skills** and understanding across periods of time. Over a series of lessons, each new session begins by rehearsing some of the key points from the previous one. **Assessment** of what took place in one lesson enables the next one to be planned more accurately by using evidence about the way that the children responded to the tasks, answered questions and completed the work. Consequently, progress in learning is reinforced from one session to the next as the threads of learning are woven together and teaching becomes more sensitive to children's needs.

All lesson planning takes note of the key resources that are required, both the practical items and the human assistance (teaching **assistants** or voluntary parental help). If equipment requires special training or there are **health and safety** factors to consider, these are taken into account when planning the lesson, as even commonly used resources can pose dangers if procedures are not correctly followed. Lesson plans often contain a list of significant words and expressions, especially subject-related ones. The extent to which key spellings are made available to pupils and the extent to which they try to spell the words unaided or with the aid of a word bank is a decision that has to be made by each teacher. The majority of teachers encourage children to try and spell words for themselves before asking an adult. Subject-related terms require special explanation.

The **inclusion** of each child is an essential factor for teachers to consider when planning a lesson or session, which might entail preparing separate tasks for the less able children or modifying the lesson so that they are able to find success in an elementary task, while the more able extend their learning through more challenging activities. If less able children are extracted from the lesson for tuition purposes, teachers have to take account of the way in which they will be incorporated into the lesson on their return.

Assessment criteria, linked closely to learning objectives, are normally noted in the planning to provide indicators by which pupil progress and attainment can be judged. Although it is impossible to observe every child closely during each lesson, teachers often employ a straightforward categorisation to indicate how pupils engaged with the knowledge demands: coped comfortably, struggled to cope, require more challenge. The three categories provide a starting point for a more sophisticated evaluation of progress, which normally relies on an assessment of children's written output after they have handed in the work (sometimes referred to as 'summative' assessment).

The final phase of a lesson (the **'lesson review'**) allows the teacher to summarise what has been achieved, draws together the threads of learning that have characterised the lesson, including **mistakes and misconceptions**, offers pupils the opportunity to share with others in the class what they have done and achieved, and indicate what will follow in the next lesson.

Further reading

Butt, G. (2003) *Lesson Planning*, London: Continuum.

Hayes, D. (2000) *The Handbook for NQTs (Primary)*, London: David Fulton, unit 4.

O'Hara, M. (2004) *Teaching 3–8*, 2nd edn, London: Continuum, section 3.

Reece, I. and Walker, S. (2000) *Teacher Training and Learning: A Practical Guide*, Sunderland: Business Education Publishers.

LESSON REVIEW

The process of lesson review or 'plenary' (a term denoting that the whole class or group is present and involved) is an important part of the learning process, as it gives an opportunity for the teacher to encourage pupils to **talk** about their work, draw together the key points from the lesson and point out **mistakes and misconceptions** and errors.

Reviewing lesson outcomes does not have to be prolonged. Teachers sometimes use the plenary to go through the lesson's key vocabulary list or ask selected pupils to explain the way they have worked out a problem or tell the rest of the class what they have found out or achieved. Occasionally it involves one child speaking on behalf of the collaborating group to explain what they have decided or summarise the results of their efforts. Children also love the opportunity to show off their models, charts, pictures and drawings, though the plenary is not necessarily used solely for 'show and tell'. Other plenary approaches include children saying what surprised or pleased them about what they have done, what problems they encountered or **reading** an extract from a piece of written work.

Teachers have a key role in bringing to a halt the work being undertaken by the children, gathering the class together with minimum disruption and enthusing about pupils' achievements. Whichever method (or combination of methods) is used to involve pupils, teachers endeavour to receive every contribution enthusiastically. Very young or shy children also need to feel that they have contributed towards the review phase, even if they have not actually spoken; this is often achieved by asking for a show of hands about different aspects of the lesson, to which all children can contribute, or finding a child who has done well and letting all the children bask in the reflected glory. There are many occasions when these final moments of a lesson are used to remind the children of what is following the break or during the next lesson and to end positively by celebrating all that has been achieved. In these ways, a plenary session not only reinforces learning but also provides the whole class with a sense of fulfilment.

Further reading

Petty, G. (2004) *Teaching Today*, 3rd edn, Cheltenham: Stanley Thornes, chapter 40.

LITERACY

Fundamentally, a literate person is someone who is able to read and write, and the term 'literacy' largely replaced the more general word 'English' in primary schools around the end of the twentieth century to describe the process by which children become literate. The teaching of literacy has always been a priority in primary schools, but in recent years this priority has been given additional impetus through a large number of government-initiated **curriculum** reforms and the use of national **testing** as a crucial indicator for school success. This emphasis has been particularly pronounced in England.

Literacy in primary education is principally concerned with the process of **communication** between pupil and pupil or pupil and adult. The more opportunity that children have to communicate verbally and make use of well-informed adults who will inspire and motivate them, the faster is their progress towards linguistic competence. Teachers work hard to encourage children to see themselves as active in their own learning, rather than as passive recipients of information. Research into the literacy development of young primary children has focused on the important contribution made by the school and the home and confirmed the importance of spoken language as a prerequisite to proficiency in written language. Young children are faced with the considerable challenge of grasping the concept that printed text is the means of representing recorded speech; they must also understand that writing provides the vehicle by which the conversion from spoken to written form takes place. Some pupils face considerable difficulties in comprehending the connections between spoken and written language, not least the fact that words are units of meaning and punctuation conventions are signposts that they must use to negotiate the written code. Statistically, these difficulties are more prevalent in boys than in girls.

Within any class of children there will be considerable variation in the previous experience of the spoken and written word. Some children come from linguistically rich homes, in which there are active verbal exchanges promoted by loquacious adults. Other children come from homes where there is little emphasis on **reading** and a restricted vocabulary range is employed by adults. Some children speak a different first language from English; in such instances English is referred to as an additional language (EAL). Studies suggest that many EAL children are effective decoders of print but may struggle with the rhythm of words and find it hard to grasp the deeper meanings of text. Teachers have to take close account of pupils' different language experiences when planning and teaching.

The concept of a *literacy hour* is rooted in the Dearing Review of the National Curriculum in England and Wales (Dearing 1993) and based on an assumption that pupils should receive 180 hours of English teaching each year. The literacy hour has received official support through the publication of a national literacy strategy, NLS (DfEE 1998c). The 180 hours of teaching provides for five hours of literacy teaching each week over the thirty-six weeks of the school year, or one hour per day. The NLS framework for teaching recommends that each lesson consist of four elements that have to be kept in balance. The first element, led by the teacher with the whole class, is based on scrutinising a specific portion of text ('shared text' work). The second element, also led by the teacher, focuses on individual key words for 5- to 7-year-olds and sentences for 7- to 11-year-olds. The third element is independent **reading**, writing or word work for 5- to 7-year-olds while the teacher works with children on tasks associated with the chosen text ('guided text' work), while for 7- to 11-year-olds the teacher works closely with at least one group on the significance and use of sentences from the text. Finally, the whole class is assembled for the **lesson review** to celebrate what has been learned.

The literacy hour framework is posited on a firm commitment to a view of learning, in which children learn incrementally, with each piece of learning being dependent upon previous mastery. Many teachers have modified the literacy hour framework to allow greater flexibility, based on concerns about the fact that children working independently do, in fact, require adult support and intervention, and the limited opportunity for extended forms of writing in the short time available. Some teachers dispense with the plenary to allow more time for the main written task.

Many literacy subject leaders discover that although there is a need to develop a programme for teachers to engage in systematic language teaching, even a carefully designed programme can be uninspiring for children unless the teaching environment emphasises the usefulness and **enjoyment** to be gained from the endeavour. Children who have been under-stimulated at home or who struggle constantly with learning to read and write take a lot of persuading that the effort is worthwhile. Unlike some other aspects of learning, weak literacy cannot easily be concealed by children and if problems persist, they quickly become demoralised. The considerable challenge for teachers of younger pupils is that if children are still finding difficulty by the end of KS1, they will probably continue to be academically handicapped throughout their primary schooling and beyond.

Teaching **assistants** exercise an important role in supporting the needs of children that struggle with literacy. Pupils who are deemed to be underachieving are sometimes given additional 'booster' classes as a means of enhancing their competence and gaining better results in national tests.

Further reading

Bearne, E. and Grainger, T. (2004) 'Raising boys' achievement in writing', *Literacy*, 38, 3, pp. 156–8.

Dearing, R. (1993) *The National Curriculum and its Assessment: Final report*, London: School Curriculum & Assessment Authority.

Department for Education and Employment (1998c) *The National Literacy Strategy*, Sudbury: DfEE Publications.

Hancock, R. and Mansfield, M. (2001) 'The literacy hour: a case for listening to children', in J. Collins, K. Insley and J. Soler (eds) *Developing Pedagogy: Researching practice*, pp. 96–108, London: Paul Chapman/Open University.

Latham, D. (2002) *How Children Learn to Write*, London: Paul Chapman.

Meek, M. (2004) 'Readings about readings', *Changing English*, 11, 2, pp. 307–17.

OFSTED (2003b) *Yes He Can: Schools where boys write well*, Reference HMI 505, London: The Stationery Office.

MEMORY

Memorising is a complex phenomenon, the most familiar aspect being an *active working memory* that pupils use immediately after they see or hear something. Some psychologists refer to this form of memory as a temporary storage facility where information is located until the brain can process the information into what is commonly referred to as *short-term memory*, which is effective for brief periods of time but does not accommodate complete retention. Thus, children may appear to learn something one day but forget it by the next and have difficulty transferring the information to the second type of memory, popularly known as *long-term memory* (permanently stored). In extreme cases a child will have difficulty grasping information for long enough in the active working memory to transfer it to the short-term memory. However, when memory works well, **knowledge** will be transferred from the active to the short-term and eventually to the long-term memory with minimum intellectual effort. There is general agreement that brain development and memory are closely related to the amount and quality of sleep that children get each night.

Both 'episodic' memory (memory for events) and 'semantic' memory (memory for facts) are significant for young learners. Some children who are brain damaged at birth struggle to recall episodic events from their everyday life with any reliability but are still capable of gaining average grades in work that relies on semantic memory, particularly in speech and language, **reading** and writing, and recall of well-ordered facts.

Children with memory strengths are easy to identify because they can accommodate large amounts of information and retain it effortlessly from a variety of sources. While such children may participate well in class discussions and offer interesting perspectives on complex issues, they may struggle to do well in tests, especially if it involves writing answers down. These pupils (more often boys than girls) present a considerable challenge for teachers and may, in exceptional cases, require additional adult support or regular access to IT support materials.

The way that pupils use what they have absorbed influences the reinforcement of concepts and **skills**. Children who struggle with memory weaknesses may appear to understand a concept, yet need a considerable amount of repetition, careful explanation and opportunities to explore ideas through problem solving and investigations. A common way in which teachers are alerted to a pupil's weak memory is when the child's written work is characterised by poor sequencing, missing words and inadequate grammar, despite the fact that the child can articulate his or her ideas. For these children, any sort of written work seems to hinder the process of organising their thoughts. If pupils have problems in absorbing information that is communicated verbally or are simply poor listeners they need to have directions explained and visually reinforced (with a diagram, for instance). If pupils have poor visual recall they may forget what they have read or been shown and need to have their learning supported through careful explanation and 'hands-on' experiences.

Teachers are regularly faced with determining whether children cannot remember because they are unable to do so or because they are unwilling to give the subject sufficient attention. Problems can also be created by the teacher's inadequacy to explain clearly, use appropriate vocabulary and inspire children, which in turn leads to a low-key **learning climate**, tedium and reduced motivation. Children are more likely to remember and understand when the topic is interesting and relevant to them.

There are a number of strategies that teachers use to build memory in primary-aged children. The first is to offer children opportunities for regular practice (for instance, in learning sets of numbers or lists of spellings). Second, teachers utilise the odd moments to remind the children about key facts and engage them in simple **activities** to reinforce the concepts. Third, **reading** well-loved books serves as a memory tool for pupils; in particular, reading aloud exposes them to language that will be of long-term benefit. When younger children ask the teacher to read a book again and again, the repetition assists memory of the story, sequencing of events and the satisfaction that they receive from grasping the plot. Fourth, teachers stimulate children's memories by enquiring what happens next or asking them to summarise what has happened so far and making a game of retelling the whole story by moving from child to child, each one making a small contribution.

Rhyming is an important language skill that encourages memory growth as well as teaching letter sounds, and is most commonly employed in poetry. Well-written prose, especially amusing pieces, is greatly enjoyed by primary pupils and can also be memorised. Once mastered by the majority, speaking the passage in unison allows less confident children to be included within the group enterprise and conceal individual shortcomings. Using multiple and entertaining ways to study enhances learning for all children, but especially for those with poor recall, as the combination of different and captivating approaches literally makes the work 'memorable'.

Further reading

Miller, A. *et al.* (2005) *A Through the Years Look at Memory*, Sesame Workshop. On-line. Available: http://www.sesameworkshop.org/parents/advice (accessed May 2005).

Setley, S. (1995) *Taming the Dragons: Real Help for Real School Problems*. Online. Available: http://members.aol.com/susans29/book.html (accessed April 2005).

MISTAKES AND MISCONCEPTIONS

The Victorian politician E. J. Phelps is credited with coining the maxim: 'the man who makes no mistakes does not usually make anything' in a speech at Mansion House, 24 January 1899 (*Penguin Dictionary of Quotations*). There is, of course, a difference between genuine errors made in the legitimate pursuit of a goal and errors that result from weak application to the task. Mistakes can be categorised under four broad headings: slips, misunderstandings, misconceptions and misapplication. Slips result from a lack of concentration and momentary lapses. For example, a young child might reverse letters or numbers. Misunderstandings lead to adopting an incorrect approach and, as a result, an inappropriate outcome. For example, a child may confuse numbers on the x- and y-axes of a graph. Misconceptions lead to confusion, as the insights and grasp of basic principles that are necessary for completion are inadequate. For example, a child may not understand the relationship between heat loss and the materials used for insulation. Misapplication occurs when, despite possessing the **knowledge** and practical strategies, they are not employed correctly. For example, a child may know how to use a dictionary but always start the search at the beginning instead of estimating the position of the word and turning to approximately the area in which it is located. Some teachers are inclined to spend more of their time dealing with relatively minor slips and misunderstandings, rather than the more profound misconceptions and misapplications.

To teach in a way that prevents pupils from developing any misconceptions (sometimes called 'faultless communication') is desirable but difficult in practice, and teachers have to accept that pupils will make some generalisations that are not correct. Sometimes, pupil misconceptions remain hidden unless teachers make a specific effort to disclose them, so a style of teaching that seeks to expose and rectify misconceptions through careful questioning and encouraging pupils to share their concerns openly is essential.

Advice given in the National **Numeracy** Strategy, NNS (DfEE 1999b) suggests that during the last phase of the lesson it is appropriate for teachers to work with the whole class to sort out any misconceptions when identifying their progress, to summarise key facts and ideas and what to remember, to make links to other areas of work, discuss the next steps and, where appropriate, set **homework** tasks. Results from the Diagnosis Teaching Project, conducted at Nottingham University's Shell Centre for Mathematical Education by Mike Askew and Dylan William, indicate that learning is more effective when common misconceptions are addressed in teaching. Two important issues are significant. The first is that addressing misconceptions during teaching improves pupils' achievements and long-term retention of mathematical concepts. Allowing the children to make their mistakes and then clarifying the position through constructive discussion seems to be more effective than drawing attention to a misconception before giving the examples. The second is that the intensity and degree of engagement with a task that pupils demonstrate in a collaborative group discussion is much more of an important influence on their learning than the amount of time spent on the task. Intensive discussions usually involve spending much longer on small but important teaching points, but this approach results in a much higher level of long-term retention than in situations where more **curriculum** content is covered superficially over the same period of time.

Further reading

Askew, M. and William, D. (2004) for the DfES, *The Standards Site*, Guide for your professional development: Unit 2 appendices, London: The Stationery Office.

Department for Education and Employment (1999b) *The National Numeracy Strategy*, London: The Stationery Office.

Makins, V. (1997) *The Invisible Children: Nipping failure in the bud*, London: David Fulton.

Spooner, M. (2004) *Errors and Misconceptions in Mathematics at Key Stage 2*, London: David Fulton.

MONITORING PROGRESS

Monitoring is a process by which children's work is regulated through close and active attention from teachers and support staff. Monitoring is closely associated with **intervention**, a process that follows monitoring through which teachers offer specific guidance and direction to pupils to correct errors, challenge their thinking and focus their attention on a specific area of work. Perceptive monitoring of pupil progress is an essential component of teaching, as there is a close correlation between how well it is carried out and the quality of children's learning. Monitoring and intervening allow teachers to offer **feedback** that will assist children in formulating ideas, understanding the work they are engaged in, and helping them to make sense of their learning. Fostering intrinsic **rewards** (self-satisfaction) as well as extrinsic rewards (based on adult satisfaction) impresses upon pupils that work is worthwhile for its own sake and not merely to please and satisfy others. Another important dimension of monitoring is that it is a means by which teachers ensure that pupils concentrate on the task they are undertaking and behave appropriately during **lessons**.

Under formal test conditions, the process of monitoring consists of ensuring that pupils conform to the required conditions (silence, individual working, etc.). However, in the vast majority of primary classroom learning situations, monitoring involves close observation of children as they grapple with tasks and respond to the demands made of them. Monitoring of work in response to children's requests for clarification leads to active intervention and the provision of appropriate feedback to them about the direction and quality of their work. Monitoring is more straightforward when teachers have clarified the **expectations** for pupils in advance of starting the tasks or **activities** and explained what constitutes satisfactory work.

When adults and children enjoy a comfortable working relationship, then constructive and sensitive criticism that results from monitoring acts as an **encouragement** and stimulus to pupils as they grapple with concepts and master practical challenges. If the monitoring is perceived by pupils as an attempt to 'catch them out' it leads to defensiveness and resentment. Many teachers invite pupils to be self-critical and evaluate their own or other pupil's work ('peer assessment') as an important contribution to the sense of shared endeavour.

Further reading

Angelle, P. (2004) 'Monitoring progress through feedback', *School Effectiveness and School Improvement*, 15, 1, pp. 115–20.

Headington, R. (2000) *Monitoring, Assessment, Recording, Reporting and Accountability*, 2nd edn, London: David Fulton, chapter 2.

MORAL DEVELOPMENT

Morality is a term applied to issues about caring relationships, universal principles that regulate forms of behaviour, right (virtuous) and wrong (inappropriate) conduct, and character. It is closely related to 'ethics' and forms part of the (non-statutory) **citizenship** curriculum in primary education. During the formative years at school, children's needs are not purely academic, but also social, spiritual and emotional. There are strong indications that while examination results are improving, there is a concomitant increase in drug-dependency, sexually transmitted diseases, self-harm, dissatisfaction with school among sections of the community and an expanding group of disaffected youngsters who resort to extreme forms of behaviour. Even children of primary school age are not immune from the impact of social division and strife. One of the aims of primary education is to help pupils to understand their place in society and encourage them to empathise with the views of others. Children can also be enthused to discover their own strengths, passions and gifting.

One of the UK government slogans, 'Use your head, teach', is one indicator of a move towards teaching as being, first and foremost, a profession requiring intelligent and knowledgeable members. However, there is unease among primary practitioners that the emphasis on academic attainment may be viewed by the public and politicians as incompatible with demonstrating and practising a caring and **nurturing** attitude towards children. For primary educators, pressure to achieve standards means that there is sometimes a tension between the time and effort expended in striving for higher test results and the attention paid to moral and ethical issues.

Adults that work in schools are not directly responsible for children's moral development and every primary teacher is conscious about trespassing on areas that are rightly the business of parents. Nevertheless, each time a child is admonished by a teacher, told how to behave or presented with choices, an ethical position is being established and a moral statement is being made. One way and another, deliberately or incidentally, teachers have an influence on the development of children's characters and are therefore locked into a position in which they exercise moral authority. Parents appear to recognise increasingly that children need and benefit from spiritual influences, as manifested through the popularity of schools with a religious foundation or strong moral ethic.

Primary educators grapple with questions about what form of education will help to develop young citizens who are not only academically sound but also wise and morally discerning in their decisions. In doing so the educators have to balance curriculum demands with the requirement to promote acceptable standards of behaviour. The imposition of a code of conduct shaped by a school discipline policy may bring about positive changes in pupil behaviour while constraints are in place but fail to provide the moral certainty that will lead to appropriate choices about lifestyle when children move outside the school influence. No teacher wishes to educate young people to be reckless and foolish, yet recklessness and foolishness have become all too familiar in society. It is clear that **knowledge**, examination success or even an intelligent understanding of issues cannot create a civilised and just society unless it is underpinned by more deeply seated moral imperatives.

Adults that work in primary schools care deeply for the pupils they consider to be 'their' children and want them to do well in their studies, to prosper in their relationships and to be satisfied with their successes and endeavours. Teachers and assistants want to use their influence to reveal something profound to children about life and its meaning and help them to appreciate that with perseverance and determination they can not only achieve commendable academic standards but also discover something about their personal worth and the worth of others.

Further reading

Day, C. (2004) *A Passion for Teaching*, London: Routledge, chapter 2.

Fisher, R. (2001) *Values for Thinking*, Oxford: Nash Pollock.

Sanger, M. and Osguthorpe, R. (2005) 'Making sense of approaches to moral education', *Journal of Moral Education*, 34, 1, pp. 57–71.

Tirri, K. (1999) 'Teachers' perceptions of moral dilemmas at school', *Journal of Moral Education*, 28, 1, pp. 31–47.

MOTIVATION FOR TEACHING

Surveys about motivation for teaching conclude that altruism, a love for children, a desire to help pupils learn and the pleasure associated with the job are highly significant factors for new recruits to the profession. People decide to become primary school teachers because they feel that it is a useful and worthwhile way to spend their working lives through making a positive contribution to the well-being of society. Research shows that many of the key factors that provide the initial spur for becoming a primary teacher are rooted in caring, self-fulfilment and the positive impact it has on young people's lives. Studies based on the views of trainee teachers reveal that their motivation rests on a belief that they can not only contribute to children's academic progress but also influence their social and **moral develop-**

ment. These altruistic desires do not mean that teachers are uninterested in good working conditions, a respectable salary and opportunities for career enhancement, but that nothing can match the satisfaction that comes from making a significant difference to the life of each child.

One of the challenges associated with an educational climate in which success is largely measured through quantitative test results is that it may be at the expense of the caring and **nurturing** atmosphere that many primary educators extol. Advocates of this 'child-centred' approach to education claim that the principle of caring for all of a child's development needs forms the bedrock of a successful education. Child-centred educators argue that when teachers' practice is based on an ethic of care it provides the motivation and commitment for them to persevere and helps to compensate for the exhausting effects that the intensification of their work has created in recent years.

In an attempt to recruit a larger number of teachers, the web site of the Training and Development Agency, TDA (the government body responsible for monitoring the recruitment and training of teachers) is now replete with stimulating statements such as 'Teaching is like no other job. It is as inspiring, challenging and unique as each child you teach' and 'Talk to teachers, pick up the exhilaration they feel' and 'You will be working ... with other intelligent and like-minded people.' This emphasis is a response to concerns that the previous recruitment campaign relied too heavily on the belief that altruism was the prime motivating factor for aspiring teachers. The TDA was concerned that it might deter potential applicants who were seeking a career that offered intellectual satisfaction, good conditions of service and personal fulfilment, rather than one that required self-sacrifice (http://www.useyourheadteach.gov.uk).

The retention of teachers is considerably more problematic than their recruitment, and the number of teachers that withdraw during training or who qualify but fail to remain in teaching for more than a few years has created a considerable problem for the government. Studies carried out during the early years of the twenty-first century indicate that around one-third of trainee teachers qualify but do not enter teaching; a further one-fifth leave the profession within three years. In total, almost one-half of new teachers leave the profession within five years. A mismatch between the aspirations of new teachers and the external demands placed on them when they are appointed is the most common reason offered for quitting. In particular, the plethora of paperwork tasks, the closely prescribed **curriculum**, scrutiny of teaching methods and the **testing** regime have been cited as principal reasons for disillusionment.

One of the paradoxes about teacher recruitment and retention is that the effort to improve the financial inducements for teachers has created a focus of attention on the pecuniary benefits of the job (which generally fall below those in many other professional settings) and away from the personal satisfaction element. This emphasis is perplexing, as personal satisfaction is the single most important motivating factor for the majority of qualified teachers and aspiring teachers.

Further reading

Gilbert, I. (2002) *Essential Motivation in the Classroom*, London: Routledge.

Hayes, D. (2004b) 'Recruitment and retention: insights into the motivation of primary trainee teachers in England', *Research in Education*, No. 71, May, pp. 37–49.

McLean, A. (2003) *The Motivated School*, London: Paul Chapman.

Moran, A., Kilpatrick, R., Abbott, J., Dallat, J. and McClune, B. (2001) 'Training to teach: motivating factors and implications for recruitment', *Evaluation and Research in Education*, 15, 1, 17–32.

Spear, M., Gould, K. and Lee, B. (2000) *Who Would be a Teacher? A review of factors motivating and demotivating prospective and practising teachers*, Slough: National Foundation for Educational Research.

Thornton, M., Bricheno, P. and Reid, I. (2002) 'Students' reasons for wanting to teach in primary school', *Research in Education*, 67, pp. 33–43.

NUMERACY

Numeracy is the **ability** to use number in calculations, including counting. However, since the introduction of a national strategy for numeracy in primary schools, some teachers use the term as short-hand for all work in mathematics. The National Numeracy Strategy, NNS (DfEE 1999b) has two main aims: first, to improve the teaching of mathematics in the classroom; and second, to improve the management of numeracy at school level. The NNS is supported by a document, the *Framework for teaching mathematics*, which is intended as a working document for teachers, providing yearly teaching programmes to help them set appropriately high **expectations** for their pupils and understand how pupils should progress through the primary years. It also outlines appropriate teaching methods. The guidance is not statutory, but it sets out a very clear and precise strategy which schools are expected to follow. The guidance makes clear that it is the responsibility of the governing body and the head teacher to manage the overall direction of the school and the setting of high standards of pupil **achievement** for staff and children.

To achieve the required objectives, the NNS promotes the use of a daily mathematics lesson to provide a practical structure of time and class management, based on a three-part framework. The lesson begins with oral work and mental calculation using whole-class teaching, frequently referred to as the mental–oral phase. The central lesson phase is used to introduce new topics or consolidate previous work, clarify **learning objectives** and offer the opportunity for pupils to implement their knowledge and rehearse their under-standing by practising mathematical examples (traditionally known as 'doing sums'). The final phase (referred to as the plenary) is to allow teachers to draw together what children have learned and to deal with any **mistakes and misconceptions** or misunderstandings. Many teachers use the final few minutes of a session as an opportu-nity to celebrate success, identify areas of confusion and indicate the direction of future learning.

Mathematical development in young children is, to an extent, influenced by social and contextual factors. Parental attitudes towards the subject and the general absence of mathematics featuring in conversations at home, other than those involving basic counting, mean that many children come to pre-schooling and the reception class with an underdeveloped sense of the subject. Other children view mathematics as being detached from real life. Despite these reservations, however, children entering school may also bring with them a fund of insight into different aspects of mathematics, such as numeral recognition, simple addition, subtraction and sharing. Tea-chers encourage pupils to explore the implications of their existing knowledge through **play** and shared experiences. Although older primary-age children may be able to work out computations cor-rectly and score good marks in national tests, they are not necessarily able to apply their mathematics to problems and investigate unfami-liar situations that would provide evidence of deeper understanding.

Teachers pay close attention to a number of issues when planning for and teaching mathematics. First, recognising that the time they spend in eliciting existing pupils' **knowledge** and understanding helps to clarify future learning needs. Second, being sensitive to the fact that the children may have a dearth of experience in using mathematical language and must be exposed gradually to key voca-bulary with careful explanation and practical involvement to reinforce concepts. Third, ensuring that the emphasis on formal teaching of number is not at the expense of investigative work and does not deprive children of opportunities to find out things through direct experience. Fourth, offering younger pupils a chance to explore ideas, sensitive to the fact that without active teacher involvement this opportunity does not in itself guarantee understanding. Fifth, translating perceptions into mathematical notation and symbols is a major challenge for many pupils, some of whom will struggle to grasp the significance of mathematical notation. Sixth, talking to children about work in mathematics to foster interest and learning. Finally, using mathematics to solve genuine problems and promote a belief in children that the subject has relevance for everyday living.

Studies indicate that primary teachers who are prepared to spend time dwelling on key areas of understanding and exploring the implications are more successful than those that speed along in a vain attempt to 'cover' the **curriculum** content. Teachers who are pre- pared to ask challenging questions, give pupils time to think and offer their own insights, and use a variety of reinforcing strategies (repeti- tion, worked examples, **collaboration** and problem solving) cultivate the most highly motivated and mathematically astute children.

Further reading

Askew, M. and William, D. (1995) *Recent Research in Mathematics Education 5–16*, London: HMSO/OFSTED.

Askew, M. and William, D. (2004) for the DfES, *The Standards Site*, Guide for your professional development: Unit 2 appendices, London: The Sta- tionery Office.

Suggate, J., Davis, A. and Goulding, M. (2001) *Mathematical Knowledge for Primary Teachers*, 2nd edn, London: David Fulton.

NURTURING

One of the longstanding questions about influences on human development has centred on a debate about whether nature (what a person seems to be disposed towards) or nurture (the environment in which children are raised) has the most pronounced impact. There is general agreement that both factors are significant, though opinions differ about which influence is the more powerful. The 'nurture' school of thought was championed by American psychologists, who argued that behaviour is learned and modifiable through experience. The 'nature' school of thought came to the forefront in the early to mid-twentieth century among European biologists such as Konrad Lorenz, best known for his pioneering work on imprinting in young animals. The controversial aspect of nature theory is the claim that behavioural tendencies are instinctive and cannot be changed by life experience. The implication of this claim for parents and teachers is that children are predisposed to particular actions and attitudes that cannot easily be remedied through intervention. Unfortunately, this argument has been used to maintain that certain races are inferior and justify certain types of anti-social behaviour by arguing that it is merely a reflection of what comes naturally to the people concerned.

Marjorie Boxall pioneered the setting up of nurture groups in the London Borough of Enfield in the early 1970s as a response to social deprivation and its consequences for children in school. Boxall argued that without adequate nurturing, the fabric of society is at risk, for with each generation there are fewer people to provide good nurturing and more children who have been deprived of it. She has been particularly keen to promote nurture groups that provide children with social and emotional experiences that are necessary as a prerequisite for formal school learning. In support of Boxall's view, school inspectors increasingly acknowledge that formal education is enhanced when schools provide high-quality nurturing environments. A nurturing environment is not incompatible with high standards of attainment and **expectations**.

The majority of primary teachers, especially those working with young children, are comfortable with the nurture theory, pointing out that there appears to be a causal link between weak progress, poor behaviour and troubled family backgrounds. In school, a nurturing environment depends upon a welcoming and warm atmosphere where the academic, developmental, behavioural and emotional needs of each pupil are all considered to be important. At the same time, work patterns for pupils are set at an appropriate level and the work content is meaningful and presented creatively so that children find the work satisfying and enjoyable. Most primary teachers are highly motivated by the responsibility for children's welfare that is attached to the job.

Nurture also extends to a concern for adults. A supportive pastoral climate for all members of the school community is an essential characteristic of primary schools, such that a distinctive feature of effective schools is the quality of relationships between teachers, support staff, parents and visitors. In turn, this caring attitude provides an example and role model for the children. In such circumstances, every aspect of school life exudes purpose and **celebration** of genuine effort and success, with the concomitant high morale and enthusiasm that is engendered.

Nurture has **health and safety** implications. For instance, some children come to school with little or no breakfast and benefit from the availability of food through pre-school 'breakfast clubs' and the like, leading to an improvement in behaviour and concentration. Similarly, the development of **homework** clubs and childcare facilities after school provides security for otherwise vulnerable children. An important aspect of nurture is respecting pupils' right to privacy and opportunity to sit quietly and undisturbed where practical to do so. The fostering of mutual respect between adults and children has been shown to lead to an improvement in behaviour and a more purposeful **learning climate**.

Extra-curricular provision promotes the development of a variety of social skills, such as teamwork, children helping each other to succeed and learning to take turns. A more informal setting increases the likelihood that children will initiate conversations (as happens in the home) rather than the adult-initiated discourse that characterises much of school life. The practice of gathering children together in a circle ('**circle time**') encourages pupils to contribute ideas safely, knowing that others are likely to listen and acknowledge their contribution. These nurturing opportunities are often a forerunner of more open discussions and collaborative tasks, by which ideas can be voiced and opinions exchanged without rancour.

Further reading

Boxall, M. (2002) *Nurture Groups in School: Principles & Practice*, London: Paul Chapman.

Clark, C. M. (1995) *Thoughtful Teaching*, London: Cassell.

Oberski, I., Ford, K., Higgins, S. and Fiher, P. (1999) 'The importance of relationships in teacher education', *Journal of Education for Teaching*, 25, 2, pp. 135–50.

ORACY

Oracy is based on the root word 'oral', shorthand for the speaking and listening that takes place during collaborative sessions. Its educational value is predicated on a belief that allowing children the space and time to **talk** together about a topic of common interest, and thereby combining their **knowledge**, understanding and wisdom, leads to a more satisfactory outcome than with one person working alone. Speaking and listening forms an integral element of communicating with others and is a fundamental part of **literacy** education because research shows that exploratory talk is an effective way of using language to think, which forms one of the principal building blocks of literacy. Where there is effective discussion it leads to significant gains in pupils' ability to recall, understand and respond to deeper meanings that are found in literature. In the UK, a number of government publications offer support in the area of speaking and listening to complement the objectives for **reading** and writing set out in the NLS, *Framework for teaching* (DfEE 1998c). The materials reflect the requirements for teachers to extend and reinforce speaking and listening in every subject area, building on and extending the approach outlined in *Teaching Speaking and Listening in Key Stages 1 and 2* (QCA 1999). The document places a lot of emphasis on the potential for learning when children are given properly constructed opportunities to explore issues, make decisions, experiment with ideas and draw conclusions through working together rather than singly. Oracy is not included in the **learning objectives** of the primary literacy strategy, although it is central to the teaching process to ensure a successful outcome.

To promote listening, children are encouraged to wait their turn while another child is speaking and carefully attend to what others are saying. Effective listening involves more than hearing the words and understanding their meaning. It also entails observation of the speaker's body language, registering the feelings and perceptions that lie behind the words, being sensitive towards verbal clues and making inferences from the tone of voice. The skill can be improved and refined by the teacher modelling careful listening by repeating or summarising for the benefit of the whole class what a child has said and giving selected children the opportunity to do the same. There are also a variety of fun ways used by primary teachers to improve pupils' listening skills, such as the 'repeat after me' game where the children echo the leader's statements using the same tone of voice. During **circle time** discussions pupils can maintain eye contact and have more opportunity to adjust to what a classmate is saying and understand why it is being said.

In addition to organising pupils in pairs or groups to assist their oracy development, teachers perform one or more of three teaching roles during speaking and listening sessions: as an expert, as a facilitator, as a participant. As an expert, teachers provide insights and advice while the children discuss things. As a facilitator teachers ensure that they have prepared the ground by explaining the purpose of the exercise, reminding children of the rules and steering them towards reaching a conclusion. As a participant teachers are involved as a temporary member of the group, contributing ideas and suggestions.

Further reading

Grugeon, E., Dawes, L. and Smith, C. (2000) *Teaching Speaking and Listening in the Primary School*, London: David Fulton.

Johnson, J. (1993) 'The National Oracy Project', *Spoken English*, 26, 1, pp. 25–38.

National Literacy Trust (2005): http://www.literacytrust.org.uk/Database/oracy.html.

ORGANISING FOR LEARNING

Organising for learning involves teachers preparing for **lessons**, ensuring that appropriate resources are available and setting out the classroom so that children can work efficiently. Whereas the *management* of learning is largely confined to the period of active teaching, the majority of organising happens before lessons commence and facilitates their smooth operation.

One of the most important areas of a teacher's responsibility involves organising resources, including working space, equipment and consumables. The provision has to be appropriate to the tasks undertaken by pupils, though **enquiry**-based activities (e.g. investigations in science, problem solving in mathematics) require a more diverse range of resources owing to the less predictable direction that learning might take. The availability of resources is also important. Equipment must be stored safely but conveniently. Not only must consumable items (such as paper) be readily available, but also pupils have to be informed about when they can be used and for what purpose, as there are financial and practical implications if resources are abused. Incorrect use of tools can lead to expensive breakages and also deprive other pupils of the opportunity of using them. The higher the risk factor, the more immediate the adult presence, high standard of discipline and training about the correct use of equipment need to be.

Large-space activities (e.g. for PE, dance and drama) and 'design and make' tasks (especially in design and technology) carry significant resource implications: adhesive tape and pots have to be distributed in advance; clay has to be accessible; tables have to be relocated; and so on. Similarly, equipment has to be checked in advance of PE lessons; drama 'props' have to be put in position; the floor space has to be cleared before a dance session; computers have to be switched on, programs set up and paper trays filled for printing. If arrangements are not in hand, the lesson stutters because the process of organising resources absorbs the time and effort that would have gone into active teaching, the exception being when the involvement of the children in the organisation forms an important part of the lesson. For example, pupils may be asked to arrange equipment or furniture as a component of their **play**.

Despite modern architectural designs and advances in materials and construction techniques, few classrooms are ideal for every **teaching approach**. Pupils spend long periods of time in the room that they consider to be a 'second home' and a consideration of their needs is a priority. Whether a classroom is brand new or a Victorian edifice, the children need to be able to move around comfortably and safely. Teachers eliminate the majority of hazards by ensuring that the room is orderly and having a place for every item; they view the classroom as a busy workshop rather than a lounge.

Organising the room also involves decisions about seating. Most teachers allocate children a specific place for the majority of lessons unless they are moved for a particular purpose, such as working collaboratively on an art project or collaborative craft activity. A minority of teachers give pupils complete freedom about where they sit or may allow children to sit where they prefer for a few days at the start of the year until the children's self-discipline and inclination to work become apparent, when changes are made accordingly. Seating arrangements can make an educationally important difference to the quality of learning. For instance, seating pupils in rows rather than grouping them tends to foster an improvement in children's concentration levels and work output, though it does not facilitate group activities. There are some advantages in creating a horseshoe pattern of seating as this design allows every child to see every other child during class discussions or question-and-answer sessions; however, few primary school classrooms are sufficiently large to allow for such a configuration. If teachers use a board or visual forms of technology to illustrate what they are teaching, children have to be seated in such a way that they can see and hear clearly.

Many teachers take account of **friendship** factors in organising seating, though if children sit with their friends around nests of tables it can result in them spending too much time on 'off-task' conversation. On the other hand, pupils are more likely to cooperate with those to whom they relate well. If friends are separated they may be tempted to wander across the room to each other, send hand signal messages or even call out openly. Although a seating arrangement where friends sit together is popular with children, it can create organisational complications when pupils of similar academic strength need to be grouped. Most teachers try to strike a balance between keeping friends together in situations where grouping does not rely principally on **ability** factors (such as in artwork) and separating them where this is necessary because of the differentiated requirements of tasks and activities. The structured patterns of **literacy** and **numeracy** lessons do not leave much room for manoeuvre, as pupils are together at the start and conclusion of the lesson and separated into ability groups for the rest of the time.

Most teachers have a basic pattern of organisation for activities, but vary the set-up according to the circumstances. For instance, tables may be placed together for the purpose of sharing resources when working on a large-scale project. Children may need to move around the room to complete a series of tasks in a given time, each task located in a different part of the room. There are also practical factors to be taken into account if children require more space for wheelchair access or specially adapted working surfaces for children with limited upper-body mobility. In addition, all schools now have a range of computers, interactive whiteboards and other equipment to support learning. If there is a computer suite situated away from the classroom, supervision of children to and from the room has to be considered. If computers are located in classrooms, managing fair access for all pupils is a priority, as more assertive children are inclined to dominate their use. Teaching **assistants** are frequently involved in supervising and advising children about effective use of technology, especially computers.

Effective organisation has to take close account of **time management**. Teachers have to 'think ahead' by deciding in advance what is essential, what is necessary and what is non-essential. They then decide what is urgent and what can wait. Obviously the combination of 'essential' and 'urgent' has to be tackled first; all else can wait. However, if too many tasks become essential and urgent, it acts as a warning to teachers that they are failing to plan sufficiently far in advance, though in the intensity of school life there are occasions when unexpected events conspire to upset the most carefully laid plans.

Further reading

Bennett, S. N. and Blundell, D. (1983) 'Quantity and quality of work in rows and classroom groups', *Educational Psychology*, 3, 2, pp. 93–105.

Dean, J. (2001) *Improving Children's Learning: Effective teaching in the primary school*, London: Routledge, chapter 1.

Hastings, N. and Chantrey Wood, K. (2002) *Reorganizing Primary Classroom Learning*, Maidstone: Open University Press.

PARENTAL INVOLVEMENT

Parents' interest and involvement in their children's learning is widely recognised as having a significant impact on the extent to which children realise their full potential. Pupils with parents who are involved in their education tend to have fewer behavioural problems, achieve better academic performance and are more likely to complete secondary school than pupils whose parents are uninvolved. Parental interest in school means that parents are more closely aware of school and classroom activities and able to coordinate their efforts with teachers. Studies have also indicated that pupils with highly involved parents tend to receive greater attention from teachers, who are therefore more likely to identify problems that inhibit children's progress. Liaison with parents has become a necessary and important part of every teacher's role, especially those working with young children and pupils with special educational needs.

Warmth and affection in the parent–child relationship is related to positive outcomes for children, including higher **self-esteem**, better levels of **communication** and fewer psychological problems. Parental warmth is even found to encourage children's use of social support and proactive, problem-focused coping strategies. Conversely, insufficient levels of parental support foster feelings of alienation, expressions of hostility and aggression, low morale and anti-social behaviours. The publication *Every Child Matters* (DfES 2004e) suggests that 'The bond between the child and their parents is the most critical influence on a child's life. Parenting has a strong impact on a child's educational development, behaviour and mental health' (p. 39). Head teachers and governors/board members of schools are acutely aware of the need to maintain an open relationship with parents: engaging and involving them through newsletters; providing information about educational initiatives; canvassing their opinions about key issues where appropriate; and actively supporting parent–teacher association meetings.

All adults that work in primary school are required to help in promoting partnerships with parents and other members of the community by acknowledging how experience and learning are shaped by cultural and linguistic heritage, gender, family and community.

Every person working closely with children must keep confidential the information they possess about them and their families, and only use it in the pupils' best interests. Most inspections of schools include a consultation with parents and (sometimes) a questionnaire to ascertain their satisfaction with the quality of education and school–home communication.

In circumstances where there is more than one school in the locality from which to choose, parents principally base their choice on oral information from other parents and a visit to the school to satisfy themselves about the prevailing climate and quality of education. Parents also gain information about the school from written information produced by schools and the latest school inspection report (paper copy or electronic).

Further reading

Arthur, J., Davison, J. and Lewis, M. (2005) *Professional Values and Practice: Achieving the standards for QTS*, London: Routledge, chapter 5.

Department for Education and Skills (2004e) *Every Child Matters*, London: The Stationery Office.

Desforges, C. and Abouchar, A. (2003) *The Impact of Parental Involvement, Parental Support and Family Education on Pupil Achievement and Adjustment: A literature review*, Research Report 433 for the DfES, London: The Stationery Office.

Feiler, A. (2003) 'A home visiting project for reception children predicted to experience literacy difficulties', *British Journal of Special Education*, 30, 3, pp. 156–62.

Holden, A. and Cullingford, C. (2003) 'An analysis of parent-teacher relations in primary schools', *Education 3–13*, 31, 3, pp. 41–8.

Kenner, C., Arju, T., Gregory, E., Jessel, J. and Ruby, M. (2004) 'The role of grandparents in children's learning', *Primary Practice*, 38, Autumn, pp. 41–4.

PASSION

Passion is used to describe teachers' emotional commitment to connect them to the children and their colleagues. Without passion the work of a teacher can become lacklustre and lose all sense of intimacy. Teachers that are keen to inspire, motivate and engage with their pupils, both relationally and in communicating the wonder of the subject they are teaching, are invariably passionate about the job.

Passionate teachers consider their pupils to be immature human beings trying to make sense of life, rather than mere recipients of information. Children are seen as curious and creative beings with the potential for advancement that sensitive adults can help to unlock and promote. Passion in teaching gives priority to the needs of individuals and their desire to explore new areas of learning; it is therefore the antithesis of a standardised and system-driven view of primary education. Some educationists argue that the requirement for teachers to 'perform' in response to government agendas absorbs time and energy that threatens to squeeze spontaneity and passion out of teaching in a thrust to meet targets.

Passion in teaching may also be expressed through an enthusiasm and commitment to a subject area. This form of passion is typically associated with secondary education where teachers spend a lot of time teaching one or two subjects to a wide range of pupils, but the increasing emphasis on subject expertise in primary schools and the emphasis on **curriculum** and **leadership** have increased its significance. Passion of itself will not guarantee an appropriate and suitable education or children learning. However, a **learning climate** in which characteristics such as empathy, compassion, commitment, patience and spontaneity are used in harness with subject expertise provides the optimum conditions for progress. Passion for a subject elicits a comparable response in children if there is an atmosphere of trust and sincere respect existing between the teacher and the taught.

Passionate primary teachers vary in personality and approach, but if pupils sense that teachers have a genuine commitment towards them and a sincere desire to help them, they are invariably more positive about learning than children taught by a technically proficient teacher in an emotionally detached manner. Such caring is signalled in many and various ways, in particular the teacher's tone of voice, willingness to listen and natural behaviour. Passion *in* teaching and *for* teaching is not about pity or allowing pupils to please themselves but about making learning a worthwhile experience all of the time, pleasant for much of the time and wonderful some of the time. It is adults conveying to children that because they are cared for, everything possible will be done to make life in school happy and fulfilling.

Further reading

Day, C. (2004) *A Passion for Teaching*, London: Routledge.
Fried, R. (1995) *The Passionate Teacher: A practical guide*, Boston: Beacon Press.

O'Quinn, E. and Garrison, J. (2004) 'Creating loving relations in the class-room', in D. Liston and J. Garrison (eds) *Teaching, Learning and Loving*, pp. 49–64, London: Routledge.

PHONICS

The phonics method is probably the best known and widely used method to teach **reading** and writing in the English language. It relies on children first being taught the alphabet, learning the names of the letters and the sounds they make. Once they have learnt the letter sounds, they begin to blend two letters together to make simple words, then three letters, then four, and so on. Eventually the words combine to create simple sentences. Phonics is generally applicable to teaching pupils during their first few years of formal education, though it can be useful in teaching an older primary child who has experienced learning difficulties.

Even though children need to be read to in school and at home, and pick up familiar words and phrases from daily life, a programme of targeted tuition is still necessary, of which phonics forms an integral part. Teachers use two broad approaches. In *analytic* phonics the teacher builds up the sounds to make a word, which is shown to the child at the same time; for example, a teacher might sound out the letters of 'f–l–a–g' and then ask the child to repeat the word. In *synthetic* phonics the children learn forty-four sounds of letters or groups of letters before being encouraged to look at books containing the words. Most teachers use a balanced combination of the two approaches.

Some reading specialists argue that the spelling-to-sound correspondences of English are so confusing that blending and sounding out is likely to lead to confusion rather than enlightenment; however, the majority of educationists believe that phonics has an important role to play in learning to read. Whatever method of phonics teaching is favoured, there is agreement among educators that for young children to learn to read effectively they need access to books containing common words that are interesting to them and capable of being sounded out. However, learning the sounds and their blends is not always very exciting, so teacher input and time spent on practice tends to be short and employ imaginative approaches supported by visual stimuli, puppets and pictures. Children can be so busy concentrating on sounding the words and blending the sounds that they do not think about their meaning, so teachers have to remind children about the significance of words, relate them to the accompanying pictures and use example sentences that include the word or words. Reading becomes more meaningful as children master the connection between different sounds and become familiar with the written words through stories, rhymes and songs. Most children want to learn to read and enjoy seeing concrete signs of progress; phonics is a systematic method by which this advancement can be realised.

Further reading

Cook, M. (ed.) (2002) *Perspectives on the Teaching and Learning of Phonics*, Royston: United Kingdom Reading Association.
OFSTED (2001) *Teaching of Phonics*, Reference HMI 329, London: The Stationery Office.
Strickland, D. S. (1998) *Teaching Phonics Today*, Newark, DE: International Reading Association.

PLAY

Play has an important role in early learning and serves as a development tool because it helps in the establishment of social relations, an understanding of natural and physical properties and the development of fine and gross motor **skills**. Play also assists children in utilising spoken and other non-verbal forms of language effectively. It offers pupils in school opportunities to converse meaningfully with other children and understanding that their words and actions can evoke a variety of responses in their peers. There is a considerable body of evidence to support the view that play helps to develop children's **imagination** and ultimately helps them to distinguish between fantasy and reality.

The social aspect of play is useful in developing self-control, a consideration for others and empathy. Children benefit from regular **interaction** with their peers from an early age, learning to share, negotiate and understand the world. Whereas new entrants to school tend to concentrate on their own concerns, a variety of play experiences help them to view events from the perspectives of other children and create a sense of their own self-worth through the regular contacts they enjoy. Children's play is nourished when adults provide or inculcate ideas that children can use as starting points for harnessing the power of their imaginations and **creativity**.

Jean Piaget, the Swiss psychologist, has had a considerable impact on the way that teachers perceive play in learning. In trying to classify how concept development takes place from early childhood to adulthood, Piaget argues that as children grow physically and intellectually, they expand the limits of their play in stages. The first stage is *sensorimotor play* in which infants and toddlers experiment with bodily sensations and motor movements involving objects and people. As children grow older and gain more motor skills (ability to manipulate objects and their own bodies), they also start to see the world in symbolic terms and begin to understand the social function of objects. Thus, they feed their teddy bears pretend food with a spoon or offer a grown-up an invisible drink in a cup. The second stage is *symbolic play* when children use simple objects to represent more sophisticated ones. A 3- or 4-year-old may use a coat as a superhero's cape and a cardboard roll as a light sabre. The space beneath a living-room chair becomes a cave and the stairs substitute for a mountain. By the age of 4 or 5, children's ideas and experiences with their immediate family and the wider social world provide material for imaginative games. Many new entrants to primary school are fascinated by construction play, building and spontaneously exuberant games, such as chasing.

Piaget refers to the next stage of play as *mastery* when children gain increasing **control** of their bodies and actions, while simultaneously incorporating imaginative forms of play. For example, mastery of riding a tricycle becomes a motorbike stunt in the child's mind. By the time they leave the Foundation Stage (for pupils aged 4 to 5 years) and enter the more formal period of primary schooling in **Key Stage** 1 (for pupils aged 5 to 7 years) children begin to develop an interest in formal games with **rules**, two or more sides and explicit activities in which issues of fairness become increasingly significant. As they mature children begin to think more abstractly, being dependent on what they can envisage and work out in their minds, rather than relying on visual stimuli and physical contact with resources. Thus, whereas a 5-year-old boy may count on his fingers to work out an addition sum, an 8-year-old is likely to be able to calculate similar problems in his head without recourse to practical aids.

Adults responsible for young primary-age children take account of the different forms of play when organising and monitoring activities. For instance, *parallel play* describes a situation where pupils play side by side, but with little or no **interaction**. Teachers in the Foundation Stage are particularly alert to pupils who regularly prefer to play alone, as this separateness is more typical of pre-school children. A desire for isolation during play is perfectly normal, providing it is not excessive, as a balance of social and solitary play is necessary for all children. Pupils benefit from the social learning that is gained through sharing and cooperating with other children during *group play* and it may signal a problem if children insist on playing on their own for most or all of the time. Playing will normally involve conversations (real or imaginary), taking turns, organising sequences of events and sharing. Elements of *imaginary play* are also significant for older primary pupils engaged in producing spontaneous drama sequences and acting out contrived scenes.

Break times in primary schools are often referred to as 'playtime', during which time children are told to 'go and play'. This *enforced* form of play, with the uncertainties of climate and physical hazards, contradicts the notion that play should always be spontaneous, stress-free and valuable for learning. Unlike school playtimes, the time, place and location of the play that occurs outside school hours is normally chosen by the children and not by adults. Either way, regular opportunities to play are essential for children's development, as deprivation can result in maladjustment and personality defect in later years.

Further reading

Broadhead, P. (2004) *Early Years Play and Learning*, London: Routledge.
Casey, T. (2005) *Inclusive Play: Practical strategies for working with children aged 3 to 8*, London: Paul Chapman.
Clouder, C. and Rawson, M. (2003) *Waldorf Education*, Edinburgh: Floris Books.
Moyles, J. (ed.) (2005) *The Excellence of Play*, Maidenhead: Open University Press.
Orr, R. (2003) *My Right to Play*, Maidenhead: Open University Press.
Thomson, S. (2003) 'A well-equipped hamster cage: the rationalisation of primary school playtime', *Education 3–13*, 31, 2, pp. 54–9.

PROFESSIONALISM

Arguments about whether or not teaching is a profession, comparable with (say) doctors and lawyers, have raged for many years. Only a generation ago, secondary teachers were paid more than primary teachers in the belief that their superior subject knowledge justified the differential because it enhanced their professional status. Contrarily, new secondary teachers were not required to possess a qualified teacher certificate until 1971, some years after this stipulation applied to primary teachers. Since that time, all new members of the teaching profession are expected to have a minimum level of teaching ability, formally recognised by a teacher-training provider. The document *Qualifying to Teach* (DfES/TTA, 2002) stresses that teachers' professional **values** and practice include having high **expectations** of all pupils, respecting their social, cultural, linguistic, religious and ethnic backgrounds, being committed to raising educational standards and showing concern for their development as learners. The establishment of standards for qualified teacher status and what amounts to a national scheme for teacher training (in the UK) helps to safeguard overall competence. The academic content of courses and the use of research to support and enhance approved teaching methods have also been the subject of considerable attention, with close monitoring of primary teacher's subject knowledge, especially in the teaching of **literacy**, **numeracy** and IT. More recently, the increase in numbers of teaching **assistants** in primary schools and the arguments about their role as substitute or ancillary teachers has reignited a debate about what constitutes professional competence.

As professionals, teachers are bound by formal and implicit codes of ethics that specify how they are to fulfil their duties and obligations with respect to the education they provide. Being bound by the same code, and having similar levels of competence and training, helps to promote a sense of collegiality and consistency across the teaching profession. The existence of General Teaching Councils (GTCs), established through the Teaching and Higher Education Act (England and Wales) 1998, largely supersedes previous attempts to define professional behaviour. The GTC for Northern Ireland was established under the auspices of the Education (Northern Ireland) Order 1998. The newly established GTCs are modelled on the Scotland TC that has been in existence since 1965.

GTCs are statutory, self-regulating professional bodies for teachers. They seek to raise the quality of teaching by maintaining and promoting the highest standards of professional practice and conduct in the interests of teachers, pupils and the general public. It is a legal requirement for teachers with Qualified Teacher Status to be registered with the respective GTC. Trainee teachers and overseas teachers qualify for provisional registration. Although teaching councils monitor behaviour nationally, it is for school governors/board to determine initially whether a teacher's conduct is acceptable and adjudicate in cases where it appears to be unsatisfactory.

One of the functions of a GTC is to investigate and hear cases against registered teachers through its disciplinary committees. Even if teachers have not been convicted of an offence in court, inappropriate behaviour in and out of school may constitute unprofessional conduct or incompetence that indicates unfitness of character to be a registered teacher. Teachers can be reported to the GTC for offences as diverse as repeatedly failing to hand in planning and assessment files to the head teacher for monitoring; demonstrating overt insensitivity to children with special needs; or using inappropriate language in front of pupils and colleagues. Removal from the register is rare, other than in extreme circumstances. Teachers who are de-registered may ask for reinstatement after an appropriate length of time, though this request is not necessarily acceded to.

The establishment of a professional code of conduct not only takes into account factors such as level of expertise, knowledge and **skills** and minimum qualifications, but also behaviour. The need for an acceptable standard of behaviour is necessary because, in addition to their academic expertise, primary teachers act as models or examples to their pupils and local communities. In this regard, a teacher's attitude and demeanour is an important contributor; welcome attributes include being positive about life in general, avoiding the temptation to moan and giving due consideration to other people's ideas. Practical considerations for teachers necessitate arriving in good time for school, relating well to other members of staff, using their time productively during the day and earning a reputation as an effective practitioner. Codifying acceptable behaviour for members of the teaching profession involves transparent monitoring and appraisal by an external body such as the local authority to ensure consistency of practice and interpretation of legislation amongst its members.

To safeguard and enhance their professional knowledge, all practitioners are expected to take responsibility for their own **professional development**, keep up to date with significant education research and innovations in teaching, and understand their role in relation to agreed school policies and practices, including pastoral responsibilities, personal safety matters and bullying.

Further reading

Department for Education and Skills/TTA (2002) *Qualifying to Teach: Professional Standards for Qualified Teacher Status and Requirements for Initial Teacher Training*, Circular 02/02, London: TTA.

Gordon, P., Perkin, H., Sockett, H. and Hoyle, E. (1983) *Is Teaching a Profession?* Bedford Way Paper 15, London: University of London Institute of Education.

GTC web site: www.gtce.org.uk

Hargreaves, D. H. (1999) 'The knowledge-creating school', *British Journal of Educational Studies*, 47, pp. 122–44.

Hayes, D. (2001a) 'Professional status and an emerging culture of conformity amongst teachers in England', *Education 3–13*, 29, 1, pp. 43–9.

Hoyle, E. and John, P. (1995) *Professional Knowledge and Professional Practice*, London: Cassell.

Kirk, D. and MacDonald, D. (2001) 'Teacher voice and ownership of curriculum change', *Journal of Curriculum Studies*, 33, pp. 551–67.

Silcock, P. (2002) 'Under construction or facing demolition? Contrasting views on English teacher professionalism from across a professional association', *Teacher Development*, 6, 2, pp. 137–55.

Silcock, P. and Brundrett, M. (2002) *Achieving Competence, Success and Excellence in Teaching*, London: Routledge.

PROFESSIONAL DEVELOPMENT

The quality of teaching impacts upon the lives and welfare of thousands of pupils. As they gain experience, teachers are expected to enhance their professional knowledge, improve their classroom practice, learn new skills and increasingly contribute to the school's academic performance. One of the greatest challenges for teachers is that there is no universally agreed definition of a progressive pedagogy (science of the art of teaching) on which to base professional development, other than one that refers to pupil test scores.

The belief that it is possible to 'spot' a good teacher is deeply engrained in the profession; heads, **induction** tutors and governors quickly conclude whether a new teacher has a promising future. The influence of subjective opinions (as opposed to using set criteria) to assess a teacher's potential is relevant from the beginning of the training process. Thus, in determining whether candidates are suitable to begin training, interviewers have to make an initial assessment of their suitability as to whether the candidates have the academic and personal qualities to succeed. In particular, careful note is taken of whether the candidates will relate well to children and have the tenacity and temperament to cope with classroom life.

Teachers not only persevere to improve their competence through self-evaluation at the end of a **lesson** or series of lessons (**reflection** *on* action) but are constantly evaluating their practice during their teaching (reflection *in* action). Newly qualified teachers tend to use the **teaching approach** that they developed during training or modelled on an experienced teacher whom they admired. However, primary teachers change in many ways during the process of their careers as they gain promotion and encounter a range of pedagogic challenges. They become more experienced in the sense of having taught for a longer time, learning new **skills** and improving old ones. Teachers extend the reaches of their intellect, change the focus of their energies and learn how to survive the demands of school routines. Most teachers become more caring, wise and sanguine, though a few become discouraged and exhausted. Many take advantage of the internal promotion opportunities. A small number become head teachers. A feature of the UK in the early twenty-first century is that the number of teachers remaining in the classroom until retirement age has fallen and with it their accumulated wisdom and experience.

The concept of an evidence-based profession has become rooted in educational vocabulary and policy. The need for teachers to provide verifiable evidence that children have benefited directly from their teaching has been integral to advancement, so teachers have to be able to point to measurable aspects of pupil learning. The implementation of a pay 'threshold' scheme for internal promotion to advanced skills' teacher, intended to keep excellent practitioners in the classroom, has had mixed results. The vast majority of teachers applying for enhancement have been successful, casting doubt on the principle of advancement on the basis of excellence. There is considerable disagreement among practitioners as to whether going through the threshold makes any appreciable impact on the quality of their teaching. With the increased emphasis upon certification in society, many teachers undertake further study to acquire advanced diplomas and academic qualifications. The establishment of a National College for School Leadership (NCSL) for preparing and training aspiring subject leaders, deputy head teachers and head teachers is another indication that professional advancement is increasingly dependent on external verification.

Further reading

Bubb, S. (2004) *The Insider's Guide to Early Professional Development*, London: Routledge.

Clandinin, D. J. and Connelly, F. M. (1995) *Teachers' Professional Knowledge Landscape*, New York: TC Press.

Jackson, P. W. (1992a) *Untaught Lessons*, New York: Teachers College Press.

Jackson, P. W. (1992b) 'Helping teachers develop', in A. Hargreaves and M. G. Fullan (eds) *Understanding Teacher Development*, pp. 62–74, London: Cassell.

Neil, P. and Morgan, C. (2003) *Continuing Professional Development for Teachers*, London: Kogan Page.

PUNISHMENT

Despite every effort to ensure that pupils learn in a stable, supportive environment, situations inevitably arise from time to time when deliberate and wilful wrongdoing invites punishment through the use of a recognised sanction, such as withdrawing privileges. Some educators are uneasy with the use of the word punishment and many teachers feel that the need to punish a child says as much about their own failure to maintain order or motivate pupils as it does about the child's behaviour. Teachers normally give children a number of warnings before punitive action is taken (akin to receiving yellow cards in a sporting event before being sent from the field if the poor conduct continues), so pupils have opportunity to exercise self-constraint and redirect their efforts.

The use of a punishment assumes a teacher's correct interpretation of the circumstances under which the misdemeanour took place. Whereas a case of (say) direct rudeness or wilful disobedience is clearly the responsibility of the individual pupil, many conflict situations that involve several young children lead to claims, counter-claims, accusations and defensiveness when an adult intervenes. Consequently, the allocation of punishments has to take account of the **context** as well as the bare facts of the case. Adults in school have to be certain of where the responsibility for blame lies, as strong emotions are stirred in children when they are wrongly accused; yet they may not feel able or have the confidence to argue the case. Some children cry or protest vehemently at perceived injustice, but many of them suppress their feelings for fear of creating further problems or incurring the adult's wrath. For instance, it is understandable if children feel a sense of injustice if the teacher keeps in the whole class at playtime because of the naughty behaviour of a small number of children. Teachers have to be perceptive to the impact that their decisions have on pupils, allow for children to explain and to ask questions for clarification. All teachers are faced with the challenge of balancing sensitivity about children's feelings with decisiveness in curbing inappropriate behaviour.

The intentional use of force as a form of punishment was abolished in all maintained schools in 1986 and corporal punishment was terminated in independent schools in 1996 to be replaced by the Schools Standards Framework Act 1998 (operational from September 1999). No member of a school staff is entitled to administer a physical punishment, even if parents have said they are happy for it to happen. Any teacher who did so would be in breach not only of contract but of the Human Rights Act 1998. Corporal punishment includes not only the use of the cane, strap or slipper, but also slapping, rough handling, shaking, pinching, prodding, pulling children's hair, pushing, tying pupils up, taping their mouths and throwing missiles at or towards them. Although the use of force is sometimes required to deal with aggressive behaviour or protect a child from harm, it must be done with due regard to the circumstances. Teachers have to maintain a sense of proportion as to the amount of force to be used (if any) in situations where the safety of a pupil is deemed to be in jeopardy and use the minimum amount required such that the desired result is achieved.

Any teacher using physical force unreasonably against pupils may be liable to a civil action for assault and could also face disciplinary action from the employing authority and/or the school governors. The case would almost certainly be referred to the General Teaching Council (GTC). The types of force that might be justified and those that are not advisable to use are described in Circular 10/98 (DfEE 1998d). However, there is no legal definition of 'reasonable force', so it is difficult for adults to be sure where the boundaries of reasonableness lie and the degree of force that is legally acceptable, especially when the pupil's age, mental condition, disability and gender are taken into consideration. Teachers are not permitted to use threatening language at any time, regardless of the provocation.

Further reading

Department for Education and Employment (1998d) Circular 10/98, *Section 550A of the Education Act 1996: The use of force to control or restrain pupils*, Sudbury: DfEE Publications.

Goldstein, S. E., Tisak, M. S. and Brinker, S. R. (2003) 'Children's judgements about common classroom punishments', *Educational Research*, 45, 2, pp. 189–98.

Harrop, A. and Williams, T. (1992) 'Rewards and punishments in the primary school: pupils' perceptions and teachers' usage', *Educational Psychology*, 7, 4, pp. 211–15.

Weijers, I. (2000) 'Punishment and upbringing: considerations for an educative justification of punishment', *Journal of Moral Education*, 29, 1, pp. 61–73.

PUPIL LEARNING

Human learning is highly complex and not fully understood. Learning comes in a variety of forms, sometimes involving the intellect, sometimes the emotions, and sometimes both. Far from being a smooth and continuous process, it is a difficult concept to define; nevertheless, there is general agreement that the process benefits from well-informed and capable teaching. One explanation about learning that receives support from medical evidence is that different types of learning are associated with the right and left parts of the brain. The left part deals principally with language acquisition, sequences, analysis and number; it works to process information and responds best to structured and sequenced learning. The right part of the brain interprets images, looks for patterns, creates metaphors and strives to synthesise and consolidate information. Interplay between the two parts of the brain appears to be necessary for the development of deep understanding, creative expression and problem solving.

The education psychologist Jerome Bruner proposed three ways in which children learn: namely, through enactive, iconic and symbolic stages. The enactive stage is characterised by an active engagement in doing things. The iconic stage is characterised by children's use of images and pictures. The symbolic stage is one in which children can reason and think abstractly. Even in a single lesson it is sometimes necessary for children to pass through the enactive stage to explore a phenomenon before they can cope with the iconic or enactive stages. For instance, a class of 8-year-olds may require an opportunity to explore randomly the relationship between a series of numbers prior to being taught the mathematical rule that applies. Similarly, 10- and 11-year-olds may benefit from being given time to create sounds using a variety of musical instruments before receiving specific **instruction**. Active engagement assists children in their search for meaning, especially in understanding the meanings behind the symbols they later employ in their work, such as map symbols, mathematical nomenclature and figures of speech. Teachers have to decide how long to allow pupils to employ enactive (exploratory) and iconic (visual representations) strategies before expecting them to engage with an abstract task (without the support of learning aids).

Pupil learning that consists of **memory** without understanding has limited value. For example, children might be systematically taught to read words correctly, recite multiplication tables or chant a religious creed, but unless they grasp their meaning and significance the depth of learning remains shallow. Learning that is purely functional, such as knowing how to subtract two numbers, has limited usefulness unless it can be employed in a genuine life situation (such as shopping).

Learning can also be experiential, such as exploring a woodland copse and absorbing its sights, scents and sounds. Some forms of pupil learning relate to the acquisition of practical **skills**, such as the correct use of equipment, utilising technology or accessing resource books. Other types of learning involve understanding procedures and require practice in following a sequence, such as manipulating computer software. Yet other forms of learning relate to problem solving, such as in design and technology, that requires time for ideas to be explored and practically put to use.

Children learn best when they are given opportunity to use a range of tactile senses, visual stimuli, careful listening, **enquiry**-based activities, conversation and paper and pencil exercises, supported by teacher explanation and reinforced through individual or group activities. Innovative and imaginative learners learn particularly effectively when they have the opportunity to use the full range of their senses and ask questions about why things happen. Learners that are more analytical tend to process information by studying a range of possibilities closely, thinking deeply and reflecting on the issues involved, before developing their own ideas and comparing them with what they observe happening. Pragmatic learners first speculate and make suggestions before finding out if their ideas work in practice, then adjust their ideas accordingly. Dynamic learners learn best when they have a chance to experiment with ways in which they can use their present level of information and surmise about other possibilities. Teachers have to take account of these different learning preferences when they plan **lessons**, such that there is sufficient freedom to satisfy the innovative pupil, sufficient intellectual challenge to satisfy the analytical pupil, sufficient opportunity for practice to satisfy the pragmatic pupil and sufficient investigation to satisfy the inquisitive pupil. Teachers also have to take account of the needs of children with **special educational needs** (SEN) and those for whom English is not the primary tongue.

Whatever **teaching approach** is employed by teachers, the most productive learning consists of absorbing facts, understanding principles and being able to use knowledge in a practical **context**. All children need to be given the opportunity to transfer what they have learned to new situations; this is often the acid test for whether or not deep learning has been achieved. Even if all the group or class appear to have grasped the principles and ideas, some children will retain what they have learned; others will require regular reminding and updating. However, the more that children can see the relevance and usefulness of their learning, the more likely it is that they will engage enthusiastically with the lesson content and retain what they need to know.

An important element of a teacher's role is to ascertain the extent and thoroughness of children's learning. The influential Russian psychologist Lev Vygotsky (1896–1934) maintained that a child follows the adult's example and, after initially receiving a lot of help, advice and support, gradually develops an ability to do the task or activity without help or assistance (e.g. Vygotsky 1978). His most famous work, *Thought and Language*, published shortly after his death, developed for the first time a theory of language development that described the development of language and logical thinking in young children in the course of their interactions with adults and the world around them; one of his tenets is that thought and language is inextricably linked. Vygotsky famously referred to the difference between what children can achieve with help from a more knowledgeable teacher (adult or child) and what they can do without guidance as the 'zone of proximal development' (ZPD). The active intervention and support of adults in children's learning as they try to narrow the ZPD is equivalent to scaffolding placed around a house as it is constructed. As a child grasps the concept and gains the necessary understanding, the amount of scaffolding can be reduced. Once the child is in a position to progress independently the scaffolding is removed completely. Consequently, it is vital that teachers are aware of children's existing knowledge and understanding and able to identify their limitations. Teachers gain this information when they get alongside children, converse with them, ask questions, allow them to respond, offer advice and explanation, and discuss the next steps in the learning process.

Pupils learn more productively when teachers adopt a positive attitude towards them and acknowledge that in searching for creative solutions there will be setbacks and need to be times of consolidation through repeated practice. All children benefit from being given an opportunity to discuss what they are doing and where it fits into their present understanding, as regardless of how carefully presented and interesting teachers make the lesson material, little learning of note takes place unless pupils engage mentally with the subject matter and make sense of things for themselves. Pupils will often complete their work simply because they are given it to do by a teacher; but the mere completion of tasks to occupy the space of a lesson does not ensure thorough learning has occurred.

Effective learning is also influenced by motivation and self-image. Some children are capable of finishing work and gaining personal satisfaction from it, regardless of the tick or comment at the bottom of the page; the majority, however, are strongly influenced by adult approval and thrive on praise. Learning is enhanced when children work cooperatively and show a willingness to persevere and concentrate. The prevailing norms and expectations of the school and classroom are significant in promoting or inhibiting effective learning.

Not all learning leads to academic outcomes. Social learning is essential if children are to understand the significance and application of empathy, sympathy and the courage of their convictions. Both as part of the formal **citizenship curriculum** and informally through regular interaction, teachers encourage pupil **collaboration** and help children to learn a variety of strategies that can be applied to interpersonal relationships and other social situations.

Further reading

Bentham, S. (2004) 'Learning and teaching styles', in E. C. Wragg (ed.) *Teaching and Learning*, pp. 72–86, London: Routledge.

General Teaching Council for England (2003) *Social interaction as a means of constructing learning: The impact of Lev Vygotsky's ideas on teaching and learning*. On-line. Available: http://www.gtce.org.uk/research/vygotskyhome. asp (accessed April 2005).

Heylighen, F. (1993) 'Epistemology: introduction', in F. Heylighen, C. Joslyn and V. Turchin (eds) *Principia Cybernetica Web* (Principia Cybernetica, Brussels). On-line. Available: http://pespmc1.vub.ac.be/REFERPCP.html (accessed May 2005).

Howe, M. J. A. (1999) *A Teacher's Guide to the Psychology of Learning*, 2nd edn, Oxford: Blackwell.

MacGilchrist, B. (2003) 'Primary learners of the future', *Education 3–13*, 31, 3, pp. 58–65.

Smith, A. (1996) *Accelerated Learning in the Classroom*, Stafford: Network Educational Press.

Vygotsky, L. S. (1978) *Mind in Society: The development of higher psychological processes*, Cambridge, MA: Harvard University Press.

Wallace, B. (2002) 'Don't work harder, work smarter', in B. Wallace and R. Bentley (eds) *Teaching Thinking Skills Across the Middle Years*, pp. 1–24, London: David Fulton/National Association for Able Children in Education.

PUPIL MOTIVATION

Children are not born with a particular view of themselves or their level of self-worth; it is something that they develop over the years, shaped through their relationships with family and friends and their wider social experiences. Although teachers cannot alter the way that children in their class have been or are treated by adults outside school, they make a significant contribution to their well-being by concentrating their efforts in six areas. First, finding out what children already know and understand. This process necessitates talking to the children, listening to what they say, checking previous school records, and observing how they approach tasks and use their existing **knowledge** and understanding. Second, modelling a positive attitude towards learning by celebrating success, commiserating with failure, being enthusiastic about discovering new facts, specifying alternatives, and offering help and guidance whenever possible. Third, giving close personal attention to children who are struggling, restless or bored, remembering that most disaffection is caused by the perceived irrelevance of the work or fear of failure. Fourth, involving children in learning by discussing the lesson purpose, establishing manageable learning targets and inviting them to comment on the quality of their work and effort. Fifth, acknowledging pupils' points of view and feelings. Finally, emphasising that success is attainable and worth cherishing.

Although primary-aged children generally respond well to the enticement of external **rewards** (extrinsic motivation) teachers have to maintain a balance between these incentives and a child's inner desire to do well (intrinsic motivation). It is commonly the case that pupils make an instinctive assessment early in the lesson about whether the content is interesting and respond accordingly. Although most children comply with the teacher's instructions without offering outward dissent, the prevalence of mundane tasks and activities limits their desire to strive for success. Effective teachers do not merely pass on information to their pupils, however skilfully, but try to instil a thirst for learning in them by making the lesson content appealing.

Studies suggest that the extent of children's satisfaction with their education experience decreases with age and drops considerably when they reach secondary school. Thus, a large majority of primary pupils think that school is a positive experience; this contrasts with about one-quarter in secondary schools who feel similarly enthusiastic. When measuring pupils' views about the relevance of what they learn and retain while in school, the motivation gap between the primary and secondary phases is even more pronounced. As pupils who retain a sense of curiosity and are at ease about their lives in school are more likely to be strongly motivated, teachers and assistants have a significant responsibility to create a dynamic learning environment in which children can prosper and enjoy what they are doing. In top-performing primary schools there is a serious effort to achieve academic success without sacrificing an investigative spirit and spontaneity.

A number of pupils need to be given a stronger sense of their own worth, as some children view themselves as powerless and gradually adopt an attitude of helplessness. Adults in school help such children to gain a stronger sense of self-worth and empowerment by giving them opportunities to assume positions of trust and responsibility. Motivation is not only important for academic work but also in preparing children to cope with the demands of life when they move on from primary school.

Further reading

Cullingford, C. (2002) *The Best Years of their Lives? Pupils' Experiences of School*, London: Kogan Page.

Hayes, D. (2003) *A Student Teacher's Guide to Primary School Placement*, London: RoutledgeFalmer.

Woods, P. (1990) *The Happiest Days?* London: Falmer, introduction and chapter 1.

QUESTIONING

The use of questioning in teaching as a means of enhancing children's learning is widely used by teachers in whole-class and large group situations. Questioning serves five broad purposes. First, it offers teachers an opportunity to engage directly with pupils and establish a positive rapport with them. Second, it stimulates pupils to think hard by posing a variety of questions that elicit considered responses from them. Third, on the basis of their answers it gives teachers the opportunity to assess the depth of understanding possessed by pupils. Fourth, it helps children to learn from others as they listen to what is said and adjust or evaluate their own understanding accordingly. Fifth, it allows teachers to identify areas of pupil misunderstanding for clarification or remedial action. Questioning also has the potential to serve wider purposes. The effective use of questions encourages children to ponder and reflect on issues and problems as a means of aiding their conceptual development, opening up fresh areas of the topic for consideration and thereby stimulating pupil initiative, **creativity** and innovation.

Questions can be of low cognitive level designed to funnel pupils' responses towards the desired answer rather than promoting higher levels of **interaction** and cognitive engagement. Teachers sometimes 'shoot' a question from pupil to pupil until a child answers correctly, but many children need to consider their answers and time has to be allowed for the mental processing to take place, which in practice necessitates short pauses. The wait time increases as pupils grapple with 'higher-order' questions that make children think more deeply and consider carefully what they say.

Questions that are principally intended to involve children in the-lesson rather than extend learning are likely to be ones that every child can answer and have only one correct answer (a 'closed' question), sometimes asked orally and sometimes carried out through formal written means (a 'test'). Questions that encourage children to think deeply tend to be open ended (i.e. inviting a variety of possible responses) and invite speculation, with supplementary questions to extend understanding. Questions to open fresh insights tend to be of the 'just imagine if' or 'suppose that' type, incorporating the use of allegory, stories and notable events to fascinate the children. Questions to stimulate initiative invite pupils to solve problems in mathematics, and to design, construct and investigate in craft, science or design technology.

A **learning climate** of which questioning is an integral part allows children time to grapple with complex issues and to make genuine errors while they do so. To promote this kind of climate, the best teachers share their curiosities with pupils and reveal their doubts when they are unsure of an answer. They stimulate pupil interest by bringing into school unusual items and fascinating books that foster a sense of mystery and wonder, and encourage children to do the same. As a way to promote higher self-esteem and recognition, some teachers urge older primary children with knowledge about a hobby or pastime to act as experts among their peers by being in the 'hot-seat': talking to the class about their interest and handling questions that are put to them.

When dealing with a wide **ability** range, teachers find that it is preferable to start with more straightforward questions as a means of involving all pupils, rather than beginning with conceptually challenging ones that limit the number of children that can participate. However, questions that are too simple may be perceived by the children as babyish, create a lacklustre atmosphere and even invite ridicule. The excessive uses of factual (right or wrong) questions that end abruptly and have no connection with the work that follows are educationally limiting. Teachers of young children have to be cautious about using too many rhetorical questions, especially when dealing with young children, who tend to offer verbal responses when the teacher is merely thinking out loud.

As with all verbal exchanges, the use of inappropriate vocabulary – whether too advanced, too vague or too specialised – confuses and puzzles children. A common failing among inexperienced teachers is to express questions poorly; include subsidiary questions within the main question; and the use of double negatives. More experienced teachers avoid framing questions in a way that alarms pupils; instead, they employ a bright tone of voice and open **body language** to reassure the children.

Inexperienced teachers sometimes use a question-and-answer approach as a substitute for direct teaching when it would be better to *tell* the children rather than spend time asking large numbers of undemanding questions to tease out the answers. Telling children facts rather than asking questions is enlivened by the use of pictures, short poems, rhymes, spontaneous role play and employment of computer technology to illustrate and clarify points. In making decisions about the balance between 'ask them' and 'tell them', teachers have to take account of the fact that although questions are an important teaching tool, they are more akin to grains of pepper on a meal than lashings of gravy, so fewer and better questions are preferable to perfunctory ones.

For children to answer questions successfully, they need rapid access to what they already know and the confidence to risk being incorrect. However, a child who appears unable to answer may have stored the **knowledge** away and, in the pressure of the moment, been unable to draw it out from **memory** or may be weighing up other options rather than offering a predictable response. Teachers have to be alert to the fact that a pupil who is always enthusiastic about answering questions is not necessarily more able or intelligent than a timid child who is reticent about offering a response.

Further reading

Bullock, K., Stables, A. and Sahin, C. (2002) 'Teachers' beliefs and practices in relation to their beliefs about questioning at key stage 2', *Educational Studies*, 28, 4, pp. 371–84.

Mroz, M. and Baumfield, V. (2002) 'Investigating pupils' questions in the primary classroom', *Educational Research*, 44, 2, pp. 129–40.

Petty, G. (2004) *Teaching Today*, 3rd edn, Cheltenham: Stanley Thornes, chapter 14.

Wragg, E. C. and Brown, G. (2001) *Questioning in the Primary School*, London: Routledge.

READING

Reading is a multifaceted process involving word recognition, comprehension and fluency, as well as personal motivation. It is the foundational skill for all school-based learning. About 5% of pupils learn to read effortlessly and one-quarter learns to read without any great difficulty when they are given formal **instruction**. There are four main approaches to reading. (1) The 'look and say' method, where children learn to recognise whole words or sentences rather than individual letter sounds. (2) **Phonics**, which relies on children learning the names of the letters of the alphabet and the sounds they make, then blending two letters together to make simple words, followed by three letters, four letters, and so on. (3) An 'experiential' approach using the child's own words to help him or her read. The child provides a word or sentence for the adult to write down and in due course writes the words independently and reads them aloud. (4) The 'context' method that involves using books selected by children in the belief that they will be more enthusiastic about reading a relevant text that interests them. Some books are specially written to support this method of learning, consisting of a longer sentence on one side of the page for the adult and one or more words on the opposite page for the child.

Although there is no single reading programme that meets all the learning needs of pupils, the most effective ones focus on the mastery of word recognition but also on comprehension, the former without the latter resulting in what is described as 'barking at print'. Teachers in school regularly share books with children, including so-called Big Books (physically big, with large print so that a group of pupils can see to read in unison), introduce and explain reading strategies, refer to letters of the alphabet and sounds by name and generally establish a **literacy**-rich environment. Teachers also promote pupil interest by reading their favourite stories, using language games and play activities, and encouraging children to see links between writing and reading.

Despite the fact that reading and writing abilities continue to develop throughout life, the most important period for literacy development is during the early **childhood** years from birth to 8 years, with regular exposure to books and stories being a crucial factor in learning to read. Parents can prepare their children to read by spending time with them, talking to them about interesting things in the world, telling and reading stories to them, and asking and answering their questions. As a result, by the time most children start the reception year at age 5 years they will have learned a lot about spoken and written forms of language; played, explored and made discoveries at home and in other settings; and watched, listened to and interacted with adults and other children.

Initial reading instruction involves helping children to understand meanings from print and giving them frequent opportunities to read simple words and be exposed to spelling–sound relationships. Children also need to learn about the structure of the alphabetic writing system and understand the structure of spoken words. Progress depends on children having a working understanding of how sounds are represented alphabetically and sufficient practice in reading a range of texts. They need gradually to extend their vocabulary, self-check their comprehension of a passage and possess strategies to correct mistakes, as well as a desire to read for a variety of purposes (information, pleasure, instructions).

The ability to read is acquired without undue difficulty by children who have normal or above-average language **skills** and have had experiences in early childhood that fostered their motivation and provided exposure to a variety of forms of literature. However, over one-half of children face more considerable challenges in learning to read; for a minority of pupils reading is one of the most difficult tasks they will have to master throughout their schooling. Many pupils who are poor readers when they first attend primary school are likely to be struggling three or four years later; most of these pupils will find advanced reading skills difficult and therefore be disadvantaged when they move into the top of the primary school. The majority of poor readers are capable of increasing their reading skills to average levels through intervention programmes that combine knowledge of phonics, fluency development and reading comprehension strategies.

Further reading

Graham, J. and Kelly, A. (2000) *Reading Under Control*, London: David Fulton.

Gregory, E. (1996) *Making Sense of a New World: Learning to read in a second language*, London: Paul Chapman.

Nation, K. and Snowling, M. J. (2004) 'Beyond phonological skills: broader language skills contribute to the development of reading', *Journal of Research in Reading*, 27, 4, pp. 342–56.

Poskiparta, E. (2003) 'Motivational–emotional vulnerability and difficulties in learning to read and spell', *British Journal of Educational Psychology*, 73, 2, pp. 187–206.

Stainthorp, R. and Hughes, D. (2004) 'What happens to precocious readers' performance by the age of eleven?', *Journal of Research in Reading*, 27, 4, pp. 357–72.

RECORDING

Formal records of pupil progress in the form of marks, grades and indications of curriculum coverage and attainment are maintained by teachers to aid **lesson planning** and assist them in transmitting information to parents, the next teacher and providing data for secondary school colleagues. Assessments of progress are carried out in one or more of six ways. (1) Asking specific questions and noting the children's responses to them. (2) Monitoring the way that children undertake their regular work. (3) Talking individually to children about their work (conferencing). (4) Giving groups of children problems or investigations to solve collaboratively. (5) Marking/grading work completed in class. (6) Setting specific tests/tasks under formal conditions. However, it tends to be data from the last two categories that are recorded and teachers are faced with decisions about precisely what should be written down and in what detail. Managing elaborate recording systems and storing large amounts of material is time consuming and teachers have to be careful that the effort they expend is not at the expense of lesson preparation and other responsibilities.

Records about children are confidential and disclosure of information to anyone other than a colleague or the parent/guardian is not permitted. Generally, if the information is factual (e.g. spelling test scores), there is less need for privacy than if a teacher writes a subjective view of a child's personality or behaviour. A written record of these more intimate details is usually only necessary when a child is being formally monitored because of concerns about his or her conduct or progress. Storage and security of sensitive records is handled through the school's central administrative system.

Parents are interested in their children's social as well as academic progress. This balance of interests is particularly well expressed through the Foundation Curriculum, for children aged 4 to 5 years, that attends to the emotional well-being of children, their attitude and disposition to learning, socialising, concentration and persistence, as well as the more obviously academic **achievements**. Parents and teachers value qualities such as team spirit, perseverance, kindness and patience, viewing them as essential attributes if children are to attain to their full potential and eventually become thoughtful, responsible adults. However, these personal characteristics are much more difficult to record than measurable attainment and teachers have to ensure that their disposition towards individual pupils (favourable or otherwise) does not cause them to be biased in the way they express their views.

Further reading

Cavendish, S. and Underwood, J. (1997) 'Keeping track: observing, assessing and recording in the learning relationship', in N. Kitson and R. Merry (eds) *Teaching in the Primary School*, pp. 85–101, London: Routledge.

Ditchfield, C. (2004) 'Assessment, recording and reporting on children's work', in K. Jacques and R. Hyland (eds) *Professional Studies: Primary phase*, pp. 51–62, Exeter: Learning Matters.

Wachter, J. C. (1999) *Sweating the Small Stuff*, London: Sage/Corwin Press.

REFLECTION

It is generally acknowledged that the concept of reflection originated with Dewey (1933), when he studied the actions involved in learning new **skills**. Dewey concluded that there are two basic sorts of actions, the first type being routine action, governed by routine, habit or **expectations**; the second type being reflective action, involving flexibility and self-appraisal, influenced by the social conditions. Dewey's original publication in 1910, *How We think*, made a unique impact on education. He wrote this book for teachers and the first edition became the 'Bible' of progressively minded educators. In recent years in the UK, Andrew Pollard and Sarah Tann (1987) popularised the concept of teacher reflection through their much acclaimed publication *The reflective practitioner*, suggesting that there are four characteristics of reflective teaching. The first characteristic implies an active concern with the aims and consequences of an action, as well as with means and technical efficiency. The second characteristic combines implementation skills with attitudes of open-mindedness, responsibility and wholeheartedness. The third characteristic is a cyclical or spiralling process, in which teachers continually monitor, evaluate and revise their own practice on the basis of what they perceive to be its strengths and shortcomings. The final characteristic of reflective teaching is based on teacher judgement, partly by self-reflection and partly by insights extracted from other areas of education. Despite the fact that 'reflection' is normally used as a noun (the reflection) it can also be viewed in the form of an adverbial clause (i.e. behaving reflectively). That is, an intelligent consideration of existing practice should be a continuous process (reflecting *during* practice) as well as a later event (reflecting *on* practice). Schon (1983) famously referred to this distinction as reflection *in* action and reflection *on* action.

The principal benefit attached to reflecting during and on practice is that it is a contributing factor towards teaching effectiveness. It is also an antidote to an instrumental (clinical/technicist) view of improvement that is characterised by the systematic enhancement of individual teaching skills, an approach well represented in the pages of competence checklists currently used in schools and teacher-training institutions. The process of reflection acknowledges that it is important for teachers to think hard about their work and exercise professional judgement about classroom practice, rather than meekly complying with externally promoted priorities.

The debate about **effectiveness** of teaching is sometimes represented as a choice between pragmatism and reflective practice. Thus, pragmatists argue that the only serious consideration is what works in the classroom when measured against formal criteria (such as those used during school **inspections**), while exponents of reflective practice argue that teachers need to engage thoughtfully with issues. However, this dichotomy is unhelpful, as the most effective practitioners are able to employ an itemised list of separate skills and competencies to evaluate practice, yet still maintain a reflectively critical and robust approach to their work. Teachers may improve in implementing a national strategy or new initiative but be hindered in reaching their potential if they are not given opportunity to think, comment, challenge, negotiate and exercise professional autonomy.

The situation for trainee teachers is particularly challenging in that in each school placement situation they need to identify and implement strategies, routines and ways of doing things that are acceptable in the specific school, rather than make their own unfettered decisions about priorities. Trainees are suspicious of vague ideas about 'being reflective', which, though useful as a guide for discussion about the job of teaching, do not help them to find ways of surviving and prospering in the classroom. Furthermore, inexperienced teachers do not always have the confidence to analyse teaching situations critically, in the belief that more experienced and qualified colleagues on the staff know what is best. While it is important for trainee teachers to replicate the good practice that they observe in other teachers, an unthinking acceptance of what they observe and subsequent attempt to reproduce the method or technique in their own teaching do not encourage them to adapt the method for a different teaching purpose.

Pupils also need time to reflect. Opportunities to pause for the purpose of inculcating a sense of wonder in children and addressing challenging issues have, in some schools, been superseded by routine and repetition, often in the form of tedious worksheets. Primary teachers can also be tempted to tell the children what they ought to know instead of allowing them opportunities to enquire, **play** and investigate; or to prescribe learning so closely that curiosity, the urge to ask questions and scrutinise evidence are diminished. The end result of a regulated **curriculum** and objectives-driven **lessons**, policed through national **testing**, may be a generation of children that feel disengaged from learning and fail to see its relevance for their lives.

Further reading

Chown, A. (1994) 'Beyond competence?', *British Journal of In-service Education*, 20, 2, pp. 161–80.
Dewey, J. (1933) *How We Think*, New York: D. C. Heath.
Ghaye, A. and Ghaye, K. (2004) *Teaching and Learning Through Critical Reflective Practice*, London: David Fulton.
Pollard, A. (2005) *Reflective Teaching*, 2nd edn, London: Continuum, chapter 1.
Pollard, A. and Tann, S. (1987) *Reflective Teaching in the Primary School*, London: Cassell.
Schon, D. A. (1983) How Professionals Think in Action, New York: Basic Books.
Zeichner, K. M. and Liston, D. P. (1996) *Reflective Teaching: an introduction*, Mahwah: Erlbaum Associates.

REPORTING

Reporting pupil progress in written or verbal form is a key issue for primary educators. It is often mistakenly believed that reporting is principally for the benefit of parents when, in fact, the main recipients are the pupils, who require **feedback** from teachers about their progress so that they can feel involved in developing strategies to build upon their strengths and combat their weaknesses. Reporting to pupils is therefore an essential element of the formative side of **assessment**, providing them with information that gives an indication of the work quality and ways to improve it. Reporting to pupils about their achievements is best carried out immediately, with the child present. Younger children are not always able to grasp the implications of adult comments, so some teachers use visual aids, such as stickers or stars to reinforce approval.

All teachers are required to provide a report on pupils' progress on at least one occasion per year. The process of reporting is principally by means of a written set of comments sent directly to the parents or guardians and through an organised face-to-face meeting with them to discuss the children's attainment. With the advent of national tests and levels of pupil attainment in English and mathematics, parental interest in scores and grades has been heightened. Whereas at one time it was adequate to inform parents about progress in general terms (excellent/good/satisfactory etc.), quantifiable measures are now of considerable significance, accentuating differences in attainment between children. Nevertheless, parents are also interested in the child's social development, **friendship** patterns and attitude towards learning. The best reporting systems provide up-to-date and accurate information so as to give conscientious parents a clear idea about the assistance that their children might benefit from at home. Primary school teachers have to strike a balance between providing sufficient information to satisfy the curiosity and 'need to know' of parents and overloading them with detail.

Accurate **recording** and reporting pupil progress is also important for the teacher who will next teach the class and who will be interested in receiving information about the children's academic achievements so that the teacher can plan and prepare appropriate work for them. However, some teachers pay limited attention to the reports that they receive from the previous teacher, preferring to carry out their own informal assessments on which to make judgements as the new school year unfolds. On transfer to secondary education, the reporting procedures must be sufficiently rigorous to assist the receiving teachers in allocating pupils to the most appropriate group or ability set.

Further reading

Advisory Centre for Education (1999) *The communicating school: Reaching parents through the annual report, school prospectus, pupil reports and more*, London: Advisory Centre for Education.

Headington, R. (2000) *Monitoring, Assessment, Recording, Reporting and Accountability*, 2nd edn, London: David Fulton, chapter 5.

REWARDS

The concept of rewards is deeply embedded in pupils and adults working in primary schools and its use is rooted in a belief that behaviour can be altered through the use of external stimuli. Thus, the adult requests a response from pupils by asking a question or requesting the completion of a piece of work, children respond to the adult's satisfaction (by giving a correct answer or completing the task) and the adult then rewards the child by offering praise, a tick on a page, a star on a chart, etc. The teacher may decide to reward successful and hardworking pupils by permitting them to do something more pleasurable (such as choosing a game to play, selecting a book, being first in the queue). Consequently, pupils become dependent on pleasing an adult in order to gain favour and satisfaction, and the cycle of events continues. The potential limitation to this approach is that over time children view success largely in terms of pleasing the teacher rather than satisfying themselves.

In an important study, two education psychologists, Harrop and Williams (1992) carried out a study into reward and **punishment** in the primary school and found that primary pupils' views about suitable rewards were different from those of teachers. Out of ten options, teachers selected 'being praised in front of other pupils' (which the children placed seventh), giving merit or house points (which the children placed ninth) and mentioned in **assembly** (which the children placed fifth) as the top three incentives. By contrast, pupils' top three options were 'parents being informed about good behaviour' (which teachers placed eighth), good written comments on work (which teachers placed fourth) and good marks (which teachers placed ninth). Harrop and Williams' study showed that whereas teachers tend to believe that adult approval *within* school, such as public praise and merit points, constitutes the most powerful reward, children tend to see the greatest rewards in terms of adult approval *outside* school (notably, parental satisfaction). A similar pattern emerged when teachers' and pupils' views about the most effective punishments were compared. Whereas pupils ranked parents being informed, being prevented from going on a school trip and being sent to see the head teacher as the three most powerful sanctions, teachers selected being told off publicly, informing parents and being told off in private as the top three. The most significant contrast between teachers' and pupils' views about punishment concerned the significance of school trips, which pupils ranked second and teachers placed ninth.

Incentives and rewards place pupils into a relatively passive role. Too much incentive reduces the internal drive to achieve self-satisfaction; too little incentive creates a staid **learning climate**. The most effective teachers first encourage children to be proud of their

175

achievements and then affirm the quality of their success through the use of external rewards. A common practice is for the teacher's approval for an individual piece of work to contribute towards a whole-group or whole-class reward.

The rewards that teachers and assistants most value are firmly rooted in successful classroom practice and the knowledge that they have contributed towards the academic and social development of pupils. The sight of happy and contented children enjoying their school work and getting on well with their peers provides the most powerful incentive for everyone associated with primary education.

Further reading

Harrop, A. and Williams, T. (1992) 'Rewards and punishments in the primary school: pupils' perceptions and teachers' usage', *Educational Psychology*, 7, 4, pp. 211–15.

Marshall, M. (2001) *Discipline without stress, punishments or rewards: How teachers and parents promote responsibility and learning*, Los Alamitos, CA: Piper Press.

RITE OF PASSAGE

The rite of passage model is posited on the principle that the possession of satisfactory teaching ability is not sufficient to guarantee new teachers an acceptance into the social fabric of school life. They also need to respond appropriately to the expectations of personal behaviour demanded by existing cultural norms, such that all new personnel are required to demonstrate a willingness to learn about the procedures and priorities that characterise the school and be ready to contribute to the shared practices. The attitude and behaviour of trainees and new teachers after their arrival is noted and evaluated by the indigenous staff, especially in primary schools, which are intimate working environments and where agreed conduct and staff relationships are essential to maintain harmony.

Trainee teachers have to face many of the challenges encountered by qualified staff, but have less influence upon determining priorities for classroom practice than newly appointed qualified teachers. Trainees also have to grapple with the emotionally exhausting task of being encultured into new school settings, in which they learn to behave as a staff member and deal acceptably with children in the classroom. Successful negotiation of this rite of passage relies both on the trainee's own attitude and on the decisions that are made by tutors and host teachers, which will vary with circumstances. Consequently, the ease with which trainee teachers are able to negotiate their rite of passage depends partly on the way they recognise and respond to the school's priorities and partly on the host teachers' capacity and willingness to assist them in the process. Some trainee teachers unintentionally upset their hosts by making ill-advised comments or damaging someone's feelings or being insensitive to the school's prevailing ethos. Every new teacher has to persevere, stay positive and accept that colleagues have enough concerns of their own than to spend all their time supporting novices.

In a landmark study about the rite of passage, Eisenhart *et al.* (1991) argue that to be accepted by the existing staff, new teachers have to pass through at least three stages, referred to as separation, transition and incorporation. Trainee teachers and new members of staff have to lose their grip on previous cultural norms, grapple with the requirements of the new situation during a transitional 'adjusting' period and finally become assimilated into the new culture. There are a number of contextual factors that affect the process of being encultured. First, the effect of existing practices that are taken for granted by the existing staff but are largely unknown by newcomers. Second, the different personal factors reflected in the images that new teachers have of themselves and their beliefs about teaching. Third, the methods and strategies used in teaching. Fourth, the quality of mentoring transmitted through coaching, discussion and the provision of emotional support. With so many diverse factors to negotiate, it is not surprising that trainee teachers on placement require a length of time to acclimatise to the prevailing school climate before they can make significant headway in their teaching.

Training providers (such as university faculties of education) make a significant contribution in preparing trainee teachers to demonstrate their enthusiasm, courtesy and dependability, and sharpening their instructional competence; however, it is the host teachers that offer the most informed advice about how trainees can best adjust to the new school setting. As a result, negotiating their rite of passage depends on how well the trainee teachers grasp what is important to the existing staff and respond accordingly. Trainee teachers may settle with ease into one school placement yet struggle in another, depending on their willingness and capacity to accommodate the way things are done there and respond in a way that is seen as appropriate.

Newly qualified teachers (NQTs) are allocated an **induction** tutor from among the staff to provide guidance and advice during the crucial first year of teaching. Experienced teachers that transfer from another primary school after a successful job interview are faced with a similar time of adjustment as they gradually absorb the school's priorities and settle into the school community. However, they have already been thoroughly inculcated into familiar primary school practices and as a result the rite of passage is considerably eased.

Further reading

Bubb, S. (2003) *The Insider's Guide for New Teachers*, London: Kogan Page.

Campbell, A. and Kane, I. (1998) *School-Based Teacher Education: Telling Tales from a Fictional Primary School*, London: David Fulton.

Eisenhart, M., Behm, L. and Romagno, L. (1991) 'Learning to teach: developing expertise or rite of passage?', *Journal of Education for Teaching*, 17, 1, pp. 51–71.

Hayes, D. (2003) *A Student Teacher's Guide to Primary School Placement*, London: RoutledgeFalmer, chapters 3, 4 and 5.

RULES

Every primary educator wants to work in an orderly environment that provides for the welfare and safety of all pupils. Although there is a consensus that a teacher's main goal is to educate and not to punish, when the **behaviour** of a child comes into conflict with the rights of other pupils, corrective action is necessary for the benefit of the individuals concerned. Accordingly, pupils are governed by the policies and regulations set out in a school's code of conduct and discipline procedures. Parents are also encouraged to become familiar with the school system, to be supportive of its aims and reflect them in their daily **communication** with their children and others in the community.

Rules are statements that translate principles about appropriate conduct and behaviour into practice. Good rules can be understood by pupils and adults and provide a shared understanding of what is permissible and what is proscribed. Most schools develop a set of rules that apply to all pupils, regardless of where they are on the premises. Individual teachers establish additional rules that are specific to the classroom in which the children spend the majority of their time, often drawn up after discussion with them. Additional rules cover conduct on educational visits and other trips outside the school grounds, with particular reference to **health and safety** issues. Rules can be expressed in terms of what children are not allowed to do; however, the most influential ones are expressed in terms of what *should* be done and the type of behaviour and conduct that is expected. For instance, a rule that states 'walk along the corridor' is considered more effective than one that states 'do not run along the corridor'.

The problem with strictly applied rules and accompanying sanctions is that they fail to take account of specific circumstances. Thus, a normally placid child who throws a tantrum and bursts into tears requires a different response from the miscreant who tries to manipulate a situation by contrived fits of temper and exaggerated crying. Experienced teachers regularly discuss and clarify with children the importance and implications of self-control and do not allow themselves to be emotionally blackmailed by defiant or devious pupils.

The renowned primary educator Ted Wragg notes that school life without any rules would be chaotic and dangerous. He draws attention to the breadth of rules that commonly govern school life and categorises them under nine headings: movement, talking, work-related, presentation, safety, space, materials, social behaviour, clothing/ appearance. Wragg also argues that rules should not be viewed separately from *relationships* because the question of rules is closely bound up with, but also distinct from, that of interpersonal issues. He also argues that the relationship between two or more people is to some extent affected by the rule conventions under which it is operating.

Many schools use a system to reward positive behaviour, by which well-behaved children are allowed a period of free-choice activities during Friday (sometimes referred to as 'golden time'). Unacceptable behaviour that does not improve after an initial warning by an adult may result in the pupil staying inside during the break. In more severe cases children may lose golden time and spend the time discussing with an adult what they did wrong and setting themselves targets for improving their behaviour. A continued infraction of the rules may mean that the child's parents are contacted and asked to come into school to discuss the situation with the class teacher or head teacher and initiate an agreed plan of action to remedy the situation.

Further reading

Pollard, A. (2005) *Reflective Teaching*, 2nd edn, London: Continuum, chapter 6.

Rogers, B. (1998) *You Know the Fair Rule*, London: Pitman.

Wragg, E. C. (2004) 'The two Rs: rules and relationships', in E. C. Wragg (ed.) *The Routledge Reader in Teaching and Learning*, pp. 60–71, London: Routledge.

SELF-ESTEEM

Self-esteem is a state of mind controlled by what a person believes about the way that others view that person. The associated terms, 'self-belief' and 'self-concept' and 'self-efficacy', indicate a state of mind controlled by how a person views him- or herself and are considered by some educationists to be more useful terms than self-esteem as they can be linked to verifiable achievement rather than opinion. Nevertheless, high self-esteem contributes to a state of what is referred to as 'relaxed alertness' in learning, which in turn allows pupils to evaluate their strengths and weaknesses and increases the likelihood that learning will be deep rather than superficial.

Adults play an important role in influencing children's self-esteem. For example, two teachers monitor children's work and offer suggestions for improvement: the first teacher depresses the pupil by focusing solely on errors; the second brings about the desired change by the use of carefully chosen words, precise guidance and suitable **target setting** for achievement. It is obvious which of the two approaches is more likely to bring about enhanced learning.

Pupils with low self-esteem are less willing to take risks in learning and may spend their time and energy completing straightforward tasks that lead most directly to the reward of adult praise and a tangible record of success (such as a tick, a positive written comment, a house point). Although this strategy brings about a temporary boost in self-esteem, it can also lead to a situation where children avoid difficult tasks and rely heavily on external stimuli to boost their sense of well-being. Virtually all primary-aged children are optimistic about being in a school situation or learning environment that caters for their needs, spends time and effort in helping them to learn and gives them opportunities to do exciting things. However, less confident children require careful **nurturing** if they are to break free from doing and saying only those things that they believe will elicit support and approval from others.

The renowned American educationist Lilian Katz suggests that parents and teachers can strengthen and support a healthy sense of self-esteem in children in at least seven ways: (1) Help them to build healthy relationships with peers. (2) Clarify their own **values** and those of others that may differ. (3) Offer them reassurance that support is unconditional. (4) Appreciate rather than merely praise their interests; avoid flattery. (5) Offer them opportunities to face challenges as well as to have fun. (6) Treat them respectfully, take their views seriously and offer meaningful **feedback**. (7) Help them to cope with setbacks and use the information and awareness they gain to future advantage.

Self-esteem is also significant for teachers, as confidence is an important factor in effective teaching. When teachers feel secure in their ability to do the job effectively, this assurance is translated into a belief that pupils will respond appropriately; as a result pupils sense the teacher's authority and are more likely to be compliant. Primary teachers tend to judge their own worth as persons in terms of their success at work; perceived inadequacies affect every aspect of their lives, both outside as well as inside school.

Further reading

Collins, M. (2001) *Because We're Worth It: Enhancing self-esteem in young children*, London: Lucky Duck/Paul Chapman.

Katz, L. G. (1995b) *How Can We Strengthen Children's Self-Esteem?*, University of Illinois, ERIC Clearinghouse on Elementary and Early Childhood Education. On-line. Available: http://www.kidsource.com/kidsource/content2/Strengthen_Children_Self.html (accessed July 2005).

Maclellan, E. (2005) 'Should we raise pupils' self-esteem?', *Education 3–13*, 33, 1, pp. 7–12.

O'Flynn, S. and Kennedy, H. (2003) Get Their Attention, London: David Fulton.

SKILLS

The development of skills in teaching and learning is a vitally important component of primary education. A skill can be described as the capacity to do something well and perform certain tasks competently, normally acquired through training and experience. Skill acquisition involves the mastery of a variety of specific abilities that combine to create the key skill that is being mastered. Thus, the skill of accessing information through the Internet requires that pupils have first gained the **ability** to use a computer mouse, select from menus, and so on. Skills may also relate to a natural ability that is refined through study, practice and expert tuition; for example, a child may improve a natural ability in drawing or running or number work through coaching and adult guidance. **Thinking** skills can also be developed in pupils by promoting discretion, judgement, understanding and sensitivity to **context** through the use of individual and group activities designed for the purpose.

One of the key decisions for teachers is whether mastery of basic skills should take place prior to the main task; or that competence in the skills should emerge as a result of doing the task and mastering each skill as it is needed. For example, pupils may be taught how to access a dictionary, but only regular use to discover the meaning of words allows a child the opportunity to come to grips with the complexities of the procedures. At the other extreme, a skill with a potential safety risk must be securely mastered before exploiting it; for example, it would be reckless to allow a young child to discover how to use a saw purely by experimenting with it! Teachers are constantly making decisions about the extent to which they monitor each step of the pupils' experiences and how much they step back and permit children to negotiate their own pathway through the work.

Teachers have to be clear about the appropriate teaching skills to employ for each occasion, though these intentions have to be tempered by a willingness to modify them in the light of what takes place during the session. Direct transmission teaching (DTT) involves imparting **knowledge** and understanding to pupils. The success by which this transmission is achieved depends upon teachers presenting the information in an orderly manner, using appropriate vocabulary, engaging the children by using varied tones of voice and speed of delivery, and employing visual aids where appropriate. A second teaching skill is interactive transmission teaching (ITT) that is also based on direct transmission but includes interludes for questions and answers. ITT is a more difficult teaching skill than DTT because the teacher has to switch between imparting information and handling pupils' answers as they respond to the questions that arise. Good teachers make sure that children can distinguish between genuine questions and rhetorical (think aloud) questions that do not require a response from them. Without such safeguards teachers have to handle a large number of unsolicited answers, especially from younger pupils. The third teaching skill that teachers employ is participative teaching (PT) where they encourage active pupil participation, not only in the form of answers to questions but also in providing insights, suggestions and examples. PT requires a considerable amount of teaching skill because it provides the most opportunities for disorder, as pupils may not possess the experience or self-discipline to wait for their turn, listen to the ideas of classmates and maintain a suitable noise level. Teachers have to work hard to clarify the **rules** about when and how the pupils can make contributions and how they should respond courteously to the views of others.

Regardless of the skills involved, teachers have to take account of pupils' abilities, experience and speed of working, offering them the opportunities to employ familiar skills in different learning contexts or to grapple with relevant and challenging new ones. If pupils are asked to investigate or solve problems, the range of skills has to be identified beforehand by the teacher to ensure that pupils can make an earnest attempt to tackle the challenge without being hampered by ignorance of the skills needed to succeed. For example, if pupils were asked to produce designs for a proposed school garden, they would need to be equipped with skills that enabled them to plan, draw and measure and the thinking skills necessary to envisage possibilities, in addition to knowledge of plants and soil conditions.

Further reading

Gunning, S., Gunning, D. and Wilson, J. (1981) *Topic Teaching in the Primary School*, London: Routledge, chapter 2.

Smith, G. F. (2004) 'Thinking skills', in E. C. Wragg (ed.) *Teaching and Learning*, pp. 105–22, London: Routledge.

SPECIAL EDUCATIONAL NEEDS

Pupils are considered to have special educational needs (SEN) if they display a learning difficulty or possess a disability that either prevents or hinders them from making use of educational facilities that are normally provided in schools for children of their age. It is estimated that around 20% of all pupils suffer from a special educational need at some time in their school careers. The need may be temporary and have minimal impact on the child's education, or more serious and chronic. Children having special educational needs require educational provision that helps them to develop their potential, achieve the greatest independence and eventually be able to exercise a full role in the community. While the education of pupils with SEN, whether in special or in ordinary schools, is broadly similar to that which is provided for other children, they are more likely to require access to specialist provision, teaching techniques and facilities. If pupils' needs necessitate formalised intervention, the **Code of Practice** for SEN is activated.

The education of children with SEN has assumed an increasingly high profile in primary education and had an impact on the work of every practitioner. At the same time it is unfortunate that the acronym SEN has become a label for children, rather than a means of focusing on their specific needs; consequently, unsatisfactory expressions such as 'SEN children' have found their way into the lexicon. If children's learning needs have been formally identified, involving the parents, head teacher, educational psychologist and local education authority, and are deemed to require specialist help within mainstream schooling, a formal statement is issued by the local authority. The statement describes the nature and parameters of the support, which frequently means receiving help from a teaching assistant (also referred to as a Learning Support Assistant, LSA). Owing to the additional cost incurred, the statementing process is often protracted.

Pupils for whom a statement of special needs has been drawn up have attracted the label of 'statemented children', though the statement referred to concerns the nature of the educational provision and is not intended to be a description of the child. Ideally, if there is a pupil who has been formally identified as having special needs, a teaching assistant will become available to support the pupil for part or all of the day, depending on the nature and severity of the need. However, the concept of one adult remaining in very close proximity to a single needy child throughout the day has become outmoded, unless the child's needs are so extreme (e.g. blindness) that such a continued adult presence is necessary.

Even if pupils benefit from specialised or individual **instruction** from an LSA in a particular subject area in which they struggle (notably, literacy) it does not necessarily involve their removal from regular class activities and segregation from social activities, as there are stigmas attached to being seen as 'different'. The strategy of removing children from mainstream activities can also reinforce pupils' perceptions of their low status and may damage their **self-esteem** and confidence, though some pupils enjoy the exclusive attention. The move towards more integrative and inclusive practices that keep all children physically together as far as possible has become more evident in some schools, with appropriate **differentiation** of the work content. Nevertheless, being taken out of the classroom for specific teaching on a one-to-one basis or in very small groups is still commonplace for younger primary-age children who need extra support, especially in reading.

Some pupils struggle with regular work to such an extent that they are not even able to reach the first level of the National Curriculum, in which case there exist a set of indicators known as the P scales to record their **achievement**. The P scales are divided into eight levels from P1 (the lowest) to P8 (the highest), though the first three levels (P1, P2 and P3) are not subject specific. In extreme cases, children may only have a tentative grasp of people, events and objects and rely heavily on tactile senses (e.g. through touching) to elicit a response, whereby P1 would be an appropriate level.

The presence of pupils with SEN in mainstream classes often benefits the overall learning climate owing to the sense of caring and cooperation that it engenders. The exception to this trend concerns children who suffer from emotional and behavioural problems, in which case the disruption and additional demands placed on the teacher and the adverse impact on pupil learning are seen to act against the best interests of the majority and have led to calls for a re-evaluation of the **inclusion** policy.

Further reading

Department for Education and Skills (2004b) *Removing Barriers to Achievement*, London: The Stationery Office.

Greenwood, C. (2004) *Understanding the Needs of Parents: Guidelines for effective collaboration with parents of children with SEN*, London: David Fulton.

McNamara, S. and Moreton, G. (1997) *Understanding Differentiation*, London: David Fulton.

Rose, R. (2000) 'Creating the conditions for inclusion in primary schools in the UK', Paper presented at the International Special Education Congress 2000. On-line. Available: http://www.isec2000.org.uk/abstracts/papers_r/rose_1.htm (accessed April 2005).

Szwed, C. (2004) 'The developing role of the primary SENCO', *Primary Practice*, 37, Summer, pp. 36–42.

STEINER–WALDORF SCHOOLS

Although the majority of state-funded schools are concerned principally with enhancing academic standards, two specific types of school are also closely associated with promoting a spiritual dimension in education. First, in the UK, schools within the Church of England or Roman Catholic traditions that provided an elementary education for underprivileged people during the nineteenth century; these 'foundation' schools retain close control over the teaching of religious education. (In recent years other denominations and world faiths have established schools that reflect their own spiritual and moral priorities.)

The second type is schools associated with the person of Rudolph Steiner, known as Steiner or Waldorf–Steiner or Steiner–Waldorf schools. In 1913 Steiner built a 'school of spiritual science' in Switzerland, which was the forerunner of the present-day schools. The name Waldorf is derived from the school that Steiner was asked to open in 1919 for the children of workers at the Waldorf–Astoria cigarette factory in Stuttgart, Germany. The first US Waldorf school opened in New York in 1928 and there are now more than 600 Waldorf schools in over thirty-two countries with approximately 120,000 pupils of primary and secondary age.

Steiner designed the **curriculum** of his schools to emphasise the relation of human beings to nature and natural rhythms, including an emphasis on festivals, myths, ancient cultures and various celebrations. He was driven by a conviction that practical **skills**, such as playing a musical instrument, weaving, wood carving, knitting and painting, were an essential part of a child's education. He believed that each human being is composed of body, spirit and soul, and that children pass through three seven-year stages from birth to the age of 21, so that the education provided at each stage should be appropriate to the 'spirit for each stage'. As Steiner believed that it is the spirit that comprehends **knowledge** and the spirit is the same in all people, regardless of mental or physical differences, he was a pioneer in educating the mentally and physically handicapped (as people were then described), which today is referred to as a policy of **inclusion**. One of the more unusual parts of the course of study involves something Steiner called 'eurythmy', an art of movement that tries to make visible what he believed were the inner forms and gestures of language and music.

Advocates of Steiner–Waldorf education claim that as children grow up, they gain the characteristics that make them human because seeds of experience are sown that germinate, grow strongly through **nurturing** and later come to fruition. Education is therefore concerned with the whole person and not merely the growth of the intellect.

Further reading

Carroll, R. T. (2003) *The Skeptic's Dictionary: A collection of strange beliefs, amusing deceptions and dangerous delusions'*, London: John Wiley & Sons.

Clouder, C. and Rawson, M. (2003) *Waldorf Education*, Edinburgh: Floris Books.

Edmunds, F. (2004) *An Introduction to Steiner Education*, Vancouver: Sophia Books.

TALK

To ensure that talk is effective and useful for learning, pupils have to be taught how to speak meaningfully to one another, listen carefully to what others have to say, respond constructively and express their own views succinctly. Throughout this complex social and intellectual process, children gradually come to acknowledge that views other than their own exist and understand that their own opinions and judgement are open to scrutiny and, perhaps, criticism. The extent of teacher involvement depends upon the nature of the talk. If the teacher intervenes too much, talking becomes fragmented; if intervention is minimal, the talk may stray too far from the intended topic or dissolve into a series of trivial comments.

If learning through talk is to be educationally valuable for primary-aged children, a number of factors must be in place. First, a positive **learning climate** must have been developed such that children are supported and encouraged to share ideas. Second, children must be inculcated into **thinking** hard about what they learn. By posing interesting and speculative questions, encouraging children to think aloud and offer alternative explanations for events and phenomena, teachers gradually foster a more inquisitive attitude and thirst to discover more. Third, children must understand the rules for taking turns and offering their opinions, and learn strategies for expressing ideas openly.

Three opportunities for talk are commonly used in primary schools: discussion, debate and dialogue. *Discussion* is a form of group **interaction** in which pupils talk between one another about an issue or a relevant topic that raises questions. In a discussion the talk consists of advancing and considering closely a variety of perspectives on the given issue. Discussion therefore requires that the children know enough about the subject to offer an opinion, suggest alternatives or summarise a position. In a classroom setting it is essential that issues under discussion lie within children's direct experience or the scope of their **imagination**.

Debate follows more closely prescribed **rules** than discussion and is more carefully structured. It needs to be formally organised and is most suitable for older primary pupils. Prior to the debate, children need time to acquire information about the topic, talk informally to one another and record some of their findings in a form that can be later shared. The search for information can also be extended into **homework** tasks. During the debate, children who have volunteered to speak are given a period of time (say three minutes) in which to share their ideas without interruption. The rest of the class have to sit patiently until the contribution has been concluded before being given time to think of a question to ask or a comment to make. Once the questions and comments are exhausted, another speaker is allowed the same amount of time to present information and ideas from a different perspective. The teacher has to monitor the time, note key comments, draw together the different threads of the debate, thank the main participants and summarise learning points.

Dialogue is a conversation between two or more persons in which both make a necessary verbal contribution to maintain the exchanges. In addition to social dialogue ('small talk') two forms of dialogue are promoted in primary education. The first form is 'critical dialogue', when issues are interrogated. The second is 'creative dialogue', when solutions to problems are being sought. Adult–pupil dialogue forms an essential element of learning, though in the majority of classrooms most talk is initiated by and sustained through the adult, with pupils responding to what the teacher says rather than being an equal participant in the exchanges. In pupil–pupil dialogue, some pupils are naturally garrulous and may dominate conversations to the detriment of more thoughtful children. Other pupils find it difficult to express themselves and yet others prefer to remain silent rather than to expose their inadequate grasp of the subject matter. Teachers take all these factors into account when planning their strategies for encouraging talk for learning.

There are numerous practical methods for promoting talk in class, some of which are more manageable than others. It is common for children to be invited by the teacher to recount an experience, comment on an issue, express an interest or concern, offer advice, provide facts, explain how something can be done or suggest alternatives. It is less common for teachers to encourage children to argue forcibly or counter a prevailing view or tell jokes. On occasions, pupils spontaneously wonder out loud, make ribald comments, call out answers or make humorous remarks that are considered to be outside the bounds of acceptable behaviour and thereby invite discipline measures to be taken. However, within a collaborative problem-solving session or investigation, all such forms of speaking may be accommodated within the group discussion; even the occasional frivolous comment can provide a useful diversion from the intensity of the formal exchanges and 'oil the wheels' of the talk.

Pupils can only talk about a topic if there is something worthwhile that warrants being addressed, such as the merits of a cause, the correctness of a decision or the ethics of a controversial issue. Younger children may be encouraged to talk about ways to share toys or whether it is right to speak to strangers in the street. Older pupils may talk about issues of fairness, equality and the employment of classroom sanctions. Children of all ages can contribute to a discussion about local issues (such as a proposed road scheme), national issues (such as how to care for the elderly) and world issues (such as conservation).

An active dialogue (whether critical or creative) is also important within a school staff as a means of enhancing team spirit, generating ideas, clarifying decisions, explaining procedures, transmitting messages, supporting learning and sharing joys and disappointments. Head teachers of successful schools invariably encourage open dialogue to raise morale and foster a vibrant and inclusive learning community.

Further reading

Black, L. (2004) 'Teacher-pupil talk in whole-class discussions and processes of social positioning within the primary school classroom', *Language and Education*, 18, 5, pp. 347–60.

Department for Education and Skills (2003c) *Speaking, listening, learning: Working with children in KS1 and KS2*, Annesley, Nottingham: DfES Publications Centre.

Dillon, J. T. (1994) *Using Discussions in Classrooms*, Maidenhead: Open University Press.

Eke, R. and Lee, J. (2005) *Using Talk Effectively in the Primary Classroom*, London: Routledge.

Myhill, D., Jones, S. and Hooper, R. (2006) *Talking, Listening, Learning: Effective talk in the primary classroom*, Maidenhead: Open University Press.

TARGET SETTING

There are three sorts of targets commonly used in primary education. The first type is *quantitative*, relying on numerical data from test scores, both internal and external to the school. For instance, a target might be set for a certain percentage of children in the school to reach a certain score in English or mathematics; or for all children in the same class to be capable of spelling a particular list of words. The second type of target is *qualitative*, based principally on a teacher's subjective evaluation of pupils' work, but incorporating factors such as behaviour and the general ambience of school life. For example, the target might be for pupils to use computer software or to walk quietly inside the building. The third type of target is based on *pupils' evaluations* of their own progress and ways to improve it. These targets are internal to the classroom, negotiated between the teacher and pupil, sometimes recorded formally by the teacher except in the case of older children, who maintain their own records. Targets must be realistic, manageable and challenging, based on evidence of previous attainment and informed by regular assessment of attainment and gaps in **knowledge**.

Although, in theory, targets are regularly reviewed by the teacher and then modified in the light of new learning and progress, the process of bespoke target setting for each child, adjusting teaching to assist pupils to meet their individual targets and subsequent assessment that their learning is secure in that area of study, is difficult in practice. Teachers simply do not have sufficient time to keep accurate track of the progress of thirty or more pupils. There are also three other factors associated with effective target setting of which teachers have to take account. First, targets that are too general are difficult to monitor because it is hard to know when they have been achieved; second, targets that are too specific tend to narrow children's perspectives and lead to rote learning; third, some targets are more to do with improvement than with mastery. The third point is significant because the concept of lifelong learning implies that although there may be identifiable stages in the process, there is no end to the extent of improvement. Many aspects of learning for primary-age children involve 'getting better' rather than 'concluding the learning'. For example, all pupils need to persevere constantly to improve their spelling and presentation, so a target expressed as 'get better at spelling' is unsatisfactorily vague; a more helpful target would be to identify a specific set of words that have to be mastered by a given date.

Adults in primary education also employ targets as a means of monitoring their own progress. For example, trainee teachers identify and then strive to gain competence in their weaker or less well-developed areas of teaching to achieve qualified status. Judgements about a teacher's competence are directly aligned to pupil achievements in formal tests and indirectly to how effectively a particular member of staff contributes to the team endeavour. Targets for both pupils and adults tend to consist of *immediate ones* associated with success in classroom practice and *end-product ones* in demonstrating long-term outcomes.

Further reading

Bremner, I. and Cartwright, D. (2004) 'Target setting in primary schools: the big squeeze', *Education 3–13*, 32, 1, pp. 4–8.

Smith, R. (2002) *Creating the Effective Primary School*, London: Routledge/ TES., chapter 4.

Wyse, D. (2001) 'Promising yourself to do better? Target-setting and literacy', *Education 3–13*, 29, 2, pp. 13–18.

TEACHER ROLE

The teacher's role has many facets but is dominated by functional aspects, including **curriculum** implementation, planning lessons, assessing pupil progress and compiling reports. Motivating factors such as altruism, compassion, a love for children and the fulfilment of working in a school environment sometimes have to be subordinated to these pragmatic concerns. Only a little more than a half of a primary teacher's time is spent actively teaching; the remainder of the time is occupied by attending meetings, administration and other school duties (such as supervising pupils in the playground). In the past, teachers could isolate themselves by staying in their classrooms, the extent of contact with colleagues depending on personal inclination. Today, teachers must be willing and able to work as team members, in the belief that multiple contributions allow for a deeper engagement with issues and appropriate solutions than working singly does. There is much for teachers to learn by observing a colleague at work but they have to be cautious about trying to replicate his or her actions without ascertaining the educational **values** that underpin them.

All teachers exercise the role of guardian, setting and maintaining a rule framework, making their **expectations** about behaviour clear to pupils and encouraging them to accept responsibility for their own actions. This social dimension of the teacher's role is crucial to success in developing a positive attitude by convincing children that they have more to gain than to lose by behaving well. The guardian role means dealing with infringements in a way that reflects their level of seriousness, anticipating disruption and taking pre-emptive action and using sanctions according to agreed procedures. Effective teachers lead like a shepherd rather than drive like a cattle rancher.

A teacher has to be influential beyond the classroom door in areas of personal relationships with support staff, contact with parents and visitors, demonstrating initiative with respect to **health and safety** issues and being a positive presence around the school. Teacher as guardian also involves protecting weaker and more vulnerable children from harm (such as bullying) and helping them to develop strategies to become more self-sufficient and confident. For trainee teachers the demands of this wider role can be a little over-whelming, their priority being rooted in effective classroom practice; however, the standards required for successful completion of their training depend on being sensitive to the other dimensions of the role.

Despite the many other calls on teachers' time, classroom teaching lies at the heart of their work. Teachers learn to gain children's attention, both by insisting that they listen and concentrate, and by making the work interesting and appealing. They convey their enthusiasm during the teaching episode, offer clear and precise explanations, ask relevant questions and invite pupils to think for themselves. Many teachers describe the thrill they experience when a child becomes excited about an aspect of learning, as they grasp the point and glimpse its implications.

Monitoring progress is an essential aspect of the teacher role. Every teacher has to become expert in diagnosing the extent of children's understanding, the areas where they lack comprehension and the best methods for remedying the situation. All monitoring depends on close observation of children, careful listening to what they say, and skilful **questioning** to gain insight into their beliefs and ideas. The best teachers do not merely discover where children's problems lie, but investigate why they have occurred and how to remedy them.

Six key influences have the potential to influence the effectiveness of a primary teacher's work. First, the intense pace of life in school, lack of opportunity for thoughtful **reflection** and the need constantly to prioritise tasks due to heavy workloads. Second, having to cope immediately with daily occurrences such as resolving disputes between pupils, responding to parental concerns, caring for injured children and carrying out running repairs on equipment. Third, offering sup-port to colleagues in an effort to maintain staff harmony and promote **collegiality**. Fourth, the shortage of time to achieve all that needs to be accomplished, regardless of how long and hard they work. Fifth, owing to the busyness of school life, the disconnection and reduced opportunities for liaison with other adults that sometimes occurs. Sixth, the organisational demands that result from the combined impact of meetings with colleagues, contacts with parents, harnessing and managing resources, planning the teaching programme, sorting out visits and special events, and liaising with teachers in other schools. The network of responsibilities that comprise the teacher role mean that the successful management of the multiplicity of demands requires teachers to be vigilant in evaluating and adjusting each day's differing priorities, while maintaining the regular timetable of teaching and associated duties.

Further reading

Carlyle, D. and Woods, P. (2002) *Emotions of Teacher Stress*, Stoke-on-Trent: Trentham.

Fenstermacher, G. D. (2004) 'The concept of manner and its visibility', in E. C. Wragg (ed.) *The Routledge Reader in Teaching and Learning*, pp. 123–35, London: Routledge.

Hayes, D. (2001b) 'Don's Diary: a life in the day of a primary teacher', *Curriculum*, 22, 1, pp. 2–16.

Helsby, G. (1998) *Changing Teachers' Work*, Buckingham: Open University Press.

Teacher Training Agency (2003) *Being a Teacher*. On-line. Available HTTP: www.useyourheadteach.gov.uk (accessed December 2004).

Woods, P. and Jeffrey, B. (2002) 'Teacher identities under stress: the emotions of separation and renewal', *International Studies in Sociology of Education*, 23, 1, pp. 89–106.

TEACHING APPROACH

A teaching approach consists of the methods and strategies that teachers employ to help pupils learn effectively and reflects the beliefs that they hold about the nature of learning. Thus, one teacher may believe that pupils learn best when they are motivated by opportunities to explore ideas as a group, while another teacher may be convinced that they learn best when working alone with tasks closely targeted to their individual needs. Again, one teacher may employ a considerable amount of direct teaching, utilising question and answer supported by repetition of facts, while another teacher employs a problem-solving method in which children are encouraged to raise their own questions and seek their own solutions. One teacher's style may be informal and strongly interactive, using **humour** and repartee, while another teacher might adopt a more detached approach, eschewing familiarity.

Primary educators are in a position to create, support and maintain challenging learning environments for all pupils and apply their professional expertise to promote learning by their knowledge of the **curriculum** and employment of a range of pupil **assessment** strategies to identify and address individual needs and differences. Every teaching approach is based upon an understanding of human development and also a grasp of learning theory and its practical implementation. The best teaching approaches provide for the flexibility to change a lesson's direction if it becomes apparent that this is necessary, accommodate the needs of faster and slower workers and draw the lesson or session to a satisfactory conclusion.

One of the most marked ways in which teaching approaches differ is in the use of discipline. One teacher will adhere strictly to the agreed behaviour code and employ sanctions systematically, with minimal regard for the particular circumstances, while another teacher will avoid the use of sanctions wherever possible, relying on verbal persuasion and warnings. Whatever approach is adopted, the best teachers speak naturally to children and not at them; take a sincere interest in what the children say; respond strongly when necessary but do not shout or humiliate a child; place explanation ahead of sanctions; and publicly acknowledge good behaviour. An effective approach also refuses to be ruffled by events and focuses on positive actions. The very best teachers allow children space to grow and develop and encourage them to express doubts, uncertainties and reservations. They use questions skilfully to help their pupils explore issues. They offer advice and suggestions and promote a learning ethos in which children are convinced that nothing is beyond their reach if they try hard enough. In this regard, an experienced and highly successful former primary head teacher in England, Sir David Winkley, compares a successful teaching approach to good jazz, claiming that good teaching is both structured and improvised, making use of the finest instruments and themes available, but deploying them in personal, original ways.

The decisions associated with determining the kind of approach that practitioners adopt is influenced by a variety of factors, including their personality, training, natural talents, disposition and school policies. However, the recommended teaching approaches relating to the National **Literacy** Strategy (NLS) and National **Numeracy** Strategy (NNS) have colonised other areas of teaching such that lessons follow a similar pattern: a teacher-led introduction to the whole class, followed by specific teaching; guided and independent tasks for groups of children; a summary of key lesson points.

Most primary teachers place considerable emphasis on their relationship with pupils as a way to enhance the quality of teaching and learning, but do so on the understanding that the ultimate arbiter is the adult, not the child. The majority of teachers embrace the principle that although pupils should make *some* decisions, adults, with the ultimate responsibility for academic standards and social behaviour, have the final say. The nature of the relationship depends to a large extent on how much teachers want their pupils to be actively involved in their learning and think about the work rather than merely complying with an insistence to do it. Although primary teachers are commonly heard to say that they want their pupils to be responsive and offer their own opinions, the pressure to cover the curriculum and achieve good test results (especially for older pupils) can thwart such aspirations.

Adopting a teaching approach also involves fundamental questions about classroom organisation and class management. At one level teachers find that it pays to teach the whole class together as much as possible, as it saves time and avoids the need to repeat the same set of instructions and explanations to different groups of children. On the other hand, the wide ability range and maturity level within a class mean that teachers need constantly to be sensitive to the differences that exist in pupils' concentration span, grasp of concepts, vocabulary and previous learning experiences. Consequently, teachers normally use a mixture of whole-class, group work and individual work according to circumstances and what they are seeking to achieve. Ultimately, all teachers have to respond to the individual needs of children, but for organisational purposes they tend to group pupils in ways that facilitate ease of working. In English and mathematics the grouping is normally on the basis of pupil attainment; in other subjects it is on a social or practical basis (such as access to resources).

Further reading

Egan, K. (2005) *An Imaginative Approach to Teaching*, San Francisco: Jossey-Bass.

Siraj-Blatchford, I. and Sylva, K. (2004) 'Researching pedagogy in English pre-schools', *British Educational Research Journal*, 30, 5, pp. 713–30.

Turner-Bissett, R. (2003) 'On the carpet: changing primary teacher contexts', *Education 3–13*, 31, 3, pp. 4–10.

Winkley, D. (2002) *Handsworth Revolution: The odyssey of a school*, London: Giles de la Mare.

TESTING

A regime of testing has emerged in recent years where pupils' grasp of specific pieces of **knowledge** and information has been scrutinised to its limits. As a consequence, teachers' efficiency has been measured in terms of examination outcomes, with the result that primary education has become more narrowly focused in a bid to raise attainment scores in mathematics and English. There is ample evidence to show that this emphasis has been at the expense of more creative and innovative approaches.

Nearly all primary-aged pupils in mainstream schools in the UK are required to undertake national tests during year 6 (aged 10–11 years). The tests are popularly referred to as SATs, based on the concept of a standard assessment task when national testing was first introduced in the early 1990s. However, they are more correctly referred to as National Curriculum Tests, NCTs, though the acronym is rarely used. A few children are exempt from the requirement to take SATs because of their exceptional learning difficulties. In England children were also formally tested at the end of Key Stage 1 (KS1) in year 2 when they were approximately 7 years of age. However, since 2005, teachers' own judgements of how pupils are progressing forms the principal source of evidence. The decision to modify the testing regime followed a successful pilot scheme in schools which revealed that teacher assessment, in conjunction with a more flexible test, reflected pupil **achievement** and potential more accurately than raw test results. Children still sit the Key Stage 1 National **Curriculum** Tests in English and maths, but not at a fixed time and with an emphasis on work that is carried out throughout the year. Key Stage 1 national tests in English and maths are marked within each school and each school's results are then made available locally. Key Stage 2 (KS2) national tests in English, maths and science are marked externally and the school's results are published nationally. In a few areas, tests of various types for those seeking grammar school places are marked externally but the results are kept confidential. In Wales, Key Stage 2 national tests in English and Welsh, maths and science became optional from 2005. New **skills** tests in **numeracy**, **literacy** and problem solving are likely to be mandatory from 2008. In Northern Ireland, transfer tests in English or Irish, maths and science and technology for those seeking grammar school places are marked externally and the results kept private; however, these tests are due to end in 2008. In Scotland, national tests in English and maths are given, corresponding roughly to Key Stages 1, 2 and 3. Pupils are not tested at a specific age or stage, but at the discretion of teachers when they consider the children ready to do so. The tests are marked internally and the results are not made known publicly.

The results of the KS2 tests in England contribute to national league tables of school performance; however, many head teachers bitterly oppose the significance attached to them. The tables are widely published and form the focus of considerable attention from parents and the community, as well as local and national government agencies. Although parents undoubtedly take a great interest in the position in the table of local schools, numerous surveys suggest that many parents feel that their children are under too much stress because of the excessive numbers of tests, the accompanying expansion of **homework** and the impact of school work on family life. Testing and retesting for the purpose of **reporting** pupil performance, the pressure on teachers to 'teach to the test' and the imposition of a rigidly prescribed subject content are viewed by many educators as an unsatisfactory way to help children gain all the necessary life skills they need to achieve their full potential in a rapidly changing world.

Further reading

Hall, K., Collins, J., Benjamin, S., Nind, M. and Sheehy, K. (2004) 'Saturated models of pupildom: assessment and inclusion/exclusion', *British Educational Research Journal*, 30, 6, pp. 801–17.

Noddings, N. (2004) 'High stakes testing: why?', *Theory and Research in Education*, 2, 3, pp. 263–9.

Reardon, T. (2004) 'Key stage 2 tests: what the teachers really think', *Education Journal*, 79, pp. 28–30.

THINKING

Over the past ten or fifteen years there has been a surge of interest about the use of thinking **skills** as a means of improving the quality of learning in classrooms. The direct teaching of strategies to aid thinking helps to develop pupils' abilities in problem solving, investigations and forms of **enquiry** that can be applied across all areas of learning and are relevant to the needs of every child, including preschoolers and new entrants. Thinking skills and strategies open new avenues for intellectual growth that allow academically capable children to be acknowledged for developing ideas and ways of working that are complex, original and insightful.

Thinking for learning presents challenges for primary teachers who work within a predetermined timetable and school-wide agreement about **learning objectives**. Teachers may want to promote children's capability as creative thinkers but feel constrained by the limitations imposed by a need to conform to the timetable requirements. A teacher may be anxious to offer pupils more opportunities to grapple

with ideas, think hard about their implications and produce innovative solutions, but hesitate to do so for fear of falling behind in
covering the **curriculum** and distorting the plans agreed jointly
with colleagues or detracting from preparing pupils for formal
testing.

An important dimension of primary education is for children to
move beyond the point where the sole aim is to complete the given
task, and become evaluators of their own and others' ideas and opinions as well. In doing so, primary-age children have to understand
the difference between constructive arguing and quarrelling. Victor
Quinn, a specialist in critical thinking, suggests that there are four
central kinds of arguments that teachers and parents need to promote
in children: (1) *Empirical* arguments about matters of fact. (2) *Conceptual* arguments about what words mean and how ideas relate. (3)
Evaluative arguments about attitudes and judgements and moral concerns with the needs and interests of others. (4) *Logical* arguments
about making connections and disciplined thought. Steve Higgins
and Jennifer Miller from the University of Newcastle (DfES 2005)
classify thinking skills' programmes and approaches into three broad
categories. The first they refer to as a *philosophical* approach, where
there is an emphasis on questioning and reasoning, particularly when
this is undertaken by a group of children or the whole class. Thus, an
issue or question is identified by the teacher and/or pupils that might
be solved or elucidated through discussion. The teacher takes the role
of facilitator and supports or challenges the discussion and pupil reasoning. The leading example of thinking in this category is 'philosophy
for children', an approach to learning developed in the United States
by Matthew Lipman in the 1960s. The second approach to thinking is
through *brain-based learning*, drawing on research into how the human
brain works and its implications for teachers and schools. Two of the
more famous names associated with this approach are Edward de Bono
and Eric Jensen, both of whom claim that teaching approaches in
schools have not sufficiently utilised information about the brain's
functioning. Ideas about accelerated learning and multiple intelligences
(see under **Emotion**) draw on brain research to inspire techniques or
activities that can be used in the classroom. The third approach is *cognitive intervention*, where teaching strategies to promote pupils' thinking
are based on activities and techniques for the purpose that the teacher
devises.

Most educators agree that the approaches and techniques associated with thinking skills need to be integrated or 'infused' into
lessons rather than taught as separate skills or through lessons that

are solely for the purpose. However, **circle time**, an approach by which children have an opportunity to express considered views openly and without censure, is one occasion when thinking skills can be specifically developed within a non-threatening and familiar setting.

Further reading

Costello, P. J. M. (2000) *Thinking Skills and Early Childhood Education*, London: David Fulton.
Department for Education and Skills (2002) *Time for Standards: Reforming the school workforce*, London: The Stationery Office.
DfES: http://www.standards.dfes.gov.uk/thinkingskills/
Fisher, R (1990) *Teaching Children To Think*, London: Blackwell.
Kelly, P. (2004) *Using Thinking Skills in the Primary Classroom*, London: Paul Chapman.
MacGilchrist, B. and Buttress, M. (2005) *Transforming Learning and Teaching*, London: Paul Chapman.
Quinn, V. (1997) *Critical Thinking in Young Minds*, London: David Fulton.
Simister, J. (2004) 'To think or not to think', *Improving Schools*, 7, 3, pp. 243–54.

TIME MANAGEMENT

Successful time management for school staff is essential to facilitate the arranging of teaching and learning. Every teacher finds that unless priorities are established and acted on decisively, the hours slip past and essential things remain untouched while trivial issues that emerge unexpectedly take precedence. Well-ordered routines contribute to higher standards in learning and help to reduce stress levels; consequently, making optimum use of the time available benefits both children and adults. One characteristic of successful primary teachers is being able to organise and manage their time effectively and efficiently. The best teachers are skilful in making the best use of the available opportunities; they seem to achieve more than their colleagues and produce work of a higher standard despite being busier.

Teachers learn to think ahead by deciding what is essential to do, what is necessary and what is non-essential. It is then possible for them to determine what is urgent and what can wait for attention. To avoid being overwhelmed, teachers tend to categorise tasks mentally under a series of headings, such as not urgent and minor, urgent but minor, urgent and significant, not urgent but significant. It is not worthwhile for teachers to spend time on doing things that are neither urgent nor significant, even if they are interesting; on the other hand, urgent tasks that are relatively unimportant still have to be dealt with as quickly as possible. If tasks are urgent and significant they assume the highest priority; the numerous other things to do simply have to wait and cannot serve as an excuse for inaction. If too many tasks are pressing and significant, it acts as a warning that too little time has been left before the deadline; use of a planning schedule with interim targets helps to avoid last-minute panics. Effective time management means that the majority of essential tasks are non-urgent because sufficient time has been left for them to be dealt with. In the hurry and scurry of school life there are occasions when unexpected events conspire to upset the most carefully laid plans, but practitioners have to be diligent to avoid being caught out too often. Regardless of the backlog of tasks, health and safety issues always receive precedence.

Teachers often find that the completion of forms, lists and other mundane tasks is more time consuming than expected. Senior teachers and the head teacher in particular have to be careful that they do not get submerged in paperwork tasks at the expense of being active around the school. The availability of teaching **assistants** allows teachers to delegate some of the time-consuming tasks that would otherwise detract from responsibilities for planning, preparation, teaching, **assessment** of pupils' work and curriculum **leadership**.

Each evening teachers mentally compile a list of things that need to be done before school begins, during the lunch break and after school. For example, a telephone call about arrangements for an educational visit can only be made out of lesson times. Information may be needed from pupils at the start of the day about numbers who wish to participate in a particular event, or the teacher may have to tell pupils about changes in the timetable. If a parent has requested a brief informal discussion with a member of the staff after school, it has to be made a priority over other jobs. The balance of each day is different and unexpected events can disrupt the best-laid plans; nevertheless, thinking and planning ahead is crucial to teaching success. Hard work and enthusiasm cannot compensate for poor time management.

Further reading

Brown, M. and Ralph, S. (1994) *Managing Stress in Schools*, Plymouth: Northcote House.

Carlyle, D. and Woods, P. (2002) *Emotions of Teacher Stress*, Stoke-on-Trent: Trentham.

TOPIC WORK

Department for Education and Skills (2003d) *Raising Standards and Tackling Workload: A national agreement*, London: The Stationery Office.
Heyda, P. (2001) *The Primary Teacher's Survival Guide*, Portsmouth: Heinemann, chapter 5.
Papworth, M. (2003) *Every Minute Counts*, New York: Continuum.
Timperley, H. and Robinson, V. M. J. (2000) 'Workload and the professional culture of teachers', *Educational Management and Administration*, 28, 1, pp. 47–62.

TOPIC WORK

The **curriculum** in primary schools requires teachers to provide pupils with a breadth and depth of learning, giving adequate time and attention to the teaching of core subjects (English, mathematics and science) while still providing sufficient attention to a worthwhile study of other subjects and religious education. Some schools choose to organise the teaching of history, geography, art, design and (sometimes) physical education within 'topics' or subject-related themes that incorporate **knowledge** from a cross-section of subjects. Unlike the regular teaching of core subjects, a topic approach is based on the principle that learning is not formulaic and does not need to be confined within subject boundaries but is more eclectic and arbitrary. The ultimate form of child-directed learning is found in free **play**.

Examples of topics include road safety, homes, exploring the school grounds, mini-beasts (small creatures) and colours. Thus, a topic on road safety with 8-year-olds might involve aspects of geography (road layouts, planning routes), mathematics (speed and direction), ICT (maps), drama (acting out road-crossing scenes) and art/design (designing warning posters). A topic based on a colour (green, say) with reception-age children might incorporate science (natural and artificial objects), art (painting an imaginary scene based on shades of green), literacy (talking about scary green monsters), geography (the shape of hills) and science (wildlife in fields). Some topics are more *thematic* in nature and have a heavy emphasis on a particular subject, notably history, geography or RE. Pupils explore the theme using art, design, dance, drama and IT as tools to create links across the subjects. Thus, 11-year-olds might explore a history theme using ICT to reproduce a historical event; dance to examine the cultural factors that impinged on the event; and discussions about issues associated with conflict through religious education and **citizenship**.

Topic work is closely associated with the concept of an integrated day where the conventional timetable is set aside in favour of a more flexible way of organising learning. Unlike formal teaching situations that are dominated by systematic **instruction** and where teachers make the vast majority of decisions about lesson content, tasks and learning outcomes, an integrated day permits pupils more choice about what they learn and how they learn it. Instead of the closely monitored **lessons** with a prescribed internal lesson structure and specified **learning objectives**, an integrated day allows pupils to follow a variety of lines of **enquiry**. The teacher establishes the broad parameters of study in advance, but children's spontaneous interests and 'need to know' are accommodated and encouraged. The advantages associated with the integrated day include the chance to give pupils sufficient time to explore issues, work at their own pace and pursue more directly what interests them about the topic. Because teachers do not lead through the lesson step by step, they are free to monitor progress, offer advice to the children and concentrate on individual needs. The disadvantages associated with an integrated topic day include ensuring that resources are available to meet every contingency, the need to maintain detailed records to keep track of pupil progress and checking that during the day (or days) a child is experiencing a wide range of learning opportunities. Topic work frequently involves group work and the production of displays and performances as means of presenting findings. Children are almost invariably motivated by the freedom to explore and be creative that topic work offers.

Further reading

Gunning, S., Gunning, D. and Wilson, J. (1981) *Topic Teaching in the Primary School*, London: Routledge

Katz, L. G. and Chard, S. C. (2000) *Engaging Children's Minds: The project approach*, Stamford, CT: Ablex.

Pinder, R. (1987) *Why Don't Teachers Teach Like They Used To?* London: Hilary Shipman, chapter 11.

VALUES

Values are fundamental beliefs or principles that determine attitudes towards human behaviour. They guide judgements about what is right or wrong and focus attention on what is important. In schools, values are fundamental expressions of what practitioners think and believe, and reflect the personal concerns and preferences that help to frame their relationships with pupils and adults. There are five key values in which education is grounded: spiritual, cultural, environmental, aesthetic and political. These values are expressed in terms of personal values with relation to self, moral values with respect to others and social values with regard to the impact on the community.

A generation ago, a leading education writer (Jeffreys 1971) claimed that the history of human thought indicates that people will always recognise the need for values that are timeless because they provide standards by which changes of manners, customs and beliefs can be judged and in the light of which the future can be planned. The same author also underlines the point that teachers must combine personal morality with impartial justice, as freedom of thought does not mean the right to hold any sort of random viewpoint. Consequently, the values that teachers bring to the classroom should not be casual beliefs but the result of careful consideration and informed **thinking**.

As the prime satisfaction for primary teachers is the joy of interacting with children and the ways they can affect their young lives, rather than a desire for monetary rewards or status, their value position is rooted in a need to love and care, to serve, to empower and to benefit their pupils. Consequently, primary teachers are constantly evaluating their work through interrogating the fundamental purpose of what they are doing as educators. **Emotion** plays a crucial part in defining teachers' value positions and, therefore, their relationship and engagement with children and their learning.

Primary educators are in a unique position to nurture the intellectual, physical, emotional, social, and civic potential of each pupil by respecting the worth of each child and offering academic and practical support and encouragement. Owing to the position of trust they hold in the community they are serving, it is generally true that almost every primary educator strives to embody honesty, diplomacy, tact and fairness in their dealings with others and professional conduct in their jobs. Teachers endeavour to establish and maintain clear standards of behaviour, conscious of the fact that they are role models for children and for less experienced colleagues. They help pupils to reflect on their own learning and connect it to their life experiences, engage children in activities that encourage diverse approaches and solutions to problems, while providing a range of ways for them to demonstrate their abilities. In effect, teachers view the classroom as a microcosm of what wider society should become, where pupils develop the capability to analyse, synthesise, evaluate, communicate effectively and demonstrate compassion towards others.

Further reading

Arthur, J., Davison, J. and Lewis, M. (2005) *Professional Values and Practice: Achieving the standards for QTS*, London: Routledge, chapters 1–3.

Cole, M. (2004) *Professional Values and Practice for Teachers and Student Teachers*, 2nd edn, London: David Fulton.

Eaude, T. (2004) *Values Education: Developing positive attitudes*, Birmingham: National Primary Trust.

Hargreaves, A. and Fullan, M. (1998) *What's Worth Fighting for in Education?* Maidstone: Open University Press.

Hawkes, N. (2005) *How to Inspire and Develop Values in the Classroom*, Cambridge: LDA/Living and Learning.

Haydon, G. (1997) *Teaching About Values*, London: Cassell.

Jeffreys, M. V. C. (1971) Education: Its nature and purpose, London: Allen & Unwin.

WEB SITES

The official site of the Department for Education and Skills in England is found at http://www.dfee.gov.uk/. This site gives general information about the education system; National Curriculum support materials and guidelines; resources for teachers and students; legislation and regulations; policy documents; on-line publications and circulars; research reports summaries and recent news. The Welsh Office web site at http://www.wales.gov.uk deals with most government issues in Wales and gives access to information provided by the Education Department (in English and Welsh). General information about education in Scotland, links to related sites and news is at http://www.scotland.gov.uk. Information about the Department for Education in Northern Ireland contains plans and strategies; statistics; circulars; on-line documents; inspection reports; information for parents and students; assessment results. Access to the Northern Ireland Network for Education is at http://www.deni.gov.uk.

INDEX

NOTE: Page numbers in italic indicate the entry for a subject.